D0875681

CENTRAL STATISTICAL OFFICE

NATIONAL ACCOUNTS STATISTICS

SOURCES AND METHODS

Edited by
RITA MAURICE
(Central Statistical Office)

LONDON
HER MAJESTY'S STATIONERY OFFICE
1968

A

Published by
HER MAJESTY'S STATIONERY OFFICE

To be purchased from
49 High Holborn, London w.c.1
423 Oxford Street, London w.1
13A Castle Street, Edinburgh 2
109 St. Mary Street, Cardiff CF1 1JW
Brazennose Street, Manchester 2
50 Fairfax Street, Bristol BS1 3DE
258–259 Broad Street, Birmingham 1
7–11 Linenhall Street, Belfast BT2 8AY
or through any bookseller

Price £2 5s. 0d. net

SBN 11 630061 2

Preface

This book provides a description of the national accounts for the United Kingdom. It describes the structure of the official accounts and the preparation of the estimates included in them. The description does not attempt to enable the reader to reconstruct the estimates, but is intended to enable him to better appreciate their significance and to assess their reliability. The aim is to show how the estimates fit into the national accounting framework and to indicate the source of the information. In many cases, when statistics are prepared by other departments, a more detailed description of their preparation is published by the department concerned.

The first such description of the national income statistics—*National Income Statistics: Sources and Methods*—was published by the Central Statistical Office in 1956. The plan of this book follows closely that of its predecessor. The two introductory chapters provide a description of the main concepts underlying the United Kingdom official statistics. There follows a short survey of the estimates of the national income aggregates (Chapter III) and a description of the arrangement of the published tables (Chapter IV). Subsequent chapters deal with various aspects of the national accounts, and there are separate chapters on the accounts for each sector of the economy (the personal sector, companies, public corporations, central government and local authorities).

In the twelve years since the earlier volume, many changes have been made and the amount of published information has been greatly expanded. The annual Blue Book, *National Income and Expenditure*, remains the basic publication, but it has grown from the fifty-three tables of the 1955 Blue Book described in *National Income Statistics: Sources and Methods*, to the eighty tables of the 1967 Blue Book described in the present volume. The first major change in this period was the inclusion of estimates of capital consumption in the 1956 Blue Book; since 1964 estimates of capital stock have also been given (see Chapter XII). The other major change has been the incorporation of financial accounts within the system (see Chapter XIV). More important, outside of the Blue Book, a system of quarterly accounts has been built up which includes all the basic summary tables; and the main quarterly series are published on a seasonally adjusted as well as an unadjusted basis. The descriptions of the estimates cover both the quarterly and annual figures and a separate section (in Chapter III) describes the methods of seasonal adjustment. An associated development was the publication in 1961 of the first official detailed input-output tables for 1954 which are consistent with the national accounts; the first summary tables for 1963 are described in Chapter IV. The present regular official publications are summarised at the beginning of Chapter IV.

The description given in this book relates to the national accounts as presented in the 1967 Blue Book, *National Income and Expenditure, 1967* (HMSO, September 1967); and it covers in detail the estimates for the eleven years 1956 to 1966 for which figures are given in the 1967 Blue Book tables. In addition, important points relating to earlier years are mentioned and sufficient information for earlier years is given to provide—together with the previous book—a description of the estimates for all years since 1946. Where estimates are quoted, they are taken from the 1967 Blue Book even if revised estimates have been published subsequently. Where additional references are given, these relate (unless otherwise stated) to other official publications by Her Majesty's Stationery Office.

Developments subsequent to the 1967 Blue Book and up to the beginning of 1968, have been noted, but not fully described. The national accounts are continually being developed as new items have to be provided for, additional information becomes available, and methods of estimation are improved. It is therefore inevitable that a description of this kind is quickly overtaken by events. As in the past, the notes to each Blue Book will bring up to date the descriptions contained in the following pages. The main current developments which are likely to lead to changes are the re-basing of the constant price estimates on 1963 instead of 1958 and the introduction of the revised Standard Industrial Classification.

The United Kingdom system of national accounts generally follows the principles recommended for international use by the United Nations in *A System of National Accounts and Supporting Tables* (New York, 1964) and the Organisation for Economic Co-operation and Development in *A Standardized System of National Accounts* (Paris, 1959). The United Nations' recommendations are at present in course of being revised and a number of changes are to be made. Corresponding changes may be made to the United Kingdom accounts if suitable data are available and the new presentation is considered appropriate for this country.

The national accounts estimates are compiled and published by the Central Statistical Office, but it will be evident from reading this book that they are to a large extent derived from the statistical work of other departments. In the case of confidential data, such as tax assessments and census of production returns, the work of analysis and summarisation is necessarily carried out by the department receiving the information. Many branches of the government statistical service and the Bank of England have also contributed extensively to the preparation of this volume and their help is gratefully acknowledged. Within the Central Statistical Office, the work of preparing this volume has in fact extended over three years and many different members of its staff have made valuable contributions to it. Their work is acknowledged with appreciation. It will also be obvious to readers of the previous book that we have built very largely on the work of those who prepared the first *Sources and Methods;* without this our task would have been immeasurably greater.

RITA MAURICE

Central Statistical Office
March 1968.

iv

Contents

Chapter I

The Conceptual Framework of National Income and Expenditure Statistics

NATIONAL INCOME, PRODUCT AND EXPENDITURE

The national income is a measure of the money value of goods and services becoming available to the nation from economic activity. It can be regarded in three ways: as a sum of incomes derived from economic activity, which can be broadly divided for example between incomes from employment and incomes from profits; as a sum of expenditure, the main distinction being that between expenditure on consumption and expenditure on adding to wealth (or investment); or as a sum of the products of the various industries of the nation. These three aspects of the national income help to explain both the ways in which the statistics are normally presented and the ways in which the estimates are compiled. The present chapter describes the three methods of approach and the relations between them.

The analysis of national income statistics is not confined to the subdivision of the national aggregates into the various forms of income, product or expenditure. It extends to the compilation of accounts for particular broad groups within the nation—the sectors of the economy—and thus throws light on the transactions between the sectors. This form of analysis is described as national accounting, and this method of presentation of national income statistics is described in Chapter II.

The aggregation of incomes

As a measure of the value of goods and services available to the nation, the national income is not simply an aggregate of all incomes. It includes only those incomes of residents of the nation, whether individual or corporate, which are derived directly from the current production of goods and services. Such incomes can be described as incomes of factors of production, or more shortly, as *factor incomes*. Other forms of income, for example retirement pensions or family allowances or receipts of private gifts, cannot be regarded as payments for current services to production; they are paid for out of factor incomes, through national insurance, through taxes, or by gifts, and are described as *transfer incomes*. Payments for which no goods or services are received in return, such as taxes, are *transfer payments*. The national income, being the total value of goods and services becoming available, cannot include both factor incomes and transfer incomes. It is measured by the sum of factor incomes.

One important form of income—interest and dividends—is susceptible to alternative treatments. It may be regarded as a factor income earned by the

1

owner of capital, or as a transfer payment out of the factor income earned by the enterprise employing the capital. In the former case, the national income would include interest and dividends as one item of factor income and undistributed profits of enterprises as another. In the latter case, the entire profits of enterprises are regarded as factor incomes, and the payments of interest and dividends as transfer incomes paid out of these profits. The aggregate national income is the same in both cases. A particular form of interest—interest on the government debt—is in both cases regarded as a transfer payment for a different reason: namely, that the national income would otherwise not be independent of the means of financing government expenditure, as it is of the means of financing producers' expenditure. Having arisen from financing past government expenditure (often in war) government debt interest cannot, without straining language, be regarded as corresponding to currently produced goods and services. In United Kingdom statistics the second of the treatments described above is adopted and payments of interest and dividends out of profits are regarded as transfer payments. The standard system of national accounts prepared by the United Nations[1] at present adopts the first treatment, but this is likely to be changed in the revision of the standard system which is now in progress. The United Kingdom treatment shows the factor income arising from current production of goods and services, irrespective of the ownership of capital and has the advantage of providing a more simple analysis of the contribution of each industry to the national income. It also has the advantage of showing one of the determinants of changes in the income from ownership of capital.

The national income of the United Kingdom is the income of residents of the United Kingdom. Some of this income arises as a result of economic activity abroad, or property held abroad, while some income arising within the United Kingdom is paid to non-residents. To arrive at the national income of United Kingdom residents the net income from abroad has to be added to the factor incomes arising in this country. The distinction between domestic income and national income is discussed in detail below.

The aggregation of products

The sum of domestic factor incomes measures the total output of goods and services within the country, described as the domestic product. Two points should be noticed. Firstly, the domestic product can be regarded as the sum of the products of industries or productive enterprises within the country, but it is the sum only of the factor incomes earned in each industry or enterprise. It is essentially a sum of the values added at each stage of production. The value of the product of the weaving industry, in this sense, consists of the wages, salaries and profits of the weavers, but it does not include the value of the yarn used in production, and so is not equal to the selling value of the cloth. Secondly, it follows that the domestic product includes only the factor incomes arising within the country; it does not include the value of imported goods and services, which are part of the domestic products of other countries.

The domestic product describes the total of domestic factor incomes. As in the case of incomes, to arrive at the national product net income from abroad has to be added to the domestic product.

---

[1] *A System of National Accounts and Supporting Tables,* United Nations (New York, 1964).

The aggregation of expenditures

The national income has been defined as the value of goods and services becoming available to the nation. Hence it can be measured not only as a sum of incomes but also by summing expenditures on these goods and services.

National expenditure can be broadly divided between consumption and adding to wealth (or investment). Consumption is taken to comprise all kinds of current expenditure on goods and services, whether by individual consumers or by collective bodies, including the government.

Adding to wealth is taken to mean the net increase in the stock of capital assets. Assets in this sense comprise both physical assets—the stock of factories, machinery, houses and so on—and financial assets in the form of holdings of securities and other claims, and in the form of currency or bank deposits, including foreign exchange. But every financial asset or claim is necessarily a liability to someone else, including currency which is regarded as a liability to the issuing authority. Hence, within the nation, financial assets must be taken to be offset exactly by financial liabilities. Adding to wealth, or investment, by the nation as a whole thus means net additions to the nation's stocks of physical assets together with any net addition to the total claims by residents of the nation on residents of other nations, in the form of gold, foreign exchange, holdings of shares in non-resident enterprises, trade credits, etc. There are, of course, forms of wealth which do not come within this definition of the stock of capital assets. Some—such as the health of the population, its technical knowledge, its heritage of literature and music—are not capable of measurement. Others—such intangible assets as patents, copyrights, concessions, leaseholds and goodwill—fall within the sphere of accountancy and might be measured, but in fact no attempt is made to specify changes in them.

Just as the national income is not simply an aggregation of all incomes, and the national product is not an aggregation of the selling values of all goods sold, so the national expenditure is not the aggregation of all purchases. It is defined so as to exclude the transactions that occur when a commodity (such as yarn for weaving) or a service (such as the carriage of yarn from spinner to weaver) is sold for the production of some finished commodity (a shirt). This involves drawing a distinction between final and intermediate purchasers and transactions. The shirt is a final product; its purchaser—the consumer—is a final purchaser, and his purchase in the retail shop is a final transaction and part of final expenditure. The transactions conducted between the spinner and the weaver, and between the weaver and the transporter are intermediate transactions. All purchases of goods and services for use in current production and subsequent resale are intermediate purchases. Goods added to stock between the end of one accounting period and the next are, however, an exception; additions to stock must be regarded as additions to wealth within the accounting period and therefore as final expenditure. To avoid duplication, only final purchases are included in the aggregate of national expenditure.

In the simple case of the shirt this distinction gives rise to little difficulty. It is less easy to determine the boundary between final and intermediate purchases in considering transactions of the government or purchases of capital assets. The solutions adopted are described later.

The treatment of international transactions

National expenditure is thus another aspect of the national income and national product. All three concepts are ways of regarding the total value of goods and services becoming available. In a closed economy, with no foreign trade, the national product and national expenditure would be different aspects of the same collection of goods and services. In an open economy, identification of the specific goods and services is rendered more difficult because many final goods contain imported material; final expenditure on such goods thus generates income and product not only in the home economy but also in the foreign country from which the imported material has been bought. Similarly part of the national product is sold to other countries. National expenditure and national product cannot therefore be identified as a tangible collection of goods and services.

National expenditure as was said above, may be regarded as comprising the nation's consumption and its investment, including as investment additions to its wealth overseas. One form of investment is, therefore, an excess of exports of goods and services over imports, which is necessarily accompanied by an increase in the nation's wealth (except where international transfers occur, a case dealt with below). This increase in wealth, or net investment abroad, which may take the form of increased holdings of foreign exchange or other financial claims on non-residents, or of increased holdings of physical assets abroad, is a part of national expenditure as defined. In the reverse case, an excess of imports is financed by drawing on the nation's wealth, or net foreign disinvestment.

From the point of view of this discussion, income received from economic activity or property held abroad is regarded as equivalent to exports; it is another means of acquiring financial assets. Income paid abroad is equivalent to imports. Thus: Exports of goods and services *plus* Income from abroad
equals Imports of goods and services *plus* Income
paid abroad *plus* Net investment abroad.

In estimating national expenditure, it is not in fact practicable, except by rather elaborate methods, to eliminate the import content from each kind of final expenditure, for example, from consumers' expenditure. The statistics from which the estimates of consumption and investment are derived relate to the total value of the final goods and services concerned, including their import content, and the estimate of national expenditure is arrived at by subtracting from this total value of final products the total value of imported goods and services.

Thus the national expenditure is equal to total expenditure by residents of the nation on all final goods and services, including their import content—a total described as domestic expenditure—*plus* total exports and income received from abroad *less* total imports and income paid abroad. It is identical with the value of goods and services becoming available as a result of the nation's economic activity, and thus with the national income and national product.

So far, only a passing reference has been made to international transfer payments, such as grants and gifts. These may be inter-governmental grants, such as aid to developing countries, or private donations, such as remittances by emigrants to their relatives at home. It would not be unreasonable to treat receipts of such gifts as part of the national income; they clearly add to the nation's ability to buy goods and services (unlike transfers or gifts between members of the nation). It may be said that the direct effect of such gifts on national income and expenditure is the same as the effect of property income from abroad, which is included as a component of the national income. It is, however, more appropriate to treat the national income as a measure of the goods and services becoming available to the nation through its own economic activity. This limitation allows the inclusion in national income of income from abroad, which is a measure of the yield of productive assets held abroad; it does not allow the inclusion of international transfers, the value of which cannot be described as a measure of the receiving nation's economic activity.

Receipts of such transfers, of course, add to national expenditure by increasing consumption or national wealth, for example, by increasing the foreign exchange reserves. The equality between national expenditure and national income is preserved by setting the value of international transfers received *less* transfers to other countries against expenditure in the form of additions to overseas assets. The specific consumption or increase in specific forms of wealth resulting from gifts is included in the detailed statistics of national expenditure, but has to be offset against the increase in national wealth as in the table below.

The identity of national income, product and expenditure

The relation between the three idential aggregates may be summarised as follows:

Relation between national income, product and expenditure

Income or product	Expenditure	
Domestic factor incomes = domestic product	Consumption (including its import content) *plus* Adding to domestic wealth (including its import content)	
	= Domestic expenditure	
plus Net income from abroad	*plus* Exports of goods and services (including their import content) and income from abroad	*plus* Net investment abroad
	less Imports of goods and services and income paid abroad	*less* Net transfers from abroad
National income or product = National expenditure		

The identities between the aggregates are, then, tautologies resulting from the definitions, not propositions about economic behaviour. Many of the conceptual problems that arise in defining these aggregates and in classifying their components can be solved only by arbitrary or conventional methods. It is not suggested that the methods applied in the official statistics for the United Kingdom are the only correct solutions, nor indeed that they are the best solutions at all times and for all purposes. The concepts that the statistics are designed to measure are themselves abstractions from the complicated realities of economic life, and the statistics may often appear remote and artificial until experience has been gained in their use as instruments for interpreting actual economic situations.

The consumption of fixed assets

To each of the three identical aggregates there corresponds a 'gross' and a 'net' concept. The process of production and the passage of time involve a gradual using up of the nation's productive assets—its buildings and machinery. This capital consumption, or depreciation, should clearly be taken into account in calculating the net annual additions to the nation's wealth, and should therefore be regarded as a deduction from income, product and expenditure—from income and product, because the using up of assets is a necessary cost of earning the income or producing the output (analogous with, although less easily measured than, the cost of raw materials); from expenditure, because depreciation of capital represents a reduction in the value of the national wealth. For two reasons, however, the main aggregates are shown before deducting any such provision. Firstly, the replacement of physical assets can be, within limits, postponed: hence it is useful to measure the total supply of goods and services becoming available, even though to preserve the nation's assets intact some part of the total must be allotted to replacement, or provisions for future replacement, of existing assets. For some purposes, it is more useful to know the total output of capital goods than to know only the net increase in the stocks of such goods after allowance for depreciation. Secondly, estimates of depreciation, or capital consumption, can be made only on the basis of convention or of some arbitrary principle of calculation. They do not represent actual transactions and are thus of a different nature from most of the other estimates in the national income statistics. The allowance for capital resources used up in production depends upon judgements about the timing of the services rendered by capital assets and is not a unique quantity. Hence the statistics at present published for the United Kingdom give precedence to measurements of 'gross' income, product and expenditure, before making allowance for that part which should be allotted to the maintenance intact of the nation's fixed assets. To preserve the true significance of the expressions national income, national product and national expenditure, the terms used to describe the estimates before deduction of capital consumption are 'national income *plus* depreciation', 'gross national product'[2] and 'gross national expenditure'. The estimates after deduction of capital consumption are described as 'national income', 'net national product' and 'net national expenditure'. In the published tables the terms generally used are 'gross national product' for the gross concept and 'national income' for the net concept.

Total personal income

Another commonly used aggregate of some importance is the total of personal incomes. It has been pointed out that the national income is defined to represent the aggregate of incomes arising from current production of goods and services *plus* net income from abroad. It is, however, convenient also to measure the simple aggregate of all incomes accruing to persons resident in the nation, whether derived from current production or by transfer of income from others through taxation or through receipts of interest and dividends. This aggregate is greater than national income *plus* depreciation to the extent that such transfer

---

[2]The gross national product is 'gross' only in the sense that no deduction is made for depreciation. It is still 'net' in the sense that it is free of duplication, including only values added in production.

incomes from public authorities (which include interest payments as well as national insurance benefits and similar grants) are included in personal income as well as the personal incomes which are taxed to provide them; it is smaller than national income *plus* depreciation to the extent that trading enterprises of all kinds retain some of the income arising from current production (or from abroad) for their own investment or for paying their own taxes.

Total personal income may be greater or less than national income *plus* depreciation, and changes in total personal incomes may also be significantly different from changes in national income *plus* depreciation. The relationship between the two may be summarised as follows:

Total personal income
less Personal income from transfers from public authorities
plus Undistributed income of corporations (including additions to reserves)
plus Taxes on income paid by corporations
plus Income of public authorities from trading, rent, dividends and interest
less Interest on public authorities' debt
equals National income *plus* depreciation

This is the way in which the aggregate national income would be built up if income from interest and dividends were regarded as a factor income. A presentation on these lines is included in the standard tables published by the United Nations[3] and one is also shown for the United Kingdom in the Blue Book (Table 9 of the 1967 Blue Book).

DEFINITION OF PRODUCTION
AND THE EXTENT OF IMPUTATION

It was said at the outset that the national income includes only those incomes, whether individual or corporate, which arise from economic activity. The problem then arises of delimiting the field of production or economic activity. In the widest sense, production might be taken to cover all activities resulting in useful goods and services. Such a definition would raise great difficulties of measurement. The domestic services of housewives, for example, and the week-end carpentry of householders, are not exchanged for money; they could be given only an assumed value which would necessarily be very arbitrary. In computing a money measure of the nation's production, it is most convenient to confine attention to activities yielding goods and services which can be given a value which is not wholly arbitrary. This means substantially those goods and services which are in fact exchanged for money.

This is already a very broad definition—much broader than the sense in which production is often used. It includes not only the output of physical commodities from extractive and manufacturing industry but also the activities of transport and communication, wholesale and retail distribution, the other service industries, and the work of civil servants, local government employees and the Forces.

In practice, the definition used in the United Kingdom statistics extends a little beyond this to cover certain kinds of activity which are not actually exchanged for money. The principal example is the provision of owner-occupied

---

[3]*A System of National Accounts and Supporting Tables*, United Nations (New York, 1964).

houses. No money actually passes between the owner and the occupier of a house when they are the same person, but the services of the building do nevertheless have a value equivalent to the net income which could be obtained by letting the building commercially. A figure based on this approach is included in the reckoning of the national income. In effect the owner-occupier is divided into two separate transactors: it is supposed that as owner he lets the building to himself as occupier for a certain rent. This process of inventing a transaction is known as 'imputation'.

Imputation is confined to the very small number of cases where a reasonably satisfactory basis for the assumed valuation is available. In general this can occur only where the imputed transactions in question are closely similar to a group of transactions in which money actually passes. Hence the flow of goods and services which contribute to the national income and product is limited to those goods and services which are *customarily* exchanged for money. Thus in the case of owner-occupied houses, a basis of valuation can be obtained because there are many commercially rented buildings. An imputed value for certain forms of employees' income in kind (such as free or cheap coal for miners, food and lodging for domestic servants and the Forces) is also included in the national income. Farm produce consumed by the farmer and his own household is included at an imputed value. Finally, a value is imputed for the services of certain buildings owned and occupied by public authorities (such as schools, hospitals). These are the only significant cases of imputation in the United Kingdom statistics of national income and expenditure. To omit some of these imputed items entirely might lead in some circumstances to misleading conclusions. For instance, if the income in kind of the Forces were omitted from personal income and expenditure, then a substantial increase in the size of the Forces would in itself appear to cause a substantial fall in consumers' expenditure. If a large number of rented houses were sold to their occupiers, the omission of imputed rent would lead to an apparent decrease in national income and product due merely to a change in ownership unrelated to any actual decrease in goods and services.

It should be observed that whenever an income is imputed, a corresponding expenditure must simultaneously be recorded. The inclusion in the owner's income of the value of an owner-occupied house must be balanced by an imagined payment of rent by the owner-occupier *qua* occupier. The inclusion in the income of domestic servants of free food must be balanced by an imagined equal expenditure by domestic servants on food. Both aspects of the imaginary transaction must be recorded in order to preserve the identity between income, product and expenditure.

Although the statistical arguments against extending the scope of imputation seem overwhelmingly strong, it must be admitted that the restriction of the estimates substantially to money transactions limits their significance in certain contexts. For example, the fact that the unpaid activities of housewives are excluded from the national income will vitiate in some degree any comparison between different countries or different periods if the amount of work done by housewives is substantially different. Thus, when more housewives go out to work this increases the national income and product but no allowance is made for any accompanying loss of their services in the home.

Another example may be found in the treatment of consumers' durable goods such as motor cars, washing machines or pianos. It would be theoretically possible to include in production the services rendered by such goods over the period of their useful lives, which is often many years. In this case the owner of these goods would be regarded as a producer and it would be necessary to impute a hire charge to himself as user in the same way as for owner-occupied houses. Although such goods are sometimes rented, there is little basis for estimating such a charge, and no imputation is made. The boundary of production is drawn where the goods are handed over to the buyer, and in effect their consumption is supposed to take place immediately. The disadvantages of this procedure are obvious. People may temporarily reduce their purchases of durable and semi-durable goods, such as cars, washing machines and clothing, to a comparatively low level without reducing correspondingly their actual use of such goods. The wearing out of existing goods is not fully replaced. In such circumstances, the figures for consumption, being restricted to new acquisitions, may give a very misleading impression of the reduction in the standard of living of consumers. These are among the limitations which should always be remembered in interpreting national income statistics.

FORMS OF INCOME

The national income includes only those incomes, whether individual or corporate, which arise from economic activity. Excepting income from abroad, such incomes are those arising from domestic production of goods and services and are described as factor incomes, since they are regarded as the earnings of factors of production. The classification of factors of production presents a good many difficulties in economic theory. Economic activity, or production, results from the combination of factors of production in various ways. The classification of factor incomes is dictated by convenience rather than by purely theoretical considerations.

In the broadest sense, factor earnings may be described as earnings from work and the use of property, or as employment income and profits. Employment income includes wages and salaries and the pay of the Forces; it is taken to include also certain supplements to employees' incomes such as contributions made by employers to national insurance and to superannuation schemes. The term profits includes all surpluses from trading, that is, any excess of operating receipts over operating expenses, by any producing enterprise whether publicly or privately owned. For traditional and statistical reasons 'rent'—the operating surplus derived from the ownership of land and buildings—is separately classified, although it differs little from any other form of profit.

The distinction between employment incomes and profits cannot be made in the case of incomes of persons working on their own account or in partnership; such incomes are therefore separately classified as income from self-employment. In practice, it is possible to distinguish profits only in the case of 'impersonal' enterprises. These can be subdivided between privately owned corporate enterprises (companies), public corporations (chiefly the bodies administering the nationalised industries) and other publicly owned trading enterprises.

The forms of income comprising the national income, as presented in the United Kingdom statistics, are given below. But the classification is not one that allows any precise division between the earnings of different kinds of factors of production.

Income from employment:
   wages
   salaries
   pay of the Forces
   supplements to employment income (employers' contributions)
Income from self-employment: a mixture of employment income and
    profit income
Profit incomes from domestic production, earned by:
   companies
   public corporations
   other public enterprises
Rent
Property income from abroad
less Property income paid abroad

The total of these incomes, after deducting stock appreciation and capital consumption, is the national income. The national income does not include any gains from the appreciation in value of assets, in particular, the appreciation of producers' stocks and work in progress (see page 17). Nor does it include gains from running down the value of fixed assets and not replacing them (capital consumption, see page 16).

THE CLASSIFICATION OF FINAL EXPENDITURE

Four groups of economic entities which buy goods and services produced in the United Kingdom may be distinguished:

   United Kingdom private households and organisations
   United Kingdom producers, or trading concerns
   United Kingdom public authorities
   Non-residents of the United Kingdom.

Consumers' expenditure

Private households or individuals buy all sorts of things—food, hair-cuts, clothing, motor cars—for their own private use and enjoyment. Since it was decided, for the reasons given above, that (except for houses) it is impracticable to measure the services rendered by consumers' durable goods over their useful lifetime, the value of consumers' expenditure must be computed at the point where the goods and services are handed over to the consumer. The purchase of these goods and services constitutes 'personal expenditure on goods and services' or, for short, *consumers' expenditure*. Also included in this category is the expenditure of associations of householders or private non-profit-making organisations serving persons, for example, clubs, charities and universities.

The acquisition of houses and land is not included in consumers' expenditure. Houses are regarded as productive assets, the house owner being therefore a producer. As mentioned above, the owner-occupier is regarded as a producer who sells the services of his house to himself at an imputed rent and the imputed rent is included in consumers' expenditure. Land also is a productive asset from which the owner may receive a rent income.

Producers' purchases

Next may be considered the purchase of goods and services by producers, whether companies, unincorporated businesses, public corporations or other public trading bodies. Most such purchases are of goods and services for use in the course of production, for example the flour bought by bakers for use in the production of bread. In such cases the purchase is regarded as an intermediate and not as a final purchase (as pointed out on page 3). The ultimate purpose both of producing the flour and of using it in the bakery is the production of bread for sale to the consumer; it is only at this stage that final expenditure is measured. Although these intermediate transactions are eliminated in estimating the national aggregates of final output and expenditure, the study of the changes in inter-industry transactions in intermediate goods and services is of great importance and interest. Some of these transactions are shown in tables in the Blue Book which display the inter-relationships between the inputs and outputs of the principal industries and the effects on different industries of changes in final expenditure.

Not all purchases of goods and services by producers, however, are for use in current production. Firstly, the producer may buy buildings, machinery, vehicles or plant which will give services to production over a number of years. This form of expenditure is described as *fixed capital formation*. To the extent that it exceeds the wearing out or depreciation of existing assets, it represents an addition to wealth and is described as net fixed capital formation. As already pointed out, (on page 6), in the official United Kingdom statistics attention is concentrated on gross fixed capital formation. Secondly, goods of the same kind as the materials used in production may be bought in excess of the amount currently used. In this case the producer's stocks of materials, his assets, will rise; he is adding to wealth or investing by *capital formation in stocks*. His assets may also be increased by additions to his stocks of unsold finished goods and by additions to work in progress, which are included in this form of expenditure.

Both these forms of expenditure by producers, capital formation in fixed assets and in stocks, form part of gross national expenditure because they add to wealth. By definition all capital formation is made by producers, since consumers are assumed in effect to use up goods and services as soon as they buy them. Thus they cannot accumulate stocks and the existence of consumers' durable goods other than houses is neglected. The purchase of new houses forms part of fixed capital formation because the houses are regarded as productive assets.

Public authorities' expenditure

Another group of purchases of goods and services is formed by the expenditure of public authorities, that is, the central government and local authorities. In the course of organising collective services, such as defence, justice, health and education, the public authorities purchase the services of their salaried officials, and many goods such as aircraft, office furniture, hospital equipment and textbooks. The services to the public which result from these purchases are rendered free, or nearly free, and so do not appear in consumers' expenditure. Nevertheless it is clearly desirable that, in reckoning the national income, the work done by teachers, judges, etc., as well as by those who make the necessary equipment for their work, should not be excluded. This may be achieved by regarding public authorities as collective bodies providing free public services for collective consumption by the community. Since these services of public authorities are not sold, they can be valued in money only by adding up the money spent by the public authorities in buying the services of teachers, health service employees, the Forces, and other public servants, together with the materials used (military equipment, blackboards, the rent of buildings, drugs, paper, etc.).

In the same way, public authorities' expenditure on fixed assets, such as buildings or fire engines, is part of national capital formation. However no account is taken, because of lack of information, of any additions to their stocks of consumable stores apart from strategic stocks and stocks held by government trading enterprises. It should, however, be noted that purchases of military equipment, however durable, are not regarded as capital formation; nearly all defence expenditure is treated as current expenditure—as consumption in a wide sense.

A more difficult problem is the treatment of government services which are services not to the citizens as ultimate consumers (for example of food, defence or justice) but to producers, for example advisory services for industry, or that part of the expenditure on the maintenance of roads which might be regarded as serving industry. It has been argued that services of this kind should be regarded as intermediate products and so excluded from final expenditure. Such a treatment would involve the complications of estimating the benefits received by various industries and it is not adopted in the United Kingdom statistics.

The argument that some government services are of the nature of intermediate rather than final products may indeed be pressed further. Although it appeals to common sense to regard publicly provided education, or parks and museums, or the health service as final products comparable with similar goods and services normally paid for in cash, yet the case is not so clear with some other government activities. For example, the services of civil servants engaged in drafting legislation might well be regarded as essentially an intermediate service required for the functioning of the present economic system. The whole apparatus of defence might be regarded in the same light. If this view were accepted, a large proportion of government activity would not feature directly as final output or final expenditure at all, although it might be considered as part of the cost of production of all other goods and services. In practice, however, there seems to be no generally acceptable way of drawing the line between 'final' and 'intermediate' forms of government activity, and all government activity is therefore treated as final. Sufficient detail is provided to enable the reader to distinguish between those activities which he might wish to regard as genuine final activities and those which he would prefer to treat as intermediate, or as what have been described as 'regrettable necessities'.

Exports and imports

The treatment of international transactions in the estimation of national expenditure has already been described on pages 3 to 5.

To sum up, the categories of final expenditure are classified as follows:

Consumers' expenditure on goods and services

Domestic fixed capital formation (gross or net)

Capital formation in stocks and work in progress

Current expenditure by public authorities on goods and services

Exports of goods and services and income from abroad
less Imports of goods and services and income paid abroad
the total being equal to National expenditure (gross or net).

VALUATION PROBLEMS:
MARKET PRICES AND FACTOR COSTS

The various forms of final output, considered from the point of view of the purchasers, are most appropriately valued at the prices which the purchasers actually pay, the import content being deducted as a single total from the sum of the various expenditures. The aggregate value of the goods and services consumed or added to the nation's wealth will not in general, however, be equal to the sum of factor incomes arising from production. The final expenditures as recorded cover any *taxes on expenditure* (broadly, what are generally known as indirect taxes, such as Customs and Excise duties) imposed on the goods and services concerned. Such taxes on expenditure are paid at one stage or another by the producers or merchants (for example, import duties paid by the importer, purchase tax paid by the wholesaler). Again, the prices paid by the final user fail to cover the total factor incomes if the producers receive a government *subsidy* (for example, the subsidies, deficiency payments or guaranteed prices paid in respect of many farm products). Such taxes and subsidies are reflected in the final or market price paid by the purchaser. But taxes accrue to, and subsidies are paid by, the government not the producer, and cannot be identified with any specific goods or services which the government provides or receives in return. Thus although indirect taxes form part of producers' costs, they do not form part of the income of factors of production. Similarly, although subsidies form part of the income of factors of production, they do not form part of the prices which the final purchaser pays.

There are therefore two different ways of valuing national expenditure and the national product; at *market prices*, including all taxes on expenditure, subsidies being regarded as negative taxes, or at *factor cost*, representing only the sum of the incomes of factors of production. The two methods lead to different totals which may also show different movements over time.

In the official statistics for the United Kingdom, the national product is usually expressed at factor cost in the sense that it is the sum of domestic factor incomes *plus* net income from abroad. The components of national expenditure are shown at market prices, the basis on which the statistics are naturally compiled. Total national expenditure is shown at factor cost, the estimate at factor cost being arrived at by deducting taxes on expenditure from, and adding subsidies to, the estimates of total national expenditure at market prices. National expenditure at factor cost is thus identical with the sum of domestic factor incomes *plus* net income from abroad, and with national product at factor cost.

Some authorities prefer to express the aggregate national product and national expenditure at market prices. For example, international recommendations suggest that 'It is more useful to reserve this abbreviated expression [gross national product] for the gross national product at market prices'[4] and the United States follows this procedure in published tables. And although in the

---

[4] *A Standardized System of National Accounts*, Organisation for European Economic Co-operation (Paris, 1959).

United Kingdom tables the main emphasis is on the aggregates at factor cost, market price aggregates are also shown in the Blue Book.

Both methods of valuation have their uses and both are well established by tradition. Broadly speaking, the justification of market prices is that they represent the relative value to the individual of different goods and services, on the usual assumption that the price paid for each commodity is proportional to its marginal significance. Thus an increase in the domestic product at market prices, other things being equal, can be regarded as indicating *prima facie* an increase in the 'economic welfare' of the community. On the other hand, valuation at factor cost displays the composition of national product or expenditure in terms of factors of production employed, the contributions of the factors being measured by the incomes that they receive. Valuation at factor cost may therefore be useful in connection with problems of the allocation of resources. The choice between the two presentations thus depends on the purpose for which the statistics are used.

Although no serious statistical problem is involved in estimating the total of taxes on expenditure or subsidies, their allocation between the different industries contributing to the national product, and between the different goods and services making up national expenditure, presents substantial difficulties of estimation in certain cases. The allocation of such taxes and subsidies to each industry is somewhat arbitrary and in the United Kingdom statistics the contribution to national product is shown as the sum of factor incomes. However, the taxes and subsidies are allocated between the different categories of final expenditure. Since the incidence of some of these taxes (for example, the tax on petrol used by business, or local rates on business premises) is spread in indeterminable proportions over most goods and services, the adjustment to factor cost cannot be carried through in full detail and is necessarily somewhat arbitrary even for the broad groups in which final expenditure is shown.

The justification of each method of valuation is subject, however, to many qualifications which seriously limit the significance of the conclusions to be drawn from the statistics. Valuation at market prices would provide a measure of changes in 'economic welfare' if final products whose market prices are equal contributed equally to welfare. But the presumption of any such equality is clearly open to doubt when any actual comparison is attempted between different periods or countries. It is distorted by differences in the distribution of income, by differences in taste, and by the difficulty of comparing the increments of welfare resulting from equal increments of government expenditure, consumers' expenditure, and investment. Hence if any considerable change occurs in these elements of the economic structure, it is difficult to conceive of statistics of national income affording in any precise sense a measure of economic welfare.

National income statistics are widely used as measures of national productivity, or for problems connected with the distribution of resources. But the factor cost measure, which is relevant to the consideration of these problems, also has important limitations. The relative rewards of factors of production in different industries or at different times are influenced by the degree of monopoly and by limitations on the free movements of factors. Moreover the existence of taxes and subsidies placed on the use of particular factors of production, or on commodities incorporating the factors, necessarily influences their relative cost to the producers employing them and thus the distribution of factors between different uses.

These qualifications are introduced to show that the meaning to be attached to the aggregate of national income, product or expenditure is essentially arbitrary and limited. The comprehensiveness of the aggregates is limited by convenience and convention; the valuations placed on goods and services are monetary values determined in imperfect markets and even if adjusted to constant prices, do not provide precise measures of changes either in welfare or in productivity. Nevertheless, the significance of the broad trends shown by the aggregates is often unmistakeable. Moreover, the interest of national income statistics lies also in the detailed analysis of transactions; although only limited significance can be attached to the aggregates, yet the components from which these aggregates are built up are, for the most part, actual money flows representing the main currents of economic activity. This emphasis on the relationships between the various parts of the economy is the basis of the national accounting approach, described in the next chapter.

THE DEFINITION OF THE NATION

National aggregates

So far, little indication has been given of what is meant by the United Kingdom, in describing the way in which its national income is compiled. Broadly, the national income, product and expenditure are the income, product and expenditure of those persons, enterprises and institutions which are regarded as United Kingdom residents. Most of the national income or product arises from economic activity within the United Kingdom, but some income accrues to United Kingdom residents as a result of economic activity abroad or property held abroad, while some income arising in the United Kingdom is paid to non-residents. For example, the income originating within the United Kingdom includes the profits of companies which are subsidiaries of overseas companies; these profits are part of property income paid abroad, and are not part of the national income of the United Kingdom. National expenditure differs from expenditure within the United Kingdom by including expenditure on exports and excluding expenditure on imports.

The definition of 'residents' is discussed on pages 436 to 438. For the moment, two important points may be noted. In the first place, United Kingdom residents include some persons whose economic activity is in fact carried on abroad. Thus the United Kingdom product includes the activity of ships and aircraft owned in the United Kingdom and of members of the Forces and government officials stationed abroad. Similarly, work done by members of other countries' Forces, or staffs of embassies stationed in the United Kingdom, is not included. Secondly, a problem arises in applying criteria of residence to business enterprises which operate abroad. The principle followed here is to regard such enterprises as divided into two parts, whether or not this conforms with the actual organisation of the enterprise: an overseas branch or subsidiary which is resident overseas and a head office which is resident in the United Kingdom. The profit earned by the overseas branch or subsidiary is regarded as originating overseas but accruing to the head office in the United Kingdom and is part of property income from abroad, whether or not it is remitted to the United Kingdom. Unremitted profits form part of net investment abroad.

Domestic aggregates

Domestic income and product is the value of goods and services produced by United Kingdom residents. It may be regarded as the income from economic activity of United Kingdom residents, as opposed to their income from property held abroad. The profits of branches and subsidiaries of overseas companies which are resident and operate in the United Kingdom are included; these branches and subsidiaries are the 'property' of their head offices overseas and their profits form part of property income paid abroad. Except in so far as the economic activity of some United Kingdom residents is in fact carried out abroad (examples are given above) domestic income is the income originating from economic activity in the United Kingdom.

Domestic product differs from national product by the amount of net property income from abroad. In the standardised system of national accounts prepared by the United Nations, the definition of the difference between domestic and national product is slightly different from that in the United Kingdom accounts. Domestic product is there defined as the income from economic activity rendered to resident producers. This includes the income paid to foreign residents working for United Kingdom resident producers and excludes the income paid to United Kingdom residents who are working for non-resident producers. In the United Kingdom accounts, income from employment is included in domestic income if the employee is resident, whether or not the producer for which he is working is resident. For the United Kingdom the difference in definition is small and the effect on the accounts is negligible. The treatment in the national accounts is consistent with that in the balance of payments accounts.

The term domestic expenditure is used to describe final expenditure by United Kingdom residents, both consumers and producers. It comprises consumption by persons and by public authorities and domestic capital formation. It thus differs from domestic income or product by the inclusion of imports and the exclusion of exports.

MAINTAINING CAPITAL INTACT

The national income may be measured by the nation's consumption *plus* any net increase in its assets or wealth. The measurement of changes in the nation's wealth raises two problems, rather similar in character, which cannot be avoided in even the most summary presentation of the statistics. These are the problems of valuing the consumption of fixed assets, or depreciation, already referred to above, and of valuing the change in assets in the form of stocks and work in progress—the problem of 'stock appreciation'.

Capital consumption

It was pointed out above that the national income and the change in wealth cannot be measured unless allowance is made for the gradual wearing out by use and obsolescence of the nation's fixed assets; and that the estimates given in the United Kingdom official statistics give precedence to gross concepts which do not purport to allow for the using up of capital assets. The difficulty arises from the fact that the cost of using fixed capital obviously cannot be measured directly; it is not represented by actual transactions.

In business accounting, this unrecorded element in current costs of production is met by provisions for depreciation. However, such provisions are generally not of the kind needed for national income accounts. They are frequently made by reference to the original cost of the asset; that is they provide for the setting aside of the original money outlay during the assumed life of the asset. Such provisions are comparable to the amortisation of a debt, rather than to a measure of the extent to which the assets are used up in each year. This is, indeed, the only approach possible if precise figures are required. Only in long periods of stable prices would the aggregated depreciation provisions be adequate for measuring capital consumption.

For the national accounts it is essential that the current charge for the use of assets should be calculated in terms of current prices, the prices at which other transactions in the accounts are measured. Capital consumption allowed for in estimating net national product must be related to the current value of resources used up in production. During or after a period of substantial changes in prices, the provisions made by business accounting become inappropriate for national income measurement. Valuation at current prices is the only way of securing internal consistency between the cost of using capital and other current costs of production; it is also the only way of treating consistently the uses of different kinds of assets.

The estimates of capital consumption are described in Chapter XII. They are based on broad assumptions about the expected lives of capital assets and their pattern of utilisation. It is rarely feasible to take account of changes in expectation of life on account of obsolescence and no allowance has been made. Assets have been assumed to render their services in equal amounts in each year of their life—the 'straight line' basis of depreciation.

Stock appreciation

The second problem arises in measuring the change in national wealth represented by changes in stocks. The concepts adopted for the measurement of national income and wealth require a measure of the change in stocks valued in the same way as other transactions in the system, that is at the prices of the period concerned. Business accounting methods, which provide most of the statistics actually used for reckoning incomes and changes in stocks, adopt a convention which results in a rather different valuation in times of substantial changes in prices. In this case, however, it is possible to make a rough adjustment for the difference between business accounting methods and the objectives of national income measurement.

In the measurement by normal accounting methods of the profit earned by a trading enterprise in a given period, the stocks taken over from the preceding period are treated as a purchase, while the stocks handed on to the following period are treated as a sale. As a result, any increase in the value of stocks between the beginning and end of the period will enter into the accounting profit, along with the excess of sales to outsiders over the sum of purchases from outsiders, payments to labour and depreciation charges. Expenditure during the year in purchasing materials is allowed as an operating expense only to the extent that the money value of stocks and work in progress at the beginning of the year is maintained. Any increase in stocks resulting from purchases in excess of this will appear as a form of investment.

If this definition of profit were accepted in national income measurement, it would mean that any increase over a year in the money value of stocks would be treated as 'adding to wealth', even if the physical volume of stocks remained constant. But for a measurement of income and stock changes consistent with the other flows dealt with in the system of national income statistics it is desirable that 'additions to wealth' should include only additions to wealth arising from the economic activity of the period; any increase in the physical volume of stocks should be included, but not an increase in the money value of stocks due to a rise in the prices at which stocks are valued. The effect of normal accounting methods is that in times of rising prices the money value of stocks increases by more than the physical volume valued at the prices of the year, and book profits thus incorporate an amount which from the present point of view must be regarded as a capital gain, not as income. The difference is described as *stock appreciation*. In reckoning the national income, product and expenditure, the estimated amount of stock appreciation is subtracted from the estimate of incomes and stock changes derived from accounting data. The stock change, after this adjustment, is described as the *value of the physical increase in stocks*. If prices are rising, stock appreciation is positive; if prices are falling, it is negative.

The estimates of stock appreciation are described in Chapter XIII, where there is a fuller treatment of this problem. The estimates of stock appreciation are only hazardous approximations and cannot be presented in much detail. Hence the adjustment is shown only for the major sectors of the economy. Further, the unadjusted accounting data of profits are more appropriate for many kinds of economic analysis than the adjusted data which represent more nearly the national income concepts. The unadjusted data are closer to profits as normally reported and have their influence on business policy; for interpretation and pre-diction of trends, the unadjusted data may prove more valuable than the adjusted estimates. Hence, wherever possible, both sets of data are provided.

Chapter II

The Framework of National Accounts

The main object of Chapter I was to explain the general significance of the concept of total national income and the relationship between the three ways of regarding it—as a sum of incomes, of expenditures or of products. It follows that the statistics can be presented in the form of a balanced account, showing for example the various kinds of national expenditure on one side of the account, and the forms of income on the other, the two parts adding to the same total.

A natural extension of this method of presentation of an account for the economy as a whole is to show balanced tables, or accounts, summarising the transactions of particular groups or entities within the economy. Thus the economy can be divided into branches or sectors and a set of accounts presented for each. The accounts for a sector represent a significant grouping of transactions displaying one aspect only of the economic activity of the nation. They thus stand between the accounts of aggregate national income and expenditure on the one hand and, on the other, the accounts which are, or could be, drawn up by enterprises or individuals for their own purposes. The principal advantage of such a framework is that it displays the relationships between the different parts of the economy, and the different forms of economic activity, in a way which the statistics of aggregate national income and expenditure alone cannot do. The organisation of the statistics into a set of national accounts is the framework on which is built the presentation of the statistics for the United Kingdom in the Blue Book.

The division of the economy into sectors is a primary feature of a national accounting system. There are various ways in which the economy may be divided. The essential elements, however, are: a *personal* or household sector serving primarily to display the transactions of members of the community in their capacity as final consumers; a sector, the accounts of which record the transactions of *productive enterprises,* whether publicly or privately owned; a sector for the transactions of the organs of *government*, both central and local, with the rest of the economy; and a sector, which may be described as the *overseas sector* or *the rest of the world,* the accounts for which record international transactions, that is transactions between residents and non-residents. The boundaries of some of these sectors may be drawn in various ways, and these essential sectors may be subdivided in greater or less detail.

A national accounting system requires, also, a method of classifying transactions which can be applied consistently to the various forms of economic activity. This introduces into the statistical method the kind of discipline and

19

order necessary in commercial accounting, although the principal consideration in the classification of transactions for national accounting must always be to serve the purpose of economic analysis.

There are two points of view from which transactions are classified. In the first place, different types of account are established, each corresponding to a particular kind of economic activity. Thus all economic activity and all transactions can be regarded as relating to one of three headings; production, consumption and adding to wealth. A production account records the transactions involved in the production and supply of goods and services. A consumption account (or income and expenditure account) records the current expenditure out of the income generated in production or received by transfers. An account for adding to wealth (or capital account) records the use of the savings derived from an income and expenditure account.

Secondly, all transactions can be divided between requited payments made for the supply of goods or services including the services of factors of production, or for the transfer of financial assets; and unrequited payments or transfers, such as taxes on income or capital, grants and gifts. The importance of this distinction is that only the requited payments enter into the national income and expenditure as defined above; the transfer payments represent a redistribution of the national income without adding to its total. Transfer payments thus appear only in the accounts for the individual sectors of the economy and not in the aggregate national income and expenditure. For example, the income of the government, regarded as an administrative apparatus and excluding its trading activities, consists wholly of transfer payments and does not appear in the national income.

The choice of sectors, the content of the accounts displayed, and the classification of transactions can be varied, and there are in fact significant differences between the systems used in different countries. The methods used in the United Kingdom are described below.

DEFINITION OF THE SECTORS

The sectors should be so defined that each constitutes a group of entities similar to one another in general characteristics affecting economic behaviour. Any grouping is bound to involve some loss of detail; the practical objective is a reasonable compromise between a mass of particulars and a grouping so broad as to obscure important differences. In practice the scope for possible multiplication of sectors is restricted by the extent of available information to a narrower range than might seem desirable.

The main sectors into which the United Kingdom economy is divided are:
> Personal sector
> Corporate enterprises:
> > Companies
> > Public corporations
> Public authorities:
> > Central government
> > Local authorities
> Overseas sector

A separate chapter of this book deals with each of these sectors.

For some purposes a consolidation of the central government's transactions with those of local authorities is appropriate, and the combination of these two sectors is referred to as 'public authorities'. For example, in analysing expenditure on the social services, the combined expenditure of all public authorities needs to be considered. Again, local authority rates are an important part of total taxes on expenditure. But the importance to economic activity of the policy decisions, especially of the budgetary decisions, of the central government justify its separation as a sector and the separate presentation of its accounts. The public authorities sector is the sector described as 'general government' in the system of national accounts prepared by the United Nations[1].

For other purposes again, it is appropriate to group public corporations with public authorities and draw a distinction between the private and public sectors of the economy:

> Private sector:
>> Personal sector
>> Companies
> Public sector:
>> Public corporations
>> Central government
>> Local authorities
> Overseas sector

Although the public corporations are productive enterprises and are run largely independently of the government, their financial affairs are interlocked with those of the government and their policy is affected by political and social considerations which do not have the same significance for privately owned productive enterprises. Sections of the Blue Book give tables summarising the transactions of public authorities and the public sector, and these tables are described in a separate chapter of this book.

A slightly different division of sectors is also necessary for the analysis of financial flows, when the activities of financial intermediaries and those providing financial services need to be distinguished from those of other productive enterprises. The division of sectors then used in the United Kingdom accounts is:

> Personal sector
> Industrial and commercial companies
> Financial companies
> Public sector
> Overseas sector

No attempt is made at present to distinguish the activities of financial intermediaries within the personal sector, such as stock jobbers and brokers. Financial companies are further sub-divided into:

> Banks
> Other financial institutions

and, on occasion, other financial institutions are further subdivided to show separately the transactions of insurance companies and superannuation funds.

Personal sector

The accounts for the personal sector record primarily the transactions of households and individuals considered as final consumers. The transactions of the other domestic sectors also record, in the last resort, the economic activities of individuals, but of individuals acting as members of collective enterprises and

---

[1] *A System of National Accounts and Supporting Tables*, United Nations (New York, 1964).

institutions. In practice, however, it is impossible to isolate entirely the transactions of households and individuals as such, and the personal sector includes
certain other elements.

The income of the personal sector necessarily includes the whole income (after
deducting trading expenses) of self-employed individuals such as farmers, professional people and individual traders and partnerships. It would be preferable, of course, to separate the transactions of such unincorporated businesses
from the purely personal transactions of their proprietors. Indeed, in every
unincorporated business for which adequate books are kept (especially for
partnerships), some attempt is made to distinguish between the income taken
out of the business by the proprietor or the partners and the income retained in
the business. In practice, it is impossible to obtain comprehensive data, or even
reliable sample data, which would make such a division possible in the national
accounts. But even if accounting data were available, it is open to question
whether the resulting division between 'distributed' and 'undistributed' income,
which must rest on an inherently arbitrary statement of transactions within the
business, would have real significance for economic analysis. Consequently, the
saving of self-employed persons, which is a substantial element in the total
saving of the personal sector, necessarily includes an indistinguishable amount
of saving reinvested in the business by the proprietor which, in the case of a
company, would be regarded as undistributed profit. This extension of the
personal sector affects primarily the capital account. The current expenditure of
the personal sector is very close to what would normally be understood as
personal or consumers' expenditure; but its capital account includes a substantial element of productive, or business, transactions.

The personal sector also includes private non-profit-making bodies serving
persons, such as universities, certain private schools, churches, charities and
social clubs. It would be preferable to treat these bodies as a separate sector
but the necessary information is not available; failing this, they must be regarded
as 'collective persons'. Further, the life funds of life assurance companies and
the funds of occupational superannuation schemes are regarded as the collective
property of the policy holders and members of the schemes. Again, a number of
items in the personal sector accounts are affected and alternative treatments
might be adopted. A separate account for these funds is given in the Blue Book.

Companies

Companies are privately controlled corporate enterprises resident in the United
Kingdom. Together with public corporations, they comprise the bulk of productive enterprises. The remaining productive enterprises consist of unincorporated businesses, which are included in the personal sector, and trading enterprises within the central government and local authority sectors. A separate
sector is established for companies, rather than for all privately owned productive enterprises, because of the difficulties described above in distinguishing
between the business income and personal income of proprietors of unincorporated enterprises.

The company sector includes some productive enterprises which provide
financial services and act as financial intermediaries. In analysing the financial
transactions of the various sectors it is necessary to separate the transactions
of these intermediaries and the company sector is therefore divided between
industrial and commercial companies and financial companies. Financial

companies comprise companies within the industry classification 'Insurance, banking and finance' with the exception of property companies, which deal in physical assets rather than financial assets. They are divided into three groups:

(a) *Banking sector*. This sector comprises the United Kingdom offices of three main groups of banks: deposit banks; accepting houses and overseas banks; and the discount market. They are distinguished from other financial institutions mainly because deposits with them are regarded as forming part of the money supply.

(b) *Insurance companies and superannuation funds*. Although the life funds of life assurance companies and the funds of superannuation schemes are regarded as the collective property of their policy holders and members of the schemes within the personal sector, the various financial transactions of the funds are attributed to financial companies. The net increase in the funds, which is part of the saving of the personal sector, is regarded as a financial asset of the personal sector and a liability of the company sector, which provides funds for companies to invest. These financial transactions are a very important part of the total transactions of financial companies and are therefore shown separately in some tables.

(c) *Other financial institutions*. These comprise the remaining financial companies.

Public corporations

Public corporations have controlled a sizeable proportion of the United Kingdom economy since the nationalisations of 1945-1951. They differ on the one hand from companies in that they are not privately controlled and their aims may not include the maximisation of their profits. They differ on the other hand from public trading departments in their relative financial independence and freedom from detailed control by the government. However, the distinction between public corporations and other public enterprises is not always clear-cut; for example, the Atomic Energy Authority might have been regarded as a public corporation rather than as part of the central government. There have also been some changes in classification, notably that of the Post Office in April 1961 when its financial arrangements were altered. Changes in the scope of the company sector and the public corporations sector as a result of successive acts of nationalisation and denationalisation must be kept in mind; for some purposes it is more appropriate to combine the two sectors. A list of public corporations is given in the annex to Chapter VIII.

Central government

The central government sector is defined in a wide sense. Besides the various departments of the government of the United Kingdom and the Northern Ireland government, it includes various funds for which separate accounts are kept. In particular, it includes the National Insurance Funds, of which the income and expenditure are determined by the central government. It also includes a number of publicly constituted boards and the like, which, while not government departments in the ordinary sense, are financially dependent upon and effectively controlled in major matters by the government. Important examples are the regional hospital boards and the Atomic Energy Authority.

Also included are certain productive or trading enterprises financed directly
from the accounts of the central government, such as the Forestry Commission
and the Royal Ordnance Factories.

Local authorities

This sector consists of all local government authorities which have power to
raise funds by means of rates or levies. It includes all levels of administrative
authorities and also local authorities with special functions such as river boards,
water boards and so on. The trading activities of local authorities are included
in this sector. By far the most important is the provision of housing, but there
are also other trading activities such as water supply and passenger transport.

Overseas sector

The accounts for the rest of the world cover the transactions of non-residents
with residents of the United Kingdom. The detailed definition of residents is
discussed on pages 436 to 438. The accounts for this sector are essentially the
transactions shown in the balance of payments accounts.

Other subdivisions

It will be realised that each of these sectors represents a very large and not in
fact wholly homogeneous group of individuals, enterprises or institutions. Much
further subdivision can be imagined, and could usefully be presented in a systematic way were the information available. For example, it would be highly
desirable to divide the personal sector between income groups or by social class
and to separate the private non-profit-making bodies serving persons. Again, the
company sector might be divided between large and small firms or between
quoted and unquoted companies. National accounts could also be devised for
particular geographical areas. The overseas sector could be divided by regions,
in a similar way to the analysis of the official statistics of the balance of payments.

   Productive enterprises may be divided by industry, and a good deal of industry
analysis is presented in the Blue Book. However, the published industrial analyses
generally cut across sector boundaries and relate to productive enterprises in
all sectors. Insufficient information is available to provide a complete set of
accounts for each industry, but this is in any case generally of less interest than
the industry analysis for all sectors combined.

TYPES OF ACCOUNT

Traditionally three main kinds of account have been used in national income
accounting, corresponding to the three functions into which economic activity
may be divided: production, consumption and adding to wealth. For each
function there is a particular kind of account, and these accounts are not very
different from the types of account used in business accounting, which are
similarly described.

Economic function	*Type of account*
Production	Production, or operating, or trading account
Consumption	Income and expenditure, or current, or appropriation account
Adding to wealth	Capital, or saving and investment account

The alternative names given to the same type of account have little special significance. In addition, a fourth type of account is also included in the United Kingdom accounts: the financial account which deals with transactions in financial assets. These transactions may be included in the capital account but it is often convenient to show them in a separate account as they deal with transactions in financial assets and liabilities as opposed to physical assets.

It is formally possible to establish each of these four accounts for each sector of the economy and for the economy as a whole. The United Kingdom statistics do not provide a set of accounts which is complete in this way, both because the information is not available and because the accounts are not all of equal interest and importance. A brief description of the types of account is given below.

Production account

This account corresponds roughly to the trading account of a firm. The main elements on the expenditure side are the current costs of production such as materials, rent, cost of services, wages and salaries, and taxes on expenditure. The receipts side comprises principally the receipts from current sales together with any subsidies received and any additions to the value of stocks and work in progress. The balance is trading profits. All factor incomes originate on the expenditure side or in the trading profits shown on a production account.

The production account is clearly appropriate only to an enterprise. A production account could, however, be constructed for the personal sector or for public authorities as well as for the company sector and public corporations since, as shown above, these sectors include a certain proportion of enterprises. In the statistics for the United Kingdom, the only individual sector for which a separate production account is at present shown is public corporations, mainly because of lack of the necessary information for other sectors. However, the main table of aggregate national income and expenditure (Table 1 of the 1967 Blue Book) is in effect a production account for the United Kingdom as a whole. This table may be regarded as summarising the activity of the economy considered as a giant enterprise: it shows, in consolidated form, the expenditure incurred on purchasing the services of all factors of production and the receipts in the form of sales to final purchasers (the different forms of final expenditure). Hence the factor incomes received by each sector may be regarded as flowing from the production account of the economy as a whole.

Production accounts for institutional sectors of the economy are of less interest than those for individual industries or groups of industries. Each sector includes productive enterprises of very varied kinds but the production accounts of enterprises within an industry are more similar and the production account for an industry shows up significant relationships. Input-output tables bring together production accounts for individual industries and show the relationships between them. Input-output tables are not prepared for each year as part of the regular national accounts of the United Kingdom, both because their preparation requires much detailed information and because they are not a necessary step in compiling the national income accounts. However, the input-output tables which have been published are fully integrated with the national income accounts, so that the relationships can be followed through to the national accounts. Primary inputs (that is, those inputs which are not the outputs of any other industry) and final demand are defined in the same way as in the

B

national income accounts and the industry groups correspond to those used in the national income statistics. Fully detailed official input-output tables for the United Kingdom have been published for only one year—1954[2]. More detailed tables will be published for 1963 and the 1967 Blue Book included a summary input-output table for that year, a short description of which is given in Chapter IV. It is proposed to construct detailed input-output tables at more frequent intervals in the future.

Income and expenditure account

The income (or trading profits) derived from the production account of a trading enterprise is carried into its income and expenditure account. In the case of a corporate enterprise this is better described as an appropriation account, in which the receipts of income, both from its own production account and from other sources, such as investments, are shown as distributed to the shareholders, the debt-holders, or, in taxes, to the government. What remains, the undistributed profit, is the enterprise's saving. The sectors which consist wholly of productive enterprises (the company sector and the public corporations sector) show no current purchases of goods and services on income and expenditure account since such enterprises are not regarded as final consumers. Their expenditure consists wholly in the redistribution of income by transfer payments of interest and dividends or grants, or by taxes. The purchases of goods and services of a productive enterprise are wholly on production account or on capital account.

The analogous income and expenditure account of persons may appear different in content, mainly because the relative importance of the items is very different, but most of the entries are basically similar. Income includes the trading profits of unincorporated enterprises and the factor income of employed persons, income from employment. Some income is also received from investments but in addition other current transfers, mainly grants from the government, are an important source of income. There is a big difference on the expenditure side because persons are final consumers and the bulk of the outlay is devoted to consumers' expenditure. Payments of interest are much less important and in the United Kingdom accounts, as often elsewhere, they are not shown as part of expenditure, but income from interest is estimated net of these payments. The other important item in expenditure is taxes and a balance of saving remains.

The income and expenditure account of public authorities brings in as income only a small amount of trading profits and the main receipts are taxes. The bulk of the outgoings consists of current expenditure on goods and services (final expenditure) and transfer payments, the latter going chiefly to the personal sector. Again a balance of saving, which is sometimes negative, remains.

Income and expenditure accounts are drawn up for all the main domestic sectors in the United Kingdom statistics. Each results in an excess (or a deficit) of current income over current outgoings which is carried forward as a form of saving (or dis-saving) to the capital account.

Capital account

The sum of the saving of each sector carried from the income and expenditure account to the capital account represents the total of national saving available

[2]*Input-Output Tables for the United Kingdom, 1954*, Studies in Official Statistics: No. 8, (1961).

for adding to wealth. The capital account for the nation as a whole shows the sum of saving of the several domestic sectors as a receipt, together with any net capital transfers received from the rest of the world. The total receipts are balanced by the additions to wealth, both in the form of physical assets (fixed assets or stocks) and financial assets, in the form of financial claims on the rest of the world.

The capital account for each sector shows as receipts the saving on its income and expenditure account, capital transfers received both from other domestic sectors and from overseas and financial liabilities contracted to other sectors. This is balanced by capital transfers paid, the increase in the sector's physical assets, and financial assets acquired in the form of claims on other sectors.

It is often convenient to restrict the capital account to the acquisition of physical assets and to show only one net item for financial assets acquired *less* liabilities contracted. This is the balance of capital receipts over capital payments. Financial transactions are then shown separately in the financial account, which is discussed below. This practice is followed in the Blue Book for the personal and company sectors but the capital accounts for public corporations, central government and local authorities also include details of financial transactions. Conceptually, the sum of the net acquisition of financial assets for the domestic sectors is equal to the net acquisition of financial claims on the rest of the world. For convenience, physical assets held abroad are included with financial assets and the sum of the net acquisition of financial assets for all sectors is then equal to net investment abroad.

Financial account

The net acquisition of financial assets is the balance carried forward from the sector capital account to the sector financial account. Conceptually, the sum of each sector's transactions in financial assets and liabilities is equal to this balance. The financial account shows the change in various financial liabilities, such as borrowing, the issue of securities, and trade debt; and in various financial assets such as loans made, deposits with banks and holdings of stocks and shares. Financial assets are in every case balanced by a corresponding liability. When the country is considered as a whole, financial transactions between residents cancel out and only transactions between residents and non-residents remain.

Financial assets are classified primarily according to the character of the asset, such as whether it is short or long-term and whether or not it is marketable, but the nature of the sector issuing the asset is also important and in most cases can be identified. Overseas assets are generally classified on a sector basis because of their importance in considering international capital movements. The classification of financial assets is described in detail in Chapter XIV. The financial account for each sector shows the net transactions in each type of asset and no attempt is made to show the individual sectors between which the transaction takes place. For marketable securities the matching of individual sellers and buyers, who may or may not be in different sectors, is in any case largely a matter of chance.

The Blue Book system of accounts

The system of sector accounts shown in the Blue Book is summarised in the table on the next page. In addition, current and capital accounts are given for public authorities and current, capital and financial accounts for the public sector.

The system of national accounts

Table numbers relate to the 1967 Blue Book

	Type of account			
	Production	Income and expenditure	Capital	Financial
United Kingdom	Table 1 rearranged as on page 62	Table 1 with the addition of current international transfers	Table 6	Table 79
Personal sector		Tables 2 and 22 (income and expenditure account)	Table 23	Table 74
Companies		Table 30[1]	Table 31	Tables 75, 76 and 77
Public corporations	Table 36 (operating account)	Table 37[1] / Table 3[1]	Table 38	
Central government		Tables 4 and 41 (current account)	Table 42	
Local authorities		Tables 5 and 45 (current account)	Table 46	
Overseas sector	Table 7 (international transactions)			Table 79

[1]Appropriation account.

A single account is given in the Blue Book for international transactions, combining elements of a production account (imports and exports of goods and services which generate factor incomes in the rest of the world or in the United Kingdom, respectively); elements of an income and expenditure account (income from profits or property, and current transfers, paid or received); and elements of a capital account (net investment abroad and capital transfers). For consistency with the rest of the national accounts, the account of international transactions should be presented as the account of the rest of the world with the United Kingdom. Thus United Kingdom exports should be treated as payments, being expenditure by the rest of the world generating factor incomes in the United Kingdom in the same way as expenditure by United Kingdom consumers generates factor incomes. United Kingdom imports should appear as receipts, being expenditure by the United Kingdom generating factor incomes in other countries. However, for convenience the account is presented from the United Kingdom point of view and United Kingdom credits are shown first as receipts from the rest of the world, and are followed by debits as payments to the rest of the world.

A separate table shows international financial transactions. This is presented as the account of the rest of the world with the United Kingdom. It is also the financial account for the United Kingdom as a whole.

Balance sheets

For a complete accounting system, the accounts of transactions in a particular period need to be supplemented by balance sheets showing the assets and liabilities held at the beginning and end of the period of account. The income arising in any period and the additions to wealth in that period can then be related to the stock of assets held at the outset. The balance sheet for the whole economy shows the stock of physical assets, in the form of fixed assets and stocks of materials, work in progress and unsold goods, and financial assets and liabilities in the form of financial claims on and liabilities to the rest of the world. The balance sheet for a sector shows in addition the financial claims on and liabilities to the other sectors of the economy.

The compilation of national and sector balance sheets has developed more slowly and less comprehensively than that of accounts of the corresponding flows. It is complicated by the problems of valuation of assets. The estimates have to allow not only for the depreciation of fixed assets from wear and tear in their use, but also for changes in valuation arising from changes in prices. The market value of financial assets in particular may change considerably over time. For comparability with the various accounts of transactions, the initial assets need to be valued at current market values. In order to reconcile assets held at the outset with additions to wealth in the period and assets held at the end of the period it is necessary to take account of appreciation and depreciation of assets during the period of account.

The Blue Book does not contain full national or sector balance sheets. However, it does contain estimates for the stocks of physical assets other than land. Estimates are given of the net capital stock of fixed assets at current replacement cost for each sector of the economy. The capital stock of fixed assets at constant replacement cost is also analysed by industry. These estimates are described in Chapter XII. The book value of stocks of materials, fuel, work in progress and unsold goods is also given by sector and by industry. The book value differs from the current replacement value in that goods will frequently be valued at their purchase price and, depending upon the period for which stocks are held, this will in part relate to the prices of earlier periods. However, the difference is usually small and would normally be well within the margin of error of the book value figures. The annual publication *United Kingdom Balance of Payments* includes estimates of United Kingdom external assets and liabilities. There are also various estimates of holdings of financial assets by certain sectors and institutions which are published in *Financial Statistics*. The available information, both official and unofficial, has been brought together by Revell and his associates who have compiled both national and sector balance sheets for the United Kingdom for the years 1957 to 1961[3].

TYPES OF TRANSACTION

As pointed out on page 20, transactions, or money flows, may be divided between requited and unrequited payments. Each group may be further subdivided by reference to the purpose of the payment and the circumstances in which it is made. Thus requited payments may be divided between payments for goods and services, payments to factors of production (wages, salaries, profits or rental income) and payments for financial assets (loans, securities, money claims, etc.). Some types of transaction may occur either on current or on capital account, according to their nature; for example, purchases of goods and services may be on current account (consumption) or on capital account (adding to wealth in the form of physical assets). Considerations of this sort suggest the following classification of transactions, which may be imputed, showing also the types of account in which they may feature:

Type of transaction	*Accounts in which appearing*
Requited payments	
Purchases and sales of goods and services	Production, income and expenditure, capital, international
Payments to factors of production	Production, income and expenditure
Payments for financial assets	Capital, financial
Capital consumption	Production, capital
Unrequited payments (*or transfers*)	
Taxes on expenditure	Production, income and expenditure, capital, international
Subsidies	Production, income and expenditure
Interest and dividends	Income and expenditure, international
Grants	Income and expenditure, capital, international
Taxes on income	Income and expenditure, international
Taxes on capital	Capital, international
Saving	Income and expenditure, capital, international
Net acquisition of financial assets	Capital, financial, international

This classification of transactions runs through the whole system of national income tables and the different types of flows are normally distinguished in each table. The main principles of the classification should be clear from the earlier discussion. Their detailed application to the transactions of each sector is explained in later chapters.

---

[3]Jack Revell assisted by Graham Hockley and John Moyle, *The Wealth of the Nation*, Cambridge University Press, 1967.

The articulation of national accounts

It is evident that each payment from an account is also a receipt in another account. For example, the payment of personal income tax appears on the payments side of the personal income and expenditure account and as a receipt in the central government current account. Wages are paid from the United Kingdom production account to the personal income and expenditure account. A few transactions, such as payments by households to domestic servants and the imputed rent of owner-occupied houses, appear as payments and receipts in the same account, but this is because the income and expenditure account of the personal sector (like that of public authorities) incorporates elements which should more strictly be transferred to production accounts. A system of national accounts in which every payment reappears as an identifiable receipt in another account is said to be *articulated*. Articulation is helpful to the estimator and to the understanding of the national accounts. However, it is essential neither to the formulation nor to the presentation of the accounts. Complete articulation is often impossible in practice because of lack of information and the detailed inter-sector flows are often of much less interest than the total flows between one sector and all other sectors combined. The United Kingdom accounts are only partly articulated. In particular, no attempt is made to present articulated financial accounts.

Relation of national accounts to commercial and other accounts

The national accounts, of course, resemble the accounts kept for their own purposes by the individuals, enterprises and institutions which make up the sectors. Thus the central government keeps for administrative and Parliamentary purposes a large number of accounts of different kinds. Individual local authorities keep revenue and capital accounts which are aggregated, with relatively minor adjustments, to form the relevant parts of the national accounts. Public corporations publish accounts annually, and companies deposit with the Registrar of Companies their appropriation accounts and balance sheets. In many cases, however, these accounts do not give the items required for national accounting purposes, or are insufficiently comprehensive. There are other cases where no accounts exist at all, or at least are not available to the estimator, for example, the income and expenditure transactions of private households. Parts of the national accounts thus represent not a summation of records actually kept but a reconstruction of what such a summation would contain if accounts were kept on certain principles. The estimator must frequently decide what kinds of transactions to include in any particular account.

In making decisions of this kind it has always to be borne in mind that the ultimate purpose of the statistics is to measure quantities which are of significance for economic analysis. For this purpose transactions must be defined and classified not on purely formal criteria but in such a way as to group together transactions which are essentially similar in their nature, causes or effects. It is recognised, however, that no single accounting framework is likely to be ideal for all kinds of analysis or in all circumstances. The purpose of the accounting framework is to provide a convenient, consistent and orderly method of presenting a mass of statistical information. But it is important that enough detail should be shown to enable the user to make such alternative arrangements of the data as may seem useful for the solution of particular problems.

Chapter III

National Income and Expenditure Estimates: General Review

1. INCOME AND EXPENDITURE AT CURRENT PRICES

In subsequent chapters a fairly detailed description will be found of the sources and methods used for the various categories of income, product and expenditure. The statistical structure is essentially synthetic; in building it up, a great variety of statistical sources, both official and unofficial, is drawn upon. The quality of the resulting figures can be judged only by reference to the quality of their component parts, bearing in mind however that at many points checks can be applied because of the inter-relationships of the concepts measured. The present chapter gives only a summary review of the sources and of the ways in which they are used.

One of the major objects of the system of national income and expenditure statistics is to throw light on the inter-relationships between various forms of economic activity—for example, between profits and capital formation, between the balance of payments and consumers' expenditure, between personal savings and personal disposable income. It may indeed be maintained that the study of these inter-relationships is more important than a knowledge of the aggregates; little is gained by precise knowledge of the size of the gross national product, although it is important to have accurate information about changes in it from year to year and about changes in its make-up. The importance of the study of inter-relationships means that internal consistency between the sources used for different items in the accounts is a major consideration in the choice and use of data and in any judgment about the reliability of the conclusions drawn from the information.

From the conceptual identities brought out in Chapter I, it is clear that the major aggregates of national income and national expenditure may be approached by estimating output, income or expenditure. Until the 1930's it was necessary to rely almost wholly on estimates of income. The early work of Bowley and Stamp[1] was based very largely on income data, especially wage statistics and tax assessments. A different approach was made by Flux[2], using estimates of industrial output from the census of production. The first attempt to reconcile aggregates derived from income data with independent estimates of the components of final expenditure was made by Clark.[3]

---

[1] A. L. Bowley, *The Division of the Product of Industry*, 1919. A. L. Bowley and Josiah Stamp, *The National Income 1924*, 1927.

[2] A. W. Flux, 'The National Income', *Journal of the Royal Statistical Society*, Vol. XCII, Part 1, 1929. A similar estimate is made in the *Report of the Census of Production 1907*, Cd. 6320.

[3] Colin Clark, *National Income and Outlay*, 1937.

The series of official estimates which began in 1941 [4] was based primarily on income data although items of expenditure other than capital formation (both in fixed assets and stocks) were directly estimated. It was only at the beginning of the 1950's—mainly because of the development of new sources of information about expenditure on fixed assets and stocks—that it became possible in the official estimates to use basically independent sources for all, or almost all, forms of income and of expenditure. Some of these estimates, especially those for certain categories of stocks, are still rough and unsatisfactory.

Estimates of income

Statistics based on tax assessments are the major source of the annual statistics of income. This source has always been very extensively drawn upon in British national income statistics for non-wage incomes, especially since its use was developed in the early work of Lord Stamp. [5] The low tax exemption limit (the effective limit from 1965/66 to 1967/68 was £283 per annum) brings almost all income earners within the field of review for income tax. The development by the Inland Revenue of the statistical analysis of the tax assessment records has made possible a very substantial extension of the detail which can be derived from these records and of the accuracy with which they can be adapted to national income concepts. Thus Inland Revenue tax data are the source for the estimates of company profits, of most of the income from self-employment, of part of rent income, and of *aggregate* wages and salaries.

In total, about three-quarters of the annual estimate of gross national product from the income side, that is the estimate of factor incomes, is derived from tax assessment data.

The Inland Revenue data on *wages and salaries* provide both quarterly and annual information as PAYE deductions are made throughout the year. The annual data are supplemented by various other sources. As tax data can be analysed only by financial units and not by establishments, they do not permit as satisfactory a division of income by industries as the statistics of wage and salary payments in the detailed censuses of production, and the statistics of average earnings and numbers employed collected by the Ministry of Labour. These latter sources are therefore used to provide an industrial analysis of the total. They are also used, together with the census of population, for making separate estimates of wages and salaries. Supplementary information on employment incomes in specific industries can also be drawn from other sources, such as the accounts of the central government and the census of distribution.

Tax assessment data for *profit incomes* provide only annual estimates and are not available for the latest periods. Other and less comprehensive data are used for making quarterly and recent annual estimates of profit incomes. The main supplementary source of information on company trading profits is the quarterly sample inquiry made by the Inland Revenue. In addition, forecasts of profits for their latest accounting years are provided by certain companies and preliminary reports on assessments are made by tax inspectors. The supplementary data on income from self-employment is much weaker; no quarterly figures are available

---

[4] *An Analysis of the Sources of War Finance and an Estimate of the National Income and Expenditure in 1938 and 1940*, Cmd. 6261.

[5] Josiah Stamp, *British Incomes and Property*, 1916.

B*

and only a relatively small proportion of unincorporated businesses is covered by forecasts or preliminary reports.

Statistics of the trading surplus of public corporations are taken from their published accounts and quarterly estimates are based on returns made by the major corporations. The annual trading surplus of central government and local authority trading enterprises is taken from their trading accounts. Quarterly figures for the central government trading surplus are based on departmental returns and for local authorities smooth quarterly changes are assumed.

Part of the estimate of income from rent is taken from the rent element of the estimate of consumers' expenditure on housing which is now based on the Family Expenditure Survey. Tax assessment data are also used in estimating the rent income of the private sector. The rent income of the central government and local authorities is estimated from their accounts. The rent income of farmers is estimated by the agricultural departments from the sources used for calculating the income of farmers. The quarterly estimates of rent income are very largely interpolated and projected.

The estimates of property income from abroad are taken from the balance of payments accounts and are based on a variety of sources, including the Board of Trade inquiry into overseas direct investment, government accounts, Bank of England records and information supplied by oil companies.

While the annual estimates of factor incomes are based mainly on tax assessments, the estimates of transfer incomes draw upon a variety of sources. The figures of receipts of interest and dividends which involve the public sector are taken mainly from accounting data and departmental returns. Estimates of receipts by companies are to a large extent built up from estimates of holdings of financial assets and interest rates. The net receipts by the personal sector are estimated as a residual from estimates of the receipts and payments of all other sectors. The other important transfer incomes are grants from public authorities to the personal sector, such as national insurance benefits; this part of personal income is based on central government and local authority accounting data and departmental returns.

Estimates of expenditure

In contrast to the estimates of factor income, estimates of final expenditure are necessarily based on a large variety of sources; consequently there is less assurance of internal consistency.

The sources used for estimates of *consumers' expenditure*, in particular, are very heterogeneous. For expenditure on food, the two major sources are the regular sample surveys of household expenditure on food conducted by the Ministry of Agriculture, Fisheries and Food (the National Food Survey) and detailed statistics, compiled by the same Ministry, relating to supplies of the main foodstuffs which are expressed originally in quantities and valued mainly at average values taken from the National Food Survey. For expenditure on alcoholic drink, Customs and Excise data are used. The estimates of expenditure on tobacco are based on trade sources. For clothing, household goods and a number of other commodities, retail sales statistics compiled by the Board of Trade are used; the method is usually to derive a base-year estimate from census of distribution statistics, adjusted to include direct sales to consumers by wholesalers and manufacturers and to exclude sales to businesses and public authorities, and to use the sample of returns made monthly to estimate changes from the base period. The same method is used for expenditure on catering and on motor vehicles, the estimates being based on the special Board of Trade inquiries into these trades.

Estimates of expenditure on fuel and light, travel, communication services and entertainment draw heavily on the information collected by the departments responsible for the regular published statistics. For a number of other goods and services, the Family Expenditure Survey is used. A number of other methods— some being little more than conjectural—are used for other forms of consumers' expenditure.

Certain general points may be observed about these estimates of consumers' expenditure. Firstly, it will be realised that the data used do not all refer strictly to expenditure by consumers—that is, generally, to retail sales. Some series for food and the series for alcoholic drink relate to supplies coming forward at some earlier stage, mainly farm and manufacturing output and withdrawals from bond. Thus changes in the series used may sometimes reflect changes in the stocks held in the distributive chain beyond the point of recording, rather than genuine changes in consumers' expenditure, and there may be errors in timing. Secondly, a proportion of many classes of consumer goods and services is bought on business account and must not be included in consumers' expenditure; the basis for an accurate estimate of such business purchases rarely exists but an estimate must be made when, as frequently happens, the original data relate to the total expenditure on a particular class of goods or services. Any expenditure by public authorities has similarly to be excluded. Thirdly, the use of a variety of independent sources increases the risk of overlapping or of omissions; errors in one item are not necessarily compensated in other items as they are when an overall measure of total expenditure is used. Overlapping or omissions may arise, for example, where Board of Trade statistics are used to provide estimates of expenditure on commodities in the base year, while subsequent changes in expenditure are estimated from changes in sales by individual kinds of business. The second and third of these factors will generally have less effect on the estimates of year-to-year changes than on the general level of consumers' expenditure.

The estimates of *fixed capital formation* and of changes in *stocks and work in progress* are more homogeneous. For private industry the major sources are the annual censuses of production, and the annual inquiries into the distributive and service trades carried out by the Board of Trade. Quarterly sample inquiries provide the basis for the quarterly figures and of the latest annual estimates before the results of the annual inquiries become available. The annual inquiries are supplemented by more detailed information when there is a detailed census of production, a census of distribution or a more detailed inquiry for a particular industry.

For private industry outside the field of these inquiries however, various sources, some far from satisfactory, must be used. The main private fixed capital formation not covered by the inquiries is in dwellings. The level of these estimates is based on an estimate of expenditure derived from numbers of houses under construction and average prices, and the changes are based on estimates of building output obtained from returns made by contractors. For the public sector, the estimates of capital formation by the central government, local authorities and public corporations are all based on their accounts; for the most recent periods and for changes within the year, departmental returns are used.

The estimates of capital formation thus rest heavily on accounting data about expenditure. Such data, being derived basically from the same records as the statistics of profits, are most likely to afford consistency between the income and expenditure estimates. This is particularly important because of the interest taken in the relationships between profits and fixed capital formation. On the other hand, reliance on accounting data means that the definition of fixed capital formation depends on the accounting conventions used and no very clear classification can be given of the types of assets which are treated, at the margin, as capital goods.

The statistics of *public authorities' current expenditure on goods and services* are also based on accounting data and departmental returns. Estimates for the central government are derived from the various Exchequer and departmental accounts. But the very detailed and accurate basic data must be extensively rearranged to fit the concepts used in the national income accounts. Much the same applies to the estimates of local authority expenditure which are summarised in *Local Government Financial Statistics*, although the basic data provided are in this case both less detailed and in some respects closer to the national accounting categories required. The rearrangement in both cases involves elements of estimation at certain points.

The statistics of *exports* and *imports of goods and services* are taken from the balance of payments accounts. Exports and imports of goods are based on the *Trade Accounts* figures of the value of goods leaving and entering the United Kingdom, with certain adjustments in respect of valuation and coverage to obtain figures on the required basis. The estimates of exports and imports of services are based on a variety of sources, the main ones being the government accounts, Bank of England records, shipping and civil aviation statistics, the Board of Trade's International Travel Survey and the series of inquiries conducted by the Board of Trade into the overseas transactions of United Kingdom companies.

The estimates of expenditure on transfers are built up from a variety of sources. Payments of interest and dividends made by the public sector are based mainly on accounting data and departmental returns. Dividend payments by companies are based on Inland Revenue data supplemented by information from the Stock Exchange Council. Interest payments by companies are estimated partly from statistics of holdings and interest rates. No complete estimate is available of payments by the personal sector, although estimates are made of certain items.

The other main current transfer payments concern public authorities and the estimates are based on accounting data and departmental returns. These are the tax payments by the various sectors to public authorities and grants made by public authorities to the personal sector. Where it is necessary to allocate total payments of taxes on income between different sectors, or to differentiate between the tax actually paid in a year and the tax liability in respect of the income arising in the same period, special estimates are made by the Inland Revenue.

The stage at which transactions are recorded

The general question of the point in time at which transactions ought to be recorded may be of considerable importance for interpreting individual series and for achieving internal consistency between the various estimates. The sale of an article involves the placing of the order by the buyer, the delivery of the article, the rendering of an account by the seller, and the actual payment by the buyer; these operations often take place on different—sometimes widely different—dates. It is necessary therefore to decide which of these events is to count as the transaction for the purpose of the national accounts, since it is clear that in any given period the value of transactions on one basis will not necessarily be the same as on another. Further, the same basis should be adopted throughout the accounts, so that the various transactions are mutually consistent. Even so, in practice difficulties arise because transactions are not recorded simultaneously as a receipt and as a payment, even when both are on one basis: transmission of orders and payments takes time and middlemen cause delays.

In practice, the choice is generally between two bases of accounting—the cash (or payments and receipts) basis, on which transactions are recorded when money passes; and the accruals (or payable-receivable) basis, on which transactions are recorded when the expenditure is incurred. The principle adopted in the national accounts is, so far as possible, to record transactions as taking place at the time when the expenditure is incurred. This is the principle required for estimation of the gross domestic product and the other national income aggregates. The national income is a measure of the goods and services becoming available. It is more appropriate for the components of final expenditure to reflect demands made on these goods and services and for the factor incomes to represent amounts arising from the production of these goods and services rather than to show the cash flows in the period. The difference between accruals and cash payments is then regarded as a financial transaction, reflecting changes in debits and credits. For transfers, cash flows are more often used because the national income aggregates are not affected and the presentation is also more simple.

The adoption of the accruals principle creates certain difficulties. Indeed, since the information most easily available for different groups of transactions is not itself on a uniform basis, the adoption of any one principle is bound to raise problems of adjustment in some part of the field. However, the number of points at which serious difficulty arises is fairly limited. Information derived from commercial accounts, such as company profits, is already in substance on the desired basis because the payable-receivable basis is that mainly used in ordinary commercial accounting. In other cases, such as wages, although the available information generally relates to cash payments, there is no reason to believe that there is frequently any large difference between one basis of measurement and another. One difficult case is that of government purchases of goods and services (other than payments of wages and salaries). For reasons connected with the maintenance of Parliamentary control, the main accounts of the central government are recorded entirely on a cash basis (see page 255). Trading accounts on a commercial basis are indeed available for government trading activities and are used in the national accounts in preference to the cash accounts whenever possible; but for most of the expenditure by the central government, records are available only on a cash basis. When there are known to be marked differences between the timing of the cash transactions in the government accounts and the recording of transactions in the accounts of other sectors, adjustments have been made to the government accounting figures.

Difficulty also arises over the recording of capital expenditure on fixed assets. For certain classes of asset, in particular building work, the construction of the asset extends over a considerable period. The problem is to ensure that the amount of work done during the accounting period, which generates factor income, is matched either by capital expenditure on the part of the purchaser (which can generally be taken to include progress payments), or by an increase in work in progress on the part of the producer, without duplication or omission. With the information available, the consistency is necessarily imperfect.

Inconsistencies may also arise from the means of recording imports and exports. These are normally included in the balance of payments accounts when they enter or leave the United Kingdom, and generally no adjustment is made for timing differences between the declaration of trade by importers and exporters and the time of change in ownership. In particular, for imports there may be differences between the time when goods are included in the estimates of stock-building and when they are counted as imports, and between the time when expenditure on imported fixed assets is charged to capital account, which may be when progress payments are made, and the time when they are counted as imports. Corresponding timing discrepancies may occur with exported goods.

While the accruals principle is applied in the recording of most final expenditure and factor income, it is less generally applied to transfers. All transfers in which the central government is concerned are recorded on a cash basis in the government accounts and, as far as possible, the transactions are recorded at the same time in the accounts of other sectors. The estimates of tax payments are, however, supplemented by annual estimates of tax accruals in the period. Dividends are also included when they are paid and the figures are supplemented by annual estimates of additions to dividend reserves by the corporate sector. Other interest payments are, however, recorded on an accruals basis and, for example, interest on bank deposits and on deposits with building societies, is assumed to be earned throughout the period of the deposit.

The extent of the inconsistency arising from the use of differing bases of accounting may not be very serious for periods as long as a year, except perhaps when there are marked changes in trend in the components. But the presence of such inconsistencies is relatively more important for the quarterly statistics.

Some discrepancies in timing may arise not from the method of recording but because the statistics do not relate exactly to the national accounting period. The national income statistics relate in principle to calendar quarters and calendar years. But, for example, the estimates of consumers' expenditure based on retail sales statistics relate to a weekly rate of expenditure which is not affected by the number of days in the calendar quarter. The PAYE returns which are used in estimating wages and salaries relate to receipts in a period of thirteen or, on occasion, fourteen weeks and the estimates may be affected by variations in the time-lag between the deduction of tax and its receipt by the Inland Revenue. The basic tax assessment data used for profit incomes relate to accounting years and so may the census of production returns which are used for annual estimates of fixed capital formation and changes in stocks and work in progress. Although the annual profits estimates take account of the variations in accounting years, the estimates of capital formation do not. It so happens that, since most accounting years end with the last or first calendar quarter, the weighted average terminal date of accounting years is near the end of the calendar year. It is nevertheless possible in certain circumstances, especially when prices change rapidly, that the results for these aggregations of accounting years may differ significantly from the actual experience during the calendar year.

The central government accounts relate to the government's financial year, ending 31 March, but most elements in the government accounts are recorded on the basis of shorter periods and reasonably good estimates can be made for calendar years.

Consistency of estimates: the residual error

It will be seen that the greater part of the statistical structure derives from three major annual sources: Inland Revenue data of tax assessments, the censuses of production and distribution and associated inquiries carried out by the Board of Trade, and the central government accounts. Each of these sources is used at many points throughout the system. These three main sources are supplemented by a variety of others. One point about the combination of these sources should be noticed. It seems reasonable to suppose that the tax assessment data and the data collected in the Board of Trade inquiries are derived from what is broadly a common method of accounting. Thus the important set of relationships between profits, fixed capital formation and changes in the value of stocks, so far as the latter two are derived from the inquiries, can be regarded as well established.

The problems of internal consistency between different types of records have an important bearing on the reconciliation between the largely independent estimates of aggregate income and aggregate expenditure. It is, of course, always possible to manipulate the least reliable estimates so that complete reconciliation of the totals is achieved; until 1953 this was always done. In view of the development of the statistical sources, it was felt, however, that it was no longer reasonable to presume that the whole discrepancy is more likely to be due to one item than to another. The error may arise, for example, not from incompleteness or inaccuracies in basic data but from an undetectable lack of simultaneity in timing which there is no reason to attribute to any one particular component. An adjustment is still made when there is reason to attribute a discrepancy to a particular item but no attempt is made to allocate all the discrepancy and the residual discrepancy between the income and expenditure estimates is shown as a *residual error*. It is presented as though it were an unknown item, positive or negative, of income. This is purely for convenience of presentation, and does not imply that the estimates of expenditure are regarded as superior in accuracy to the estimates of income.

The reliability of the estimates

It is essential that a system of statistics of national income and expenditure, or of national accounts, should be comprehensive; an estimate must be included for each item that appears in a balancing account. The estimator could not establish a system of national income statistics at all if he were compelled to restrict his presentation to those components in the system which are soundly based on accurately recorded facts. It is inevitable that the published statistics should include a number of figures for which the evidence is relatively weak. It is, however, the duty of the estimator to warn the users of the statistics about the weakness of some of the figures presented. The object is that the user should not (except at his own risk) draw substantial conclusions about the state of the economy from differences between components, or differences between one year and another in the value of a given component, when there is a good chance that such differences may be due solely to errors in estimation.

It will be clear from the summary review of the data used that it is impossible to calculate statistical margins of error of the kind that are derived from random samples for any of the aggregates or for most of their components. It is however possible, from knowledge of the data, to form very rough and mainly subjective judgments of the range of reasonable doubt attaching to the estimates. This is done in the chapters concerned with the detailed estimates. Wherever possible these judgments are standardised by the use of uniform gradings, as follows:

Margin of error

A ± less than 3 per cent
B ± 3 per cent to 10 per cent
C ± more than 10 per cent

The terms 'good', 'fair' and 'poor' are used at some points in the text and are broadly equivalent to the categories A, B and C. Like margins of error derived from random samples, these judgments do not represent absolute certainty. They may be taken to mean that, in the opinion of the estimators and in their present state of knowledge, there is, say, a 90 per cent chance that the true value of the figures referred to lies within the limits set by the grading.

It has not in fact been found possible to attach gradings to every individual series nor to apply them in a fully standardised way. A description is usually given of the reliability of the figures for the later years shown in the Blue Book. The figures for the most recent years are often preliminary estimates and thus more uncertain than the figures for earlier years and a separate assessment of the latest estimates is also given where appropriate. Generally, the figures for only the most recent year are less reliable. In some cases, however, the description of sources will show that the reliability of an estimate for a given year improves over a much longer period; for example, the statistics based on tax assessments are subject to revision for a number of years after the first provisional estimates are made. In other cases some earlier year, such as 1958, represents a benchmark year because of the taking of a detailed census. In the Blue Book summary tables the figures for the earliest years shown, generally for years before 1948, are much less reliable than those for later years because of the development of new sources of information. Also the figures for 1938 are subject to much more uncertainty than those for post-war years.

The gradings are applied to the absolute values of the various components. It is generally true to say that the absolute error in the *change* from year to year is likely to be less than might appear from the errors attached to the absolute values. Nearly always, when a figure is attributed to an item about which there is much uncertainty, consideration is paid to the probable change from the previous year. This implies that the error in the absolute figures, whatever it may be, is likely to be in the same direction in all years. The deviations between the estimates and the facts are likely to consist partly of a bias which is more or less constant from year to year, and partly of a more random element. This is another way in which the margins of error shown here differ from those attaching to random samples.

Those major aggregates of which the components are drawn from a variety of sources (such as total consumers' expenditure, or total fixed capital formation) contain some very reliable estimates and some exceedingly weak ones. The proportionate error attaching to the aggregates is likely to be less than the weighted mean of the proportionate errors attached to the components. This is so not only because the errors in the components are likely, at least in part, to offset each other, but also because the estimate of each major aggregate is to some extent controlled by the relationships between income and expenditure.

The gradings are attached to the annual figures appearing in the Blue Book. They are not necessarily any indication of the reliability of the basic statistics from which the Blue Book figures are derived. It frequently happens that a margin of error arises not in the basic statistics but in the various adjustments required to adapt the basic statistics to national accounting concepts. For example, for some items of consumers' expenditure, reliable figures exist of the total supply of a class of goods, but considerable uncertainty arises in the proportion to be attributed to consumers' expenditure and the proportion to be attributed to business purchases. Again, much of the margin of error attaching to the estimates of company profits arises not from the basic data derived from tax assessments but from the adjustments required to adapt the basic statistics to a definition consistent with the conceptual framework of the national accounts.

The gradings do not rule out the possibility of subsequent revisions resulting in new estimates differing from the old by more than the margin of error attributed here. Firstly, as pointed out above, the gradings are intended to represent a probability, suggested as 90 per cent, and not a certainty. Secondly, the gradings represent an opinion arrived at with present knowledge—that is, on the basis of all the information now available and on an appreciation of the extent of the unfilled gaps in the information. New sources of information, for example new kinds of statistical returns, may however make it apparent that the estimate of an item for some years past was even further from the truth than the estimators thought likely. For example, the first Board of Trade inquiry into the motor trades led to upward revisions to the estimates of consumers' expenditure on cars and motor cycles. Thirdly, substantial revisions are sometimes necessary because of changes in definition. Some of these are required because an internal inconsistency of definition comes to light—an element of duplication or a gap between different parts of the accounts. Other changes in definition may be made in order to achieve consistency with international conventions.

One final point must be made bearing on the reliability of the statistics. No attempt is made to round off the estimates beyond the nearest £ million. It will be evident from the discussion of the degree of reliability that many estimates, stated to the nearest £1 million, must in fact be regarded as correct only to the nearest £5 million or even, for large items, to the nearest £50 million. The choice between rounding off and apparent but often spurious precision is a matter on which different views may be held. The arguments determining the presentation in the national accounts of figures which have the appearance of more precision than the evidence warrants are: (a) the accumulation of rounding errors, which sometimes occurs when a number of rounded figures are added together, is avoided; (b) the presentation of rounded figures often distorts differences over time, or between items; (c) some of the estimates in the tables are fairly precise; if the item is small (say less than £50 million), rounding, even to the nearest £5 million, would unnecessarily distort what they show; yet if such series remained unrounded, the major aggregates of which they are components (including the national income itself) would retain an apparent precision which they do not in fact possess. In presenting figures to the nearest £ million, the rounding is always such that the components add to the total, so that the accounts balance. In particular, the quarterly estimates, both before and after seasonal adjustment, add up to the calendar year figures. Also, the rounding is made consistent throughout the sector accounts.

If these reservations are borne in mind, the following table summarising the reliability gradings of the major components may be of value. The gradings relate to the latest year. Although the estimates for the latest year are less reliable than those for earlier years, they are not sufficiently so to warrant a lower grading, except in the case of company profits which depend upon tax assessments available only after two or three years.

Reliability of annual estimates of major components at current prices

A ± less than 3 per cent
B ± 3 per cent to 10 per cent
C ± more than 10 per cent

Income:	
Income from employment:[1];	A
Income from self-employmen	B
Gross trading profits of companies	B
Trading surplus of public corporations	A
Gross trading surplus of other public enterprises	B
Rent	B
Net property income from abroad	C
Expenditure:	
Consumers' expenditure:[1];	A
Public authorities' current expenditure on goods and services	A
Gross domestic fixed capital formation:[1];	B
Value of increase in stocks and work in progress:[1];	C
of which—stock appreciation	C
physical increase	C
Exports of goods and services:[1];	A
Imports of goods and services:[1];	A
Taxes on expenditure	A
Subsidies	A
Gross national product	A

[1]For a detailed grading of the components see subsequent chapters.

2. EXPENDITURE AND OUTPUT AT CONSTANT PRICES

For many purposes, the comparison of estimates of gross domestic product over time is of more interest when the effects of changes in prices are eliminated. Accordingly, estimates are made of the gross domestic product and its main components in each year, revalued at the average prices of a selected base year. There are two general methods of estimating gross domestic product at constant prices: the expenditure method and the production method.

The expenditure method consists in estimating at constant prices all the components of final expenditure on goods and services—consumers' expenditure, public authorities' current expenditure, gross domestic fixed capital formation, the value of the physical increase in stocks and work in progress, and exports—and deducting estimates of imports of goods and services at constant prices. The production method consists in adding together the contributions of all industries to the gross domestic product, that is their net output including depreciation, valued at base year prices. All industries are included, whether they produce goods or services and irrespective of whether they produce raw materials or intermediate products for use by other industries, final products for investment or consumption or for export, or—as often happens—some combination of these. If complete, accurate and detailed information about all transactions were available, the two methods should, in theory, lead to the same answer.

Both of these methods are used in the United Kingdom to estimate gross domestic product at constant prices annually and quarterly. Estimates of gross domestic product revalued at constant prices by categories of final expenditure are summarised in Table 14 of the 1967 Blue Book. Detailed estimates of consumers' expenditure and of capital formation are shown in other sections of the Blue Book. Estimates of changes in gross domestic product at constant prices, subdivided by industries, are given in Table 15 of the 1967 Blue Book. More detailed estimates for manufacturing industries are given in the tables on the index of industrial production published in the *Monthly Digest of Statistics* and the *Annual Abstract of Statistics*. The expenditure and output estimates are both related to the same base year, the year of the latest detailed census of production for which results are available. The base year for the 1967 Blue Book estimates was 1958; earlier estimates were based on 1954 and 1948. The base year will be changed to 1963 when the detailed results of the 1963 census of production become available.

Direct estimates of gross domestic product at constant prices cannot be made from income data. Although wages and salaries may be deflated by an index of wage and salary rates, this provides a measure of only part of net output which docs not take full account of changes in labour productivity. The only satisfactory revaluation of profit incomes is obtained by taking the difference between deflated gross output and deflated inputs including labour costs, which is not distinct from the output estimate. The various types of factor income might be deflated by changes in the prices of the goods and services on which the income is spent; but not all income is immediately spent, and until income is spent it cannot be identified with actual goods and services. However, since by definition total factor income equals total expenditure on the gross domestic product at current prices, the price index derived by dividing the expenditure-based estimate at current prices by the corresponding estimate at constant prices can be treated as a currently weighted price index applicable to total factor income. The estimate of gross domestic product at constant prices obtained in this way differs from the expenditure estimate only by the deflated value of the residual error (the difference between the income and expenditure estimates of gross domestic product at current prices). It provides no information on changes in the deflated values of separate components of factor income, but it does provide an alternative estimate of gross domestic product at constant prices which may be compared with the results of the direct measures of expenditure and output.

The estimates of the gross domestic product at constant prices adhere, of course, to the definitions laid down in Chapter I. But the compilation of estimates of expenditure and output in real terms gives rise to a fairly distinct set of conceptual and practical problems. The main problem is to determine the appropriate unit in which each component of the domestic product is to be measured. The need for general principles of measurement is particularly felt in connection with the output of services—as opposed to goods—including the services provided by public authorities. A brief account of these conceptual problems and of the solutions adopted is necessary to an understanding of the nature of the estimates.

General principles of measurement

The domestic product (defined on page 7) comprises all goods and services which result from economic activity; and this activity is deemed to take place within a certain boundary—known as the boundary of production. In accordance with this definition, it may be stated as a general principle that the goods and services which comprise the domestic product should be measured at the points at which they cross the production boundary (except for any additions to stocks and work in progress during the period which are of course included in the domestic product); final goods and services should in other words be measured at the points at which they finally emerge from the production process.

Generally speaking, this is also the point at which the final purchase takes place. In the case of most goods—as opposed to services—there is not much difficulty in determining the appropriate measure of changes in output; the quantity and the unit of measurement, as well as the price per unit, are usually stated at the time of purchase. It is useful, indeed, to remember that the purchase or sale of goods and services is generally governed by a (frequently unwritten) contract which specifies the nature of the commodity, the unit and the conditions of the sale. Thus, in cases such as the provision of personal services, where the unit of output is not immediately obvious, the appropriate measure can usually be determined by considering what the producer is under contract to provide, or what the final purchaser in fact obtains, during the period in question.

The same criteria cannot readily be applied to services that are provided by public authorities for the benefit of the community as a whole. Payments made by the central government and local authorities to the police, the Forces, civil servants, teachers and doctors, and the associated purchases of various materials —uniforms, munitions, surgical equipment, etc.—are treated as forms of final expenditure in estimating national expenditure at current prices. The process of production does not, however, stop short at this point, but extends to the maintenance of law and order, the provision of defence, the processes of government administration, the provision of education and medical attention, and so on. When public authorities pay for labour and materials, this is not an end in itself but enables them to provide certain services for the benefit of the community. The fact that specific charges are not usually made to the consumers of the services is not a sufficient reason to exclude them. The production process is therefore assumed to include the provision of such services, which are valued, at current prices, at the cost of the labour, materials, etc. used in producing them.

As most of the services provided by public authorities are not bought or sold in any market, but are provided free of charge—or with only a nominal charge unrelated to the quantity obtained—it is not possible to apply the criterion of the market contract. Thus there are inherent difficulties in measuring, at constant prices, the output of government services, the exact nature of which cannot be precisely determined. Sometimes it is helpful to consider the methods used in measuring analogous services produced under private enterprise; but it is difficult to imagine any homogeneous units in which it would be possible to measure year-to-year changes in defence or civil administration. The units that are available are often not homogeneous; for example, an increase in the number of pupils in schools may be accompanied by a decline in the attention received by each pupil rather than a proportional increase in output, unless there is a corresponding increase in the number of teachers. In general, the solution adopted has been to use changes in numbers employed as an indicator of changes in output. The implied assumption of no change in productivity is obviously not satisfactory since it takes no account of the use of more modern equipment, such as computers. The problem has been discussed at a number of international conferences without any generally acceptable solution being reached. In some countries, the assumption has been made that productivity in the public services increases at the same rate as productivity in all other industries, or in all other service industries. The appropriate productivity change is, however, difficult to assess and in the United Kingdom accounts the assumption of no change in productivity has been preferred. This is equivalent to taking the purchase of labour and materials by public authorities as being at the production boundary. It provides an estimate consistent with revaluing expenditure by public authorities on wages and salaries by calculating the amount which would have been spent had there been no changes in rates of pay.

This leads to another general problem in the measurement of gross domestic product at constant prices. The unit of measurement for each good or service should be as homogeneous as possible in order to preserve the proper distinction between price changes and quantity changes. Any improvement in quality, such as a shift towards higher quality television sets and cars, should be included in the measurement of the quantity change and should not be reflected in the price change.[6] Any changes in the amount, or quality, of services purchased with the product should be taken into account in the measurement of the quantity change. Improvements in quality and increased proportions of higher quality goods may be better allowed for by estimating quantity changes from changes in value divided by a price index rather than by using changes in quantitative measures of output. In either case, the units need to be narrowly enough defined to remain as homogeneous as possible; a quality change will not be accurately reflected in a deflated value series if the price index does not relate to goods of a sufficiently detailed and constant specification. Considerable problems arise when one type of good is replaced by an entirely different type, and it may then be impossible to obtain a satisfactory estimate of the associated change in the quantity or price level. If performance is improved without a corresponding increase in price, what in effect is an increase in output may be ignored and the increase in gross domestic product will be understated. On the other hand, it often happens that the introduction of a new product is made the occasion for an upward price adjustment; such price increases may be left out of account and, if so, the increase in gross domestic product will be overstated. Also, the price indices should, but may not always, represent changes in the prices actually paid; for example goods may be bought at a discount or the price indicators may relate only to particular markets which may be changing in relative importance.

---

[6]See J. L. Nicholson, 'The Measurement of Quality Changes', *The Economic Journal*, Vol. LXXVII, September 1967.

The measure of the change in gross domestic product at constant prices necessarily depends upon the year chosen as the base. Relative prices change over time and different relative prices result in a different measure of the change in gross domestic product. Changes in quantities are associated with the changes in relative prices and the pattern of prices in the base year ought not therefore to be too different from that of the current year. A compromise has to be made between the comparability obtained by measuring changes over a number of years in terms of the same base year and the need to measure changes in terms of up-to-date relative prices. In the United Kingdom accounts the base year has been determined by the year of the detailed censuses of production and is changed about every five years. Estimates for all years are shown in terms of one base year, and although the expenditure estimates have generally been re-calculated in detail when the base year is changed, the output estimates have merely been linked to the new base year without detailed recalculation of the earlier years.

The expenditure approach

The methods used in estimating the various components of expenditure at constant prices are so far as possible consistent with the measures of output. More detailed descriptions will be found in subsequent chapters dealing with the corresponding current price estimates.

There are various methods of obtaining estimates of expenditure at constant prices. The most usual method is that of deflating estimates of expenditure at current prices, derived from the original source, by an index of price changes. This method is used for about two-fifths of consumers' expenditure. Over three-quarters of public authorities' current expenditure on goods and services is revalued in this way, including over two-fifths which is expenditure on wages and salaries deflated by an index of changes in wage and salary rates. The same method is also used for most of the value of the physical increase in stocks and work in progress, for over half of exports of goods and services and for about two-fifths of imports of goods and services. For a fair proportion of the components of expenditure, including nearly half of consumers' expenditure, the basic data consist of estimates of the actual quantities of goods purchased; the estimates of expenditure at constant prices are derived by attaching appropriate base-year weights to the indicators of quantity. This method is also used for some of the estimates of changes in stocks, for over two-fifths of exports of goods and services and over half of imports of goods and services. For expenditure on services changes in expenditure at constant prices are frequently represented by an independent, and often somewhat arbitrary, indicator of changes in the quantity of services obtained. This method is used for some services purchased by consumers and for expenditure on certain services by public authorities; for the latter the indicator of changes in services obtained is generally the numbers employed.

The price indices implicit in any comparison between estimates of expenditure at current prices and estimates at constant prices reflect the methods by which changes in quantity are measured. In some cases, the movement in the implied price indices may not be the same as the movement in actual prices charged, because the latter may not relate to identical commodities or services in every year. In other cases, for example many of the estimates for services, the index of prices implied by the estimates is influenced by the arbitrariness of the measures of changes in quantity. The implied price indices are based on weights of the current year and provide a direct measure of price changes only between the current year and the base year. Comparisons other than with the base year may be affected by changes in the pattern of expenditure, which however are generally more important over longer than over shorter periods.

The expenditure method provides estimates of gross domestic product, sub-divided by categories of final expenditure, which are valued at market prices in the base year. Estimates of the gross domestic product at factor cost are derived by subtracting estimates of total taxes on expenditure *less* subsidies, valued at base-year rates, from the estimates at market prices. Formerly estimates were made of each of the various forms of final expenditure at factor cost, but this procedure was dropped in favour of the present practice because the estimates of total taxes on expenditure *less* subsidies are more reliable than separate estimates for each category of final expenditure.

The estimates of indirect taxes at constant rates of tax present little difficulty. About half the total—the taxes on alcoholic drink, tobacco and hydrocarbon oils—is estimated by multiplying the physical quantity of the taxable goods by the rates of tax which applied in the base year. For *ad valorem* duties the pro-portion of tax to market price in the base year is applied to the expenditure at constant prices in other years on the items concerned. The net rent or rateable value on which local authority rates are based is changed only occasionally; after allowing for these changes the procedure for estimating rates at constant prices is the same as for taxes charged on the basis of quantity. Estimates for subsidies are more of a problem and the methods used are approximate. The largest item, agricultural subsidies, consists mainly of payments to farmers of the difference between guaranteed prices for various agricultural products and actual prices in the market. The estimate at constant prices is obtained by applying the subsidy per unit for each product in the base year to the quantities marketed in other years. The central government and local authority subsidies for housing are revalued by reference to the subsidy per house in the base year and subsequent changes in the stock of such houses. The revaluation is carried out in rather less detail quarterly than annually.

Estimates of gross national product at market prices and at factor cost are obtained by the addition of net property income from abroad, which is revalued at constant prices simply by dividing it by the price index implied by the estimates of imports of goods and services at current and constant prices. This procedure gives a measure of the change in the worth of the net income flow for purchasing imported goods and services. The treatment is possible only because the net flow has always been inwards; a different method of deflation would have to be adopted for a net outward flow. In the United Kingdom accounts no attempt is made to revalue separately the gross flows of property income from abroad and property income paid abroad. The problem of revaluing this income at constant prices reflects the difficulties of using the income approach, referred to above (page 45).[7]

---

[7]See J. L. Nicholson, 'The Effects of International Trade on the Measurement of Real National Income', *The Economic Journal*, Vol. LXX, September 1960.

The production approach

The production method starts from the estimated contribution of each industry to the gross domestic product in the base year. The year-to-year changes in output, estimated by various measures of changes in the quantity of output, are combined with weights proportional to the estimated contribution to the gross domestic product in the base year. Changes in the gross domestic product are thus estimated by a base-weighted quantity index and the result is expressed as an index with the base year as 100.

The base-year weights are the estimated values of net output including depreciation but excluding stock appreciation. These estimates are subdivided in the degree of detail necessary to provide estimates for the different sections of each industry, which are further subdivided in proportion to the estimated net output for each individual product.

It is then necessary to decide, in the light of the general principles mentioned above, the most suitable indicator to represent the movements in the output of each product. It is seldom possible to obtain a direct measure of changes in net output (that is, gross output *minus* input) as sufficient information is not normally available to enable both gross output and input to be estimated at constant prices. In practice, therefore, the change in net output is generally represented by a measure which relates to gross output, including the contributions of earlier stages of production. Any change, therefore, in the ratio of net to gross output at constant prices would result in the measure being, to that extent, inaccurate. For example, if a manufacturing firm decides to install its own electricity generating plant, the resulting increase in its net output would not be reflected in the measure of gross output of manufactured goods. Changes in the ratio of net to gross output can also be caused by changes in the amount or quality of workmanship incorporated in the product; by economy or extravagance in the use of materials; by changes in the degree of integration of industry; or by changes in costs of advertising or payments for other services per unit of output. Precise information about such changes is not usually obtainable.

Moreover, even the figures of gross output are not generally available for every grade and quality in which each commodity is produced; and without this kind of detail estimates of total output at constant prices cannot be entirely accurate. There may indeed be changes in quality or design from one year to another which are not susceptible of measurement; and sometimes, of course, entirely new commodities are produced. Difficulties of this kind are inherent in comparisons over time. In compiling the series for individual products it is frequently necessary to make approximations and adjustments because of discontinuities in the data. The practical aim has been to make full use of all the detailed information which is available, or obtainable, and to marry the indicators to the weights in such a way as to obtain the maximum coverage of each industry, while avoiding duplication. The methods are summarised below. Full details of the weights and indicators used, together with further explanations of the methods used for particular industries, will be found in Chapter V.

The estimates from the production side incorporate the constituent indices of the official index of industrial production, which covers mining and quarrying, manufacturing industries, construction, and gas, electricity and water; these industries account for about half the gross domestic product. The problems involved in measuring changes in the output of industries covered by the index of industrial production are discussed in detail in the published description of the index[8] which also contains full details of the statistics used in compiling the index. Indicators of quantities of goods produced account for nearly half of the total weight of the index. Next most important are deflated values of output which account for just over one-third. Where no satisfactory measure of output is available, the indicator is generally the quantity of materials used but in a few cases the number of persons employed has to be used.

The application of the production method to industries outside the scope of the index of production was developed by the Department of Applied Economics of Cambridge University before official estimates were published.[9]

For agriculture, estimates are made of the value of net output at constant prices. Estimates are made of the values of gross output and of all items of input at constant prices. The difference between the estimate of total output and the estimate of total input, both at constant prices, provides the required estimate of net output.

There remain the industries providing various kinds of services, namely: transport and communication; distributive trades; insurance, banking and finance; professional and scientific services and miscellaneous services (Orders XIX to XXIII of the *Standard Industrial Classification, 1958*). In all these industries, the general aim has been to use, wherever possible, a direct measure of output in terms of the actual quantity of goods handled, or of services rendered, in conformity with the general principles outlined above (page 44). The services of retail distribution, for example, are measured by the volume of turnover; those of passenger transport by the number of passenger miles, and of goods transport by the number of ton miles; the services of building societies by the number of mortgage advances. For most of public education and health services and also for public administration and defence, employment is used as an indicator of output. For example, the services of the Forces and of the police are represented by indices of changes in the numbers employed which allow for changes in the numbers employed in the various grades.

It must be admitted that many of the indicators which are intended to represent changes in output provide only very rough measures of changes in the output of the industries in question. But even a crude measure of output is assumed to be preferable to an index based on the cost, at constant prices, of the factors of production engaged in producing the output. The latter method is only used *faute de mieux*, for example in public services, where it is difficult to find any suitable measure of services rendered.

The relative importance of the various types of indicators used in the annual estimates of output is summarised in the table at the top of the next page.

The production method is used in compiling estimates of the gross domestic product, subdivided by industry of origin, at constant factor cost. No attempt is made to estimate the gross domestic product, by industry of origin, at constant market prices. The allocation of indirect taxes and subsidies between different industries producing the gross domestic product would, indeed, be somewhat arbitrary; for example purchase tax, which is paid at the wholesale stage, might be allocated either to wholesale distribution or to the industries producing

---

[8] *The Index of Industrial Production: Method of Compilation*, Studies in Official Statistics, No. 7 (1959) and *Economic Trends*, March 1962.

[9] See W. B. Reddaway, 'Movements in the Real Product of the United Kingdom,' *Journal of the Royal Statistical Society*, Vol. CXIII, 1950; and C. F. Carter, 'Index Numbers of the Real Product of the United Kingdom,' *ibid*. Vol. CXV, 1952.

Type of indicator	Percentage of total weight
Net output at constant prices......................................	4
Output indicators:	
Quantity of output of goods	22
Quantity indicators for services rendered	12
Value of output of goods revalued at constant prices................	18
Value indicators for services rendered revalued at constant prices	22
Input indicators:	
Quantity of material inputs	7
Employment	15
	100

the taxable goods. And taxes levied on imported goods account for about two-fifths of total taxes on expenditure. These difficulties are less important in some other countries, where estimates at market prices are made, than they are in the United Kingdom.

Consistency of estimates at constant prices

In principle, the expenditure and output approaches to the measurement of gross domestic product at constant prices should lead to the same answer. So also should the income estimate, since the income and expenditure approaches aim to measure the same aggregate at current prices and the income data are revalued by the overall price index implied for expenditure. In the absence of full and accurate information there are many reasons why the three methods must be expected to give different results. Various approximations have to be used at all stages and could give rise to differences. These have been outlined in the description of the methods given above.

Although the estimates obtained by the expenditure and output methods are largely independent every effort has been made in applying them to achieve mutual consistency. Thus the same principles have been followed in measuring the expenditure at constant prices on, and the output of, all final goods and services; wherever a choice has had to be made between using one method of measurement, or one set of data, rather than another (for example, physical quantities or deflated values), arbitrary differences have been avoided; and where estimates of expenditure at current prices are deflated for changes in prices, the price index is, wherever possible, of the Paasche type, using current-year weights, since this is consistent with the Laspeyre type of quantity index, using base-year weights.

In a few instances, the same basic statistics have been used in both sets of estimates. But in general the information used for the two methods is different, as explained above; it is only if an industry has no input from other industries that the two methods coincide. Thus an index of the change in net output at constant prices, at the last stage of production, would not be expected to show the same movement as an index of expenditure at constant prices on the final goods in question, which covers the output of all stages of production.

A detailed reconciliation of the two sets of results would be possible only if sufficient information were available to determine the contribution of each industry to each item of final expenditure. It would require a detailed input-output matrix for each year, which would have to be translated into constant prices. Since it is not yet possible to make this reconciliation, there is no way of determining which method is the more reliable, and one answer cannot be regarded as more accurate than the other.

Although the results of the three approaches are not the same, the table below shows that agreement of estimated changes is fairly close, especially when taken over a long period. One noticeable feature of this table is the frequency with which gaps between the different series in one year disappear or even change sign a year later. This suggests that many of the discrepancies in the year-to-year movements may be the result of timing differences between the three sets of data.

Gross domestic product at constant factor cost

1958 = 100

	Based on expenditure data	Based on income data	Based on output data		Based on expenditure data	Based on income data	Based on output data
1948	78·0	78·8	79·8	1958	100·0	100·0	100·0
1949	80·4	82·2	82·6	1959	103·5	104·0	104·5
1950	83·0	84·5	85·7	1960	108·7	111·3	110·1
1951	86·0	87·2	87·6	1961	112·7	114·1	112·1
1952	86·0	87·2	87·0	1962	113·7	115·2	113·5
1953	90·0	90·1	90·5	1963	118·4	120·3	117·3
1954	93·2	94·1	94·3	1964	125·3	127·7	124·4
1955	96·4	98·1	97·5	1965	128·6	131·8	127·6
1956	98·3	98·9	98·4	1966	130·6	133·3	129·6
1957	100·2	100·3	100·1				

Source: 1967 Blue Book, Table 8

As might be expected, the differences between the three estimates are more marked for quarterly changes than for annual changes. In particular, the expenditure and output approaches may from time to time show markedly different quarterly movements because the index of industrial production, which makes up half of the output estimates, is designed to estimate the rate of production and to allow for variations in the number of working days; nearly all of the expenditure data relate in principle to the calendar quarter, without adjustment for variations in its length.

Reliability

As has already been implied, it is very difficult to judge the reliability of the estimates at constant prices. Estimates of this nature are to some extent arbitrary and a guide to their reliability can only be given in the context of the principles adopted in their compilation. The accuracy of the estimates depends partly on how much expenditure or output has changed; for the base year there is no difference between the current and constant price estimates and the estimates become less reliable the further they are from the base year. The following remarks are no more than a very general guide to the reliability of the annual estimates, given in terms of the gradings described on pages 39 to 41.

The estimates of final expenditure at constant prices are less reliable than the estimates at current prices, except where the estimates at constant prices are based on detailed quantities purchased, because of uncertainties surrounding the process of deflation by price indices. The table below gives the reliability grading in terms of the absolute values in £ million at constant prices of the various components. The gradings in the table are appropriate to a year, say, three or four years away from the base year. The estimates for the latest year are less reliable than those for the latest year but one, but not sufficiently so to warrant a separate grading.

Reliability of annual estimates of major components at constant prices

Consumers' expenditure	A
Public authorities' current expenditure on goods and services	B
Gross domestic fixed capital formation	C
Value of physical increase in stocks and work in progress	C
Exports of goods and services	B
Imports of goods and services	B
Adjustment to factor cost	A
Gross domestic product	A

The errors in the year-to-year changes, as opposed to the absolute values, are greater for the estimates at constant prices than for those at current prices (see page 40) and the reliability of the estimates of changes is less over longer periods. The estimates of changes in consumers' expenditure at constant prices are measured more accurately than those in other forms of final expenditure because the estimates are based to a larger extent on detailed quantity information. The estimates of changes in part of public authorities' current expenditure on goods and services and on gross fixed capital formation are weakened by the variable nature of some of the goods purchased which makes it difficult to distinguish quantity changes from price changes. A weakness of the estimates of changes in exports and imports of goods is that the statistics of quantities for some commodity headings are not comparable over time because their commodity content may change. For some of the items in exports and imports of services the units to be revalued are difficult to specify.

The reliability of the estimates made by the production method varies considerably from one industry to another. For the estimated movements in output, the description of the margins of error must be interpreted as applying to the error in the absolute annual index, based on 100, and not to the percentage change shown by that index.

The index numbers for agriculture, mining, manufacturing industries, and gas, electricity and water, are probably the most reliable. The accuracy of indices of the output of these industries over periods of up to, say, five years may be described as good, and over longer periods as fair. The reliability of the indices for construction, transport and communication and the distributive trades over relatively short periods of up to, say, five years, but depending partly on the extent of the changes, may be described as fair. The reliability of the indices for the other four orders of the *Standard Industrial Classification, 1958* (insurance, banking and finance; public administration and defence; professional services; and miscellaneous services) varies a great deal between the different subdivisions of each group and depends, to some extent, on acceptance of the underlying concepts. For each of these groups as a whole, and allowing for compensation between errors in the estimates for constituent sections, the indices covering periods of not more than say, five years, may be regarded as fair. It must, however, be remembered that, outside the field of the index of industrial production, many of the estimates for the latest year and some of the estimates for the previous year may subsequently be revised, as the basic data gradually become available.

3. SEASONALLY ADJUSTED ESTIMATES

For each of the quarterly measures of gross domestic product, estimates are made of the regular seasonal fluctuations in the series and the measures are published on a seasonally adjusted basis. Some of the sector accounts are also adjusted for seasonal fluctuations. The general principles followed in making these adjustments are the same throughout the accounts and the discussion of them is therefore brought together in this section.

General principles of seasonal adjustment

Descriptions of various methods of calculating seasonal adjustments will be found in most elementary textbooks on statistical methods.[10] The method most commonly used in the United Kingdom national accounts is the ratio to moving average method, which in its simplest form comprises four basic stages:

(i) The original series is first adjusted to eliminate, as far as possible, the effects of certain special factors which would otherwise obscure the normal seasonal fluctuations. Examples of such special factors are the exceptionally severe winter of 1963, the anticipation of tax changes, and strikes.

(ii) The trend in this adjusted series is estimated by calculating moving averages.

(iii) Percentage deviations of the adjusted series from the trend are calculated for each quarter and the average of these deviations for the same quarter in successive years is taken to represent the average seasonal adjustment factor for that quarter.

(iv) The seasonal adjustment factors are applied to the adjusted series and the special factors are then added back to arrive at the seasonally adjusted estimates of the original unadjusted series.

The method is applied with varying degrees of sophistication, according to the size and regularity of the seasonal fluctuations in the original series. For example, some series are adjusted to allow for the date of Easter, which may fall within the first or second quarters of the calendar year, but most series are not; the calculation of the seasonal adjustment factors may allow for trends in the seasonal factors over time; exceptionally large deviations from the trend may be excluded from the calculation of the average seasonal adjustment factors; the calculation may be based on as long a period as ten years, or it may be restricted to a few years, especially, for example, when the source of the information has changed or where the coverage of the series has been revised. In some cases, where the seasonal fluctuation is relatively small and the level of the series has not changed significantly, the seasonal adjustments may be calculated from absolute

---

[10]See, for example, R. G. D. Allen, *Statistics for Economists*; Taro Yamane, *Statistics, An Introductory Analysis*; P. H. Karmel, *Applied Statistics for Economists: A Course in Statistical Methods*.

rather than percentage deviations. For a few series, for example, stock appreciation, there appear to be no regular seasonal fluctuations and no seasonal
adjustment is made.

Many of the seasonal adjustment calculations are done on electronic computers using more refined versions of the basic method described above. The
method most commonly employed is a variant of Method II of the United States
Bureau of the Census.[11] A set of computer programmes developed by the Board
of Trade is also used. The simplest ratio to moving average method, giving one
average seasonal adjustment over the period, is also used a good deal, partly
because of the limitations of the basic quarterly data.

It is not possible to devise a unique set of seasonally adjusted figures; the
estimates depend upon the methods used and are to some extent subjective. The
series will differ according to the length of the period on which the seasonal
adjustment calculations are based, and according to the method of calculation.
The estimates for the latest quarters are particularly uncertain as the seasonal
adjustment has to be based on fluctuations in previous years and the pattern of
seasonal fluctuation may change. More commonly, it has to be decided whether
to use for the latest year the average seasonal adjustment in recent years or a
projection of the trend in that ratio. The original unadjusted series are subject to
error and the adjustment for seasonal factors adds a further uncertainty.

Throughout the national accounts, seasonal adjustments are calculated on
component series, in as fine detail as is judged appropriate. The published
seasonally adjusted series are the sum of the seasonally adjusted components.
The application of this procedure ensures that the quarterly accounts balance
in the same way as the annual ones. Also, in all cases the seasonally adjusted
estimates for each calendar year are themselves adjusted before publication to
sum to the total of the unadjusted estimates for the calendar year. This procedure
is followed even when the basic data relate to the government financial year
ending in the first quarter. Most of the public sector data are on this basis and the
sum of the seasonally adjusted estimates for the financial year may differ from
the basic unadjusted data.

Income

The seasonally adjusted income estimates are built up in much less detail than
those for expenditure which are described below. Within wages and salaries, that
part of the estimate which is based on PAYE returns, and accounts for over 90
per cent of total wages and salaries, is seasonally adjusted as one series, generally
using the variant of Census Method II. The quarterly estimate for the civil
service requires no seasonal adjustment and the other items are seasonally
adjusted in total. A small seasonal adjustment is made for fluctuations in payments to the Forces. Employers' contributions are not adjusted: there appears to
be no quarterly variation in national insurance and health contributions and
quarterly estimates of other contributions are interpolations of annual figures.
The series for company profits is seasonally adjusted in total, and so is the series
for the trading surplus of public corporations. No seasonal adjustment is made
to the trading surplus of other public enterprises, or to income from rent. There
is little information on quarterly variations in income from self-employment and

---

[11] Julius Shiskin, *Electronic Computers and Business Indicators*, Occasional Paper 57,
National Bureau of Economic Research, New York, 1957.

the series for farmers' income and income of professional persons are largely interpolated. The quarterly indicators used to estimate the income of other sole traders and partnerships show some seasonal fluctuations and the series is seasonally adjusted as one item.

Expenditure

The seasonally adjusted estimates of expenditure are built up in considerable detail. Much of this detail for the constant price estimates is published. At current prices the seasonally adjusted estimates are built up in less detail and only the estimates of total consumers' expenditure, exports and imports of goods and of services, total final expenditure and gross domestic product are published.

The seasonally adjusted estimates of consumers' expenditure at constant prices are built up from 38 separate seasonally adjusted components, and 13 separate components are published. The seasonally adjusted current price estimates, which are published only in total, are built up in the same detail, except that for a few series where the value of expenditure has been affected by tax changes the seasonal factors calculated for the constant price estimates are assumed to apply to the current price series. This assumption is satisfactory because there are no seasonal fluctuations in the relevant price indices.

Central government current expenditure on goods and services at constant prices is divided into three parts for seasonal adjustment. Expenditure on defence and on the national health service are seasonally adjusted separately. No adjustment is made to the remaining expenditure which does not show regular seasonal fluctuations. Current expenditure on goods and services by local authorities is seasonally adjusted in two parts: education and other. One estimate is published of the total of public authorities current expenditure on goods and services at constant prices. An estimate is calculated at current prices, based on one seasonal adjustment of the total, but is not separately published: it is used in compiling the published estimate of total final expenditure at current prices.

Expenditure at constant prices on gross domestic fixed capital formation is seasonally adjusted in over 40 separate component series for the analysis by industry group, the types of asset being considered separately for most industry groups in order to provide consistent estimates for the asset analysis. In the sector analysis, eight series are adjusted separately within public authorities, and 15 within public corporations; the private sector series is then derived as a residual from the total determined by the industry analysis. The seasonal adjustment of estimates of the physical increase in stocks is carried out for 18 separate series within manufacturing, and for eight other series in the distributive trades and other industries. All of these adjustments are worked out from the quarterly variations in the total of stocks held at constant prices, and not from the changes in the total. For the compilation of the seasonally adjusted estimates of total final expenditure at current prices the overall seasonal adjustments from the constant price series for fixed capital formation and the value of the physical increase in stocks are applied to the current price estimates as there are no significant seasonal fluctuations in prices; these seasonally adjusted series are not separately published.

Estimates of exports and imports of goods are seasonally adjusted in total. These estimates of course relate to exports and imports as measured for the balance of payments; the Board of Trade publish detailed seasonally adjusted figures of exports and imports as they appear in the *Trade Accounts*. The main groups of services—government, shipping, civil aviation, travel and the rest—are seasonally adjusted separately; the estimates are made separately and in the same detail at constant and current prices. Most of the components of the current price series are published in the balance of payments accounts.

The adjustment to factor cost at current prices is built up from three main parts: central government taxes on expenditure and total subsidies are adjusted separately and local authority rates require no adjustment since the estimates relate to accruals and not to cash receipts. The constant price estimates for the earlier years were built up in the same detail but from 1963, when more information became available, an adjustment is also made in much greater detail for the main central government taxes.

Output

Separate seasonally adjusted estimates are published for eight industry groups: agriculture, forestry and fishing; mining and quarrying; manufacturing; construction; gas, electricity and water; transport and communication; distributive trades; and other services. The quarterly series for gross domestic product is a weighted average of these components. Forms of the ratio to moving average method of seasonal adjustment are used throughout, a variant of Census Method II being used for many of the series.

For agriculture, it is virtually impossible to measure work done on a quarterly basis and the quarterly figures are interpolations of the annual series (see page 88). Quarterly unadjusted index numbers are estimated for forestry and fishing and these two series are seasonally adjusted separately.

For the index of industrial production industries, monthly unadjusted and seasonally adjusted series are also published in the *Monthly Digest of Statistics*, and the quarterly series are simple averages of the monthly figures. A general description of these series has been published with the description of the index.[12] Manufacturing industry is seasonally adjusted as one series. Mining and quarrying, construction, and gas, electricity and water are adjusted separately.

Transport and communication is seasonally adjusted as a whole, as are the index numbers for the distributive trades. Within the series for other services, insurance, banking and finance, professional and scientific services and miscellaneous services are seasonally adjusted separately. There is virtually no seasonal fluctuation in the series for public administration and defence and ownership of dwellings and no adjustments are made to them.

Sector accounts

In addition to the estimates of gross domestic product, some of the sector accounts are published on a seasonally adjusted basis. The personal income and expenditure account is seasonally adjusted and published in *Economic Trends* and the *Monthly Digest of Statistics*. The additional seasonal adjustments required for this account are to income from current grants from public authorities, income from rent, dividends and net interest, and payments of United Kingdom taxes on income. The seasonal adjustment to income from current grants is not large: it is based on separate consideration of regular quarterly

---

[12]*The Index of Industrial Production: Method of Compilation*, Studies in Official Statistics, No. 7, 1959.

fluctuations in national insurance benefits and in grants from the central government, and in grants from local authorities. The seasonally adjusted receipts of rent, dividends and net interest are derived as a residual from seasonally adjusted estimates of the rent, dividend and interest flows between the other sectors. The seasonally adjusted estimates of total United Kingdom tax payments are built up from seasonally adjusted estimates of the various categories of tax, allowing where possible for changes in the rates of taxation.

The company appropriation account is published on a seasonally adjusted basis in *Financial Statistics*. Rent and non-trading income is mainly estimated on an accruals basis and is not seasonally adjusted. The published series for income from abroad, dividends on ordinary shares, other interest payments and profits due and taxes paid abroad are each seasonally adjusted in aggregate. United Kingdom tax payments are adjusted in two parts: the payments of tax made to the Inland Revenue and the tax deducted from payments of dividends, which is a negative item within the published figure of tax payments. In 1966 the seasonal pattern changed because of the introduction of corporation tax and the change in arrangements for taxation of dividends and interest.

Seasonally adjusted estimates of the net acquisition of financial assets of the personal sector, companies and the public sector are published in *Financial Statistics*. The two accounts just described provide seasonally adjusted estimates of private sector saving and the public sector estimate is obtained as a residual. Total saving is equal to total investment, including net investment abroad, apart from the residual error. Seasonally adjusted estimates of gross fixed capital formation, the value of the increase in stocks and the residual error are obtained for the estimates of gross domestic product. The seasonally adjusted estimates of net investment abroad are taken from the balance of payments accounts. No seasonal adjustments have been made to capital transfers because the amounts involved are not large. A combined figure is published for capital formation in fixed assets and in stocks and work in progress by each of the three sectors mainly because the seasonal adjustments to the latter are very approximate; the two forms of capital formation are in fact adjusted separately. An overall adjustment is used consistent with that for all sectors combined, and with that for fixed capital formation at constant prices by the public and private sectors.

Chapter IV

Published Tables

1. THE ORGANISATION OF PUBLISHED TABLES

THE BLUE BOOK TABLES

The presentation in the Blue Book of the statistics of national income and expenditure follows so far as possible the systematic exposition of sector accounts described in Chapter II, but incorporates, in addition, a number of other tables which are not formally a part of the national accounting structure. The arrangement of the 1967 Blue Book is as follows:

General tables

    I. *Summary tables.* This section contains the basic national accounts.

    II. *Expenditure and output at constant prices.* This section contains summary tables showing the major components of expenditure at constant market prices and of output, by industry groups, at constant factor cost.

    III. *Industrial input and output.* In this section are assembled certain tables showing an analysis by industry, as opposed to an analysis by sector.

Sector tables

    IV. *The personal sector.* This section is devoted to a detailed analysis of certain aspects of the income, expenditure and saving of the personal sector. The capital account is also given.

    V. *Companies.* This section shows appropriation and capital accounts both for industrial and commercial and for financial companies. An industrial analysis of trading profits is given for all companies.

    VI. *Public corporations.* This section gives operating, appropriation and capital accounts for public corporations. The appropriation and capital accounts are analysed by industry.

    VII. *Central government.* This section gives current and capital accounts for the central government. The National Insurance Funds are included in the central government but a separate account is also given for them.

    VIII. *Local authorities.* This section gives current and capital accounts for local authorities.

    IX. *Combined public authorities.* This section gives accounts for central government and local authorities combined, together with some analysis of expenditure on goods and services, tax receipts and subsidies.

    X. *Public sector.* This section contains accounts for central government, local authorities and public corporations combined, together with a detailed functional analysis of their combined expenditure.

Capital and financial accounts

XI. *Capital formation.* The first group of tables in this section brings together data on gross domestic fixed capital formation by sector, industry and type of asset. Estimates are given of capital consumption and capital stock. In subsequent tables investment in stocks and work in progress is analysed by sector and industry.

XII. *Financial accounts.* The summary table brings together the capital accounts of the various sectors to show the derivation for each sector of the net acquisition of financial assets. Subsequent tables show the changes in individual forms of assets and liabilities within this net total, so far as they can be identified.

The tables in sections IV-XII and the sources of information used, are described in detail in succeeding chapters of this book. Many of the tables in sections I-III are drawn from these fuller tables and are described in the relevant chapters. Following sections of this chapter give some description of the tables in sections I-III, with special attention to those tables which do not receive full treatment elsewhere.

Selected tables from the Blue Book are also published in the *Annual Abstract of Statistics.*

THE WHITE PAPER TABLES

The national income and balance of payments White Paper which is published just before the Budget is presented to Parliament in March or April. It contains preliminary estimates of the first eight summary tables given in the Blue Book.

Preliminary estimates are also given for shortened versions of the following 1967 Blue Book tables:

Table 14. Expenditure and output at 1958 prices

Table 15. Index numbers of output at constant factor cost

Tables 27 and 28. Consumers' expenditure

Tables 54, 58 and 59. Gross domestic fixed capital formation

Tables 69 and 70. Value of physical increase in stocks and work in progress

Included in the notes are preliminary estimates of depreciation.

THE QUARTERLY TABLES

The quarterly tables follow as far as possible the arrangement of the annual tables. All the main summary tables given in the Blue Book are presented quarterly, with summarised versions of the other tables included also in the White Paper. The tables, listed below, are published quarterly in *Economic Trends* with a commentary. Tables A to D and J to M are also published in the *Monthly Digest of Statistics,* and Tables F and G in *Financial Statistics.* The appropriation accounts of companies and public corporations, which are combined in Table E, are also shown separately in *Financial Statistics.*

Tables A, B, D, F, J, K, L and M have been published on a consistent basis from 1955. Table C is carried back only to 1958. The remaining accounts published in *Economic Trends* (Tables E, G, H and I) have all been carried back to 1961. The appropriation account for companies has, however, been published from 1960 and that for public corporations from 1959. A long run of figures is given each year in the October issue of *Economic Trends*.

The arrangement of the quarterly tables differs slightly from that in the Blue Book, because of differences in presentation and in the amount of information available. Table A relates to the gross domestic product, while Table 1 of the Blue Book relates to the gross national product. All the expenditure tables include estimates at current and constant prices, and the constant price estimates are seasonally adjusted. Factor incomes (Table B) and the personal income and expenditure account (Table D) are also seasonally adjusted. The seasonally adjusted appropriation account for companies is shown in *Financial Statistics*.

The main difference between the quarterly and annual tables arises in the treatment of additions to reserves. The annual accounts include estimates of changes in reserves for dividends and interest and for taxes on income. In the quarterly accounts dividends and taxes on income are estimated on a payments basis, and no provision is made for changes in reserves, which are therefore included in the quarterly estimates of saving.

Quarterly financial accounts on the same basis as the annual tables have been published from 1963 in *Financial Statistics*. All of the tables in the financial accounts sector of the Blue Book are published quarterly, except the table showing the acquisition of the financial assets of the public sector by other sectors. However, all the quarterly information necessary to compile the latter table is available in *Financial Statistics*. A summarised version of the table on the net acquisition of financial assets is also published on a seasonally adjusted basis. *Financial Statistics* also contains much of the basic material, some of which is available monthly, from which the financial accounts are assembled.

2. THE SUMMARY TABLES

Table 1. Gross national product

Table 1 in the Blue Book contains a summary presentation of the national income and expenditure. One part of the table shows the expenditure flows which generate the gross national product, these flows being expressed at market prices but adjusted at the foot of this part of the table to factor cost. The other part shows the different kinds of income payment arising from the economic activities which result in production.

Gross national product, 1966

£ million

Expenditure		Factor incomes	
Consumers' expenditure.........	24,116	Income from employment	22,437
Public authorities' current expenditure on goods and services ..	6,391	Income from self-employment[1]	2,470[2]
Gross domestic capital formation:		Gross trading profits of companies[1]	4,646[2]
Fixed capital formation	6,635	Gross trading surplus of public corporations[1]	1,038
Value of physical increase in stocks and work in progress..	209	Gross trading surplus of other public enterprises[1]	98
Total domestic expenditure at market prices	37,351	Rent[3]	1,949
Exports and property income from abroad	8,640	Total domestic income before providing for depreciation and stock appreciation	32,638
less Imports and property income paid abroad	− 8,455	*less* Stock appreciation.........	−351
		Residual error	−160
less Taxes on expenditure	− 5,596	Gross domestic product at factor cost	32,127
Subsidies.....................	558	Net property income from abroad	371
Gross national product (gross national expenditure at factor cost)	32,498	Gross national product (national income and depreciation)	32,498

Source: 1967 Blue Book, Table 1

[1]Before providing for depreciation and stock appreciation.
[2]After deduction of payments of selective employment tax and before allowing for refunds or premiums due but not yet received.
[3]Before providing for depreciation.

This table contains the elements of what was described as the United Kingdom production account (page 25). The table may be regarded as a consolidated account of the productive activity of the economy as a whole considered as a giant firm. The items of income may then be considered as payments by the firm to the different factors of production which it employs. These payments are carried forward as receipts into the income and expenditure accounts of the different sectors and represent their whole receipts from production, to which may be added other receipts from grants and other unrequited flows. The items of expenditure are receipts by the firm from all sales of goods and services to final users. These sales are made, so to speak, to the sectors, including residents abroad, purchasing goods and services and appear in their expenditure either on income and expenditure account or on capital account.

Some rearrangement of Table 1 is, however, required if it is to be used as a production account. Imports of goods and services, and taxes on expenditure, which appear in Table 1 as deductions from final expenditure at market prices, should be shown as payments by the firm to residents abroad and to the public authorities sector, respectively. Consumers' and public authorities' expenditure abroad is not a sale from the United Kingdom production account or a payment out of this account, and must therefore be excluded from final expenditure and from imports. Property incomes paid to and received from abroad are treated as transfer payments and do not flow through the United Kingdom production account; they are therefore omitted. Purely as a matter of convenience stock appreciation is treated as a sale by the firm and not as a deduction from incomes.

Table 1 of the Blue Book, rearranged in the form of a production account, is shown in the table below.

United Kingdom production account, 1966

£ million

Receipts		Payments	
Consumers' expenditure at home	23,709	Income from employment	22,437
Public authorities' current expenditure on goods and services at		Income from self-employment ..	2,470
		Gross profits and other trading	
home	6,223	income	5,782
Gross domestic capital formation	6,844	Rent	1,949
Stock appreciation	351	Imports of goods and services ...	6,550
Exports of goods and services ...	6,939	Taxes on expenditure	5,596
Subsidies.....................	558		
		Total payments	44,784
		Residual error	−160
Total	44,624	Total	44,624

Source: 1967 Blue Book, Tables 1, 7 and 27 and unpublished estimate

Table 1 as set out in the Blue Book, however, is designed as a summary table of all the main flows leading up to the total of gross national product at factor cost which is generally regarded as the most significant aggregate. The aggregates shown in the production account above, on the other hand, have no particular significance in the system.

The items in Table 1 are shown gross, before providing for depreciation. An estimate of capital consumption is given at the foot of the table and deducted from the gross national product to arrive at the national income.

Tables 2 to 5. Income and expenditure accounts

Summary tables 2 to 5 need not be described at length since they are all explained in detail in subsequent chapters:

Table 2. Personal income and expenditure—this is the income and expenditure account of the personal sector (see Chapter VI).

Table 3. Corporate income appropriation account—the combined appropriation accounts of companies (see Chapter VII) and public corporations (see Chapter VIII). It is not strictly a consolidated account because interest and dividend payments between companies and public corporations have not been eliminated.

Table 4. Current account of central government including National Insurance Funds—the income and expenditure account of central government (see Chapter IX).

Table 5. Current account of local authorities—the income and expenditure account of local authorities (see Chapter X).

Table 6. Combined capital account

This table brings together the capital accounts for all sectors of the economy. A capital account is included in each of the sector sections of the Blue Book and the sector accounts are described in subsequent chapters. The presentation of the combined capital account differs from that of the sector accounts in that stock appreciation is deducted from receipts and only the value of the physical increase in stocks is shown on the payments side of the account. In the national accounts the gain arising from the appreciation of stocks is a capital gain and not part of income; to be comparable with the valuation of investment in fixed assets, the investment in stocks and work in progress must be valued at current prices (see pages 17 and 18).

Table 6 shows separately the receipts on capital account of each sector from savings, which are the excess of current income over current outlay, brought forward from Tables 2 to 5. The savings of persons, companies and public corporations, as explained in the notes on the tables from which they are drawn, are estimated after deducting accruals of taxes arising from each year's income, since it is felt that accruals—rather than taxes actually paid which may relate to the income of earlier years—are the more significant charge against the current year's income. On the other hand, the savings of the central government are reckoned after crediting only the taxes actually received. The difference between the tax accruing on the income of the tax-paying enterprises and the taxes actually paid is treated as though transferred from the appropriation accounts of the enterprises not to central government but to a notional tax reserve; it is nevertheless a source of funds for temporary investment. Hence the payments into this reserve are shown as receipts in Table 6. The analogous differences between provision for dividends and interest and actual payments are treated in the same way and the additions to dividend and interest reserves are also shown as receipts in Table 6. The figures of savings are before providing for depreciation and stock appreciation, and stock appreciation is deducted as a separate item. When the sector capital accounts are combined, capital transfers between sectors cancel out and the receipts in Table 6 therefore include only capital transfers from abroad. For the private sector, no distinction is made between current and capital transfers from abroad and capital transfers from abroad relate to receipts by the central government.

Conceptually, the total of savings after deducting stock appreciation, together with capital transfers from abroad, represents the total funds available for gross investment. However, there are discrepancies between the income and expenditure data from which the estimates of savings are derived as a residual. The overall difference between the income and expenditure data, the *residual error*, has to be brought into the table in order to preserve the balance between total receipts and total payments. The nature of the residual error is explained on page 39. It is presented as a form of income (positive or negative) and thus of savings, which is not attributable to any sector.

The payments in Table 6 represent the gross investment, or additions to wealth, for the nation as a whole. Investment is measured gross in the sense that it is before deduction of depreciation on domestic fixed assets. Gross investment takes three forms: domestic investment in fixed assets (such as plant and buildings), investment in stocks and work in progress (materials, partly finished products and goods awaiting sale) and net investment abroad. The first two represent investment in physical assets and the latter is regarded as investment in financial assets, although it does include investment in physical assets held abroad. The estimates of gross domestic fixed capital formation and of the value of the physical increase in stocks are described in Chapters XII and XIII respectively. Net investment abroad represents the net increase in the value of overseas assets acquired by United Kingdom residents *less* the net increase in the value of assets in the United Kingdom acquired by non-residents. It is equal to the current balance in the balance of payments accounts, except in the years 1947 to 1951 when certain capital grants from overseas governments were not taken into account in arriving at the current balance. Net investment abroad is taken from the international transactions account (Table 7) and is further described in Chapter XV.

The total of investment may be related to the size of the gross national product; the amount of investment is a measure of the resources applied to the renewal and expansion of the nation's productive assets at home and abroad. The comparison shows at the same time the proportion of income devoted to saving as distinct from current consumption. The total of investment may also be related to the initial stock of assets to show the extent of the increase in the national wealth.

An alternative arrangement of the sector capital accounts is given in the section on financial accounts (Table 72 of the 1967 Blue Book) and described in Chapter XIV.

Table 7. International transactions

This is a combined account which incorporates items from the United Kingdom production account and from the current and capital accounts of the domestic sectors. It sets out in very summary form the principal elements in the balance of payments. The account is described in detail in Chapter XV.

Table 8. Gross domestic product at factor cost

This table brings together the various estimates of gross domestic product at factor cost. They are shown in index number form, with the base year for the constant price estimates as 100.

The estimate of gross domestic product at current prices based on expenditure data is given in Table 1. The corresponding estimate based on income data is equal to the sum of factor incomes and can be derived from Table 1 by deducting stock appreciation from total domestic income.

The estimate of gross domestic product at constant prices based on expenditure data is given in Table 14. The estimate based on income data is derived by deflating the income estimate of gross domestic product at current prices by the price index for gross domestic product implied by the current and constant price estimates based on expenditure data. This price index is given in the table on index numbers of costs and prices (Table 16) as the index of total home costs. The estimate based on output data is given in the table on index numbers of output at constant factor cost (Table 15).

Table 9. Shares in the gross national product

Two alternative analyses are presented of the distribution of the gross national product between categories of income. The right-hand side of the table on page 61 (Table 1 in the Blue Book) shows the gross incomes received by factors of production before redistribution through payments of dividends and interest and transfers, or taxes on income. For some purposes it is more convenient to show the distribution of the gross national product after such transfers. In the first part of Table 9, therefore, factor incomes are still shown before deducting taxes on income, but transfers in the form of current grants from public authorities (national insurance benefits, etc.) and receipts of dividends and net interest, are added to personal income; the income of companies and public corporations is then shown after net payments of dividends and interest, and a negative income is shown for public authorities. In the second part of Table 9, the redistribution is carried a stage further; taxes on income are deducted from the income of the personal sector and from the incomes of companies and public corporations. The income attributed to the personal sector thus becomes its disposable income after accruals of taxes on income; and that attributed to companies and public corporations is equal to the gross savings of these sectors.

Table 10. The composition of final output

This table shows the primary input content of total final output at market prices, divided between factor incomes, imports and taxes on expenditure *less* subsidies. Total final output is the value at market prices, of home produced and imported goods and services available for private and public consumption, investment and export. It is equal to total final expenditure and the residual error is included in it.

Table 11. Gross national product by industry

This table shows the gross national product divided by industry of origin; it shows the total factor incomes originating in each industry, before providing for depreciation and stock appreciation. The total of factor incomes originating in each industry is equal to the net output or value added of that industry, that is its contribution to the gross national product, *plus* stock appreciation. Stock appreciation is included in each industry's contribution because of the difficulties of making separate estimates for each industry. The table is a summary of Table 17 which shows, where possible, the separate forms of factor income.

Table 12. Gross national product by category of expenditure

In this table estimates of expenditure are given at both market prices and factor cost (that is, with taxes on expenditure subtracted and subsidies added). The estimates of domestic expenditure at market prices are the same as those in Table 1. The estimates of exports of goods and services at market prices are taken from Table 7, as are the estimates of imports of goods and services. The estimates at market prices of gross domestic product and gross national product shown in this table thus include all United Kingdom taxes on expenditure *less* subsidies. They include taxes on expenditure levied on imports, in addition to taxes on the various components of the gross domestic product.

c*

The view may be taken that market prices of imports, as of other goods, must include any taxes which they attract, since it is the price including duty which the purchaser has to pay, and which therefore affects substitution at the margin between different commodities, whether home produced or imported[1]. Thus, the estimates at market prices of the gross domestic and national products, which exclude imports, should also exclude taxes on imports. This definition does not conform to that proposed by the United Nations[2] and the estimates published in the Blue Book follow the international definition in order to facilitate comparisons. Estimates conforming with the alternative definition can be obtained by using the figures of taxes on expenditure levied on imports published in the notes to the Blue Book. These figures are of the amounts paid in customs duty on imports of merchandise arriving in the country or on withdrawals from bond. The figures include the duties on the quantities withdrawn from bond during the year and not those on the quantities actually imported during the year in such cases as tobacco, when the duties are normally paid on withdrawal from bond. The temporary charge on imports from 1964 to 1966 is included. Excise duties, such as purchase tax, on imports are not included, since separate figures are not available but the amounts involved are relatively small. An allowance is deducted for payments of export rebate in respect of hydrocarbon oil duty.

The estimates at factor cost in the lower part of the table involve allocating taxes on expenditure and subsidies between the various forms of final expenditure. The allocation of taxes and subsidies used in this table is taken from Table 50. Some of the difficulties of making this allocation are explained on page 327 and the allocation must be regarded only as an approximation. In particular, it is not practicable to allocate taxes and subsidies specifically to stockbuilding: hence the factor cost of the increase in stocks is combined with that of fixed capital formation.

Table 13. Gross national product by sector and type of income and employment by sector

This table shows the contribution of the production activity of each sector of the economy to the gross national product and gives estimates of numbers employed in each sector. The changes in the figures for the sectors are affected by changes in classification, principally the incorporation of businesses and nationalisation or de-nationalisation of companies. In particular, there is a break in the series from April 1961 when the Post Office is treated as a public corporation instead of as a central government trading enterprise.

The contribution to gross national product is divided between income from employment, income from self-employment, profit incomes and rent. The factor incomes are distributed according to the sector of employment and not according to the sector to which they are paid.

Total income from employment is estimated mainly from tax assessment data; the estimates are described in Chapter VI. Income from employment

---

[1] A fuller discussion of the problem is contained in 'National income at factor cost or market prices?' by J. L. Nicholson, *Economic Journal*, Vol. LXV, June 1955.

[2] *A System of National Accounts and Supporting Tables*, United Nations, New York, 1964 and its forthcoming revised edition.

arising within the public sector is estimated independently in constructing the public sector tables and the remainder is attributed to the private sector. Income from employment paid by public corporations is shown in their operating account (Table 36), which is described in Chapter VIII. Most of the wages and salaries paid by public authorities form part of current expenditure on goods and services, which is analysed in Table 48; other payments by public authorities are shown in a footnote to that table, which is described in Chapter XI. The remaining income is taken to be that paid by employers in the private sector, including any income from employment by non-residents. The income of domestic servants employed by private households and income from employment arising from the activity of private non-profit-making bodies serving persons are part of consumers' expenditure (see Table 27) and arise entirely in the personal sector. These amounts are shown separately in the table; the estimates are described in Chapter VI. All the income from employment in agriculture is also attributed to the personal sector. This is in line with the treatment of profit income from agriculture, all of which is included in income from self-employment. The remainder of income from employment is divided between unincorporated businesses (the personal sector) and companies, mainly on the basis of an Inland Revenue analysis of taxable income by category of employer.

The various forms of trading income other than rent arise in different sectors, and there is no problem of allocation. Income from self-employment, however, includes all income of farmers, even if their business is incorporated, and all of this income is attributed to the personal sector.

Income from rent is estimated in total for the economy, as described in Appendix I. Rent income received by the public sector is shown in the current accounts. The allocation of the remainder between the personal sector and companies for earlier years is very approximate, being based on a largely arbitrary allocation of rent income from various groups of property between the sectors (see Appendix I). With the abolition of income tax under Schedule A, more information became available from assessments under Schedule D from 1964/65 and the estimation of rent income for the personal sector and companies for the later years is more accurate.

This table also includes a section showing estimates of employment by sector. The estimates are of employment at mid-June of each year and are therefore only approximately comparable with the estimates of income given in the table. The total working population in employment in the United Kingdom is taken from the mid-year estimates published by the Ministry of Labour and by the Ministry of Health and Social Services, Northern Ireland. In these estimates a part-time worker is counted as one person.

Estimates of employment in the public sector are based on various sources. For public corporations, the figures are based mainly on data in the annual reports of the corporations. Most of the information for the central government is provided by the Treasury and the health departments. For local authorities a large proportion of employment is covered by the figures, published annually in the *Ministry of Labour Gazette*, of numbers employed in Great Britain by local authorities and police forces; these figures are then adjusted to allow for estimated double counting of part-time employees, such as teachers in evening classes, who are included in another sector. The Ministry of Health and Social Services, Northern Ireland provides details of numbers employed in the public sector in Northern Ireland.

The estimates of employment in the private sector are residuals and thus include any differences between the method of measuring total employment and the methods used for estimating employment in the public sector. In particular, the estimates include some who, at mid-June, are neither in jobs nor registered as wholly unemployed; all these are included in the estimate for the private sector. The division of employment between the public and the private sectors can therefore only be regarded as approximate. Because sufficient information is not available it is not possible to allocate employment in the private sector between the personal sector and companies.

A fuller analysis of employment, for the years 1957 to 1961, is given in an article published in the December 1962 issue of *Economic Trends*.

3. EXPENDITURE AND OUTPUT AT CONSTANT PRICES

Table 14. Expenditure and output at 1958 prices

Table 14 shows each major category of final expenditure revalued at constant market prices. The methods of deriving these estimates are summarised in Chapter III and are described in subsequent chapters where the current price estimates are described. The treatment of taxes on imports is the same as that in Table 12 (see page 65) and the estimates at market prices of gross domestic and gross national product include taxes levied on imports. Estimates of gross domestic and gross national product at constant market prices excluding taxes levied on imports may be derived by using the figures of taxes levied on imports at constant prices given in the notes to the Blue Book.

Net property income from abroad is revalued at constant prices by dividing it by the price index implied by the estimates of imports of goods and services at current and constant prices (shown in Table 16). Property income from abroad and property income paid abroad are not revalued separately.

The estimates of gross domestic product at factor cost are derived by subtracting estimates of total taxes on expenditure *less* subsidies revalued at 1958 average rates from the estimates of gross domestic product revalued at average 1958 market prices. The various forms of final expenditure are not estimated separately at constant factor cost because of the statistical difficulties involved. The estimates of total taxes on expenditure *less* subsidies at constant rates are more reliable than separate estimates for each category of final expenditure. They are a necessary step in arriving at the estimates of gross domestic product at factor cost, but this does not necessarily imply that they are in themselves of economic significance.

Table 15. Index numbers of output at constant factor cost

This table shows the contributions, revalued at constant prices, of different industries to the gross domestic product. The methods of deriving these estimates are summarised in Chapter III and described in greater detail in Chapter V.

Table 16. Index numbers of costs and prices

The index numbers of total home costs per unit of output are derived by dividing the estimate of the gross domestic product at current factor cost based on expenditure data (Table 1) by the estimate of the gross domestic product at constant factor cost based on expenditure data (Table 14). Alternative estimates of the index numbers of home costs per unit of output would be obtained by using the other estimates of gross domestic product shown in Table 8.

The index numbers of income from employment per unit of output are derived by dividing the estimate of income from employment by the estimate of the gross domestic product at constant factor cost based on income data. The result is expressed as an index, taking the quotient for the base year of the constant price estimates as 100.

The index numbers of gross profits and other trading income per unit of output are derived in the same way. The estimate of gross profits and other trading income, after providing for stock appreciation, is divided by the estimate of the gross domestic product at constant factor cost based on income data and the result is expressed as an index, taking the quotient for the base year of the constant price estimates as 100.

The estimate of gross domestic product at constant factor cost to which the incomes are related is shown in index number form in Table 8. It is obtained by dividing the income estimate of gross domestic product by the index of total home costs. The estimate based on income data is used, rather than that based on expenditure or output, because the numerator and denominator are then consistent. The index for total home costs is thus a weighted average of that for income from employment and that for gross profits and other trading income, the weights being the relative importance of the two forms of income in the base year.

Each price index is the result of dividing an estimated total for the year in question at current prices by a corresponding total revalued at constant prices. The index number for any year is therefore based on the weights of that year, and provides a direct measure of the change in prices between that year and the base year. Comparisons other than with the base year may be affected by differences in the weights which are generally more important over longer than over shorter periods. Where the information is considered sufficiently accurate, the indices are given to one decimal place.

Total final output is the value at market prices of home produced and imported goods and services available for private and public consumption, investment and export.

4. INDUSTRIAL INPUT AND OUTPUT

Table 17. Gross domestic product by industry and type of income

This table, which is summarised in Table 11, shows the composition by industry group of the gross domestic product and the forms of factor income originating in each industry. The total of factor incomes is divided where possible between wages, salaries, employers' contributions to national insurance and to superannuation funds, etc., income from self-employment, gross trading profits of companies, and gross trading surplus of public corporations and other public enterprises. The full analysis cannot, however, be estimated for every industry. Thus, in some cases, all forms of income from employment (wages, salaries and employers' contributions) are combined. In others, two or more forms of trading income (income from self-employment, company profits, trading surplus of public corporations and trading surplus of other public enterprises) are combined. The treatment of rent is explained below under the heading 'Insurance, banking and finance (including real estate)'.

The total of factor incomes generated in each industry is identical with the net output or value added of the industry *plus* stock appreciation; that is, the excess of the value of the goods and services produced by the industry over the cost of goods and services used in production, before provision is made for the depreciation of fixed assets and for stock appreciation. In this context, the value of goods produced is reckoned at factor cost, that is, it excludes any taxes on expenditure paid by the producer and any subsidy received by him from public authorities is not deducted.

The table gives an analysis by only broad industry groups, because comparable data are not available to provide a finer industry classification. In the case of income from employment the unit of classification is normally the establishment while the estimates of trading income are generally based on the financial unit used for tax purposes. It is thus possible, where a company is engaged in two or more activities, for example manufacturing and distribution, for the employment income arising from these activities to be allocated to each of them while the profits are unavoidably allocated to only one industry group. The difference in classification is not likely to have a significant effect on the estimates for the groups shown, although some error may arise in the allocation of trading income between manufacturing and distribution.

The estimates of income from employment by industry are described in Chapter VI, pages 133 to 140. The estimate for 'Other services' is a residual between the estimates made for other industries shown and the total based on Inland Revenue statistics; as such it is subject to a wide margin of error. The estimates of trading income by industry for public enterprises are built up from the accounts of the various enterprises. For private enterprises, the estimates are based on the industry analyses of the profit incomes charged to tax, which are made by the Inland Revenue, and published in the annual reports of the Commissioners. The incomes charged to tax for each industry group are adjusted as far as possible to the definition of trading income required for the national accounts and the adjustments described in Chapters VI (pages 145–7) and VII (pages 223–6) are distributed over the various industry groups. In the case of insurance, banking and finance, the gross profits and other income are shown before the required adjustment for net interest receipts, which is shown separately to arrive at the trading income excluding net interest receipts, as defined for the national accounts (see pages 204 to 206).

The definition of the various branches of industry follows the *Standard Industrial Classification, 1958*, as listed below.

Agriculture, forestry and fishing. Order I. The rent of farm land and buildings, both paid and imputed is included in trading income.

Mining and quarrying. Order II.

Manufacturing. Orders III–XVI.

Construction. Order XVII. Building work done by the direct employees of public authorities and of undertakings in transport and communication is not classified to those industries, but is included here. Building work done by the direct employees of gas, electricity and water undertakings is included under 'Gas, electricity and water'.

Gas, electricity and water. Order XVIII. See note on 'Construction'.

Transport. Order XIX, apart from communication (Minimum List Heading 707).

Communication. The remainder of Order XIX.

Distributive trades. Order XX.

Insurance, banking and finance (including real estate). Part of Order XXI. For an explanation of these figures see Chapter VII, page 205. Included here, for real estate is the rent income arising from (a) land and buildings rented to trading concerns or public authorities, even though the owners of the property may be a concern primarily engaged in some other industry, such as a manufacturing concern, (b) buildings owned and used by public authorities, other than for their trading activities. The imputed income from owner-occupation of trading bodies is not included: this is regarded as part of trading profits. Also excluded is the income from the letting or owner-occupation of dwellings, which is shown separately. The rent income from farm land and buildings, both paid and imputed, is also excluded from the rent income of real estate and is included with income from self-employment and other trading income under 'Agriculture, forestry and fishing'. Employment income arising in real estate is included here only if it arises in a business concern classified to this industry. Other employment income arising in real estate is included under the main activity of the concern.

Ownership of dwellings. Part of Order XXI. Rent income, actual or imputed, from the ownership of dwellings, and of property occupied by non-profit-making bodies. Any employment income arising from this activity is included under the main activity of the concern. This form of income is shown separately from the other income generated in Order XXI because of its special interest and because much of the income is received by individuals, including owner-occupiers. The corresponding income from owner-occupied trading property is included in the trading income of each industry.

Public administration and defence. Order XXIV. The services rendered are measured by the wages and salaries of civilian employees, pay in cash and kind of the Forces, and employers' contributions.

Public health services. Part of Order XXII. Health services provided by public authorities, measured by the wages, salaries and employers' contributions in respect of staff employed. The fees of hospital consultants are included but not the remuneration of general practitioners and dentists, who are regarded as being self-employed.

Local authority educational services. Part of Order XXII. Educational services provided by local authorities, measured by the wages, salaries and employers' contributions in respect of staff employed (see page 139).

Other services. Order XXIII and the remaining parts of Order XXII. The wages, salaries and employers' contributions paid in respect of domestic servants employed by private households and in respect of employees of private non-profit-making bodies serving persons, which are included in Order XXIII, are shown separately in Table 13.

Table 18. Wages and salaries in manufacturing industries

This table supplements Table 17 and provides further details of the distribution by industry of wages and salaries in manufacturing industries, defined as in the *Standard Industrial Classification, 1958.* Reference is made to it on page 135.

Estimates of the average numbers of wage earners and salary earners employed throughout the year in all manufacturing industries are also given in this table. However, the estimates of the number of salary earners are not precisely comparable with the estimates of salaries. The figures of salaries include rough estimates of the amounts paid in fees to directors, whereas the estimates of numbers do not include those directors paid by fee only. An estimate is given in the footnote to the table of the average salary, excluding directors' fees, in the latest year.

INPUT-OUTPUT TABLES

The three provisional input-output tables for 1963 which are included in the 1967 Blue Book were designed to bring up to date the tables previously published for the year 1954[3]. The tables are a revised version of those originally published, together with additional tables and commentary, in the August 1966 issue of *Economic Trends*. The tables follow the same conceptual framework as the summary tables previously published for 1954, which can be referred to for a discussion of the definitions and concepts used. However, there are three changes in presentation. First, a little more industrial detail is shown in the tables for 1963 than in the original summary tables for 1954. Secondly, stock appreciation has been eliminated from the figures. Thirdly, the expenditure of public authorities is shown in a more gross form than in the 1954 exercise. The study for 1963 also differs from the one for 1954 in that it is not based on a full analysis of the census of production for the year in question. Such a census was taken for 1963, but only provisional and summary results were available when these tables were prepared. The tables in the 1967 Blue Book are thus provisional, pending the publication of more firmly based and more detailed input-output tables, based on the full results of the census of production for 1963.

The tables for 1963 were designed to provide statistics for use in broad economic studies only. They were derived partly by an 'up-dating' process, which is described below and, because of the limitations of this process, they are not suitable for use in detailed industrial studies; even for the broad industry groups shown, they should be used with caution.

For agriculture, forestry and fishing, coal mining, mineral oil refining, and the gas, electricity and water industries, the figures for inputs and outputs were computed primarily from departmental statistics for 1963. For the remaining industries, which include most of manufacturing, the estimates of input and output were derived by up-dating the 1954 input-output table in the following way. First, gross output free from duplication for each industry group (that is, excluding sales between establishments within the industry group) was estimated from the provisional results of the census of production for 1963. The extent of this duplication could be estimated only roughly since detailed figures of inputs to industry were not available. Second, final expenditure at sellers' prices, estimated from national accounts data, was deducted from these gross output totals to give estimates of total intermediate output for each industry group (that is, the row totals to the right of the inner matrix of intermediate transactions shown in Table 19). Third, column totals of this inner matrix were

---

[3] *Input-Output Tables for the United Kingdom, 1954*, Studies in Official Statistics, No. 8, 1961.

estimated by deducting net output and net taxes on expenditure from the non-duplicated gross output totals. Fourth, the 1954 inputs to each industry group, revalued at 1963 prices, were adjusted *pro rata* so as to add up to the column totals. Fifth, these estimated inputs on the 1954 pattern were summed horizontally and compared with the independent estimates of row totals of intermediate output described above. Differences between the two estimates of intermediate output were eliminated by a repeated process of *pro-rating* both horizontally and vertically until the inner matrix balanced. The end-result is a set of intermediate transactions consistent with given estimates of total inputs of goods and services and of total intermediate sales of goods and services. This process depends on an initial assumption that trends in the total industrial usage of each commodity group are applicable to each of the individual user industries, but this assumption is eventually modified in the *pro-rating* process.

Imports were allocated to industries and final buyers according to the description of the imported commodity. Thus, metalliferous ores were allocated to metal manufacturing and textile fibres to the textiles, leather and clothing industry group. For certain commodities, for example copper bars and sawn timber, which are used by more than one industry group, the allocation can only be very rough until the full detail on industrial usage becomes available from the census of production. The final detailed tables, when they are produced, will include an import matrix showing the commodity composition of each industry group's imports, and also a commodity/industry matrix showing the commodity composition of each industry's inputs, from which industry/industry and commodity/commodity matrices can be derived.

Whilst using the same conceptual framework and definitions as the 1954 study, it cannot be certain that full allowance has been made for all the statistical changes which have taken place since the 1954 study, nor for the fact that the departmental statistics used for 1963 are not always completely consistent with the census of production information because of differences, for example, in timing and classification. Thus although the tables do provide figures corresponding to those for 1954, particular caution should be exercised in making comparisons at the detailed level. Such comparisons may also be affected by the relative position of the two years in the business cycle.

The value of each industry group's output is measured at market prices and free from duplication, that is, it excludes that part of the output of each establishment which is sold to other establishments within the same industry group. This makes the output of the industry group independent of its structure and organisation.

The value of the output of the transport and distributive trades (part of the output of 'Services') is measured by the gross margin on the goods and services transported or sold. It thus equals the incomes generated *plus* the cost of goods and services used by these industries in providing their services; it does not include the factory value of the goods transported or distributed. In effect, manufacturers and overseas suppliers are regarded as selling their outputs direct to the industries or final buyers who in reality buy from the distributor; the latter is treated as an agent who sells only his own services. The gross output of the manufacturing industries includes any value added (net output) by their merchanting activities but not the selling value of the goods merchanted.

All sales and purchases of goods produced are measured in terms of sellers' value (the amount received by the seller) as distinct from purchasers' value (the amount paid by the purchaser). Transport charges are considered as sales by 'Services' to the user. Thus, for example, sales by 'Services' to persons comprises (*a*) consumers' expenditure on travel, communications, entertainment and all other services, and (*b*) the value of the services rendered by the transport industry and the distributive trades in handling goods purchased by persons from industry and in handling imports bought by persons. The principal advantage of recording all transactions at sellers' prices and not at the price paid by the purchaser is that the figures of sales both to other industries and to final buyers within each row are on the same price basis and are, as far as possible, comparable.

Taxes on expenditure and subsidies paid or received by a producer are, with the exception of excise duties on drink and tobacco, treated as being paid by the producer selling the taxed or subsidised goods, that is, as positive or negative inputs respectively. Thus, agricultural subsidies are treated as a negative primary input in column 1 of Table 19. The excise duties on drink and tobacco have been treated as taxes on consumers. For consistency with the treatment of transport and distributive services, customs duties and purchase tax paid by wholesalers on marketed goods, which enter directly into final output without further processing in the United Kingdom, are treated as if they were paid directly by the final buyer. They therefore appear only in columns 17 to 19 of row 19 in Table 19. Sales by final buyers (row 17) include sales by industry and public authorities of second-hand vehicles, ships and plant and machinery for scrap or to personal consumers, or for export. They also include payments by persons to the central government for goods and services provided under the national health service, and fees paid by persons to both central and local government for various services. Sales abroad by public authorities are also included.

The value of the physical change in stocks and work in progress in column 20 of Table 19 represents the value of the physical change in the stocks of goods *produced* by the various industries or imported. The estimates, therefore, differ from the figures in the section of the Blue Book on capital formation which represent the change in all kinds of stocks *held* by the various industries. The allocation of stocks to the producing industry is inevitably approximate.

In Table 19 stock appreciation is not included in the figures of total output nor in the figures of gross profits and other trading income. This treatment differs from that followed in the summary input-output flow table for 1954 where stock appreciation was shown in a separate column and included in both total output and primary input, but not in intermediate or final output. Since stock appreciation has to be eliminated from the flow table before it can be inverted and before the various supplementary input-output tables can be prepared, it is now thought preferable to present the main input-output flow table adjusted in this way. The new presentation makes it possible to record all inputs on a current price basis; it is also somewhat less complex.

The estimates of stock appreciation on goods *held* by the different industry groups in 1963 are given below. These estimates of stock appreciation represent for each industry group the difference between the figures of gross profits and other trading income, after deducting stock appreciation, given in Table 19, and the corresponding figures before deducting stock appreciation, given in the table on gross domestic product by industry and type of income (Table 17).

	£ million
Agriculture, forestry and fishing	28
Coal mining	2
Other mining and quarrying	—
Food, drink and tobacco	36
Mineral oil refining	—
Other chemicals and allied industries..................	1
Metal manufacture	10
Engineering and allied industries	42
Textiles, leather and clothing	37
Other manufacturing	10
Construction	8
Gas, electricity and water	7
Services	31
Total stock appreciation	212

Table 19. Summary input-output transactions matrix, 1963

This is the basic inter-industry transactions matrix. In the table, the United Kingdom economy is divided into fourteen broad industry groups. Estimates are given for each industry of its purchases (for use in current production) of the goods and services produced by each of the other industries, of the services of factors of production and of imports; and of the sales of its products as inter-mediate output to other industries and as final output to the personal sector, public authorities, capital formation and for export. All the transactions are valued at ex-factory, or sellers' prices, and not at purchasers' prices.

This table is linked to the estimates of gross domestic product in the following ways:

	£ million
Income from employment (the total in column 23 of row 20)	18,145
plus Gross profits and other trading income and the residual error (the total in column 23 and 21)	8,582
equals Gross domestic product at factor cost..............	26,727
Total final expenditure or output (the total in column 22)...	36,179
less Imports of goods and services (the total in column 23 of row 16)	—5,964
less Net taxes on expenditure (the total in column 23 of row 19)	—3,488
equals Gross domestic product at factor cost..............	26,727

The columns in the table show the estimated extent to which each of the fourteen industry groups was dependent on other industries and on imports for its supply of inputs on production account in 1963. From the figures in each column can be deduced the inputs required on average by each industry to produce £100 of final demand.

Table 20. Total requirements per £100 of final industrial output in terms of gross output, 1963

On the assumption that the inputs required by each industry group are the same for each unit of its output, the average relationships between the inputs (both direct and indirect) and the outputs of the different industries in 1963 can be derived from the intermediate transactions in Table 19. The indirect inputs are those required at earlier stages of production for the production of the direct inputs. These relationships are given in this table in the form of estimates of the outputs (both direct and indirect) required on average to produce £100 of final output by each industry group in 1963. They were obtained by inverting the matrix of coefficients derived from the values of the intermediate transactions in Table 19. These relationships may not be the same as the marginal relationships which would apply for changes in output, but are nevertheless a useful approach to the assessment of the effect of changes in output of one industry on the demands of other industries.

Table 21. Total requirements per £100 of final industrial output in terms of net output, 1963

For many purposes it is more convenient to present the results of Table 20 in a different form so that the contribution of each of the different industries, of imports and of taxes on expenditure *less* subsidies, to the output of a particular industry group adds to 100 per cent. The figures are derived by applying the appropriate ratios of net output to gross output to the figures for each industry given in Table 20.

Chapter V

Output at Constant Prices

1. CONCEPTS

As stated in Chapter III, there are two general methods of estimating the domestic product at constant prices. The production method, the subject of this chapter, arrives at the gross domestic product by adding together the contributions of all industries, that is their net output including depreciation.

'Industries' in this sense covers all economic activity and includes not only industries like coal mining or engineering, which produce goods, but also those which provide services. The service industries are defined to include not only industries such as transport or banking but also government and public administration. The contributions of all these industries are included whether they produce goods or services for final use in consumption or investment or intermediate products for use by other industries. The definition of the production boundary is discussed in Chapter I.

The contribution of each industry to the domestic product is its 'net output', that is the value of its gross (or total) output *less* any materials or services it has acquired from other industries or has imported. For example, the value of the gross output of the weaving industry will include the value of the yarn bought from the spinning industry and it may also include the value of services provided by banking, advertising and so on; the value of these materials and services has to be deducted in order to arrive at its net output. Net output in this sense includes provision for depreciation but excludes stock appreciation. It differs from the census of production concept of net output in the calculation of which not all inputs of services are deducted. The net output of each industry consists of the services of the factors of production engaged in that industry and equals the sum of the factor incomes (wages, salaries and profit incomes) earned in the industry after deducting stock appreciation. The total of the net output of all industries is called the gross domestic product—the value of the goods and services produced during the period in question; the product is described as 'gross' because depreciation has not been deducted. The estimate of gross domestic product thus derived is measured at factor cost; it excludes taxes on expenditure and includes subsidies.

The measurement of net output at constant prices

Conceptually, net output should be estimated at constant prices by revaluing at constant prices both the gross output and the inputs of materials, fuel, services and so on, and subtracting the latter from the former. This is known as 'double deflation'. In practice this method is difficult to apply because it requires a great deal of information. Unless full information on all transactions is available at frequent intervals the method can give unreliable results, as the output and input data must be consistent and relate to the same period. This applies especially if net output is small in relation to gross output. The double deflation method is in

77

fact used in United Kingdom statistics only for estimating the net output of agriculture. It is used for agriculture, not only because this is an industry for which there is sufficient information available, but also because it is an industry in which the relationship of net output to inputs and gross output can vary significantly from one year to another owing to weather conditions. Changes in inputs or gross output would therefore not give a satisfactory indication of changes in net output.

Net output at constant prices may be estimated by the use of changes in other series to indicate the changes in net output. Provided that the ratio of net output to gross output remains unchanged at constant prices, changes in net output at constant prices will be measured by changes in gross output at constant prices. This approach, of finding some indicator which will reflect changes in net output, is adopted in the United Kingdom statistics for all industries other than agriculture. This method of estimating changes in net output is simpler than that of double deflation and may in practice be more accurate.

The most frequently used indicator is gross output. Changes in the ratio of net output to gross output in individual industries can be caused by many factors, such as changes in production methods, variations in the products made and materials used, and changes in services supplied by other industries. It is likely that some of the errors introduced by the operation of these factors in individual industries will be somewhat reduced in the aggregate for all industries. For example, if an intermediate process is transferred from one industry to another this does not necessarily alter the combined amount of work done, and if the gross output indicator overstates the change in the net output of one industry for this reason, the error may be offset by an understatement of the change in the net output of the other industry. Nevertheless, it should be realised that the use of gross output as an indicator is a substitute for what is really required. The resulting estimates may understate the true increase in net output where there is a change towards more processing per unit of output and economy in the use of materials.

Changes in net output may also be estimated by changes in inputs. The input chosen is generally materials used and this is subject to the same sort of limitations as gross output. Where production processes are improved and economies are made in the use of materials, changes in materials used may underestimate changes in net output. Employment is sometimes the input indicator but it is used as little as possible because it does not take account of any increases in productivity and therefore tends to underestimate increases in net output.

Technological change occurs only slowly, so that changes in gross output can be taken as a sufficiently good approximation to changes in net output so long as the basic estimate of net output is revised sufficiently frequently. Periodic revision of the basic estimates of net output takes account of changes in the relationship of net output to gross output and inputs and prevents continuing bias in the results.

Problems of measurement

In the case of industries whose outputs consist of physical products—as opposed to services—there is usually no great difficulty in determining appropriate measures of changes in output at constant prices. The quantity and the unit of measurement, as well as the price per unit, are usually stated at the time of purchase. Changes in output at constant prices can usually be estimated from the physical quantities of goods produced or from the value of output deflated by an index of price.

Greater difficulties arise, however, with the measurement of the output of service industries for which there may be no obvious physical units. For some service industries, such as transport or distribution, measures of output suggest themselves fairly readily: the output of transport can be measured in terms of the miles travelled and the distances over which goods are transported; the output of the distributive trades may be estimated by the volume of turnover. But the output of financial concerns (banks, building societies, etc.) is difficult to define, since the commodity mainly dealt with is money itself. For example banks, as well as keeping customers' accounts and providing other services, act as intermediaries in channelling funds between lender and borrower. The provision of these financial services requires the employment of people and other organisational arrangements, and it is necessary to allow for changes in their output if the gross domestic product is to be measured. In such cases the change in the services provided may have to be indicated by some series associated with these services, such as the deflated value of bank advances which is used as an indicator of the change in part of the services provided by banks.

Special problems arise in the case of services provided by public authorities for the community as a whole, including public health and education and public administration and defence. The fact that these services are provided free of charge, or with only a nominal charge, means that it is not possible to apply the criterion of the market contract to define the nature of their output. Sometimes it is helpful to consider the methods used in measuring analagous services produced under private enterprise and some such measures are used; for example changes in the provision of certain local authority health services are indicated by changes in the number of cases. However, where units are available to indicate changes in the output of services their relationship to these services tends to be variable. For example an increase in the number of pupils in schools might represent a decline in the quality of education rather than an increase in the amount of education, if there was no corresponding increase in the number of teachers. Conversely, an increase in the number of teachers might be associated with lower output per teacher rather than a proportionate increase in the quality of education. In other cases, it is difficult to suggest any possible units, for example for defence and civil administration. In general, the solution adopted has been to use changes in the numbers employed as an indicator of changes in output. The assumption that this implies, of no change in productivity, is obviously not satisfactory although it seems the best approach with our present knowledge.

Even when the unit of output is easily determined, considerable difficulties arise in practice in measuring changes in output over time. The unit of output needs to be narrowly enough defined so that the units are homogeneous throughout the period. Improvements in quality need to be allowed for and, for example, changes in the amount or quality of services provided with a product need to be taken into account. Problems arise when there are changes in the range of goods produced and new products come on to the market.

Where comparisons are made over a number of years the well-known 'index number problem' also arises. The combined estimates of changes in net output at constant prices reflect the relative prices of all goods and services in the base year. There is generally no reason for preferring the relative prices of one year to those of another, but almost certainly the choice of one rather than another will affect the result. There is thus no one result that is 'correct'. In practice a choice has to be made between continuity and the use of up-to-date relative prices. Continuity is achieved by retaining the same base year. Though changes in relative prices cannot be taken into account during this period and the appearance of new products is difficult to allow for, any bias in the estimates is unlikely to become serious if the base year is changed at sufficiently frequent intervals. The relative prices are more appropriate if the base year is changed frequently. In practice this is difficult to do because, so long as changes in net output are estimated by indicators, the information required for the base year is much more detailed than that required for other years.

When the base year is changed it is possible to provide two measures of the output at constant prices between the new and the old base year; one using the relative prices of the old base year and the other the relative prices of the new base year. Such a comparison was made for the industrial production industries when the base year was changed from 1948 to 1954[1]. However, there is no unique solution to the problem of which estimate to use. In practice, the United Kingdom official estimates now keep to the old base year for the period up to the new base year, and relate to the new base year for the period starting with the new base year. The estimated changes are linked to a common reference base for convenience, without calculating any special links between estimates calculated on different base years.

2. THE PUBLISHED TABLES

Since the United Kingdom estimates of output at constant prices are estimated almost entirely by the use of indicators to represent changes in net output at constant prices, they are presented in the form of estimated changes, rather than in terms of estimated values. The relative movements in the indicators are combined using as weights the value of net output in each industry in the base year. The results are presented in the form of index numbers where, for each industrial Order and for all industries, the net output in the base year is taken as 100.

The estimates of output at constant prices are prepared and published on the basis of the *Standard Industrial Classification, 1958*, which is followed so far as possible throughout the national accounts. The classification is divided into 24 sections, or Orders, and each Order is further subdivided into Minimum List Headings for the separate industries making up the industrial Order. For example, Order XIX, transport and communication, includes railways, road passenger transport, sea transport, air transport and so on. The table of the weights and indicators used for the estimates of output at constant prices, which is given as an annex to this chapter, follows the Orders and Minimum List Headings of the *Standard Industrial Classification, 1958*. As well as these 24 Orders, the ownership of dwellings is also distinguished separately from real estate within the insurance, banking and finance Order, as elsewhere in the

---

[1]*The Index of Industrial Production: Method of Compilation*, Studies in Official Statistics, No. 7, 1959.

national accounts. This is because of its special interest and because much of the income, actual and imputed, is received by individuals, including owner-occupiers.

The Blue Book table

The Blue Book includes one table (Table 15 of the 1967 Blue Book) on output at constant prices which gives index numbers of output at constant factor cost for 17 industrial groups and for all industries combined. The estimates have been prepared on a consistent basis from 1948. All of the industrial Orders outside of manufacturing are separately shown and so is the ownership of dwellings. More detail for the industries covered by the index of industrial production is given in the *Annual Abstract of Statistics* and, for the most recent years, in the *Monthly Digest of Statistics*.

The estimates are shown related to the latest base year as 100. For the 1967 Blue Book the base year was 1958. The base year is governed by the year of the latest detailed census of production and will be changed to 1963 when the detailed results of the census for that year become available. Although the estimates for all years are related to the latest base year, estimates for earlier years were compiled on an earlier base. The estimates of changes in output for the years 1948 to 1958 were compiled using 1954 weights; those for the years from 1958 onwards were compiled using 1958 weights. When the base year is changed to 1963 figures for the years from 1963 onwards will be compiled using 1963 weights.

The quarterly table

Quarterly estimates of output at constant prices were first published in 1966 and have been compiled back to 1958. The estimates are published quarterly on a seasonally adjusted basis in *Economic Trends*, with the quarterly article on national income and expenditure, and in the *Monthly Digest of Statistics*.

The estimates are compiled and presented in the same way as the annual figures, but the data available for the quarterly estimates are generally in less detail than for the annual estimates. Some of the industrial Orders are therefore combined before they are presented in the quarterly table, and the table gives estimates for only four groups outside of industrial production, compared with eight given annually. As in the case of the annual estimates, more detail on the industries covered by the index of industrial production is published in the *Monthly Digest of Statistics* and changes in the output of these industries are estimated monthly as well as quarterly. The process of adjustment to remove the effects of normal seasonal movements is based on the ratio to moving average method (see Section 3 of Chapter III).

3. STATISTICAL SOURCES

WEIGHTS

The indicators of changes in net output in each industry are combined using weights based on the relative contribution made by each industry to the gross domestic product, as measured by its net output in the base year. The starting point for the calculation of the weights is the analysis of the gross domestic product by industry and type of income which is given in the Blue Book (Table

17 of the 1967 Blue Book). This gives an analysis of factor incomes, differing from the required concept of net output only by the inclusion of stock appreciation. The difference was not allowed for in calculating the weights for 1958 when it was very small.

The weights for 1958 are generally consistent with the figures given in the 1962 Blue Book, the estimates available at the time when the weights were compiled. However, the Blue Book table gives figures by only broad industrial groups and a breakdown into at least Minimum List Headings is required to provide sufficiently detailed weights for the estimates of output at constant prices. Also the analysis contains a large group under 'Other services', which cannot be satisfactorily subdivided because the estimate of income from employment in these industries is derived as a residual between the total for all industries, which is based mainly on Inland Revenue data, and the estimates for individual industries, which are obtained from a variety of independent sources. The industrial analysis of wages and salaries and of profits made by the Inland Revenue provides consistent figures for all industries in detail approximating to that of the Minimum List Headings. For the 1958 weights it was used to subdivide, and in some cases to adjust, the industrial analysis given in the Blue Book in order to obtain detailed estimates on a consistent basis. The Inland Revenue analysis is based on a classification of financial units as opposed to the classification by establishments which is the aim of the Blue Book table. The difference in classification affects the weights but is not likely to reduce the accuracy of the estimates of changes in net output. The main effect of using Inland Revenue data is to increase the weight for manufacturing and reduce the weight for miscellaneous services. A further adjustment which was made to the Blue Book analysis for the 1958 weights deserves to be mentioned. The weight for transport and communication (road goods transport) was increased to cover all 'C' licence transport by making appropriate transfers from the weights for other industries employing these vehicles (manufacturing, construction and the distributive trades). This adjustment was made because the indicator used relates to road goods vehicles employed in all industries.

The analysis of factor incomes provided only the total weight for the industrial production industries. Within these industries the detailed weights were compiled from the results of the detailed census of production. Although the data are independent, every effort was made to produce weights which related to the same definition of net output. For the calculation of the weights, industries were subdivided into Minimum List Headings and within that into specialist groups of the *Standard Industrial Classification, 1958.* The weight for each industry was apportioned between the several products or product groups made by the industry in order to provide appropriate weights for the output series used as indicators. Where it was not possible to measure the output of all the products of an industry it was assumed that the uncovered portion moves with one or more of the indicators which are available.

Where a breakdown of the weights within Minimum List Headings was required for industries outside of industrial production, and this was not provided by Inland Revenue data, the further sub-division necessary was generally made on the basis of gross receipts, for example within railways and postal services and telecommunications. In the case of the distributive trades the weights within Minimum List Headings were estimated from the information on gross margins provided by the latest census of distribution. Gross margins on turnover

are not an exact measure of net output since net output is obtained after deduction
of payments to other industries for services such as rents, advertising and transport, but they are the best guide which is available.

One other aspect of the weights which needs to be mentioned concerns the
insurance, banking and finance industry where the treatment differs from that
elsewhere in the national accounts. In order that changes in the financial services
provided by this industry should be included in estimating the gross domestic
product, the weight for insurance, banking and finance included their net
receipts of interest which are one of the means of paying for these financial
services. In accordance with national accounting definitions, the net output
weights of other industries were estimated before receipts and payments of
interest and thus the industry weights contained a certain amount of duplication.
There is no very satisfactory basis for allocating the amount of net interest
included for insurance, banking and finance against the weights of the other
industries. The procedure adopted was to deduct from the weight for all industries the weight for net interest, by proportionately reducing the weight for
each Order (including ownership of dwellings) except for the Orders covering
insurance, banking and finance and public administration and defence.

The 1958 weights, scaled to add to 10,000 for convenience, are shown in detail
in the annex to this chapter. The weights were first calculated in value terms as
estimates of the factor incomes in the base year. The following table summarises
the weights for 1958 scaled to add to 10,000. Column (1) shows the weights
implied by the analysis of factor incomes shown in the 1962 Blue Book. Column
(2) gives the weights after the adjustments have been made and summarises the
weights shown in the annex. Column (3) gives the calculated weights further
adjusted to allow for the deduction for net interest, as described above. These
are the weights used in combining the Orders to produce the overall index
number; no separate series of index numbers is calculated for the net interest
adjustment.

Net output, 1958

Weights per 10,000

	Blue Book analysis (1)	Calculated weights (2)	Weights adjusted for net interest (3)
Agriculture, forestry and fishing.........	443	444	429
Mining and quarrying	360	351	339
Manufacturing.......................	3,540	3,659	3,534
Construction	600	616	595
Gas, electricity and water	266	264	255
Transport and communication	799	884	853
Distributive trades....................	1,263	1,162	1,122
Insurance, banking and finance	603	604	604
Professional and scientific services.......	} 1,468 {	704	680
Miscellaneous services		648	627
Public administration and defence.......	622	628	628
Ownership of dwellings	346	346	334
Net interest adjustment	−310	−310	—
	10,000	10,000	10,000

INDICATORS

A list of the series used from 1958 in both the annual and the quarterly estimates is set out in the annex to this chapter. Where a series is available both annually and quarterly it is listed once only, under the annual heading. Where an annual series is not available quarterly, the substitute quarterly indicator is shown.

Agriculture

The large amount of price and quantity data available for agriculture makes it possible to use the double deflation method for this industry. Some 250 items of output and 400 items of input are separately distinguished each carrying its own base-period price weight. A three-year price average (for the farm years 1954/55 to 1956/57) is used for the purposes of revaluation to reduce the effect of fluctuations arising from weather conditions and other factors. The resulting estimates of net output at constant prices for the June to May farm years are allocated to calendar years in the proportion 7:5. For example the estimate for 1965 is 5/12 of that for the 1964/65 farm year *plus* 7/12 of that for the 1965/66 farm year. A full description of the method and indicators used is given in an article in the March 1960 issue of *Economic Trends*. However, since this article was published, estimates have been made of the output of agricultural contractors and have been included in the index for agriculture, in accordance with the *Standard Industrial Classification, 1958*. Estimates of depreciation are added back to make the estimates consistent with the definition of gross domestic product.

Mining and quarrying; Manufacturing; Construction; and Gas, electricity and water

These industries are covered by the official index of industrial production. Activity in these industries was measured for a considerable time before the work of attempting to measure the output of other industries was begun in the early 1950's. The index of industrial production has a significance independent of its role as a constituent part of the index of gross domestic product at constant prices. It draws on very extensive data consisting to a considerable extent of information on physical outputs or closely related series. It is prepared and published monthly and provides an important economic indicator. A full description of the index has been published elsewhere[2].

As shown in the annex, the index of production covers just under half of the gross domestic product. Within this field the relative importance of the various industrial groups is shown in the table on the next page.

In the construction of the index some 880 different series are used. Most of these are for calendar months or periods of four or five weeks. Nearly a quarter of the total weight, however, is carried by quarterly series, some of the more important of which are supplemented by monthly series which are used before the quarterly figures become available and also to estimate movements within quarters. Adjustments are made in the series for calendar periods to eliminate the effect of variations in their length, so that the index estimates changes in the average weekly rate of production in each month.

Figures of output are the most frequently used indicators, but in some cases statistics of material inputs are used and, in a very few, employment series. For

[2]*The Index of Industrial Production: Method of Compilation*, Studies in Official Statistics, No. 7, 1959 and *Economic Trends*, March 1962.

Net output, 1958

	Orders of *Standard Industrial Classification, 1958*	Weight per 1,000
II	Mining and quarrying	71·7
III	Food, drink and tobacco	86·0
IV	Chemicals and allied industries	67·8
V	Metal manufacture	68·5
VI	Engineering and electrical goods	166·9
VII	Shipbuilding and marine engineering	21·8
VIII	Vehicles	79·1
IX	Metal goods not elsewhere specified	42·1
X	Textiles	58·2
XI	Leather, leather goods and fur	4·1
XII	Clothing and footwear	29·5
XIII	Bricks, pottery, glass, cement, etc.	28·1
XIV	Timber, furniture, etc.	19·9
XV	Paper, printing and publishing	54·7
XVI	Other manufacturing industries	21·6
XVII	Construction	125·9
XVIII	Gas, electricity and water	54·1
		1,000

some industries it is judged more satisfactory to use as indicators series of the deflated values of deliveries or production rather than physical measures in terms of quantities of the goods produced. Such series are used for the engineering and construction industries which produce a range of products so varied in type or specification that no suitable units are available for measuring overall output in physical terms. For the purpose of the construction of constant price series use is made of the extensive series of index numbers of wholesale prices for the output of finished products, or of special cost indices. The proportions of the total weight of the index of industrial production represented by the various types of indicator are:

	Percentage of total weight
Output indicators:	
Quantities delivered or produced	48
Value of deliveries or sales revalued at constant prices	35
Input indicators:	
Quantities of major materials received.................	14
Number of persons employed	3
	100

Transport and communication

This is an industry group for which suitable indicators of gross output are readily available. For most of the main forms of transport, figures of passenger miles and of freight ton-miles constitute the basis of the system of indicators employed.

In the case of road goods transport, the indicator used is an estimate of the ton-mileage of all road goods vehicles. The weight for this indicator has therefore been increased by transfers from other industries employing 'C' licence vehicles, though strictly the work done by these vehicles should be included with the industries which own them (see page 82).

For sea transport it is necessary to allow for the work done on cross-voyages as well as on voyages between this country and abroad. The annual inquiry of the Chamber of Shipping provides estimates of gross receipts of British operated tankers and dry cargo vessels which are deflated by indices of freight rates.

The communications industry is quite well covered by volume indicators of various kinds.

Distributive trades

The indicators for this industry are based on the volume of turnover, that is on turnover at constant prices. Where wholesalers mainly supply retailers, as is the case for most consumer goods, wholesale as well as retail distribution of these categories is represented by the indices of the volume of retail trade. Other wholesale dealing in materials is represented where possible by indices of deliveries, and otherwise by indices of production or consumption of the various materials. The activities of export merchants are represented by a number of indices of the volume of groups of United Kingdom exports and re-exports.

Insurance, banking and finance

As far as possible in this industry specific indicators of activity are used. For life assurance business the indicator is derived by deflating the expenses of handling life assurance; this is the same series as is included in consumers' expenditure at constant prices. For other forms of insurance the indicators are generally the excess of premiums over claims, deflated by an appropriate price index.

Banks are regarded as providing financial services to borrowers in addition to that of keeping customers' accounts, etc. The indicators of output for the latter are the number of cheques cleared and total deposits deflated. For financial services the indicator is bank advances deflated. Similar types of indicators are used for other financial institutions.

Property management is included in this Order; the indicator used is the stock of commercial and industrial buildings.

Professional and scientific services

The greater part of the weight for this Order is accounted for by public education and health services. As explained on page 79, the output of these services is represented by employment indicators, with the exception of local authority health services for which the indicators are on an output basis, for example number of patients attending clinics. For a large part of the remaining services in this group there is little information on output and for some of these also employment indicators are used.

Originally output indicators of various kinds were used to measure changes in the volume of output even in those areas where the problems of measurement are greatest as, for example, public education and health services. Such series as number of pupils in schools and number of bed-days in hospital were used, either by themselves or in conjunction with series for the numbers employed. Indicators of this type proved unsatisfactory and have been abandoned, partly because of the difficulty of finding indicators which bear a constant relationship to output and also because of the need to keep the output estimates consistent with the expenditure estimates (see Chapter III). It was obviously necessary to revalue expenditure on wages and salaries by public authorities by methods consistent with those used to measure output. Revaluing expenditure on wages and salaries at constant prices by calculating the amount that would have had to be spent if there had been no increases in rates of pay, gave different results from the indicators of output. The present practice, therefore, with a few minor exceptions, is to measure output in public education and health by reference to the numbers employed. Wherever possible, however, the figures used are not crude totals of staff but are weighted to take account of changes in the numbers in different grades or ranks. The assumption is thus made that the 'output' of a senior employee bears the same relation to that of a junior as their respective salaries bear to each other, and that within a particular grade or rank there is no change in output per head from year to year.

Miscellaneous services

Most of the services in this group, which are largely final services provided by the private sector, are covered by gross output indicators. Many of the services are provided virtually entirely to personal consumers, and the indicators for these are taken from the estimates of consumers' expenditure on these services at constant prices.

Public administration and defence

The output of this Order consists of the direct services of the armed forces and women's services, civil servants, etc. and it is estimated from changes in employment. Originally such output indicators as are available, for example the number of beneficiaries under social security schemes, were used but they were abandoned for the same reasons as for public education and health services (see above). Separate indicators representing the various grades of staff are used. For example, 25 series are used for the Army, covering officers and other ranks, with separate series for men and women. Because of this treatment productivity is assumed to be unchanged within each grade of employment, any change in output per head being due to a change in the composition by grade of the total number employed.

It should be noted that this industry is defined as in the *Standard Industrial Classification, 1958* and does not include the activities of persons employed by public authorities but classified to other industries; for example, ordnance factories are included in manufacturing and the national health service is included in professional and scientific services.

Ownership of dwellings

Ownership of dwellings is shown separately and is defined as the contribution to the gross domestic product made by the stock of dwellings. It is measured by consumers' expenditure at constant prices on rent, including imputed rent of owner-occupied houses.

Quarterly indicators

The quarterly indicators are selected so as to reflect the movements of the annual indicators as closely as possible. In many cases the same indicator is used. In some cases it has been possible to select alternative series covering the same industry. For example, the annual indicator for rail passenger transport is based on the number of passenger miles; these statistics are not available quarterly, but an alternative indicator, the aggregate number of passenger journeys, is available quarterly. This is probably inferior to the annual series but is thought to be the best substitute available. In other cases quarterly indicators for closely related industries are used. For example, the quarterly indicator for the airport services industry is the combined indicators for the other parts of the air transport industry. Some industries, such as 'Other transport and storage' are represented in the quarterly index by the quarterly indicators for the other industries within the same industrial Order.

The quarterly indicators are used only to estimate changes within the year. For completed years the quarterly index for each industry Order has been adjusted to bring its level to that of the annual index. For current quarters a provisional adjustment is made for each Order using the final adjustment to the preceding year's figures as a guide. Final adjustments are made when the annual indices for each Order are available, and the quarterly estimates are revised to agree with the annual figures. In the table opposite the quarterly series are shown as published in the October 1967 issue of *Economic Trends*, and as they would have been at that date if the quarterly rather than the annual indicators had been used where the two differ. It will be seen that the difference between the two series, that is the overall final adjustment, is not large and does not change much from year to year.

These adjustments are made at Order level and the overall index for each quarter is produced by combining the results for each Order, using the same weights as for the annual index.

The extent to which each industry group is covered by quarterly information comparable to the annual data varies considerably. For industrial production the quarterly index of production is consistent with the annual index. For agriculture, where a large part of output consists of crops grown and harvested once a year, there seems to be no satisfactory way of allocating the annual output to particular quarters within the farming year. In this case therefore the quarterly figures used are interpolations of the farming year figures. Transport and communication is fairly well covered by quarterly information, and for the distributive trades all the annual indicators are available quarterly. For insurance, banking and finance, although several of the annual indicators for banking and finance are available quarterly, there are no corresponding quarterly series for insurance, which is therefore covered quarterly partly by a series for net acquisition of financial assets by insurance companies, and partly by an employment indicator. For professional and scientific services, and public administration and defence, the quarterly indicators are total employment in each industry; these series are similar to those used in the annual estimates except that the latter incorporate more detailed information about the numbers in each grade of staff. Miscellaneous services are well covered by quarterly data, although some of the quarterly estimates of consumers' expenditure which are used as indicators are only interpolations and projections of the annual figures.

Index numbers of gross domestic product at constant factor cost
1958 = 100
Seasonally adjusted

		After final adjustment (as published)	Before adjustment
1963	1st quarter	112·6	112·2
	2nd quarter	116·5	116·1
	3rd quarter	119·1	118·7
	4th quarter	121·0	120·6
	Year	117·3	116·9
1964	1st quarter	122·6	122·1
	2nd quarter	124·2	123·7
	3rd quarter	124·8	124·3
	4th quarter	125·9	125·4
	Year	124·4	123·9
1965	1st quarter	127·6	127·0
	2nd quarter	126·7	126·0
	3rd quarter	127·6	126·9
	4th quarter	128·8	128·1
	Year	127·6	127·0
1966	1st quarter	130·2	129·4
	2nd quarter	129·5	128·7
	3rd quarter	130·0	129·1
	4th quarter	128·8	127·9
	Year	129·6	128·8

4. RELIABILITY

The reliability of the estimates should be considered in the light of what they are intended to achieve. The object of the calculation is not to measure the absolute level of output, but changes in the level of output. Even if full and complete information were available, the statistical and conceptual problems involved in the calculation of constant price estimates and index numbers would still remain. It must be realised that an estimate of this nature is to some extent an arbitrary measure, and its movement should only be interpreted in the light of the conventions and solutions adopted in its compilation, as for example the use of base-year weights and the restricted definition of output for public services. However, if these limitations are realised then the measure of change in output over one period can reasonably be compared with that for another period.

A guide to the reliability of the estimates of output can thus only be given in the context of the principles adopted in its compilation, that is, whether the data available are adequate for this purpose. Judged by this standard it is possible to give a general guide in terms of the index numbers based on 100 (not the percentage change in the index numbers). The reliability of the indices for

D

agriculture, mining, manufacturing industries and gas, electricity and water over periods of up to say, five years, may be described as good in terms of the reliability gradings described on pages 39 to 41. Those for construction, transport and communication and distributive trades are fair. The reliability of the indices within the other four Orders varies a good deal and depends greatly on the underlying concepts. Accepting the conceptual approach, the indices for the Orders as a whole, allowing for compensation between errors in the estimates for constituent sections, can be regarded as fair. The reliability of the overall index of output, as based on the concepts used in its compilation, can be described as good. However, it must be remembered that, outside of the field of the index of industrial production, many of the estimates for the latest year and some of the estimates for the previous year may subsequently be revised, as the full data gradually become available.

The quarterly index of output is necessarily less reliable than the annual index. The quarterly indices for the latest year are more liable to error since they are in part based on provisional information and are subject to adjustment when the full annual data become available. The estimates for the latest quarter are less reliable than those for earlier quarters because not all the information is available in time for the first published estimates.

ANNEX

INDICATORS AND WEIGHTS USED FROM 1958 IN ESTIMATING
THE GROSS DOMESTIC PRODUCT AT CONSTANT FACTOR COST

Standard industrial classification			Weight per 10,000	Annual indicator	Quarterly indicator (if different from annual indicator)
Order	Mini- mum List Head- ing	Industry			
I		*Agriculture, forestry, fishing*	*444*		
	001	Agriculture and horticulture	421	Net output of all holdings at constant prices	Interpolation and projection of the annual figures (see page 84)
	002	Forestry	2	Forest area, Great Britain	Represented by the two following indicators
			2	Area planted	
			2	Production of hardwood	
			2	Production of pitwood and softwood	
	003	Fishing	13	Landings of British taking: weighted total of different types of fish	Landings of British taking: unweigh- ted total
			2	Imports of oil from British whale fisheries	Represented by the preceding indi- cator
II		*Mining and quarrying*	*4,890*	Index of industrial produc- tion[1]	
III-XVI		*Manufacturing*			
XVII		*Construction*			
XVIII		*Gas, electricity and water*			
XIX		*Transport and communication*	*884*		
	701	Railways		British Railways: Number of passenger miles:	
			36	Ordinary tickets	Number of passen- ger journeys
			2	Early morning tickets	
			6	Season tickets	
				Number of freight net ton miles:	
			45	Merchandise and minerals	
			39	Coal and coke	
			11	Parcels receipts, deflated	Parcels and mails, receipts deflated
			6	Mail: numbers of letters and parcels posted	

[1] See *The Index of Industrial Production: Method of Compilation,* Studies in Official Statistics, No. 7, 1959 and *Economic Trends,* March 1962.

Standard industrial classification			Weight per 10,000	Annual indicator	Quarterly indicator (if different from annual indicator)
Order	Minimum List Heading	Industry			
XIX cont.		Railways (*cont.*)	1	Number of parcels handled by British Railways collection and delivery service	Represented by the remainder of the Order
			3	Quantity of freight handled by British Railways collection and delivery service	
			8	London Transport railways: number of passenger miles	Number of passenger journeys
	702	Road passenger transport	18	London Transport road services: number of passenger miles	All operators: total number of passenger journeys
			20	Transport Holding Company road services: number of passenger miles	
			86	Other operators: number of passenger journeys	
	703	Road goods transport	170	Number of ton miles for all road goods transport, including 'C' licence vehicles	Index of ton miles
	704	Sea transport		Freight receipts of vessels in foreign trade deflated by indices of freight rates:	
			33	Tankers	
				Dry cargo:	
			65	Liners	Total dry cargo
			11	Tramps	
				Passenger movement by Commonwealth ships (assumed that proportion of passengers carried by British ships is constant):	
			2	Between U.K. and continent	
			13	Between U.K. and other countries	
			6	Vessels in coastal trade: arrivals and departures of Commonwealth ships with cargo (net tonnage)	
	705	Port and inland water transport	55	Total arrivals and departures of shipping at U.K. ports (net tonnage), representing port services	
			4	Inland waterways: net ton miles	

Standard industrial classification			Weight per 10,000	Annual indicator	Quarterly indicator (if different from annual indicator)
Order	Mini- mum List Head- ing	Industry			
XIX *cont.*	706	Air transport		All scheduled services:	
			17	Number of passenger miles	
				Number of short ton miles:	
			2	Mail	
			3	Freight	
			7	Non-scheduled services: available capacity (short ton miles)	
			2	Total flights between the U.K. and abroad *plus* twice internal flights, re-presenting airport services	Represented by the remainder of air transport
	707	Postal services and telecommuni- cations		General Post Office:	
			69	Number of letters and parcels posted, parcels and letters weighted 7:1	Number of machine-counted letters and number of parcels
			1	Number of money orders issued	
			4	Number of postal orders cashed	
			13	Number of pensions and allowances paid [2]	
			1	Number of broadcast re-ceiving licences issued [2]	
			2	Number of inland telegrams	
			3	Number of overseas tele-grams	
				Number of telephone ex-change connections:	
			14	Business	Represented by the remainder of the Order
			17	Residence	
				Number of telephone calls:	
			23	Trunk	
			21	Local	[3]
			2	International	
			1	Number of telex calls	
				Number of private wire rentals:	
			4	Telephone	
			2	Telex	
			3	Number of telegrams handled by cable companies	Represented by the remainder of the Order
	709	Miscellaneous transport services and storage	33	Number in employment	

[2] Representing agency services.
[3] Quarterly figures of local calls are estimates.

Standard industrial classification			Weight per 10,000	Annual indicator	Quarterly indicator (if different from annual indicator)
Order	Mini-mum List Head-ing	Industry			
XX		*Distributive trades*	*1,162*		
	810	Wholesale distribution	245	Volume index of retail sales, representing wholesalers supplying mainly retailers	
			40	Deliveries of petroleum products for inland consumption	
			1	Consumption of newsprint	
			7	Home deliveries of paper and board	
			11	Deliveries of cotton and mixture cloth and fibres, representing merchant converters	
			42	Volume of U.K. exports of various categories of goods, representing export trade of merchants	
	820	Retail distribution	598	Volume index of retail sales	
			5	Deflated cost of national health service prescriptions	
	831	Dealing in coal, builders' materials, grain and agricul-tural supplies	32	Coal consumed by main classes of user	
			29	Index of industrial production for construction (Order XVII)	
			16	Deflated value of farmers' purchases of feedingstuffs	⎫ Interpolation and ⎬ projection of the
			4	Deflated value of farmers' purchases of fertilizers	annual figures ⎭
			6	Wheat and oats milled	
			3	Arable acreage under seed	⎫ Interpolation and
			8	Livestock on agricultural holdings	⎬ projection of the annual figures ⎭
	832	Dealing in other industrial materials and machinery	2	Consumption of iron ore	
			17	Consumption of various metals	
			17	Deliveries of timber	
			3	Production of hides and leather	
			16	Consumption of cotton and wool yarns, etc.	
			1	Consumption of jute	
			28	Deflated value of deliveries of various categories of machinery	
			1	Receipts of iron and steel scrap by steel works and foundries	

Standard industrial classification			Weight per 10,000	Annual indicator	Quarterly indicator (if different from annual indicator)
Order	Mini-mum List Head-ing	Industry			
XX *cont.*		Dealing in other industrial materials and machinery (*cont.*)	4	Consumption of scrap copper, zinc and lead	
			1	Consumption of waste paper	
			1	Consumption of crude rubber	
			8	Production of chemicals and dyestuffs	
			5	Deflated value of imports of oils	
			11	Total volume of U.K. exports	
XXI		*Insurance, banking and finance*	*604*		
	860/1	Insurance	83	Consumers' expenditure on life assurance at constant prices	
			3	Accident insurance: premiums paid deflated by consumer price index	From 1963: two indicators, weighted equally:
			25	Fire insurance: premiums paid *less* claims deflated by price index for gross domestic capital formation	(i) Number in employment in Order XXI
			8	Marine, aviation and transit insurance: premiums paid *less* claims deflated by average of unit value indices for imports and exports	(ii) Net acquisition of financial assets by insurance companies deflated by F.T. —Actuaries index of share prices
			25	Motor vehicle insurance: premiums paid *less* claims deflated by price index of vehicles	
			20	Miscellaneous insurance: premiums paid *less* claims deflated by consumer price index	Up to 1962: number in employment in Order XXI
	860/2	Banking	101	Number of cheques cleared	
			27	Total bank deposits deflated by consumer price index	
			6	Amount remaining invested in national savings deflated by consumer price index	
			11	Bank advances deflated by consumer price index	
	860/3	Finance		Building societies:	
			4	From 1965: number of mortgage advances Up to 1964: value of mortgage advances deflated by price index of houses with vacant possession	

Standard industrial classification			Weight per 10,000	Annual indicator	Quarterly indicator (if different from annual indicator)
Order	Mini- mum List Head- ing	Industry			
XXI cont.		Finance (*cont.*)	4	Value of mortgages out- standing ⎤ deflated by consumer price index	
			4	Total liabilities ⎦	
			18	From 1965: number of trans- actions on London Stock Exchange Up to 1964: number of bar- gains marked on London Stock Exchange	
			18	Stamp duty on share transfers deflated by index of share prices	Represented by the preceding indicator
			17	New capital issues deflated by capital goods price index Hire purchase finance com- panies:	
			8	New credit extended ⎤ deflated by durable goods price index	
			8	Balance of credit out- standing ⎦	
	860/4	Property owning and managing, etc.	20	Transfer costs of land and buildings at constant prices, representing estate agents, etc.	
			146	Stock of commercial and in- dustrial buildings, represen- ting real estate industry	Interpolation and projection of the annual figures
			48	Parts of 860/3 and 860/4 not covered above, represented by the remainder of the Order	
XXII		*Professional and scientific services*	704		
	871	Accountancy services		Number of Schedule D tax assessments:	
			7	Individuals	
			12	Partnerships	Number in employ-
			16	Number of tax assessments on companies: From 1966/67: corpor- ation tax Up to 1965/66: income tax	ment in Order XXII (one indicator for the Order)
	872	Educational services	161	Weighted index of teachers in grant-aided schools and establishments	

Standard industrial classification			Weight per 10,000	Annual indicator	Quarterly indicator (if different from annual indicator)
Order	Minimum List Heading	Industry			
XXII cont.		Educational services (cont.)	10	Number of university lecturers	
			100	Others employed in education	
	873	Legal services	41	Weighted average of various kinds of cases tried in Courts of Justice	
			4	Number of grants of probate	
	874	Medical and dental services	144	Index of hospital staff, based on staff costs	
			1	Ante-natal, post-natal and child welfare clinics: number of patients	
			3	Home-nursing: number of patients	
			1	Health visits: number of patients	Number in employment in Order XXII (one indicator for the Order)
			3	Home helps: number of cases	
			5	Midwives: number of home confinements	
			5	Ambulance service mileage	
			8	School medical service: number of children inspected	
			34	Number of doctors on the Executive Council services list, representing general practice	
			13	Weighted average of number of dental treatments	
			26	Number employed in other medical services	
	875	Religious organisations	15	Number in employment	
	879	Other professional and scientific services	95	Number in employment	
XXIII		*Miscellaneous services*	648		
	881	Cinemas, theatres, radio, etc.	24	Number of admissions to cinemas	
			11	Weighted average of radio and television licences current	
			30	Consumers' expenditure on sport and other entertainment at constant prices	
	882	Sport and other recreations	16		

D*

Standard industrial classification			Weight per 10,000	Annual indicator	Quarterly indicator (if different from annual indicator)
Order	Mini- mum List Head- ing	Industry			
XXIII cont.	883	Betting	15	Consumers' expenditure at constant prices	
	884	Catering, hotels, etc.	183	From 1960: index of catering turnover deflated Up to 1959: estimated total expenditure at constant prices	
	885 886	Laundries Dry cleaning, etc. }	44	From 1963: index of turnover deflated Up to 1962: consumers' expenditure at constant prices	
	887	Motor repairers, garages, etc.	95	From 1963: index of motor trades' total turnover deflated Up to 1962: series for new registrations, licences current, and deliveries of motor spirit	
	888	Repair of boots and shoes	9	Consumers' expenditure at constant prices	
	889	Hairdressing and manicure	30	Consumers' expenditure at constant prices	
	891	Private domestic service	50	Number in employment	Interpolation and projection of the annual figures
	899	Other services	141	Number in employment	
XXIV		*Public adminis- tration and defence*	*628*		
	901	National govern- ment service	238	Armed services and women's services: weighted index of strength	
			152	Non-industrial civil servants: weighted index of staff	
			34	Industrial civil servants: number in employment	Number in employ- ment in Order
	906	Local govern- ment service	42	Police: weighted index of strength	XXIV (one in- dicator for the
			10	Fire service: weighted index of strength	Order)
			152	Other local government service: number in employment	
		Ownership of dwellings	*346*	Consumers' expenditure on rent at constant prices, representing house owner- ship and occupation (see page 87)	
		Adjustment for net interest	*—310*	See page 83	

Chapter VI

The Personal Sector

1. GENERAL DESCRIPTION

The personal sector is made up mainly of households and individuals resident in the United Kingdom as distinct from corporate businesses or organs of government. It includes individuals living in hostels and other institutions as well as those living in private households. The sector extends beyond households and individuals to include unincorporated private businesses of sole traders and partnerships such as farms, retail shops and independent professional men. It also includes private non-profit-making bodies serving persons and private trusts.

Unincorporated private enterprises

The businesses of sole traders and partnerships of individuals do not have a legal existence distinct from the persons who are their members and their activities are therefore included in the personal sector. Their activities would account for most of an operating account of the personal sector, if one were prepared and published. Within the income and expenditure account, their inclusion affects the total of personal income. Their income, which is described as income from self-employment, in effect includes the undistributed as well as the distributed profits of these businesses. These two elements cannot be distinguished statistically nor probably by many of the individuals concerned, even with access to their accounts. The undistributed profits of these businesses form part of personal saving.

The capital account is the account most affected by the inclusion of these businesses in the personal sector. Personal saving includes the equivalent of their undistributed profits before providing for depreciation and capital gains or losses due to stock appreciation. Estimates of stock changes for the personal sector are entirely attributable to changes in stocks of unincorporated enterprises. The fixed capital formation of the personal sector, apart from that in land and existing buildings and in dwellings, is also mainly attributable to these businesses.

Individual farmers and partnerships, which would in any case be included in the personal sector, account for most of the agricultural enterprises. For statistical convenience, agricultural companies are grouped with them in the personal sector and are not included in the company sector (see page 142).

Private non-profit-making bodies serving persons

These comprise universities, direct grant and other non-profit-making schools and colleges, churches, charities, clubs and societies, trade unions, friendly societies and private housing associations. They are included in the personal

99

sector even though they may be incorporated under the Companies Acts. Co-operative societies and building societies are not included here, but are treated as corporate businesses and included in the company sector. Private non-profit-making bodies serving persons are regarded as groups of persons acting collectively for mutual benefit. Only that part of their income which is derived from other sectors—mainly income from property or investments—is an addition to personal income. Personal donations to such bodies and grants by them to individuals are like gifts from one person to another and do not enter into total personal income or current expenditure. The estimates of donations to such bodies from other sectors, which should be included in total personal income or in receipts of capital transfers are, however, incomplete. Transfers from public authorities, such as government grants to universities and schools, are included in current grants from public authorities and in capital transfers. Contributions by companies to charities have been estimated from Inland Revenue data, but the estimates cover only contributions not allowed as a business expense and no information is available about contributions included in business expenses. The expenditure of these bodies on goods and services, chiefly the pay of their employees, is treated as part of consumers' expenditure. The income of their employees is, of course, also included in income from employment on the other side of the personal income and expenditure account.

It would be desirable to provide a separate account for these bodies, to show transactions between them and the main part of the personal sector, but at present there is insufficient information to do this. The accounts of non-profit-making institutions serving other sectors, for example trade associations and private research associations established by industry, are similarly consolidated with the accounts of the sector concerned.

Private trusts

These are trusts, other than those for charitable purposes which are covered in the previous paragraph, normally created by individuals and usually for named beneficiaries. They include, for example, trusts created by a deceased person through his will to provide for a widow or children and trusts created during life to provide for dependent relatives.

Life assurance and superannuation funds

The life funds of life assurance companies and the funds of superannuation schemes are considered to be the collective property of the policy holders and members of the schemes in the personal sector. This treatment of the funds affects a number of items in the personal sector accounts.

Since the funds are regarded as the collective property of persons, the income of the funds which does not arise from premiums paid by persons is included in personal income. Personal income includes employers' contributions which are paid directly to the schemes; an estimate of these contributions is included in income from employment. The rent, dividend and interest income of the funds is included in personal sector receipts of rent, dividends and interest.

The schemes are regarded as providing a service to consumers; the service of covering life risks. Consumers' expenditure therefore includes the administrative costs (wages, commissions, rents, etc.) of the schemes, together with the share of profits allocated to the life assurance companies and their shareholders.

Premiums paid by persons, in excess of the costs, etc. mentioned in the preceding paragraph, and claims received by them are not shown in the personal income and expenditure account because they do not change the balance of personal income and expenditure; they affect only the form in which persons hold their assets. For example, contributions to the funds result in a larger amount of assets being held by the funds, but do not affect the total of personal assets. This treatment is satisfactory so long as interest is centred on the accounts of the personal sector as a whole, but the treatment conceals some redistribution of income within the personal sector. Thus personal income, in the presentation now adopted, includes elements of income accruing to persons which are not currently received in cash (employers' contributions to pension schemes and the property income of life funds and pension funds), and ignores some incomes which are in fact received (pensions and other benefits from life assurance and pension schemes).

An alternative arrangement of the income of persons, designed to show the distinction between direct income from current work and property on the one hand and, on the other, income from current grants, pensions, life assurance benefits, etc. (some of which may be regarded as deferred income from work or property), is given in a table in the Blue Book (see page 114). Another alternative form of presentation would be to show amounts of premiums and claims as separate current transfers in the personal income and expenditure account and the net increase in the funds as an imputed interest payment from the company sector to the personal sector. The rent, dividend and interest income of the funds would then be treated as a receipt of companies.

A revenue account for the funds, showing separately the various items involved is given in Table 24 of the 1967 Blue Book and described below (page 113).

The capital transactions of the funds are, however, included with those of financial companies. The financial account for the personal sector includes a single entry for the net increase in the funds and any capital formation by the funds and their various transactions in financial assets are attributed to financial companies (see page 413).

2. THE PUBLISHED TABLES

INCOME AND EXPENDITURE ACCOUNT

The income and expenditure account is the main table for the personal sector. It is included in shortened form in the summary tables of the Blue Book and in detail in the section on the personal sector. The detailed account presented in the 1967 Blue Book is shown on the next page.

This table provides an analysis of personal income by type of income and not by type of recipient. A large proportion of persons receive more than one form of income; some wage and salary earners may receive both income from employment and income from national insurance benefits in the course of one year; probably a majority of persons in receipt of dividend and interest income also receive income from some other source.

Personal income and expenditure account, 1966

£ million

Income before tax		Expenditure	
Wages	11,935	Consumers' expenditure.........	24,116
Salaries	8,185		
Pay in cash and kind of H.M.		Transfers abroad (net)	62
Forces	513	Taxes paid abroad	8
Employers' contributions:			
National insurance and health...	902	United Kingdom taxes on	
Other......................	902	income:	
		Payments	3,646
Total income from employment ..	22,437	Additions to tax reserves	35
Professional persons[1]	449	National insurance and health	
Farmers[1]	595	contributions	1,797
Other sole traders and partner-			
ships[1]	1,426	Total current expenditure	29,664
Total income from self-employ-			
ment[1]	2,470	Balance: saving before providing	
		for depreciation and stock ap-	
Rent, dividends and net interest:		preciation	1,844
Receipts by life assurance and			
superannuation funds	870		
Other receipts	2,728		
Total	3,598		
Current transfers to charities from			
companies	30		
National insurance benefits and			
other current grants from public			
authorities	2,973		
Total personal income[1]	31,508	Total	31,508

Source: 1967 Blue Book, Table 22

[1]Before providing for depreciation and stock appreciation.

Income from employment

This includes all wages and salaries including certain forms of payment in kind *less* certain specific expenses of employment, and the pay and allowances in cash and kind of H.M. Forces. It also includes payments by employers regarded as supplements to wages and salaries; these are (a) employers' contributions to the national insurance scheme, to the national health service and to the Redundancy Fund, and (b) employers' contributions to pension schemes, together with compensation payments for injury, etc. Income from employment, thus defined, represented nearly three-quarters of total personal income in 1966. A fuller description is given on pages 119 to 128.

Income from self-employment

This is the income of persons from unincorporated businesses, namely farmers, professional people (but not those who receive salaries), shopkeepers and other sole traders and partnerships. Such personal incomes, broadly those assessed to income tax under Schedule D as profits of a trade, profession or vocation, must be regarded as a combination of labour income and profits, and there is no way of distinguishing between these two elements. This is important because differences in the relative importance of these mixed incomes, in 1966 nearly one-twelfth of total personal income in the United Kingdom, may affect any comparison of the distribution of income between the factors of production from one period to another or between one country and another. It must also be noted that although these incomes are computed, as for income tax, after deducting all business operating expenses (except provision for depreciation), they must cover not only the personal expenditure of the recipients but also any amounts retained in the business for expenditure on fixed assets and stocks. For a fuller description see pages 142 to 147.

Rent, dividends and net interest

This represents an estimate of the total property income received by the personal sector. Rent is defined as income arising from the ownership of land and buildings (including the imputed rent of owner-occupied dwellings estimated in the way described on page 162), *less* expenditure on repairs and insurance. Dividends represent the actual amounts received in the year (not the amounts payable out of current year's earnings of companies, for which an estimate is made in the appropriation account of companies—see page 210). The major item is interest and dividends on securities of public authorities, public corporations and companies (resident and non-resident). The total also includes dividends on purchases from co-operative societies, interest on shares and deposits with building societies, and interest on bank deposits. All figures of income from these sources are estimated before deduction of tax.

The income from investments and other property of private non-profit-making bodies serving persons, of private trusts, of the life funds of assurance companies and of superannuation funds, is included here. That of the life assurance and superannuation funds is shown separately.

Personal income from rent, dividends and net interest appears as a combined item in the national accounts tables. This is because the data at present available do not permit satisfactory estimates of the separate items of personal income from these sources. The total receipts of rent income by all sectors, which equals total payments, is estimated as part of total domestic income. Payments of dividends and interest can be estimated for all sectors other than the personal sector, and so can the combined receipts of rent, dividends and interest. From total payments *less* receipts by other sectors, the rent, dividends and net interest receipts of the personal sector can be obtained as a residue. The method of calculation is illustrated on the next page.

Like all figures obtained as residues, the estimate of personal income from rent, dividends and net interest cannot be regarded as accurate. Also, with this method of calculation the estimate is not subdivided between different forms of income. There is, for example, no estimate of personal receipts of company dividends or of income from overseas investments. However, an estimate of rent income received by the personal sector is made for the distribution of gross national product by sector (see page 67), although up to 1964 there was little information and the estimate for the earlier years is approximate.

The estimate of income from rent, dividends and net interest is after deduction of interest payments by the personal sector. Estimates can be made of certain main items of interest paid by the personal sector, and such estimates are made in order to improve the analysis of personal income. The estimates are described on page 114.

The allocation of property income, 1966

	1966 £ million	Table in 1967 Blue Book
A. Payments		
Rent	1,949	Table 1
Interest and dividend payments[1]:		
By companies[2]	2,652	Table 30
By public corporations	476	Table 37
By central government[2]	1,041	Table 41
By local authorities	600	Table 45
Payments abroad by companies:		
Profits due abroad net of United Kingdom tax	220	Table 30
United Kingdom tax on profits due abroad	190	Table 30
Property income from abroad (payments by overseas sector)	1,496	Table 7
Total payments	8,624	
B. Receipts by all sectors except personal sector		
Companies:		
Rent and non-trading income[2]	1,351	Table 30
Income from abroad	1,362	Table 30
Public corporations:		
Rent and non-trading income	91	Table 37
Income from abroad	8	Table 37
Central government:		
Rent	96	Table 41
Interest and dividends, etc.[2]	673	Table 41
Local authorities:		
Rent	604	Table 45
Interest, etc..	67	Table 45
Property income paid abroad (receipts by overseas sector)	774	Table 7
Total receipts by all sectors except personal sector	5,026	
C. Receipts of rent, dividends and net interest by personal sector		
(A *less* B)	3,598	Table 2

[1]Including payments abroad.

[2]Excluding in each case estimated payments to, or receipts from, other units within the same sector (for example, national debt interest paid to other central government departments, company dividends paid to other companies, etc.).

Current transfers to charities from companies

This item represents the income of charities contributed by companies and identifiable from Inland Revenue data. The estimates cover both covenanted and uncovenanted contributions not allowed as a business expense.Those contributions which are allowed as a business expense for taxation purposes, that is contributions made primarily for the benefit of employees, are not covered.

National insurance benefits and other current grants from public authorities

These incomes are all transfer payments, both to persons and to private non-profit-making bodies serving persons, which are derived not by services to production, but by grants from the central government, including the National Insurance Funds, or from local authorities. Although this form of income should be limited to current grants, these are taken to include death grants, injury benefits and post-war credits, which might be regarded as capital payments. But less ambiguous forms of capital grants, such as war damage compensation and grants to universities towards the cost of buildings and equipment, are excluded. The largest component of current grants, in 1966 well over half the total, is national insurance benefits; of the other items, the most important are supplementary benefits, family allowances, and war pensions and service grants. The complete list will be found in the current accounts of the central government and local authorities (Tables 41 and 45 of the 1967 Blue Book). They are described under the various services provided by public authorities, in Chapter XI.

These payments, with one exception, are confined to payments in cash as distinct from benefits in kind such as the provision of education or the services of doctors. The exception is that the net cost to public authorities of school meals, milk and welfare foods provided free or at subsidised prices, is included here as though it were a cash grant to persons. The allocation of expenditure of this kind between government and consumers presents some difficulty. A practical advantage of the treatment adopted here is that all expenditure on food for use by households is recorded under consumers' expenditure; and changes in the level of consumers' expenditure are not affected by variations in the scale of provision by the government for school meals and welfare foods.

Consumers' expenditure

Personal expenditure on goods and services would be a more precise, although unwieldy, description of this item. It is often loosely described as 'personal consumption' or just 'consumption', but these terms are in some ways misleading. The essential points in the general definition of consumers' expenditure are:

(a) It covers all expenditure by the personal sector, including private non-profit-making bodies serving persons, on goods and services for current use. It does not cover the whole of national expenditure on consumer-type goods and services: it excludes all business expenditure which is reckoned as current costs of production and expenditure by public authorities which is part of their final expenditure. Such expenditure on consumer goods and services can often be estimated only very roughly. Certain purchases by workers of tools or special clothing, which are deducted from employment income, as noted on page 126, are regarded as business expenditure and excluded from consumers' expenditure. Business expenditure on cars, meals, etc., which is allowed as a business expense in computing income for tax purposes of both employed and self-employed persons, is also excluded. Expenditure by employers which is regarded as income in kind of employees and included in personal income is, however, included. This relates mainly to expenditure on food, including meals in canteens and meal vouchers, and accommodation which may be provided free or at reduced prices. Income in kind is defined on page 125.

(b) It includes expenditure on durable goods, for instance motor cars, which from the point of view of the individual might more appropriately be treated as capital expenditure. The only exception is the purchase of land and dwellings and costs incurred in connection with the transfer of their ownership, which are treated as personal capital expenditure. It would be possible to treat all personal purchases of durable goods as capital expenditure. However, this would involve, first, reckoning as consumers' expenditure the annual value or benefit derived from such goods, which could be related to the rate of interest and of depreciation, and secondly, imputing a corresponding amount of income. This is in fact done for dwellings. But there exists a basis for the imputation in the rents paid for dwellings which are let, and in the estimated annual values used for rating purposes. For other durable goods the calculation would be almost entirely fictitious. Although some imputations have been suggested, the common international practice is to reckon all consumers' expenditure, except that on the purchase of land and dwellings, as current expenditure. Nevertheless, in interpreting the pattern of consumers' expenditure and personal saving, the separation of purchases of durable goods from goods more rapidly consumed can be of great importance, and the items which might be regarded as goods of a capital nature are so far as possible shown separately.

(c) Consumers' expenditure does not include free services, such as education and the health service, provided by public authorities. These are treated as current expenditure by public authorities—as collective consumption. But consumers' expenditure includes the cost of private purchases of analogous services, for example private education, and also the payments made by patients for goods and services provided under the national health service. A reduction in consumers' expenditure may thus be directly linked with an increase in the extent of public provision of such services. However, the net cost to public authorities of school meals, milk and welfare foods, provided free or at subsidised prices, is included in consumers' expenditure, so that consumers' expenditure includes their total cost (see page 105).

(d) Expenditure must be understood as the acquisition of goods and services rather than actual disbursements of cash in the period of account. It relates to the total value of goods acquired whether paid for outright or not. Thus when consumers buy on hire purchase or other forms of credit much of the payment may occur after the transaction is recorded. Similarly, contributions to Christmas or holiday funds are not regarded as expenditure until goods or services are actually acquired. This treatment, of course, has a bearing on the measurement of personal saving. An increase in the amount of consumer debt outstanding will, other things being equal, be associated with lower personal saving.

When credit is extended by the retailer, the goods acquired are valued at the total amount charged by the retailer, including any amount charged for the provision of credit. Hence consumers' expenditure may be said to comprise not only the cash price of such goods but also the interest charge and the administrative costs of supplying the goods on credit. However, when credit is extended by a hire purchase finance company, the cost of that credit is separated and is not included in consumers' expenditure but is treated as an interest payment.

(e) The estimates of consumers' expenditure include purchases of second-hand as well as of new goods, *less* the proceeds of sales of used goods. The sale of second-hand goods between consumers does not in itself affect the total of consumers' expenditure. But the total must include purchases by consumers of second-hand goods from other sectors (for example of second-hand cars from business concerns, or of army surpluses from the government), and also the costs incurred in the transfer of used goods when the goods are bought from a dealer (dealers' margins and handling and reconditioning costs).

The estimate of consumers' expenditure, more than that of any other major magnitude in the national accounts, is built up commodity by commodity from a variety of sources. The classification and the sources from which estimates are made are described on pages 147 to 202. The method of brick by brick estimation implies that considerable efforts may often be required to estimate individual forms of personal expenditure which are in themselves of little economic significance, but which must be measured solely to estimate total expenditure. Some gaps and some duplications are almost inevitable as there is no adequate check on the aggregate other than the check afforded by the balance between national income and national expenditure in total.

The estimates of consumers' expenditure in the Blue Book are presented for a number of categories of goods and services valued both at current and at constant market prices (see page 117). The same information is given quarterly for a much more limited number of categories.

Transfers abroad (net)

This item represents net transfer payments by persons to the rest of the world in the form of migrants' remittances, gifts, etc. The figure is taken directly from the balance of payments accounts where it is entitled 'Private transfers'. The item includes gifts of goods sent by parcel post, payments by United Kingdom residents to their dependants overseas and transfers of funds by missionary societies and charitable institutions. Some of the payments included, for example legacies and assets transferred by migrants, should strictly be treated as capital transactions. Some transfers may also relate to companies and not to the personal sector, but such transfers are thought to be small. The item, although small, is shown separately in the accounts of the personal sector because it falls into a separate category of transactions (voluntary transfers to and from overseas residents).

Taxes paid abroad

This item represents payments of taxes to overseas governments by the personal sector on property income from abroad. The estimate is made by the Inland Revenue on the basis of the relief given against United Kingdom tax. The item is small but is shown separately because it falls into a separate category of transactions.

United Kingdom taxes on income

Taxes paid by the personal sector consist mainly of income tax and surtax. Up to 1966 they also included a small amount (about £3 million) of profits tax payable by Lloyd's underwriters and farming companies (included in the personal sector). From 1964 the estimated amount of income tax on short-term capital gains, collected under Schedule D, is excluded from this item and included with taxes on capital. In respect of years before 1947, small amounts of profits tax and excess profits tax were also charged on sole traders and partnerships.

Tax deducted at source by companies, public corporations or public authorities on dividends and interest paid to the personal sector is included here. Such taxes are regarded as falling on those receiving the dividends and interest, not on the companies or public authorities paying them. Thus persons are regarded as receiving dividends and interest payments gross, before deduction of tax. The estimate of tax payments by persons takes into account not the standard rates of tax which are deducted at source, but the actual taxes paid by persons. The actual tax payments are, of course, determined by the level of the total taxable income of the recipients and therefore the amount of tax falling specifically on dividends and interest cannot be ascertained (see page 328). The estimates include the tax paid on the investment income of the life funds of life assurance companies and of superannuation funds, which are regarded as the property of the personal sector.

Most persons pay income tax at the same time as they receive their income, by deduction from wages or salaries under 'Pay-as-you-earn' (PAYE) or by deduction at source from dividend and interest payments. For them, accrual and payment of tax can therefore be regarded as simultaneous. Traders and professional men, on the other hand, are generally assessed, like companies, by reference to the profits earned in an earlier period; it is therefore assumed that such persons, like companies, establish a reserve against future payments of tax, although it is doubtful whether many in fact do so. Surtax payments also lag behind the income on which the liability is normally measured. An estimate is therefore made of additions to tax reserves representing the excess of tax accruing on the year's income over actual tax payments, and arising wholly from incomes from self-employment and from incomes chargeable to surtax. No allowance is made for the effect on the difference between accrual and payment of tax of the delay in making repayments of income tax. To treat total tax accruals as a charge against income before the amount of saving is calculated, although corresponding with accounting realities in the case of companies, may be regarded as somewhat fictitious for the personal sector; for some purposes it may be more realistic to treat the additions to tax reserves as a part of personal saving. They are so treated in the quarterly accounts because no quarterly estimates of additions to reserves can be made.

The estimates of tax payments by the personal sector are made by the Inland Revenue from the records of tax collected under the various schedules of income tax, most of which can be allocated directly between the different sectors, and from the separate records of surtax collection. Under the new system of company taxation the taxes paid by the personal sector from 1966 approximate fairly closely to the total of income tax and surtax payments. Where tax is deducted at source the estimates relate as far as possible to the amounts withheld rather than to receipts by the Inland Revenue. The reliability of the estimates of payments is good. The estimates of accruals and therefore of additions to tax reserves are based on a further analysis of income tax and surtax assessments by the year in which the income arose.

National insurance and health contributions

This comprises both flat rate and graduated contributions from employers, employed, self-employed and non-employed persons. It will be remembered that employers' contributions are included in personal income, and the total of national insurance and health contributions is thus treated as a direct tax falling on the recipients of income from employment and self-employment, and not as a tax on the employer. The figures are taken from the central government accounts and are described on page 265.

Balance: saving before providing for depreciation and stock appreciation

This important element is obtained as a residue or balancing item; it is the difference between the estimate of total personal income on the one hand and the total of consumers' expenditure, transfers abroad, tax accruals and national insurance contributions on the other. Its accuracy, therefore, depends on the accuracy of these other items in the personal income and expenditure account. Since personal saving is a relatively small difference between two large aggregates which are themselves subject to error the estimate of personal saving is particularly uncertain. However, the estimates of changes in saving are unlikely to be grossly erroneous even though the absolute level of saving may be open to significant error.

There is some check on the movements of the personal savings figure, although not one independent of the residual method of calculation, in that the saving of the personal sector should be equal to the excess of total investment (in fixed assets, stocks and net investment abroad) over the aggregate saving derived from the other sectors and capital transfers from abroad. The residual error, which is treated as a form of income not matched by identifiable expenditure, appears as a form of saving in the combined capital account (Table 6 of the 1967 Blue Book) and shows that the estimates of total investment and aggregate saving do not in fact balance perfectly. If an error in the figure of the saving of the personal sector arises from an error in the items of factor income (income from employment and self-employment) or final expenditure (consumers' expenditure) then the residual error is affected by an equal amount.

It is possible for the absolute level of personal saving to be in error without the residual error being affected, if an error in personal income from employment and self-employment or consumers' expenditure is associated with an equal error in fixed capital formation or the increase in the value of stocks. For example, if consumers' expenditure were too high and fixed capital formation were the same amount too low, the residual error would not be affected but personal saving would be too low. In the earlier estimates made for periods before 1948 there was little direct evidence about fixed capital formation or stockbuilding which were estimated largely as balancing items and incorporated the errors which for subsequent years are shown as the residual error. An error in the level of personal saving may also arise from errors in the estimates of transfer income and payments; the error would then be associated with an equal and opposite error in the saving of other sectors.

An independent but, as yet, very rough check on the estimate of personal saving is provided by the estimates of transactions in financial assets. The excess of personal saving and net receipts from capital transfers over expenditure on fixed assets and stocks represents the net acquisition of financial assets. An independent estimate of the net acquisition of financial assets can be built up from individual estimates of transactions in the various forms of financial assets. In recent years there has been a big increase in the information available about financial transactions (described in Chapter XIV) and from 1963 an approximate indication is available for nearly all the major items. A comparison of the two estimates of personal saving (before providing for tax reserves) can be made from the 1967 Blue Book for the years 1965 and 1966 as follows:

The personal sector

Alternative estimates of personal saving[1]

	£ million	
	1965	1966
Balancing item in personal income and expenditure account[1]	1,895	1,879
Net acquisition of identified physical and financial assets *plus* net payments of capital transfers	2,427	2,410
Difference (net acquisition of unidentified assets and liabilities and statistical discrepancy).................	532	531

[1]Before providing for depreciation, stock appreciation and additions to tax reserves.

The estimate of saving derived from the net acquisition of financial assets is too high in so far as increases in some forms of financial liability are not recorded; in particular, trade and other credit received by the personal sector. On the other hand, it is too low in so far as acquisitions of financial assets are not recorded. The balancing item in the personal income and expenditure account is too low because there is inadequate information on transfers between the company sector and the personal sector, in particular on transfers to the private non-profit-making bodies in the personal sector. In so far as the residual error in these two years is due to errors in income from employment and self-employment or consumers' expenditure, the balancing item in the personal income and expenditure account is too high. On a quarterly basis, there is evidence that part of the residual error is attributable to the personal sector items because there is a distinct seasonal pattern in the residual error which appears to be associated with a seasonal pattern in the difference between the two estimates of personal saving. In the first quarter of the year the residual error is generally a large negative (that is income considerably exceeds expenditure) and the estimate of saving from the personal income and expenditure account appears to be higher than that obtained from the financial account, whereas in the other quarters it appears to be lower[1].

In addition to the unreliability surrounding the figures of personal saving, the following considerations are important for interpreting them:

(a) The estimates necessarily include not only personal saving as it might be generally understood but also the whole saving of self-employed persons, although part of the latter, if it could be distinguished, might be better regarded as business rather than personal saving. There is no unique way of dividing the income of the owner of an unincorporated business, even notionally, between salary, distributed profit and undistributed profit. Estimates are made of the amount of fixed capital formation and of the value of the increase in the stocks of unincorporated enterprises, and as a convenient hypothesis these expenditures might be regarded as a first charge on profits, and excluded from personal saving. This would not necessarily, however, bear much relation to reality since such capital formation may often be financed not out of profit but by borrowing from other persons or other sectors. An estimate for stock appreciation attributable to the personal sector is, however, made and can be excluded from the

[1] See 'More Light on Personal Saving', *Economic Trends*, April 1965.

saving of the personal sector. Saving also includes provision for depreciation both by unincorporated enterprises and in respect of buildings owned by the personal sector.

(b) The estimates include the collective saving done by non-profit-making bodies, including charities, and private trusts.

(c) Saving by means of life assurance and superannuation schemes is included. The excess of the income of life assurance and superannuation funds from premiums, etc. and from property, over benefits paid and administrative costs, etc., is included in personal saving (see page 100). An estimate of this form of saving is given in the revenue account of the funds (Table 24 of the 1967 Blue Book).

(d) Another difference from what might be the popular interpretation of personal saving is that saving by the purchase of durable goods (other than land and houses) is excluded since these purchases are treated as consumers' expenditure.

National income statisticians in other countries where estimates of personal saving are attempted are confronted by similar problems. There are, certainly, ways in which the estimate of personal saving might be improved. The first way, which is constantly being pursued, is the improvement of the estimates of personal income and expenditure. For example, to build up estimates of consumers' expenditure to a reliable total is important not only because the aggregate is significant in itself, but also because it is essential, in present conditions, for a reliable estimate of saving.

The second approach is the study of the changes in financial assets and liabilities held by persons. For many of these, reliable statistics have existed for some time, although in some cases there are difficulties in separating the assets held by persons from those held by other sectors. However, this information has been of limited use in explaining the year-to-year fluctuations because there has been little or no information on some important forms of assets and liabilities most likely to be affected by substantial fluctuations in the level of personal saving. In recent years there has been a big increase in the information available about financial transactions. From 1963 it is possible to make at least rough estimates of two important variable items—holdings of government securities and holdings of company and overseas securities. These new estimates have led to the alternative estimates of saving in 1965 and 1966 given above. However, there is still insufficient information on the various short-term assets and debts of unincorporated businesses and of trade and other credit provided by companies to persons, which may be important in arriving at estimates of personal saving by this method. The improvement of the financial information is continuing and the available information is set out in the financial account for the personal sector (Table 74 of the 1967 Blue Book).

A third approach is the collection of information on saving by a sample survey of persons. Some results have been published[2] of a series of such surveys conducted by the Oxford Institute of Statistics and a survey for 1955 conducted

---

[2] See H. F. Lydall, *British Incomes and Savings*, Blackwell, 1955, describing the first of these surveys (that made in 1952); and articles on this and subsequent surveys in the *Bulletin of the Oxford Institute of Statistics*, February 1955, May 1955, August 1955 and May 1958.

by the Central Statistical Office. The method is, however, a difficult one to use for the estimation of total saving, first because most saving is done by relatively few people and it is difficult to obtain a satisfactory sample; secondly because the questions asked are inevitably complicated and the response tends to be inadequate; and thirdly because the figures cover the saving of households only and exclude the saving of individuals living in institutions and, more important, the 'collective' saving of private trusts and non-profit-making bodies.

OTHER BLUE BOOK TABLES RELATING TO THE PERSONAL SECTOR

The standard national accounts for the personal sector are the income and expenditure account (described above), the capital account (described below) and the financial account (described in Chapter XIV). In addition there are a number of other Blue Book tables relating to the personal sector which are designed to show in more detail particular aspects of personal transactions.

Tables 17 and 18. Industrial analysis of personal income

Income from employment is analysed according to industry. The analysis showing the contribution of each major industry group to the gross domestic product (Table 17) shows also where possible the division into wages, salaries and employers' contributions to national insurance and to superannuation schemes, etc. A more detailed analysis (Table 18) shows separately the wages and salaries (but not employers' contributions) in each of fourteen manufacturing industries. A similar analysis by industry for income from self-employment is not made because of uncertainty about the industrial composition of the adjustments to the Inland Revenue figures; for most of the industry groups in Table 17 income from self-employment is combined with the gross trading profits of companies. An analysis of the incomes of the self-employed (individuals and partnerships) which are charged to tax in industries classified by financial units (and thus not completely comparable with the analysis of income from employment for establishments in Table 17 of the Blue Book) is, however, shown in the annual *Report of the Commissioners of Inland Revenue*. For example, the 110th Report (Cmnd. 3508) gives figures in Tables 41 to 44 for assessments made in 1965/66.

Table 23. Capital account

Receipts on capital account for the personal sector are the saving and additions to tax reserves carried forward from the personal income and expenditure account, together with receipts from capital transfers. Up to the early 1950's capital transfers received by the personal sector were mainly war damage compensation paid by the central government. In 1955 and 1956, the most important item was compensation payments made under the Town and Country Planning Acts of 1954, but these declined rapidly and by 1960 were unimportant. The most important item in the early 1960's was central government capital grants for education which are grants made to universities and other private non-profit-making bodies. Other items of importance in later years are grants to farmers, mainly for farm improvements and field drainage, and local authority grants for the conversion and improvement of housing. Receipts are shown net of payments, but payments have been very small. The 1966 total of £155 million was made up as shown below.

	£ million
Education	104
Agriculture	19
Housing..........................	18
Other...........................	18
less Payments	—4
Total	155

Payments on capital account for the personal sector are fixed capital formation, the increase in the value of stocks, and taxes on capital. The basis of the estimates of gross domestic fixed capital formation is described in Chapter XII and that of the increase in the value of stocks in Chapter XIII. The only taxes on capital from 1955 to 1963 were death duties; from 1964 the estimated amount of tax on short-term capital gains and from 1966 payments of capital gains tax are included. The balancing item in the account is the net acquisition of financial assets including net investment abroad; an analysis of financial transactions is given in the financial account for the personal sector, described in Chapter XIV.

Table 24. *Revenue account of life assurance and superannuation funds*

This table is a revenue account for life assurance and superannuation funds which are regarded as the property of the policy holders and members of the schemes in the personal sector (see page 100). Life assurance includes industrial as well as ordinary business, including that of collecting societies. All life assurance business is included and attributed to the personal sector even though some may be undertaken for other sectors. In the case of unfunded super-annuation schemes—principally the superannuation schemes for national government service employees, police and firemen—the table includes the benefits actually paid in the year, both in contributions of employers and in pensions and other benefits paid. These items also include some redundancy payments made by employers and compensation payments by employers to injured employees or their dependants.

The estimates for life assurance and insured pension schemes are derived from the summary accounts of assurance companies and collecting societies, published in the *Annual Abstract of Statistics* (for example, Tables 364 and 370 of the 1967 issue). The estimates for non-insured funds are based mainly on Inland Revenue data and the published accounts of public enterprises. For non-insured funds and private unfunded schemes, use has also been made of the surveys of occupational pension schemes undertaken by the Government Actuary. Account is also taken of information collected from their members by the Institute of Actuaries and the Faculty of Actuaries in Scotland.

The contributions of employers are those included in income from employ-ment; the estimates are described on pages 126 to 128. The contributions of employees, individual premiums, etc. consist of employees' contributions to superannuation funds and individual payments to life assurance companies and collecting societies, including payments by the self-employed. Payments to life funds are obtained by deducting from the total amount of premiums paid the estimated amount of employers' contributions to superannuation schemes insured with life companies. Rent, dividend and interest receipts are estimated before payment of tax which is included in administrative costs, etc. The figures for pensions and other benefits paid include lump sum payments, payments to widows and dependants, surrenders, etc., so far as ascertainable, as well as annuities to policy holders and retired employees. The estimates of administrative costs, etc. are described on page 181. The balancing item, the 'Net increase in funds', is part of personal saving, and is shown in the financial accounts as a transaction between the personal sector and financial institutions. The financial transactions of the funds are shown separately in the analysis of financial transactions by sector and type of asset (Table 73 of the 1967 Blue Book).

Table 25. Categories of personal income

A method of classifying personal income is given, alternative to that in Tables 2 and 22. It is designed to distinguish (a) cash income from imputed income and income in kind; (b) pensions and other benefits from life assurance and superannuation schemes on the one hand, from income derived from work and property on the other; and (c) the income of households (including unincorporated businesses) from the income of 'collective persons'. The object of the third of these distinctions cannot be fully realised; the income of life assurance and superannuation funds is distinguished but, because of lack of information, the income of private non-profit-making bodies and private trusts generally cannot be separated from the income of households.

Some of the items require further explanation:

(a) *Rent, dividends and interest.* In Table 2, only a single net figure is given of receipts from rent, dividends and interest *less* payments of interest. For Table 25 this figure is divided between cash receipts of households and private non-profit-making bodies, imputed receipts of households and private non-profit-making bodies (rent of owner-occupied dwellings and accrued interest on national savings certificates) and cash receipts of life assurance and superannuation schemes (shown separately in Table 24). Estimates are made of the main categories which can be identified of interest payments by households and private non-profit-making bodies and added to the net figure of their cash receipts to give an estimate of gross receipts. About half of the total payments of £668 million for 1966 was accounted for by mortgage interest paid to building societies. The remainder covered mortgage interest paid to local authorities and general insurance companies, interest on bank advances and hire purchase charges paid to hire purchase finance companies (but not those paid to household goods shops).

(b) *Imputed income and income in kind* are, as far as possible, distinguished from the cash income of households, including H.M. Forces, and private non-profit-making bodies.

(c) *Current grants from public authorities* are divided to show separately retirement pensions and similar payments. A comparison can thus be made between income from all kinds of pensions and income from work and property.

(d) *Pensions and other benefits from life assurance and superannuation schemes* are those shown separately in the revenue account of the funds (Table 24) described above. In the national accounts such receipts are not treated as personal income, but are regarded as transfers within the personal sector (see page 101).

(e) *Adjustment for life assurance and superannuation funds.* The total income of households and private non-profit-making bodies, including pensions and other benefits from life assurance and superannuation schemes (as shown in

Table 25) falls short of total personal income (as defined in Table 2) by the extent to which such pensions, etc. fall short of receipts by the life assurance and superannuation funds from employers' contributions and property income (see page 100).

Table 26. Distribution of personal income before and after tax

This table provides an analysis of personal income, from all sources, by ranges of total income before and after tax. It is based mainly on the income surveys of the tax returns of individuals now carried out annually by the Inland Revenue. The incomes of husband and wife are counted as one income, as for tax purposes.

The income of individuals as defined for income tax purposes differs in a number of ways from the definition of personal income in the national income accounts. The main difference in coverage is the inclusion in the Inland Revenue returns of all pensions and all annuities except the non-taxable capital element of purchased life annuities. On the other hand, employers' contributions to national insurance and superannuation schemes are excluded.

The incomes shown in the classification by ranges include the following in addition to income covered by the Inland Revenue data:

(i) Incomes below the effective exemption limit, except the incomes of persons receiving less than £50 a year

(ii) Supplementary benefits and those national insurance benefits and grants which are not liable to tax (unemployment, sickness, maternity, injury, disablement and death benefits and grants)

(iii) Scholarships and other educational grants

(iv) Income in kind of domestic servants and agricultural workers

Estimates of each of these items have been allocated to what seem to be the most appropriate income ranges.

It is, however, impossible to allocate the whole of the income of the personal sector by income ranges and the following main components of income are excluded from the classification by ranges:

(a) The 'collective' income received from other sectors by private non-profit-making bodies, by private trusts and by life assurance and superannuation funds. This comprises investment income and also grants by public authorities to universities, schools, etc. and gifts by companies to charities. Pensions and annuities, etc. paid out by life assurance and superannuation funds and trusts are, however, included.

(b) Income directly received by, or imputed to, individuals which is not regarded as income in the Inland Revenue returns either because of its non-taxable nature, or because it is specifically exempt from tax:

(i) Income in kind other than that of domestic servants and agricultural workers

(ii) The imputed rent of owner-occupied dwellings or, before 1963, the amount by which the imputed rent exceeded the income tax valuation

(iii) The difference between the estimated income of farmers and the sum of their tax assessments

(iv) Certain non-taxable grants from public authorities (school meals, milk and welfare foods and industrial services for the disabled)

(v) Accrued interest on national savings certificates

(vi) Dividends of co-operative societies

(vii) Post-war credits

(viii) Employers' contributions to national insurance and superannuation schemes

(c) Incomes of persons receiving less than £50 a year.

(d) Deductions from income which are allowed for in the Inland Revenue returns but not in the estimation of personal income:

(i) That part of the income of self-employed individuals which is covered by capital allowances

(ii) That part of employees' contributions to superannuation schemes which is allowable as a deduction for income tax purposes; and, before 1961/62, part of employees' contributions to national insurance

The classification by ranges also excludes mortgage interest (except from 1967/68 that on option mortgage schemes), bank interest and other loan interest allowable as a deduction for tax purposes. The estimates of personal income are net of all interest payments.

The difference between total personal income and the total income shown by ranges, which in the table is called 'Income not included in the classification by ranges', is mainly the sum of the above categories (a) to (d) *less* the total of pensions and annuities, etc. derived from private superannuation schemes and the taxable portion of purchased life annuities. The incomes shown in the distribution by ranges include these pensions and annuities, and exclude most of the corresponding contributions and premiums. These constitute transfers within the personal sector and do not affect total personal income (see page 100).

The income allocated by ranges is over 80 per cent of total personal income. The unallocated balance might of course be allocated by arbitrary hypothesis, but it seems preferable to confine the table to those forms of income for which there is at least some direct evidence of the distribution.

The table also shows the number of incomes. The combined income of a married couple is counted as one income, but juveniles receiving separate incomes, even though partially dependent on their parents, are treated as receiving separate incomes. The number of incomes in each year is estimated by deducting from the total population of the United Kingdom the estimated number of married couples, the estimated number of persons with no income and those having incomes of under £50 in the year. The latter includes, for instance, schoolchildren with casual earnings and persons with small investment incomes. The estimate cannot be precise and there is no check from the income tax records because the number of persons with incomes in the year below the effective exemption limit is not directly recorded. The numbers relate to all persons receiving incomes for the whole or any part of the year. A woman who is single, widowed or divorced for part of the year is counted as having a separate income of the amount received while she was single, widowed or divorced. For this reason, and also because others have incomes for only part of the year if they start work, retire or die, the number of small incomes is larger than it would be if incomes were measured by their annual rates at a given point of time.

The distribution of incomes above the income tax effective exemption limit is based on the income surveys carried out by the Inland Revenue, of the tax returns. The Inland Revenue conducts detailed quinquennial surveys of a sample of incomes which are described in the annual *Report of the Commissioners of Inland Revenue*. The table in the 1967 Blue Book is based, for 1959, on the survey for 1959/60 described in the 105th Report and, for 1964, on the survey for 1964/65 described in the 109th Report. Figures for other years were previously based on projections from the last available quinquennial survey, but this method proved unreliable. From 1962/63 annual surveys, similar to the special quinquennial surveys but smaller in coverage, provide a basis for estimating the distributions each year. Provisional estimates for the latest year are based on the first results of the latest survey (in the 1967 Blue Book figures for 1965 are based on first results of the 1965/66 survey) and estimates for the earlier years are based on the final results of earlier surveys (in the 1967 Blue Book 1963 figures are based on final results of the 1963/64 survey). Incomes below the income tax effective exemption limit are mainly those of the retired, old age pensioners, juveniles and part-time workers; their total income is roughly estimated from, for example, the total amount of retirement pensions and the numbers and average earnings of juveniles, allowing for overlapping with the income tax field.

It will be noticed that the total amount of income tax and surtax payable by persons, as shown in this table, differs somewhat from the total of tax accruals in the corresponding years as shown in the personal income and expenditure account (Table 2). The reasons for this difference are that in this table:

(i) Interest paid by building societies is included in the distribution of income by ranges net of tax paid at the composite rate by building societies; the tax is not included in the individual tax returns and is therefore excluded

(ii) Certain categories of personal income, mainly the 'collective' income referred to above, are omitted from the distribution of income by ranges and the tax falling on this income is therefore excluded

(iii) The rates of tax imposed by the Budget of the year are applied to the income of the whole calendar year, although in fact the income received in the first quarter will have borne tax at the rates set by the previous Budget

(iv) The tax shown is the gross amount, before deduction of relief in respect of overseas taxation on income received from abroad, and thus approximates to the combined total of United Kingdom and overseas tax

Tables 27 and 28. Consumers' expenditure

Two tables are provided showing consumers' expenditure in detail. The general definition of consumers' expenditure is given on page 105; the system of classification and the methods of estimation are described on pages 147 to 202. Table 27 shows the detail of consumers' expenditure at current market prices and Table 28 shows estimates in the same detail (apart from the combination of catering, wages and salaries paid by non-profit-making bodies and insurance with other services) of expenditure revalued at constant prices.

The price index implied by the estimates for total consumers' expenditure on goods and services at current prices and the corresponding estimates at constant prices is shown in the table on index numbers of costs and prices (Table 16 of the 1967 Blue Book). The price index for any year is therefore based on the weights of that year and provides a direct measure of the change in prices between that year and the base year. Comparisons other than with the base year may be affected by differences in the weights, which are generally more important over longer than over shorter periods.

Table 29. Taxes on expenditure and subsidies allocated to consumers' expenditure

This table shows estimates of the taxes and subsidies attributable to specific categories of consumers' expenditure, together with an overall estimate of total taxes on expenditure and subsidies attributable to consumers' expenditure. The estimates show which categories of expenditure are most heavily taxed and subsidised, and make it possible to estimate the demands on factors of production arising from different forms of final expenditure by consumers.

The taxes allocated to various specific categories of consumers' expenditure are listed below.

(a) *Food (household expenditure)*. Receipts from protective duties on food and feedingstuffs, purchase tax on confectionery, ice cream and certain beverages, *less* an allowance for meals provided by catering establishments, income in kind, business expenditure and expenditure by public authorities.

(b) *Alcoholic drink*. Receipts from Customs and Excise duties *less* the same proportionate allowance for business expenditure as is used in estimating consumers' expenditure. Purchase tax on cider and perry and liquor excise licences.

(c) *Tobacco*. Total receipts of Customs and Excise duties on tobacco *less* an allowance for business expenditure.

(d) *Housing*. Estimates of local authority rates accruing on domestic property and property occupied by private non-profit-making bodies are allocated to rent, rates and water charges. Water charges are regarded as payment for a service, not as a tax. Part of protective duties and purchase tax on materials for maintenance and repair work is allocated to maintenance, repairs and improvements by occupiers.

(e) *Fuel and light*. Part of the receipts from the duty on kerosene and gas oil.

(f) *Clothing; Durable goods; Other household goods; Chemists' goods; Miscellaneous recreational goods; Other miscellaneous goods*. Receipts from protective duties, the temporary charge on imports and purchase tax falling on items within these categories, with a proportion deducted for purchases other than by consumers where this seems appropriate. The allocations for these groups are largely conjectural. Nearly all of the Customs and Excise duties on matches is allocated to consumers' expenditure on other household goods. Payments for dog and gun licences are allocated to miscellaneous recreational goods.

(g) *Running costs of motor vehicles*. The part of receipts from duties on hydrocarbon oils which is estimated to be from personal expenditure on petrol and oil. The part of receipts from motor vehicle licences, driving licences, driving test fees and Ministry of Transport vehicle test certificates which is included in the estimates of consumers' expenditure.

(h) *Travel*. Receipts from duties on hydrocarbon oils in respect of public service vehicles and part of similar receipts in respect of taxis. Licences for public road passenger vehicles.

(i) *Communication services*. Part of the Post Office contribution to the Exchequer.

(j) *Entertainment and recreational services*. Estimated purchase tax receipts on radio and television sets rented by consumers, entertainments duty up to 1960, television licence duty from 1957 to 1963, and up to 1960 that part of broadcast licence revenue retained by the Exchequer. The remainder of the payments for radio and television licences is regarded as payment for a service, not a tax.

(k) *Other services (including catering)*. Part of the receipts from protective duties on food and feedingstuffs and purchase tax on confectionery, ice cream and certain beverages. Estimated purchase tax on goods used in the repair of radio and television sets. Taxes on betting and bookmakers' and gaming licences.

That part of stamp duties on cheques and transactions in stocks and shares which is estimated to be paid by persons. Estimated fines and fees paid by persons to central government.

(l) *Income in kind not included elsewhere*. A small part of the receipts from protective duties on food and feedingstuffs, purchase tax on confectionery, ice cream and certain beverages.

In 1966, the proportion of payments of selective employment tax attributed to consumers' expenditure is based largely on input-output statistics for 1963. Payments made by those industries which do not qualify for a premium or refund of tax, broadly the service industries, have been allocated between the various categories of consumers' expenditure. Payments qualifying for a subsequent premium or refund, for example those by manufacturing industry, have not been allocated to categories of consumers' expenditure.

A similar allocation of taxes is carried out for the other types of final expenditure and the remaining amounts of tax not directly allocated are distributed proportionately between the types of final expenditure, after certain adjustments have been made to exclude readily identifiable components which contain no indirect taxes (see page 327). The amount of tax so distributed to consumers' expenditure is shown as tax 'Not allocated to categories'.

Subsidies are allocated in the same way as taxes. The subsidies allocated to various specific categories of consumers' expenditure are listed below.

(a) *Food (household expenditure)*. The agriculture and food subsidies *less* allowances for meals provided by catering establishments, income in kind, business expenditure and expenditure by public authorities.

(b) *Rent, rates and water charges*. All the housing subsidies.

(c) *Travel*. From 1960 part of the subsidy to the railways is allocated to consumers' expenditure according to the proportion of passenger receipts from consumers to total railway receipts for passenger and freight services. From 1965 half the subsidy for air navigation services. Nearly all of the remaining subsidies to transport and communication.

(d) *Other services (including catering)*. Part of the agriculture and food subsidies.

(e) *Income in kind not included elsewhere*. A small part of agriculture and food subsidies in respect of income in kind of H.M. Forces, merchant seamen and fishermen.

QUARTERLY TABLES

Personal income, expenditure and saving

This table is a summarised version of the personal income and expenditure account in the Blue Book. Income from self-employment is combined with income from rent, dividends and net interest because the quarterly information available does not permit satisfactory separate estimates to be made. There is no quarterly information on taxes paid abroad which are interpolated and grouped with transfers abroad. The estimates of United Kingdom taxes are restricted to tax payments, since the taxes are based on annual income and it is not possible to make quarterly estimates of tax accruals. The estimates of saving therefore include any additions to tax reserves. The estimates have been prepared on a consistent basis from 1955 and the series are seasonally adjusted. Unadjusted estimates for 1954 have also been published in the January 1958 issue of *Economic Trends*.

Consumers' expenditure

This table is a summarised version of the two Blue Book tables on consumers' expenditure, giving estimates at both current and constant prices for a restricted number of categories. The constant price estimates are seasonally adjusted. The estimates have been prepared on a consistent basis from 1955. Unadjusted estimates at current prices have been published back to 1945 and at constant prices back to 1948 but have not been kept up to date. Revised quarterly estimates for certain items of consumers' expenditure for the years 1948 to 1954 were last published in the October 1962 issue of *Economic Trends*.

3. STATISTICAL SOURCES: INCOME FROM EMPLOYMENT

To those receiving income from employment, this income is the reward for labour services contributed to production; to producers paying the income, it is the cost of obtaining those services. To these two ways of conceiving income from employment there correspond two kinds of analysis: the first leads to a division of total income from employment between forms of income—wages, salaries, pay of the Forces, etc.; the second leads to a division of the total by industry of origin.

Forms of income

The forms of income described as income from employment are as follows:
(a) Wages and salaries in cash, including directors' fees. These comprise amounts paid in cash by employers to employees *plus* any amounts deducted at source on behalf of employees such as payments of tax, employees' contributions to national insurance and superannuation contributions *less* any cash payments by employers to employees for expenses incurred as part of their employment which are allowed as a deduction for tax.
(b) Income in kind of civilian employees, comprising the imputed vàlue of certain goods and services supplied by employers to employees free or at reduced prices.
(c) *less* Expenses of employment borne by employees and not recovered from their employers, but allowed as a deduction for tax; for example, allowances for tools and clothing.
(d) Pay, cash allowances and income in kind of the armed services, women's services, and the reserve and auxiliary forces.
(e) Employers' contributions to the national insurance scheme, to the national health service and to the Redundancy Fund.
(f) Employers' contributions to superannuation schemes and pension funds.
(g) Certain compensation payments to employees for losses sustained in the course of their employment, or on its termination through redundancy.
The table opposite shows how the estimates of income from employment for 1966 given in the 1967 Blue Book were built up from these seven different types of payment.

Employers' contributions, items (e) to (g), are treated as part of the price at which labour services are sold, as well as of the price at which they are bought, and are included in income from employment. Employers' contributions to national insurance are treated as though they were a tax deducted at source from the employees' income. Similarly, employers' contributions to superannuation schemes are treated as a part of employees' income which is compulsorily saved. Even so, total income from employment does not represent the total cost of employing labour; the estimates of income in kind are not comprehensive (see page 125) and income from employment does not cover costs which benefit the employer rather than the employee, such as costs of recruitment and training, and the provision of amenities at places of work.

Forms of income from employment, 1966

	£ million
(a) Wages in cash	11,863
Salaries in cash	8,203
(b) Income in kind of civilian employees	234
(c) *less* Expenses of employment borne by employees	−180
Total wages and salaries	20,120
(d) Pay, cash allowances and income in kind of H.M. Forces	513
(e) Employers' contributions to national insurance and health	902
(f) Employers' contributions to superannuation schemes	862
(g) Employers' compensation payments, etc.	40
Total income from employment	22,437

Distinction between wages and salaries

Only a limited importance can be attached to the separation of wages from salaries in the national accounts. The distinction is necessarily arbitrary and no clear dividing line can be drawn, but it nevertheless has certain practical uses.

The distinction is in fact made in some of the statistical sources largely because the processes of wage settlement are more highly organised than those for the determination of salaries. Until information was collected in the post-war censuses of production, accurate information about salary earnings was confined to national government service and a few other industries. The distinction made in the national accounts is derived primarily from that used in the census of production under which separate information on earnings is provided for operatives and for administrative, technical and clerical employees. The census of production defines administrative, technical and clerical employees as including managing and other directors in receipt of a definite wage, salary or commission; managers, superintendents, and works foremen; research, experimental, development, technical and design employees (other than operatives); draughtsmen and tracers; editorial staff, staff reporters, canvassers, competition and advertising staff; travellers; and office (including works office) employees. Operatives are defined as comprising all other classes of employees.

So far as possible, the line of division for the industries outside the census of production has been drawn in accordance with the division used in the census. Shop assistants do not fit easily into either category and have been treated by

E

some authorities as wage earners and by others as salary earners. In the national accounts they are treated as wage earners. Policemen and firemen are also treated as wage earners. For most industries outside the scope of the census of production, there is little information on the proportions of wage earners and salary earners except from the results of the 1951 and subsequent censuses of population, which are used for the national accounts estimates. Some information on the overall division between wages and salaries has been collected in the income surveys carried out by the Inland Revenue but no industry analysis is available and the information has not so far been used in preparing the estimates for the national accounts.

General methods of estimation

Total income from employment is estimated almost wholly from tax data[3], but for the analysis between wages and salaries and by industry a number of different sources are used. The industrial analysis of the tax data is not used because it is based on the financial unit, whereas the conceptual basis of the industrial breakdowns in the national accounts is the establishment. Other sources, of which the most important are the detailed censuses of production and Ministry of Labour statistics, provide an industrial classification based on establishments, and for most industrial groups give a basis for the separation of wages and salaries. There is little direct information about wages and salaries for part of Order XXII and for Order XXIII of the *Standard Industrial Classification, 1958* which are grouped together as 'Other services' and their wage and salary bill is taken to be the residual difference between the total derived from tax data and the sum of the independent estimates for all other industries. Any discrepancy between these different sources therefore falls into the group 'Other services'.

Estimates of the numbers of wage earners and salary earners are given only for the total of manufacturing industries; these are shown in Table 18 of the 1967 Blue Book, referred to on page 112, and described below, page 135. Although for some other industries estimates of average earnings are used to build up the total wage and salary bill, for some of the major industry groups it is impossible to identify at all accurately either the average number of persons receiving income from employment in the course of the year or the total number of recipients, which may be very different. Because of differences in the definition of numbers employed, and differences in classification, it is unsafe to divide the wage or salary bill given in the Blue Book by the numbers employed as reported in other sources, for example the Ministry of Labour statistics of employment. The main interest in the national accounts is necessarily in the aggregate wage and salary bill and, wherever possible, data about the total annual wage or salary bill are used in preference to data about weekly earnings per head. For information about average hourly or weekly earnings per head, reference should be made to the Ministry of Labour statistics of average wage and salary earnings and standard rates of wages.

The methods of estimating total income from employment are described below. The independent methods used for the analysis by industry, and for the division between wages and salaries, are described on pages 133 to 140.

---

[3]Most of this material is published annually in the *Report of the Commissioners of Her Majesty's Inland Revenue*, for example, data for 1965/66 and earlier years in Tables 50 to 52 of 110th Report, Cmnd. 3508.

ESTIMATION OF TOTAL INCOME FROM EMPLOYMENT

Wages and salaries in cash

The incomes of the great majority of wage and salary earners are above the exemption limit for 'Pay-as-you-earn' (PAYE). Under this system income tax is deducted at source by the employer, and employers have to make returns of the pay and tax of all their employees with incomes above the PAYE exemption limit. It is thus possible to obtain reliable and almost complete information about wages and salaries paid in cash from the PAYE deduction cards, or machine statements and the related returns, sent by employers to local tax offices after the end of the financial year. The checking of the returns with employers, to ensure that they are complete and accurate, and the central collection and tabulation of the information, now takes about ten to eleven months before the information is virtually complete. This means, for example, that almost final figures relating to the financial year 1965/66 were available about February 1967. For the last nine months of the latest year shown in each Blue Book, the quarterly estimates, as described below, are used.

To arrive at a complete estimate of wages and salaries in cash, the following adjustments must be made to the figures derived from PAYE returns.

(a) *Earned income below the PAYE limit.* The PAYE system of tax deduction normally operates only for incomes above a specified limit which has varied from time to time in line with changes in personal allowances. For the financial year 1967/68 the limit was £5 5s. 0d. a week, or, for monthly paid employees, £22 15s. 0d. a month. These amounts are the approximate weekly and monthly equivalents of the minimum annual income on which any liability to tax can arise. The effective limit from 1965/66 to 1967/68 was £283 per annum. Should the pay for any one period rise above the limit, a deduction card must be completed by the employer and the whole of the pay received in that year from the current employer will then be recorded, even though the pay in subsequent periods may fall below the limit. So long as the pay remains below the PAYE deduction card limit, the income is not recorded. The estimate of incomes below the limit is based on estimates of the numbers concerned and their average annual earnings. It covers chiefly the earnings of juveniles and women working part-time.

(b) *Incomplete returns.* PAYE deduction cards are not always obtained from farmers in respect of all their employees, or for all domestic servants even though the income may be above the deduction card limit, most often because it is known that no tax has to be deducted. For these two groups, additions are made to the tax assessment data based on the independent estimates for agricultural workers and domestic servants described on pages 134 and 140.

(c) *Pensions.* Pensions, but not lump sums, paid by central government, by local authorities and by privately financed funds, excluding payments direct to pensioners by life assurance companies, are included in the PAYE returns if the pension is above the tax deduction card limit or if the pensioner has other income sufficient to produce some liability to tax. In estimating the wage and salary bill from PAYE statistics it is therefore necessary to make a deduction for such pensions. The estimate of the amount of pensions paid under PAYE is mainly based on the income surveys, which from 1962/63 have been carried out annually by the Inland Revenue.

(d) *Adjustment to calendar year.* The financial year data from tax deduction cards are adjusted to a calendar year basis by using the quarterly estimates described below.

The adjustments to the PAYE figures for 1966 in the 1967 Blue Book are:

	£ million
PAYE estimates, adjusted to calendar year....................	20,126
Earned income below the tax deduction card limit, other than in agriculture and domestic service	310
Income in cash of agricultural workers and domestic servants in excess of that included in PAYE estimates................	50
less Pensions of retired employees included in PAYE estimates....	−420
Wages and salaries in cash, before deduction of tax	20,066

No adjustment is made to the figures derived from PAYE returns in respect of the lump sum compensation payments on loss of office which are included; these payments are regarded as part of income from employment.

Quarterly estimates of wages and salaries in cash

From 1954/55 to 1959/60 quarterly estimates of wages and salaries paid under PAYE were based as follows. A sample of the tax deduction cards for 1954/55 was taken and an analysis was made of the pay and tax up to the end of each quarter of that year. Adjustments were made for subsequent quarters according to the changes in quarterly receipts of tax, allowing for the effects of changes in rates or allowances.

The 1954/55 analysis covered only about half the total pay, as a considerable number of employers use variations of the tax deduction cards which do not show pay quarter by quarter but only the annual total. From the second quarter of 1960 an additional inquiry was therefore made. A sample of the employers using cards which do not show details of pay was asked to provide quarterly figures of pay and tax, and the results were grossed up to give total pay by this group of employers. An analysis was also made for 1960/61 similar to that for 1954/55 to give an estimate of the pay on normal tax deduction cards. These two results were used together to give an estimate of total quarterly pay under PAYE in 1960/61.

Estimates of quarterly pay since 1960/61 are based on a comparison of information from the following sources:

(a) Weekly figures of receipts of PAYE tax from employers which provide an estimate of the amount of PAYE tax deducted in each quarter and thus of the wages and salaries paid.

(b) A continuation of the sample of employers taken in 1960/61. Returns are received quarterly from about 1,800 employers who have mechanized accounting systems, and whose payroll covers a quarter of total wages and salaries.

An additional source available from January 1963 is:

(c) The Ministry of Labour monthly index of average earnings in manufacturing and some other industries, coupled with estimates of numbers of employees in employment.

The quarterly estimates are revised when the annual financial year totals of pay become available from PAYE returns.

The quarterly adjustments to the PAYE estimates are interpolated and projected, unless any information is available which suggests a departure from the trend, for instance a change in the tax deduction card limit. These quarterly figures allow for estimated seasonal variations in some of the items included.

Income in kind of civilian employees

Estimates for the following items are included:

(a) Board and lodging, food and other items provided by farmers for agricultural workers. The estimates are provided by the agricultural departments.

(b) Coal provided free or at concessionary rates to miners and other colliery employees. The estimates are provided by the Ministry of Power.

(c) Food and lodging received by domestic servants. Rough estimates are included in the calculation of the wage and salary bill.

(d) Food provided for merchant seamen and fishermen. Rough estimates are included in the calculation of the wage and salary bill.

(e) Imputed rent of housing provided free by other employers and rates paid by employers. Estimates are based on the Family Expenditure Survey.

(f) The net cost to employers of meal vouchers and meals provided in canteens. Estimates have been made using the results of the Ministry of Labour inquiry into employers' total labour costs in 1964 and other sources.

(g) The net cost to employers of food and accommodation provided for staff in catering establishments other than canteens. The value is assumed to be about five per cent of consumers' expenditure on meals and accommodation in these establishments.

Quarterly estimates are interpolated and projected.

Additional items might be included if more information were available. In general, all receipts in kind, such as the uniforms provided for many transport workers, might be included where they are of direct benefit to the employee, for example by allowing him to reduce his own expenditure on clothes, and can be regarded as part of the employer's labour costs. The same applies to the special travel concessions enjoyed by many transport workers and to certain recreational facilities and health services provided by employers. Those receipts in kind which may be regarded as protection against the specific drawbacks of the job should not, however, be included. The dividing line is difficult to draw in logic, and probably impossible to draw in practice. Hence a rather restricted definition is adopted here, which, in particular, excludes all clothing except in the case of the Forces.

An inquiry into employers' total labour costs in 1964 was made by the Ministry of Labour[4]. This inquiry covered items of income in kind other than those included in the estimates, for example health services, transport and clothing. But the inquiry related to only one year and covered only manufacturing and certain non-manufacturing industries. It therefore did not provide sufficient information to extend the coverage of the estimates of income in kind. The purpose of the inquiry was to ascertain the total labour costs incurred by employers, and the inquiry therefore also covered such items as recruitment and training costs, which are a labour cost to the employer but cannot be regarded as part of the employee's income.

---

[4]See *Ministry of Labour Gazette*, December 1966 and March 1967.

Expenses of employment borne by employees

The amounts allowed by the Inland Revenue, in charging income tax under Schedule E, as a necessary expense of employment are excluded from personal income. They cover expenditure by an employee not refunded by an employer on, for example, tools, special clothing, subscriptions to learned societies, and in certain cases, such as commercial travellers, travelling in the course of the work. Expenses of travelling between home and work are not covered. The estimates are based on information provided by the Inland Revenue.

Pay in cash and kind of H.M. Forces

The estimates are compiled from returns furnished quarterly by the service departments on the same basis as the figures published subsequently in the *Appropriation Accounts*. The following payments in cash are included:

(a) Pay and cash allowances of British officers and men in the armed forces (but not of Commonwealth, including colonial, and other troops) whether on general service or serving in the Ministry of Defence or other government departments.

(b) Pay and allowances of members of the nursing services and women's services.

(c) Pay and allowances of reserve forces, and territorial and cadet forces.

Pensions and retired pay of former ('non-effective') members of the Forces are excluded, being treated, like other unfunded pensions, as employers' contributions. Employers' contributions to national insurance are treated in the same way.

Income in kind is measured by the cost of issues of food and clothing. Nothing is included for lodging.

Pay to members of the Forces on release leave, pensions and grants awarded for death or disability and extended service bounties are excluded and treated as current transfers by public authorities to the personal sector.

Employers' contributions to national insurance and health

This item covers employers' contributions to the national insurance scheme (both flat rate and graduated contributions), the industrial injuries scheme, the national health service and, from 1965, the Redundancy Fund.

Selective employment tax, paid from 1966 together with flat rate national insurance contributions, is regarded as an indirect tax falling on employers, and is not included. The estimates are taken from the central government accounts (see page 287). Quarterly figures are based on returns prepared by the Government Actuary's Department.

Employers' contributions to superannuation schemes

Employers' contributions to superannuation and pension schemes are treated as supplements to wages and salaries and hence as savings out of employees' current income. Consequently the pensions actually received by retired employees are regarded as a transfer within the personal sector and excluded from personal income. Some employers, however, including the central government, pay non-contributory pensions to their retired employees, as and when they become due, without making current provision for future pension liabilities. It would be desirable in these cases to include in income from employment not pensions paid to past employees, but the currently accruing liability to pay pensions in the future to present employees. Unfortunately, no measures of this liability exist, except for the General Post Office, and as an unsatisfactory alternative the pensions currently paid are included instead in income from employment. These represent a considerable underestimate because of the growth both in numbers of civil servants and in average pay. However, these pensions, like contributions to funded pensions schemes, are reckoned as a current expense by the employer, so that the balance between national income and expenditure is maintained. Employers' contributions to superannuation schemes thus consist predominantly of current contributions to schemes by employers, but include also an element of actual pensions paid.

There are several ways in which employers can operate contributory pension schemes for their employees, for instance by a privately operated fund or by a scheme arranged with a life assurance company. Small private funds often take cover against particular contingencies with a life assurance company but are still treated as privately financed. Pension arrangements may also be classified according to the tax treatment of the employees' contributions, in three ways:

(a) 'approved funds' under which the employees' contributions are treated as an expense and allowed in full as a deduction from income for income tax purposes;

(b) schemes arranged directly with a life assurance office under which the employees' contributions are given only life insurance relief;

(c) unapproved pension schemes where the contributions of both the employer and employee are taxed as the income of the employee and tax relief is given only to the extent that it is due under the ordinary rules for life insurance relief.

The sources of information for employers' contributions to superannuation funds and pension schemes operated by public authorities and the larger public corporations are the published accounts of the bodies concerned. For private employers and the smaller corporations, estimates are made by the Inland Revenue from two sources:

(a) since 1954, a regular series of returns by tax inspectors of the accounts of privately operated funds, which are analysed in detail;

(b) the annual review of life assurance business[5], which gives figures for occupational schemes, including reinsured funds.

Use has also been made of the surveys of occupational pensions schemes undertaken by the Government Actuary[6], information collected from their members by the Institute of Actuaries and the Faculty of Actuaries in Scotland, and the Ministry of Labour inquiry into employers' labour costs in 1964.

In the absence of other information, quarterly figures are interpolated or projected.

The main constituents of the figure of total employers' contributions to

---

[5] See for example, *Life Assurance in the United Kingdom 1962-66*, issued by the Life Offices' Association, the Associated Scottish Life Offices and the Industrial Life Offices Association.

[6] For details of the latest survey, relating to 1963, see *Occupational Pension Schemes: A New Survey by the Government Actuary, 1966*.

superannuation schemes for 1966, given on page 121, are as follows:

	£ million
Contributions to superannuation schemes:	
National health service and teachers	83
Local authorities (excluding police and firemen)	56
General Post Office[1]	43
Other public corporations and privately financed schemes..	270
Schemes operated through life assurance companies........	180
Actual pensions, including lump sums, paid:	
Central government:	
Civilians[2]	63
H.M. Forces......................................	82
Police and firemen[2]	25
Private industry (nominal figure)	60
Total	862

[1]Although there is no funded scheme an estimate of the
annual liability is entered in the trading accounts of the
Post Office before striking the trading surplus.
[2]Pensions paid *less* employees' contributions.

The figures in all cases cover (a) payments to widows and orphans where provision for such payments is incorporated in the scheme, and (b) lump sum payments on death or retirement as well as annuities.

Employers' compensation payments

This item includes certain compensation payments not included in the wage and salary bill or in the figures for pensions, etc. paid out. Some compensation payments paid on loss of employment are subject to income tax and are therefore included in the estimates of the wage and salary bill. The payments which are not subject to income tax are most conveniently included in income from employment and regarded as an operating expense in computing trading profits or surplus. An alternative treatment would be to regard them as current transfers; this would have the drawback that the payments would have to be treated as appropriations of profits. Estimates are included for compensation paid to injured employees or to their dependants apart from payments under the national insurance and industrial injuries schemes; certain compensation payments by public corporations to former employees; compensation paid for personal injury to 'third parties'; and payments to employees under the Redundancy Payments Act, 1965 which are not recovered by rebates from the Fund. For public corporations, estimates are made on the basis of information given in their published accounts. For other enterprises use has been made of the Ministry of Labour inquiry into total labour costs in 1964. For other years and for industries not covered by the inquiry only very rough estimates can be made of employers' liability payments outside the statutory schemes.

Quarterly figures of employers' payments to employees, *less* rebates from the Fund, under the Redundancy Payments Act are provided by the Ministry of Labour. Other quarterly figures are interpolated and projected.

ANALYSIS OF INCOME FROM EMPLOYMENT BY INDUSTRY
AND DIVISION BETWEEN WAGES AND SALARIES

As explained above, the division of income from employment between industries, and the separation between wages and salaries by industries and in total, are derived from a variety of sources independently of the estimate of total income from employment. These sources, and the methods used, are now described.

Sources of information for individual industries

The census of production provides information on mining and quarrying, manufacturing industries, construction (except in 1950), and gas, electricity and water supply. The detailed censuses include statistics of average numbers employed and total annual earnings separately for operatives (wage earners) and administrative, technical and clerical workers (salary earners) which are the basis for the Blue Book estimates of the wage and salary bill in the industries covered by the censuses for those years. A census giving this information was taken for each year from 1948 to 1958 and for 1963. The 1958 Census was based on the revised *Standard Industrial Classification*, 1958, while earlier censuses were based on the 1948 Classification. The census estimates include allowances for small firms from which full returns were not required and for firms making unsatisfactory returns. The census of production is described briefly in Appendix II. After 1958 the figures from the detailed censuses have been used as benchmarks and preliminary estimates for years between detailed censuses have been made for most of the industries covered from estimated changes in the numbers employed and in average wage and salary earnings (see pages 134 to 136). The estimates for 1959 to 1962 were obtained in this way and then adjusted in the light of the results of the 1963 census of production.

The census of distribution provides figures of the wage and salary bill for the distributive trades, but wages and salaries are not distinguished separately. A census covering both wholesale and retail distribution was taken in 1950 and censuses covering retail distribution were taken for 1957, 1961 and 1966. The census results provide a check on the estimated wage and salary bill based on estimates of numbers employed and average earnings.

Apart from the production industries and distributive trades the only groups for which direct estimates of total pay can be obtained from independent sources are the public corporations and the main branches of central government service—the national health service and non-industrial salaried staffs engaged in public administration and defence, for which estimates are obtained from the *Appropriation Accounts* or analogous returns. For some of the public corporations calendar year figures have to be estimated from published financial year totals.

For most of the remaining industries, statistics of the wage and salary bill are compiled by making estimates, first, of the number of wage and salary earners employed, and secondly, of average earnings. This method is used mainly for agriculture, some forms of transport and communication, insurance, banking and finance, local government service, and, in part, for miscellaneous services.

Numbers employed

The comprehensive source of information for total numbers employed in Great Britain is the regular Ministry of Labour statistics of employment. For the

E*

national accounts, figures from the Ministry of Health and Social Services, Northern Ireland are added to obtain estimates for the United Kingdom[7]. This information is generally supplemented by the censuses of population[8] to give the division between wage earners and salary earners which is not shown in the Ministry of Labour statistics. From 1948 the Ministry of Labour estimates of numbers in employment are derived mainly from the exchange of national insurance cards of persons insured as employees. From the June exchange of cards and supplementary returns from employers, an estimate is made by the Ministry of Labour for each industry of the total number of insured persons in the category of employees at the middle of each year. By deducting the numbers registered at employment exchanges as wholly unemployed at the same date, an estimate is made of the number employed. For production industries these estimates are kept up to date by monthly returns from a sample of employers of numbers employed, defined as 'on the payroll'. With other supplementary sources estimates of average annual employment in each industry can be made.

Certain problems arise in using these statistics of employment to form estimates of the wage and salary bill consistent with the estimates based on the census of production and other sources:

(a) Although efforts have been made to ensure that each establishment is classified to the same industry in the Ministry of Labour statistics, the census of production and all other relevant official returns, in accordance with the Standard Industrial Classification, nevertheless, certain differences have not been completely resolved. Differences may arise partly from differences in the extent to which ancillary activities are separated and classified to other industries, or from a time lag in re-classifying firms in Ministry of Labour records. The estimates of the wage and salary bill based on the censuses of production are lower than those which would be obtained by using Ministry of Labour data for the census industries. With the controlling total of the aggregate wage and salary bill in all industries being derived from PAYE returns, the difference is offset by a difference of the same size and opposite sign in the wage and salary bill for one or other of the non-manufacturing industries. A rough allowance for the difference is made in estimating the wage and salary bill for transport and the distributive trades; any remaining difference is included in the residual estimate for 'Other services'.

(b) The average number employed, as derived from the Ministry of Labour statistics, is based on the number insured *less* those registered as wholly unemployed. This is not necessarily the appropriate number by which to multiply the average wage or salary as given in the sources described below to arrive at the aggregate of wages or salaries paid during the year, because the average number employed, on this definition, is not necessarily the average number receiving pay. At any one time there may be persons with current insurance cards not registered as wholly unemployed and yet away from work because of temporary unemployment, sickness, trade disputes or voluntary absenteeism or because

---

[7]A description of the methods of estimation is given in the *Ministry of Labour Gazette*, May 1966. The figures are published monthly in the *Ministry of Labour Gazette*. Corresponding figures for Northern Ireland are published six-monthly in the Northern Ireland *Digest of Statistics*.

[8]*Census 1951, England and Wales*: Industry Tables; *Census 1961, England and Wales*: Industry Tables, Part I; *Census 1961, Scotland*, Volume VI, Part II: Industry Tables. The results of the 1966 census were not available for the 1967 Blue Book.

they are temporarily not seeking work. In using these statistics for calculating the wage and salary bill, adjustments are made for the incidence of sickness, but a margin of error remains in the computation.

(c) For many industries outside the census of production there is no information apart from that in the 1951 and subsequent censuses of population to show changes in the proportions of wage earners and salary earners.

Wage earnings

For each year from 1948 to 1958 and subsequently for years when there has been a detailed census, the census of production provides information. The other principal source of data about average wage earnings is the inquiry carried out regularly by the Ministry of Labour each April and October since 1947[9]. These inquiries have been used to provide information on changes in average wage earnings after 1958 in the industries covered by the census of production. In addition to covering part of mining, manufacturing, construction and gas, electricity and water, these inquiries also cover part of transport, communication, certain miscellaneous services and public administration. The inquiries are voluntary, and the response, although high, is not complete in the industries covered. The returns show the aggregate amounts earned in the week of inquiry by wage earners, including the proportionate amount of any bonuses, before deduction of income tax and insurance contributions. The number of persons at work during all or part of the week is also reported. Similar information is also available for agriculture, coal mining and for some other parts of transport. The half-yearly figures of average weekly earnings are converted into average annual earnings by interpolation, using the Ministry of Labour monthly indices of changes in recognised rates of wages. Up to 1963 no allowance could be made for seasonal changes in earnings. From 1963 the Ministry of Labour monthly inquiry into average earnings [10] also provides information between half-yearly inquiries.

For the distributive trades, there is little information about average wage earnings, and an estimate is made based on the recognised time rates[11] for various classes of workers. Any such estimate is liable to substantial error because of ignorance of the distribution of workers between the various classes, the amount of part-time work, and the incidence of overtime and bonuses. The estimates for the distributive trades have, however, been checked against the data about the total wage and salary bill in the censuses of distribution, referred to above.

Agricultural earnings, which include payments in kind, are estimated by the agricultural departments from regular sample surveys. These inquiries cover payments by farmers to casual workers who may at other times of the year be engaged in non-agricultural occupations, or not gainfully employed. The seasonal movement of workers into agriculture may lead to errors in estimates of the wage bill in the industries to which such workers normally belong if these estimates are based on earnings data for only certain weeks in the year. These seasonal movements in employment are one factor making it difficult to estimate the wage bill as a whole from an industrial classification of workers

[9]See, for example, *Ministry of Labour Gazette,* February 1968.
[10]Described in the *Ministry of Labour Gazette,* March 1967.
[11]See, for example, *Time Rates of Wages and Hours of Work, 1st April 1967.*

based on their principal employment combined with data about earnings relating to particular weeks in the year or to standard rates of pay.

Salary earnings

For each year from 1948 to 1958 and subsequently for years when there has been a detailed census, the census of production provides information on the industries covered. From 1955, an annual inquiry into salary earnings has been made by the Ministry of Labour each October. From 1959 it has covered the census industries, public administration and certain other services[12]. Returns show the number of administrative, technical and clerical staff employed in the last pay-week of October, and total salaries paid in the month to those paid monthly, and in the last pay-week in the month to those paid weekly; from this information total average salary earnings on a weekly basis are derived. These figures are used to give an estimate of the annual change in average salary earnings for the census of production industries in years for which no information on salaries is provided by the census.

Outside the census of production industries and nearly all forms of public employment, little information is at present available about salary earnings. The estimates made for individual industries are very insecure but the estimate of total salaries is absolutely as reliable as that of total wages in that the two estimates add up to the total wage and salary bill. The principal methods used are:

(a) If an estimate is available of the total wage and salary bill in an industry or part of an industry, and an estimate has been made, by the methods described above, of the total wage bill, then the salary bill is taken as the difference. This is done for local government service, for which data about total remuneration are available from *Local Government Financial Statistics*, and for the major nationalised transport undertakings, figures for total remuneration being obtained from their annual accounts.

(b) Analogy with the average level of salary earnings in those industries for which statistics exist—generally the census of production industries.

Directors' fees are included, though not separately distinguished, in the PAYE figures of wages and salaries. They are not, however, included in the sources already mentioned from which the estimates of salaries by industry are constructed. Rough estimates have therefore to be made for each industry of the amounts received by directors paid by fee. Figures for 1951 were based on details from the 1951 census of population which gave the number and distribution by industry of people of the status of 'general managers, directors, etc.' and on the assumption that the average director's fee in 1951 in each industry was about £550 per annum. Comparable figures for other years have been estimated assuming that the amount paid in directors' fees has changed proportionately to the salary bill. The reliability of the estimates is poor.

Distribution by industry of other forms of income from employment

The Ministry of Labour 1964 inquiry into employers' labour costs has been of general use in allocating by industry the forms of income from employment, apart from wages and salaries. Some forms of *income in kind* such as miners' coal are peculiar to one industry; others, such as canteen meals, have to be allocated

---

[12]See, for example, *Ministry of Labour Gazette*, March 1968.

over a wide range of industries. The deduction for *expenses of employment* is allocated in proportion to the total wage and salary bill. The values of total *employers' contributions* for individual production industries are available from the 1963 census of production. *Employers' contributions to national insurance and health* are for the most part allocated in proportion to numbers of men, women and juveniles employed, and according to information from PAYE returns on amounts paid in graduated contributions. *Employers' contributions to pension schemes* and *compensation payments* are allocated as follows:

(a) the Ministry of Labour provides an analysis by industry for employers' payments under the Redundancy Payments Act;

(b) separate figures of other payments by industry are available for the public services and the nationalised industries;

(c) estimates for the industries covered by the census of production and the labour costs inquiry are then made;

(d) payments are allocated to industries not covered by (b) and (c) in proportion to the wage and salary bill.

The following table shows the analysis by industry of total employers' contributions in 1966, as estimated for the 1967 Blue Book:

	£ million
Agriculture, forestry and fishing	20
Mining and quarrying	50
Manufacturing	540
Construction	102
Gas, electricity and water	45
Transport and communication	168
Distributive trades	148
Insurance, banking and finance	128
Public administration and defence:	
National government service	180
Local government service	77
Public health and local authority educational services	154
Other services	192
Total	1,804

SOURCES USED FOR WAGES AND SALARIES
IN INDIVIDUAL INDUSTRIES

This section describes the sources used for estimating wages and salaries industry by industry. The Roman numerals refer to the Orders of the Standard Industrial Classification as revised in 1958. At this revision some items were reclassified to different Orders, and the figures for earlier years have been adjusted as far as possible to the 1958 Classification. The description relates to the estimates of wages and salaries in cash, excluding directors' fees. The estimates of income in kind relating to specific industries are also covered.

The methods described for the latest year are normally the methods used in each Blue Book for the latest year shown, for which figures are sometimes not available on as reliable a basis as for earlier years.

In general the methods used to obtain estimates of total numbers employed throughout the year and the number of wage earners and salary earners are first described. Where this is followed by a description of the methods used to estimate the average wage and the average salary, it is to be assumed that the wage bill and the salary bill have been estimated by multiplying numbers employed by average earnings. Wherever direct methods are used to estimate the wage bill and salary bill they are described after the methods used for numbers employed. The reliability of the estimates is indicated on page 141.

I Agriculture, forestry, fishing

Agriculture. Estimates of the numbers employed are provided by the agricultural departments, based on information derived from the agricultural census, in which returns are made by farmers and growers occupying more than one acre of crops and grass. The figures refer to all persons employed in farming irrespective of whether they receive a cash wage, excluding the farmer, his wife, and any schoolchildren, but including casual workers. Wage earners are distinguished from salary earners; the latter include farm managers, foremen and bailiffs. The numbers employed are greater than those shown by the Ministry of Labour statistics which relate only to persons insured as employees, and exclude partners of the main occupier and some other working relatives who insure themselves as self-employed persons.

The average wage and average salary are calculated by the agricultural departments from regular sample surveys of earnings carried out by officers of the departments. In the year ended 30 September 1966 the sample visited in England and Wales comprised 4,250 holdings representing about three per cent of the holdings employing workers. These inquiries provide reliable information.

The estimates of average earnings include the value of income in kind, which amounted to about £8 million in 1966. In the case of unpaid family workers an income is attributed equal to that received by paid workers of corresponding age, sex and occupation[13].

Forestry and fishing. Total numbers employed are Ministry of Labour figures *less* numbers temporarily unemployed. The number of salary earners is taken to be about 4,000 in each year. For years before the latest, the total wage and salary bill is estimated from PAYE statistics, arbitrarily split between wages and salaries in such a way as to produce, in conjunction with the figures of numbers employed, reasonable figures of average earnings. For the latest year estimates are based on (a) changes in numbers employed, (b) changes in wage rates and (c) changes in average salary earnings based on changes in salaries in other industries.

II Mining and quarrying

Coal mining. Figures of changes in the numbers employed since the latest detailed census of production are taken from the Ministry of Power *Statistical Digest*. For the latest two years, numbers are estimated from the changes in the Ministry of Labour employment figures.

---

[13]For a detailed account of the inquiries reference should be made to an article by H. Palca and I. G. R. Davies 'Earnings and Conditions of Employment in Agriculture' *Journal of the Royal Statistical Society*, Series A (General), Vol. CXIV, Part 1, 1951. See also articles in *Economic Trends*, May 1962, and annually in the *Ministry of Labour Gazette*, for example October 1967.

The wage and salary bill in the detailed censuses of production is used as a benchmark. An addition is made for coal provided free or at concessionary rates to employees, which amounted to about £24 million in 1966. For other years, wages paid in collieries operated by the National Coal Board are taken from the Board's annual accounts, with an addition for wages paid on capital account and wages paid in collieries not operated by the National Coal Board. Figures for the latest year are estimated from information collected by the National Coal Board. The estimate of the salary bill is based on the change in the total amount of salaries paid on revenue account by the National Coal Board as given in their annual accounts. Figures for the latest year are estimated from information collected by the National Coal Board.

Other mining and quarrying. Figures from the detailed censuses of production are used as benchmarks. For other years figures for numbers of wage earners employed are taken from the Ministry of Power *Statistical Digest*. For the latest two years numbers are estimated from the changes in the Ministry of Labour employment figures. The wage and salary bill is estimated from (a) changes in numbers employed and (b) changes in average wage earnings and average salary earnings from the earnings inquiries of the Ministry of Labour.

III to XVI Manufacturing industries

The latest detailed census of production figures of numbers employed are projected according to the change in the Ministry of Labour figures for employment and for the ratio of manual workers to administrative, technical and clerical employees. The wage and salary bill is estimated since the latest detailed census of production for each manufacturing industry from (a) changes in numbers employed and (b) changes in average wage earnings and average salary earnings from the earnings inquiries of the Ministry of Labour.

These sources provide the figures of wages and salaries for each of the Orders III to XVI and the total number of wage earners and of salary earners in all manufacturing industries which are shown in the Blue Book (Table 18 of the 1967 Blue Book).

XVII Construction

Numbers employed are a projection from the latest detailed census of production figures, made according to the change in the employment figures collected by the Ministry of Public Building and Works, which have a coverage similar to that of the census of production.

The wage and salary bill is estimated since the latest detailed census of production from (a) changes in numbers employed and (b) changes in average wage earnings and average salary earnings from the earnings inquiries of the Ministry of Labour.

XVIII Gas, electricity and water

Gas and electricity. Figures from the detailed censuses of production are used as benchmarks. For other years, figures of numbers employed and of wages and salaries are taken from the Ministry of Power *Statistical Digest*; an addition is made to the figures for electricity in respect of a small number of workers in transport undertakings who are excluded from these figures but included in the census. For the latest two years, numbers are estimated from changes in the Ministry of Labour employment figures and estimates of the total wage and salary bill are obtained from the annual reports of the public corporations concerned or from departmental sources. The wage bill is estimated from changes in the Ministry of Labour figures of numbers employed and average wage earnings, and the salary bill is taken to be the difference between the wage bill and the total.

Water supply. The latest detailed census figures of numbers employed are projected according to changes in the Ministry of Labour employment figures. The wage and salary bill is estimated from (a) changes in numbers employed and (b) changes in average wage earnings and average salary earnings from the earnings inquiries of the Ministry of Labour.

XIX (part) Transport

British Transport Commission (up to 1962). Up to the end of 1962, when the British Transport Commission was dissolved, the wage and salary bill of all British Transport Commission employees in Order XIX was estimated as a whole. Figures of numbers employed were taken from the annual accounts of the British Transport Commission, with a deduction for those not in Order XIX. The split into wage earners and salary earners was estimated from information given in these accounts. An estimate of the total wage and salary bill was provided by the British Transport Commission, from which estimates of the parts not in Order XIX were deducted. Average wage and average salary earnings were estimated from the figures of average earnings of different grades of British Railways staff given in the annual accounts. These were multiplied by the figures of numbers employed to give total wages and total salaries; small adjustments were made to bring this total to the figure for the total wage and salary bill.

British Railways Board and London Transport Board (from 1963). From 1963 the numbers of wage earners and salary earners employed by the British Railways Board and London Transport Board are estimated from figures given in their annual accounts, with a deduction for staff not in Order XIX.

Figures of total wages and salaries are also given in their annual accounts, from which the estimated part not in Order XIX is excluded. The wage bill is estimated from figures of average wage earnings, which are given half-yearly in the *Ministry of Labour Gazette* for British Railways staff and London Transport staff and corresponding figures of numbers employed. The salary bill is taken to be the difference between the wage bill and the total.

The wage and salary bill for others previously employed by the British Transport Commission is included from 1963 with road passenger transport and road haulage contracting or the rest of transport.

Road passenger transport and road haulage contracting. Numbers employed are Ministry of Labour figures *less*, up to 1962, the numbers employed in these activities within the British Transport Commission, and, from 1963, the numbers employed in road transport by the London Transport Board. The proportions of wage and salary earners are derived from the 1951 and subsequent censuses of population. Average wages are derived from the average wage earnings inquiries of the Ministry of Labour. Average salaries are taken to be the same as for the British Transport Commission up to 1962, and from 1963 the same as for the British Railways Board.

Shipping. Details are received from the Registrar General of Shipping of the numbers of seamen afloat; officers (salary earners) are distinguished from ratings (wage earners). Estimates are made of the number of seamen temporarily ashore and persons employed in shore establishments. For the latter, the proportions of wage and salary earners are estimated by reference to the 1951 and subsequent censuses of population.

There is little information on average wages and salaries except for basic rates, and the average earnings of seamen employed by the nationalised transport undertakings. For years before the latest, the total wage and salary bill is estimated from PAYE statistics, arbitrarily split between wages and salaries in such a way as to produce, in conjunction with the figures of numbers employed, reasonable figures of average earnings. For the latest year estimates are based on (a) changes in numbers employed, (b) changes in wage rates and (c) changes in average salary earnings based on the changes in the general level of salaries in other industries.

Dock labour. The annual report of the National Dock Labour Board provides statistics of the numbers and pay of all classes of dock workers, including those working on daily or half-daily engagements. These figures relate to wage earners only.

Rest of transport. Ministry of Labour numbers employed are used for the whole of land and air transport *less* the numbers in the activities already covered above *plus* an estimate of the number of persons employed in transport organisations classified to manufacturing (Orders III to XVI) in Ministry of Labour statistics but excluded from the census of production. The proportions of wage and salary earners are derived from the 1951 and subsequent censuses of population.

The average wage is assumed to be the same as for the part of transport covered by the wage earnings inquiries of the Ministry of Labour. The average salary is taken to be the same as for the British Transport Commission up to 1962, and from 1963 the same as for the British Railways Board.

XIX (part) Communication

Post Office. The Post Office and Treasury provide figures of numbers employed for both industrial and non-industrial staff. Numbers employed in the Post Office Savings Bank and in the factory departments, as shown in the Post Office *Estimates* up to 1961 and from then on in the Post Office accounts, are excluded since these are not classified to Order XIX. Industrial staff *plus* messengers, postmen and cleaners are treated as wage earners; all other staff are treated as salary earners, including counter hands and switchboard operators.

Up to 1960/61 the total wage and salary bill of the Post Office for financial years was obtained from the *Appropriation Accounts*; calendar year figures were obtained by interpolation. The Treasury, from returns submitted by the Post Office, provided figures of the total remuneration of non-industrial staff from which estimates of the pay of non-industrial staff in the Post Office Savings Bank and factory departments, and of messengers, postmen and cleaners were deducted to give the salary bill. The wage bill was taken as the difference between the salary bill and the total.

From the financial year 1961/62 the Post Office has provided figures of total wages and total salaries for those employees included in Order XIX.

Rest of communication. Ministry of Labour figures of numbers employed for postal services and telecommunications are used *less* the numbers in the Post Office. The proportions of wage and salary earners and the average wage and average salary are assumed to be the same as for the Post Office.

XX Distributive trades

Ministry of Labour numbers employed are used *plus* an allowance for persons employed in distributive and selling organisations and head offices classified to manufacturing in the Ministry of Labour statistics but excluded from the census of production. The proportions of wage and salary earners are estimated from the 1951 and subsequent censuses of population. Shop assistants are treated as wage earners.

Apart from recent Ministry of Labour inquiries into the average earnings of selling staff in retail distribution, the only information available on average wages and salaries relates to minimum and recognised wage rates. Year-to-year movements in earnings are roughly estimated by reference to changes in these rates and to changes in the level of earnings in other industries. Reference is also made to the changes shown by PAYE statistics of total wages and salaries in the distributive trades. A small addition is made to the wage bill to allow for the earnings of any part-time assistants, not included in the Ministry of Labour figures of numbers employed.

The censuses of distribution provide a partial check on the wage and salary bill for certain years. The census of distribution for 1950 covered both the wholesale and retail trades but the censuses for 1957, 1961 and 1966 covered retail trade only.

XXI Insurance, banking and finance

Ministry of Labour figures of numbers employed are used. The proportions of wage and salary earners are estimated from the 1951 and subsequent censuses of population.

For years before the latest, the total wage and salary bill is estimated from PAYE statistics, arbitrarily split between wages and salaries in such a way as to produce, in conjunction with the figures of numbers employed, reasonable figures of average earnings. For the latest year, estimates are based on (a) changes in numbers employed, (b) changes in wage rates and (c) changes in average salary earnings based on the changes in the general level of salaries in other industries.

XXIV Public administration and defence

National government service. The Treasury provides figures of numbers employed for both industrial and non-industrial staff of government departments. Industrial staff *plus* messengers, lift attendants, storemen, etc. who are included among non-industrial staff, are treated as wage earners; the remaining non-industrial staff are treated as salary earners. Average wage earnings are taken from the inquiries of the Ministry of Labour. The salary bill is based on figures provided by the Treasury of the pay of non-industrial civil servants, excluding those employed in the Post Office, the Forestry Commission and the Stationery Office, but including those in the other branches of government outside the definition of national government service. Estimates of the pay of these employees must therefore be deducted. A further deduction is made for the pay of messengers, etc. and an addition is made for salaries paid by the government of Northern Ireland.

Local government service. Ministry of Labour figures of numbers employed are used *less* an estimate of those engaged in building and civil engineering work (see Order XVII). The proportions of wage earners and salary earners are estimated from the 1951 and subsequent censuses of population. Average wage earnings are taken from the inquiries of the Ministry of Labour.

For years before the latest two, the wage and salary bill is based on financial year figures obtained by the Ministry of Housing and Local Government from local authorities in England and Wales of the remuneration of staff classified by type of service, which are published in *Local Government Financial Statistics.* Amounts paid to staff employed in education, health, transport, building, etc. are deducted to get an estimate of the remuneration of staff in local government service as defined in the *Standard Industrial Classification, 1958.* This is then increased to allow for local authorities in Scotland and Northern Ireland. The amount paid in wages is estimated by multiplying the number of wage earners by the average wage. This is deducted from the total wage and salary bill to arrive at an estimate of the salary bill. For the latest two years the total wage and salary bill is estimated from the results of a quarterly sample inquiry (see page 318).

XXII (part) Professional and scientific services

Public health services. The numbers of wage and salary earners in the national health service and the amount of their pay are estimated from information given in the accounts published under the National Health Service Acts, supplemented by information from the Ministry of Health and the Scottish Home and Health Department.

Numbers employed in the local authority health services are estimated from information in the annual reports of the Ministry of Health. Home helps employed in the local authority health services are included.

Estimates of the wage and salary bill are made from information supplied by the Ministry of Housing and Local Government on remuneration of staff employed by local authorities in England and Wales, classified by type of service (see Order XXIV, Local government service, above). The split into wages and salaries is estimated from information given in the annual reports of the Ministry of Health.

Local authority educational services. Estimates of the number of teachers employed by local authorities and their salaries are provided by the Department of Education and Science and the Scottish Education Department. An addition is made for other salaried employees, including staff employed in the administration of local educational services, clerical staff, staff employed in school canteens and school health service staff. An addition is also made for Northern Ireland, which includes the salaries of teachers paid direct by the Ministry of Education for Northern Ireland. Except for these, teachers and other staff employed in direct grant schools and other non-maintained schools and establishments are excluded. The number of wage earners (cleaners, caretakers, canteen workers, etc.) is estimated from the Ministry of Labour figures of numbers employed by local authorities in education departments. The total wage and salary bill is estimated from the information provided by the Ministry of Housing and Local Government and information published in *Local Government Financial Statistics* (see Order XXIV, Local government service, above). Total salaries are deducted and the wage bill is taken as the residual.

XXII (part) Professional and scientific services and XXIII Miscellaneous services

Other services. Numbers employed are obtained as a residue by deducting the total numbers employed in the industries already covered from the total numbers employed in the United Kingdom derived from the figures of the Ministry of Labour and Ministry of Health and Social Services, Northern Ireland. An addition is made for uninsured part-time workers. The proportions of wage earners and salary earners are roughly estimated from the 1951 and subsequent censuses of population. The wage and salary bill is derived as a residue, being the difference between the estimate of the total wage and salary bill based mainly on Inland Revenue statistics, and the sum of the estimated wage and salary bills for the industries already covered. Any discrepancy between income from employment derived from tax data and from other sources therefore falls into this group and the estimate is subject to a wide margin of error. The wage and salary bill is divided between wages and salaries using the estimated numbers of wage earners and salary earners and average wages and average salaries in other industries.

Separate estimates for the following two items within this group are given in the analysis of income by sector of employment (Table 13 of the 1967 Blue Book).

(i) *Private domestic servants.* The census of population provides the numbers employed for those years in which a census was taken. For other years the numbers are estimated from changes in Ministry of Labour employment figures. The figure for 1961 derived from the census is about a quarter higher than the Ministry of Labour figure. All employees are taken to be wage earners.

Little is known of the average wage earnings of domestic servants. As mentioned on page 123, a large number of those employed have no PAYE deduction cards and consequently tax assessment data cannot be used to estimate the wage bill. Following sample inquiries by the Social Survey covering, among other things, personal expenditure on domestic servants, average earnings in 1957, including income in kind, were estimated to be about £230 per annum. Later figures are based on changes in the section of the index of retail prices for domestic help, and board and lodging allowances in other occupations. The estimates appear to be reasonably consistent with grossed up estimates obtained from the Family Expenditure Survey of personal expenditure on domestic services generally (including window cleaning, etc.), but both series are subject to a wide margin of error.

It is assumed that one-tenth of all domestic servants are employed by businesses and nine-tenths by persons. The figures for the personal sector in the analysis of income by sector and the amounts included in consumers' expenditure relate to nine-tenths of the total.

(ii) *Services to private non-profit-making bodies serving persons.* A rough estimate of the wage and salary bill paid by these bodies is derived from (a) PAYE statistics, which are classified not only by industry but also by type of employer, (b) the reports of the Registrar of Friendly Societies, from which estimates are made of salaries paid by trade unions and friendly societies, (c) the reports of the University Grants Committee giving wages and salaries paid in universities and (d) information provided by the Department of Education and Science on the pay of teachers in direct grant schools.

RELIABILITY

In the table opposite an attempt is made to classify the estimates of the wage and salary bill in each industry according to their reliability, as described on pages 39 to 41.

Reliability of annual estimates of income from employment[1]

A ± less than 3 per cent
B ± 3 per cent to 10 per cent
C ± more than 10 per cent

SIC Order	Industry	Wages		Salaries		Wages and salaries		Wages and salaries, 1966 £ million	
		Years before latest	Latest year	Years before latest	Latest year	Years before latest	Latest year	Wages	Salaries
I	Agriculture	B	B	B	B	B	B	263	35
	Forestry and fishing	C	C	C	C	B	C	32	5
II	Coal mining ...	A	A	A	A	A	A	427	53
	Other mining and quarrying[2]	B	B	B	B	B	B	42	10
III to XVI	Manufacturing[2]	B	B	B	B	B	B	4,922	2,368
XVII	Construction[2] ...	B	B	B	B	B	B	1,311	365
XVIII	Gas, electricity and water[2] ...	A	B	A	B	A	B	263	178
XIX	Transport	B	B	C	C	B	B	973	359
	Communication...	A	B	A	B	A	B	278	159
XX	Distributive trades	C	C	C	C	B	C	1,031	1,067
XXI	Insurance, banking and finance.....	C	C	B	B	B	B	49	664
XXIV	National government service ...	B	B	A	B	A	B	125	478
	Local government service	C	C	C	C	B	C	318	261
XXII (part)	Public health services	B	B	A	B	A	B	191	403
	Local authority educational services	C	C	B	B	A	B	137	675
XXII (part) and XXIII	Other services...	C	C	C	C	C	C	1,573	1,105
	Total wages and salaries	A	A	A	A	A	A	11,935	8,185
Pay in cash and kind of H.M. Forces..................						A	A	513	
Employers' contributions: National insurance........						A	A	902	
Other....................						B	B	902	
Total income from employment						A	A	22,437	

(1)For the significance of the reliability gradings see pages 39 to 41.
(2) In years for which results of a detailed census of production are available, grading is A throughout; other years as shown.

The estimates of the aggregate wage and salary bill and of total income from employment are considered to be good. The chief source of error in these aggregates arises from the adjustments explained on pages 123 to 126, which are made to the basic PAYE data. The reliability of each of these adjustments is poor. The estimate of the aggregate for the latest year is less reliable than those for earlier years partly because full information from PAYE data is not available, but the same grading is given. The percentage error in the estimate for the latest year, as revealed by the later PAYE statistics, has in recent years been less than 1 per cent.

Two general points should be noted. One element of uncertainty arises from the attempt to separate wages and salaries. For several non-manufacturing industries little is known about the relative amounts received by wage earners and salary earners; the estimates of the combined wage and salary bill for these industries are more reliable than the separate estimates of the wage bill and the salary bill. A second general element of uncertainty arises from the marginal adjustments, which are made to the basic data for each industry, to allow for directors' fees, income in kind and expenses of employment (see pages 125-6 and 132-3). The reliability of the total estimates of these adjustments is poor and their allocation to the various industries is very rough.

4. STATISTICAL SOURCES: INCOME FROM SELF-EMPLOYMENT

This class of incomes, which incorporates elements of both labour income and profit income, may be described either as income from self-employment to distinguish it from the income of employees, or as income of unincorporated enterprises to distinguish it from the income of companies and public corporations. Its place in the accounts of the personal sector is described on page 102. Income from self-employment is divided into three groups: income of farmers, professional earnings, and income of other sole traders and partnerships. Income from farming is estimated from data collected by the agricultural departments and the other two forms of income are estimated from Inland Revenue data.

Income of farmers

Income of farmers consists of the income from agriculture, horticulture and direct retailing of occupiers of holdings of one acre or more. Before 1954, holdings in Northern Ireland of one quarter of an acre to one acre were also included. Most farmers are sole traders or in partnerships, but because of the method of estimation, the profits of the companies engaged in farming are included in income of farmers, and excluded from the profits of companies in the accounts of the company sector. Income earned by farmers with smaller holdings is included with the income of other sole traders and partnerships. These definitions are adopted so as to secure consistency in coverage with the data on farm incomes published by the agricultural departments.

Income from farming represents the reward of the manual and managerial labour of farmers and their wives and the return on their capital. Income from the ownership of land and buildings, including the income imputed to farmers owning the farms on which they work, is, however, excluded from income from farming and treated as part of rent income. This treatment therefore differs from that of imputed rent of trading property which is included in trading profits and not under rent.

The figures are based on estimates by the Ministry of Agriculture, Fisheries and Food, the Department of Agriculture and Fisheries for Scotland, and the Ministry of Agriculture for Northern Ireland. The departments estimate the value of income from farming for accounting years ending in May. Estimates for the last complete farm year, together with forecasts for the current farm year, are published in the White Paper[14] issued each spring in connection with the determination of farm prices under the Agriculture Acts of 1947 and 1957.

The estimate of income from farming is built up from very detailed estimates of output and expenditure. The industry is treated as one large national farm; this affects the treatment in the accounts of the numerous transactions occurring between farm and farm, either directly or by way of merchants and processors. Where home grown agricultural produce appears on the expenditure side of the account, as do purchases of home grown feed cereals under feedingstuffs, that produce also appears on the revenue side; but where the expenditure side is on a net basis, for example by excluding unfinished livestock reared in the United Kingdom, the revenue side excludes them also. Either method avoids double-counting of profits from the same produce at different stages of growth or marketing. All farms are treated as though they were tenanted and transactions of farmers in their capacity as landlords are excluded. The items of cost which are deducted from gross receipts are labour costs, rent and rental value of land and buildings (as though all farms were tenanted), interest, purchases of goods and services from other industries or from abroad and provision for depreciation of equipment. The calculation for 1965/66 is shown in the table below.

Calculation of income from farming 1965/66

£ million

Revenue		Expenditure	
Milk and milk products	412½	Labour	312½
Fatstock:		Rent and interest	146
Cattle	272	Machinery:	
Sheep	85	Depreciation	90½
Pigs	211½	Repairs	73½
Eggs	179½	Fuel and oil.................	50
Poultry and other livestock	87½	Other.......................	24
Grain	222	Feedingstuffs	476½
Other farm crops	137	Fertilisers	120
Horticultural products	181½	Other.......................	214
Other credits	40		
		Total	1,507
Total	1,828½		
Farming grants, subsidies and sundry receipts	99	Net income from farming	468½
Increase in the value of farm stocks and work in hand	48		
Total	1,975½	Total	1,975½

Source: Cmnd. 3229, Appendix II, Table B

[14] For example, *Annual Review and Determination of Guarantees 1967*, Cmnd. 3229, issued in March 1967, gives detailed estimates for 1965/66 and forecasts for 1966/67.

The agricultural subsidies appear in the table in two ways. Those paid in implementation of price guarantees, that is the 'deficiency payments', appear under commodity receipts; the direct subsidies, such as those on fertilisers, lime and ploughing up grassland, come under farming grants and subsidies. Revenue includes the value, at average realisation prices of produce sold, of produce not sold but consumed on the farm; in the mid-1960's the value of this produce is estimated to have been about £30 million and the net income arising from it about £8 million. The expenditure items are gross in the sense that they include some capital expenditure, for example farm labour used in improving the farm, but this capital expenditure is balanced by an item on the revenue side under 'Other credits'. The interest item relates to farmers' borrowing from banks, merchants and hire purchase finance houses in their capacity as tenant farmers. The increase in the value of farm stocks and work in hand consists of the difference between the beginning and end of the year in the book values of livestock and growing crops, together with tillages, harvested crops, feedingstuffs on hand, etc. No estimate is made of any change in the value of manurial residues in the soil.

For the national accounts, the estimates of income from farming made by the agricultural departments have to be increased in two respects. Interest paid on borrowed working capital is not treated as an expense and no provision is made in expenses for depreciation. The adjusted farm year figures are then converted to calendar years. The figure for 1965, for example, is taken to be equal to 5/12 of the income earned in the farm year 1964/65 *plus* 7/12 of the income earned in the farm year 1965/66. This simple conversion may lead to error in estimating the income for a particular calendar year.

Quarterly estimates of income from farming are included in published estimates for 'Other personal income'. The quarterly figures are a smooth interpolation of the calendar year totals. For the latest quarters a projection is made from the latest crop year figure, adjusted to normal weather conditions.

Income of professional persons

Professional earnings include all the earnings of individuals and partnerships assessable to income tax under Schedule D from the carrying on of professions where the profits made depend wholly or mainly on personal qualifications. They exclude the profits of business consisting wholly or mainly in the making of contracts on behalf of others or in the giving of commercial advice relating to contracts, which are included in 'Income of other sole traders and partnerships'. Thus, this item covers the earnings of doctors, dentists, lawyers, artists, journalists and architects working on their own account, including earnings of general practitioners and dentists practising under the national health service, but excludes the profits of brokers and estate agents. It also excludes the salaries of members of the professions chargeable to tax under Schedule E and thus excludes the salaries of all doctors who are whole-time hospital employees, of nearly all teachers, and the pay of H.M. Forces.

The main source of information for professional earnings is the statistics of assessments to tax collected by the Inland Revenue; these relate to the total amount of profits assessable to income tax under Schedule D. Before 1952 an addition was made for profits tax and excess profits tax which were deducted for tax purposes in arriving at the Schedule D profits. The profits are before deduction of depreciation, as required for the national accounts. The statistics have much the same general characteristics as those of company profits derived from the same source and described on pages 217 to 219, to which reference should be made for a more detailed description of the methods of using these tax assessments. The terms used in Inland Revenue data are explained in Appendix III.

For the years up to and including the last year but two shown in the Blue Book, the figures are based on the assessments to income tax under Schedule D, Cases I and II, made in the income tax year following the year of profit. Up to 1966 all assessments were recorded; thereafter a five per cent sample of all assessments of profits under £10,000 is taken each year, together with all assessments of £10,000 or more. There are several reasons why the assessments do not cover the earnings of the calendar year precisely. First, about ten per cent of the income tax assessments for all unincorporated businesses made in the year relate to earlier years. Secondly, although Schedule D assessments are, broadly speaking, based on the profits of the previous year, this is not always true; for instance, when a business starts or finishes, some of the assessments are based on the current year's profits. Probably some five to eight per cent of the assessments for unincorporated businesses are on the basis of the current year, but since delay in securing information often retards such assessments, this includes some duplication with the late assessments and this error may offset the first. Thirdly, assessments based on the previous year are based on the profits of the accounting period ending at any time in the previous income tax year; in practice, this gives an average year for profits centred on, and mostly falling within, the calendar year, because about four-fifths of the accounting years of unincorporated businesses end either in the fourth or first quarter of the calendar year. In the case of companies, the quarterly sample returns provide information on which to adjust the accounting year figures to a calendar year basis, but this information is not available for unincorporated enterprises and no adjustment is made.

For the last two years shown, the Inland Revenue estimates are based on incomplete data. The data comprise three series of reports. The first report gives a preliminary estimate of the profits of the current year for traders whose profits normally exceed £10,000. The second report is submitted when accounts are received and the third when the trader's tax liability has been agreed; the second and third reports cover all traders whose profits are £10,000 or more and a one per cent sample of the remainder. Similar reports for companies, and the ways in which they are used, are described in detail in Chapter VII.

Because of the very large number of cases for which data are not available in advance of actual assessment, the estimates for the last two years are subject to substantial later amendment. For the last year but one the coverage of the data in respect of professional earnings is fairly good—about half of total earnings—but for the latest year it is very limited—less than ten per cent—and the estimate for that year must therefore be regarded as highly provisional.

For the national accounts estimates a number of adjustments have to be made to the Inland Revenue figures.

(a) *Under-assessment of income.* That some understatement of income occurs in tax returns is borne out by the figures published by the Inland Revenue of taxes and penalties charged in cases that have come to light. There must obviously be other cases so far undetected and the figures published in the national accounts include an arbitrary addition on this account.

(b) *Contributions to superannuation schemes.* An addition is made for the government contribution to the national health service superannuation scheme for general practitioners and dentists.

(c) *Owner-occupied property.* Trading profits are taken to include the income from owner-occupied property. When this income was taxed under Schedule A, the net Schedule A value was deducted in arriving at trading profits under Schedule D and had to be added back. This adjustment is not required for the years after 1961.

(d) *Interest.* Interest paid on bank advances and certain other interest payments are allowed by the Inland Revenue as an expense in arriving at the assessment of profits. In the national income accounts such interest is regarded as a share of profits, not as a payment to a factor of production. An estimate of the amount paid—consisting of interest on bank advances, on trade bills and acceptances, and on hire purchase debt—has therefore to be added back to the Inland Revenue estimate of profits.

(e) *Capital gains.* After 1963 certain short-term capital gains were assessed to income tax under Case VII and from 1965/66 it was possible for certain long-term capital gains, normally assessed to capital gains tax, to be included in income tax assessments. These amounts are excluded.

Quarterly estimates of income of professional persons are included in published estimates for 'Other personal income'. The quarterly figures are generally a smooth interpolation of the annual figures, but when additional information is available it is taken into account. For example, changes in the income of general practitioners and dentists under the national health service can be identified from the central government accounts and are incorporated in the estimate for the appropriate quarter.

Income of other sole traders and partnerships

The income of other sole traders and partnerships includes all income of unincorporated enterprises assessed under Schedule D except income classified under farming or professional earnings. This group includes agents, for example agents working on commission, unless there is a contract of service with a single employer. Where there is such a contract, for example in the case of most salesmen working on commission, the whole income is normally assessed under Schedule E and is treated as income from employment.

The main source of information on earnings of other sole traders and partnerships is the statistics of assessments to tax collected by the Inland Revenue, and the estimates are made in the same way as those described above for the income of professional persons. The estimates for the last two years, which are based on incomplete data, are less reliable than those for professional earnings since the data for the last year but one cover only about 20 to 25 per cent of total profits and for the latest year less than five per cent.

As in the case of professional earnings, a number of adjustments have to be made to the Inland Revenue figures.

(a) *Under-assessment of income.*

(b) *Owner-occupied property.*

(c) *Interest.*

(d) *Capital gains.*

These four adjustments are discussed above. Two further adjustments are also made.

(e) *Smallholders.* An estimate is added for the incomes of smallholders which are excluded from the agricultural returns on which the estimate of income from farming is based. This covers income from agricultural holdings of less than one acre. The estimate is very rough. In the mid-1960's it amounted to about £30 million a year.

(f) *Jobbers.* The income of jobbers on the stock exchange and of some other dealers in financial assets is derived from the difference between the buying and selling prices of securities. In so far as these margins are not included in the estimates of expenditure on making financial transactions, the gain of the financial dealer should be regarded as a capital gain and not as part of his trading income, for the estimates of income and expenditure to be consistent. An estimated deduction is made from the income assessed to tax under Schedule D for the exclusion of these gains. An alternative treatment would be to regard these gains as a charge for a financial service. This would involve adjustments to the figures of financial transactions, to company profits and to consumers' expenditure, which would be difficult to make accurately and therefore this treatment has not been adopted in the accounts.

The quarterly estimates of income of other sole traders and partnerships are included in published estimates for 'Other personal income'. The annual industrial analysis made by the Inland Revenue provides separate estimates for manufacturing, construction, transport and communication and the distributive trades. For these categories quarterly income is assumed to vary respectively with movements in the index of manufacturing production, the value of building work done, the index of output at constant prices for transport and communication, and the index of sales by independent retailers. For other categories quarterly income is taken as a smooth interpolation of the annual figures.

Reliability

The estimate of income from farming is built up from very detailed figures and, for all but the latest year, the estimate should be fairly reliable. However, alternative estimates derived from a sample of farm accounts sometimes differ considerably in level and there is uncertainty about the calendar year as opposed to the farm year estimates. The annual estimates should therefore be regarded as in category B of the gradings described on pages 39 to 41.

The reliability of the estimates of the general level of incomes of professional persons and other sole traders and partnerships is not high, for the reasons given above. It is thought that the margin of error lies within the range of category B. The estimates of year-to-year changes are somewhat more reliable, except for the last two years shown.

5. STATISTICAL SOURCES: CONSUMERS' EXPENDITURE

SUMMARY OF SOURCES FOR ESTIMATING CONSUMERS' EXPENDITURE

A general description of what is covered by consumers' expenditure is given on page 105. The quarterly and annual estimates of consumers' expenditure at current and at constant prices are built up commodity by commodity from a variety of independent sources. The source which is chosen for a particular commodity or service is the one which in the light of available information is judged to provide the most reliable estimate of the level and changes in expenditure on that commodity or service.

Three general sources are available for estimating consumers' expenditure:

(a) statistics of supplies;

(b) sample surveys of consumers' expenditure;

(c) statistics of sales by retail shops and other outlets.

These are discussed in general terms below.

(a) Statistics of supplies

Statistics of supplies may relate either to total output *plus* imports *less* exports, or to deliveries from one stage of production or distribution to the next, for example deliveries to wholesalers. Supply statistics usually relate to well defined commodity groups, which is an advantage in building up commodity estimates of expenditure, but several adjustments may have to be made to them before they provide estimates of expenditure by consumers. Allowance should be made for any changes in distributors' stocks and for losses or wastage in distribution. If possible, supplies of a product which are used for further manufacture must be distinguished from supplies of the same product which are bought direct by consumers. On the other hand, care must be taken that newly developed products are not missed from the estimates through lack of statistical information. Short period supply statistics are mostly recorded by quantity and although information may be available on average retail values, these values may not relate to the quantity measures in which the supplies are recorded. Factors then need to be devised for converting one measure of quantity into the other. Where supply statistics are in value terms an allowance—sometimes rather uncertain—has to be made for the appropriate mark-up necessary to convert factory, wholesale or import values to the amount paid by the consumer. Finally, deductions may have to be made for business purchases at the retail stage.

The main use of supply statistics is in estimating consumers' expenditure on food (in conjunction with data from the National Food Survey) and on alcoholic drink. Detailed information relating to supplies of many foodstuffs is compiled by the Ministry of Agriculture, Fisheries and Food, based on import and export statistics, on the statistics of agricultural output collected by the agricultural departments and on returns from manufacturers and processors. These statistics are mostly expressed in quantities which are valued mainly by average values taken from the National Food Survey. These average values reflect the prices actually paid by consumers. The estimates of consumers' expenditure on alcoholic drink are based on statistics of the quantities on which duty is paid, multiplied by estimated average retail values.

(b) Sample surveys of consumers' expenditure

An alternative approach is that of direct and continuous inquiry among a sample of consumers. This method has four distinct advantages: firstly, it is comprehensive in its coverage of the goods and services bought by the households or persons surveyed; secondly, it excludes business expenditure; thirdly, it measures the flow of consumers' goods and services at the time of purchase and at the prices paid by the consumers; fourthly, it can provide, subject to sampling fluctuations, a detailed and flexible commodity analysis of expenditure.

It may also permit an analysis by different categories of consumers, for example, in different income groups.

But there are problems and limitations in using sample survey data for estimating consumers' expenditure. Firstly, records of spending kept by households in such surveys tend to show a significantly higher rate of spending in the first few days than in subsequent days and the problem arises as to where the true level of expenditure lies. Secondly, the fact that some of the people who are approached in a survey do not for one reason or another co-operate fully is likely to introduce some bias into the results, the nature and extent of which is difficult to assess. Thirdly, since the most convenient place to approach people for detailed information about their spending is in their homes, surveys of consumers' expenditure generally relate to households and do not cover residents of hotels and other institutions. In estimating consumers' expenditure from surveys an addition must therefore be made for the spending of the non-household population; this spending, however, is generally small in relation to the expenditure of households. Fourthly, there are difficulties in obtaining from a continuous household survey reliable information on expenditure while away on holiday. A fifth problem arises from the fact that people do not fully record their expenditure on certain items, notably alcoholic drink and tobacco.

A further important limitation in using moderate-sized sample surveys for estimating consumers' expenditure is that sampling fluctuations may obscure the changes in expenditure, particularly from quarter to quarter. These fluctuations tend to be greater for the more expensive items, which people do not buy often. While quarterly changes in expenditure on, for example, most foods may be satisfactorily estimated from a moderate-sized survey, bigger surveys may be needed for estimating quarterly changes in expenditure on items such as cars, central heating or the more expensive articles of clothing.

Three continuous surveys are available for estimating consumers' expenditure, or parts of consumers' expenditure: the National Food Survey of the Ministry of Agriculture, Fisheries and Food; the Family Expenditure Survey of the Ministry of Labour; and the International Passenger Survey of the Board of Trade. The field work for the Family Expenditure Survey and the International Passenger Survey is carried out by the Government Social Survey.

The National Food Survey[15] was started in 1940 to provide an independent check on food consumption and expenditure during the war and was used mainly to get information about standards of nutrition in the lower income groups. Urban working-class households were the principal groups studied until 1950, when the survey was extended to cover the whole population and analyses of expenditure by social class and by family composition were added. The survey covers household expenditure on food and does not include meals and snacks bought away from home, purchases of sweets and chocolates, ice cream or most soft drinks. Each household participating in the survey records for one week the quantity and the value of food bought. In 1966 about 14,000 households were approached of which about 7,500 responded fully. The survey is used extensively, together with statistics of supplies, in estimating consumers' expenditure on food. A major use is for data on average prices paid by consumers.

---

[15] *Household Food Consumption and Expenditure*: annual reports of the National Food Survey Committee.

The Family Expenditure Survey[16] was started in 1957 to meet a variety of needs. Information about the pattern of expenditure is required by the Ministry of Labour to provide weights for the index of retail prices. As well as using the survey for the estimates of consumers' expenditure, the Central Statistical Office use the information from the survey to study the redistributive effects on income of taxation and social benefits. The survey, which like the National Food Survey is taken continuously throughout the year, is not confined to expenditure on food but covers expenditure on all goods and services by all members of the household, whether the goods and services are consumed inside or outside the home. Members of each household participating in the survey record for two weeks the value of their expenditure and give particulars of their income. From 1957 to 1966 about 5,000 households were approached in the course of a year, of which about 3,500 co-operated fully; the number approached was increased to about 10,000 in 1967. Because of the comparatively small size of the sample before 1967, sampling errors for many items were rather high and only limited use could be made of the survey for estimating consumers' expenditure. Generally, the survey was used only for annual estimates.

The International Passenger Survey[17] was started in 1961 as a continuous sample survey of passengers travelling on the short sea and air routes between the United Kingdom and the continent of Europe, and on the long air routes beyond Europe. In 1964 the survey was extended to cover passengers on the long sea routes beyond Europe. Information is given by passengers—both residents of this country and of other countries—on their nationality, country of residence, purpose of visit, length of stay, and expenditure in the country visited. The main purposes of the survey are to provide information on migration and on the balance of payments by enabling estimates to be made of expenditure by United Kingdom residents while travelling abroad and the expenditure of foreign tourists, etc. in this country.

(c) Statistics of sales by retail shops and other outlets

A third approach is to collect statistics of sales by retailers and other outlets selling goods and services direct to consumers. The method is usually to collect statistics monthly or quarterly from a sample of outlets and use these to project forwards the statistics obtained from a more detailed inquiry or census. The Board of Trade publishes monthly statistics on the sales of retailers, caterers, motor traders, laundries and dry cleaners, and hairdressers. Full censuses of distribution and other services were taken for 1950 and 1961 and sample censuses for 1957 and 1966. Detailed inquiries were made into the catering trades in 1960 and 1964 and into the motor trades in 1962 and 1967. (See Appendix II.) The effective sample may not be a strictly random one since response may vary between different kinds and sizes of business, but the sample can be stratified by kind and size of business and the results combined according to the census figures for the individual kinds and sizes of business.

---

[16] *Family Expenditure Survey: Report for 1957–59; Family Expenditure Survey: Report for 1960 and 1961*, and annual reports thereafter. The results of a similar inquiry were published in *Report of an Enquiry into Household Expenditure in 1953–54*. Earlier surveys were made on specific items of expenditure and a survey of total expenditure of working class households was made in selected weeks of 1937–38.

[17] Results are published in the *Board of Trade Journal;* the methods are described in the issue for 23 March 1963.

This approach shares with continuous sample surveys the advantage of measuring the flow of goods and services at the time of purchase and at prices actually paid by purchasers. Within the field covered by outlet statistics all commodities are covered and there is no duplication. Outlet statistics usually include some sales to businesses but since businesses buy more from wholesalers than from outlets directly serving consumers, this is not generally as troublesome a problem as it may be with statistics of supplies.

The sampling unit in outlet statistics is a retail organisation selling to hundreds of customers instead of, as in consumer surveys, an individual household or purchaser. Consequently a sample of outlets can cover a far higher proportion of the population's spending at the types of outlet to which the sample relates than can be covered by a consumer survey of practicable size. Provided that full coverage of big outlets is secured each quarter and that the smaller outlets in the sample make returns reasonably consistently quarter by quarter, then outlet statistics can be expected to measure short-term trends of expenditure more reliably than consumer surveys or (if several uncertain adjustments are made to them) statistics of supplies. In the longer term, considerable attention must be paid to the problem of keeping the sample representative of all outlets in the field covered; in particular, of keeping a representative balance between established and newly opened shops. A census, with its detailed enumeration of outlets, provides a periodic check on the sampling frame but it is a costly operation to carry out frequently.

The available outlet statistics do not cover the whole range of consumer goods and services, and some types of outlet are not covered, such as manufacturers, farms and wholesalers having direct sales to consumers, boarding houses, social clubs selling alcoholic drinks to their members, street traders and newsvendors.

A difficulty of using outlet statistics as a source for estimates of consumers' expenditure is that retailers and other outlets cannot be expected to provide a commodity analysis of their sales every month or quarter; a considerable task is undertaken by the retailer in providing information for broad commodity groups in periodic censuses. The method of estimating commodity figures from outlet sources is therefore to project forwards the commodity figures from the last census, after these have been adjusted to exclude business purchases and to accord with the classification of consumers' expenditure. The indicators for projecting these commodity figures are constructed from the monthly or quarterly figures of sales by various kinds of retail business (including mail order businesses). In so far as retailers or other outlets specialise in particular goods or services they can be classified to their main kind of business—furniture shops, clothing shops, hairdressers, etc.—and their total sales provide indicators of the trend of sales of particular commodity groups or services. Even where retailers do not specialise, they may be able to provide separate sales figures for departments of their business and these can be combined, by using appropriate weights derived from the census, with the sales indicators of the specialist shops to provide a single index for the value of sales of each commodity group or service. Indices of this kind are used to estimate consumers' expenditure on clothing and footwear, household durable goods, household textiles, soft furnishings, hardware, chemists' goods, some recreational goods and miscellaneous goods. In addition, indices of catering turnover are used to estimate expenditure on meals and accommodation outside the home.

Indices of this kind are only approximate measures of the trend of sales of a particular commodity group or service. The tendency for retail trade to become less specialised, for example for furniture shops to sell domestic appliances, for clothing shops to sell soft furnishings and in general for shops to sell a wider variety of goods without necessarily keeping departmental records, makes the indicators less reliable as a source for commodity estimates between censuses. Thus indices of sales by various kinds of retail business do not provide a fully satisfactory means for projecting forwards the commodity figures of a census, though they do provide appropriate indicators for projecting forwards the kind of business figures.

A combined index of the total turnover of retailers and other traders is less subject to these disadvantages. Because of its wide coverage a combined index of the turnover of retailers, caterers, and other service traders, derived from census and monthly statistics collected by the Board of Trade, provides a good indication of the quarterly changes in total expenditure in the field they cover. However, the analysis by outlet that is inherent in building up to this total is less useful than the analysis by commodity group. It may become possible to combine the overall outlet statistics with an analysis by commodity based on other statistics but there is at present a gap between the level of the estimates derived from these outlet statistics and the higher level built up commodity by commodity from the various sources, including to some extent retail sales, which is used for the national accounts. This gap cannot be entirely eliminated by adjustments to bring the 'outlet' total and the 'commodity' total to a common definition.

Basic sources used for the estimates of consumers' expenditure, 1966

Basic sources	Percentage of total consumers' expenditure, 1966	
	Annual estimates	Quarterly estimates
Statistics of supplies:		
Production, imports and exports (including food valued by means of the National Food Survey)	10	10
Quantities on which duty paid	6	6
Sample surveys of consumers' expenditure:		
National Food Survey (supported by statistics of supplies)	12	12
Family Expenditure Survey	13	—
International Passenger Survey.....................	1	1
Statistics of sales by retail shops and other outlets:		
Retail sales	18	18
Caterers' turnover	5	5
Sales by other outlets	11	11
Trade sources	9	9
Miscellaneous sources:		
Direct estimates.................................	14	5
Indicators of quarterly changes in annual estimates	—	10
No firm basis:		
Quarterly figures interpolation of annual figures	—	12
Annual and quarterly figures	1	1
Total	100	100

In addition to the outlet statistics discussed above, other statistics are returned by organisations directly serving consumers. They are used to estimate consumers' expenditure on coal, coke, electricity, gas, rail and road travel and admissions to cinemas.

Summary of sources

The sources used for 1966 are summarised in the annex to this chapter. The annex is further summarised in the table on the preceding page, which shows the relative importance in the estimates for 1966 of the basic sources discussed above. Where information is available quarterly the annual estimates are a simple addition of the quarterly estimates.

REVALUATION OF CONSUMERS' EXPENDITURE AT CONSTANT PRICES

Ideally, in revaluing consumers' expenditure at constant prices, purchases of every grade and size of every commodity and of every type of service which has a separate price should be revalued at their price in the base year, after allowing for changes in quality since the base year. In practice, information does not exist for revaluing consumers' expenditure in such detail but it is nevertheless revalued in very considerable detail, many hundreds of estimates being revalued separately. Adjustments for changes in quality are limited because of the difficulties of taking objective account of these changes. Since, with technological advance, the quality of products tends to improve, the estimates of consumers' expenditure at constant prices probably tend to understate the true growth in standards of consumption.

The same base year is retained in the national accounts for a number of years, the base year being determined by the year of the last detailed census of production. The estimates in the 1967 Blue Book are based on 1958; the base year will be changed to 1963 when the detailed results of the 1963 census of production become available.

The methods used for estimating expenditure at constant prices depend on the methods used for the current price estimates. Where the estimate at current prices is one of quantity multiplied by current average value, the estimate at constant prices is the same quantity multiplied by the average value in the base year. Where the current price estimate is in value terms only, it is deflated by an appropriate price index. The indices most widely used for this purpose are components of the index of retail prices[18]. The index does not, however, cover the whole range of consumers' expenditure, and other indices have to be used or estimated where necessary. If no other appropriate price index is available the general consumer price index implied by the estimates of consumers' expenditure at current and constant prices on all other goods and services is used. Where the current price estimate is a benchmark estimate projected forwards by separate indices of volume and of price, the constant price estimate is obtained by projecting the estimate for the base year by the index of volume only. All these revaluations are carried out in as great detail as possible.

---

[18]See *Method of Construction and Calculation of the Index of Retail Prices,* Studies in Official Statistics, No. 6, 4th edition 1967.

The relative importance of these three methods for estimating consumers' expenditure at constant prices in 1966 is shown in the table below. A description of the method used for each specific item is given in the detailed description below (pages 155 to 186).

Methods used for revaluing at constant prices consumers' expenditure, 1966

Method of revaluation	Percentage of total consumers' expenditure at current prices, 1966
Quantities multiplied by average values in base year......................	42
Base year estimates projected forwards by an index of volume............	14
Current price estimates deflated by:	
Index of retail prices..	24
Other price indices	16
No firm basis (including deflation by the general consumer price index)....	4
Total consumers' expenditure..	100

THE CLASSIFICATION OF CONSUMERS' EXPENDITURE

There are several ways of classifying the items of consumers' expenditure by groups and it is clear that there is no one classification which would meet the needs of all users of these figures. The classification adopted in United Kingdom statistics is mainly by object, distinguishing for example food, housing, clothing, travel, insurance. A broad distinction is preserved between major durables and other goods, and between goods in general and services. But the distinction is not complete; for example the category of durable goods excludes hardware and some costly goods such as jewellery and watches, expenditure on which may be influenced by considerations similar to those affecting goods classified as durable. The durable goods category is intended to cover those goods which constitute a volatile element in consumers' expenditure and goods which are relatively costly and which are generally available on credit terms. The United Kingdom classification differs somewhat from those used internationally: estimates are prepared for the United Nations and the Organisation for Economic Co-operation and Development on the basis of the classifications which they use.

A classification by producing industries, as defined in the Standard Industrial Classification, is required for input-output analysis and is estimated in particular years for this purpose. But there are considerable difficulties in analysing consumers' expenditure in this way, for example in distinguishing between expenditure on metal and on plastic goods.

A problem of classification arises when a composite product or service is bought by the consumer. The principal case is expenditure in hotels, restaurants, canteens etc., where the consumer is buying not only food and drink but also the services of the staff and the other facilities provided by the establishment. Separate figures are given of household expenditure on food; food purchased from catering establishments is included in the item 'Catering (meals and accommodation)'. Estimates of total personal expenditure on food, including the purchases of food by caterers for consumption on or off the premises, are however given in the notes at the end of the Blue Book. However, all personal expenditure on alcoholic drink is included in the category 'Alcoholic drink' because purchases from catering establishments for consumption off the premises are much more important than in the case of food, and expenditure cannot be satisfactorily divided.

The expenditure categories relate to purchases of new goods only, except in the case of motor vehicles. Except for vehicles, it is assumed that second-hand goods are purchased mainly from other consumers and the net effect of these purchases on total consumers' expenditure is equivalent to the dealers' margins on the sale of second-hand goods. The estimate of purchases *less* sales is included in the category 'Other services'.

In general, expenditure imputed as a counterpart to income in kind is allocated to the appropriate expenditure category according to the type of good or service received. Exceptions are the estimated values of food and clothing issued to the Forces and auxiliary services and of food supplied to merchant seamen and fishermen; these values are included in the separate category 'Income in kind not included elsewhere'.

The sources used for estimates of expenditure generally include, without any possibility of separation, purchases in the United Kingdom by non-residents. A deduction is made for the total of these purchases so that the total of expenditure relates only to United Kingdom residents. Correspondingly, an estimate is made of personal expenditure in foreign countries by United Kingdom residents and included in total consumers' expenditure. Neither item can be allocated between commodities and both are treated as adjustments to the total. Hence exact figures are not available of expenditure by United Kingdom residents on each commodity or service.

The classification used in the 1967 Blue Book, together with notes on methods of estimating each item is given in the following pages.

SOURCES AND METHODS FOR ESTIMATING CONSUMERS' EXPENDITURE ON SPECIFIC ITEMS

The following pages describe in detail the methods of estimation used for the eleven years 1956 to 1966 covered by the 1967 Blue Book. As far as possible, where different methods were used for earlier years, the time of the change in methods is indicated and some account is given of the methods on which the figures for earlier years depend. In the immediate post-war years a good deal of information was available from rationing statistics and other information on controls. For details of the methods of preparation of estimates from this information, reference should be made to the previous description of the estimates[19].

1. Food

Expenditure on food may be for food prepared within the household or for food provided by caterers. The published tables on consumers' expenditure show household expenditure on food, but combined estimates of household and other personal expenditure on food are given in the notes at the end of the Blue Book.

---

[19] *National Income Statistics: Sources and Methods*, Studies in Official Statistics, No. 3, 1956.

Also, the item of expenditure 'Income in kind not included elsewhere' includes the estimated value of food issued to the Forces and to merchant seamen and fishermen. In the following paragraphs the methods used to estimate both household expenditure and other personal expenditure on food are described.

The item 'Food (household expenditure)' comprises all food and non-alcoholic beverages bought at retail by households for consumption in the household or elsewhere. Food withdrawn by farmers, other commercial food producers and retailers for their own consumption is treated as household purchases. Domestic poultry keeping and food cultivation in gardens and allotments are not regarded as commercial enterprises and nothing is included for the food produced.

Other personal expenditure on food forms part of the item 'Catering (meals and accommodation)'. The latter item includes the full value to the consumer of meals taken in hotels, restaurants, etc. but it is only the estimated amounts paid by caterers for their food supplies which are classified as other personal expenditure on food. Other personal expenditure on food is therefore equivalent to purchases of food by catering establishments for consumption on or off the premises. Catering establishments include both commercial and non-commercial establishments, for example cafes, restaurants, hotels, fish and chip shops, canteens, office dining-rooms, schools (providing school meals and school milk) and communal establishments such as orphanages. An adjustment is made to exclude amounts charged to business accounts, which are currently assumed to be nearly three per cent of the annual expenditure in catering establishments. It is assumed that all payments for meals in canteens and office dining-rooms are made out of personal income and that such payments cover at least the cost of the food. The value of food bought with luncheon vouchers is included in the estimates of other personal expenditure on food. Payments by public authorities for food consumed in hospitals, prisons, borstal institutions, residential schools and homes for the aged are excluded; this expenditure is part of public authorities' current expenditure on goods and services.

Extensive use is now made of the National Food Survey, which provides continuous information on the quantity and value of food bought by housewives and gives a guide to the proportion of recorded supplies which is appropriate to consumers' expenditure as defined for the national accounts. As increasing use has been made of the survey, estimates for recent and for earlier years have been revised. Before 1952, however, the scope of the survey was limited and does not provide a basis for detailed revision of the figures; therefore no estimates for individual commodity groups are available before 1952 consistent with those for later years, although the estimates of total consumers' expenditure on food for the years 1946 to 1951 have been adjusted to bring them approximately into line with the revised figures for later years.

Generally, the National Food Survey is used for estimating quantities where supply statistics are unsuitable either because of the use of the food at several stages of manufacture or because information on wastage, stock changes, etc. is limited. But the estimates which are based on the survey are reconciled with available statistics of supplies. About half of the estimates of household expenditure on food are now based on the results of the survey including the estimates of expenditure on bread, flour and cake, meat other than bacon or ham, meat products, most canned foods, sugar, potatoes and other vegetables, tea, coffee and some fresh fruits. The calculation of household expenditure from the National Food Survey excludes expenditure by people resident in catering establishments or institutions or serving in the Forces. An adjustment is also incorporated in the calculation to reflect the reduction in total household expenditure when holidays are taken away from home.

The balance of the estimates of household expenditure on food is based as far as quantities are concerned on statistics of supplies, that is imports and farm and manufacturing output, adjusted for exports and for amounts used in further processing, stock changes, wastage, etc. This balance covers both household and caterers' purchases of the foods concerned and a division between the two types of purchases is estimated from information from a variety of sources on meals taken outside the home.

All of the quantity estimates of household purchases of food which are based on the National Food Survey, and many of those which are based on supply data, are valued by means of average values taken from the National Food Survey so that the survey is the basis for most of the valuation of household expenditure on food. These values represent the average prices actually paid by consumers, except that milk under the National Milk Schemes and other welfare foods are valued at the cost, if any, to the consumer *plus* the additional cost met by the government. Quantities consumed on farms are valued at the prices which would be received by the farmer if the goods were sold. Food bought for consumption in catering establishments is valued at the estimated prices paid by the caterer. School milk is valued at the cost to the government.

For the constant price estimates consumers' expenditure on food is generally revalued commodity by commodity at the average unit values of the base year. But in the case of fresh fruit and vegetables (other than potatoes), where the composition of each of the broad groups of varieties and the quality of their components change radically from quarter to quarter in the year, consumers' expenditure on each group of varieties is revalued at the average value for that group in the corresponding quarter of the base year. For the purposes of this revaluation the average value for the base year as a whole is varied over the quarters of the base year according to the average seasonal pattern of several years. Detailed revaluation of the food estimates before 1955 raises many uncertainties because of rapid changes in the quality of foods during the period of derationing; therefore only approximate estimates are available of the total of expenditure on food at constant prices before 1955.

The following paragraphs describe the sources used to estimate expenditure on the individual food groups shown in the 1967 Blue Book.

Bread and cereals. Bread, flour, cakes, biscuits, cereal breakfast foods, oatmeal, rice, barley products, semolina, pasta, sago, tapioca, arrowroot, cornflour, custard and blancmange powders.

Estimates of expenditure on this group are calculated from information received on deliveries and utilisation of flour, together with returns from manufacturers of their production of biscuits, cereal breakfast foods, oatmeal, cornflour, and custard and blancmange powders. Imports and exports of cereal products are also available. For bread, flour and cakes, from 1953 purchased quantities are derived from the National Food Survey. All the above information is in terms of quantity. Price data are obtained from the National Food Survey for most of the items in this group, and from trade price lists for a few standard articles, such as oatmeal, and custard powder.

Meat and bacon. Meat, offal, bacon and ham, canned meat, poultry, game and rabbits, sausages, other meat products.

Estimates of expenditure on carcase meat and offal, sausages and other meat products are based for home production on quantities derived from slaughtering statistics and for imports and exports on quantities derived from the *Overseas Trade Accounts of the United Kingdom* (*Trade Accounts*) with adjustments for known stock changes. The results of the National Food Survey are used as a guide in estimating the proportions of meat going to the various end-uses. Before mid-1954 quantities were derived from rationing statistics. The quantities have been valued throughout at average prices recorded by the National Food Survey, due allowance being made for the difference between carcase weight and the weight as purchased by the consumer.

A similar procedure has been adopted for bacon and ham. Imports and home production of canned meat are known. The quantity available is analysed into main varieties and valued at estimated average prices based on the National Food Survey, with allowance for the amount of meat removed from cans and sold sliced.

The estimate of expenditure on poultry, game and rabbits is based on the production estimates of the agricultural departments and import statistics from the *Trade Accounts*. The seasonal pattern of purchases is indicated by the National Food Survey, but an adjustment is necessary to allow for the exceptional demand at Christmas, when survey field work is usually interrupted. The results of the National Food Survey are also used to indicate the division of purchases between households, caterers, and manufacturers, and for average prices.

Fish (*including shell fish*). Fresh, frozen, cured and canned fish, and fish products.

The basic information about fresh and frozen fish consists of figures of British landings, supplemented by particulars of fish not of British taking from the *Trade Accounts*. Returns of the production of cured fish are available. In estimating consumers' expenditure, allowance is made for fish going to fish fryers (treated as caterers), which is valued separately.

Quantities of canned fish are known from manufacturers' returns of home production and import statistics. They are valued at prices based on the National Food Survey.

Oils and fats. Butter, margarine, lard, other edible fats.

Figures are available for the production of butter (derived from milk used), margarine and cooking fats, and imports are derived from the *Trade Accounts*. Deductions are made for quantities used in the manufacture of other foods (including butter blended with margarine). Estimated prices are based on the results of the National Food Survey.

Before 1954, the imports, production and distribution of all these commodities were controlled; prices were known, and estimates were based on rationing statistics.

Sugar, preserves and confectionery. Sugar, syrup and treacle, jam, marmalade, fruit curd, mincemeat, honey, chocolate and sugar confectionery, and table jellies.

For sugar, the basic commodity of this group, information is available on total supplies, but little detail is known of the use of sugar in manufactured products. Consumption estimates for sugar and for syrup and treacle are based on the National Food Survey. Before September, 1953, there were detailed statistics of supplies and allocations of sugar, and prices were controlled.

Estimates of expenditure on jam and marmalade, fruit curd, mincemeat and table jellies are based on production figures from manufacturers, and import statistics. Prices are based on the results of the National Food Survey.

For chocolate and sugar confectionery, the trade association supplies figures of despatches by manufacturers to the home market together with estimates of the retail value of the products.

Dairy products. Liquid and condensed milk, cream, cheese, eggs.

Estimates of sales of full-priced liquid milk are based on information supplied by the Milk Marketing Boards. The quantities of milk provided under the school milk and the National Milk Schemes are known; they are valued at their total cost to public authorities before deduction of receipts. The cost of school milk is part of non-household expenditure on food. The net cost to public authorities of school milk and the National Milk Schemes is treated as a grant to persons, so that the item appears on both sides of the personal income and expenditure account.

For condensed milk, cream and cheese, estimates are available of home production (based on milk used) and of imports. Consumption estimates are based on supplies and on data from the National Food Survey. The total home production of eggs is estimated by the Ministry of Agriculture, Fisheries and Food, and imports are obtained from the *Trade Accounts.* Deductions from total supplies are made for eggs for hatching and for processing, and for the quantities produced by domestic poultry keepers. Prices are based on the National Food Survey.

Fruit. Fresh, canned, dried, frozen and crystallized fruit; nuts.

Potatoes and vegetables. Potatoes and potato products; fresh, canned, dried and frozen vegetables; pickles and sauces.

The methods used for estimating expenditure on these two groups can conveniently be considered together. Estimates of consumption are derived from the agricultural departments' estimates of crops harvested, and from particulars of imports, deducting allowances for waste and for use by manufacturers and interpreting the result in conjunction with the results of the National Food Survey.

Particulars of the production and stocks of canned and frozen fruit and vegetables are available from the trade, and imports are obtained from the *Trade Accounts.* Details of the production of pickles and sauces, analysed by type, are provided by manufacturers, and retail prices are calculated from trade price lists.

In order to allow for variations in the fresh fruit and vegetables available at different times of the year, expenditure is revalued at prices of the corresponding quarter of the base year.

Beverages. Tea, coffee, cocoa, soft drinks.

The results of the National Food Survey are used in estimating household expenditure on tea. Estimates are also available of the total quantity of tea entering into consumption.

There is reliable information on the production of coffee essences and powders, and on cocoa powder and drinking chocolate supplied to the home market. For roast and ground coffee, quantities purchased by households and prices are taken from the National Food Survey.

Manufacturers of soft drinks provide figures of the quantities produced, and these are valued at prices based on trade price lists.

Other manufactured foods. Infant and invalid foods, welfare foods (for example, cod liver oil, orange juice) and miscellaneous manufactured foods, of which the most important are ice cream, canned soups and condiments.

Expenditure on welfare foods is valued at the net cost to the government *plus* the cost to the consumer, in the same way as milk supplied under national schemes.

Estimates are available from manufacturers of their production of some types of infant and invalid foods, canned soups, and ice cream. For the remaining items in the group the information is much more limited, depending largely on material collected during the early post-war years. Consumption of these items does not vary much and prices are available from trade price lists and from the National Food Survey.

2. Alcoholic drink

The group covers alcoholic drink bought by consumers from retailers and in public houses, hotels, restaurants and other commercial catering establishments, and alcoholic drink bought by non-profit-making clubs. The drink bought by consumers in commercial catering establishments is valued at the prices paid by the consumer including any charge for serving it; the alcoholic drink bought by clubs should be valued at the prices paid by the clubs but separate information on these purchases is not regularly available and no allowance is therefore made for the reduced prices at which the clubs usually buy. As a compensating factor, data on the average value of draught beer which is used in the estimates relates to prices in public bars and the allowance which is made for the additional charges in other bars, restaurants, etc. is probably too small.

Apart from expenditure on cider and perry, the estimates of expenditure on alcoholic drink are based on the quantities withdrawn from bond (more precisely, on the quantities on which duty is paid) during the quarter multiplied by average values. The delay between payment of duty and date of purchase for consumption is usually ignored. During this period there may be some building up or running down of manufacturers' or distributors' stocks out of bond which would, incorrectly, be recorded as consumers' expenditure. However, statistics collected by the Board of Trade on the turnover of public houses and off-licences, and on changes in the stocks of wine and spirit merchants and off-licences, give an indication of any unusual movement in these stocks, for example in anticipation of changes in the rates of duty. When it appears that the stocks changes have been exceptional, the estimates of consumers' expenditure are adjusted to exclude them.

Beer (including ale, stout and lager). The consumption of beer is measured by the net quantity of beer, including imported beer, on which duty is paid during the quarter, as published in the *Monthly Digest of Statistics*. The price of beer varies between districts, between different bars in the same public house, between types of beer and according to whether it is sold on draught or in bottle. Particulars of quantities sold, and of average prices, for each category of beer are obtained from trade sources and are used to estimate the value of total expenditure. Of the total, an allowance which is assumed to be two per cent is deducted for expenditure charged to business accounts.

There are several ways in which expenditure on beer might be revalued at constant prices. The simplest method is to multiply the number of bulk barrels consumed in any year by the average price per bulk barrel in the base year. This method makes no allowance for changes in quality as measured by the strength or average gravity of the beer. Another possibility is to use the standard barrel as the unit of consumption and revalue by using the average price of a standard barrel in the base year. This method takes full account of changes in quality but tends to give an unreliable measure of the change in real expenditure because it presupposes that alcoholic content is the sole criterion by which consumers' satisfaction is measured. The method of revaluation which has been adopted is a compromise between the two described above. The price index used is based on the average of the price indices for a bulk barrel and a standard barrel calculated separately for each category. The same general principle is used in compiling the index of retail prices[20].

Spirits. The consumption of spirits is obtained by adding retained imports on which duty is paid to the net quantity of home produced spirits on which duty is paid *less* the amount used for medical or scientific purposes. Monthly information on the quantities of the different types of spirits is given in the *Monthly Digest of Statistics.* Home consumption of rum and brandy is available separately. Consumption of whisky is assumed to correspond to the series for home produced mature spirit, while gin is taken as 95 per cent of immature spirits (home produced *plus* imported).

The average price per proof gallon of spirits sold by the glass is considerably higher than of spirits sold in bottle and, in valuing the quantities of each type of spirits, assumptions must be made about the proportions sold in these two ways. Since there is no direct information on these proportions, an element of uncertainty is introduced into the estimation of expenditure on spirits, but in judging how the proportions may be changing account is taken of the relative trends in the turnover of public houses and of off-licences, as shown in the Board of Trade statistics of catering turnover and retail sales. Prices of spirits sold by bottle and by glass are based on off-licence lists and on information collected for the index of retail prices. Of total expenditure on spirits an arbitrary proportion (taken to be ten per cent up to March 1965 and eight per cent from April 1965) is deducted for purchases charged to business accounts.

Expenditure at constant prices is obtained for each of the five types of spirits by valuing the quantities sold by the bottle and by the glass at their respective average prices in the base year.

Imported wines. Monthly information on the quantities of imported wines on which duty is paid is published in the *Monthly Digest of Statistics,* for the categories: foreign heavy wines, foreign light wines, Commonwealth heavy wines, Commonwealth light wines and sparkling wines.

Each category of wine is valued at an average of prices given in off-licence lists, converted to prices per gallon. An addition is made for service charges on wine served in bottle in restaurants, and by glass. As in the case of spirits, assumptions have to be made about the proportions of wine sold with and without service charges.

Of total expenditure on imported wines, a proportion (assumed to be the same as for spirits) is deducted for purchases charged to business accounts.

Expenditure at constant prices is obtained for each category separately by valuing the quantity of wine at the average price calculated for the base year.

---

[20] *Method of Construction and Calculation of the Index of Retail Prices,* Studies in Official Statistics, No. 6, 4th edition 1967.

F*

British wines. The quantity charged with duty is published in the *Monthly Digest of Statistics* and expenditure is calculated by applying an average price to these quantities. Expenditure at constant prices is obtained by valuing the quantity of wine at the average price calculated for the base year.

Cider and perry. The production of cider and perry is reported quarterly to the Ministry of Agriculture, Fisheries and Food, and expenditure is estimated by applying average prices derived from off-licence lists to the quantities produced. Expenditure at constant prices is obtained by applying average prices in the base year.

3. Tobacco

Quarterly estimates of consumers' expenditure on home manufactured tobacco products (including Cavendish manufactured in bond) are supplied by the trade. The quantities of imported tobacco products are obtained from the *Trade Accounts*. Estimates of the average retail prices paid for all tobacco products are provided by the trade.

Tobacco bought between 1947 and 1958 under the coupon scheme for old age pensioners was valued at its full retail price *less* the cost of the scheme to the government, as obtained from Customs and Excise. An estimate provided by the trade of the proportion, by weight, of tobacco consumed by old age pensioners in the form of cigarettes was the basis for the allocation of the amount to be deducted between cigarettes and pipe tobacco.

Expenditure at constant prices is obtained by valuing sales of the main types of cigarette and of other tobacco separately at the average prices of the base year.

4. Housing

This item relates to land and dwellings used by persons for residential or recreational as opposed to business purposes, and land and buildings used by private non-profit-making bodies serving persons.

The item consists of three main parts:

rent, including imputed rent of owner-occupiers;
rates and water charges;
maintenance, repairs and improvements by occupiers.

Nothing is included for persons living in hotels, boarding houses, etc. because the rent element of their expenditure is included in expenditure on 'Catering (meals and accommodation)'. Rent for holiday flats, bungalows, caravans, etc. is also included in the latter item.

Rent. From 1964 the annual estimates of rent are based on the Family Expenditure Survey. They are made up of:

(i) The rent of rented accommodation, excluding any element of rates, and the ground rent paid by owner-occupiers. Since 1964 information has been collected in the Family Expenditure Survey on the rateable values of all types of dwellings; this has provided a basis for distinguishing the rent element from the rates element in payments by tenants to landlords. Additions are made for site rents of owner-occupied caravans based on estimates by the National Caravan Council of numbers of caravans and special survey information on average rents.

(ii) The imputed rent of owner-occupiers. Information collected in the Family Expenditure Survey since 1957 on the rateable value of owner-occupied dwellings provides a basis for imputing a total rent to owner-occupiers. This imputed rent is the rateable value adjusted for changes since the last valuation in the general level of rents as shown by the index of retail prices.

(iii) The imputed rent of rent-free accommodation. The estimates for this item, which is included as income in kind, have been derived since 1964 from the Family Expenditure Survey in the same way as for the imputed rent of owner-occupiers.

A rough addition is made for the rent paid by or imputed to private non-profit-making bodies.

The quarterly estimates of rent are mainly based on interpolation of the annual changes in the aggregate rateable value of domestic property in Great Britain to represent quantity changes, and on the rent component of the index of retail prices to allow for price changes.

Rates. From 1964 the annual estimates of consumers' expenditure on rates are calculated from the statistics of aggregate rateable values of domestic property and poundages published in *Rates and Rateable Values in England and Wales* and *Rates and Rateable Values in Scotland.* Roughly half the total rates paid in Northern Ireland, as shown in *Northern Ireland Local Authority Rate Statistics*, are taken to be domestic. An adjustment has been made in the estimates from 1966 to take account of the rate rebate for low income households. An addition is made for water charges not included in the rate poundages. A rough addition is also made for the rates and water charges paid by non-profit-making bodies.

Quarterly estimates are based on interpolation and projection of the annual figures of aggregate rateable value together with interpolation and projection of the change in the poundage based on movements in the rates and water charges component of the index of retail prices.

For the period 1956 to 1963 estimates of rent, and of rates and water charges were derived from the Ministry of Labour household expenditure inquiry for 1953-54 and a Social Survey inquiry for 1955, projected forwards by the figures of the aggregate rateable value of domestic property in England and Wales as an index of quantity, and the rent, rates and water charges components of the index of retail prices as an index of price. Figures of aggregate rateable value of domestic property were not available for Scotland before 1962 or for England and Wales before 1956. Estimates of the stock of dwellings (in numbers) were used as an index of quantity for projecting the results of the 1953-54 and 1955 household inquiries backwards over the period 1946 to 1955.

These methods produced estimates for 1964 which were much lower than the present estimates. The estimates for the years up to 1963 were therefore revised upwards, the revisions being gradually tapered down to zero in 1939.

Estimates of rent and rates at constant prices are obtained by projecting the base-year figures forwards by an index of the aggregate rateable value of domestic property. Quarterly figures are interpolated and projected.

Maintenance, repairs and improvements by occupiers. This covers expenditure by tenants and owner-occupiers, including the cost of materials bought by the occupier. The estimates include the purchase of paint, paint brushes, wallpaper and other do-it-yourself tools and materials; the purchase and erection costs of garages, sheds, greenhouses, etc.; the installation of central heating in existing dwellings (but not electric unit plan storage heaters, which are classified under 'Radio, electrical and other durable goods'); and contractors' work on maintenance, repairs and other improvements. Expenditure on improvements other than that assisted by local authority grants is included, even though it might be better treated as capital expenditure, because the information available does not permit a division between improvements and repairs and maintenance. Expenditure by insurance companies on the repair of private dwellings and buildings of non-profit-making bodies is included and so are the management expenses of insuring these buildings where the premiums are paid by the occupiers. (For the general treatment of insurance, see item 20 on page 181.)

The estimates for repairs, maintenance and improvements are uncertain; they are in general based on the Family Expenditure Survey but account is also taken of the statistics of work done on house repairs, covering expenditure by both occupiers and landlords, collected by the Ministry of Public Building and Works. Information from various sources on the installation of central heating is also used. Separate annual estimates are made from the survey of purchases of materials and of contractors' work. Since some expenditures by individual households are very big, particularly on contractors' work, the sampling errors of the estimates from the survey have been high, although the increase in the size of the sample will reduce them. The changes in expenditure are consequently difficult to judge and the figures are subject to considerable revision as longer runs of results become available from the survey. A rough addition is made for expenditure by non-profit-making bodies on repairs, etc. to their buildings and for the expenditure of insurance companies on repairs under consumers' policies. Quarterly figures are interpolated and projected on the basis of the quarterly pattern of expenditure shown over several years by the survey.

The estimates are revalued at constant prices by means of the 'Charges for repairs, etc.' and 'Materials for home repairs, etc.' sections of the index of retail prices. A rough index has been compiled to allow for changes in the costs of central heating installation.

The management expenses of insuring the structure of dwellings, where premiums are paid by the occupier, are calculated as follows. The ratio of expenses to premiums for fire insurance, taken from the summarised annual accounts of insurance companies, is applied to annual estimates of the premiums paid by consumers for insuring the structure of dwellings, based on the Family Expenditure Survey. A rough addition is made for the buildings of non-profit-making bodies. Quarterly figures are interpolated and projected. As no price index is available for the costs of managing the insurance, the estimates are revalued at constant prices by means of the general consumer price index.

5. *Fuel and light*

Consumers' expenditure on fuel and light covers expenditure on all forms of fuel and power used for domestic heating, lighting and power, but not the cost of hiring equipment. Most of the material on which the quarterly estimates are based is published annually in the *Statistical Digest* of the Ministry of Power.

Coal. Estimates of consumers' expenditure in Great Britain are based mainly on returns made by coal merchants to the Ministry of Power. The returns give details of house coal, anthracite and boiler fuel (other than coke) supplied by merchants, mainly to domestic consumers, but they include some disposals to shops, offices and other partly or entirely non-residential establishments. These disposals are adjusted to the definition of consumers' expenditure by deducting estimates of the non-personal element and adding part of the coal sold to large non-industrial establishments to cover such consumers as private non-profit-making schools and charitable institutions. Estimates for Northern Ireland are based on colliery despatches of house coal to Northern Ireland.

Expenditure on each type of coal, anthracite and boiler fuel is calculated by applying estimated average delivered prices to the estimated quantities going to consumers. In addition, the full value of all coal supplied free or at reduced prices to miners and other colliery employees is included. For national accounts purposes, this coal is valued at pithead prices and is included in income in kind.

Consumers' expenditure on coal is revalued at constant prices by applying appropriate average values in the base year to the quantity used by consumers in each of the categories of coal, anthracite and boiler fuel (other than coke).

Coke and premium smokeless fuels. Estimates of consumers' expenditure in Great Britain on these fuels are based upon disposals by merchants, gas works and coke ovens to domestic consumers, and include an arbitrary allowance for the personal element in supplies of coke to the non-industrial sector. Consumption in Northern Ireland is allowed for by adding 2 per cent to the figures for Great Britain. Prices are estimated from a sample of quotations for different areas of Great Britain. Expenditure at constant prices is obtained by applying the average price in the base year to the quantities for each year.

Electricity. From 1948 consumers' expenditure is taken as sales by the public electricity supply to domestic consumers in Great Britain, *plus* an estimate representing the personal element in sales to farms, *plus* 10 per cent of sales to combined domestic and commercial premises *plus* 1 per cent of sales to non-industrial premises. The total so obtained is increased by $1\frac{1}{2}$ per cent to allow for consumers in Northern Ireland. Sales are priced according to statistics of average revenue per unit for sales to domestic consumers.

Consumers' expenditure at constant prices is obtained by applying the average revenue per unit from domestic sales in the base year to the number of units sold to consumers in each year. The estimates of expenditure at constant prices are thus proportional to the number of units of electricity consumed. Under the two-part tariffs which are widespread in the electricity industry, the average cost to the consumer of a unit of electricity falls as the quantity consumed rises; this is reflected in the price index which can be derived by dividing the estimates of consumers' expenditure at current prices by the estimates at constant prices. The component of the index of retail prices, on the other hand, is based on changes in the prices of fixed quantities of electricity and is thus independent of changes in the quantity of electricity consumed. If this index were used to revalue consumers' expenditure on electricity at constant prices, the resulting estimates would not be proportional to the number of units of electricity consumed.

Gas. Consumers' expenditure in Great Britain is taken as sales to domestic consumers *plus* 1 per cent of sales to non-industrial premises. The total for Great Britain is increased by $1\frac{1}{2}$ per cent to allow for consumers' expenditure in Northern Ireland. The average price used is the average revenue per therm recorded by the Gas Council for sales to domestic consumers.

Expenditure at constant prices is obtained by applying to the number of therms sold the average revenue per therm in the base year. Again two-part tariffs are widespread and, as with electricity, the average cost to the consumer of a therm of gas under such tariffs falls as his consumption rises.

Other fuels. Estimates of the quantity and value of paraffin, fuel oil and liquid gases bought by consumers are provided by a trade source. Expenditure on fuel oil and liquid gases at constant prices is obtained by applying to the quantities bought the average price in the base year. From 1962 expenditure on paraffin at constant prices has also been obtained in this way; up to 1962 the appropriate section of the index of retail prices was used to revalue the current price estimates. There are no statistics of expenditure on wood and the figures are guessed; the amount involved is thought to be relatively small.

6. Clothing

Footwear. This includes all boots, shoes, slippers, etc. but excludes socks and stockings (included under 'Other clothing'), repairs and repair materials.

Other clothing. This includes all kinds of garments, dress materials, millinery, knitting wool, haberdashery, etc., and an allowance for the making-up of consumers' own materials. It excludes expenditure on repairs and alterations. In the Blue Book the figures are divided between 'Men's and boys' wear' and 'Women's, girls' and infants' wear'; haberdashery, etc. is included in the latter.

From 1950 estimates of consumers' expenditure on clothing and footwear are based on monthly statistics of retail sales, which are used to project benchmark figures in the way described on page 150. The benchmark estimates are derived from the commodity analysis of sales given in the censuses of distribution, after adding sales direct to the public by manufacturers and wholesalers and estimated sales in Northern Ireland, and after deducting estimated business purchases and allowing for some differences in classification between the commodity analysis of the national accounts and of the census. Adjustments have been made to bring the estimates for the years before 1950 into line with those for later years.

The clothing and footwear component of the index of retail prices provides the basic data for revaluing the expenditure at constant prices.

7. Durable goods

This category covers those goods which are relatively costly and which are generally available on credit terms. The category has been defined in the light of the information available and consequently excludes certain goods which could satisfy these criteria, for example expensive crockery and glassware, jewellery, watches and items of clothing such as fur coats.

Motor cars and motor cycles, new and second-hand. Purchases *less* sales by consumers of motor cars, motor cycles, three-wheeled motor vehicles, motor scooters and mopeds.

Estimates from 1962 are based on the Board of Trade inquiries into the motor trades. The inquiry for 1962 provided the basis for an estimate of the sales in that year of all types of new and used motor vehicles *less* purchases by motor traders of new vehicles from other traders and of used vehicles from all sources. This estimate is carried forwards by the results of the Board of Trade monthly inquiry into the motor trades. From these figures are deducted the estimates which are made for the national accounts of investment in road vehicles (capital expenditure by the public sector, by companies and by persons on business account). From the resulting estimates of personal expenditure on motor vehicles are deducted personal exports of motor vehicles which are included in the export figures.

Before 1962 the estimates for cars and motor cycles were made separately. The estimates of expenditure on cars for the years 1954 to 1961 were made as follows. A benchmark estimate of total expenditure on new cars was made for the year 1960 from an analysis by make and engine capacity of registrations of new cars in Great Britain and from published data on retail prices, excluding purchase tax, in the benchmark year. This provided estimates for 1960 of the average values excluding purchase tax of new cars in broad engine capacity ranges and these were applied to quarterly figures of the numbers of new registrations for the engine capacity ranges from 1954 onwards. The resulting volume series, after grossing up to a United Kingdom basis, was converted to an expenditure series at current prices by means of an index of prices of new cars excluding purchase tax. Additions were then made for purchase tax and for delivery charges. From these estimates of total expenditure on new cars were deducted rough estimates of investment in cars (capital expenditure by the public sector, by companies and by persons on business account). Rough additions were made for dealers' margins on sales of used cars.

The estimates of capital expenditure were made as follows. Comprehensive figures were available of capital expenditure on road vehicles as a whole; information was also available on expenditure on buses and rough estimates were made of expenditure on other commercial vehicles, based on numbers registered. Subtracting expenditure on buses and other commercial vehicles from total capital expenditure on road vehicles left, as a residual, an estimate of capital expenditure on cars. These figures covered purchases of new and used vehicles *less* sales of used vehicles. The difference between the estimate of total purchases of new cars and the estimate of capital expenditure on cars therefore represented an approximation to purchases of new cars by consumers together with the value (other than dealers' margins) of used cars sold by business to consumers. Rough additions were made for dealers' margins.

For the years from 1948 to 1961 the estimates of consumers' expenditure at current and constant prices on new motor cycles, including scooters, mopeds and three-wheeled vehicles, were based on production and import data *plus* estimated distributors' margins and the appropriate purchase tax. An arbitrary deduction of 2 per cent was made for business expenditure. Rough additions were made for dealers' margins on sales of used motor cycles.

The current price estimates from 1962 are revalued at constant prices by using an overall price index obtained by weighting together separate price indices for motor cars, motor cycles, etc., and dealers' margins on second-hand vehicles. The price index for cars is derived from estimates of consumers' expenditure at current and constant prices obtained by a continuation of the methods used up to 1962. For motor cycles and dealers' margins on second-hand vehicles components of the index of retail prices are used.

Charges on hire purchase transactions in motor vehicles are excluded from consumers' expenditure. These charges are paid almost entirely to finance companies and are treated in the national accounts as interest payments by persons, which are a deduction from personal income from rent, dividends and net interest (see page 103).

Furniture and floor coverings. Furniture, mattresses and floor coverings.

Radio, electrical and other durable goods. Radio and television sets; record players; tape recorders; musical instruments; household appliances such as electric and gas fires, electric unit plan storage heaters, paraffin heaters, washing machines, cookers, refrigerators, vacuum cleaners, sewing machines, lawn mowers; perambulators; and pedal cycles. Separate estimates of expenditure on pedal cycles are given in the notes at the end of the Blue Book. Expenditure on renting such goods is excluded; rent of radio and television sets is included in 'Entertainment and recreational services' and of domestic appliances in 'Other services'. Expenditure on repairs of all these goods is included in 'Other services'.

From 1950 estimates of consumers' expenditure on these items are based on monthly statistics of retail sales, projecting forwards benchmark figures from the censuses of distribution in the same way as for clothing. Fairly extensive adjustments have to be made to the census headings corresponding to the group 'Radio, electrical and other durable goods', to bring the census headings into line with the national accounts classification. The relevant census headings are: electrical appliances, etc.; radio and television sets, etc.; cycles and cycle accessories; perambulators; and gas appliances. Additions are made for estimated sales of paraffin heaters, lawn mowers and sewing machines, and deductions for estimated sales of gramophone records, cycle accessories and minor electrical goods.

The estimates before 1950 were based on other sources and were originally made on a different commodity classification. Adjustments have had to be made, some of which are rather uncertain, to bring the estimates into line with the present classification and to make them consistent with those for later years.

The estimates are revalued at constant prices by means of appropriate items from the household durable goods component of the index of retail prices.

8. Other household goods

Household textiles, soft furnishings. Comprises soft bedding (blankets, sheets, pillows), cushions, furnishing fabrics, and household textiles.

Hardware. Comprises hardware, pottery, glassware, cutlery, minor radio and electrical goods, and cycle accessories.

The estimates for these two categories are based on monthly statistics of retail sales, projecting forwards benchmark figures from the censuses of distribution in the same way as for clothing.

The adjustments which have to be made to the benchmark figures to allow for differences of classification between the commodity analyses of the national accounts and of the census are more extensive for hardware than for other items based on retail sales. Deductions, some of which are uncertain, have to be made from the census figures for sales by hardware shops of the following goods: gas appliances, lawn mowers, paraffin and paraffin heaters, builders' and decorators' supplies, household cleaning materials, paint, wallpaper, and other do-it-yourself tools and materials; and additions have to be made for minor electrical goods and cycle accessories. Moreover, the indicators for projecting forwards the benchmark figures for hardware, based mainly on sales by specialist hardware shops and the hardware departments of department stores, are not very satisfactory, both because the sales figures do not correspond very closely to the national accounts category and because of the difficulty of allowing for changes in the sales of hardware by general stores. An adjustment is, however, made to the indicators in order to exclude sales of paraffin by hardware shops. The estimates for hardware are therefore not considered sufficiently reliable to be shown separately in the main Blue Book tables on consumers' expenditure. However, it is recognised that for certain purposes it is important to have separate estimates even though they are subject to rather wide margins of error and the estimates are given separately in the notes at the end of the Blue Book.

The estimates before 1950 were based on other sources and were originally made on a different commodity classification. Adjustments have had to be made, some of which are rather uncertain, to bring the estimates into line with the present classification and to make them consistent with those for later years.

The estimates are revalued at constant prices mainly by items from the household durable goods component of the index of retail prices.

Matches. The quantities of home produced and imported matches charged with duty are published in the *Monthly Digest of Statistics.* These quantities are multiplied by the estimated average value in the base year to produce a value series at constant prices. This in turn is converted to current prices by the matches component of the index of retail prices. A deduction of 10 per cent is made to allow for expenditure by public authorities and business concerns. The estimates are given separately in the notes at the end of the Blue Book.

Soap and other cleaning materials. This group includes hard, soft and toilet soap, soap and detergent powders and flakes, scourers, polishes, soda, disinfectants, etc. Car cleaning materials are in principle classified under 'Running costs of motor vehicles' but some expenditure on these materials is likely to be included in these estimates.

From 1957 the estimates of expenditure are based on the Family Expenditure Survey. Before 1957 the estimates were based on production data and other information supplied by the trade. The general level of these estimates has been adjusted slightly to make them consistent with the estimates for later years.

Separate estimates are made for (i) soap and soapless detergents and (ii) other cleaning materials, which are separately revalued at constant prices by items from the miscellaneous goods component of the index of retail prices.

9. Books, newspapers and magazines

Books. Estimates of consumers' expenditure are based on quarterly trade estimates of the value of sales by book publishers to the home market, including books published by H.M. Stationery Office. An addition for the value of imported books is based on import statistics. An estimated distributors' mark-up is applied, but no allowance is made for changes in stocks. An arbitrary deduction of two per cent is made for business purchases. Deductions for expenditure by maintained schools are based on information for England and Wales published in *Education Statistics*[21] with an approximate allowance for expenditure in Scotland based on numbers of pupils. Deductions for expenditure by public libraries have been based from 1962/63 on information for England and Wales published in *Public Library Statistics*[21], and before 1962/63 on information from the Library Association published in the *Annual Abstract of Statistics.*

The estimates are revalued at constant prices by the books component of the index of retail prices.

Newspapers. Estimates of expenditure are made separately for the following nine types of newspapers: (i) national morning; (ii) national evening; (iii) national Sunday; (iv) other national weekly; (v) provincial morning; (vi) provincial evening; (vii) provincial Sunday; (viii) other provincial weekly; (ix) all others. The estimates are calculated from figures of circulation per issue and prices now given half-yearly in *British Rate and Data.* The figures are assumed to apply throughout the half-year, but where information is available from other sources on changes in price within the half-year these are allowed for. In the

---

[21] Published by the Institute of Municipal Treasurers and Accountants and Society of County Treasurers.

first seven categories expenditure is calculated quarterly by multiplying together the circulation per issue, the number of issues per quarter and the price of every recorded newspaper. Account is taken of newspapers starting or ceasing publication. Expenditure on (viii), other provincial weekly newspapers, is based on a benchmark estimate projected forwards by changes in the circulation and prices of a sample of this type of newspaper. The estimates for (ix), all other newspapers, are based on a benchmark estimate projected forwards by changes in the estimates for categories (v) to (viii). All estimates for current quarters have to be projected forwards provisionally on the basis of past trends until information from *British Rate and Data* becomes available.

It is assumed that purchases of newspapers by public authorities and business firms are balanced by purchases of technical papers by the personal sector. This is an arbitrary assumption for which there is no statistical evidence.

In estimating expenditure at constant prices, the base-year estimate of expenditure on each of the nine types of newspaper is projected forwards by the total circulation of that type of newspaper.

Magazines. All periodicals other than newspapers. Miscellaneous publications, such as HMSO papers, maps and time-tables are also included.

Estimates are made separately for (i) children's comics and magazines; (ii) women's weekly magazines; (iii) women's monthly magazines; (iv) other magazines, subdivided into about eight categories according to the number of issues per year; (v) miscellaneous publications.

Figures of circulation per issue of children's comics and magazines are provided half-yearly by the publishers. Figures of circulation per issue of women's and other magazines are given annually in *Flanan's Press Guide*. Prices are taken from *Willing's Press Guide*. The figures of circulation per issue and of price are interpolated for the quarters of the year on a smooth trend. Expenditure is calculated quarterly by multiplying together the estimated circulation per issue, the number of issues per quarter and the estimated price of every recorded magazine. A rough addition is made for expenditure on miscellaneous publications. Estimates for current quarters are projected forwards provisionally on the basis of past trends until information from press guides and the trade becomes available.

In revaluing expenditure at constant prices the base-year estimate of expenditure on each of the categories of magazine is projected forwards by the total circulation of this category.

10. Chemists' goods

This group comprises expenditure on drugs, medicines and medical goods, toilet requisites and toilet preparations (excluding toilet soap but including cosmetics). It excludes drugs, etc. supplied under the national health service, whether or not these are paid for in part by consumers. Payments by consumers for national health service prescriptions are classified under 'Other services'.

The estimates are based on monthly statistics of retail sales, projecting benchmark figures from the censuses of distribution. Additions to the benchmark census figures are made for sales of chemists' goods by service trades such as hairdressers and by manufacturers and wholesalers direct to the public. Additions are also made for private purchases of spectacles, surgical appliances, etc. and for sales in Northern Ireland. Deductions are made for sales of toilet soap, for chemists' receipts under the national health service and for sales to businesses.

Chemists' receipts under the national health service are included in the unadjusted census figures but excluded from the monthly statistics of retail sales.

The estimates are revalued at constant prices using a combination of selected components of the index of retail prices.

11. Miscellaneous recreational goods

This group consists of three main parts: (i) miscellaneous recreational equipment; (ii) horticultural goods; and (iii) domestic pets.

(i) *Miscellaneous recreational equipment.* Caravans, yachts, boats, gramophone records, toys and sports goods, photographic and non-medical optical goods including developing and printing of film, miscellaneous goods connected with arts, crafts and hobbies, not specified elsewhere.

Total expenditure on new caravans is calculated annually from the numbers produced for the home market multiplied by their estimated average retail value including delivery charges; no adjustment is made for changes in distributors' stocks. Half of this total is attributed to consumers and half to commercial caravan parks and other business users. The quarterly number of hire purchase contracts for new caravans compiled by Hire Purchase Information Limited is used as an indicator of quarterly changes within the year and of changes since the last annual estimate. Expenditure at constant prices is obtained by multiplying the number of caravans attributed to consumers by the estimated average value in the base year. Estimates of purchases *less* sales by consumers of second-hand caravans are included under 'Other services'.

Expenditure on yachts and boats is not yet satisfactorily represented in the estimates. Nothing is included specifically at present; but in so far as yachts and boats are bought from retailers and classified as recreational equipment they will be included within the estimates based on the censuses of distribution and statistics of retail sales. Expenditure on other miscellaneous recreational equipment, apart from gramophone records, is based on monthly statistics of retail sales, projecting benchmark figures from the censuses of distribution consisting of expenditure on photographic goods *plus* half the estimate of expenditure on toys, sports goods and leather goods. The remaining half of the census estimate for toys, sports goods and leather goods is regarded as coming within the group 'Other miscellaneous goods'. For gramophone records, estimates are based on quarterly figures of manufacturers' sales adjusted for wholesale and retail margins and purchase tax. Expenditure is revalued at constant prices by means of appropriate indices obtained from the components of the index of retail prices.

(ii) *Horticultural goods.* Flowers, seeds, plants, etc. and miscellaneous garden equipment not specified elsewhere.

The annual estimates are based on the Family Expenditure Survey and on statistics of imports and home output of flowers, bulbs and seeds. Quarterly figures are interpolated and projected.

Expenditure is revalued at constant prices by means of a rough index of average values of various types of horticultural products which is specially compiled.

(iii) *Domestic pets.* Purchase and upkeep of domestic pets of all kinds, domestic poultry, racing and riding horses; pet foods; veterinary goods and services; dog and gun licences.

The most important component of this group is pet foods. A benchmark estimate for prepared pet foods derived from the census of production is projected forwards annually by a volume index based on production data and a price index consisting of the 'Food for animals' component of the index of retail prices. An allowance is added for bird seed and other foods. Quarterly figures are interpolated. The estimates are broadly consistent with the results of the Family Expenditure Survey although, because of wide variations in expenditure on pet foods between households, the sampling errors of the survey are high for this item. Expenditure at constant prices is obtained by projecting forwards the estimate for the base year by the index of volume.

With the exception of dog and gun licences (for which figures of receipts are available) there is little reliable information for the rest of the group. Account is taken of the results of the Family Expenditure Survey in estimating expenditure on the remainder, but the sampling errors of the survey for these items are high.

12. Other miscellaneous goods

Stationery and writing equipment, paper goods, umbrellas and walking sticks, handbags and purses, etc., travel goods, clocks and watches, jewellery, penknives, smokers' requisites, pictures, frames, vases and miscellaneous fancy or ornamental articles for personal or domestic use.

The quarterly estimates for this group are based on statistics of retail sales projecting benchmark figures from the censuses of distribution consisting of estimates of sales of jewellery, stationery and half of the sales of toys, sports goods and leather goods. Expenditure at constant prices is obtained by deflating the current price series using information about the price movements of fancy goods, stationery and jewellery.

13. Running costs of motor vehicles

This group comprises (i) petrol and oil, (ii) maintenance, repairs, spare parts and accessories, (iii) garage rents, (iv) motor vehicle insurance, (v) motor vehicle and driving licences, (vi) driving lessons, (vii) Ministry of Transport driving tests, and (viii) Ministry of Transport tests of roadworthiness.

(i) *Petrol and oil.* Quarterly figures of the price, quantity and value of oil and of the various grades of petrol used for private motoring are provided by the trade. Expenditure at constant prices is obtained by applying the average price in the base year to the quantity of oil and of each grade of petrol.

(ii) *Maintenance, repairs, spare parts and accessories.* This group includes the expenditure of insurance companies on repairs under consumers' policies. A benchmark estimate of consumers' expenditure on the group, for which there is little reliable data, is projected forwards by the estimated quantity of petrol bought by consumers as an index of volume, and by the 'Maintenance of motor vehicles' section of the index of retail prices as an index of price. Expenditure at constant prices consists of the estimate for the base year projected by the index of volume.

(iii) *Garage rents.* Estimates are based annually on the results of the Family Expenditure Survey. Quarterly figures are interpolated and projected.

(iv) *Motor vehicle insurance.* This comprises the management expenses of insuring consumers' motor vehicles. (For the general treatment of insurance, see item 20 on page 181.) The ratio of expenses to premiums for insuring motor vehicles of all kinds, taken from the summarised annual accounts of insurance companies, is applied to annual estimates of the premiums paid by consumers, based on the Family Expenditure Survey. Quarterly figures are interpolated and projected. As no price index is available for the costs of managing the insurance, the estimates are revalued at constant prices by means of the general consumer price index.

(v) *Motor vehicle and driving licences.* Estimates of consumers' expenditure on motor car and motor cycle licences are based annually on the Family Expenditure Survey and interpolated quarterly on the basis of Ministry of Transport returns of total receipts by licensing authorities for motor car and motor cycle licences. Figures of receipts in Great Britain for driving licences are also available quarterly from the Ministry of Transport and additions are made for receipts in Northern Ireland. All of these are taken to be personal. Expenditure on motor vehicle and driving licences is revalued at constant prices by means of index numbers compiled from changes in the licensing rates.

(vi) *Driving lessons.* A benchmark estimate based on information supplied by the Motor Schools Association of the number of pupils attending driving schools is projected backwards and forwards by an index of the number of people taking driving tests in order to obtain estimates of the number of pupils attending driving schools each year. Expenditure at current or constant prices is obtained by multiplying together the estimated number of pupils, the estimated average number of hours of tuition per pupil and the estimated average current or base-year cost per hour of tuition. Quarterly figures are interpolated and projected with an adjustment when exceptional weather conditions have occurred.

(vii) *Driving test fees.* Figures of receipts of driving test fees are available annually from the Ministry of Transport. All of these receipts are taken to be from persons. Quarterly estimates are interpolated and projected. Expenditure is revalued at constant prices by an index of the changes in test fees.

(viii) *Ministry of Transport tests of roadworthiness.* Quarterly figures of the number of initial tests carried out and the number of cars which failed the test are provided by the Ministry of Transport. Expenditure at current prices is obtained by multiplying (a) the number of cars tested by the cost of the test, (b) the number of cars which passed the test by the cost of the Ministry of Transport certificate, and (c) the estimated number which are re-tested by the estimated average cost of re-testing and the cost of the certificate. At present all the expenditure is assumed to be personal because newer cars do not have to be tested and business expenditure is thought to be small. In estimating expenditure at constant prices, the number of cars tested is multiplied by charges in the base year.

14. Travel

Rail. The estimates of consumers' expenditure on rail travel are based annually and quarterly on figures of passenger receipts by the British Railways Board and London Transport Board. Additions are made for travel in Northern Ireland, and deductions based on the National Travel Survey of the Ministry of Transport are made for public authorities' and business expenditure.

Receipts for each of the main fare categories on British Rail and London Transport railways are revalued at constant prices by indices of estimated average receipts per passenger mile. The resulting estimates at constant prices are thus proportional to the estimates of passenger miles travelled in each of the fare categories.

Bus, coach and tram. Expenditure on these forms of travel is taken from annual and quarterly statistics of passenger receipts compiled by the Ministry of Transport and published in the *Monthly Digest of Statistics*. To the figures as published, which relate to Great Britain, 2 per cent is added for expenditure in Northern Ireland and an arbitrary allowance of 3 per cent is deducted for public authorities' and business expenditure.

Expenditure is revalued at constant prices separately for travel by London Transport, local authorities' transport and other road operators' transport. The corresponding index numbers of the average level of fares on bus and coach services are used, as prepared by the Ministry of Transport and published in *Passenger Transport in Great Britain*.

Other travel. This consists of travel by (i) taxis and private hire, including contract hire, cars; (ii) air; (iii) sea; and (iv) car ferries.

(i) *Taxis and private hire cars*. A benchmark estimate of consumers' expenditure on taxis and cars hired with driver has been made for 1964, based on the results of the National Travel Survey. This estimate is projected backwards and forwards on a smooth trend broadly in line with changes in the number of taxis licensed to give estimates of expenditure at constant prices. These estimates are revalued at current prices by means of the implied consumer price index for expenditure on the running costs of motor vehicles. Expenditure on the hire of self-drive cars is still largely guessed before 1961. Subsequently, the results of the Family Expenditure Survey form the basis of the estimates at current prices. These current price estimates are also revalued at constant prices by the price index for the running costs of motor vehicles. Quarterly figures are interpolated and projected.

(ii) *Air*. Estimates from 1964 of quarterly expenditure on travel (including emigration) by air between the United Kingdom and places abroad other than the Irish Republic are based on the results of the Board of Trade International Passenger Survey. Expenditure is revalued at constant prices by means of an index of average fares based on the average revenue per passenger mile of British European Airways and British Overseas Airways Corporation.

For years before 1964 annual expenditure (excluding emigration) has been calculated from estimates of the number of residents returning to the United Kingdom from visits abroad, the average length of journey, and average fare per passenger mile, using as a benchmark the figures for 1964 based on the International Passenger Survey. For 1962 and 1963 the numbers of United Kingdom residents returning from non-business visits abroad have been derived from the Board of Trade International Passenger Survey. For earlier years it has been assumed that some two-thirds of the numbers on European routes and one-third of the numbers on other routes were United Kingdom residents travelling for personal reasons. Rough estimates of the average length of journey on European and non-European air routes were made from the total number of passenger journeys (whether by residents or non-residents), classified broadly according to country of embarkation. The average fare per passenger mile of journeys on European routes was taken to be equivalent to that for journeys by BEA; for journeys outside Europe the average BOAC fare was taken. Expenditure by emigrants before 1964 has been calculated from numbers, as shown in the annual reports of the Overseas Migration Board, multiplied by average fares on international services derived from the accounts of BOAC and BEA. Estimates of expenditure have been revalued at constant prices by using the average fares per passenger mile for the base year instead of those for the current year.

Expenditure on travel by air between the United Kingdom and the Irish Republic is calculated annually from the number of visits, the average length of journey and the average fare per passenger mile. The total number of non-business visitors arriving in the Irish Republic from the United Kingdom is taken from statistics published annually in the *Irish Trade Journal*. The average length of journey is calculated from statistics of air travel between Dublin and the United Kingdom given in the *Irish Statistical Abstract* and the BEA average fare per passenger mile is applied. Quarterly figures are interpolated on the basis of the total passenger movement by air between the United Kingdom and Ireland. Expenditure at constant prices is estimated by using the average fare per passenger mile in the base year instead of that in the current year.

Expenditure on air travel within the United Kingdom, including travel between Great Britain and Northern Ireland, the Isle of Man and the Channel Islands, is obtained annually by applying the BEA average fare per passenger mile on domestic services to total passenger miles on domestic services as published in the *Monthly Digest of Statistics*. About 40 per cent of this expenditure is taken to be personal. Quarterly figures are interpolated. Expenditure at constant prices is obtained by applying the rates in the base year to the estimated passenger miles flown.

(iii) *Sea*. The annual estimates of expenditure on travel to European countries and local journeys are based on passenger receipts of ships owned by the British Railways Board together with an adjustment for United Kingdom residents travelling on other shipping lines to the Continent and for business travel. This adjustment is based on a comparison for 1965 between numbers travelling by British Rail ships and estimates from the International Passenger Survey of the numbers of United Kingdom residents travelling on the short sea routes for purposes other than business. Local journeys include travel between Great Britain and Northern Ireland, the Irish Republic, the Isle of Man, the Isle of Wight and the Channel Islands. Quarterly figures are interpolated on the basis of numbers of United Kingdom residents travelling on the short sea routes for non-business reasons as recorded by the International Passenger Survey. Expenditure at constant prices is obtained by deflating the current price estimates by an average fare index derived from British Railways Board statistics of passenger receipts and passenger journeys.

For the long sea routes information was available up to 1959, from detailed ships' manifests required under the Merchant Shipping Acts, on the number of journeys by United Kingdom residents and emigrants analysed by class of fare and route. Detailed estimates of expenditure at current and constant prices were built up by combining the number of journeys with estimated average fares derived from shipping companies' leaflets. Expenditure by United Kingdom residents and by emigrants were calculated separately. In 1960 the ships' manifests were simplified and supplemented by a card system for recording information about United Kingdom and Commonwealth passengers. These cards did not yield information in sufficient detail to enable the earlier system of estimating expenditure to be continued. Consequently for the years 1960 to 1963 the estimates of expenditure at constant prices were derived by projecting the 1959 estimates of expenditure by United Kingdom residents and emigrants by the total number of journeys in each category. The resulting series was converted to a series at current prices by means of a weighted index of fares, the weights being based on the detailed information for 1959.

Following the amendment of the merchant shipping regulations, sea cards were not required for Commonwealth citizens travelling on the long sea routes, so that after 1963 statistics which distinguished United Kingdom residents and emigrants from other travellers were no longer available. From 1964 onwards, therefore, the number of journeys is taken as twice the number of United Kingdom residents returning from non-business trips abroad on the long sea routes as recorded quarterly in the International Passenger Survey. Numbers of emigrants are provided annually by the General Register Office. In calculating the index of fares used to convert the volume series to current prices, the weights for the major routes are now based on the numbers of travellers and emigrants in the current year.

The proportion of expenditure by United Kingdom residents travelling on the long sea routes which is assumed to be personal has been progressively increased from 25 per cent in the immediate post-war years to 60 per cent at present on the basis of information derived from the International Passenger Survey on purpose and place of visit. All expenditure by emigrants is taken to be personal. Quarterly figures are interpolated and projected.

Expenditure on day trips is calculated quarterly by multiplying numbers of passengers (estimated from Board of Trade statistics of 'no passport' excursions) by average fares, based on British Railways Board and shipping companies' leaflets. Expenditure at constant prices is calculated by multiplying the number of passengers by the average fare in the base year.

The quarterly estimates of expenditure on pleasure cruises are calculated by multiplying the numbers of passengers travelling on cruises, which are provided by the Board of Trade, by estimated average fares, which are based on shipping companies' leaflets. Expenditure at constant prices is calculated by multiplying the numbers of passengers by the average fare in the base year. All expenditure on pleasure cruises is assumed to be personal.

(iv) *Car ferries*. This item covers the transport of accompanied cars by rail, sea and air, internally and to other countries. All of the expenditure is taken to be personal.

Estimates of expenditure on internal rail ferries are based on statistics provided by the British Railways Board of numbers of cars carried and total receipts from these services. Of the total, half is assumed to relate to the cost of transporting cars as distinct from the fares of the occupants which are included with rail travel. The estimates are revalued at constant prices by multiplying the number of cars carried by the average cost of transport in the base year.

The numbers of cars transported on sea routes to and from the Continent are provided annually by Customs and Excise. An estimate of cars owned by non-residents, assumed to be a quarter of the total number departing, is deducted. The average fares are based on statistics, provided by the British Railways Board, of the numbers of accompanied cars and receipts on British Rail's Continental sea services. Estimates for other sea routes (Northern Ireland, Irish Republic, Isle of Wight, Channel Islands, etc.) are based on annual figures provided by the British Railways Board of their receipts for accompanied cars. The estimates for Continental and other sea routes are both revalued at constant prices by means of an index of the average fares on British Rail's Continental sea services.

Annual expenditure on air ferries at current and constant prices is estimated by combining figures of the volume of traffic in ton miles provided by the Board of Trade with estimates of the average fares per ton mile.

Quarterly figures for car ferries are interpolated and projected.

15. Communication services

Postal. Postage on correspondence and parcels and the poundage on postal and money orders.

Estimates of the volume of traffic and of total expenditure at current and constant prices are made quarterly by the Post Office for the three main categories of postal services, namely correspondence, parcels and remittance services. Estimates of the number of parcels and the average postage per parcel are made on the basis of a sample which in 1967 comprised 0·2 per cent of traffic. Total expenditure on parcel post is calculated from the number of parcels multiplied by the average postage per parcel. The total poundage on money and postal orders is obtained as part of the routine accounting system. Expenditure on correspondence is arrived at by deducting expenditure on parcels and remittance services from total postal receipts. On the basis of sample surveys this is further divided between registration fees, recorded delivery service, pools correspondence, postcards, newspapers and samples, printed papers, and letters. Broad assumptions are made about the percentage of total expenditure which is personal for each of the three main categories of postal services. These percentages are, however, subject to a margin of error.

Expenditure at constant prices on parcels is obtained by applying the average postage per parcel in the base year to the estimates of the volume of traffic. Expenditure on remittance services is obtained by multiplying the total poundage by the ratio of average poundage in the base year to average poundage in the current year. Expenditure on correspondence is revalued at constant prices by means of an index of the average expenditure per item for each type of correspondence.

Telephone and telegraph. Telephone charges, telegrams and cablegrams.

Estimates of expenditure on telephone rentals and calls at current and constant prices are prepared quarterly by the Post Office. A quarterly record of telephone subscribers classified by the Post Office into residence rate subscribers and business rate subscribers forms the basis of the allocation between personal and business expenditure. It is not known to what extent rentals of telephones installed in private residences and calls made from them may be part of business expenditure and no deduction is made. It is assumed that all calls made from public call boxes are personal although it is realised that a small, though unknown, number are business calls.

For those subscribers without STD (subscriber trunk dialling) facilities the number of local calls per subscriber is estimated from a sample analysis of telephone accounts, and the number of trunk calls and their average value from a sample analysis of operator-controlled trunk calls. Since 1962, when STD facilities started to become generally available to private subscribers, the total number of STD call units per subscriber, covering both trunk and local calls, has been estimated from a sample of telephone accounts. A call unit is an accounting unit valued in 1967 at 2d. From this information—on the number of subscribers, the number of calls or call units per subscriber, the rental and call charges *plus* the receipts from public call boxes—estimates of consumers' expenditure at current prices are calculated. These are converted to constant prices by dividing by current-weighted price indices.

Counts of telegrams are available quarterly and continuous sampling of the traffic since 1956 makes possible an analysis of its main characteristics. In particular an allocation between personal and business traffic can be made. The average price of a telegram, also derived from the sample of traffic, is then applied to the numbers to give estimates of consumers' expenditure at current prices. Prior to 1956, periodic samples were used as a basis for estimates of consumers' expenditure. Consumers' expenditure at constant prices is obtained by deflating the current price estimates by a price index of telegram tariffs.

16. Entertainment and recreational services

Cinema. Admissions to cinemas.

Figures of box office takings by cinemas in Great Britain have been compiled quarterly by the Board of Trade since 1950. After adding two per cent for takings in Northern Ireland, these provide the figures of consumers' expenditure on cinema admissions. The estimates are revalued at constant prices by the 'Admission to cinemas' component of the index of retail prices.

Other. This item consists of four parts: (i) other admissions and recreational services, (ii) renting of television and radio sets, (iii) relay of vision and sound, and (iv) television and radio licences.

(i) *Other admissions and recreational services.* That is, admissions to theatres, concert halls, sporting events, dance halls, skating rinks, exhibitions, and all other places of public amusement; hire of horses, pleasure boats; and other recreational services.

From 1957 annual estimates are based on the results of the Family Expenditure Survey. The estimates are not derived quarter by quarter from the survey because of sampling fluctuations but the annual estimates are broken down according to the quarterly pattern of expenditure shown over several years by the survey. Figures for the latest quarters are projected provisionally.

Before 1957 the estimates were based on tax receipts for the forms of entertainment which bore tax but there was little information on which to base the estimates for other amusements, which were largely guessed.

The estimates are revalued at constant prices by items from the 'Other entertainment' section of the index of retail prices.

(ii) *Renting of television and radio sets.* A benchmark estimate from the censuses of distribution is projected forwards quarterly by figures of the numbers of sets hired out as an index of volume, and by the television set rental component of the index of retail prices as an index of price. Information on the number of sets hired out by specialist rental companies is collected by the Board of Trade. Expenditure at constant prices consists of the base year estimate projected forwards by the index of volume. The purchase of television and radio sets for hiring out is part of gross domestic fixed capital formation by the rental businesses.

(iii) *Relay of sound and vision.* A benchmark estimate of expenditure on the wired relay of sound and vision, based on Post Office records of the number of subscribers multiplied by an estimated average subscription, is projected forwards quarterly by figures of the numbers of subscribers as an index of volume, and by an estimated index of price. Information on the number of subscribers to specialist relay companies is collected by the Board of Trade. Expenditure at constant prices consists of the base year estimate projected forwards by the index of volume.

(iv) *Radio and television licences.* Figures of receipts for radio and for television licences are available quarterly from the Post Office; they are revalued at constant prices by indices of the licence rates.

17. Domestic service

This includes expenditure on the wages, in cash and kind, national insurance contributions and selective employment tax for indoor and outdoor private domestic servants. It excludes expenditure ranking as business expenses, for example by doctors and dentists, and pocket money paid to au pair girls.

The figure included in consumers' expenditure corresponds to the estimate of domestic servants' income incorporated in total personal income, except for selective employment tax. A description of the estimate of income is given on page 140. Expenditure at constant prices is estimated by applying estimated average earnings in the base year to the estimates of numbers employed.

18. Catering (meals and accommodation)

This group comprises meals and accommodation in commercial establishments and meals, but not accommodation, in non-commercial establishments. Accommodation in non-commercial establishments is included in the rent paid by, or imputed to, private non-profit-making bodies (under 'Rent, rates and water charges'). Expenditure on alcoholic drink in these establishments is excluded but expenditure on other drinks is included.

The group covers personal expenditure on:
(i) meals and accommodation in hotels, holiday camps, boarding houses, restaurants (including those in retail shops), cafes, fish and chip shops, clubs, and canteens whether operated individually (for example by industrial firms) or by catering contractors;
(ii) meals in maintained schools;
(iii) school milk;
(iv) meals and accommodation in profit-making schools and, for staff only, in national health service hospitals; but meals only in universities and other non-profit-making establishments;
(v) accommodation in holiday flats, bungalows, caravans, etc.; fees for holiday caravan and camping sites.

Included in the estimates are the face value of luncheon vouchers, the net cost to employers of meals provided in canteens, and the value of food and accommodation provided free to the staff of catering establishments. These items, together with the net cost to the government of meals and milk in schools (treated as grants to persons) appear on both sides of the personal income and expenditure account. Expenditure on meals and accommodation by public authorities, for example in hospitals, prisons, borstal institutions, residential schools and homes for the aged, is not included here but forms part of public authorities' current expenditure on goods and services.

Estimates from 1964 are made as follows. For (i), monthly statistics of the turnover in Great Britain of (a) licensed hotels and holiday camps, (b) restaurants, cafes, fish and chip shops and (c) canteens are used to project forwards benchmark figures derived from the 1964 catering inquiry. Expenditure in unlicensed hotels and boarding houses in 1964 is estimated from an inquiry made by the Government Social Survey; it is assumed to change in line with expenditure in licensed hotels and holiday camps. The catering statistics include the face value of luncheon vouchers but additions are made to the benchmark figures for the net cost to employers of meals provided in canteens (using the Ministry of Labour inquiry into employers' total labour costs in 1964), for food and accommodation provided free to staff, and for expenditure in Northern

Ireland. Deductions are made for business expenditure but there is little firm evidence on which to base these deductions. For (ii), estimates are based on information collected by the Department of Education and Science on the numbers and gross costs of meals in maintained schools. The Department of Education and Science also provides the information for (iii); the milk provided in schools is valued at the cost to the government. For (iv), estimates are based on payments by staff to national health service hospitals for rent, board and lodging; on numbers of day and boarding pupils in private schools and of students in university hostels; and on information from the census of population on numbers in miscellaneous communal establishments. Rough additions are made for (v), based on surveys which have been carried out from time to time on holiday accommodation.

The estimates for the years before 1964 are based on the estimates by the Ministry of Agriculture, Fisheries and Food of 'Other personal expenditure on food' (described on pages 155 to 160) together with estimates derived from Inland Revenue statistics of wages, salaries and gross profits in hotels and catering firms and information collected by the Department of Education and Science on the cost of school meals.

Expenditure in all years is revalued at constant prices by an index of the cost of food, derived from the estimates by the Ministry of Agriculture, Fisheries and Food of non-household personal expenditure on food at current and constant prices, price indices of the miscellaneous goods and services assumed to be bought by hotels and catering establishments, and a specially constructed index of average earnings in hotels and catering establishments. The estimates at constant prices are not shown separately because of uncertainties in revaluing the service element of meals and accommodation by the index of average earnings.

19. Wages, salaries, etc. paid by private non-profit-making bodies (excluding catering)

This item covers the wages, salaries, national insurance contributions and selective employment tax paid to or on behalf of their employees by private non-profit-making bodies serving persons. The general treatment of these bodies is described on page 99. The institutions covered in this item are universities, direct grant and other non-profit-making schools and colleges, churches, charitable institutions, trade unions, friendly societies, social clubs, etc. Wages and salaries paid by non-commercial catering institutions are excluded since they are an element of consumers' expenditure on 'Alcoholic drink' and 'Catering'. The item appears on both sides of the personal income and expenditure account. Fairly detailed annual information is available for universities, direct grant schools, trade unions and friendly societies; the remainder of the estimate is based on annual PAYE statistics from the Inland Revenue. Quarterly figures are interpolated and projected.

Expenditure is revalued at constant prices by an index of wages and salaries.

20. Insurance

This group covers life assurance, insurance of the contents of dwellings, accident and miscellaneous insurance. Insurance of the structure of dwellings is included in 'Maintenance, repairs and improvements by occupiers' and of motor vehicles in 'Running costs of motor vehicles'.

The estimates of consumers' expenditure in each year on all forms of life assurance are taken to be the sum of the expenses of management and shareholders' surplus appropriate to life business transacted within the United Kingdom by life assurance and industrial assurance companies, collecting societies and superannuation funds established in the United Kingdom. The estimates are mainly derived from the summarised accounts of these institutions but the expenses of superannuation funds are estimated from Inland Revenue data.

A general explanation of the treatment of the funds of these institutions is given on page 100. The estimate of consumers' expenditure on life assurance in 1964, the latest year for which full information was available for the 1967 Blue Book, is related to the estimate of the 'Administrative costs, etc.' of life assurance and superannuation funds given in the revenue account of the funds (Table 24 of the 1967 Blue Book, see page 113) as follows:

	£ million
Consumers' expenditure on insurance (Table 27)......	238
less Expenditure on insurance of contents of dwellings, accident and miscellaneous insurance............	−18
Consumers' expenditure on life assurance, etc.........	220
plus Payments of United Kingdom taxes on the investment income of the funds	70
Administrative costs, etc. of life assurance and superannuation funds (Table 24).....................	290

The estimates of consumers' expenditure on other forms of insurance are similarly taken to be the sum of the management expenses and the increase in 'additional' reserves appropriate to business transacted within the United Kingdom. Repairs and replacements of the objects insured are included in consumers' expenditure on the items concerned. In estimating consumers' expenditure on insuring the contents of dwellings, the ratio of expenses to premiums for fire insurance, taken from the summarised annual accounts of insurance companies, is applied to annual estimates of the premiums paid by consumers for this insurance, based on the Family Expenditure Survey. Consumers' expenditure on accident and miscellaneous insurance is taken to be 5 per cent of the expenses of these forms of insurance as derived from the summarised accounts of insurance companies. Quarterly figures are interpolated and projected.

As no price index is available for the costs of managing the insurance, the expenses of management are revalued at constant prices by the general consumer price index.

21. Other services

The estimates for some of the items in this group, which amounted in total to some £1,070 million in 1966, are weak and separate figures for them are not shown in the Blue Book tables. However, to give an indication of their relative importance, a figure (rough in some cases) of current expenditure in 1966 on each item is shown below against the appropriate sub-heading.

(i) *Medical services to private patients* (£40 million). This item consists of the fees paid by private patients (and by insurance companies on behalf of private patients) to doctors, dentists, nurses, chiropodists, osteopaths, etc., and fees charged by private nursing homes. Annual estimates are broadly based on the Family Expenditure Survey which, however, shows high sampling fluctuations for this item. Some allowance must also be made for the possibility that households containing a sick person do not respond well to the survey. Independent studies provide an occasional check on the estimates. Quarterly figures are interpolated and projected. The revaluation of expenditure at constant prices is guessed.

(ii) *The national health service* (£30 million, but £55 million in 1964 when there were prescription charges). This item consists of all payments by persons for goods and services provided under the national health service; that is, hospital, specialist and ancillary services (including private beds in national health service hospitals), pharmaceutical services (including prescription charges), general dental services and supplementary ophthalmic services. The figures are obtained from the published annual accounts (see page 302, item 22). Quarterly figures are interpolated and projected. The estimates are revalued at constant prices in the same way as public authorities' expenditure on goods and services on these items of the national health service (see page 358).

(iii) *Private education and training* (£65 million). Schools and other educational establishments are regarded as providing a composite service to consumers (see page 154). The part of expenditure included in this item covers tuition fees only; it excludes expenditure on food and accommodation. The tuition fees included in the item are those which are paid to profit-making institutions or persons, that is, profit-making schools and profit-making educational and training services of all kinds, such as correspondence courses, foreign language tuition, tennis coaching, etc. Direct grant schools and all independent senior schools which are recognised as efficient by the Department of Education and Science are taken to be non-profit-making and fees paid to them are not included in this item (the wages and salaries of their employees are included in item 19 above). Benchmark estimates of tuition fees paid to other independent schools in 1959/60 based on published information on fees and numbers of pupils (separately for boys and girls, and in two age groups) are projected forwards annually by indices of the numbers of pupils in these age groups at the schools. The resulting volume series are converted to series at current prices by annual price indices of tuition fees at samples of the appropriate kinds of school. Quarterly figures are interpolated and projected. Expenditure at constant prices consists of the estimates for the base year projected forwards by the indices of volume. Rough additions, based on information from the Family Expenditure Survey, are made for consumers' expenditure on tuition fees for other profit-making educational and training services.

(iv) *Laundry, launderettes, dry cleaning and dyeing* (£110 million). The annual estimates from 1957 are based on the Family Expenditure Survey. Because of sampling fluctuations, quarterly estimates are based on the average quarterly pattern of expenditure shown over several years by the survey. Estimates for the latest quarters are projected. In estimating expenditure before 1957 use was made of the Ministry of Labour household budget inquiry for 1953-54 and various special surveys carried out by the Social Survey. Expenditure is revalued at constant prices by the appropriate sections of the index of retail prices.

(v) *Miscellaneous repair services* (£120 million). This item covers repairs to footwear, clothing, radio and television sets, domestic appliances, cycles, furniture, watches, etc. The annual estimates from 1957 are based on the Family Expenditure Survey and quarterly figures are interpolated and projected. In estimating expenditure before 1957, use was made of various special surveys carried out by the Social Survey, and the Ministry of Labour household budget inquiry for 1953-54. Expenditure is revalued at constant prices by appropriate sections of the index of retail prices.

(vi) *Second-hand goods* (£20 million). This item comprises the dealers' margins on the transfer of ownership of second-hand goods other than motor vehicles. It is assumed that all the goods are transferred between consumers, so that purchases *less* sales are equal to the dealers' margins. Expenditure on second-hand caravans is estimated quarterly from the number of hire purchase contracts for used caravans compiled by Hire Purchase Information Limited, and the estimated average dealers' margin. It is assumed that the number of used caravans bought on hire purchase represents half the total number of used caravans bought and that purchases of used caravans on business account are negligible. Estimates at constant prices are based on numbers multiplied by the estimated average dealers' margin in the base year. Benchmark estimates of the dealers' margins on sales of other second-hand goods are based on information from the censuses of distribution, allowances being made for establishments not covered by the census (mainly auction sale-rooms) and for sales in Northern Ireland. Estimates for years between censuses are based on the trends in total expenditure on second-hand goods shown by the Family Expenditure Survey. Quarterly figures are interpolated and projected. A price index corresponding to the index used for deflating expenditure on new furniture is used to estimate expenditure at constant prices.

(vii) *Hire of domestic appliances* (£5 million). This comprises gas and electricity meter rents and the hire of appliances from the gas and electricity boards. Annual information on the revenue received for these items is published in the Ministry of Power *Statistical Digest*. It is assumed that the ratio of personal to total expenditure on these items is the same as the ratio of domestic consumers to the total number of consumers. Quarterly figures are interpolated and projected. Expenditure is revalued at constant prices by the price indices for gas and electric cookers in the index of retail prices.

(viii) *Miscellaneous household services* (£35 million). This item comprises removals, storage, chimney sweeping, window cleaning, etc. Rough estimates of expenditure on this group of services have been based on the results of various sample surveys, but the item is mainly guessed.

(ix) *Hairdressing, manicure, beauty care* (£170 million). The annual estimates are based on the Family Expenditure Survey. Because of sampling fluctuations, quarterly estimates are based on the average quarterly pattern shown over several years by the survey. Estimates for the latest quarters are projected. In estimating expenditure before 1957 use was made of special sample surveys and of the Ministry of Labour household budget inquiry for 1953-54. Expenditure is revalued at constant prices by the appropriate section of the index of retail prices.

(x) *Undertaking* (£30 million). Consumers' expenditure on this item is estimated quarterly by multiplying the number of deaths by the estimated average cost of a funeral. Expenditure at constant prices is estimated by multiplying the number of deaths by the average cost in the base year.

(xi) *Betting and gaming* (£200 million). Consumers' expenditure on betting is the cost to persons taking part of all forms of gambling activity. It is thus measured by the amount staked *less* the part returned in the form of winnings, that is the net loss incurred. This net loss is in turn equivalent to the net takings of persons engaged either wholly or part-time in the industry *plus* the amount taken by the government in the form of betting duties. The item excludes, for example, raffles organised for charity. The costs of operating the premium bond scheme are excluded; they are part of public authorities' current expenditure on goods and services.

Consumers' expenditure on football pools, fixed-odds football betting, horse and greyhound race betting with bookmakers on and off-course (including betting shops), and greyhound racing totalisators is calculated quarterly from tax receipts, from which stakes can be derived. Information is available on the percentage of stakes retained by the pools promoters and by the greyhound racing totalisators. Amounts retained by bookmakers are assumed to be proportional to gross stakes. Amounts retained by horse racing totalisators are published in the annual reports of the Horserace Totalisator Board, quarterly figures being interpolated and projected. Fixed-odds football betting was not taxed before 1964 and betting with bookmakers was not taxed before October 1966. There is no firm basis for estimating consumers' expenditure on these items in earlier years; the figures included have been based on information from the annual review of the Churches' Council on Gambling.

In estimating expenditure on bingo, gaming machines, roulette, chemin-de-fer, card games in clubs, gaming in amusement arcades, fun fairs, etc., use has been made of the *Report on Enquiry into Gaming under Section 2 of Finance Act 1963* (Cmnd. 2275); the information on permits and licences published annually under the Betting, Gaming and Lotteries Act, 1963; the *Report of the Royal Commission on Betting, Lotteries and Gaming* (Cmd. 8190); the annual reviews of the Churches' Council on Gambling; and licence receipts for gaming machines and gaming premises.

Expenditure is revalued at constant prices first by adjusting for changes since the base year in rates of tax and in retention rates, and secondly by adjusting for changes in the general consumer price index.

(xii) *Fees paid to local authorities* (£110 million). This item consists of payments made by persons to local authorities for services connected with items such as education (but not school meals), care of the aged and handicapped including accommodation in houses and hostels, car parking fees, use of baths, parks, public libraries, etc. Receipts for these items are given separately each year in *Local Government Financial Statistics*. The estimate is necessarily rough as an assumption has to be made in each case about the proportion of receipts attributable to personal expenditure. Quarterly figures are interpolated and projected. Expenditure is revalued at constant prices by using a general index of wage rates.

(xiii) *Bank charges* (£20 million). A benchmark estimate of actual payments of bank charges by consumers in 1963, based on a comparison of data from the Family Expenditure Survey and from banking sources, is projected backwards and forwards by an annual index of bank debit clearings. The quarterly charges are interpolated and allocated to the second and fourth quarters of each year. Charges are revalued at constant prices by the general consumer price index.

(xiv) *Stamp duties* (£30 million). This item consists of duties on leases, mortgages, cheques, and on transfers of stocks and shares and other financial assets. Stamp duties incurred in the transfer of ownership of land and buildings are excluded; they are treated as gross domestic fixed capital formation. Annual estimates of consumers' expenditure are made by extracting the appropriate items from the figures published in the annual reports of the Inland Revenue and the *Finance Accounts of Northern Ireland*, while making assumptions about the ratio of personal to business expenditure in each case. The personal ratio for stamp duties on stocks and shares is based on analyses of transactions in financial assets. The figures of transactions in financial assets also provide the basis for the quarterly estimates of stamp duties on stocks and shares; quarterly estimates of other stamp duties are interpolated and projected. The estimates are revalued at constant prices by indices of the rates of duty, together with indices of stocks and share prices.

(xv) *Stockbrokers' charges* (£35 million). Estimates of stockbrokers' charges from 1965 are based quarterly on the statistics of transactions in stocks and shares published in *Financial Statistics* together with estimates, given in the *Stock Exchange Journal* for June 1965, of rates of commission paid on transactions. Analyses of these transactions provide a basis for estimating the proportions of total charges which are paid by the personal sector. Allowance is made for any changes in standard rates of commission as published in the *Stock Exchange Year Book*. Estimates for years before 1965 have been obtained by projecting the 1965 estimate backwards in line with total stamp duties on stocks and shares, allowing for changes in rates of stamp duty and commission. Stockbrokers' charges are revalued at constant prices by means of an index of stocks and share prices, and by changes in rates of commission.

(xvi) *Fines and fees* (£15 million). This item covers fines paid to county courts, fines for motoring offences, passport fees, etc. Receipts for these items are given separately each year in the *Appropriation Accounts*. The estimate is necessarily rough as an assumption has to be made in each case about the proportion of receipts attributable to personal expenditure. Quarterly figures are interpolated and projected. This item is not revalued at constant prices.

(xvii) *Other miscellaneous services* (£35 million). This item includes legal fees (other than those for the transfer of ownership of land and buildings which are treated as part of gross domestic fixed capital formation), pawnbrokers' charges, services of photographers, auctioneers, etc., transport of luggage and animals, cloakroom fees, subscriptions to libraries, etc. There is very little information about these items and the amounts included are guesses.

22. Income in kind not included elsewhere

This group comprises the estimated value of food and clothing issued to the Forces and auxiliary services and of food supplied to merchant seamen and fishermen. The estimates are the same as those included in personal income. The expenditure is classified under 'Other goods' in the figures of consumers' expenditure which are published quarterly. The value of the income in kind of the Forces is estimated quarterly by the service departments by analysing expenditure under different Votes. The value of the food supplied to merchant seamen and fishermen is estimated very roughly on the basis of employment in the merchant service and the fishing industry. Expenditure is revalued at constant prices by the implied consumer price index for household expenditure on food.

G

23. *Expenditure by foreign tourists, etc. in the United Kingdom*

By definition, estimates of consumers' expenditure should exclude all purchases made by non-residents. Since it is impossible to make a separate deduction for each category of expenditure, a single deduction is made for total expenditure by overseas visitors on holiday and on business, by the Forces of other countries stationed in the United Kingdom, by employees of overseas governments, and by other non-residents in this country.

The amount of the deduction for visitors is given quarterly by the 'Travel credits' in the balance of payments accounts, which is estimated from the International Passenger Survey. An additional amount representing personal expenditure by the United States Forces in this country is provided by the U.S. military authorities. The numbers of employees of overseas governments based in this country are provided by the Foreign Office, and the numbers of overseas journalists are available from the *Directory of Newspaper and Magazine Personnel and Data.* These numbers are multiplied by an assumed average personal expenditure. An additional amount should be included for the expenditure of overseas students which forms part of exports of services, but was not included for the 1967 Blue Book. A special price index for revaluing this group at constant prices has been constructed on assumptions about the kinds of goods and services bought.

24. *Consumers' expenditure abroad*

This is a further adjustment needed to complete the estimates of expenditure out of the total personal income of United Kingdom residents. Personal expenditure abroad by travellers from the United Kingdom, by members of the Forces and government employees stationed abroad must be added to the estimates of consumers' expenditure on the items listed above.

Personal expenditure abroad by United Kingdom travellers is estimated quarterly by dividing the 'Travel debits' in the balance of payments accounts between personal and business or official expenditure on the basis of information from the International Passenger Survey. This estimate excludes fare payments on travel to and from the United Kingdom, which are included in consumers' expenditure on travel.

The estimates of personal expenditure by members of the Forces in foreign countries and in NAAFI's and other United Kingdom institutions abroad are based on quarterly information on the pay of Royal Air Force and Army personnel serving abroad, and the total pay of the Navy. Assumptions—which are particularly approximate for the Navy—have to be made about the proportion of pay which is spent abroad. Information on the pay and allowances of government staff based in the United Kingdom and serving abroad is available annually from departments. Assumptions are made about the proportion of pay and allowances which is spent abroad, and quarterly figures are interpolated and projected.

Retail price indices are available for most of the countries visited and special indices have been constructed to represent the kind of goods and services likely to be bought by British travellers. These indices are weighted into a single index by the current distribution by areas of travel debits in the balance of payments accounts, adjusted for changes in exchange rates. This index is used to revalue total consumers' expenditure abroad at constant prices.

RELIABILITY

An attempt to assess the margins of error attaching to the annual estimates of the various items of consumers' expenditure, at current prices, is made in the table following. This should be read in the light of the general discussion on pages 39 to 41 of the significance of these margins of error.

For some items, estimates for earlier years are not as reliable as those for later years. For example, some of the items which have been based from 1957 on the results of the Family Expenditure Survey were based on less regular information before 1957. The grading of the estimates given here relates to the later years. The estimates for the latest year are only slightly less reliable than those for the latest year but one, although some of the most recent estimates are subject to revision as fuller information becomes available.

Apart from routine revisions of this kind there are three broad ways in which more fundamental revisions may arise:

(i) In the method of commodity by commodity estimation gaps are liable to develop in the estimates; for example items on which expenditure was at one time negligible may become significant, and when estimates for these items are brought into the accounts revisions over several years will be made to the commodity groups in which the items are classified. The effect of these revisions is usually to steepen somewhat the trend of the estimates in recent years.

(ii) Estimates which are based on statistics of retail sales and other outlets may need revision in the light of the results of a new census. These revisions may extend back almost to the preceding census.

(iii) A new and more reliable source may show that the level of an estimate is wrong. A judgement has then to be taken as to whether the changes in expenditure shown by the previous source are likely to have been reasonably correct over past years, in which case the general level of the estimates over the past years will be revised while keeping the changes unaltered; or whether the error in the estimates developed over a limited period, in which case revisions to the estimates for this period only are involved, with a consequent revision to the changes.

In general, the estimates of year-to-year changes are more reliable than might appear from the gradings allotted in the table to the absolute values of the estimates (see page 40).

Notwithstanding the large proportion of items graded B or C, the estimates of total consumers' expenditure at current prices are graded A. The superiority of the estimates of total expenditure is due to the probability that errors in the components will to some extent offset each other.

The constant price estimates are generally less reliable than those at current prices because of the impossibility of revaluing expenditure in the finest commodity detail; but it is thought that only a few of the constant price estimates are on this account markedly less reliable than the corresponding current price estimates. A special element of uncertainty arises in the estimates at constant prices, namely that limited allowance has been made for changes in quality (see pages 45 and 153).

Reliability of annual estimates of consumers' expenditure at current prices[1]

A ± less than 3 per cent
B ± 3 per cent to 10 per cent
C ± more than 10 per cent

	Grading[1]	Consumers' expenditure at current prices, 1966 £ million
1. Food (household expenditure):		
Bread and cereals	B	688
Meat and bacon	B	1,476
Fish	B	196
Oils and fats	B	245
Sugar, preserves and confectionery	B	500
Dairy products	B	810
Fruit	B	328
Potatoes and vegetables	B	602
Beverages	B	320
Other manufactured food	B	164
Total	B	5,329
2. Alcoholic drink:		
Beer	B	887
Wines, spirits, cider, etc.	B	630
Total	B	1,517
3. Tobacco:		
Cigarettes	A	1,316
Other	A	188
Total	A	1,504
4. Housing:		
Rent, rates and water charges	B	2,263
Maintenance, repairs and improvements by occupiers	C	502
Total	B	2,765
5. Fuel and light:		
Coal and coke	A	369
Electricity	A	490
Gas	A	233
Other	B	67
Total	A	1,159
6. Clothing:		
Footwear	B	356
Other clothing:		
Men's and boys' wear	B	573
Women's, girls' and infants' wear	B	1,152
Total	B	2,081

[1]For the significance of the reliability gradings see pages 39 to 41.

	Grading[1]	Consumers' expenditure at current prices, 1966 £ million
7. Durable goods:		
Motor cars and motor cycles, new and second-hand	B	773
Furniture and floor coverings	C	502
Radio, electrical and other durable goods	C	523
Total	B	1,798
8. Other household goods:		
Household textiles, soft furnishings and hardware...	C	430
Matches, soap and other cleaning materials, etc.....	B	230
Total	B	660
9. Books, newspapers and magazines:		
Books	B	92
Newspapers	A	203
Magazines......................................	B	72
Total	B	367
10. Chemists' goods...............................	C	339
11. Miscellaneous recreational goods	C	482
12. Other miscellaneous goods	C	332
13. Running costs of motor vehicles..................	C	1,052
14. Travel:		
Rail	A	179
Bus, coach and tram	A	381
Other	B	218
Total	A	778
15. Communication services:		
Postal	B	102
Telephone and telegraph	A	122
Total	A	224
16. Entertainment and recreational services:		
Cinema	A	63
Other	B	338
Total	B	401
17. Domestic service	C	104
18. Catering (meals and accommodation)	B	1,377
19. Wages, salaries, etc. paid by private non-profit-making bodies (excluding catering)	B	285
20. Insurance	B	274
21. Other services................................	C	1,070
22. Income in kind not included elsewhere	B	53
23. *less* Expenditure by foreign tourists, etc. in the United Kingdom................................	B	−242
Consumers' expenditure in the United Kingdom	A	23,709
24. Consumers' expenditure abroad	B	407
Total	A	24,116

[1] For the significance of the reliability gradings see pages 39 to 41.

ANNEX

SUMMARY OF THE SOURCES AND METHODS USED

	Estimates at current prices	
	Annual	Quarterly
1. Food (household expenditure)	As quarterly estimates	Statistics of supplies and National Food Survey
2. Alcoholic drink	As quarterly estimates	Quantities on which duty is paid multiplied by estimated average values. (Except for cider and perry for which quantities are based on production data).
3. Tobacco		
Home manufactured	As quarterly estimates	Trade source
Imported products	As quarterly estimates	Quantities imported for home use multiplied by estimated average values
4. Housing		
Rent	Family Expenditure Survey	Interpolation and projection of the annual figures on the basis of changes in the aggregate rateable value of domestic property and changes in the rent component of the index of retail prices
Rates and water charges	Aggregate rateable value of domestic property multiplied by the rate poundage	Interpolation and projection of the annual figures on the basis of changes in the aggregate rateable value of domestic property and changes in the rates and water charges component of the index of retail prices
Maintenance, repairs and improvements by occupiers	Family Expenditure Survey	Interpolation and projection of the annual figures
5. Fuel and light		
Coal and coke	As quarterly estimates	Quantities of merchants disposals multiplied by estimated average values
Electricity and gas	As quarterly estimates	Amounts billed and meter collections
Paraffin, fuel oil and liquid gases	As quarterly estimates	Trade source
Wood	No firm basis	No firm basis
6. Clothing and footwear	As quarterly estimates	Benchmark estimate based on census of distribution projected forwards by monthly statistics of retail sales
7. Durable goods		
Motor cars and motor cycles, new and second-hand	As quarterly estimates	Benchmark estimate based on Board of Trade inquiry into the motor trades, projected forwards by monthly statistics of motor trading
Furniture and floor coverings	As quarterly estimates	Benchmark estimate based on census of distribution projected forwards by monthly statistics of retail sales
Radio, electrical and other durable goods	As quarterly estimates	Benchmark estimate based on census of distribution projected forwards by monthly statistics of retail sales

ANNEX

FOR THE ESTIMATES OF CONSUMERS' EXPENDITURE IN 1966

	Estimates at constant prices
1. Food (household expenditure)	Mainly quantities multiplied by average values in base year
2. Alcoholic drink	Quantities multiplied by estimated average values in base year
3. Tobacco	
Home manufactured	Quantities multiplied by estimated average values in base year
Imported products	Quantities multiplied by estimated average values in base year
4. Housing	
Rent	
Rates and water charges	Base-year estimates projected forwards by changes in aggregate rateable value of domestic property
Maintenance, repairs and improvements by occupiers	Current price estimates deflated by appropriate sections of index of retail prices
5. Fuel and light	
Coal and coke	Quantities multiplied by average values in base year
Electricity and gas	Quantities multiplied by average values in base year
Paraffin, fuel oil and liquid gases	Quantities multiplied by average values in base year
Wood	No firm basis
6. Clothing and footwear	Current price estimates deflated by appropriate sections of index of retail prices
7. Durable goods	
Motor cars and motor cycles, new and second-hand	Current price estimates deflated by an index of prices
Furniture and floor coverings	Current price estimates deflated by appropriate sections of index of retail prices
Radio, electrical and other durable goods	Current price estimates deflated by appropriate sections of index of retail prices

	Estimates at current prices	
	Annual	Quarterly
8. Other household goods Household textiles, soft furnishings and hardware	As quarterly estimates	Benchmark estimate based on census of distribution projected forwards by monthly statistics of retail sales
Matches	As quarterly estimates	Quantities charged with duty multiplied by average value in base year and by matches component of the index of retail prices
Soap and other cleaning materials	Family Expenditure Survey	Interpolation and projection of the annual figures
9. Books, newspapers and magazines Books	As quarterly estimates	Trade source for home production and import statistics for imports
Newspapers	Circulation multiplied by price (half-yearly)	Interpolation and projection of the half-yearly figures
Magazines	Circulation multiplied by price (half-yearly)	Interpolation and projection of the half-yearly figures
10. Chemists' goods	As quarterly estimates	Benchmark estimate based on census of distribution projected forwards by monthly statistics of retail sales
11. Miscellaneous recreational goods Caravans	Production multiplied by average value	Interpolation and projection of the annual figures using number of hire purchase contracts as an indicator
Sports goods, records, toys, photographic equipment, etc.	As quarterly estimates	Benchmark estimate based on census of distribution projected forwards by monthly statistics of retail sales
Horticultural goods	Family Expenditure Survey and statistics of supplies	Interpolation and projection of the annual figures
Pet foods	Benchmark estimate based on census of production projected forwards by an index of volume based on production statistics and the food for animals component of the index of retail prices	Interpolation and projection of the annual figures
Other recreational goods	No firm basis	No firm basis
12. Other miscellaneous goods	As quarterly estimates	Benchmark estimate based on census of distribution projected forwards by monthly statistics of retail sales
13. Running costs of motor vehicles Petrol and oil	As quarterly estimates	Trade source
Maintenance, repairs, spare parts and accessories	As quarterly estimates	Benchmark estimate projected forwards by an index of volume based on the estimated quantity of petrol bought by consumers and the maintenance of motor vehicles component of the index of retail prices

	Estimates at constant prices
8. Other household goods	
Household textiles, soft furnishings and hardware	Current price estimates deflated by appropriate sections index of retail prices
Matches	Quantities multiplied by average value in base year
Soap and other cleaning materials	Current price estimates deflated by appropriate sections of index of retail prices
9. Books, newspapers and magazines	
Books	Current price estimates deflated by appropriate section of index of retail prices
Newspapers	Base-year estimate for each main type of newspaper projected forwards by circulation
Magazines	Base-year estimate for each main type of magazine projected forwards by circulation
10. Chemists' goods	Current price estimates deflated by appropriate sections of index of retail prices
11. Miscellaneous recreational goods	
Caravans	Quantities multiplied by average value in base year
Sports goods, records, toys, photographic equipment, etc.	Current price estimates deflated by appropriate sections of index of retail prices
Horticultural goods	Current price estimates deflated by an index of estimated average values
Pet foods	Base-year estimate projected forwards by index of volume based on production statistics
Other recreational goods	No firm basis
12. Other miscellaneous goods	Current price estimates deflated by appropriate sections of index of retail prices
13. Running costs of motor vehicles	
Petrol and oil	Quantities multiplied by average values in base year
Maintenance, repairs, spare parts and accessories	Base-year estimate projected forwards by index of volume based on estimated quantity of petrol bought by consumers

G*

	Estimates at current prices	
	Annual	Quarterly
Garage rents	Family Expenditure Survey	Interpolation and projection of the annual figures
Motor vehicle insurance	Family Expenditure Survey and insurance statistics	Interpolation and projection of the annual figures
Motor vehicle licences	Family Expenditure Survey	Interpolation and projection of the annual figures on the basis of total receipts by licensing authorities
Driving licences	As quarterly estimates	Receipts by licensing authorities
Driving lessons	Estimated numbers multiplied by estimated average fee	Interpolation and projection of the annual figures
Driving test fees	Receipts by central government	Interpolation and projection of the annual figures
Ministry of Transport tests of roadworthiness	As quarterly estimates	Numbers of tests multiplied by fees
14. Travel		
Rail	As quarterly estimates	Passenger receipts
Bus, coach and tram	As quarterly estimates	Passenger receipts
Taxis and cars hired with driver	Benchmark estimate projected by index of volume based on number of taxis licensed and index of running costs of motor vehicles	Interpolation and projection of the annual figures
Hire of self-drive cars	Family Expenditure Survey	Interpolation and projection of the annual figures
Air		
Overseas countries (except Irish Republic)	As quarterly estimates	International Passenger Survey
Irish Republic	Numbers of visitors from G.B. multiplied by estimated length of journey and estimated fare per passenger mile	Interpolation and projection of the annual figures using the total passenger movement between the United Kingdom and the Irish Republic as an indicator
Internal	Passenger miles multiplied by estimated fare per passenger mile	Interpolation and projection of the annual figures
Sea		
Internal and to all European countries	Passenger receipts of British Railways ships and International Passenger Survey	Interpolation and projection of the annual figures using information from International Passenger Survey as an indicator
Non-European countries— United Kingdom residents	As quarterly estimates	Benchmark estimate projected forwards by numbers of travellers from the International Passenger Survey and an index of average fares

	Estimates at constant prices
Garage rents	No firm basis for revaluation
Motor vehicle insurance	Current price estimates deflated by general consumer price index
Motor vehicle licences	Current price estimates deflated by an index of licensing rates
Driving licences	Current price estimates deflated by an index of licensing rates
Driving lessons	Estimated numbers multiplied by average fee in base year
Driving test fees	Current price estimates deflated by an index of fees
Ministry of Transport tests of road-worthiness	Numbers multiplied by fees in base year

14. Travel

Rail	Current price estimates deflated by indices of average receipts per passenger mile
Bus, coach and tram	Current price estimates deflated by indices of average fares per passenger mile
Taxis and cars hired with driver	Benchmark estimate projected by index of volume based on number of taxis licensed
Hire of self-drive cars	Current price estimates deflated by an index of the running costs of motor vehicles
Air	
Overseas countries (except Irish Republic)	Current price estimates deflated by an index of estimated average fares
Irish Republic	Passenger miles multiplied by estimated fare per passenger mile in base year
Internal	Passenger miles multiplied by estimated fare per passenger mile in base year
Sea	
Internal and to all European countries	Current price estimates deflated by an index of average fares
Non-European countries— United Kingdom residents	Numbers of travellers multiplied by estimated average fare in base year

	Estimates at current prices	
	Annual	Quarterly
Non-European countries— United Kingdom emigrants	Benchmark estimate projected forwards by numbers of emigrants provided by the General Register Office and an index of average fares	Interpolation and projection of the annual figures
Day trips	As quarterly estimates	Numbers of passengers multiplied by average fare
Pleasure cruises	As quarterly estimates	Numbers of passengers multiplied by estimated average fare
Car ferries Internal rail	Receipts by British Railways Board	Interpolation and projection of the annual figures
Sea—to Continent	Numbers of cars multiplied by estimated average fare	Interpolation and projection of the annual figures
Sea—to Irish Republic and internal	Receipts by British Railways Board	Interpolation and projection of the annual figures
Air	Volume of traffic multiplied by estimated average fare	Interpolation and projection of the annual figures
15. Communication services Postal	As quarterly estimates	Sample information obtained by the Post Office on receipts
Telephone	As quarterly estimates	Samples of residence rate subscribers' accounts and receipts from public call boxes
Telegraph	As quarterly estimates	Counts of telegrams multiplied by sample estimates of average values
16. Entertainment and recreational services Cinema	As quarterly estimates	Receipts from admissions to cinemas
Other admissions, etc.	Family Expenditure Survey	Interpolation and projection of the annual figures
Renting of television and radio sets	As quarterly estimates	Benchmark estimate based on census of distribution projected forwards by numbers of sets on hire as an index of volume and the television set rental component of the index of retail prices
Relay of sound and vision	As quarterly estimates	Benchmark estimate projected forwards by numbers of subscribers as an index of volume and an index of estimated prices
Radio and television licences	As quarterly estimates	Post Office receipts

	Estimates at constant prices
Non-European countries— United Kingdom emigrants	Numbers of emigrants multiplied by estimated average fare in base year
Day trips	Numbers of passengers multiplied by average fare in base year
Pleasure cruises	Numbers of passengers multiplied by average fare in base year
Car ferries Internal rail	Numbers of cars multiplied by average fare in base year
Sea—to Continent	Current price estimates deflated by an index of average fares on British Rail's Continental services
Sea—to Irish Republic and internal	
Air	Volume of traffic multiplied by average fare in base year
15. Communication services Postal	Estimated postal traffic multiplied by average values in base year
Telephone	Current price estimates deflated by current-weighted price index numbers
Telegraph	Current price estimates deflated by a price index of telegram tariffs
16. Entertainment and recreational services Cinema	Current price estimates deflated by appropriate section of index of retail prices
Other admissions, etc.	Current price estimates deflated by appropriate sections of index of retail prices
Renting of television and radio sets	Base-year estimate projected forwards by numbers of sets on hire as an index of volume
Relay of sound and vision	Base-year estimate projected forwards by numbers of subscribers as an index of volume
Radio and television licences	Current price estimates deflated by an index of licence rates

	Estimates at current prices	
	Annual	Quarterly
17. Domestic service	Benchmark estimate projected forwards by numbers employed as an index of volume and index of estimated average earnings	Interpolation and projection of the annual figures
18. Catering (meals and accommodation)		
Hotels, boarding houses, holiday camps, restaurants, clubs, canteens	As quarterly estimates	Benchmark estimate based on catering inquiry projected forwards by monthly statistics of catering turnover
Meals in maintained schools	Returns to Department of Education and Science	Interpolation and projection of the annual figures
School milk	As quarterly estimates	Estimates by Department of Education and Science
Staff of national health service hospitals	Government receipts	Interpolation and projection of the annual figures
Private schools and universities	Numbers multiplied by estimated average expenditure per head	Interpolation and projection of the annual figures
Other communal establishments, holiday flats, bungalows, caravans, etc.	No firm basis	No firm basis
19. Wages, salaries, etc. paid by private non-profit-making bodies	Accounts of institutions and Inland Revenue statistics	Interpolation and projection of the annual figures
20. Insurance		
Life	Insurance statistics	Interpolation and projection of the annual figures
Other	Insurance statistics and Family Expenditure Survey	Interpolation and projection of the annual figures
21. Other services		
Medical services to private patients	Family Expenditure Survey	Interpolation and projection of the annual figures
National health service payments by patients	Government receipts	Interpolation and projection of the annual figures
Private education and training		
Schools	Benchmark estimate projected forwards by numbers of pupils as an index of volume and an index of tuition fees	Interpolation and projection of the annual figures
Other educational and training services	Family Expenditure Survey	Interpolation and projection of the annual figures
Laundry, launderettes, dry cleaning and dyeing	Family Expenditure Survey	Interpolation and projection of the annual figures on the basis of average quarterly variations from the Family Expenditure Survey
Miscellaneous repair services	Family Expenditure Survey	Interpolation and projection of the annual figures

	Estimates at constant prices
17. Domestic service	Base-year estimate projected forwards by numbers employed as an index of volume
18. Catering (meals and accommodation) Hotels, boarding houses, holiday camps, restaurants, clubs, canteens Meals in maintained schools School milk Staff of national health service hospitals Private schools and universities Other communal establishments, holiday flats, bungalows, caravans, etc.	Current price estimates deflated by an index of prices
19. Wages, salaries, etc. paid by private non-profit-making bodies	Current price estimates deflated by an index of wages and salaries
20. Insurance Life Other	Current price estimates deflated by general consumer price index
21. Other services Medical services to private patients	No firm basis for revaluation
National health service payments by patients	Revalued in the same way as public authorities' expenditure on these items of the national health service
Private education and training Schools	Base-year estimate projected forwards by numbers of pupils as an index of volume
Other educational and training services	No firm basis for revaluation
Laundry, launderettes, dry cleaning and dyeing	Current price estimates deflated by appropriate sections of index of retail prices
Miscellaneous repair services	Current price estimates deflated by appropriate sections of index of retail prices

	Estimates at current prices	
	Annual	Quarterly
Second-hand goods Caravans	As quarterly estimates	Based on numbers of hire purchase contracts and estimated average dealers' margin
Other	Family Expenditure Survey and census of distribution	Interpolation and projection of the annual figures
Hire of domestic appliances	Statistics from electricity and gas boards	Interpolation and projection of the annual figures
Miscellaneous household services	No firm basis	No firm basis
Hairdressing	Family Expenditure Survey	Interpolation and projection of the annual figures on the basis of average quarterly variations from the Family Expenditure Survey
Undertaking	As quarterly estimates	Number of deaths multiplied by estimated average cost of funeral
Betting Football pools, fixed odds football betting, betting with bookmakers on and off-course (including betting shops), greyhound racing totalisators	As quarterly estimates	Based on government receipts of tax
Horserace totalisators	Horserace Totalisator Board statistics	Interpolation and projection of the annual figures
Bingo and gaming	No firm basis	No firm basis
Fees paid to local authorities	*Local Government Financial Statistics*	Interpolation and projection of the annual figures
Bank charges	Benchmark estimate projected forwards on the basis of bank debit clearings	Interpolation and projection of the annual figures, allocating charges to the second and fourth quarters
Stamp duties	Receipts by Inland Revenue	On stocks and shares: interpolation and projection of the annual figures on the basis of quarterly figures of transactions in stocks and shares. Other: interpolation and projection of the annual figures
Stockbrokers' charges	As quarterly estimates	Quarterly values of transactions in stocks and shares multiplied by estimated rates of commission
Fines and fees	Receipts by central government	Interpolation and projection of the annual figures
Other miscellaneous services	No firm basis	No firm basis
22. Income in kind not included elsewhere	As quarterly estimates	Mainly statistics from the defence departments
23. Expenditure by foreign tourists, etc. in the United Kingdom	As quarterly estimates	Mainly International Passenger Survey
24. Consumers' expenditure abroad	As quarterly estimates	International Passenger Survey and statistics of the pay of the Forces and other government employees serving abroad

	Estimates at constant prices
Second-hand goods Caravans	Estimated numbers of hire purchase contracts multiplied by average dealers' margin in base year
Other	Current price estimates deflated by a price index for new furniture
Hire of domestic appliances	Current price estimates deflated by appropriate sections of index of retail prices

Miscellaneous
  household services
  Hairdressing
	No firm basis
	
	Current price estimates deflated by appropriate section of index of retail prices

Undertaking	Number of deaths multiplied by estimated average cost of funeral in base year
Betting Football pools, fixed odds football betting, betting with bookmakers on and off-course (including betting shops), greyhound racing totalisators	Current price estimates deflated by indices of tax and retention rates and by the general consumer price index
Horserace totalisators	Current price estimates deflated by an index of retention rates and by the general consumer price index
Bingo and gaming	Current price estimates deflated by general consumer price index
Fees paid to local authorities	Current price estimates deflated by general index of wage rates
Bank charges	Current price estimates deflated by general consumer price index
Stamp duties	Current price estimates deflated by index of rates of duty together with indices of stocks and share prices
Stockbrokers' charges	Current price estimates deflated by indices of stocks and share prices, and of standard rates of commission
Fines and fees	Not revalued
Other miscellaneous services	No firm basis
22. Income in kind not included elsewhere	Current price estimates deflated by implied consumer price index for household expenditure on food
23. Expenditure by foreign tourists, etc. in the United Kingdom	Current price estimates deflated by a specially constructed price index
24. Consumers' expenditure abroad	Current price estimates deflated by a specially constructed price index

Chapter VII

Companies

1. GENERAL DESCRIPTION

The company sector comprises privately controlled corporate enterprises organised for profit and resident in the United Kingdom, and is the source of more than half of the gross national product. The main constituent of the company sector is nearly 11,000 registered public companies with a paid-up share capital of over £11,000 million and total net assets of about two and a half times that amount. More in number but smaller in total net assets are nearly 400,000 private companies, many of which are subsidiaries of public companies or of other private companies. Also included in the company sector are nearly 900 co-operative societies, engaged in production, wholesaling and retailing, with an issued share capital of nearly £300 million. And building societies, which at the end of 1966 numbered nearly 600, with an issued share capital of approaching £6,000 million.

Private companies, unlike public companies, may restrict the rights of members to transfer shares, limit their membership to between two and fifty (inclusive) and do not invite public subscription to their shares or debentures, which cannot therefore have a stock exchange quotation. Moreover, until the Companies Act, 1967, which abolished the status of 'exempt private companies', most private companies were not obliged, as are most other companies, to lodge their annual accounts and balance sheets with the Registrar of Companies for public inspection. Only about one-tenth of the private companies were non-exempt and had to lodge accounts. No distinction can be made in the national accounts statistics of profits, etc. between public and private companies.

Companies have long been liable to taxes which are not borne by individuals and unincorporated businesses, and the distinction which the Inland Revenue is obliged to make between companies and other businesses has been found convenient in national accounts statistics. Although the company sector includes a great number of small enterprises, distinguishable only by legal form from sole traders and partnerships, the main weight is carried by large enterprises with substantial capital and a high degree of permanence. Thus the 4,000 largest companies account for about three-quarters of total company profits.

The term 'companies' is, however, used for convenience rather than because it conveys any precise legal significance. Essentially, in this system of statistics, it implies (a) corporate status—a legal personality distinct from the persons who are its members, (b) private control as distinct from control by public authorities, and, with some exceptions, (c) operation for gain. Corporate status normally carries with it limited liability, but there are a few unlimited companies, and limited liability may be granted to certain partners in unincorporated partnerships.

The company sector includes private non-profit-making bodies serving companies, such as trade associations, whether or not they are incorporated. Some bodies aided by grants from the central government come into this category (see page 298). But the company sector excludes the following bodies, some of which are in fact incorporated under the Companies Act as Statutory Companies by Royal Charter, or under the Industrial and Provident Societies Act:

(a) the public corporations—mainly the bodies managing the nationalised industries;

(b) the trading enterprises of the central government and local authorities;

(c) corporate bodies treated as part of the system of public authorities but not as trading enterprises—for example, the Regional Hospital Boards, which are bodies corporate under the National Health Service Act, 1946, and the Honourable Artillery Company, incorporated by Letters Patent;

(d) private non-profit-making bodies serving persons: universities, direct grant and other non-profit-making independent schools, charities, churches, clubs and other societies, trade unions and friendly societies such as mutual insurance societies (but co-operative societies and building societies are treated as companies);

(e) agricultural companies, which, for statistical convenience, are excluded because they are included with individual farmers and partnerships in the personal sector (see page 142).

The sector accounts for companies represent the transactions of a particular kind of trading body, not the transactions in a particular area of economic activity. The area covered by the company sector changes substantially over time, because of nationalisation and denationalisation, the transfer of particular activities between government and private hands, the transfer of the residence of companies between this country and abroad, and the incorporation of unincorporated businesses. Total company profits may fall on account of nationalisation or may rise because a nationalised industry has been returned to private ownership. The table given below shows the gross trading profits of all companies (as in Table 1 of the 1967 Blue Book) and the gross trading profits of those companies that were not nationalised at any time during the period. The same considerations apply, of course, to the changes in interest and dividend payments, and other items in the company accounts. For some purposes, the more significant changes are those shown by the combined accounts of companies and public corporations, as given in the corporate appropriation account (Table 3 of the 1967 Blue Book).

Gross trading profits

£ million

	1938	1946	1950	1955	1960	1962	1963	1964	1965	1966
All companies ...	690	1,476	2,126	2,904	3,771	3,629	4,143	4,645	4,867	4,646
Non-nationalised companies	570	1,335	2,077	2,821	3,596	3,519	4,017	4,495	4,726	4,511

Source: 1967 Blue Book, Tables 1 and 34 and earlier Blue Books for figures for the years 1938, 1946, 1950 and 1955

Financial companies

For the analysis of financial transactions between the sectors, the company sector is divided into two parts, financial companies being distinguished from industrial and commercial companies. The financial companies sector comprises banks, accepting houses, discount houses, the trustee savings banks, the Investment Account of the Post Office Savings Bank, building societies, hire purchase finance companies and certain other institutions which accept deposits, unit trusts, investment trusts quoted on the London Stock Exchange, insurance companies, superannuation funds and certain special finance agencies such as the Agricultural Mortgage Corporation and the Industrial and Commercial Finance Corporation. Superannuation funds are included with financial companies even though relatively few of them have corporate status, because their liabilities are similar to those of life assurance companies. The income of financial companies is derived mainly from transactions in financial assets, that is from lending and borrowing. Broadly it is Order XXI in the *Standard Industrial Classification, 1958* with the exception of property companies, which derive their income mainly from the ownership of land and buildings. In the industrial analysis property companies are included in the industry 'Insurance, banking and finance', but in the sector analysis the relevant group is financial companies, and property companies are included with industrial and commercial companies.

A problem which has always caused some difficulty in national accounting statistics is the measurement of the contribution of financial companies to gross domestic product, consistent with that of other industries. The contribution to gross domestic product of an enterprise is measured by its 'net output'—the excess of its receipts from the sale of goods and services over its operating expenditure on goods and services from other enterprises. Net output in this sense includes provision for depreciation but excludes stock appreciation. The same definition must be applied to financial companies to reach an all industry total that can be called the total output of goods and services. But the application of this definition to financial companies produces a paradoxical result. The contribution to gross domestic product of a bank, for example, is the excess of bank charges and commissions received from depositors (the only receipt by banks directly related to the services they supply) over the operating expenses for office materials, furniture, rent, etc. (their only purchase of goods and services from other enterprises). This net output is naturally small. Moreover, the element of profit obtained by deducting wages, salaries, etc. from net output in the same way as for other industries, is usually negative; wages, salaries and purchases of goods and services from other enterprises normally exceed receipts from bank charges and commissions. The reason for this peculiarity is that banks derive their income by lending money at a higher rate of interest than they pay on money deposited with them; and in the national accounts interest receipts and payments are regarded as transfers and not as receipts and payments for a financial service. This income in a sense subsidises the provision by banks of those services for which inadequate payment is received in the form of bank charges and commissions. Other financial companies are analogous to the banks in the way in which they derive their income, many of them doing so almost entirely from the difference between the rates of interest which they charge and the rates which they themselves pay.

A possible solution is to treat all (or part) of the net receipts of interest by financial companies as being in effect a payment, in addition to bank charges, etc., for general financial services rendered. This would increase the profit incomes of financial companies to a figure nearer to that in their published accounts. At the same time it would be necessary to impute to other sectors a charge for these financial services. In so far as these purchases are made by businesses they would be treated like raw materials or any other intermediate goods: the imputed cost of financial services would be regarded as an additional cost of production, and their profit incomes would be reduced by the same amount as profits of financial companies were increased. If all financial services were rendered to businesses the problem would be reduced to that of determining whether the net interest income of financial companies should be regarded as generated in that sector or outside it.

Some financial services, however, are rendered to persons and public authorities, as customers of banks and as borrowers from banks and other financial companies. The imputed charge for these services to final consumers would therefore have to be treated as final expenditure, mainly as a part of consumers' expenditure on goods and services. To this extent the imputation would involve an increase in total final expenditure and in national income.

To carry through this kind of solution would require the allocation of the charge for financial services to specific industries and sectors. The standard international systems of national accounts[1] recommend an imputation of financial charges on these lines, amounting to the difference between the excess of investment income accruing to financial concerns over deposit interest accruing to their depositors. They suggest that imputed bank service charges be distributed in proportion to the bank deposits held by each industry or sector. However, this recommendation is likely to be changed in the revision of the international system which is now in progress. In the United Kingdom insufficient evidence is available to determine the allocation of imputed charges for all financial services between sectors and between industries. It is believed that the assumptions involved in the distribution of these imputed charges, which for all financial concerns currently amount to over £1,000 million a year, would be more misleading than the paradox of financial concerns appearing to make a steady annual loss.

The distribution of gross domestic product by industry (Table 17 in the 1967 Blue Book) sets out the position in 'Insurance, banking and finance (including real estate)' for 1966 as follows:

	£ million
Income from employment	841
Gross profits and other income	1,118
Rent..............................	459
Adjustment for net interest	−1,344
Total contribution to total domestic income........................	1,074

The second and third lines constitute profits as normally understood—except that depreciation is not treated as a current cost and that certain gains and losses on investments, treated as trading profits or losses for tax purposes, are not

---

[1] *A System of National Accounts and Supporting Tables*, United Nations, New York, 1964, and *A Standardized System of National Accounts*, OEEC, Paris, 1959.

brought into account. The definition of the rent income included here is given on page 71. The fourth line represents the deduction required so that the profits of the financial concerns can be added to those of other industries to make up the contribution of profits to national income. In the alternative system of presentation described above, under which a charge for financial services would be imputed to the customers of financial concerns, the second line unadjusted would remain as the profits of the insurance, banking and finance industry and there would be no adjustment for net interest. Part of the £1,344 million for financial services would be attributed to businesses and be deducted in some way from the profits of all other industries; and total final expenditure and national income would be greater than now shown by the part of the £1,344 million attributed to final consumers' purchases of financial services.

The distribution of trading profits of companies by industry (Table 35 of the 1967 Blue Book) shows the profits, excluding rent, of the insurance, banking and finance industry as normally understood. They are comparable with the profits shown in the second line of the table in the preceding paragraph. But, though comparable, they are smaller, because they relate to companies only and exclude the substantial number of unincorporated businesses—for example, stock-brokers—within the insurance, banking and finance industry. The adjustment for net interest is included in Table 35 along with certain other adjustments, in the item 'Adjustments'.

Life assurance companies, including industrial assurance and collecting societies, and superannuation funds are treated differently from other financial companies, since their funds are treated as the property of the personal sector (see page 100) while the business itself is in the company sector. The treatment of life assurance companies in the national accounts is thus to include that part of their profits which accrues to shareholders in company profits, while that part which accrues to policy holders in the form of bonuses is attributed to the personal sector. The income of life assurance and superannuation funds from rent, dividends and net interest is included in personal income. Consumers' expenditure includes as expenditure on life assurance the management expenses and profits accruing to shareholders of the insurance companies and the expenses of superannuation funds (see page 181). The increase in the funds forms part of personal saving which represents a claim by the personal sector on the funds. The capital formation of the funds and their financial transactions are included with those of financial companies (see page 413).

The treatment of trustee savings banks also differs from that of other financial companies because the funds of the ordinary departments are managed by the central government. Deposits with these departments are therefore regarded as national savings received by the central government and interest paid to the trustees is regarded as being paid directly to the depositors in the personal sector.

2. THE PUBLISHED TABLES

The Blue Book gives appropriation and capital accounts for all companies, and also for industrial and commercial companies and for financial companies separately. An appropriation account is also given for companies which have never been nationalised. No production accounts are available for the company sector. The appropriation and capital accounts of all companies are also published on a quarterly basis in *Financial Statistics*, together with separate capital accounts for industrial and commercial companies and financial companies.

APPROPRIATION ACCOUNT

The appropriation account in the 1967 Blue Book for all companies is shown in the table below.

Company appropriation account, 1966

£ million

Income		Allocation of income	
Income arising in the United Kingdom:		Dividends and interest: Payments:	
Gross trading profits[1][2][3] ..	4,646	Debenture interest	230
		Dividends on preference	
Rent and non-trading income.	1,351	shares	121
		Dividends on ordinary	
		shares	1,633
Total	5,997	Co-operative society dividends and interest......	51
Income from abroad[4]	1,362	Interest on building society	
		shares and deposits.....	314
		Other interest paid by	
		banks, etc.	303
			2,652
		Additions to dividend reserves	−62
		Current transfers to charities...	30
		Profits due abroad net of United Kingdom tax[4]	220
		United Kingdom taxes on income:	
		Payments on profits due abroad	190
		Payments on other profits....	567
		Additions to reserves on profits due abroad	−40
		Additions to reserves on other profits	376
		Taxes paid abroad	548
		Balance: undistributed income after taxation[1]...........	2,878
Total	7,359	Total	7,359

Source: 1967 Blue Book, Table 30

[1] Before providing for depreciation and stock appreciation.
[2] Including United Kingdom branches and subsidiaries of non-resident parent companies.
[3] After deducting payments of selective employment tax and before allowing for refunds or premiums due but not yet received.
[4] After deducting depreciation allowances but before providing for stock appreciation.

Very broadly, the appropriation account of companies corresponds with the profit and loss accounts and appropriation accounts presented by companies to their shareholders. But there are some substantial modifications to normal accounting practice both in the content of the items, for example the omission of any provision for depreciation, and in the form of presentation.

Gross trading profits

The opening entry in the account, and the chief source of company income, is the gross trading profits of all companies operating in the United Kingdom. This figure, representing earnings from production and trade in the United Kingdom, is regarded as the share of these companies in the gross national product (their factor income) and appears as one of the constituents of the national income, for example in Table 1 of the Blue Book. Profits of United Kingdom branches and subsidiaries of overseas parent companies are included and profits of overseas branches and subsidiaries of United Kingdom parent companies are excluded.

These profits may be regarded as the total surpluses carried forward from a series of production or operating accounts for each company. Such operating accounts would contain under payments the current purchases of goods and services from all other enterprises in the United Kingdom and from abroad and the purchase of labour services from the firms' own employees; under receipts they would include the total sales of goods and services *plus* increases in the value of stocks and work in progress. Four features of this definition of trading profits should be noted:

(a) no provision is made for depreciation as a current cost before reckoning profits;

(b) no provision is made for stock appreciation or depreciation (that part of accounting profits attributable to the effect of price changes on stock values) in reckoning profits;

(c) all interest payments are treated as appropriations of income, not as operating expenses deducted in reckoning profits;

(d) income from owner-occupied trading property is included.

For national income purposes, trading profits should properly be differently defined. A charge for depreciation, representing as nearly as possible the use of fixed assets during the year at the prices of the year, should be included in current operating costs before striking the profits balance. And stock appreciation or depreciation—that part of accounting profits due to the effect of price changes on stock values—should be excluded from profits. Trading profits are not defined in this way mainly because of the difficulties of estimation (see Chapter I). An approximate allocation by sector of both capital consumption and stock appreciation is published, however, in the section of the Blue Book on capital formation (see Chapters XII and XIII).

Rent and non-trading income

To companies' gross trading profits from production and trade in the United Kingdom must be added their rent and non-trading income. This item refers only to such income arising in the United Kingdom. It consists mainly of rents, other than the income arising from owner-occupied property, and interest. Since the table is a consolidated account for all companies, income of this kind received from United Kingdom resident companies is omitted and the item is confined to property income received from other domestic sectors—the personal sector, public corporations and public authorities. The income of the life funds of life assurance companies and of superannuation funds is not included as the funds are regarded as the property of the personal sector.

Among the main constituents of the non-trading income of the company sector are interest received on public debt, interest on bank advances to the personal and public sectors, and mortgage interest received from the personal sector by building societies. The bulk of this income is received by financial companies. The whole of company non-trading income is regarded as transfer income and is excluded as such from the calculation of gross domestic product and national income; it is treated as income redistributed from other sectors to companies.

Income from abroad

Company income earned abroad is estimated for the balance of payments net of depreciation provisions and foreign taxes. For the national income accounts, however, foreign taxes are added back and an offsetting payment is shown separately (see page 214). Company income from abroad, unlike gross trading profits, is thus measured after allowing for depreciation provisions. Some information on depreciation is available from the Board of Trade inquiry into overseas direct investment but it is not complete: in 1965 depreciation totalled nearly £200 million for direct investment excluding oil.

There are three main categories of income included in this item: income on portfolio investment abroad, income on direct investment, and other investment income. Income on portfolio investment abroad relates solely to remitted dividends and interest payments. Income on direct investment includes the earnings, whether remitted to the United Kingdom or not, of non-resident branches, the dividends and parent companies' share of undistributed income of non-resident subsidiaries, and interest on loans by United Kingdom parent companies to these branches and subsidiaries. Where companies have head offices in the United Kingdom but operate mainly abroad—as do many plantation and mining companies—their operations abroad are regarded as undertaken by a non-resident branch. From 1963 the net earnings of United Kingdom insurance companies from their overseas branches and subsidiaries are included in direct investment income. Previously they were included in the balance of payments accounts not as investment income but as receipts from the sale of services. This change of treatment from 1963 has not been carried backwards, however, for lack of information. Other investment income is largely the earnings of United Kingdom oil companies and of interest earned by companies on trade credits granted. Broadly speaking, the earnings of oil companies represent the surplus on current transactions of United Kingdom companies from operations abroad. Such earnings are estimated from cash flows. For various reasons, they do not correspond precisely to profits earned abroad. They include, for instance, the value of services rendered by the parent company to subsidiaries and associates abroad.

Definitions of resident and non-resident companies, of direct and portfolio investment, together with a description of the sources of the various estimates, will be found in the chapter on international transactions (Chapter XV).

Property income from abroad is now defined in the same way in the national income accounts as in the balance of payments accounts. All income from abroad is included in 'Income from abroad', and both 'Gross trading profits' and 'Rent and non-trading income' relate solely to such income arising in the United Kingdom. It is no longer necessary to include in the company appropriation account an item 'Balance of payments adjustment' such as appeared in the 1960 and earlier Blue Books. The estimates for all years have been put as far as possible on to a consistent basis although the adjustments to the years before 1958 are necessarily approximate (see page 464).

Included in the estimates of income from abroad, and correspondingly profits due abroad, are the unremitted profits of branches and subsidiaries abroad. Unless these are included the contribution of companies to gross national product and saving is incorrectly stated, for gross domestic capital formation includes the fixed capital expenditure of branches and subsidiaries in the United Kingdom of non-resident parent companies but excludes direct investment abroad by United Kingdom companies. Consequently, for the country as a whole, unless unremitted profits and dividends are taken into account, the identity that savings equals gross domestic capital formation *plus* net investment abroad would be in error.

Dividends and interest

Payments of dividends and interest include debenture interest, preference dividends and ordinary dividends. Dividends and interest paid by co-operative societies and interest on building society shares and deposits are shown separately. There is also an item of miscellaneous interest payments, nearly all of which is bank deposit interest. As on the income side of the account, dividend and interest payments by one United Kingdom company to another are excluded. Also excluded are the dividends of United Kingdom subsidiaries to their non-resident parent companies, since these are taken into account in the item 'Profits due abroad net of United Kingdom income tax'.

All dividend and interest payments are shown before deduction of income tax, although in fact companies normally deduct income tax at the standard rate before payment. Before the introduction of corporation tax, a company was assessed to income tax on the whole of its taxable income whether distributed or not. When dividends and interest were paid from this income companies were not required to account for the tax deducted from the dividends and interest paid. The 1965 Finance Act introduced corporation tax in place of income tax on company profits and required companies to deduct income tax from dividends and interest at the time of payment and remit the tax to the Inland Revenue. This system first affected company profits in accounting years ending in 1965/66 and dividends and interest paid in 1966/67.

The recipient of dividends and interest has always been assessed to tax by reference to the whole of his income, including dividends and interest before deduction of tax. In his tax assessment, allowance is made for the tax already deducted on payment by the company. Thus a shareholder liable to surtax is charged on the gross amount of a dividend before income tax was deducted. And, if a shareholder is not liable to income tax at the standard rate, he may recover from the Inland Revenue tax that has been deducted by the company. The deduction of tax at source, wherever possible, before income reaches its ultimate recipient, has been described as the keystone of the United Kingdom income tax collection system. But one result of this system is that the precise amount of tax falling on the final recipient of the income subject to tax can rarely be obtained directly from the records.

Payments of ordinary dividends other than interim dividends, and to a lesser extent of dividends on preference shares, are in most cases distributions out of income earned in a previous year. Hence companies may be regarded as making an appropriation out of the year's profits for distributions that will not in fact be made until the following year. Since for some purposes the accruals of dividends are more significant than the actual payments in the year, allowance is made by adding an item 'Additions to dividend reserves', representing any estimated excess of accruals of dividends over actual payments. Thus the figure of accruals (payments *plus* addition to reserves) is the appropriate figure to relate to profits earned in the year, and to use in making an estimate of savings, but the figure of payments is required to match the corresponding figures of receipts by other sectors.

Current transfers to charities

This item represents identified contributions by companies to non-profit-making bodies in the personal sector. The estimates cover covenanted and uncovenanted contributions not allowed as a business expense.

Profits due abroad net of United Kingdom tax

This item consists of profits, net of depreciation provisions, of United Kingdom branches of non-resident companies *plus* the share of net profits of United Kingdom subsidiaries, whether distributed or not, accruing to non-resident parent companies. In the case of United Kingdom subsidiaries of non-resident oil companies it is the net earnings remitted abroad which are included, estimates of net profits being unavailable. Some information on depreciation is available from the Board of Trade inquiry into overseas direct investment, but it is not complete: in 1964 and 1965 this was of the order of £100 million for direct investment excluding oil.

United Kingdom taxes on income

The taxes covered by this item were changed by the Finance Act, 1965, under the provisions of which companies became subject to corporation tax instead of income tax and profits tax. In earlier years, taxes on company income also included excess profits tax, which was repealed in 1946, and excess profits levy which was repealed in 1953.

The table shows two items: tax payments and additions to tax reserves. Tax payments relate to actual payments of tax in the calendar year. However, an alternative concept of tax accruals in the year, that is of tax ultimately to be paid in respect of trading and non-trading income of the year, is also of importance because it is regarded as good accounting practice for companies to set aside in their accounts the money they expect to pay in tax against the income on which the tax is assessed. For any individual company the amount to be put aside to meet taxation each year will then consist of the tax at current rates on current income *plus* any changes necessary to the previous year's tax reserves because rates of tax have changed; this will relate to the company's own accounting period. The total of such amounts, or the accruals of tax for all companies, is estimated by reference to the aggregate of accounting periods ending in the fiscal year up to 5 April; but since the average of such accounting periods is close to the calendar year little accuracy is forfeited by taking this as the accruals of tax for the calendar year. The item 'Additions to tax reserves' is simply the excess of tax accruals in the year over tax payments in the year. For most purposes the figure of tax accruals is the appropriate deduction from gross profits for the analysis of the trend of profits after tax and of saving. It often varies widely from tax payments because of changes both in the level of profits and in the rates of tax and capital allowances. In particular, the change in the tax system introduced in the Finance Act, 1965 affects tax accruals from 1965 onwards and, although there were no substantial payments of corporation tax until 1967, tax payments in 1965 especially were heavily affected by the provisions for transition from the old to the new system. Also, the withdrawal of investment allowances and the changes in initial allowances from 17 January 1966, when investment grants were introduced, increased tax accruals from 1966.

Before the change in the system of taxation, companies were subject to both profits tax and income tax. Changes in the rate of profits tax made in a Budget normally applied only to the profits made after the financial year then ending on 31 March. Assessments were raised on the profits of the company's accounting period, with different rates applied to the profits of the periods before and after the date of change of rate. Companies could therefore set aside the profits tax which would eventually be payable in full knowledge of the correct rate. Profits tax was payable one month after assessment, which might take place at any time up to six years after the end of the accounting period, but was usually made, possibly in estimated form, within a year.

Income tax, on the other hand, was assessed upon profits made by companies in their own accounting periods ending in the fiscal year up to 5 April and the rate of tax, which was fixed in the Budget normally about the end of the fiscal year, applied to profits in the whole of the accounting period ending in that year. For example, the profits earned in accounting periods ending within the twelve months up to 5 April 1963 normally formed the basis of income tax assessments for 1963/64 at the rate determined in April 1963, and the tax became payable on 1 January 1964. The profits were earned mainly in 1962 but, at the end of 1962, the tax due in 1964 might be affected by tax rates fixed in the next Budget.

Companies were assessed to income tax on the whole of their taxable income, whether distributed or not, but they were not required to account for the tax deducted from dividends and interest paid. The tax payments by companies shown in the table for the period covered by the old system are net, after deducting the amounts withheld from dividend and interest payments which in the national accounts are regarded as falling on the recipients of the dividends and interest. They therefore consist of profits tax on the whole profits and income tax on the undistributed profits only. Tax accruals likewise are the net amount that companies estimate they will have to bear after crediting the income tax at the rates current at the end of their accounting periods which they will pass on to recipients by deduction from dividend and interest payments. Hence, additions to reserves are reduced by the excess of tax at the current rate on the dividend reserves at the end of the year and tax at the preceding year's rate on the dividend reserves brought forward from that year.

For most companies, the last assessment to income tax was for 1965/66, on the basis of profits made in accounting periods ending in the fiscal year 1964/65; the first assessment to corporation tax was in 1966/67 on the basis of accounting periods ending in the fiscal year 1965/66, with corporation tax first becoming payable on 1 January 1967. Like profits tax, corporation tax is assessed on the whole of accounting periods, with apportionments on a time basis where two rates of tax are involved. Normally the rate of tax for a financial year will be fixed as for income tax, just after the end of the financial year. The tax is payable nine months after the end of the accounting period, but existing companies can continue to pay the tax after the same interval as they paid income tax. As previously, the estimate of tax accruals is made by reference to the rate of corporation tax in force during the calendar year, for example in 1967, since it was announced in November that the rate for profits earned in 1967/68 would be increased from 40 per cent to 42½ per cent in the next Budget, tax accruals for

1967 are calculated accordingly, with the higher rate applying to profits earned after 31 March 1967.

In addition, for 1966/67 and subsequent years, companies have to account for the income tax deducted generally at the standard rate from any distributions they make. In so far as this is paid to the Inland Revenue in the same year, it does not affect the tax payments of companies. In general, companies which receive income under deduction of income tax, such as interest on some government securities, local authority securities, or taxed interest or dividends from other companies, can set off the tax on that income against the income tax deductible from the distributions they themselves make. To this extent, therefore, income tax reaches the Inland Revenue only on the amount of income distributed by way of dividends and interest outside the company sector. But also, if income tax suffered by deduction on income received, other than taxed dividends received from other companies, exceeds tax deductible from interest payments, it may be set against the company's corporation tax liability; and if the company has otherwise made a loss, it may, subject to certain conditions, claim a repayment of income tax suffered. Any excess of income tax suffered by deduction on dividends received can likewise be repaid. Further, it is assumed that under the new system a gross reserve is allocated for interest and dividend payments and for the tax due on them; hence no adjustment is needed to the addition to tax reserves item for a change in the rate of tax deducted from dividends, since this is supposed to cause no change in the total allocated for distribution, but only in its apportionment between tax deducted and net distributions.

The 1965 Finance Act also contained provisions designed to ease the transition from one form of taxation to another—in particular, the making of transitional relief payments to companies who lost some of the concessions previously associated with income subject to overseas tax, and the abatement of Schedule 12 income tax in the first year to companies who were judged to have paid dividends out of income which had already borne income tax and profits tax. The net effect of these provisions was to relieve them of taxation and thus to reduce their net payments of tax, shown in the national accounts.

From 1967 company taxes on income therefore consist of corporation tax *plus* the net income tax suffered on investment income *less* receipts by companies of overspill relief in respect of overseas tax not relieved against corporation tax. In addition, tax payments include an adjustment for changes in the amount of income tax in the hands of companies. Companies deduct tax from wages and salaries under PAYE and the corresponding amounts due to be paid by companies to the Inland Revenue are paid only after an interval. The same considerations now apply to the income tax deducted from dividends and interest under Schedule 12. This adjustment is of more importance for the quarterly estimates than for the annual ones.

A footnote to the appropriation account in the Blue Book shows the tax payments and tax accruals for companies and shareholders combined. These figures are obtained by adding to the figures of taxes on companies, income tax at the standard rate deducted from their dividends and interest payments. This addition is not the tax ultimately suffered by the recipients of these payments; the rate of tax suffered by any shareholder is affected by his personal circumstances and his total income from all sources, and may therefore be higher (because of surtax) or lower (because of personal reliefs and reduced rates of tax) than the standard rate of income tax. The figures are nevertheless useful in analysing the trend of the total tax burden on loan and share capital holders.

Taxes paid abroad

This item consists of the taxes paid to overseas governments and authorities on the income of overseas branches and subsidiaries of United Kingdom resident companies, and on company income from portfolio investment abroad. Taxes which are regarded as part of operating expenses, including most mining royalties, are excluded.

Undistributed income

The residual balance carried forward to the capital account comprises the company sector's undistributed income after taxation before providing for depreciation and stock appreciation. The excess of depreciation on profits due abroad over depreciation on income from abroad is included in this item.

CAPITAL ACCOUNT

The capital account in the 1967 Blue Book for all companies is as follows:

Company capital account, 1966

£ million

Receipts		Payments	
Undistributed income after taxation before providing for depreciation and stock appreciation.....................	2,878	Gross domestic fixed capital formation	2,601
Additions to dividend reserves...	− 62	Increase in value of stocks and work in progress	403
Additions to tax reserves	336	Net acquisition of financial assets including net investment abroad	169
Capital transfers (net)	21		
Total	3,173	Total	3,173

Source: 1967 Blue Book, Table 31

The capital account is the link between the appropriation account and the financial account. The receipts consist of company gross saving, additions to dividend reserves, additions to tax reserves, and net capital transfers, the first three items being brought forward from the appropriation account. In the first half of the 1960's capital transfers consisted mainly of receipts of central government grants to assist industry *less* contributions by companies towards the capital cost of connecting their premises to the electricity supply. In the 1950's receipts of war damage compensation were also important. From 1967 this item is much more important because it includes receipts of investment grants in respect of capital expenditure after 17 January 1966.

On the payments side are gross domestic fixed capital formation and the increase in the value of stocks and work in progress; these items are described in Chapters XII and XIII respectively. Since company saving is recorded before any deduction for stock appreciation, it is the increase in the value of stocks and work in progress, and not the value of the physical increase, that must be included. The residual item, 'Net acquisition of financial assets including net investment abroad', shows the extent to which capital receipts are more or less than sufficient to pay for company capital formation. The financial accounts, shown in the financial accounts section of the Blue Book and described in Chapter XIV, show how this surplus or deficit is invested or financed.

OTHER BLUE BOOK TABLES

Appropriation and capital accounts of industrial and commercial companies and financial companies

The basic difference between these accounts and those for the company sector as a whole is the inclusion of flows between industrial and commercial companies and financial companies. In the accounts for all companies all inter-company payments are consolidated out; but for these accounts only receipts and payments within the two sub-sectors are consolidated out. In particular, receipts of dividends and interest by financial companies from industrial and commercial companies and payments of dividends and interest by financial companies to industrial and commercial companies are recorded.

The accounts for these two sectors follow the same principles as those for the company sector as a whole but some differences in treatment arise because of lack of adequate information and less detail is given. Additions to dividend reserves are not shown in the appropriation accounts and the residual saving item includes additions to dividend reserves. Additions to tax reserves are not shown separately from United Kingdom tax payments and only the United Kingdom tax accruals are given in the appropriation accounts. In the 1967 Blue Book all of the current transfers to charities were attributed to industrial and commercial companies, although it has subsequently been estimated that about one-tenth of the contributions are made by financial companies. The negative gross trading profits for financial companies arise from the exclusion of net interest receipts (see page 204).

In the capital accounts, additions to tax reserves, net capital transfers and investment in stocks and work in progress are all assumed to be negligible for financial companies; none of these items appears in the capital account for financial companies and the estimates for the whole company sector are attributed to industrial and commercial companies. For investment in stocks, little error is likely to arise from this assumption as financial companies hold only very small stocks.

Separate capital accounts for industrial and commercial and for financial companies are available only from 1959 onwards because of lack of information about gross domestic fixed capital formation in earlier years.

Appropriation account of non-nationalised companies

This account relates to companies never nationalised at any time since 1938. Because of nationalisation and denationalisation, the area of the company sector has changed from time to time, whereas the coverage of this table is the same for all years shown. From 1956 to 1966 the industries principally affected are steel and road transport. The adjustments needed to the account for all companies are provided by the Inland Revenue, except for non-trading income, to which an arbitrary adjustment is made.

Trading profits by industry

An industrial analysis of gross and net trading profits of companies operating in the United Kingdom is given in Table 35 of the 1967 Blue Book. The figures are based on the industrial analysis of tax assessments made by the Inland Revenue and published in the annual reports of the Commissioners. But some adjustments are made to bring the coverage of the figures into line with gross trading profits as defined in the company appropriation account. Estimates of profits of co-operative societies are added to the estimates for 'Food, drink and tobacco' and 'Distributive trades'. Profits of professional companies are included in 'Other services'. Many of the adjustments required to profits as assessed for tax cannot be allocated in detail by industry and form part of the general adjustments item which is necessary to bring the sum of company profits for all industries into line with the total in the company appropriation account. The adjustments are, however, distributed over broad industry groups for the analysis of gross domestic product by industry and type of income (Table 17 of the 1967 Blue Book). The figures for 'Insurance, banking and finance' show profits as normally understood, that is including net recipts of interest and dividends, and the difference accounts for a large part of the adjustments item (see page 204). Since this table is on an industry basis, these figures include property companies.

The classification used corresponds with the *Standard Industrial Classification, 1958*, but the basis of assessment to tax is necessarily the financial unit and not the individual establishment or business unit. Hence this analysis of profits by industry is not precisely comparable with, for example, the Ministry of Labour analysis of employment by industry nor with the census of production data used for the analysis of wages and salaries, both of which are based on a classification of establishments. There is, however, no reason to suppose that year-to-year changes in the profits figures for the different industries are not comparable with the year-to-year changes in other series based on establishments or business units. Moreover, it seems probable that profits figures on a financial unit basis are not appreciably different from those on an establishment basis for broad industry groups; hence the analysis of gross company profits for financial units is used for the analysis of gross domestic product by broad industry groups, given in the section of the Blue Book on industrial input and output (Table 17 of the 1967 Blue Book, see page 68).

Net profits are also shown, the figures being the profits after deducting the depreciation allowed for income tax, including initial allowances at varying rates and investment allowances. The Inland Revenue depreciation allowances are described in the annex to Chapter XII. The resulting figures of net profits differ from those which would be obtained by deducting the estimates of capital consumption made for the national accounts and shown in Table 62 of the 1967 Blue Book (see page 383).

Because of the nature of the material from which the figures are compiled, as described above, it is not possible to give this industrial analysis of profits for the most recent year.

QUARTERLY TABLES

A quarterly appropriation account for all companies is published in *Financial Statistics* and the estimates of undistributed income are divided approximately between industrial and commercial companies and financial companies. For the quarterly accounts undistributed income, or saving, is defined differently from the annual accounts and the quarterly estimates of saving include indistinguishably changes in dividend and tax reserves. The quarterly appropriation account has been published on a consistent basis from 1960. The account is seasonally adjusted. Quarterly capital accounts, dating back to 1962, are also published in *Financial Statistics* separately for industrial and commercial companies and for financial companies.

An acute problem with the quarterly estimates, which is much less important for the annual figures, is whether transfer income and payments should be measured on an accruals or on a cash basis. For instance, whether interest on company holdings of government securities, or interest on bank advances, should be included to the extent it has accrued or to the extent it has been paid. It is usual for bank borrowers to pay interest on bank advances at the end of the second and fourth quarters, so there is an appreciable difference between the two bases. The national accounts are generally on an accruals basis (see pages 36 to 39). In some cases, however, the data available do not permit quarterly estimates of accruals to be made with any confidence; in others accruals are more easily estimated than payments. A compromise solution has therefore been adopted: some items are on an accruals basis and some on a payments basis but, as far as possible, each item is treated consistently throughout the accounts so that transfers between domestic sectors cancel out. In the case of taxes on income, which are essentially assessed on an annual basis, quarterly estimates are made of payments only. Also on a payments basis are the quarterly estimates of dividends on both ordinary and preference shares, and debenture interest, which become payable on certain dates and are included in the figures at that time. As far as possible, interest receipts from the central government are recorded on a payments basis because they are included in the government accounts as they are paid. Other interest receipts and payments are generally estimated on an accruals basis.

3. STATISTICAL SOURCES: PROFITS AND OTHER INCOME OF COMPANIES

PROFITS

The main basis of the estimates of company profits is the information collected by the Inland Revenue in the course of assessing companies to income tax and, from 1965/66, to corporation tax. Most of the data required, both for the total of company profits and its analysis by industry, are derived from Inland Revenue records and estimates. A summary description of the Inland Revenue terms is given in Appendix III.

The estimation of company profits is complicated by several factors, in particular:

(a) Companies are normally assessed to tax on the basis of their incomes in their own accounting years; for the national accounts, however, figures for calendar years are required.

(b) The process of determining the level of profits of an individual company for tax purposes is often lengthy; hence the estimates for a number of recent years may be subject to continuous revision until virtually all assessments reach their final stage.

(c) Losses may be used for the relief of tax in years other than those in which they are incurred, which are the relevant years for the national accounts.

H

(d) There is inevitably a time lag between the end of a company's accounting year and the assessment of its profits by the Inland Revenue. It is some time before accounts are submitted to the Inland Revenue and there is a further lapse of time before their assessment and analysis is completed. Even if all assessments could be completed within the income tax year and all records tabulated—which in fact cannot be done (see (b) above)—there would be a gap of fifteen months between the end of the calendar year in which the bulk of the profits were earned and the earliest date at which statistics could be compiled. Consequently, for the calendar year just past no assessments are available on which to base profit estimates, and only partial data are available for the previous calendar year.

No attempt was made to deal with the first of these complications until quarterly estimates of profits became available. Since 1955 the Inland Revenue has made estimates of profits earned in each quarter of the year from returns made by a sample of companies, and these estimates have been used to adjust accounting year figures to a calendar year basis. Estimates of company profits are on this basis from 1955 onwards but no adjustments have been made to profits of earlier years. The estimate of gross trading profits in 1955 calculated on the old unadjusted basis would be £28 million, or about 1 per cent, lower than on the new basis. To circumvent the fourth difficulty—the estimation of profits before tax assessments become available—forecasts of profits for each accounting year are sent by certain companies to Inland Revenue tax districts and Inspectors of Taxes submit preliminary reports of profits when companies' accounts are received and also when they are agreed.

Accounting years

A company is normally assessed to tax on the basis of profits made in its own accounting year. The distribution of profits by companies' accounting years is approximately as follows:

	Percentage of total profits
Accounting years ending in:	
April to June	10
July to September	15
October to December	50
January to March	25

The average accounting year, weighted by amount of profits, ends about the beginning of December.

Although the bulk of the assessments made in any one year cover company profits in accounting years ending in the previous fiscal or financial year, some assessments are late and refer to earlier years. In the mid-1960's late assessments accounted for about five per cent of the total amount of company income assessed to income tax. But under income tax some assessments were on a current year basis and since delay in securing information often retarded such assessments, they included some duplication with the late assessments and the error from their inclusion partly offset the error from the inclusion of late assessments.

The quarterly profits series, which is described more fully below, provides estimates of the profits earned in each quarter by a sample of large companies. By combining the quarterly figures, it is possible to reconstruct a company's profits earned both in its year of account ending in any particular financial year, and in the nearest corresponding calendar year. The profits earned in the former are the basis of taxation assessment; those earned in the latter are the profits required for the national accounts. The ratios between the two provide a method of adjusting profits for each year of account industry by industry to a calendar year basis.

Losses

Broadly, the losses made in a particular year of account are not recorded in the assessments covering that year since firms making a loss are not liable to tax and so are not assessed. However, there are several ways in which a company can obtain relief in respect of business losses.

(a) Trading losses may be carried forward and set against trading income of the same trade in a subsequent year, or against interest and dividends brought into account as if they were trading income for corporation tax purposes.

(b) Trading losses may be set against any other income (including chargeable gains) of the same accounting period. From 1953/54 under income tax, such losses could also be set against other income of the following year; under corporation tax, they may be set against other income of the preceding year.

(c) From 1953/54 arrangements may also be made for trading losses of one company to be set against the trading income of an associate company in the same accounting period.

The losses under (a) allowed in any year of assessment on profits of the preceding year are assumed to be losses of the preceding year but one. Those under (b) are all assumed to be losses of the same year as the assessment. The losses under (c) are included in assessments made.

This method of estimation, however, may lead to error because under (a) some of the losses may have been carried forward more than one year; under (b) the loss may, since 1953, be set not against the assessment for the current year, but against that for the following, or now the preceding, year. Moreover, losses incurred by companies going steadily downhill, and never enjoying a profit against which to offset the losses, may never be recorded. Therefore the estimate of total losses may be too low, and the estimate of aggregate profits too high.

The total amount of losses is substantial—of the order of £200 million in the mid-1960's.

Stages in the estimation of profits: an example

When the national income estimates are being prepared, for example in mid-1967, the latest year for which profits figures are available based on complete statistics of assessments is the last calendar year but two (1964) and the year before that (1963) is the latest year for which the figures can be regarded as firm. Statistics of assessments are only partially complete for the last calendar year but one (1965) and there are no assessments at all for the latest year (1966).

The statistics available for each recent year—recent, that is, in relation to the time at which any particular Blue Book is in preparation—and the methods used for estimating total company profits are described in the following paragraphs. The description is written from the standpoint of the preparation of the 1967 Blue Book round about the middle of 1967.

Profits earned in 1964. A first approximation to total company profits earned in 1964 can be obtained from tax assessments made in the financial year 1965/66, which cover profits made in company accounting periods ending in 1964/65 and become available in January 1967. If the liability of a company is not agreed before the end of the year of assessment a provisional assessment is made. If this provisional assessment is too small, or part of the liability has been over-looked, one or more additional assessments will be made later; if it is too large, part of it will subsequently be discharged or repaid. Additional assessments (increases in profits) and discharges (reductions in profits) can therefore be considered separately. The amounts of additional assessments for 1964/65 will not be known until the end of 1967, but as an approximation, the additional assessments made in 1965/66 on company accounts ending in 1963/64 (the year before the accounting year under consideration) and all earlier years are added to the profits of 1964/65 by way of positive amendment. About half the amount of discharges, however, occur in the first year and nearly 80 per cent of the amount for the 1964/65 accounting periods will have been assessed by September 1966. At that point the discharges and repayments outstanding for company years ending in 1964/65 are taken as being equal to the discharges and repay-ments assessed in 1965/66 for all years before 1964/65. The figures so adjusted are taken as the final estimate of profits for company accounting periods ending in 1964/65, assessed in 1965/66, even though they include some profits for several years before 1964/65, which have been in dispute, and exclude some profits of 1964/65 which will not be agreed for years afterwards. The error introduced by these approximations is unlikely to exceed 1 per cent.

Although the profits of accounting periods ending in the financial year 1964/65 are a reasonable first approximation to the profits of the year 1964, they contain some profits earned in the last two quarters of 1963, and in the first quarter of 1965, by companies whose accounting years end in the June, Septem-ber or March quarters. The next step is designed to substitute for these profits, the profits earned in 1964 in accounting years not ending in 1964/65. For this purpose the quarterly profits sample is used. A description of the sample and its general use is given below; it is sufficient to say here that it provides an esti-mate of the profits earned in each calendar quarter by a sample of large com-panies. Both the quarterly profits sample and the population of companies as a whole is classified by industry and by the quarter in which the accounting period ends. It is possible to construct, for the quarterly sample of companies in a particular industry with accounting years ending in, say, March, both profits for accounting years ending in March, and profits for the calendar year. The ratio of these two years' profits obtained from the sample is used to convert the profits of all companies in the particular industry in question having accounts ending in March to calendar year profits. Similarly, the ratio of the sample profits in each industry and accounting year group to the profits of all companies in the same industry and with the same accounting year is used to gross up the profits of the sample companies in later years for which tax assessments are not yet available. The aggregate of the calendar year estimates of profits over all industries and all four accounting years gives the total profits estimate for the year; for example, the total of the estimated calendar year profits of companies having accounting periods ending in June, September and December 1964, and March 1965, over all industries, provides the estimate of profits for the calendar year 1964.

Profits earned in 1965 and 1966. For these two years complete statistics of tax assessments are not available. Other methods of estimation have therefore to be adopted and other information used.

(a) The Inland Revenue obtains reports from tax districts of changes in profits over the preceding year for a sample of accounts which have been received. Two reports are obtained: a preliminary report when the company's accounts are received; and a final, more detailed report, when the computation of profit or loss is agreed. From 1966/67 the reports relate to all companies whose trading income or loss, after the deduction of capital allowances, exceeds £10,000 and 1 in 20 of all other companies, serially selected. For earlier years, preliminary reports related to companies with gross profits of £2,000 or more and final reports to companies with gross profits of £5,000 or more, but to no smaller companies.

(b) In addition to these figures for companies whose accounts have already been received, the Inland Revenue in January each year asks traders whose profits are likely to be £10,000 or more and who are not in the sample providing quarterly profits figures, to forecast their profits for their current accounting year in advance of the submission of their accounts.

(c) A large sample of companies provides quarterly estimates of profits (see below).

Companies in categories (a), (b), or (c), after overlapping is eliminated, are subdivided by industry group and accounting year. For each group the ratio is calculated of profits in their accounting years ending in 1965/66 to those of the same companies in their preceding accounting year. Similar ratios are calculated for profits in 1966/67 in relation to those of 1965/66. These ratios are then linked and applied to the estimated profits in 1964/65, based on tax assessments, of all companies in these groups, to obtain estimated profits of all companies in such groups in 1965/66 and 1966/67. As before, estimates of quarterly profits are used to adjust these accounting year figures to a calendar year basis.

In June 1965, when estimates were made for the 1965 Blue Book, the proportions of total profits of companies covered by the various types of information were roughly as given below. The position at the time of preparing the 1966 and 1967 Blue Books has not been described at this point because, owing to the change in the tax system, the figures would not have been typical. The figures reflect the position before the coverage of the preliminary and final reports was changed.

	Percentage of total profits
1963 profits	
Preliminary reports based on accounts	11
Final reports based on accounts	14
Traders' forecasts	2
Quarterly profits sample.....................	48
1964 profits	
Preliminary reports based on accounts	1½
Final reports based on accounts	1
Traders' forecasts	19
Quarterly profits sample.....................	40

It is clear from the method outlined that the profits estimates for recent years have to be continually revised. Revision of the figures based on tax assessments, and the substitution with the passage of time of figures based on accounts for those based on forecasts, lead to recalculation and revision of the profits estimates.

Some pertinent points about the method used and various types of account are listed below.

(a) The cases for which accounts have been received, and still more those for which liability has been settled, will relate mainly to companies whose accounting periods end early in the tax year. This is of much greater relevance, of course, for the latest year than for the previous year.

(b) Traders' forecasts are in some cases estimates made before the end of their accounting year, and may therefore be biassed. A correction for bias is used in calculations derived from them.

(c) The figures from the preliminary and final reports based on accounts relate mainly to larger companies (see page 221) and the figures from the quarterly sample to companies with a profit of £100,000 or more. Results therefore give greater weight to the larger companies and their experience may differ from that of smaller concerns.

(d) The companies reporting quarterly are by no means a random selection, even within the strata covered. Some trades may be very much under-represented; and although an attempt is made to correct for this by weighting the figures by industry group, the error may still be considerable.

(e) The percentage changes in profits have to be applied to figures for an earlier year, 1964, which is itself partly estimated and liable to amendment.

(f) The figures relate only to traders for whom the profits of two consecutive years are known. They contain no adjustment for changes owing to new concerns starting business or old ones dropping out.

Quarterly estimates of profits

A sample of companies accounting for almost a half of total company profits supplies quarterly returns of their profits. The sample is a voluntary one and is kept up to date by periodic additions to the list of companies sampled. The sample is taken from only the largest companies with annual profits of £100,000 or more; as far as possible it includes all companies with profits of over £1 million a year. The sample companies make estimates of their profits earned in each quarter. Some companies find it difficult to assess at all accurately the profits arising in each quarter, particularly when the period of production is lengthy and when the measurement of changes in stocks may lead to errors.

The method of making quarterly estimates of profits is implicit in the procedure for adjusting estimates of profits from an accounting year to a calendar year basis. Annual estimates of profits classified by company accounting year and industry group are used as supplementary data to gross up the quarterly figures for the corresponding period of companies in the quarterly sample. The grossing up thus done industry by industry provides, on aggregation, estimates of quarterly profits of all companies. Clearly, as the annual profits estimates are derived from traders' forecasts, preliminary reports and tax assessments, they are continually revised and with them the corresponding quarterly estimates.

For the most recent quarters no supplementary data is available. For example, in 1967, when figures for the first and second quarters of the year were received from companies in the quarterly sample, no supplementary data for the year ending with these quarters was available, not even company forecasts. The procedure adopted for the most recent periods is to calculate for each industry group the ratio of profits shown in the sample for a particular quarter to those in the corresponding quarter of the preceding year and then to apply this ratio to the estimates of profits of all companies for the corresponding quarter of the previous year, which will already have been strengthened with some tax data. The advantage of this system lies in the fact that every improvement to the data for earlier years is reflected in the estimates for more recent periods. Its drawback is the amount of revision which it entails. Moreover bias may enter the estimates of changes in profits compared with the previous year obtained from the sample both because the sample is not fully random, and also because of the difficulties in measuring quarterly profits accurately.

Owing to the nature of the quarterly sample, it is not possible to use the quarterly returns to make separate estimates of profits in the various industries. In addition to the wide variations in coverage from industry to industry, the industrial breakdown differs from that of the tax assessments because in some cases a return relates to a group of companies which are assessed to tax individually.

Adjustments to Inland Revenue profits data

Because profits defined for national accounting purposes are not identical with profits assessed to tax and because the coverage of companies by the Inland Revenue is not quite that required in the national accounts tables, certain adjustments are needed.

The basic data received by Inland Revenue relate to all profits subject to United Kingdom tax and therefore to the profits of all companies operating in the United Kingdom, whether domestically owned or not, and to those companies resident in the United Kingdom but operating abroad. The definition of 'resident' for tax purposes includes branches and subsidiaries of overseas companies operating in the United Kingdom and in this respect is practically identical with the concept required for the national accounts.

For the national accounts only profits arising in the United Kingdom are estimated from this source. The profits of United Kingdom companies with operations mainly abroad, together with dividends received from overseas subsidiaries, are distinguished from profits arising from operations mainly at home. The division is not completely clear-cut and some profits of overseas branches of United Kingdom companies are included with the estimates of profits arising in the United Kingdom.

The main tabulation of company profits by Inland Revenue relates very nearly to industrial and commercial companies. The taxable profits of financial companies are separately estimated. The following adjustments are made to the main Inland Revenue estimates of the profits of industrial and commercial companies.

(a) *Profits earned abroad.* Profits earned by United Kingdom companies from operations abroad may be included with the estimates of profits arising in the United Kingdom and vice versa for operations at home. A small and uncertainly based adjustment (£4 million in 1966) is made for the balance.

(b) *Agricultural activities.* Some industrial and commercial companies obtain a small, but unknown, part of their profits from minor subsidiary activities in agriculture. It is statistically convenient to include these profits with income from agriculture and an arbitrary deduction is made (£3 million in 1966).

(c) *Professional firms.* An estimate is added of the profits of the few professional concerns which are companies, and are not included in the main tabulation.

(d) *Co-operative societies.* The profits of co-operative societies are deemed to be their surpluses before distribution of 'dividends' on sales or of interest on loans and shares. Estimates are prepared by the Inland Revenue.

(e) *Interest.* Under income tax and corporation tax bank interest and certain other interest payments are allowed as expenses in reckoning profits. In the national accounts such interest is regarded as a share of profits, not as part of operating expenditure. The amount paid under this head has therefore to be added back to the Inland Revenue profits estimates. Interest paid by companies on bank advances is estimated by applying an appropriate rate of interest to the estimated average monthly level of advances made to industrial and commercial companies. Similar methods are used for calculating interest paid by companies on trade bills and acceptances and on hire purchase debt; details of these estimates are given in the section on non-trading income on page 229.

(f) *Financial charges.* Expenditure by companies on commissions, stamp duties and other expenses connected with mortgages, capital issues and transfers of financial assets is not treated by the Inland Revenue as an operating expense, except in the case of companies whose business it is to deal in financial assets, but it is so treated in the national accounts. The estimated amount of this expenditure (over £40 million in 1966) is therefore deducted from the Inland Revenue profits estimates. New issue expenses are assumed to be five per cent of new capital issues by industrial and commercial companies. Stamp duties are divided into two categories—those on share and loan capital issued by companies, and those on the transfer of stocks and shares. Share and loan capital stamp duty is allocated between industrial and commercial companies and financial companies according to the division of new issues between the two. Stamp duty on the transfer of stocks and shares is allocated between the various sectors according to such information about financial transactions as is available. To these estimates are added allowances for stockbrokers' charges based on statistics of financial transactions and information on rates of commission.

(g) *Owner-occupied property.* Trading profits in the national accounts are deemed to include the income arising from owner-occupied trading property. When Schedule A income tax was in existence the net Schedule A value of owner-occupied property, which was deducted by Inland Revenue in arriving at trading profits under Schedule D, had therefore to be added back. Schedule A ceased to exist from the end of 1963, and therefore from then on no such addition has been needed.

(h) *War damage repairs.* This adjustment item ceased in 1964, following several years in which the adjustments were very small. War damage repairs to business property, like other repairs and maintenance, are regarded as current expenditure in the national accounts, as distinct from capital reconstructions which are regarded as capital expenditure. Expenditure on war damage repairs, however, is not allowed as an operating expense for tax purposes, but is treated as capital expenditure offset by a capital receipt. An estimate of repairs met out of war damage compensation was therefore deducted from the figure of trading profits provided by the Inland Revenue.

(i) *Evasion.* There is clearly some incentive for companies to understate their profits in order to reduce their tax liability. The extent to which this occurs is not known but it is thought to be very small. An arbitrary amount is added to the Inland Revenue estimate of profits on this account.

(j) *Nationalised industries.* Where the whole, or virtually the whole, of an industry is nationalised the Inland Revenue figures can be adjusted without difficulty to exclude profits from the date of nationalisation. An estimate of the profits for the part of the year in which the industry remained in private hands is included in the figures of company profits. Road passenger transport and iron and steel present special problems because, during the first period of national-isation, the nationalised companies did not lose their identity but continued to be assessed under their own names. These companies were excluded from the figures during the first period of nationalisation by tracing the individual assess-ments.

(k) *Bad debts.* The Inland Revenue allows a deduction for bad debts in assess-ing company profits. If the debt is between two companies, the decrease in the profits of the company incurring the bad debt is offset by the increase in the profits (or decrease in the loss) of the defaulting company. But if the default is by the personal sector, there is no such offset and the profits of the company sector are less by the extent of such bad debts. The goods and services will have been included in personal expenditure, whether paid for or not, and to balance national income and expenditure it would be appropriate to add back to company profits the bad debts between the company and personal sectors and to include an offsetting transfer to the personal sector in the company approp-riation account. This treatment has not so far been adopted, for lack of infor-mation.

(l) *Insurance claims.* Claims on non-life insurance companies are debited to the current accounts of these companies, but may be credited to the capital accounts of receiving industrial and commercial companies. This asymmetrical treatment, if no adjustment is made, causes a divergence in the estimates of gross national product and gross national expenditure. The problem can be viewed slightly differently. The gross profits of the non-life insurance companies are the difference between premiums received and (i) claims paid *plus* (ii) increase in reserves on account of accruing liability (if applicable) *plus* (iii) salaries and wages, and current expenses. The amount received by the insurance companies for the services provided is the premiums received *less* the claims paid. However, companies debit their operating accounts not with the cost of these insurance services, but with the full cost of the premiums paid. Accordingly the correct treatment, in so far as claims are credited to company capital accounts, would be for all such claims to be added back to company profits. In fact not all claims are credited to company capital accounts; if a building were destroyed by fire the claim undoubtedly would be, but if the claim is for minor damage to property or theft, the claim is often credited to current account to offset the cost of repairs or replacement. No information is available on the quantitative importance of claims credited to capital account; consequently it has not so far been possible to adjust the profits of industrial and commercial companies for them.

(m) *Business entertaining.* Expenses incurred after 6 April 1965, in providing business entertainment, other than for overseas customers, are not allowable as a deduction in computing profits chargeable to tax; for national accounting purposes such expenses continue to be deducted in arriving at profits.

(n) *Close companies.* Under corporation tax the profits of close companies include any remuneration paid to directors which is above the statutory limits laid down in the Finance Act, 1965; as all directors' remuneration is included

H*

in wages and salaries, the excess remuneration is deducted from profits in arriving at the profits figures for the national accounts.

Financial companies

As explained on page 204 the contribution of financial companies to the national income is measured by the difference between their receipts for services rendered (represented by charges and commissions) and their management expenses (salaries and wages and payments for current expenses), which may be described as their 'national income profits'. Together, 'national income profits' and net interest receipts add to profits in the more ordinary sense of the term. In what follows 'profits' in relation to financial companies is restricted to this more ordinary sense.

A major difficulty is that neither 'national income profits' nor profits in the ordinary sense are given directly by Inland Revenue data. Income tax assessments on financial companies often included interest received in full without prior deduction of tax, but they always excluded any interest from which tax had been deducted. Such investment income could well be the major source of revenue. Profits tax assessments included both kinds of interest, but also included, in a form not readily separable, the profits of many subsidiary companies engaged in other trades. Under corporation tax the position is much the same as under income tax; corporation tax assessments include interest received gross, but exclude interest received net, of income tax, although tax borne by deduction on such interest may be used, in certain circumstances, to reduce the corporation tax liability. Estimates are therefore made using various sources of information—Inland Revenue data and whatever published information is available. As a general check on the reasonableness of the estimates an appropriation account is built up for each main category of financial company.

For the London clearing banks and the Scottish and Northern Ireland banks, the Inland Revenue has figures from a series of special reports of total net income split between investment income taxed at source, trading income and gains or losses on realised investments. Gains or losses on realised investments may sometimes be large for this group; even before the introduction of capital gains tax, the difference between purchase and sale prices, although the transactions may be years apart, was charged to or allowed for income tax in the year of sale. These capital gains or losses do not correspond to any economic activity and are excluded from national income estimates of profits. Capital allowances are added to the other net income to obtain the gross profits.

For the remaining banks in this country—that is for British overseas and Commonwealth banks, American banks, other overseas and foreign banks, and accepting houses—the Inland Revenue has no special reports. A less reliable method is therefore resorted to. The net acquisition of financial and overseas assets of this group (including the discount houses) is known from their published balance sheets and other information. To this figure, to obtain an estimate of their profits, must be added their gross capital formation, interest paid on debentures and dividends (gross of tax), and taxes paid. Unfortunately, with this method, any revaluation of assets in balance sheets will give rise to error, since the profits so estimated will contain capital gains or losses. It is hoped that sometime in the future it will be possible to make a more reliable estimate of their profits, in the manner now followed for the clearing banks.

The profits of these two groups of banks, estimated in these different ways, are aggregated to obtain an estimate of the gross trading profits of all banks. Finally, to estimate the 'national income profits' of banks, their receipts from interest and dividends *less* interest paid on their deposits are subtracted from their total profits. The method of estimating these net interest receipts is described below. However, for this calculation interest receipts and payments between banks and financial companies, or between one bank and another, are not eliminated, in contrast to the consolidation made in estimating non-trading income for the sector.

This indirect method of estimating 'national income profits' by subtracting net interest receipts (without consolidation) from estimated total profits is also used for insurance companies, hire purchase finance companies, and 'other finance companies'.

The estimates of the profits of the trustee savings banks are taken from their published reports. The estimated profits of building societies are based on tax assessments, together with information from the reports of the Registrar of Friendly Societies. The estimates for insurance companies are based partly on Inland Revenue data and partly on Board of Trade sources.

The profits of hire purchase finance companies are derived from estimates of their undistributed net income, as stated in their annual reports. To obtain an estimate of gross trading profits, debenture interest and dividends (gross of tax), taxes paid, and capital allowances are added to their undistributed net income. Estimated net interest receipts, consisting of earnings on hire purchase debt *less* interest paid on bills discounted, on borrowing and on deposits, are then subtracted from the estimated gross trading profits to obtain an estimate of 'national income profits'. This procedure is not satisfactory because the undistributed income in such companies' reports relates to different accounting years, includes the earnings of subsidiaries located abroad, and may also include the earnings of domestic subsidiaries not engaged in hire purchase finance.

For the remaining financial companies the chief source of the profits estimates is the Inland Revenue data, described above, but the estimates are very unreliable.

The estimates of the 'national income profits' of the different categories of financial company are then aggregated to obtain the estimates for all financial companies.

RENT AND NON-TRADING INCOME

The rent and non-trading income of all companies is simply the sum of that of industrial and commercial companies and that of financial companies, with receipts and payments between these two sectors eliminated. It is convenient to describe the receipts of the two sectors separately. Most of the information on which the estimates of non-trading income are based is published in *Financial Statistics*. The estimates of non-trading income are all prepared on a quarterly basis. Rent is estimated quarterly by interpolation and projection of the annual figures.

Industrial and commercial companies

Rent and non-trading income of industrial and commercial companies consists of rent; interest on public sector debt—British government securities, Treasury bills, tax reserve certificates, local authority securities, mortgages, bills and temporary money; interest on deposits with banks, discount houses, hire purchase finance companies and building societies; and debenture interest and dividends on investments in financial companies.

The figure for rent refers only to the rent income from land and buildings let to a tenant. The figure required is the total rent received *less* rates, water charges, insurance, provision for repairs and other current expenses. Up to 1963 the estimation of rent income for companies was very approximate, being based mainly on a rough allocation by sector of rent income from various groups of property (see Appendix I). With the abolition of income tax under Schedule A, Schedule D assessments cover the whole of rent and not just the excess rents and provide much more reliable information on the rent income of companies. In future, statistics arising from corporation tax will also provide information on this item, which in 1966 amounted to nearly £200 million.

Estimates of interest on government securities and Treasury bills are based upon partial information about company holdings derived from analyses of company accounts. The estimates are poor but the amounts involved are thought not to be very large. For government securities the average yield on medium and long-dated securities, as calculated by the Bank of England, is applied to average quarterly holdings. For Treasury bills, variations in cash receipts are allowed for by applying the estimated proportion of total bills held by industrial and commercial companies to total interest paid by the government. Estimates of interest earned on tax reserve certificates are also based upon the information available on holdings and the rate of interest.

Interest on local authority debt held by industrial and commercial companies is estimated from information obtained from a sample of local authorities about the amounts of local authority debt, other than quoted securities, held by various sectors of the economy. An appropriate interest rate is applied to these holdings. Interest on quoted local authority securities is thought to be very small and is ignored.

Interest received on bank deposits by industrial and commercial companies is derived as part of the estimate of interest paid by banks. Total interest paid by banks and discount houses on their deposits is calculated by applying an appropriate rate of interest paid on deposit accounts to the estimated average monthly level of such accounts. A separate calculation is made for the group consisting of British and Commonwealth banks, American banks, other foreign and overseas banks, and accepting houses, since the banks in this group allow a higher rate of interest on deposits than the clearing banks. The amount of interest received by industrial and commercial companies is estimated on the assumption that the proportion of deposit accounts held by industrial and commercial companies is the same as the proportion of all deposits (current and deposit accounts) held by them. Interest received by industrial and commercial companies on deposits with hire purchase finance companies is similarly estimated using the breakdown of deposits provided by the hire purchase finance companies.

Other interest and dividends on investments in financial companies are believed to be small; an arbitrary amount is included.

Financial companies

It is important to note that the rent and non-trading income of financial companies excludes the receipts of the life funds of life assurance companies and superannuation funds. This has a significant effect on many of the estimates.

Rent received by financial companies, excluding the life funds of life assurance companies and the funds of superannuation schemes, is small; an arbitrary allowance is made for it. The non-trading income of financial companies consists mainly of interest on bank advances, trade bills and acceptances, mortgage advances, government and local authority securities, Treasury bills, local authority bills and temporary money, hire purchase debt, and interest and dividends received from investments in industrial and commercial companies.

Interest received on bank advances from the various sectors of the economy is calculated by applying appropriate rates of interest to the average monthly levels of advances. It is assumed that banks charge local authorities and public corporations bank rate *plus* one half per cent, companies bank rate *plus* one per cent, and the personal sector bank rate *plus* one and three-quarters per cent. In 1966 this interest accounted for nearly one-third of the total rent and non-trading income of financial companies.

A similar method is used for estimating interest received by banks, accepting houses and discount houses on their holdings of bills and acceptances: an average bill rate is applied to their average quarterly holdings. The allocation of this sum between payments by industrial and commercial companies and by the personal sector is arbitrary.

Mortgage interest received by building societies is obtained quarterly from a sample of building societies, and is available annually from the reports of the Registrar of Friendly Societies. Almost all of the interest is received from the personal sector. In 1966 this interest accounted for one-fifth of the total rent and non-trading income of financial companies.

Interest received by financial companies on government securities is estimated by applying the average yield on medium and long-dated government securities, as calculated by the Bank of England, to average quarterly holdings. The application of such an average rate is arbitrary and the procedure is therefore unsatisfactory; also, holdings may be stated at book values or, in a few cases, at nominal values which differ from the market values to which the yields relate. A similar method is used for estimating interest received by financial companies on local authority securities. The amount of interest received on Treasury bills is estimated by applying the proportion of total Treasury bills held by financial companies to the total interest paid by the government. Interest received on local authority bills and temporary money is based on information about holdings obtained from banks and local authorities, to which appropriate interest rates are applied.

Earnings on hire purchase debt are estimated from statistics of outstanding debt. This sum is roughly allocated by sector from analyses of the types of goods against which new hire purchase credit has been advanced.

INCOME FROM ABROAD

Estimates of income from abroad received by all companies are taken from the statistics of the balance of payments. A description of the sources of the estimates will be found in the chapter on international transactions (Chapter XV) and in the annual Pink Book, *United Kingdom Balance of Payments*.

The figures in the balance of payments accounts are after deduction of foreign taxes. Estimates of taxes paid abroad are made by the Inland Revenue on the basis of information obtained when United Kingdom tax is relieved against foreign tax. Relief up to the level of British taxation is now given for all central government taxes. The estimates relate to tax payments rather than tax accruals.

Income from abroad received by industrial and commercial companies is obtained as a residual by subtracting the income from abroad received by financial companies from that received by all companies. Income from abroad of financial companies consists of two main items: (i) the profits of non-resident subsidiaries and branches accruing to financial parent companies in the United Kingdom; and (ii) interest and dividends received by financial companies on portfolio investment abroad, and interest on bank advances received from non-residents. These estimates are based partly on tax assessments.

Quarterly estimates of company income from abroad are taken from the balance of payments statistics. Quarterly estimates of taxes paid abroad are based on payments where these are known and otherwise on quarterly variations in income from abroad.

4. STATISTICAL SOURCES: APPROPRIATION OF COMPANY INCOME

INTEREST AND DIVIDENDS
All companies

The main categories of interest and dividend payments shown in the 1967 Blue Book are given in the table on page 207.

Debenture interest, although not liable previously to profits tax or now to corporation tax, has always been assessed to income tax; it is charged to income tax on the payer as part of the mechanism of collection of tax by deduction at source. Estimates of debenture interest payments up to 1964 could be made from the amount of interest and annuities allowed as a deduction in assessments to profits tax. The allowance did not relate only to debenture interest; royalties and certain other items were also not liable to profits tax and had to be excluded in making the estimates. Profits tax data provided no information on debenture interest paid by one company to another and the estimate, which had to be deducted in order to obtain the figure for the company sector, is largely guess-work. Debenture interest so estimated refers to debenture interest accrued in companies' accounting years, rather than to interest paid in calendar years. For the national accounts, estimates of payments are made assuming that interest is paid in two instalments at the end of each six months accrual period. This procedure also provides the basis for the quarterly estimates. Tax assessment data are available only with a considerable time lag and the latest estimates were based on information provided by the Stock Exchange Council. From April 1966 debenture interest, again together with royalties and other annual payments, became directly liable to income tax under Schedule 12 of the 1965 Finance Act. A monthly analysis of the tax receipts will provide the future basis for quarterly estimates of payments of debenture interest.

Estimates of dividend payments on preference and ordinary shares are also ultimately based on Inland Revenue data but, as with debenture interest, the information before the introduction of corporation tax was available only after a considerable time lag.

Before 1 April 1958, the rate of profits tax was higher on distributed profits and dividend payments could be estimated directly from profits tax data available to the Inland Revenue, after allowance for companies falling below the exemption limit for profits tax. Thereafter, dividend payments and accruals were obtainable only indirectly on a sampling basis from the final reports on companies with gross profits of £5,000 or more (see page 221), which gives less reliable results considerably in arrear. The national accounts figures were therefore estimated from Inland Revenue data supplemented by Stock Exchange data. The Inland Revenue data on preference and ordinary share dividends, like that on debenture interest, refers to dividends accruing from profits in companies' accounting years, not to actual payments in calendar years. It is assumed, as for debenture interest, that preference dividends are paid in two instalments, each at the end of its six months accrual period. The interim ordinary dividend is assumed to be paid in the year of accrual, and the final ordinary dividend in the subsequent year.

From April 1966, dividend payments became directly liable to income tax under Schedule 12 of the 1965 Finance Act. A monthly analysis of the tax receipts will provide the future basis for quarterly estimates of dividend payments on ordinary and preference shares combined.

Annual information is published by the Stock Exchange Council on announcements of dividends on preference and on ordinary shares by companies whose securities are quoted on the London Stock Exchange and corresponding quarterly information is provided to the Central Statistical Office. In addition, an analysis is made of announcements in the press to give quarterly estimates of payments by the largest companies and of the interval between announcement and payment for other quoted companies. The Stock Exchange information is the only source from which the division between ordinary dividends and preference dividends can be estimated. Only resident companies are covered, and these of course include the United Kingdom subsidiaries of non-resident parent companies. Dividends paid by investment trusts, unit trusts and by unquoted companies are not covered, and estimates are made from Inland Revenue data.

Dividends paid by United Kingdom subsidiaries to their non-resident parent companies are excluded from dividends paid by the company sector and are taken into account in 'Profits due abroad net of United Kingdom tax'. Their payments are included in the figures obtained by the Inland Revenue from their final reports and balance of payments information is used in order to exclude them. When a United Kingdom subsidiary is 100 per cent owned by the non-resident parent company, no adjustment is needed to the Stock Exchange data: the shares of the subsidiary could not be quoted, and so would not be included with those reported by the Stock Exchange Council. The Stock Exchange figures need adjustment only when the subsidiary is partially owned, and its shares may therefore be quoted.

To obtain estimates of dividend payments by the company sector, inter-company payments must be eliminated. The profits tax computations made by Inland Revenue included a specific item for dividends received from other companies whose profits were chargeable to profits tax. This made possible, with adjustment for exempt companies, an estimate of the amount of inter-company dividend payments. The Stock Exchange data relate to payments by groups of companies and an estimate of payments between groups of companies, also based on profits tax data, is deducted. Payments of dividends to life funds of life assurance companies and superannuation funds are not treated as inter-company payments since these funds are regarded as being the property of the personal sector.

Nationalisation and denationalisation also necessitate adjustments. For example, when the steel companies were nationalised in 1951 (and also in 1967) the shares were transferred from private to public ownership and distribution of dividends by these companies were then excluded from company sector dividends.

The source of information on co-operative society dividends and interest is the annual statistics of the Registrar of Friendly Societies, together with Inland Revenue data.

Annual payments by building societies of interest on their shares and deposits are obtainable from Inland Revenue sources and from the statistics published annually by the Registrar of Friendly Societies. Quarterly information is obtained from a sample of building societies. The data relate to net interest, after payment of income tax by the societies; the equivalent gross interest is estimated for the national accounts by adding tax at the composite rate paid by the societies on this interest. The estimates are on an accruals basis. Also included are interest payments on loans to the societies from the central government.

'Other interest paid by banks, etc.' covers interest paid by banks, discount houses, the special investment departments of trustee savings banks and hire purchase finance companies. In 1966 interest paid by banks and discount houses accounted for about four-fifths of the total. The method of making the estimates of interest paid on deposits is described on page 228. Interest paid to other companies is eliminated. The interest is calculated on a quarterly basis, as it accrues.

Industrial and commercial companies; Financial companies

Separate estimates for financial companies of various receipts and payments of dividends and interest are used in the course of estimating their profits (see page 226) and in building up the figures of receipts and payments for all companies (see page 228 and above). The sources of information about the various receipts and payments for financial companies are tax data, reports by the Stock Exchange Council on debenture interest and dividends, published statistics of financial assets held by financial companies, statistics of deposits with building societies, banks, discount houses and hire purchase finance companies and information on interest rates. These estimates of receipts and payments for financial companies are divided between those involving industrial and commercial companies and those involving other sectors, those involving other financial companies being eliminated. The estimates of payments by industrial and commercial companies are then made indirectly; they are equal to the total estimate for the company sector *less* that part of the company sector total which is attributable to financial companies *plus* receipts by financial companies from industrial and commercial companies.

CURRENT TRANSFERS TO CHARITIES

Information about companies' contributions to charities is provided by Inland Revenue tax data. The figures relate to covenanted and uncovenanted contributions which are not allowed as a business expense. Those contributions which are allowed as a business expense for taxation purposes, that is where the charity involved benefits employees, etc., are not covered. Between seventy-five and eighty per cent of all covenanted payments to charities are estimated to be made by companies. In addition, an allowance is made for uncovenanted contributions to charities by companies.

PROFITS DUE ABROAD NET OF UNITED KINGDOM TAX

Estimates of this item are obtained from balance of payments statistics and information about the sources of the estimates will be found in Chapter XV, which deals with international transactions.

Profits due abroad net of United Kingdom tax for financial companies are separately estimated by the Bank of England. Mostly this item consists of the profits of United Kingdom branches and subsidiaries of non-resident banks. The profits of such subsidiaries which are not completely foreign-owned are of course taken into account only to the extent that they accrue to the non-resident parent company. The profits due abroad of industrial and commercial companies are obtained as a residual, the estimate for financial companies being subtracted from that for all companies.

UNITED KINGDOM TAXES ON INCOME

Tax system up to 1964/65

Profits tax, except for small amounts due from other sectors for which both payments and accruals could be closely estimated, fell only on companies; total payments in each quarter were known from collection records, and the accruals of tax due from companies were estimated by the Inland Revenue from profits tax assessments obtained from collection records.

Income tax collection records do not distinguish between companies and other taxpayers, except for tax collected under PAYE, but most of the tax collected under the various schedules can be allocated directly between the different sectors on the basis of less up-to-date information from tax assessments. The income tax payments by companies are estimated quarterly as the difference between the total income tax paid and the estimated payments of all the other sectors.

Company income tax accruals, that is, payments *plus* additions to reserves, were estimated from the net profits (after deducting capital allowances), the non-trading income and the dividends payable, together with adjustments due to retrospective changes in tax rates. The estimates of accruals, unlike the estimates of payments, necessarily relate to the profits corresponding to the aggregate of accounting years, since this is the basis for tax assessments. There were four components:

(a) The net profits, the amount of which for the current year normally formed the basis of assessments made for the following year and payments at the beginning of the calendar year after that. The tax was estimated at the current rate even though the assessment might be at a different rate.

(b) The non-trading income, some of which suffered tax by deduction at the current rates, the remainder approximating in aggregate to the assessments for the current year at current tax rates.

(c) The dividends payable out of the current year profits, a large proportion of which would be paid in the following year, from which companies deducted tax at the rate in force at the time of payment.

(d) Adjustments of tax reserves of the preceding year, which were estimated at that year's rate of tax before the present year's rate was known. This comprised an adjustment in respect of income tax on profits of the preceding year assessable in the present year, and an adjustment for tax deductible from dividends payable out of the preceding year's profits but not actually paid before the present year's rate came into force, normally on 6 April.

Additions to tax reserves were the excess of the income tax accruals, as outlined above, and profits tax accruals over the total tax payments.

For profits due abroad separate estimates of tax accruals are made by the Inland Revenue. The estimates are made in the same way as the estimates of all taxes, based on the estimated income due abroad. Tax payments are estimated by lagging tax accruals.

For financial companies, tax accruals are also separately estimated, and accruals for industrial and commercial companies are obtained as a difference. Tax on the investment income of the life funds of life assurance companies and superannuation funds is excluded since the income of these funds is attributed to the personal sector.

An alternative basis of estimating company tax payments would be to calculate them from the income and dividend estimates, assuming that all tax is paid on the theoretically due date. This method is vitiated, however, by delays in payments and repayments of appreciable amounts of tax for various reasons, for example litigation, the effect of which cannot generally be estimated.

Tax system from 1965/66

Under the Finance Act, 1965, companies became subject to corporation tax instead of to income tax and profits tax. In addition, for 1966/67 and subsequent years, companies have to account for the income tax deducted generally at the standard rate on any distributions they make.

Corporation tax was first payable on 1 January 1967 on trading profits made in accounting periods ending in 1965/66. Total payments in each quarter are known from collection records and except for very small amounts due from other sectors, corporation tax falls only on companies. The estimated amount of tax arising on capital gains is excluded and regarded as a tax on capital. Payments of overspill relief, which are deducted, are made entirely to companies.

Income tax payments by companies continue to be estimated quarterly as a residual difference between the total tax paid and the estimated payments of all other sectors. These payments consist mainly of the adjustment for changes in the amount of income tax in the hands of companies, due to the interval between deduction of tax under PAYE and under Schedule 12 and its payment to the Inland Revenue. The adjustment is based on variations in receipts shown by collection records.

From 1965 company tax accruals are made up from the following components:

(a) The net trading and non-trading income, liable to corporation tax at current rates.

(b) The non-trading income subject to deduction of income tax at source, the tax on which can generally be set off against other tax liabilities.

(c) Adjustments of tax reserves of the preceding year which were estimated before the rate of corporation tax applicable to the preceding year's income was known.

(d) Income from abroad which is eligible for overspill relief in respect of overseas tax not relieved against corporation tax. This item is a temporary one.

The estimates of tax accruals for 1965 and 1966 were affected by the transition to the new tax system. For the compilation of tax accruals in 1965 the rate of corporation tax adopted was 40 per cent even though some companies assumed a different rate in preparing their accounts before the rate was announced in 1966. The estimates include as a negative item the excess of the income tax deducted from dividends and interest payable out of the profits of the year over the tax which companies were required to account for to the Inland Revenue under Schedule 12. Liability under Schedule 12 arose only in respect of dividends and interest paid after 5 April 1966; the tax deducted from payments before 6 April 1966 was treated as covered by the income tax charged on companies. Moreover, in the case of some dividends paid after 5 April relief was due under Section 85 of the Finance Act, 1965.

5. RELIABILITY

The accuracy of the estimates of profits is reduced by the adjustments which have to be made to the basic data, but these adjustments do not seriously affect the reliability of the changes from year to year. Profits in the three most recent years, for example the figures for 1966, 1965 and 1964 in the 1967 Blue Book, may be deemed to fall in category B of the reliability gradings described on pages 39 to 41. Profits for earlier years are in category A, but for 1954 and earlier years are less accurate than for later years because, in the absence of quarterly figures, the estimates are aggregates of data relating to accounting years. The estimates of rent and non-trading income, being built up from individual interest flows which cannot always be accurately estimated for each sector, should be regarded as in category B. The reliability of the estimates of income from abroad and profits due abroad is discussed on page 471.

The estimates of dividend payments in 1957 and earlier years are in category A but the figures fall into category B between 1958 and 1966. The estimates of interest payments on building society shares and deposits, and of co-operative society dividends and interest are in category A, but the totals of payments included in 'Other interest' are in category B. The estimates for current transfers to charities relate only to contributions not allowed as a business expense and may well be incomplete; they should therefore be regarded as in category C. The estimates of United Kingdom taxes on income are in category A but the estimates of taxes paid abroad are based on incomplete information, which relates only to tax paid up to the level of British taxation, and should be regarded as in category C. Additions to dividend reserves and additions to tax reserves, which are the difference between the estimates of accruals and payments, and the residual saving item are also less accurate, and probably fall into category B.

The above appraisal may also be applied to the appropriation accounts for industrial and commercial companies and for non-nationalised companies. However, the estimates in the appropriation account for financial companies are less reliable and should be regarded as falling mostly in category C in the latest years and category B in earlier years.

The estimates of gross and net trading profits by industry based on tax assessments may be regarded as in category A except for the latest two years' estimates (1964 and 1965 in the 1967 Blue Book) which may be deemed to fall in category B. However, not all of the adjustments to the basic data which are required to obtain estimates on national accounting definitions are allocated by industry, and in this respect the estimates are less reliable. Also, the estimation of depreciation allowances makes the net profits figures less certain than the gross figures.

These estimates of reliability relate to the data available from the taxation system in force up to 1964/65; the assessments may be different when the data from the new taxation system are in full use.

Chapter VIII

Public Corporations

1. GENERAL DESCRIPTION

The major part of this sector comprises the bodies managing the industries nationalised in the period 1946 to 1951; the phrase public corporations is used to describe both these bodies and others, such as the British Broadcasting Corporation, with certain similar features. Where public enterprises such as the London Passenger Transport Board were superseded on nationalisation, they are also included in the sector for the earlier years.

Public corporations, in the sense used here, can be defined as public trading bodies which have a substantial degree of financial independence of the public authority—generally the central government—which created them. A public corporation is thus distinguished from other types of trading body by two main characteristics. Firstly, it is publicly controlled to the extent that the Sovereign, Parliament or a Minister appoints, directly or indirectly, the whole or the majority of the board of management. Secondly, it is a corporate body free to manage its affairs without detailed control by Parliament or other elected body; in particular, its financial independence includes the power to borrow, within limits laid down by Parliament, and to maintain its own reserves. It is this second characteristic which distinguishes the public corporations from those trading bodies which are treated as part of the central government sector, such as the Forestry Commission, the Royal Ordnance Factories and the other trading bodies listed on pages 296 and 297, and from local authority trading undertakings. All the latter obtain their money from, and surrender their surpluses to, the public authority of which they form a part and to which they are responsible in detail for the conduct of their trading operations. It should be noted that this definition of public corporations has led to the transfer of certain trading bodies from the central government sector to the public corporations sector. In April 1961 the Post Office was transferred to the public corporations sector in consequence of the financial independence given it under the Post Office Act, 1961. And the operation of international airports was transferred when the British Airports Authority took over responsibility from the Ministry of Aviation in April 1966.

Public corporations thus constitute a category somewhere between direct government trading undertakings and private enterprises. They form an important group of enterprises publicly owned and managed in the public interest; but at the same time conducted, in most respects, on ordinary business lines. They tend to differ, in economic experience and behaviour, both from companies on the one hand and from government trading bodies on the other. These

237

features, combined with the importance of the public corporations in the economy, justify their segregation as a separate sector. For certain purposes, however, their accounts are consolidated with those of companies to form the corporate sector; and public corporations are also combined with public authorities to show the total transactions of the public sector of the economy.

A list of public corporations is given in the annex to this chapter. Public corporations include the activities of subsidiaries where their accounts are consolidated with those of the parent corporation.

In interpreting the year-to-year changes in the accounts of this sector, it should be remembered that the area of nationalised industry changes from time to time. It expanded continuously in the post-war years up to 1952; public corporations were responsible for less than one per cent of the gross national product in 1945 but in 1952 for over 10 per cent [1]. There was a slight reduction in its relative importance between 1952 and 1960 as a result of the denationalisation of iron and steel and road haulage undertakings, but the transfer of the Post Office from the central government sector on 1 April 1961 to the public corporations sector restored the contribution of the public corporations to the gross national product to the previous peak of over 10 per cent and it remained at over 10 per cent up to 1966. The sector was enlarged on 28 July 1967 by the setting up of the British Steel Corporation.

The publicly owned basic industries—coal, gas and electricity and the publicly owned portions of iron and steel and transport and communication—account for nearly all of the contribution of public corporations to the gross national product. Although some of the public corporations in other branches of industrial activity perform well-known and very important functions, their collective contribution to the gross national product is relatively small.

Attention is drawn to the treatment of the iron and steel and road haulage industries during the process of denationalisation. On 13 July 1953 the assets and liabilities of the Iron and Steel Corporation of Great Britain, which controlled the nationalised iron and steel companies, were transferred to the Iron and Steel Holding and Realisation Agency (apart from the liability for British Iron and Steel stock which was transferred to the Consolidated Fund and became part of the national debt). The primary object of the Agency was to sell the individual iron and steel concerns back to private hands—a process which began in 1953 when the Agency directly held investments in 71 subsidiary companies; by 1963 the Agency was left with direct holdings in only one company. The subsidiary companies, which for the most part retained their separate identities for operating and accounting purposes throughout the period of nationalisation, have been treated as part of the public corporations sector up to the date at which the Agency disposed of its direct holdings and returned the assets to private ownership.

In the case of road haulage undertakings for the carriage of freight, which were progressively nationalised during the years 1948 to 1952, the circumstances of denationalisation differed from those of the iron and steel industry but the statistical treatment was similar. As with the iron and steel concerns, the income earned by these undertakings was progressively transferred from the public corporations sector as denationalisation proceeded.

---

[1] See T. M. Ridley, 'Notes on the Extent of the Public Sector', *Journal of the Royal Statistical Society*, Series A (General), Vol. CXIV, Part II, 1951.

2. THE PUBLISHED TABLES

OPERATING ACCOUNT

The public corporations sector is the only sector for which it has so far been possible to produce an operating, or production, account—the account which corresponds roughly to the trading account of a firm.

The operating account for all public corporations combined in 1966 is presented as follows:

Public corporations' operating account, 1966

£ million

Receipts		Payments	
Sales:		Wages, salaries, etc.	2,213
	} 4,905[1]	Purchases of goods and	
Revenue sales outside sector		services	2,082
Revenue sales inside sector		*less* Increase in value of stocks	
	358	and work in progress	−41
Sales to own capital account		Taxes on expenditure:	
	151	Rates	69
Subsidies...................		Motor vehicle, catering	
		licences, etc.	8
		Gross trading surplus and rent	
		before providing for deprec-	
		iation and stock apprec-	
		iation...................	1,083
Total	5,414	Total	5,414

Source: 1967 Blue Book, Table 36

[1]The division between these two items is given for 1964 and earlier years.

This is a consolidated trading or production account for public corporations whose trading operations are wholly or substantially conducted within the United Kingdom. For example, the two airways corporations are included but the Commonwealth Development Corporation is excluded. The surplus of operating revenue over operating expenses for public corporations whose trading is wholly or mainly conducted abroad is included in the appropriation account for public corporations as income from abroad.

The operating account shows the aggregate trading results of the corporations before making provisions for, or payments of, interest and taxes on income and before making provisions for depreciation and stock appreciation. Certain adjustments are made to the published accounts of the corporations in order to arrive at figures on the basis required for the national accounts.

Receipts

Sales include the gross receipts from the ownership of land, houses and other buildings which are let; the expenditure incurred by the corporations on repairs, maintenance, etc. is included in the items on the other side of the account. Income from rent is therefore included in the balance of the account under the title 'Gross trading surplus and rent before providing for depreciation and stock appreciation'.

Sales (and purchases) exclude transactions between establishments in the same corporation but include transactions between corporations (estimated at £550 million in 1964) as well as transactions with other sectors of the economy. Sales to their own capital account are shown separately, comprising capital work done valued at cost price (cost of materials and wages) and capitalised interest charges. Capital work done by the corporations is apportioned between wages, salaries, etc. and purchases of goods and services on the payments side of the account. By including wages charged to capital account in this way, a closer estimate of the contribution of the public corporations to the gross domestic product can be obtained from the operating account.

In the case of the British Broadcasting Corporation the greater part of its receipts consists of income from the sale of broadcast receiving licences. The amount included is the gross receipts by the Post Office from the sale of licences *less* the costs of collection paid to the Post Office, and *less* the licence revenue retained by the Exchequer in the years 1946 to 1960.

The item 'Subsidies' became much more important in 1960 when the revenue deficits of nationalised transport undertakings became covered by central government subsidies. The item includes the revenue deficits of the British Transport Commission from 1960 to 1962, the British Railways Board and British Waterways Board from 1963 to 1966 and the London Transport Board in 1966. These are recorded in the accounts of both central government and public corporations as they accrue. Other corporations receiving subsidies in 1966 were the Ulster Transport Authority, the New Town Development Corporations, the Commission for the New Towns, the Scottish Special Housing Association, the Northern Ireland Housing Trust and the National Research Development Corporation. These subsidies, however, accounted for only £9 million of the total of £151 million. Various other corporations received subsidies in earlier years.

Payments

Operating expenditure as shown in the accounts of public corporations is adjusted in a number of ways for the national accounts. The main adjustments are (a) the exclusion of the unspent portion of internal provisions against future expenditure on such items as repairs; (b) the exclusion of expenditure on renewals which is treated in the national accounts as fixed capital formation for those years in which certain corporations have charged such expenditure to their operating accounts; and (c) the addition of expenditure charged by corporations to their capital accounts but not regarded as fixed capital formation in the national accounts, for example the costs of conversion of consumers' appliances to natural gas.

The increase in the book value of stocks and work in progress is entered as a deduction on the payments side of the account. This is equivalent to treating the book value of the opening stock as a purchase and that of the closing stock as a sale. Hence any element of stock appreciation due to a rise in prices during the year of goods bought is deducted from purchases and included in the figure of the gross trading surplus.

The amounts shown for taxes on expenditure consist of rates, payments in lieu of rates under Part V of the Local Government Act, 1948, motor vehicle licence duties, catering licences and stamp duty. Taxes, such as the duty on hydrocarbon oils, which are incorporated in the purchase price of goods and services are not included.

APPROPRIATION ACCOUNT

The appropriation account for all public corporations combined is presented as follows:

Public corporations' appropriation account, 1966

£ million

Income		Allocation of income	
Gross trading surplus before providing for depreciation and stock appreciation	1,038	Interest and dividends: Payments: On loans from central government	371
Rent	45	Other................	105
Non-trading income	46	Additions to interest and dividend reserves	12
Income from abroad	8	United Kingdom taxes on income: Payments	31
		Additions to tax reserves	—25
		Balance: undistributed income before providing for depreciation and stock appreciation	643
Total	1,137	Total	1,137

Source: 1967 Blue Book, Table 37

This account shows how the income of public corporations is made up and how it is allocated between interest and dividends, taxes on income and savings. It corresponds to the similar appropriation account for companies and the two tables are in fact amalgamated to give the corporate income appropriation account in Table 3 of the Blue Book (see page 62).

Income

The first two items, the 'Gross trading surplus' of the corporations operating wholly or mainly in the United Kingdom and 'Rent' represent the combined balance transferred from the operating account.

Rent represents the income, after expenses have been paid, derived from the ownership of land and buildings. As in the case of other enterprises no rent income is imputed for owner-occupied trading property and its contribution as a factor of production is embodied in the gross trading surplus.

'Non-trading income' consists of investment income, before deduction of tax at source, and miscellaneous earnings from non-trading activities. Most of this income is received from outside the sector, but no attempt is made to consolidate completely the account of public corporations by deducting, as should be done, receipts of non-trading income by one corporation from another. Finally, 'Income earned abroad' is added, being the profits of the corporations operating wholly or mainly overseas, whether remitted to the United Kingdom or not.

Allocation of income

Interest and dividends. Payments of interest on loans from central government in 1966 were made up as follows:

	£ million
Electricity Council	118
Post Office	56
British Railways Board	52
National Coal Board	41
Housing and new town corporations	26
Gas Council	20
Scottish Electricity Boards	19
Other corporations	39
Total	371

'Other interest and dividends' covers interest on stock issued by the corporations, interest on compensation stock issued to former shareholders in the undertakings and interest on short-term loans and bank overdrafts. It includes the net revenue of the Iron and Steel Holding and Realisation Agency payable to the Exchequer. This revenue was derived by the Agency from dividends received from the constituent companies (one company only by 1963) and from interest received from holdings retained in denationalised companies. Other items included are the half-yearly payments by the Bank of England to the Exchequer, dividends paid by Cable and Wireless Ltd., payments by the Independent Television Authority and the Transport Holding Company from their surplus revenue to the Exchequer, and payments by British Overseas Airways Corporation on its Exchequer dividend capital.

All interest and dividend payments are shown gross before deduction of income tax, which is regarded as falling on the recipients of interest and dividends. As in the case of non-trading income, payments of interest by one corporation to another are not deducted. For each year the difference between actual payments of interest and dividends and the amount of interest and dividends properly chargeable for the year is shown separately as an addition to, or a deduction from, reserves for future payments. The large run-down of reserves in 1962 and their rebuilding in 1963 resulted from the winding-up of the British Transport Commission and its reconstitution as five separate undertakings.

United Kingdom taxes on income. From 1965/66 corporations became subject to corporation tax which replaced income tax and profits tax. Up to 1953 corporations were also subject to excess profits levy and up to 1946 excess profits tax. It should be noted that the absence of equity capital placed the public corporations in a different position from companies in respect of liability to profits tax; the public corporations were not liable to the higher rate of profits tax payable by companies on distributed profits up to 1958. Furthermore, interest on loan capital was normally treated as a deduction from profits in arriving at the assessment for profits tax. In the case of the public corporations, only a part of such interest was deducted, the proportion being determined with reference to the pre-nationalisation proportion of loan interest to equity distributions for the former undertakings.

Taxes on income are shown in the same way as for companies and amounts withheld by deduction from interest and dividends paid are treated as tax falling on the recipients of the interest and dividends and not on the corporations. The figures of tax payments by the corporations are taken to be the amounts paid to the Inland Revenue *less* amounts of tax withheld from dividends and interest paid. The amounts withheld are estimated to have been closely matched by corresponding payments to the Inland Revenue in each calendar year up to 1965. In 1966, the new system of taxation of interest and dividends reduced the delay between deduction of tax from interest and dividend payments and payment of the corresponding tax to the Inland Revenue. As a result, tax payments in 1966 were exceptionally high and tax reserves are shown as being correspondingly reduced.

Payments of taxes on income in the year are shown separately from additions to tax reserves; these additions represent the difference between actual payments in the year and the estimated tax at current rates on the income of the year, together with any alterations to previous reserves consequent on the Budget for the year. As mentioned above, in 1966 additions to reserves include a downward adjustment due to the change in the system of taxation of interest and dividends.

The estimates are based mainly on the published accounts of the corporations but information on receipts of tax by the Inland Revenue is also used. The reliability of the figures is limited by the degree of detail shown in the published accounts. For example, tax that is unpaid at the balancing date may be included in sundry creditors and not shown separately. Tax reserves set up by the corporations in order to spread over time the tax relief given by the initial allowances for capital expenditure are usually distinguishable in the accounts and changes in these reserves are excluded.

CAPITAL ACCOUNT

The capital account for all public corporations combined is presented as follows:

Public corporations' capital account, 1966

£ million

Receipts		Payments	
Undistributed income before provision for depreciation and stock appreciation	643	Gross domestic fixed capital formation	1,447
Additions to interest and dividend reserves	12	Increase in value of stocks and work in progress......	41
Additions to tax reserves	—25	*Transactions in financial assets*	
Capital transfers (net)	11		
		Net lending to private sector	8
Transactions in financial assets			
		Net lending and investment abroad	6
Loans from central government (net).................	867		
Stock issued *less* stock redeemed	—12	Cash expenditure on company securities, etc. (net)	22
		Net acquisition of other financial assets	—28
Total	1,496	Total	1,496

Source: 1967 Blue Book, Table 38

The capital account shows the corporations' investment in fixed assets, stocks and certain financial assets and the main sources from which the investment has been financed. The account does not record transactions relating to the transfer of undertakings to or from the sector but only the transactions of corporations while they are in the sector.

Receipts

The receipts represent the sources of finance. They are as follows.

(a) *Undistributed income before provision for depreciation and stock appreciation.* This is the balance brought forward from the appropriation account.

(b) *Additions to interest and dividend and tax reserves.* These are additional financial resources temporarily available which are brought forward from the appropriation account.

(c) *Capital transfers (net).* In 1966 the main constituents of this item were contributions by consumers towards the cost of connecting consumers' premises to the electricity supply, etc. and Exchequer capital grants towards the external services of the British Broadcasting Corporation. Central government grants for civil defence works are included. In earlier years other main items were: Exchequer capital contributions such as those paid to the housing corporations and the New Town Development Corporations; in 1955 and 1956 the compensation paid to the British Transport Commission from the proceeds of the transport levy (see page 265); and in 1949 receipts of war damage compensation *less* payments of war damage contributions.

For certain years capital transfers on writing-off debt are shown separately. They represent the notional receipt from the central government of the amounts by which the capital liabilities of public corporations have been reduced as a result of capital reconstruction and writing-off debt. Details are given on page 283. The changes in these capital liabilities are also shown separately for the same years under the headings 'Loans from central government (net)' and 'Stock issued *less* stock redeemed'.

(d) *Loans from central government (net).* Under the Finance Acts of 1956 and 1958, public corporations in Great Britain ceased to raise capital by the issue of stock and from 1956 loans from the central government have been their chief source of external finance. An account of the reasons for this change is given in paragraphs 84 to 89 of the Radcliffe Report[2]. The figures are taken from the central government accounts, and are further described on pages 284 and 285.

Changes in net indebtedness to the central government arising in certain years from capital reconstruction and writing-off debt are shown separately (see pages 283 and 284).

(e) *Stock issued less stock redeemed.* For this item premiums are added to, and discounts are deducted from, the nominal value of the stock involved. Only stock issued for cash is included; stock issued to former owners of acquired undertakings is excluded. After 1955 external finance has not been obtained by the issue of stock except in Northern Ireland, as explained above.

The decrease in liability for stock as a result of writing-off debt in certain years is shown separately as 'Transfer of liability to central government'.

---

[2]*Committee on the Working of the Monetary System*, Cmnd. 827.

Payments

The investment financed by these receipts falls into the following groups.

(a) *Gross domestic fixed capital formation.* This comprises expenditure within the United Kingdom on the replacement of, and additions and improvements to, fixed assets *less* the proceeds from the sale of any fixed assets. Work done by the corporations for their own capital accounts is included. It includes interest which has been capitalised by certain corporations in respect of funds used for expenditure on fixed assets in the period before the assets came into productive use. Further details are given in Chapter XII.

(b) *Increase in value of stocks and work in progress.* This includes stock appreciation as well as the value of the physical increase in stocks. The estimates are described in Chapter XIII.

(c) *Net lending to private sector.* This item comprises loans by *less* repayments to the National Film Finance Corporation, the Sugar Board and the Housing Corporation, together with the financial support of research and development projects by the National Research Development Corporation.

(d) *Net lending and investment abroad.* This consists of net lending by the Commonwealth Development Corporation for the financing of development projects overseas, together with capital expenditure on fixed assets abroad by the British Broadcasting Corporation.

(e) *Cash expenditure on company securities, etc. (net).* This comprises cash expenditure on the acquisition of subsidiaries, trade investments and marketable securities. The expenditure has been identified only from 1964.

(f) *Net acquisition of other financial assets.* This item summarises the changes in all balance sheet entries, both assets and liabilities, not dealt with elsewhere in the capital account: for example cash, bank advances, borrowing from superannuation funds, trade credit granted, hire purchase credit given on consumers' appliances, and trade debts. It also includes the differences between the figures of government loans taken from the central government accounts and those included in the corporations' published accounts.

ANALYSIS BY INDUSTRY OF APPROPRIATION AND CAPITAL ACCOUNTS

Tables 39 and 40 of the 1967 Blue Book show the appropriation and capital accounts—but not the operating account—of public corporations grouped by industries. These tables cannot be compiled until the full accounts of the corporations are available and are therefore not given for the latest year shown in the combined tables.

The grouping of industries is shown in the following list; the corporations listed and the titles used are those in existence at the end of 1966. The corporations are each classified to one industry, except in the cases noted in the list, and in general no attempt is made to classify establishments engaged in subsidiary activities, for example railway workshops, to the industry to which they belong. This grouping of industries is used for the estimates of gross domestic product by industry (Table 17 of the 1967 Blue Book).

Fuel and power. National Coal Board, Electricity Council, Central Electricity Generating Board, Area Electricity Boards, North of Scotland Hydro-Electric Board, South of Scotland Electricity Board, Electricity Board for Northern Ireland, Gas Council and Area Gas Boards.

Iron and steel. The Iron and Steel Holding and Realisation Agency and its subsidiaries.

Transport and communication. British Railways Board, London Transport Board, British Transport Docks Board, British Waterways Board, Transport Holding Company, Ulster Transport Authority, National Dock Labour Board, National Ports Council, British Overseas Airways Corporation, British European Airways, British Airports Authority, Post Office, Cable and Wireless Ltd.

Housing and new town corporations. New Town Development Corporations, Commission for the New Towns, Scottish Special Housing Association, Northern Ireland Housing Trust, Coal Industry Housing Association (fixed capital expenditure on housing by the National Coal Board), Housing Corporation.

Other corporations. British Broadcasting Corporation, Independent Television Authority, Bank of England, National Film Finance Corporation, National Research Development Corporation, Commonwealth Development Corporation, Covent Garden Market Authority, Sugar Board, Industrial Reorganisation Corporation, Coal Industry Social Welfare Organisation, and the internal insurance funds mentioned below.

In their own accounts the public corporations exclude from their trading surpluses the surpluses accruing to the various internal insurance funds, which provide for various forms of compensation; these surpluses are the payments into the funds, which are mainly charged to the corporations operating accounts, *less* compensation payments. Such surpluses must, however, be included in the trading surplus of the public corporations sector for consistency with the transactions of the rest of the economy. To simplify comparison with the published accounts, the transactions of these internal insurance funds are, in principle, excluded in Tables 39 and 40 from the transactions of the corporations in each industry group and entered in the miscellaneous group 'Other corporations'. In practice only one corporation is so treated at the present time; payments by the National Coal Board into funds for workmen's compensation, supplementary injuries, surface damage, restoration of opencast sites, compensation for loss of office and insurance are regarded as operating expenses of the Board and as operating receipts of the group 'Other corporations'. The excess of receipts over expenses in these compensation activities, that is the increase in provisions for deferred liabilities as shown in the balance sheet, is treated as undistributed income in the 'Other corporations' group.

Sufficiently reliable estimates of additions to tax and interest reserves on the basis used in the Blue Book cannot be made for the corporations in each of the separate industries. The appropriation accounts therefore show the provision for interest and dividends and for United Kingdom taxes on income, including additions to reserves. The entries for additions to tax and interest reserves in the capital account are omitted from the receipts and the figure of 'Net acquisition of other financial assets including net investment abroad' therefore excludes any changes in financial assets associated with changes in these temporary reserves.

QUARTERLY TABLES

Quarterly appropriation and capital accounts for all public corporations combined are published in *Financial Statistics*; the figures have been published from 1959. The accounts correspond to those in the Blue Book, although the presentation is somewhat different. In the appropriation account additions to tax and to interest and dividend reserves are not specified in the allocation of income and are included in the balance of undistributed income. Hence it is not necessary to add them back as a source of funds to the receipts side of the capital account. The capital account also shows some additional detail on financial transactions, which in the Blue Book is incorporated in the section on financial accounts.

3. STATISTICAL SOURCES

Annual accounts

The basic source of information is the published accounts of the public corporations to which certain adjustments are made, as described in the previous section. When the accounts do not relate to the calendar year, some of the calendar year estimates have been derived by interpolation but others, such as the trading surplus and certain items in the capital account, are more precisely adjusted on the basis of the quarterly information. Figures for corporations set up or terminated other than at the beginning or end of a calendar year have been included in the accounts only with respect to that portion of the initial or final year in which they were operating as public corporations. Figures for the latest year shown are in some cases provisional, being compiled before the appearance of the published accounts.

Where the estimates relate to transactions with the central government, the estimates are taken from the central government accounts rather than the accounts of the public corporations, in order to achieve the consistency necessary in the national accounts. This applies to interest payments, capital grants and loans.

Quarterly accounts

Less basic data are available quarterly than annually and a certain amount of interpolation and estimation has to be undertaken, particularly for the smaller items. The series are adjusted to the aggregates for the year when the annual figures become available.

The major public corporations provide quarterly returns which show:
Gross trading surplus
Capital grants received
Gross domestic fixed capital formation
Change in value of stocks
Change in trade credit (net)
Cash expenditure on company securities, etc.
In 1966 these returns covered some 95 per cent of the total gross trading surplus of public corporations.

The items which are taken from the central government accounts are all available quarterly. Quarterly payments of taxes on income, after deduction of amounts withheld from interest and dividends paid, are calculated from information on receipts of tax by the Inland Revenue and estimates of the relevant interest and dividend payments. Payments of interest on stock issues are estimated on the basis of the dates when the interest becomes due. For the remaining small items of interest smooth quarterly changes are assumed. The quarterly estimates of rent, non-trading income and income earned abroad are all interpolated and projected on the basis of the annual figures.

The additional transactions on financial assets which are included in the quarterly capital account are based on the returns made by the corporations and by banks, superannuation funds and local authorities. Further details of financial transactions are given in Chapter XIV.

4. RELIABILITY

The reliability of the basic annual data, being mainly published accounts, can be regarded as in category A of the gradings described on pages 39 to 41. Possibilities of error arise in adjusting financial year figures to a calendar year basis, in the estimates of items in the operating account which are not always distinguishable in the published accounts, and in some of the minor adjustments for individual items, but are probably not sufficient to reduce significantly the reliability of the annual figures as a whole.

The quarterly figures, involving rather more estimation, must be rated at a lower level of reliability. Even when returned by the corporations themselves, the quarterly figures are sometimes estimated. This applies even after the quarterly figures have been adjusted to the annual totals, since there is no basis on which accurately to allocate the annual adjustment over the four quarters of the year.

ANNEX

PUBLIC CORPORATIONS SECTOR

Corporations in existence at 31 *December 1966*	*Commencing or vesting date*
British Broadcasting Corporation......................	1927
Electricity Board for Northern Ireland	1932
Scottish Special Housing Association	1937
British Overseas Airways Corporation	1940
North of Scotland Hydro-Electric Board	1943
Northern Ireland Housing Trust	1945
Bank of England[1]	1 March 1946
British European Airways	1 August 1946
New Town Development Corporations and Commission for the New Towns .... and various later dates	1 December 1946
National Coal Board	1 January 1947
National Dock Labour Board	28 June 1947
Raw Cotton Commission[2]	1 January 1948
National Film Finance Corporation (previously the National Film Finance Company).............................	1 October 1948
Ulster Transport Authority	1 October 1948
Gas Council and Area Gas Boards	1 May 1949
National Research Development Corporation..............	28 June 1949
Iron and Steel Holding and Realisation Agency and its subsidiaries[3][4]..	13 July 1953
Independent Television Authority.......................	4 August 1954
South of Scotland Electricity Board[3]....................	1 April 1955
Sugar Board...	1 January 1957
Electricity Council, Central Electricity Generating Board and Area Electricity Boards[3]	1 January 1958
Post Office...	1 April 1961
Covent Garden Market Authority.......................	30 October 1961
British Railways Board[3]	1 January 1963
London Transport Board[3]	1 January 1963
British Transport Docks Board[3].......................	1 January 1963
British Waterways Board[3]	1 January 1963
Transport Holding Company[3].........................	1 January 1963
National Ports Council	10 June 1964
Housing Corporation	1 September 1964
British Airports Authority.............................	1 April 1966
Industrial Reorganisation Corporation	21 December 1966

[1]Excluding the transactions of the Issue Department which are treated as transactions of central government (see page 252).
[2]Finally wound up on 1 January 1968.
[3]Corporations which succeeded existing corporations (see next page).
[4]The Agency's remaining subsidiary was vested in the British Steel Corporation when it was set up on 28 July 1967. The Agency was dissolved on 30 September 1967.

J

*Commencing or
vesting date*

Corporations operating wholly or mainly overseas:
Commonwealth Development Corporation (previously the
   Colonial Development Corporation) .... 16 February 1948
Cable and Wireless Ltd................................ 1 April 1950

Corporations succeeded by other corporations

Central Electricity Board, 1926 to 1 April 1948. Succeeded by the British
  Electricity Authority.

British Electricity Authority and Area Electricity Boards, 1 April 1948 to 31 March
  1955. Recreated as two separate corporations: the Central Electricity Authority
  and Area Boards, and the South of Scotland Electricity Board.

Central Electricity Authority and Area Electricity Boards, 1 April 1955 to 31
  December 1957. Reorganised as the Electricity Council, Central Electricity
  Generating Board and Area Electricity Boards.

London Passenger Transport Board, 1933 to 1 January 1948. Absorbed in the
  British Transport Commission and recreated as the London Transport Board
  on 1 January 1963.

British Transport Commission, 1 January 1948 to 31 December 1962. Recreated
  as five separate corporations: the British Railways Board, the London Transport Board, the British Transport Docks Board, the British Waterways Board
  and the Transport Holding Company.

British South America Airways Corporation, 1 August 1946 to 30 July 1949.
  Absorbed in British Overseas Airways Corporation.

Cable and Wireless Ltd., 1 January 1947 to 1 April 1950. In 1950 the United
  Kingdom assets were taken over by the Post Office; the remainder of the
  undertaking, operating mainly overseas, continued to be treated as a public
  corporation.

Iron and Steel Corporation of Great Britain, 15 February 1951 to 13 July 1953.
  Succeeded by the Iron and Steel Holding and Realisation Agency (see page
  238).

Great Northern Railway Board (Northern Ireland portion), 1 September 1953 to
  1 October 1958. Absorbed in Ulster Transport Authority.

Corporations not succeeded by other corporations

National Service Hostels Corporation Ltd., 1941 to 10 September 1956.
Festival Gardens Ltd., 16 November 1949 to 15 December 1953.
Overseas Food Corporation, 16 February 1948 to 1 April 1955.

Chapter IX

Central Government

1. GENERAL DESCRIPTION

THE SCOPE OF CENTRAL GOVERNMENT

The central government, as a sector of the economy, is defined here in a wide sense. It can be regarded as embracing all bodies for whose activities a Minister of the Crown, or other responsible person, is accountable to Parliament. One of the marks of this accountability is that such bodies submit to Parliament detailed statements of their estimated and actual expenditure and their collection of revenue. The central government includes, in addition to the ordinary government departments, a number of bodies (for example, Regional Hospital Boards) administering public policy but without the substantial degree of financial independence which characterises the public corporations; it also includes certain extra-budgetary funds and accounts controlled by departments, of which the National Insurance Funds are the most important. It should be noted in particular that the accounts of the government of Northern Ireland are combined with those of the United Kingdom government. The three main classes which go to make up the central government, as here defined, are now described in more detail.

Government departments. These comprise the Ministry of Defence and the civil departments of the United Kingdom government and of the Northern Ireland government, whose expenditure is described as expenditure on 'Supply services'. This includes all bodies, boards, committees and commissions under the aegis of government departments and whose accounting arrangements are identical with those of government departments, that is their expenditure is charged directly to supply Votes. Examples are the Monopolies Commission and the Countryside Commission. For national accounting purposes this class is divided between bodies carrying on trading activities, a list of which is given in Annex 1 on page 296, and non-trading bodies. *Estimates* are published annually in February or March for all departments, showing expenditure and some classes of receipts expected for the year beginning 1 April; the *Appropriation Accounts* show in slightly less detail the expenditure and receipts actually incurred. For most trading activities, trading accounts on a commercial (as opposed to a cash) basis are published in addition to the *Estimates* and *Appropriation Accounts.*

Bodies not administered as part of government departments but subject nevertheless to varying degrees of ministerial or departmental control. In particular, these bodies are subject to detailed financial control. In most cases they draw a sub-

251

stantial part of their income from government grants. Important examples are
the Regional Hospital Boards, the Boards of Governors of Teaching Hospitals
and the Atomic Energy Authority. There is a considerable number of other
bodies, most of which are listed in Annex 2 to this chapter. Details of the revenue
and expenditure of these bodies are generally appended in the *Estimates* and
Appropriation Accounts or appear as separate House of Commons papers, or
sometimes as Command papers (see Annex 3). Bodies in receipt of government
grants, but having also other appreciable means of financial support, for example
the universities, are treated as belonging to the company sector or to the personal
sector. The borderline here between the central government and the rest of the
economy is rather arbitrary. This problem is discussed further on page 261.

Extra-budgetary funds and accounts controlled by departments. The third main
component of the central government as defined in the national accounts
consists of a variety of funds for which separate accounts are maintained but
which are directly administered by the departments and bodies referred to in the
previous paragraphs. Examples are:

(a) National Insurance Funds
(b) Local Loans Fund
(c) Development Fund
(d) Civil Contingencies Fund
(e) Exchange Equalisation Account
(f) Post Office Savings Banks Fund
(g) Redundancy Fund

A fuller list appears in Annex 3. The accounts of most of the funds referred to in
this paragraph are included in the *Estimates* and *Appropriation Accounts* or are
published as House of Commons papers or Command papers.

The Issue Department of the Bank of England is regarded as an agent of the
central government and its transactions on behalf of the central government are
treated as though they were transactions of the central government itself.

Up to 31 March 1968 the great bulk of government revenue was ultimately
paid into the Consolidated Fund and almost all government expenditure was
paid out of issues from that Fund. The Consolidated Fund was virtually syn-
onymous with the term Exchequer, which was then the central cash account of
the government with the Bank of England and Bank of Ireland. Most transactions of the Exchequer were, however, internal to the central government as
here defined, and therefore disappear on consolidation (see next page). But a
few transactions, such as the expenses of management of and interest on the
national debt, were transactions with the non-government sector of the economy.

From 1 April 1968 the National Loans Fund was set up with a separate cash
account at the Bank of England. From that date this account contains all the
transactions connected with the national debt and the bulk of government
lending, transferred to the new Fund from the Consolidated Fund. The Consolidated Fund and the National Loans Fund between them cover nearly all
government revenue, ordinary expenditure, lending and borrowing. Throughout
this chapter the introduction of the National Loans Fund has been largely
ignored, because the description relates to the 1967 Blue Book which was based
on the previous form of accounts. And the term Exchequer is retained to describe
the central cash account of the government.

GENERAL METHOD OF ANALYSIS OF THE DATA

The transactions of the central government as here defined are recorded, usually in a good deal of detail, in the accounts of the departments, bodies and funds discussed in the preceding paragraphs. A general description of the sources is given in Section 4 of this chapter and details of the principal published accounts are listed in Annex 3. But these accounts are not presented in a form suitable for national accounting purposes. Two principal operations have to be carried out to fit the large mass of data into the national accounting framework. In the first place, the various accounts have to be consolidated so that only transactions of the government, considered as a whole, with the rest of the economy remain. Secondly, such transactions with the rest of the economy have to be classified according to the economic categories used in the national accounts.

The consolidation of accounts

In the first process—consolidation—transactions between any two parts of the central government are, with certain exceptions, eliminated. In particular, most transactions between the Exchequer and departments disappear. As an example, we may consider the case of taxes collected by the Inland Revenue. The department in due course passes the money it collects to the Exchequer. On consolidating the accounts of this department with the Exchequer account, the payment by the department to the Exchequer disappears, so that the consolidated account shows only receipts of taxes by the department. Similarly issues of money from the Exchequer to departments to finance departmental expenditure disappear in the process of consolidation, and only payments by departments made outside the central government appear in the consolidated account. Departmental receipts and payments, as recorded in the consolidated account of the central government constructed for national accounts purposes, may therefore differ significantly from the receipts and issues as recorded in the Exchequer accounts.

Other internal transactions which disappear on consolidation are:

(a) Expenditure on goods and services by one department through the agency of another; on consolidation, only the expenditure of the agent department remains. The most important example is the payments by the defence departments to the Ministry of Technology, or previously the Ministry of Aviation, for defence equipment supplied.

(b) Debt interest paid by the Exchequer to government funds, for example debt interest paid on government securities held by the National Insurance Funds.

(c) Grants between one part of the government and another, for example grants by the Ministry of Social Security to the National Insurance Funds.

(d) Lending between one part of the government and another, for example money invested by the National Insurance Funds in government securities through the agency of the National Debt Commissioners.

Internal transactions are not eliminated when the economic category of the payment by one part of the government differs from that of the receipt by the other part. Thus national insurance contributions paid by the government in respect of its employees, although effectively internal, do not disappear on consolidation but form part of government expenditure on wages and salaries, etc. Similarly, selective employment tax and other taxes on expenditure forming part of expenditure on goods and services by the government are not eliminated in the process of consolidation. Purchases by the non-trading parts of the central government from government trading bodies, for example Royal Ordnance Factories, appear both in expenditure on goods and services and in the operating receipts of the trading bodies, and thus make a contribution towards the gross trading surplus. Thus the valuation of central government expenditure on goods and services is comparable with that of private sector expenditure.

The economic classification of the central government accounts

The object of the second main process applied to the accounts of the central government is to present the transactions of the government in categories which are economically significant and to relate the government's activities to those of the rest of the economy. This calls for a reclassification of government transactions, as set out in the accounts presented to Parliament, in accordance with the principles adopted for national income accounting as a whole. Although the nature or purpose of most government transactions is fairly clear, in some cases the distinctions are not easy to draw. A principal consideration, however, is that the classification should be consistent with the treatment of these transactions in other sectors of the economy, and it may thus be influenced by the data available for other sectors. Certain problems of definition and treatment which arise in connection with the economic classification are further discussed below.

The arrangement of government transactions involves a division into the three types of account—production, current and capital—which are described in Chapter II. A production account is not published for central government, but the balance on this account (gross trading surplus and rent) is entered in the current account. Within the current and capital accounts, transactions are further divided between requited payments and unrequited payments or transfers (see page 30).

Government transactions, after consolidation, are classified into the following broad economic categories:

(a) *Receipts on current account.*
(i) Gross trading surplus and rent. These are regarded as factor incomes and make a direct contribution to the gross national product.
(ii) Current transfers. These comprise taxes on income, taxes on expenditure, national insurance contributions, interest and dividends, and grants or gifts (mainly from overseas governments).
(b) *Expenditure on current account.*
(i) Purchases of goods and services. This represents consumption by the central government and forms part of final expenditure. It includes expenditure on the wages and salaries, etc. of government employees, other than those engaged in trading activities or on capital works. Certain non-trading receipts from the sale of goods and services are deducted from the related expenditure. Payments incurred on the production account of central government trading bodies are excluded.
(ii) Current transfers. These comprise subsidies (that is transfers to the production accounts of public or private trading bodies), debt interest, and current grants (to the personal sector, local authorities and the overseas sector).
(c) *Receipts on capital account.*
(i) Capital transfers. These comprise taxes on capital and capital transfers from abroad.
(ii) Financial transactions. Receipts from the sale of government securities, receipts from national savings, other borrowing, and other financial receipts.

(d) *Payments on capital account.*

(i) Purchases of goods and services. This represents capital formation in fixed assets and stocks, and forms part of final expenditure. It covers expenditure for both trading and non-trading activities. Receipts from the sale of fixed assets are deducted.

(ii) Capital transfers. These comprise grants towards the capital expenditure of the private sector, public corporations and local authorities.

(iii) Financial transactions. Lending, the purchase of company securities, etc.

A further subdivision is made of each class of payments according to the function of the expenditure or type of service provided—a classification which differs at many points from any that might be derived from the more usual analysis according to spending departments. This functional analysis of expenditure is not shown separately for the central government, except for an analysis of current and capital expenditure on goods and services, because a considerable part of government expenditure on the provision of services is carried out through the agency of other bodies in the public sector—local authorities and public corporations. A full classification of expenditure by functional categories is therefore confined to the consolidated expenditure of the public sector, for which a two-way classification by functional and economic categories is given; this analysis is described in Chapter XI.

Basis of recording transactions

Most of the figures appearing in the central government tables refer to cash payments and receipts—like the accounts presented to Parliament from which the figures are ultimately derived[1]. They are not on a payable-receivable, or an accruals basis, although this basis would often be more consistent with the figures in the corresponding accounts of the sectors concerned in transactions with the government (see pages 36 to 39). In one or two cases, however, where the information is available it has been considered worthwhile to adjust the government cash figures to the basis of corresponding figures recorded in the accounts of other sectors. Examples are:

(a) Expenditure on subsidies to the nationalised transport undertakings, which represents the accrual of liability for this item. The item is thus recorded in the same way as it is in the accounts of public corporations, on which the estimates are based.

(b) Receipts of purchase tax, which represent the amount of tax charged by registered traders, rather than actual receipts by Customs and Excise. The adjustment is based on the fact that there is generally an average delay of about one calendar quarter between the time when traders charge the tax to their customers and make their payments to Customs and Excise.

(c) Interest on national savings certificates, where the interest accruing is substituted for the interest paid on certificates cashed. The excess of interest accrued over interest paid is regarded as part of the increase in national savings.

The counterpart of the adjustment made to the government cash figures in respect of the first two items is treated as a financial transaction—a change in debtors and creditors—and is shown in the capital account.

---

[1]For a discussion of the central government accounts from this point of view see *Final Report of the Committee on the Form of Government Accounts*, Cmd. 7969. See also *Control of Public Expenditure*, Cmnd. 1432.

A particular difficulty arises over the recording of government purchases of goods and services. For certain categories of goods and services, mainly those purchased for military defence, cash payments may misrepresent the expenditure actually being incurred, since the payments are subject to random fluctuations of timing. This difficulty is of greater significance in the quarterly accounts than in the annual accounts; the method of dealing with it is discussed below (see page 271). Irregularities in expenditure on wages and salaries may arise if increases in the pay of government employees are backdated. No adjustments are made to the cash figures in this instance because of the difficulty of estimating such adjustments and of allowing for them throughout the national accounts.

The difficulties of obtaining consistency between the government accounts and those of the rest of the economy do not arise in the case of activities for which accounts are prepared on a commercial, or payable-receivable, basis. These include not only government trading activities but also certain non-trading activities, for example the Regional Hospital Boards, for which accounts on a payable-receivable basis are prepared.

2. SOME PROBLEMS IN THE CLASSIFICATION OF GOVERNMENT TRANSACTIONS

TRADING BODIES

The major activities of government are the administration and defence of the country, the provision of various communal services, without charge or for a nominal charge, and the collection of taxes. But in addition there are branches of government mainly engaged in trading and thus akin to business enterprises, although not necessarily operating with the object of maximum profit. These trading activities have been of less importance in recent years but their treatment raises certain conceptual problems.

Government trading bodies are distinguished from public corporations (described in Chapter VIII) by the fact that the former are financially integrated with the central government, their expenditure generally being authorised by Vote on a year-to-year basis, and their cash surpluses, if any, apart from working balances which may be considerable, being returned to the Exchequer. Although the activities of these trading bodies resemble in many respects those of business enterprises, their financial integration with, and their control by, the central government bring them within the central government sector.

The criteria for distinguishing the trading activities of the central government from its other activities are:

(a) that the activity consists in production of goods and services, or in trading, of a kind which is or might be conducted by a private business;

(b) that distinct sales, either to the public or to a separate branch of the government, can be identified; and that the sales account for the major part of the production;

(c) that separate accounts of the activity are kept on a commercial accounting basis; or, failing this, that records exist from which such accounts can be constructed.

In nearly every department of the government, there are branches which recover part of the cost of the services they provide from sales to the public. Examples range from the charges for dental treatment under the national health service to the sale of postcards at the National Gallery. It is the exception, rather than the rule, to treat such activities as trading. Although prices charged may in some cases represent fairly accurately the cost of particular goods and services provided when considered in isolation, these charges are incidental to the general community service being provided by the government free of charge. The method followed is therefore to deduct the receipts from the corresponding expenditure and to enter the net expenditure in the government accounts. This treatment differs from the treatment of trading activities in that no attempt is made to calculate a profit or loss. Payments made by persons for, say, dental treatment or National Gallery postcards appear as components of consumers' expenditure.

A full list of government trading bodies is given in Annex 1 to this chapter. It should be observed that not all government establishments engaged in production of physical goods fulfil the conditions laid down above for treatment as trading bodies. Thus, although the Royal Ordnance Factories are treated as trading bodies, the Navy dockyards, R.E.M.E. workshops and Air Force maintenance units are not. Nor is the Stationery Office, because no suitable accounts are available for its printing activities and its selling activities are relatively minor. The commercial operations of the Atomic Energy Authority have been treated as a trading activity only from April 1965, when separate accounts of those operations were first published. It will be seen from Annex 1 that trading activities include not only the purchase and sale of goods and services but also the ownership and leasing of land and buildings and other fixed assets, for example Crown estates and Board of Trade factories. The government trading income from the ownership of these fixed assets is included, however, not under the heading 'Gross trading surplus' but under 'Rent', along with rent income from other government property. Income from property owned by the government and used for its trading activities is, however, included in the gross trading surplus as for private enterprises.

The distinction between the trading and non-trading activities of the government affects both the presentation of the government accounts and the measurement of national income. Payments on production account, for example the wages and salaries paid to employees engaged in trading activities, are not included in government current expenditure on goods and services, nor are trading receipts included in government revenue. But the balance of trading receipts over trading expenses, after adjustment for changes in stocks, debtors and creditors, etc., and with certain other modifications described below, is included in the central government current account as gross trading surplus.

In the national accounts profit incomes are shown before deducting provisions for capital consumption, and interest payments are treated throughout as transfer payments and not as payments of factor income (see Chapter I). In conformity with this treatment, the trading surplus of the government is reckoned before deducting any provision for depreciation or interest charges.

In the case of those trading activities where the aim is that total costs, including depreciation and interest, should be broadly covered over a period, the national accounts include a gross trading surplus equal to the overall surplus or deficit as shown in the accounts of the trading body *plus* its provision for depreciation and interest charges. Such bodies may make substantial surpluses, or deficits, in any one year which can reasonably be regarded as analogous to the profits, or losses, of private businesses, and thus as factor incomes contributing to gross national product.

J*

Some government trading activities, however, for reasons of policy are deliberately run at a loss, the prices at which the commodities or services are sold being fixed at less than the costs, including depreciation and interest, incurred in providing them. In 1966 activities of this kind were limited to the aerodromes and air navigation services run by the Board of Trade and the leasing of factories in development areas; up to 1956 Ministry of Food commodity trading was the principal example. Such deficits are not brought into the government trading surplus. The trading body is regarded as receiving on its production account a payment from the Exchequer equal to its deficit after charging depreciation and interest. The payment is regarded as government expenditure on subsidies and, in conformity with the above definition, the trading body is regarded as having a gross trading surplus exactly equal to the provision made in its accounts for depreciation and interest. The provision for depreciation is based on the original, that is the historical, cost. This treatment corresponds to that of private enterprises whose selling prices are reduced by the receipt of subsidies from the government. As a result, variations in the losses of such government trading bodies do not affect the gross national product and the other aggregates measured at factor cost. These aggregates are the same as if the commodities or services were sold at a price which exactly covered costs, including depreciation and interest.

On the other hand, where a government enterprise is able by virtue of its monopoly to fix a selling price so as to yield an overall surplus, by analogy with the subsidies just described this surplus is appropriately treated as a tax on expenditure, while only the provision for depreciation and interest is included in gross trading surplus. For those years when the Post Office could be regarded as having served as a revenue-producing instrument for the Exchequer this is the treatment adopted. From April 1956 to March 1961 however, provision was made for a fixed Post Office contribution to the Exchequer, any remaining surplus or deficit being carried forward as a change in reserves. Thus from April 1956 to March 1961 only the fixed contribution of £5 million a year made by the Post Office is regarded as a tax on expenditure, the remaining surplus before depreciation and interest being regarded as trading income analogous to that of a private enterprise and included in the central government gross trading surplus. From April 1961 the Post Office has been treated as a public corporation because the Post Office Act, 1961 changed its financial status, and its expenditure was no longer appropriated by Vote, nor were its surpluses returned to the Exchequer.

The item 'Gross trading surplus', which with 'Rent' is the contribution of central government trading activity to the gross national product, therefore consists of:

(a) the trading surpluses, before deducting depreciation and interest, of those trading bodies which aim broadly at balancing their accounts over a period;

(b) the depreciation and interest of those trading bodies aiming as a matter of policy at incurring a loss;

(c) the depreciation and interest of those trading bodies making a surplus by virtue of their monopoly position. The Post Office was included in this category for the period up to April 1956.

The distinction between these three classes is often difficult to draw; the way in which the criterion is applied in each case is noted in the list of trading bodies given in Annex 1 to this chapter.

THE CLASSIFICATION OF TAX RECEIPTS

The tax revenue of the government is classified into:

taxes on income, often described as direct taxes;

taxes on capital;

taxes on expenditure, often described as indirect taxes;

national insurance contributions, etc. regarded as a direct tax on income.

Most taxes fall clearly into one of these groups. But problems of allocation arise in certain cases.

The distinction between these different kinds of taxes is important for two reasons: (a) if a tax is treated as a payment from the capital account of, say, persons, consistency requires that it should be regarded as a capital receipt of government; if it were regarded as a current receipt of government, then government current receipts would be increased by a transfer not reflected in current payments by the personal sector; (b) taxes on expenditure, as distinct from taxes on income and capital, are regarded as an element in the prices of final goods and services having no counterpart in factor incomes.

Taxes on capital

These include death duties and, from 1964, taxes on capital gains. Included also in the years 1948 to 1954 were receipts from the special contribution, levied in 1948/49 and assessed on the basis of investment income. The special charge levied in 1968/69 is also regarded as a tax on capital. From 1967 receipts of the betterment levy on the development value of land are also included.

Both death duties and taxes on capital gains are regarded as payments from the capital account of the taxpayer, because they are assessed on the basis of capital and not of income. Death duties are payments of a once for all nature and it is a realistic presumption that the payment of death duties results in a roughly comparable diminution in the capital assets of the personal sector. To a lesser extent the same is true of taxes on capital gains although these taxes may be paid with some regularity. Since capital gains are not part of national income it is desirable to distinguish taxes on capital gains from taxes on income. The special contribution and special charge, being assessed on the basis of investment income, indirectly tax the wealth giving rise to that income; and their once for all nature makes it reasonable to suppose the payments are from capital rather than income.

Taxes on income and taxes on expenditure

The distinction between taxes on income and taxes on expenditure may cause difficulty in marginal cases. Broadly, taxes which enter into costs of production and distribution, such as taxes on tobacco and petrol, purchase tax, selective employment tax, etc. are treated as taxes on expenditure; they are operating costs, but not factor rewards. Taxes on final buyers associated with the purchase, possession or use of particular goods are also treated as taxes on expenditure, for instance motor vehicle licence duties and stamp duties on the transfer of property. But where taxes are levied on the possession or use of consumption goods, such as motor vehicle licence duties paid by consumers, they are not associated with any productive activity and they might be regarded as a direct, rather than an indirect tax. Doubt may also arise over the treatment of taxes associated with the use of capital goods, for example land and buildings. Income tax assessed up to 1963 under Schedule A is regarded as a tax on income, because it was charged in respect of the rent income attributed to the owner-occupier. But local rates are regarded as a tax on expenditure because they are in general charged in respect of occupancy.

Any fees and licences paid to the government for services which the government alone can provide, or for which there is no parallel among the services provided by private industry, are included among taxes on expenditure. Examples are passport fees, fees for applying to the courts and the transport levy raised from 1954 to 1956. Fines or penalties imposed by the government are also treated as taxes on expenditure. International recommendations suggest that fees and fines of this kind paid by consumers should be treated as a special category of transfer payments by the personal sector to the government and should not be included in consumers' expenditure [2]. This treatment has much to commend it since many such fees and fines cannot strictly be regarded as part of the market price of any goods or services. But in the United Kingdom the items have been considered not important enough to justify a separate category of transactions. Fees and receipts for services rendered in cases where the government does not enjoy a monopoly or compulsory powers, and where there is a clear link between the payment and the acquisition of goods or services, are treated as a deduction from government current expenditure on goods and services and not as a tax on expenditure. Examples are payments to dentists for treatment under the national health service and payments for the purchase of postcards at the National Gallery.

National insurance contributions, etc.

National insurance and other similar contributions from employers and employees are treated as a form of tax because the national insurance system, being compulsory, must be regarded as an instrument of public policy rather than as a trading activity comparable with private insurance schemes. The contributions are a tax on income, rather than a tax on employers' expenditure on wages and salaries, because they are associated with direct benefits to the employee; they are also, in part, paid from the employee's income. Contributions to national insurance, national health and the Redundancy Fund are all treated in this way. But selective employment tax, which is collected with national insurance contributions, is regarded as a tax on expenditure and not as a tax on income, because it is not associated with any benefit to the employee and is paid entirely by employers.

THE DEFINITION OF GRANTS

Grants have to be distinguished from subsidies, which are also unrequited payments. The distinction is that subsidies are unrequited payments to the production accounts of trading concerns, whether in the public sector, for example the British Railways Board, or in the private sector, for example farmers receiving deficiency payments. Such payments are treated as trading receipts of the recipient and have the effect of reducing his selling prices, just as taxes on expenditure increase them. Grants, on the other hand, are not direct payments into production accounts. All unrequited payments of a current nature to trading concerns are regarded as subsidies and central government current grants therefore comprise current transfer payments to local authorities, the personal sector and the overseas sector. A number of problems arise in applying these

---

[2] *A System of National Accounts and Supporting Tables*, United Nations, New York, 1964.

criteria to certain government payments which might be treated as subsidies, or as current grants, or in some other way.

Unrequited payments to trading concerns may also be of a capital nature; these are regarded as capital grants and not as subsidies. Capital grants are made to assist the financing of capital expenditure, generally on fixed assets.

Payments to grant-aided bodies

Payments to grant-aided bodies may be divided into three different categories according to the type of body being financed:

(a) Grant-aided bodies which are wholly, or almost wholly, financed by the government—although with varying degrees of independence in operation—and which are subject to the same sort of financial control as that imposed on ordinary government departments. These bodies are treated as part of the central government, as explained on page 251. On consolidation of accounts, the grants to such bodies therefore disappear and their expenditure is recorded as part of central government expenditure. This category includes, for example, the Medical Research Council, the British Council and the Atomic Energy Authority.

(b) Bodies serving industry, supported by the government but not wholly dependent on government funds nor subject to detailed financial control. These bodies are grouped with trading concerns, in the same way as trade associations and other private non-profit-making bodies serving industry. They are treated as part of the company sector, although they do not trade or produce in the ordinary sense. Examples are the British Standards Institution and industrial training boards. Central government payments to these bodies are treated as government purchases of goods and services by analogy with the treatment of expenditure on advisory services to industry (see below). The payments could be regarded as subsidies, but it is difficult to determine which branches of industry benefit and it seems simpler to restrict subsidies to direct payments to productive enterprises. The current expenditure of these bodies which is not financed by government grants is regarded as intermediate expenditure and the excess of their receipts over their current expenditure is treated as part of company trading profits.

(c) Other grant-aided bodies are those which, like the second category, are only in part dependent on grants from the government but whose functions are to provide services to persons. The universities are the principal example. These private non-profit-making bodies are treated as part of the personal sector. Government payments to them on current account are treated as current grants to the personal sector, and their current expenditure on goods and services is included in consumers' expenditure.

Annex 2 to this chapter gives a list of the main grant-aided bodies, showing to which of these three categories each is classified.

Advisory and other services to industry

The government provides certain advisory services—for agriculture, export promotion, and so on—which might otherwise be provided by private organisations on a commercial basis. The cost of these services is treated as government expenditure on goods and services. It might, however, be argued that this cost in effect represents a subsidy to industry and should be treated as such. This argument might be extended to many other services to industry rendered by the government, such as the operation of employment exchanges by the Ministry of Labour or the services of the Board of Trade and other departments in regulating industry and trade or in producing commercial or statistical information. If the cost of such services were treated as subsidies, there would be imputed subsidy payments by government to industry, balanced by a corresponding imputed cost of production, in the production accounts of industry; industry's trading profits would remain unaffected. The undesirability of extending the amount of imputation, together with the difficulty of determining which government services could reasonably be regarded as services to industry and which branches of industry benefit, rules out this method of treatment.

Grants in kind

The net cost to the central government of milk and other welfare foods, provided free or at subsidised prices, is treated not as current expenditure on goods and services but as a current grant to the personal sector. This corresponds to the treatment of local authorities' expenditure on school meals and milk, and is adopted in order that consumers' expenditure should include all expenditure on food for use by households (see page 105). The same procedure was adopted even before October 1955, when the net cost of welfare foods and milk in schools was shown as a loss in the trading accounts of the former Ministry of Food.

3. THE PUBLISHED TABLES

Four tables in the Blue Book present the central government accounts. A detailed current account for the central government as a whole is shown, a summarised version of which is included in the summary tables. Separate detailed current accounts are also given for the central government excluding the National Insurance Funds and for the National Insurance Funds. The capital account for the central government includes details of financial transactions.

Additional information is given in the sections of the Blue Book on combined public authorities and the public sector. These tables are described in Chapter XI. Current and capital accounts for the central government on the same basis as those given in the Blue Book are published in the *Financial Statement* presented to Parliament on the day of the Budget. These tables relate to the financial year just ended and the coming financial year.

CURRENT ACCOUNT

The current account for 1966 in the 1967 Blue Book is presented on the next page. The current account corresponds to the income and expenditure account or appropriation account presented for other domestic sectors. The notes in the following paragraphs describe the composition of the separate items in the table. References to income and expenditure in Great Britain apply also to the corresponding income and expenditure in Northern Ireland. References to particular departments should be taken to cover, where relevant, any other departments which had the same responsibilities in earlier years.

Taxes on income

The distinctions between taxes on income and taxes on capital and expenditure are discussed on pages 259 to 260. Taxes on income consist of receipts from *less* repayments to taxpayers, whether or not resident in the United Kingdom, of the

Current account of central government including National Insurance Funds, 1966

£ million

Receipts		Expenditure	
Taxes on income:		Current expenditure on goods and services:	
Income tax	4,119	Military defence	2,162
Surtax	210	National health service	1,158
Profits tax.................	135	Other[1]	791
Corporation tax	23		
less Overspill relief	−38	Total	4,111
Total	4,449	Subsidies[1]	476
		Current grants to personal sector:	
Taxes on expenditure:		Post-war credits...........	17
Customs and Excise duties[1].	3,617	Education[1]...............	185
Motor vehicle licence duties ..	270	Child care.................	4
less Export rebates	−96	Milk and welfare food schemes	43
Selective employment tax	307	Social security benefits:	
Stamp duties	78	National insurance	1,894
Post Office contribution to the		Other[1]	546
Exchequer	2	Employment services	29
Miscellaneous	65	Other.....................	47
Total	4,243	Total	2,765
National insurance contributions	1,613	Debt interest	1,041
National health contributions ..	166	Current grants to local authorities	1,479
Redundancy Fund contributions	18	Current grants to overseas countries and international organisations	165
Gross trading surplus[1]........	15	National insurance benefits and war pensions paid to non-residents	17
Rent:			
Temporary houses and Forces' married quarters	4		
Other.....................	92		
Interest and dividends, etc:		Total current expenditure	10,054
On loans to local authorities..	171		
On loans to public corporations	371	Balance: current surplus before providing for depreciation	
Other.....................	131	and stock appreciation	1,219
Total	11,273	Total	11,273

Source: 1967 Blue Book, Table 41

[1]These items are subdivided in the Blue Book table, as described in the notes below.

taxes listed in the table. Income tax excludes the estimated amount of tax on short-term capital gains collected under Schedule D from 1964 which is included in taxes on capital. Income tax deducted from post-war refunds of excess profits tax is excluded in earlier years. Receipts of excess profits tax and excess profits levy are also shown separately in the Blue Book table; they were negligible after 1965. Post-war refunds of excess profits tax are not deducted; they are regarded as capital transfers (see page 283). Payments of overspill relief, made in certain cases where the overseas tax rate exceeds the corporation tax rate, under Section 84 of the Finance Act, 1965, are shown separately as a deduction from this item.

The figures relate to actual receipts of tax, not to the amount of tax ultimately payable on the income earned in the year, nor to the tax legally payable during the year. As already explained on page 253, the figures shown are the amounts collected by the Inland Revenue and not the amounts received by the Exchequer from the Inland Revenue. The allocation of the total amount received between different types of income and different types of taxpayer is described on page 328. The annual reports of the Commissioners of Inland Revenue give figures of taxes on income payable in each year [3].

Taxes on expenditure

These consist of net receipts from those taxes which are treated as part of the costs of production of particular commodities, or which fall on specific kinds of expenditure (see page 259). They are divided as follows:

(a) *Customs and Excise duties.* The figures are derived from Customs and Excise returns. The table shows separately receipts from duties on beer, wines and spirits, tobacco, hydrocarbon oils, protective duties, temporary charge on imports (payable from 1964 to 1966), purchase tax, entertainments (up to 1960), television licence (from 1957 to 1963), television advertisement (from 1961 to 1964), betting, and all other items. The classification is that used in the annual reports of the Commissioners of H.M. Customs and Excise. As explained on page 255, receipts of purchase tax represent an estimate of the amount of tax charged by registered traders in the period, taken as the amount received one quarter later. The excess or deficiency of actual receipts by Customs and Excise over this amount is shown in the capital account under the heading 'Adjustment for purchase tax'. Receipts of duty on hydrocarbon oils and purchase tax are shown before deducting export rebates, which are deducted separately.

(b) *Motor vehicle licence duties.* The figures are derived from Ministry of Transport returns. These duties are collected by local authorities as agents of the Ministry of Transport and remitted through that Ministry to the Exchequer. The figures represent an estimate of the amounts received by local authorities.

(c) *Export rebates.* These are rebates of the payments of the duty on hydrocarbon oils, purchase tax and motor vehicle licence duties entering into the cost of goods exported from 26 October 1964.

(d) *Selective employment tax.* The tax became payable from 5 September 1966. It is included on a cash basis as it is paid. The figures represent total receipts *less* refunds, including the refund element of premium payments. Premium payments did not begin until 1967.

(e) *Stamp duties.* The figures are derived from Inland Revenue returns. The main items are duties on conveyance of land and houses, on transfers of stocks and shares and on cheques. A full analysis is given in the annual reports of the Commissioners of Inland Revenue.

(f) *Post Office contribution to the Exchequer.* The figures are derived from the *Finance Accounts.* The treatment of this item is discussed on page 258. It represents (a) prior to April 1956 the Post Office surplus (b) from April 1956 to March 1961 a contribution of £5 million a year as fixed for the purposes of the *Post Office Commercial Accounts* [4] and (c) from April 1961 the contribution in lieu of taxes made from the Post Office Fund.

---

[3] See for example *Report of the Commissioners of Her Majesty's Inland Revenue*, 110th Report, Cmnd. 3508.

[4] See *Report on Post Office Development and Finance, 1955*, Cmd. 9576.

(g) *Miscellaneous items.* In 1966 these consisted of:

£ *million*

(i) Fees from government permits, fines, penalties, etc. included among appropriations-in-aid of departmental expenditure. The figures are derived from analysis of the *Appropriation Accounts*. . .   39

(ii) Payments to the Exchequer by the Independent Television Authority in respect of 'additional payments' by the programme contractors under the Television Act, 1964.   21

(iii) Certain items included among Miscellaneous Revenue of the Exchequer, derived from the *Finance Accounts* and *Appropriation Accounts*   1

(iv) Licence duties retained by local authorities—mainly dog and gun licences. The figures are derived from local authority accounts. They are regarded as central government taxes because the rates are determined by the central government; the amounts are included in current grants to local authorities (see page 308).   1

(v) Tithe annuities payable by landowners to the Tithe Redemption Commission after landowners' liabilities for tithe rent charges had been extinguished by the Tithe Act, 1936. Lump sum payments by landowners in commutation of annuities are included   3

Total   65

Land development charges levied from 1948 to 1960 under the Town and Country Planning Acts, 1947 are included in this item.

Categories of taxes on expenditure no longer levied but shown for earlier years are as follows:

(a) *Transport levy.* This was imposed on certain road goods vehicles under the Transport Act, 1953, and was collected in the years 1954 to 1956. The proceeds were used to finance the payment of compensation to the British Transport Commission for the capital loss sustained by the Commission on the sale of part of its road haulage undertaking. These payments to the Commission are treated as capital grants (see page 283).

(b) *Broadcast licence revenue retained by the Exchequer.* The amounts shown under this heading represent the excess of receipts from broadcast receiving licences over the amounts actually paid to the B.B.C. for its home services and the cost of collection paid to the Post Office. From 1961 nothing was retained by the Exchequer.

National insurance, national health and Redundancy Fund contributions

This item covers contributions to the national insurance scheme (both flat rate and graduated contributions), the industrial injuries scheme, the national health service and, from 1965, the Redundancy Fund. These contributions are treated as a form of tax on income. Prior to September 1957 no direct contributions were made in respect of the national health service, although it was partly financed from the National Insurance Funds. The contributions from different types of contributor are shown separately in Tables 44 and 51 of the 1967 Blue

Book. Redundancy Fund contributions became payable by employers from 5 December 1965 under the Redundancy Payments Act. The contributions are paid with national insurance contributions. Payments of selective employment tax, collected from September 1966 with national insurance contributions, are regarded as a tax on expenditure and are not included here.

Gross trading surplus

The definition of this item is discussed on pages 256 to 258. It excludes the income arising from the ownership and letting of land, buildings, and other fixed assets which is included under 'Rent'. Income from the ownership of property used for government trading activities is included. A list of trading activities is given in Annex 1 to this chapter. The composition of the gross trading surplus in 1966 was as follows:

£ million

Trading surpluses (or losses) before deducting depreciation and interest:	
Atomic Energy Authority (trading activities)	9
Export Credits Guarantee Department	− 4
Post Office Savings Bank	−18
Other trading bodies	3
Depreciation (based on historical cost) and interest only:	
Forestry Commission	16
Royal Ordnance Factories	6
Civil aerodromes and air navigation services	3
Total	15

In conformity with the definition of the gross trading profits of banks used elsewhere in the national accounts (see pages 204 to 206), the gross trading surplus of the Post Office Savings Bank is a loss equal to its expenses of operation. This loss is offset by its net investment income. In the calculation of the trading surplus of the Royal Mint, United Kingdom coin is regarded as being sold by the Mint at cost to the central government. The purchase of the coin is reflected in 'Current expenditure on goods and services', while the increase in face value of issued coin is treated as a form of borrowing in the central government capital account. In the calculation of the trading surplus of the Forestry Commission, the increase in value of stocks of growing timber is taken to be the net cost, including depreciation and interest, of forestry operations, so that the trading surplus is equal to depreciation and interest charges. The Royal Ordnance Factories are considered to transfer their products to service departments at prices exactly equal to their costs, including an allowance for depreciation and interest.

As mentioned on page 258, up to April 1961 the Post Office is regarded as a government trading body and for the years up to 1961 separate figures of the gross trading surplus for the Post Office are given in the current account of the central government. Until March 1956 this represents only depreciation (at historical cost) and interest on the capital employed in the Post Office. From April 1956 to March 1961 the item represents the Post Office trading surplus, before deducting depreciation and interest, but after deducting the fixed contribution of £5 million a year to the Exchequer. The Post Office Savings Bank continued to be treated as part of central government after April 1961 because its funds are administered by the National Debt Commissioners.

Rent

Like the trading surplus, the rent income of the central government is a direct contribution to the gross national product. Rent income is measured after deducting the cost of repairs, etc. but before deducting depreciation and interest and the principles applied are the same as those for other sectors. Thus, in addition to rent income arising from owning and letting property, this item includes an imputed rent in respect of non-trading property owned and also occupied by the government. The government as owner is regarded as letting the building to itself as occupier, the payment of rent as occupier and the receipt of rent as owner being two parts of an imputed transaction (see pages 7 and 8). The imputed receipt is included in rent and the imputed payment in current expenditure on goods and services. Income from land and buildings owned by the government and used by government trading bodies, however, is not included under rent; as with other trading enterprises, the income contributes to the gross trading surplus.

For convenience, the rent income of the central government includes income arising from the owning and leasing of fixed assets other than land and buildings; for private trading enterprises such income is included with trading profits. Except in the case of the Atomic Energy Authority, no income is imputed for non-trading assets other than land and buildings which are owned and used by the government.

There are special difficulties involved in attempting to quantify imputed rent in respect of government-owned buildings used for non-trading purposes, such as hospitals. This is because in many cases there are no actual market rents for similar types of buildings which could provide a basis for estimation. Where market rents do not provide a basis, the imputed rents are estimated by two possible methods:

(a) an assessment of rateable value;

(b) depreciation and interest on capital employed.

Both of these methods have certain deficiencies as applied to the assets considered here. Rateable values are normally assessed on the basis of the rent at which the property might reasonably be expected to let, but in the case of these government properties the assessments of rateable values are necessarily more subjective. In the case of depreciation and interest on capital, these usually relate to original cost and are not necessarily a measure of the current use value. Nor do these charges themselves necessarily relate to all the assets in current use, since some of them may have been fully amortised. On the other hand, depreciation and interest charges may well be higher than the market rents for alternative, less suitable, uses of the property.

In practice the method adopted for any particular category of assets depends largely upon the data available, but where a choice is possible the advantage of using the same basis of imputation for groups of assets which are frequently compared, for example hospitals and schools, is borne in mind. The methods adopted are listed below. One category of assets owned, though not exclusively used, by the central government for which no imputation is made is trunk roads. Similarly, no imputation is made for other roads in the accounts of local authorities (see page 311), and nothing is included for roads in the estimates of capital consumption (see page 387). This is in accordance with the treatment of roads recommended by the United Nations[5].

The composition of rent in 1966 was as follows:

£ million

Rent from letting of property:

Ministry of Technology (buildings, plant and machinery)	5
Ministry of Public Building and Works................	3
Ministry of Defence (land and buildings)	3
Crown Estate Office	4
Board of Trade (factories)	5
Other	1

Imputed rent from owner-occupied property:

Non-trading assets of the Atomic Energy Authority....	42
Hospitals...	21
Government offices	8
Married quarters for the Forces at home	4
Total	96

Rent from the letting of property represents gross rents received *less* expenses (in so far as they can be identified) other than depreciation and interest charges. In the case of Board of Trade factories, rent is taken as equal to depreciation and interest charges; the amount by which this exceeds the net rents received is treated as a subsidy (see page 258).

Imputed rent in respect of the principal non-trading fixed assets owned and used by the central government is estimated by the following methods:

(a) non-trading assets of the Atomic Energy Authority—measured by depreciation and interest on capital employed as shown in the Authority's published balance sheet;

(b) national health service hospitals—based on the assessments of rateable values made by the Treasury valuer;

(c) government offices and buildings—based on floor space and the market rents of similar accommodation;

(d) married quarters for the Forces at home—measured by the annuities, that is interest and amortisation of capital, paid by the service departments to the Exchequer. The accommodation is financed under the Armed Forces (Housing Loans) Acts, 1949 and 1958.

A corresponding imputation of current expenditure on goods and services by the central government is made in respect of the current use of these assets. In the case of married quarters for the Forces, the amount treated as current expenditure on goods and services is the excess of imputed rent *plus* repairs and other expenses over the rents received from tenants. The amount of imputed rent is shown separately in the detailed analysis of public authorities' current expenditure on goods and services (Table 48 of the 1967 Blue Book).

An imputation of rent income was also made up to March 1962 in respect of government-owned temporary houses and schools. This was taken as equal to the

---

[5]*A System of National Accounts and Supporting Tables*, United Nations, New York, 1964.

annuities paid by the housing and education departments to the Exchequer and Ministry of Works respectively. Because the life of temporary houses exceeded the ten years envisaged at the time of construction, the period over which the annuities were paid by the housing departments was extended by several years, with a consequential reduction in the annual payment from April 1955. This resulted in a substantial reduction in 1955 to the figures for imputed rent from temporary houses, and the item disappeared after March 1962 when payment of the annuities ceased. The excess of this imputed rent for temporary houses and temporary schools over the amounts actually received from local authorities for their use is treated in the one case as part of housing subsidies (see page 327) and in the other as current expenditure on goods and services.

Interest and dividends, etc.

This consisted of the following items in 1966:

	£ million
Interest on loans to:	
The personal sector	2
Companies	21
Public corporations	371
Local authorities	171
The overseas sector	17
Investment income of extra-Exchequer funds, other than national debt interest:	
National Insurance Funds	12
Post Office Savings Bank and Fund for the Banks for Savings	17
Other interest and dividends, etc.:	
On company securities	29
Other	33
Total	673

Details of the loans in respect of which interest is received are given below in the description of the central government capital account (see pages 284 to 286). Receipts on company securities relate mainly to dividends on British Petroleum and Suez Canal shares. Other receipts of interest and dividends, etc. include the payments by the Bank of England to the Exchequer under Section 1(4) of the Bank of England Act, 1946; dividends paid by Cable and Wireless Ltd.; net revenue of the Iron and Steel Holding and Realisation Agency paid into the Exchequer from 1955 to 1967; surplus revenue of the Transport Holding Company, paid under Section 29(10) of the Transport Act, 1962; payments to the Exchequer by the Independent Television Authority under Section 13(2) of the Television Act, 1954 and Section 21(4) of the Television Act, 1964; and dividends paid on its Exchequer dividend capital by British Overseas Airways Corporation under Section 2(2) of the Air Corporations Act, 1966.

Current grants from overseas governments

This item relates to grants in aid of current expenditure. No receipts have been recorded under this heading from 1959 to 1966. Grants in kind, for example free transfers of military equipment, are excluded from the accounts. A grant is treated as current only if the expenditure which it is to finance is treated as current in the national income accounts. Since defence expenditure is treated almost entirely as current expenditure, defence aid is also treated as a current grant.

The current grants included here are:

(a) Defence aid from the United States under the Mutual Defence Assistance Agreement (M.D.A.), the Mutual Security Act (M.S.A.) and the Agricultural Trade Development and Assistance Act (United States Public Law 480), and from Canada under similar arrangements. This is the item described as 'Defence aid' in the balance of payments statistics.

(b) Grants deemed to have been received under the Benton and Moody amendments to the Mutual Security Acts of 1951 and 1952 and to the Economic Co-operation Act of 1948[6].

The sums received are recorded after deducting the United States share of the sterling counterpart of the grants. The figures are the same as those used in the balance of payments statistics, where they are included in government receipts of transfers on current account.

It should be noted that other receipts which are treated in the balance of payments statistics as government receipts of transfers on current account are included in the national income accounts as receipts on capital account where they are included in 'Net receipts from settlements, etc.' (see page 276).

Current expenditure on goods and services

Current expenditure on goods and services relates to the non-trading activities of the government. It excludes the operating expenditure of government trading bodies, although in earlier years it includes exceptionally certain administrative costs of the former Ministry of Food. It comprises:

(a) Payments for the services of employees, including employers' contributions to national insurance, superannuation, etc. The definition is consistent with that of income from employment (see Chapter VI, Section 3). Superannuation contributions include not only employers' contributions to contributory pension schemes, for example for national health service employees, but also payments of pensions under the non-contributory schemes for civil servants. For the widows' and dependants' contributory pension schemes the employers' contributions are taken to be the pensions paid *less* contributions of employees. From September 1966 selective employment tax in respect of government civilian employees is also included.

(b) Purchases of goods and services from government trading bodies, from other sectors of the economy and from abroad, other than purchases of fixed assets and of strategic stocks.

(c) Imputed rent in respect of the non-trading fixed assets owned and used by the central government. The amount of imputed rent is shown separately in the detailed analysis of public authorities' current expenditure on goods and services (Table 48 of the 1967 Blue Book). Actual payments of rent are included in (b) above.

---

[6]For description see *Arrangements for the Expenditure of Counterpart Funds derived from United States Economic Aid under Section 9(c) of the Mutual Security Act of 1952*, Cmd. 8776.

less (d) Receipts from sales of goods and services by non-trading branches of the government (other than sales of fixed assets and strategic stocks) and reimbursements of expenditure incurred by the government on behalf of other sectors. Examples are receipts from sales by the Stationery Office and charges for pay and amenity beds in hospitals. The distinction between receipts treated as sales for services rendered and as taxes on expenditure is discussed on page 260. Contributions made by the German Federal Republic towards the cost of United Kingdom forces from 1955/56 to 1960/61 are treated as a deduction from expenditure. Where the transfer of buildings and other fixed assets to overseas governments on independence does not form part of economic or military aid, and is therefore not included in current grants abroad, no deduction has been made from this item. Apart from the exclusion of purchases and sales of strategic stocks, no adjustment is made to current expenditure on goods and services for changes in the holdings of stores by non-trading branches of the government.

Current expenditure on goods and services is distinguished from capital expenditure in that the former does not create a physical asset which will provide services in the future. Some current expenditure may be of long-term benefit to the nation, not only from the standpoint of social welfare, as with expenditure on health services, but also from the economic standpoint of higher productivity, as with expenditure on technical education. Nevertheless so long as the expenditure does not create a physical asset, such as a hospital or a school, it is regarded as current expenditure. Expenditure is generally regarded as capital if similar expenditure by the private sector is so regarded. But expenditure on military equipment, however durable, is regarded as current expenditure (see page 362).

In the current account given in the Blue Book current expenditure on goods and services is analysed by sixteen functional groups, instead of the three groups shown in the table on page 263. Details of the functional classification are given in Chapter XI where the more detailed classification applied to public sector expenditure is described.

In the government accounts current expenditure on goods and services is mainly recorded on a cash basis, but for certain items cash payments may misrepresent the expenditure actually being incurred, since the payments are subject to random fluctuations of timing and are likely to be inconsistent with the transactions recorded by other sectors. The main difficulty arises in the field of defence expenditure where there are substantial and variable time lags between the submission and payment of bills for many goods and services and their actual provision. The method of dealing with the problem is, for these items, to use the cash figures for complete financial years only, making use of forecasts for the current year, and generally to assume a smooth trend of expenditure during the financial year. Thus the most recent quarterly estimates for defence expenditure on research and development and shipbuilding, for example, are based on the latest estimates available for these items of expenditure for the current financial year. Since estimates of expenditure for the latest financial year are subject to revision at various times during the course of the year, it follows that the latest quarterly estimates are also subject to periodic revision until the actual expenditure for the financial year, upon which they are ultimately based, is known. This method of measuring current expenditure on goods and services, being based on the financial year as a whole, necessarily assumes an arbitrary pattern of expenditure during the year which may not in fact reflect what is actually taking place each quarter and thus may be inconsistent with the accounts for other sectors. Nevertheless, the estimates compiled in this way are thought to be more useful than those based simply on cash payments. Quarterly cash figures continue to be used for expenditure on wages and salaries, including Forces' pay, where these can be separately identified.

Subsidies

These are payments to a producer or trader having the effect of reducing selling prices below the factor costs of production, including the financing of deficits on public trading services deliberately run at a loss. The nature of subsidy payments, and the distinction between subsidies and grants, is described on page 260. In 1966 the main subsidies shown separately in the Blue Book table were payments to local authorities and public corporations in support of their housing services (£108 million), payments in support of agriculture (204 million) and the deficit grants paid to the nationalised transport undertakings (£142 million). The revenue deficits of nationalised transport undertakings have been covered by subsidies from 1960. Payments of selective employment premiums in excess of the original tax payment are regarded as a subsidy, but the premium payments did not begin until 1967. Payments of the regional employment premium beginning in 1967 are also included in this item. A full description of each class of central government subsidy will be found in Chapter XI.

For consistency with the accounts of other sectors, expenditure on certain subsidies is recorded as liability for subsidy accrues (see page 255). This treatment is adopted for subsidies to the British Railways Board, London Transport Board and British Waterways Board (British Transport Commission until 1963), for which figures are taken from their accounts. Housing subsidies are also treated in this way; they are assumed to accrue evenly throughout the year. The excess or deficiency of subsidies accrued over payments appears in the capital account under the heading 'Adjustment for subsidies'. This is of importance mainly in the quarterly accounts.

Current grants to personal sector

These are unrequited payments or transfers to persons, and to non-profit-making bodies serving persons, included in the income of the personal sector. The item consists largely of social security benefits. The largest other item in 1966 was grants for education, which in the Blue Book table is subdivided between scholarships and maintenance allowances, grants to universities, colleges, etc., and grants to other bodies. The net cost to the government of milk and welfare food schemes is included (see page 262). From 1966 rebates to employers from the Redundancy Fund are regarded as being paid direct to persons and are included here. Current grants to non-residents—national insurance benefits and war pensions paid to recipients no longer residing in the United Kingdom—are excluded and treated as current grants paid abroad (see page 273). A full description will be found, service by service, in Chapter XI.

Debt interest

The main element of this item consists of payments of national debt interest, including interest paid to foreign governments. Interest on securities held within the central government as here defined is excluded; for example government securities held by the National Insurance Funds, the Post Office Savings Bank and the Fund for the Banks for Savings. Interest on securities held by the Issue Department of the Bank of England is also excluded (see page 252). These payments within the central government are excluded from revenue as well as from expenditure.

Debt interest includes as one of its components interest paid on national savings certificates cashed. The interest accruing on national savings certificates whether paid or unpaid is, however, substituted by adding to interest paid an amount representing the estimated increase in the government liability for accrued interest. Interest paid to depositors with the ordinary accounts of the Post Office Savings Bank and to the trustees in respect of deposits with the ordinary departments of the trustee savings banks is included. Prize money on premium savings bonds is also treated as debt interest.

Other items included in debt interest are (a) charges on drawings from the International Monetary Fund; (b) the interest element of the loan charges transferred to the Health Ministers when local authority hospitals were vested in the national health service; (c) the interest on stock issued to finance Irish land purchase, paid by the Land Purchase (1891) Account and the Irish Land Purchase Fund; (d) the interest on redemption stock issued under the Tithe Act, 1936.

Current grants to local authorities

This comprises current grants to local authorities for all services other than housing, the payments for which are treated as subsidies, and grants not allocated to specific services.

Up to March 1959 non-specific grants consisted mainly of equalisation grants. From April 1959 many specific grants were replaced by the general grant and rate-deficiency grants were also introduced. The current account of local authorities given in the Blue Book (Table 45 of the 1967 Blue Book) provides an analysis of total current grants to local authorities between those not allocated to specific services and those allocated to various specific services, such as roads, police, and so on. Details of the items included are given on pages 308 to 309. The figures are derived from the *Appropriation Accounts* and differ slightly from the corresponding figures which can be derived from the accounts of local authorities (see page) 309.

Current grants abroad

These comprise (a) grants to overseas countries and international organisations which consist mainly of grants to overseas governments under the economic aid programme; military aid and subscriptions to international organisations are also included; (b) national insurance benefits and war pensions paid to non-residents. They are described in more detail by service in Chapter XI. The same figures appear in the balance of payments accounts under the heading 'Government transfers'.

Balance: current surplus before providing for depreciation and stock appreciation

This item is the residual balance carried forward to the capital account. It represents the saving of central government on current account defined in the same way as the saving of other sectors, except in so far as the saving of other sectors is arrived at after deduction of additions to tax reserves.

CAPITAL ACCOUNT

The capital account is set out on page 275. The transactions recorded in the capital account include detailed transactions in financial assets and liabilities of various kinds as well as other capital transactions. The total net change in the financial assets of the central government can be derived from the capital account as follows (the figures relate to 1966):

	£ million
Current surplus	1,219
plus Capital transfers (net receipts)	66
less Gross capital formation	−366
Net acquisition of financial assets........................	919

This is the summary presentation of the capital account, shown in Table 72 of the 1967 Blue Book. The financial transactions of the central government are arranged in the capital account to show the central government borrowing requirement, that is its 'Net balance' (see page 278), which provides a link with the transactions recorded in the Exchequer accounts.

Taxes on capital

A general discussion of the distinction between taxes on capital and taxes on income is given on page 259. The main item is net receipts by the Inland Revenue from death duties. From 1964 the estimated amount of tax on short-term capital gains collected under income tax Schedule D is included. From 1966 receipts of capital gains tax, including the estimated amount charged and collected under corporation tax, are included. For the years 1948 to 1954 the figures also included receipts from the special contribution and the receipts from the special charge levied in 1968/69 are also regarded as taxes on capital. From 1967 receipts of the betterment levy are also included.

Capital transfers from abroad

There were no receipts in this category from 1956 to 1966. Transfers in earlier years comprise:

(a) *Grants under the European Recovery Programme and gifts from abroad.* The main item was grants, as distinct from loans, from the United States under the European Recovery Programme received from 1947 to 1951. These receipts are included in the capital account of the balance of payments accounts. Receipts under the European Recovery Programme were included in full, repayments of a proportion of the sterling counterpart being treated as capital transfers by the United Kingdom (see page 284). Gifts from the Australian and New Zealand governments in 1947 and 1949 were also included.

(b) *Sales of surplus war stores held abroad.* The last year in which receipts of this nature are recorded in the account is 1952. They were receipts from the sale of surplus war stores, mainly held abroad, to non-residents, including as far as possible sales forming part of general post-war settlements of debts and claims. The estimates are based on returns from the departments concerned with the disposal of the stores. These receipts might have been treated as a change in stocks, like sales at home of surplus war stores; instead they are treated as capital transfers because the sales in early post-war years were bound up in many cases with financial settlements. In the balance of payments accounts they are treated as current receipts.

Capital account of central government including National Insurance Funds, 1966

£ million

Receipts		Payments	
Current surplus before providing for depreciation and stock appreciation	1,219	Gross domestic fixed capital formation[1]	341
Taxes on capital	317	Increase in value of stocks:	
		Trading bodies	27
Transactions in financial assets		Strategic stocks	−2
Receipts from certain pension 'funds' (net)	64	Total	25
Northern Ireland central government[1]	14	Capital transfers:	
Adjustment for purchase tax....	−7	Capital grants to private sector:	
Adjustment for subsidies	−2		
Miscellaneous financial receipts (net) and changes in cash balances	21	Grants to universities, colleges, etc.	93
		Town and Country planning compensation	—
Net balance:		War damage compensation	3
Increase in net indebtedness to Bank of England Banking Department	44	Other	71
		Capital grants to local authorities:	
Increase in notes and coin in circulation	148	War damage compensation	1
Increase in non-marketable debt:		Other...................	81
		Capital grants to public corporations[1]	2
National savings	−202		
Tax reserve certificates	79	Total	251
Receipts from market transactions:			
Treasury bills	−10	*Transactions in financial assets*	
Government and government guaranteed securities	230	Net lending:	
		Net lending to private sector[1]	20
Direct borrowing (net) from overseas governments and institutions:		Net lending to public sector:	
		Local authorities	546
		Public corporations[1]	867
Borrowing from overseas governments............	51	Net lending to overseas sector:	
		Loans to overseas governments	95
less Repayments to overseas governments............	−48	*less* Repayments by overseas governments............	−30
Increase in holdings of interest-free notes by the International Monetary Fund	159	Drawings from United Kingdom subscriptions to international lending bodies ...	10
less Capital subscriptions to the International Monetary Fund and European Fund	−175	Other...................	2
Other.....................	−24	Total net lending..........	1,510
less Increase in gold and currency reserves	282	Cash expenditure on company securities (net)	33
		Coal compensation: issues of stock	—
Net balance	534		
Total	2,160	Total	2,160

Source: 1967 Blue Book, Table 42

[1]These items are subdivided in the Blue Book table, as described in the notes below.

(c) *Net receipts from settlements, etc.* In the early post-war years the main constituents of this item were settlements of debts and claims arising from the war. Included in 1951 and 1952 are receipts under the 'Katz-Gaitskell' agreement, which provided that part of the United Kingdom gold and dollar payments to the European Payments Union should be refunded by the United States government. The last major item is a figure of £15 million in 1953 representing receipts from the Korean Operations Pool Account, a scheme whereby the cost of maintaining Commonwealth Forces in Korea was shared among the governments concerned. The same receipts are included in the balance of payments current account.

Proceeds of iron and steel disposals

There were receipts from this source from 1953 to 1964. The figures represent total receipts by the Iron and Steel Holding and Realisation Agency (absorbed by the British Steel Corporation in 1967) from the sale of the assets of the iron and steel concerns to private owners. Receipts were partly in cash and from 1953 to 1955 partly in the form of government securities, which were passed to the National Debt Commissioners for cancellation. The excess of the Agency's cash receipts from sales over the corresponding payments into the Iron and Steel Realisation Account, administered by the Treasury, is treated as lending to the Agency, and is included in the item 'Net lending to public corporations'.

Receipts from certain pension 'funds' (net)

The components of this item are:

(a) Receipts of pension contributions from employers and employees in respect of pensions for school teachers and national health service staff *less* pensions actually paid to retired employees.

(b) The excess of the provision for pensions charged as a current cost in the Post Office commercial accounts over the pensions and gratuities actually paid to retired Post Office employees. Although the Post Office is treated as a public corporation from April 1961 the arrangements for superannuation of Post Office employees continue to be a central government responsibility and the excess of receipts from the Post Office Fund over pensions and gratuities paid is included under this heading.

(c) An imputed receipt of £88 million in 1955, representing the liability taken over by the United Kingdom government from the Indian government for the payment of pensions to certain members of the former India service and their dependants. The payments of pensions by the United Kingdom government to the members of the former India service, beginning in April 1955, are included as a deduction in this item. In return for the United Kingdom government assuming this liability, the outstanding amount of the loan from the Indian government to the United Kingdom government was reduced by £88 million which is included in the item 'Miscellaneous financial receipts (net) and changes in cash balances'.

(d) The excess of the provision made by the Forestry Commission for pensions and gratuities over payments made during the year.

Northern Ireland central government

Net sales of securities. This item covers all transactions in marketable securities by the Northern Ireland Exchequer and central government funds of Northern

Ireland. Transactions between separate parts of the Northern Ireland government disappear on consolidation, but the sale of marketable securities by a Northern Ireland fund to a United Kingdom government fund, for example the National Insurance Fund, would appear here as a positive entry and under the heading 'Receipts from market transactions' as a deduction.

Increase in other debt. This represents net receipts from Northern Ireland Treasury bills, Ulster savings certificates, Ulster development bonds, and bank advances. The increase in accrued interest outstanding on certificates and bonds is included.

Adjustment for purchase tax

This represents the excess or deficiency of purchase tax receipts by Customs and Excise over the estimated amount of purchase tax charged by registered traders in the year, which is included in the current account.

Adjustment for subsidies

This represents the excess or deficiency of the amount of subsidies accrued during the period, which is included in the current account (see page 272), over subsidy payments in the period.

Transactions in marketable securities on acquisition of the capital of certain undertakings

The following items are included:

(a) The issue in 1946 of £58 million of 3 per cent Treasury stock (1966 or after) to holders of the capital stock of the Bank of England which was transferred to Treasury ownership.

(b) The issue in 1949 of stock of a market value of £32 million to companies holding shares in Cable and Wireless Limited, as compensation for the transfer of the shares to Treasury ownership.

(c) Issues of stock between 1947 and 1956 as compensation to former colliery owners for collieries and other assets vested in the National Coal Board.

(d) Government securities redeemed in the years 1953 to 1955 in connection with the return of the iron and steel industry to private ownership. These transactions appear here as a deduction and are balanced by a positive entry under the heading 'Proceeds of iron and steel disposals'.

(e) The transfer in 1953 to the Consolidated Fund of liability for the £244 million of $3\frac{1}{4}$ per cent guaranteed stock, 1979-81 of the Iron and Steel Corporation of Great Britain (renamed $3\frac{1}{2}$ per cent Treasury stock, 1979-81). By this transfer the Exchequer became entitled to the net revenue of the Iron and Steel Holding and Realisation Agency and to the proceeds of iron and steel disposals.

(f) The transfer in 1963 from the British Transport Commission to the Consolidated Fund of liability for the £1,444 million of British Transport stock, against which has been offset a sum of £42 million representing the book value of government and government guaranteed securities transferred to the Treasury.

(g) The transfer in 1965 to the Consolidated Fund of liability for the £52 million of British Overseas Airways Corporation stock.

With the exception of item (d) all these transactions are balanced by entries on the payments side of the capital account. Items (a), (b) and (e) appear under the heading 'Acquisition of the capital of certain other undertakings' (see page 286), item (c) under 'Coal compensation: issues of stock', and items (f) and (g) under 'Net lending to public corporations'.

Miscellaneous financial receipts (net) and changes in cash balances

This is essentially the residual item in the table and therefore reflects any errors and omissions in other items in the central government accounts as presented in the published tables. The following specific items are included:

(a) The decrease in debtors (and payments in advance) *plus* the increase in creditors (and provisions) recorded in the accounts which are the basis of the published tables. During the years in which central government trading activities were of importance, the principal element in this item was the change in debtors and creditors of trading bodies. The change in debtors and creditors of certain non-trading bodies for which accounts are prepared on a payable-receivable basis, for example Regional Hospital Boards, are also included in this item.

(b) The difference arising from recording certain transactions, mainly current expenditure on military defence, on a basis other than cash payments, although the latter is the only basis on which actual accounting figures are available (see page 271).

(c) Up to 1957 the purchases of silver towards the obligation to return to the United States government the silver bullion transferred to this country under Lend-Lease arrangements were a deduction from this item. The eventual return of silver bullion (£22 million in 1956 and £7 million in 1957) was a positive entry under both this heading and 'Loan repayments to overseas governments'.

(d) The decrease in cash balances held at commercial banks by government departments and those bodies, for example Regional Hospital Boards, which are part of the central government. The balances of the Exchequer and Paymaster General held at the Bank of England are not included; they are reflected in the item 'Increase in net indebtedness to Bank of England Banking Department'. Balances held by departments with the Paymaster General and re-lent by him to the Exchequer disappear on consolidation.

(e) Increases in ways and means advances and holdings of non-market Treasury bills by certain official bodies and departmental funds which are not part of the central government sector. Examples are the Metropolitan police and, from April 1961, the Post Office.

(f) Miscellaneous items of borrowing, for example certain receipts from the sale of securities by the British Transport Stock Redemption Fund which was transferred to the Treasury from January 1963; *less* repayments of debt, such as the capital element of the loan charges transferred to the Health Ministers when local authority hospitals were vested in the national health service, and the purchase of 3 per cent redemption stock, 1986-96 by the Redemption Annuities Account under the Tithe Act, 1936.

(g) Certain miscellaneous capital receipts, such as gifts to the Exchequer.

(h) The imputed payment of £88 million in 1955, representing the part of the United Kingdom government debt to India which was cancelled under the pension arrangements described on page 276, is deducted from this item.

Net balance

The net balance is a measure of the government requirement to borrow to cover its total expenditure, including lending, in so far as it is not covered by taxation and other current and capital receipts. It is equal to government borrowing *less* any increase (or *plus* any decrease) in its holdings of gold and currency reserves. The 'Net balance' provides a link with the Exchequer accounts; it is equal to Exchequer borrowing and special transactions (net) *less* receipts from extra-Exchequer funds, etc. (see page 293). It is reckoned after deducting borrowing by the Northern Ireland central government. From 1968/69 the net balance is less than the borrowing requirement of the National Loans Fund by any surplus of the National Insurance Funds and any increase in departmental balances, etc. The remaining receipts on capital account provide an analysis of this item.

Increase in net indebtedness to Bank of England Banking Department

All transactions between the central government and the Bank of England Banking Department are included under this heading. The government has a net liability to the Banking Department of the Bank of England, which holds government debt of various kinds and at the same time has liabilities to the government, in the shape of balances of the Exchequer and the Paymaster General at the Bank of England. This item comprises the sum of the increases in assets of the Banking Department: ways and means advances, bank notes and coin, tax reserve certificates, British government and government guaranteed securities (as measured by net cash transactions), Treasury bills and Treasury interest-free notes; *less* increases in the liabilities of the Banking Department in respect of balances of the Exchequer and Paymaster General at the Bank of England.

Increase in notes and coin in circulation

This is the increase in the fiduciary note issue and issued coin *less* the increase in the holding of notes and coin by the Banking Department of the Bank of England. The Issue Department of the Bank of England is treated as an agent of the central government (see page 252). Changes in holdings by the Banking Department are reflected in the preceding item, 'Increase in net indebtedness to Bank of England Banking Department'.

Increase in non-marketable debt

National savings. This represents the increase in outstanding deposits (including accrued interest) with the ordinary accounts of the Post Office Savings Bank and the ordinary departments of the trustee savings banks, net receipts from the sale of premium savings bonds, defence bonds, national development bonds and national savings certificates, *plus* the increase in liability for accrued interest on national savings certificates. Receipts from Ulster development bonds and savings certificates appear under 'Northern Ireland central government: increase in other debt'.

It should be noted that the figures differ from the total of national savings shown in the financial account for the personal sector (Table 74 of the 1967 Blue Book) which also includes the increase in outstanding deposits with the Investment Account of the Post Office Savings Bank and the special investment departments of trustee savings banks. These deposits, unlike deposits with the ordinary accounts and departments, are not directly re-lent to the government.

The increase in holdings of government securities by investors on the Post Office register is not included; it is included under receipts from market transactions.

Tax reserve certificates. This represents net receipts from the issue of tax reserve certificates.

Receipts from market transactions

Treasury bills. This represents the increase in market Treasury bills, that is all bills outstanding other than those held by the National Debt Commissioners, the Exchange Equalisation Account, government departments and the Bank of England. The counterpart of most transactions between central monetary institutions in support of the reserves in the form of swaps against sterling is included, but bills held by the Bank of England on behalf of central monetary institutions as the sterling equivalent of foreign currency deposits are excluded; they are included under 'Other direct borrowing (net) from overseas governments and institutions'.

Government and government guaranteed securities. This represents the total cash issues of British government securities *less* redemptions, including the purchases by government sinking funds, *less* changes in holdings of government and government guaranteed securities by the Bank of England and National Debt Commissioners. The increase in the holdings of securities for the Post Office Savings Bank Investment Account is included in this item. Transactions are recorded in terms of the cash received or paid, and not in nominal values.

Borrowing from overseas governments

The main items in the early post-war years were as follows:
(a) drawings on the United States and Canadian lines of credit granted in 1945 and 1946;
(b) loans received from the United States under the European Recovery and Mutual Assistance Programmes from 1948 to 1952;
(c) the South African gold loan (£80 million in 1948);
(d) the loans from India and Pakistan (£176 million in 1948).
From 1953 to 1966 the only items which have appeared under this heading are:
(a) a drawing of £89 million in 1957 from the Export-Import Bank line of credit;
(b) in 1959 the conversion into a Treasury bond of the balance of £37 million in the German debt payment account;
(c) a loan of £18 million in 1961 from Switzerland under an agreement dated 20 October 1961[7];
(d) drawings of £51 million in 1966 from the Export-Import Bank lines of credit which were used to finance the purchase of military aircraft from the United States.

Repayments to overseas governments

This represents repayments of principal of the loans from overseas governments described above, of certain wartime loans, and payments under the Lend-Lease settlement of 1945. After 1958 the only wartime loan involved is the loan from Portugal. From 1959 the figures include repayments of debt created on the liquidation of the European Payments Union.

---

[7] *Agreement for a Loan by Switzerland to the Government of the United Kingdom,* Cmnd. 1684.

As mentioned on page 278, the figures for 1956 and 1957 include £22 million and £7 million respectively, representing the return to the United States government of the 88 million ounces of silver bullion originally transferred to the United Kingdom under Lend-Lease arrangements. The figure for 1959 includes £89 million repaid to the Export-Import Bank.

Increase in holdings of interest-free notes by the International Monetary Fund

Holdings of interest-free notes by the International Monetary Fund represent the counterpart of (a) the unused balance of the sterling portion of the United Kingdom subscription to the Fund, which is deposited in the United Kingdom against the issue of interest-free notes from the Exchequer and is available for drawings from the Fund in sterling by other countries, and (b) United Kingdom drawings from the Fund. When drawings are made from the Fund by the United Kingdom, the foreign currencies drawn are purchased for sterling and the Fund lends back the sterling to the Exchequer on the security of interest-free notes.

Capital subscriptions to the International Monetary Fund and European Fund

The figure for 1959 comprises issues of £232 million under the International Bank and Monetary Fund Act, 1959 and £4 million under the European Monetary Agreement Act, 1959. The figure of £1 million for 1960 represents a refund under the latter Act. The figure of £175 million for 1966 represents an increase in the subscription to the I.M.F.

Other direct borrowing (net) from overseas governments and institutions

This includes:
(a) any change in the sterling equivalent of foreign currency deposits by overseas central banks;
(b) deposits by the German Federal Republic made to offset part of the foreign exchange costs of stationing Forces in Germany *less* withdrawals made from time to time for expenditure in this country.

Increase in gold and currency reserves

This is the net change in the official holdings of gold, dollars and other foreign currencies, both convertible and non-convertible. Up to 1959 the change in the United Kingdom balance in the European Payments Union is also included. The figures do not reflect the transfers from the government portfolio of dollar securities to the reserves. Further details are given on page 455.

Gross domestic fixed capital formation

The estimates of gross fixed capital formation are described in Chapter XII. The definition of fixed capital formation by the central government follows so far as possible the definition applied in the private sector, except in the case of expenditure on military defence (see page 362). Sales of goods previously acquired by the government where the original acquisition would be treated as fixed capital formation, for example sales of machine tools by the Ministry of Technology, are deducted. Sales of factories on mortgage terms are also deducted at the time of sale, the loans created by these transactions being included under the heading 'Net lending to private sector'. Fixed capital formation does not include the acquisition of assets of companies which are nationalised; this is regarded as a financial transaction.

K

Up to April 1961 fixed capital formation by the Post Office is an important item. The other expenditure included here relates principally to buildings and equipment for research and development, hospitals, trunk roads and motorways, offices and other public buildings. The expenditure is analysed by eleven services in the Blue Book table; details of this classification are given in Chapter XI.

Increase in value of stocks

Trading bodies. The figures relate to the stocks of those bodies listed in Annex 1 to this chapter. The figures show the increase in the book value of stocks and work in progress and thus include any stock appreciation.

Strategic stocks. The figures relate to stocks held under the programmes for procuring strategic reserves of food and raw materials, and represent the cost of purchases *less* receipts from sales. Handling costs and other expenses incidental to the storage of strategic stocks are included in current expenditure on goods and services.

The estimates are further described in Chapter XIII. Receipts from sales of other goods are treated as deductions from expenditure on goods and services and not included here. For years prior to 1953, however, sales of surplus war stores in the United Kingdom were shown as a separate item under this heading because of their importance and special nature.

Capital grants to private sector

These items are unrequited payments regarded as paid into the capital accounts of the recipients. A detailed functional analysis of central government grants, consolidated with those of local authorities, is given in Table 53 of the 1967 Blue Book, which is described in Chapter XI.

Grants to universities, colleges, etc. From April 1962 the figures include grants by the Department of Education and Science to colleges of advanced technology. Prior to April 1962 these colleges were the direct responsibility of local authorities and their costs were included in local authorities' expenditure.

Town and Country Planning compensation. This comprises payments made by the Ministry of Housing and Local Government, the Scottish Development Department and the Central Land Board under the Town and Country Planning Acts of 1954. The compensation arises mainly from:

(a) depreciation in the value of land consequent upon the refusal or conditional grant of planning permission;

(b) the levying of development charges under the Town and Country Planning Acts, 1947, which were in general abolished for development begun on or after 18 November 1962;

(c) the compulsory acquisition of land by public authorities before January 1955 at existing-use values. The amount of this compensation was generally recouped by the Central Land Board from the acquiring authority and these recoupments have been deducted in arriving at the figures shown. Amounts paid by public authorities (usually local authorities) to the Central Land Board in such circumstances will, in general, have been treated as fixed capital formation by the public authorities concerned.

Both the principal and interest elements of compensation payments are included. Payments to local authorities under the Acts of 1947 and 1954 are excluded; they are included in 'Capital grants to local authorities'. The annuities paid out of the Votes of the Ministry of Housing and Local Government and the Scottish Development Department to the Exchequer in reimbursement of issues from the Consolidated Fund under the Acts of 1954 and the corresponding receipt of these annuities into the Exchequer are internal transactions of the central government which disappear on consolidation.

War damage compensation. This covers payments by the War Damage Commission and the Board of Trade under the War Damage Act, 1943; payments by the Ministry of Transport under the Marine War Risks Insurance Scheme; and certain payments by the Central Land Board under the Town and Country Planning Acts, 1947.

Other capital grants. Major items included here are agricultural support payments of a capital nature, mainly grants for farm improvements and field drainage, and grants by the Board of Trade under the Local Employment Acts towards expenditure on plant, machinery and buildings in development areas. Also included are post-war refunds of excess profits tax, which were relatively minor after 1955. These payments are included under this heading because their payment was conditional on their being used in developing or re-equipping the recipient's business (until the passage of the Finance Act, 1953 when only a small residue remained). The refunds were subject to tax and the figures are shown in the capital account after deduction of income tax which is excluded from tax receipts recorded in the current account.

From 1967 payments of investment grants, made in respect of capital expenditure after 17 January 1966, are included in this item.

Capital grants to local authorities

War damage compensation, under the provisions described above, and other capital grants are shown separately. All grants to local authorities treated by them as capital receipts are included. Certain grants made specifically towards capital expenditure met from revenue and treated by local authorities as current receipts are also included. A functional analysis of these grants is given in the capital account of local authorities (Table 46 of the 1967 Blue Book) and a further description of them appears in Chapter X (page 314).

Capital grants to public corporations

Capital grants to public corporations include grants to the British Broadcasting Corporation for capital expenditure in connection with external services, and grants to various public corporations for civil defence works. Compensation paid to the British Transport Commission in 1955 and 1956 for the capital loss sustained by the Commission on the sale of part of its road haulage undertaking is also included; these payments were financed mainly from the transport levy (see page 265).

Notional payments on writing-off debt in certain years are distinguished from other capital grants. The former represent one part of the transaction recorded in the capital account when government loans to public corporations have been formally written-off. The other part of the transaction appears as a repayment under the heading 'Net lending to public corporations: loans written-off'. Transactions on writing-off debt are as follows:

(a) government loans to the Overseas Food Corporation of £36 million, £1 million and £3 million written-off in 1951, 1952 and 1955 respectively;

(b) the write-off in 1962 of government loans to the Ulster Transport Authority amounting to £10 million;

(c) the write-off in 1963 of £487 million government loans to the British Transport Commission against which has been offset the transfer of £55 million in cash and securities from the British Transport Commission to the Treasury;

(d) the write-off in 1965 of £415 million government loans to the National Coal Board and £110 million of debt of the British Overseas Airways Corporation.

Capital transfers abroad

There were no payments in this category from 1952 to 1966. Transfers in earlier years covered payments to the United States government of a proportion of the sterling counterpart of aid received under the European Recovery Programme, and grants to European countries under the Intra-European Payments Agreement and the European Payments Union. Revaluation payments made by the United Kingdom on the devaluation of sterling in 1949 were included in this item. Entries arising from revaluations on devaluation in 1967 are included elsewhere in the accounts.

Net lending to private sector

This comprises loans *less* repayments of principal to the personal sector and companies. In the Blue Book table net lending to industry and trade, building societies and private housing associations are shown separately. Details of the composition of this item and its functional classification are given in Chapter XI.

Net lending to local authorities

This comprises advances, *less* repayments of principal, to local authorities from:
(a) the Local Loans Fund through the agency of the Public Works Loan Board;
(b) the Consolidated Fund to harbour authorities;
(c) the Northern Ireland Government Loans Fund;
(d) certain government departments, mainly for the financing of tunnels and bridges.

Net lending to public corporations

Net lending to public corporations covers advances *less* repayments to the bodies defined as public corporations in Chapter VIII. Most of this lending appears in the first instance as issues from and repayments to the Consolidated Fund (from April 1968 the National Loans Fund); however, such issues and repayments are made through special accounts and funds administered by the appropriate government department, and it is from such accounts that the figures of lending are taken.

There was a substantial increase in government lending to public corporations after 1955. Up to 1955 the principal recipients of loans were the National Coal Board, the Raw Cotton Commission, the housing and new town corporations and the Commonwealth Development Corporation. From 1956 certain public corporations in Great Britain ceased to raise capital by the issue of stock, and instead advances were made to them from the Exchequer, through the appropriate departmental accounts, under the Finance Acts of 1956 and 1958. The public corporations concerned were the British Transport Commission, Gas

Council, Central Electricity Authority, North of Scotland Hydro-Electric Board, South of Scotland Electricity Board, British Overseas Airways Corporation and British European Airways Corporation. In 1957, 1958 and 1959 loans to finance the deficit of the British Transport Commission are included. From 1960, however, the revenue deficit of the British Transport Commission was financed by grants which are treated as subsidies and included in government expenditure on current account. Also included is net lending by the Northern Ireland Exchequer and Government Loans Fund to the Northern Ireland Housing Trust, the Electricity Board for Northern Ireland and the Ulster Transport Authority. Amounts regarded as being lent to the Iron and Steel Holding and Realisation Agency are included in this item (see page 276).

On the vesting of certain undertakings as public corporations, principally the National Coal Board and the Raw Cotton Commission, there appeared in their opening balance sheets a liability towards the central government. The lending by the central government corresponding to these initial liabilities is not reflected here, but repayments of these liabilities are recorded in this item. In particular, the capital element of the annuities by which the National Coal Board is repaying its initial liability to the government is deducted. Increases in the amounts formerly deposited by the National Coal Board with the Exchequer as ways and means advances have also been deducted.

For certain years loans written-off are shown separately. They represent the repayment of government loans formally written-off, already mentioned under 'Capital grants to public corporations: on writing-off debt'.

Transfer of liability for stock is also shown separately for certain years. It represents the increase in liabilities of public corporations to the central government resulting from the transfer of liability for stock to the Consolidated Fund. British Transport Commission stock of nominal value £1,444 million was transferred in 1963 and British Overseas Airways Corporation stock of nominal value £52 million was transferred in 1965 (see page 277).

Loans to overseas governments

From 1950 to 1966 the principal component is loans to the less developed countries for economic development, comprising:
    (a) advances under Section 3 of the Export Guarantees Act, 1949;
    (b) advances under the Colonial Development and Welfare Acts, 1959 to 1965;
    (c) loans made by the Ministry of Overseas Development.
The figure for 1951 includes a loan of £22 million to enable Denmark to buy back kroner accumulated in London before the start of the European Payments Union. In the early post-war years the item included the cost of the United Kingdom share of relief imports into Germany and the advance of £100 million to Argentina in 1948 under the Andes Agreement.

Loan repayments by overseas governments

This represents repayments of principal of the loans and advances to overseas governments described above, together with repayment of certain advances to allied governments made during the war of 1939-45.

Drawings from United Kingdom subscriptions to international lending bodies

This item represents drawings by the International Bank for Reconstruction and Development, the International Development Association and the Asian

Development Bank from United Kingdom subscriptions. The sterling component of these subscriptions is normally re-lent to the Exchequer in the form of interest-free notes until required by the international organisation, so that except for minor timing differences the amounts shown under this heading are equivalent to subscriptions *less* the increase in holdings of interest-free notes by these bodies. The figure for 1956 also includes a subscription of £5 million to the International Finance Corporation.

Other net lending to overseas sector

This covers other loans *less* repayments made overseas. The main items included are loans to aluminium producers in Canada and certain uranium producers in South Africa and Australia. Loans to other uranium producers in Australia are included with loans to overseas governments. Loans to the Commonwealth Development Corporation, which invests in certain enterprises overseas, are included under 'Net lending to public corporations'. Other items included are purchases of United Nations bonds in 1962 and subsequent repayments, and in 1966 the servicing of loans by the International Bank for Reconstruction and Development to Rhodesia, guaranteed by the United Kingdom government.

Cash expenditure on company securities (net)

The figure for 1966 comprises expenditure of £31 million on British Petroleum shares and £1·5 million on shares and loan stock of Fairfields (Glasgow) Ltd.

Coal compensation

The last cash payments of compensation to former owners of colliery concerns transferred to the National Coal Board were made in 1955. The last issues of stock were made in 1956; these figures relate to the market value of the stock issued and not the nominal value; they are also included in 'Transactions in marketable securities on acquisition of the capital of certain undertakings' (see page 277).

Acquisition of the capital of certain undertakings

From 1954 to 1966 there were no entries under this heading. Earlier entries relate to the acquisition of the capital of the Bank of England in 1946, of Cable and Wireless Ltd. in 1949, and of the Iron and Steel Corporation in 1953. These entries are balanced by an equal amount included in the receipts item 'Transactions in marketable securities on acquisition of the capital of certain undertakings' (see page 277). Also included in 1953 is the Northern Ireland government share of the compensation paid when the Great Northern Railway Board of Ireland was jointly acquired by the government of Northern Ireland and the government of the Irish Republic (£2 million).

THE CURRENT ACCOUNT OF CENTRAL GOVERNMENT
EXCLUDING NATIONAL INSURANCE FUNDS

For certain purposes, in particular for international comparisons, it is useful to be able to distinguish the transactions of the central government sector apart from the National Insurance Funds. A simplified current account on this basis is given in the Blue Book (Table 43 of the 1967 Blue Book). The differences from the current account of the central government sector as a whole are listed below.

Receipts

(a) Receipts of national insurance contributions are excluded. Prior to September 1957 that part of the national insurance contributions transferred from the Funds towards the cost of the national health service is included. From September 1957 separate contributions to the health service became payable and appear in both tables.

(b) 'Interest and dividends, etc.' excludes the receipts of the National Insurance Funds on holdings of securities other than those of the central government. Receipts of interest on holdings of government securities are excluded from both tables.

Expenditure

(a) Current expenditure on goods and services excludes the administrative costs of the national insurance scheme and certain other costs borne by the National Insurance Funds.

(b) Current grants to the personal sector and current grants abroad both exclude national insurance benefits.

(c) Payments of debt interest include payments to the National Insurance Funds on government securities held by the Funds.

(d) The contribution of the Exchequer to the National Insurance Funds is included as a current grant.

(e) The current surplus excludes that of the National Insurance Funds.

CURRENT ACCOUNT OF NATIONAL INSURANCE FUNDS

This account (Table 44 of the 1967 Blue Book) shows the current income and expenditure of the National Insurance and Industrial Injuries Funds (see page 302).

Receipts are divided between contributions from employers, contributions from insured persons, payments in lieu of graduated contributions from 1962, the contribution from the Exchequer received through the Ministry of Social Security, and investment income. Contributions from employers and insured persons are subdivided to show receipts in respect of H.M. Forces, civilian employees, the self-employed, and persons who are not employed. Contributions to the national health service from September 1957, to the Redundancy Fund from December 1965, and payments of selective employment tax from September 1966, although collected with national insurance contributions are not paid into the Funds and are excluded from this table.

Expenditure is divided between the costs of administering the national insurance scheme and certain expenditure on training and rehabilitation (current expenditure on goods and services), expenditure on benefits (current grants to personal sector and current grants abroad) and the contribution made by the National Insurance Funds towards the cost of the national health service which was paid to the health departments until September 1957. Current grants to the personal sector are subdivided between the different types of benefit.

QUARTERLY TABLES

Quarterly estimates are compiled for both the current and capital accounts of the central government including National Insurance Funds. The current account is published quarterly in *Economic Trends* and each month with the capital account in *Financial Statistics*.

The quarterly tables are prepared on the same basis as the annual tables described above, although less detail is given. The quarterly current account has been published from 1954 and the capital account from 1958.

4. STATISTICAL SOURCES

Although nearly all the basic material used for the analysis of central government transactions is to be found in published sources, few of the figures in the national income accounts are directly identifiable in these sources. The national income accounts present the results of a fairly elaborate process first of consolidation, so as to eliminate many classes of internal transactions, then of rearrangement, so as to display the statistics in a form useful for economic analysis and so far as possible uniformly with the treatment of the rest of the economy. Moreover, almost all the detailed accounts in published sources relate to the financial year ending 31 March and have to be adjusted to provide figures for calendar years. Apart from the weekly summary of Exchequer receipts and issues, which was inappropriate for national income accounts, the only published information available for shorter periods has related to tax receipts and national savings.

The discussion below is mostly confined to a description of the annual published sources, from which the general method of analysis will be most easily appreciated. However, most of the calendar year figures in the national income accounts are derived from special quarterly returns made by departments, although, in some cases, interpolation of the financial year figures has to be used. For the latest year some of the figures shown are based on advance estimates of expenditure actually incurred, and are therefore provisional. The detailed accounts for the latest year are generally not available when the Blue Book is prepared.

THE EXCHEQUER ACCOUNTS

The Exchequer accounts, as prepared for the years up to 1967/68, are statements of the cash flows through the United Kingdom government accounts with the Bank of England and Bank of Ireland, and show Exchequer receipts and issues under headings which correspond to the requirements of Parliamentary control. The scope of the Exchequer accounts is confined to those transactions which were required by law to pass through the Consolidated Fund. The operations of the National Insurance Funds and a number of other government funds are either excluded altogether or only very partially reflected in the Exchequer accounts. Although the Exchequer accounts occupy a position of central importance, they are not a major direct source of data for the national accounts tables. This is because most Exchequer transactions are with departments and other government bodies, and are thus internal to the central government sector as defined for national accounts purposes. Exchequer transactions outside the central government sector, mainly interest on and management of the national debt and transactions in marketable securities, are however used directly in compiling the central government accounts. The Exchequer accounts are also useful in providing a framework by means of which the accounts of the departments, bodies and funds making up the central government sector can be systematically related.

The main Exchequer account published is *Finance Accounts of the United Kingdom*. The transactions recorded in these accounts may be summarised as shown below.

Summary of Exchequer receipts and payments, 1965/66

£ million

Receipts		Payments	
Taxation	8,324	Supply services	7,140
Miscellaneous receipts	820	Consolidated Fund standing services	1,316
Total revenue	9,144		
		Total expenditure	8,456
Exchequer borrowing (net receipts)	814	Consolidated Fund loans (net)	1,265
Special transactions (net)	−237		
Total	9,721	Total	9,721

Source: 1965/66 Finance Accounts

There is a natural division in the accounts between Exchequer revenue and expenditure on the one hand and the transactions leading up to the Exchequer net financing requirement on the other.

Exchequer revenue consists mainly of taxation, that is the amounts paid over to the Exchequer by the revenue departments. The *Finance Accounts* contain details of the amounts collected as well as the amounts paid over to the Exchequer. In addition to taxation, revenue consists of interest on Consolidated Fund loans and other receipts of interest and dividends; receipts from the sale of broadcast receiving licences; and other miscellaneous receipts, consisting mainly of departmental receipts (other than those used as appropriations in aid of expenditure) which are required to be paid into the Exchequer. Fuller details of the receipts paid over by departments are given in *Appropriation Accounts*.

Exchequer expenditure is divided between issues for supply services and for Consolidated Fund standing services. The bulk of expenditure is on account of supply services, that is departmental expenditure which is provided for by annual Votes by Parliament. Consolidated Fund standing services, on the other hand, are so distinguished because they have been authorised once and for all by statute as permanent charges on the Fund. These consist largely of interest on and management of the national debt, but also include payments to the Northern Ireland government in respect of reserved taxes, repayment of post-war credits, war damage compensation, and items such as the Civil List and salaries and pensions of judges.

The other transactions summarised in the table above show advances *less* repayments from the Consolidated Fund in respect of loans to industry and other loans, and the Exchequer borrowing needed to finance this lending after taking account of special transactions and the surplus of revenue over expenditure. Exchequer borrowing comprises net receipts from issues of marketable securities, Treasury bills, ways and means advances, national savings, tax

K*

**Reconciliation between Exchequer revenue and central
government receipts on current account, 1965/66**

	£ million
Exchequer revenue (Taxation *plus* Miscellaneous receipts)	9,144[1]
less Receipts on capital account:	
Taxes on capital	−296
Other (including loan repayments)..............................	−45
less Receipts from broadcast receiving licences, treated in the national accounts as trading receipts of the B.B.C. and the Post Office	−69
less Receipts from extra-Exchequer bodies, treated in the national accounts as transfers within central government.................................	−12
plus Current receipts of extra-Exchequer bodies from outside central government (excluding gross trading surplus):	
National Insurance Funds.	1,596
Other (including Northern Ireland central government)............	83
less Receipts treated in the national accounts as deductions from corresponding current expenditure	−13
plus Receipts deducted from Vote expenditure, treated in the national accounts as central government current receipts:	
National health contributions	160
Taxes on expenditure	39
less Receipts of interest and surplus revenue from Votes, treated in the national accounts as transfers within central government	−141
plus Gross trading surplus as defined in the national accounts	27
plus Rent income from letting property as defined in the national accounts ..	20
plus Excess of tax and other receipts by departments over corresponding amounts paid into Exchequer	8
plus Excess of accruals of taxes on expenditure over receipts by departments .	2
plus Imputed rent	73
Miscellaneous	3
Central government current receipts	10,579[2]

[1]As published in *Finance Accounts of the United Kingdom, 1965/66*.
[2]As published in October 1967 issue of *Economic Trends*.

Reconciliation between Exchequer expenditure and central government expenditure on current account, 1965/66

£ million

	Supply services	Consolidated Fund standing services	Total (including extra-Exchequer bodies)
Exchequer expenditure	7,140[1]	1,316[1]	8,456[1]
less Payments on capital account:			
Gross capital formation	−308	—	−308
Other (including grants and loans)	−270	−3	−273
less Payments to the B.B.C. and the Post Office from receipts from broadcast receiving licences	−69	—	−69
less Payments to extra-Exchequer bodies, treated in the national accounts as transfers within central government:			
National Insurance Funds	−297	−62	−359
Northern Ireland central government	−1	−149	−150
Other.....................................	−1	−187	−188
plus Current expenditure of extra-Exchequer bodies outside central government:			
National Insurance Funds			1,930
Northern Ireland central government			127
Other.....................................			89
less Receipts treated in the national accounts as deductions from corresponding current expenditure			−13
plus Receipts deducted from Vote expenditure, treated in the national accounts as central government receipts:			
National health contributions	160	—	160
Taxes on expenditure	39	—	39
Gross trading surplus			42
Rent			20
Other (capital receipts).....................	61	—	61
less Vote payments of interest and surplus revenue to the Exchequer, treated in the national accounts as transfers within central government			−141
less Increase in departmental balances			−9
plus Increase in accrued interest on national savings certificates			—
plus Excess of accrual of liability for subsidies over payments by departments	8	—	8
plus Imputed rent			73
Miscellaneous			6
Central government current expenditure.............			9,501[2]

[1] As published in *Finance Accounts of the United Kingdom, 1965/66.*

[2] As published in October 1967 issue of *Economic Trends.*

reserve certificates, and direct borrowing (net) from overseas governments and institutions, *less* payments to statutory sinking funds and terminable annuities due to National Debt Commissioners. Special transactions cover mainly changes in the sterling capital of the Exchange Equalisation Account and subscriptions and contributions to international financial organisations; in 1966/67 and 1967/68 advances to Votes for the purchase of military aircraft from the United States are also covered. From 1968/69 nearly all of the transactions mentioned in this paragraph are included in the accounts of the National Loans Fund and not the Consolidated Fund.

The scope of the Exchequer accounts is considerably narrower than the central government sector as a whole, which includes the transactions of the Northern Ireland government, the National Insurance Funds and a number of other funds. There are also other differences in scope because of the imputation of some transactions.

The tables on pages 290 and 291 provide a reconciliation between Exchequer receipts and expenditure and the current receipts and expenditure in the central government accounts for 1965/66, the latest year for which *Finance Accounts* was available when the 1967 Blue Book was prepared. The table on page 293 relates the Exchequer financing requirement to the net balance in the central government capital account. Similar reconciliations were included in the *Financial Statement* for 1965, 1966 and 1967. The 1968 *Financial Statement* gave a different form of reconciliation, showing the relationship of the national accounts items to the transactions recorded in the accounts of the Consolidated Fund and the National Loans Fund.

A further discussion of the relationship between Exchequer transactions and the national accounts is given in the White Paper [8] issued before the form of the Exchequer Accounts was changed for 1964/65. The earlier form of accounts is set out in the first description of the national accounts [9]. The changes in the accounts resulting from the establishment of the National Loans Fund in April 1968 have little effect on this relationship.

SUPPLY SERVICES

The larger part of government expenditure is on account of 'Supply services', authorised annually by the Appropriation Acts. The principal published sources relating to departmental expenditure are the *Estimates* published in the February or March preceding the financial year to which they refer and the *Appropriation Accounts* published from January to March after the end of the financial year which show expenditure actually incurred. During the course of the financial year revised or supplementary estimates are also published. The defence estimates and appropriation accounts are published separately from the civil estimates and appropriation accounts, which since 1962/63 have been divided into eleven classes. The classes are further divided into Votes, each of which relates to the whole, or part, of a single department's expenditure. The expenditure of the larger departments is divided into several Votes, for example ten Votes for the Army Department; for other departments one Vote covers the

[8] *Reform of the Exchequer Accounts*, Cmnd. 2014.
[9] *National Income Statistics: Sources and Methods*, Studies in Official Statistics, No. 3, 1956.

**Reconciliation between Exchequer financing requirement and
central government net balance, 1965/66**

	£ million
Exchequer borrowing *plus* Special transactions (net)	577[1]
less Surpluses lent by extra-Exchequer funds to Exchequer but not constituting borrowing from sectors of the economy outside central government:	
Departmental balances (including Civil Contingencies Fund and various deposit accounts)	45
National Insurance Funds	−30
Local Loans Fund	−3
Issue Department surplus income	−75
plus Increase in coin in circulation...	16
Transactions included as receipts (reducing borrowing requirement) or as expenditure (increasing borrowing requirement) in giving rise to central government net balance:	
Drawings from United Kingdom subscriptions to international lending bodies (excluding I.M.F.)	15
Accrued interest on national savings certificates	—
Miscellaneous	−46
Central government net balance	499[2]

[1]As published in *Finance Accounts of the United Kingdom, 1965/66*.
[2]As published in the June 1966 and subsequent issues of *Financial Statistics*.

whole expenditure, for example there is one Vote for the Inland Revenue. To a certain extent each Vote brings together the expenditure connected with a particular object or purpose. For instance, although there is one Vote for the general administrative expenses of the Board of Trade, there are separate Votes for Board of Trade expenditure on promotion of trade, exports, etc., for Board of Trade promotion of local employment, and so on. These objects or purposes are related to the classification by function given in the Blue Book (see Chapter XI). In some cases, however, a single Vote may cover a number of services, for example the Vote for the Home Office covers a range of services which are allocated to various categories in the functional analysis of public expenditure.

Each Vote is subdivided by sub-heads which generally show the subject, or economic nature, of the expenditure such as salaries and wages, fuel and light, purchase of machinery, contributions in lieu of rates. From this information the greater part of expenditure can be classified into the economic categories of expenditure used in the national accounts. With the introduction of a revised form of *Civil Estimates* in 1962/63 and of *Defence Estimates* in 1963/64, the detailed classification of sub-heads has been carried out by departments in co-operation with the Central Statistical Office, and a table showing the national accounts classification of each Vote is included as part of the published *Estimates*. These tables are summarised in the *Memorandum by the Financial Secretary to the Treasury* which is published at the same time of the year as the *Estimates*. Although at present no similar classification of appropriation accounts is published, from 1963/64 departments have been responsible for carrying out the initial classification of these accounts into economic and functional categories. This facilitates a more detailed classification of transactions than was possible from the published *Appropriation Accounts*, which normally show less detail than the *Estimates*.

Besides showing departmental payments, the *Estimates* and *Appropriation Accounts* show departmental receipts other than receipts of taxes by the revenue departments. Such departmental receipts are of two classes: (a) those which, up to limits laid down in the *Estimates*, may be appropriated in aid of departmental expenditure; and (b) the rest which must in due course be paid over to the Exchequer (as Exchequer Extra Receipts). For the national accounts the distinction between the two classes (a) and (b) is not relevant. The estimate and appropriation account for each Vote shows these receipts in some detail and this enables them to be classified by their economic category, for example interest on loans, sales of fixed assets (which are deducted from gross fixed capital formation), and receipts of rent.

To complete the picture of supply service transactions it is necessary to refer to the *Finance Accounts* which show in summary form the Exchequer issues for supply services and the departmental payments to the Exchequer (described as Exchequer Extra Receipts) referred to in the preceding paragraph. These are, however, transactions within the government and they disappear on consolidating the Exchequer accounts with the accounts of supply services.

The principal task in the analysis of supply services is therefore to sort out payments and receipts, both appropriations-in-aid and receipts payable to the Exchequer, into the economic categories used in the national accounts. Payments and receipts which disappear on consolidation of supply services with the accounts of the rest of the central government are ignored, for example, grants to the National Insurance Funds (see page 253); in place of these grants shown in the *Appropriation Accounts*, the national accounts show by virtue of the process of consolidation the full expenditure and income, other than grants, of grant-aided bodies and funds.

The *Estimates* and *Appropriation Accounts* for supply services of the Northern Ireland government follow the pattern of those for the United Kingdom government and their analysis is similar.

A special analysis has to be made in the case of trading services, for which the *Appropriation Accounts* show only cash payments and cash receipts. In some cases only a net figure is shown—either net cash surplus or net cash payment. The trading analysis is derived from *Trading Accounts and Balance Sheets* and other published accounts for trading bodies, which are listed in Annex 1.

OTHER BODIES, FUNDS AND ACCOUNTS

Besides the Exchequer accounts and the accounts of the supply services, the accounts of the various bodies and funds referred to on pages 251 and 252 are subjected to the same processes of consolidation and classification of transactions by economic categories. The internal transactions which disappear on consolidation of the whole of the central government accounts—such as grants and loans from supply Votes or from the Exchequer—are ignored. The principal published accounts are listed in Annex 3, but there are many others of lesser importance. In principle the national accounts, which aim to show transactions between the central government (as here defined) and the rest of the economy, should incorporate all the accounts of what may be described as peripheral bodies or funds. But in practice the national accounts analysis is based in some of the less important cases on the transactions between the Exchequer, or supply Votes, and these peripheral bodies and funds, instead of on the latter's transactions with the rest of the economy.

As mentioned above, there is some published information available which provides quarterly figures of tax receipts and national savings, but most of the central government quarterly figures are compiled from special returns. The main source of information is a quarterly return by all departments to the Treasury which provides an analysis of expenditure on supply services by economic categories. It also includes particulars of extra-Exchequer receipts. Special returns are also made by departments covering the income and expenditure of extra-Exchequer funds and accounts, including in particular the National Insurance Funds. The figures generally relate to cash transactions, which is the normal basis of departmental accounting, but for trading services the departments concerned provide a quarterly estimate of the gross trading surplus on a payable-receivable basis. A return is also provided in respect of the Regional Hospital Boards which gives their expenditure on a payable-receivable basis. The figures may only approximate to those required; for example, if accounts are not analysed in the full detail for calendar quarters, and if accounts are kept for periods of complete weeks rather than for calendar quarters.

Lending from the Consolidated Fund is mainly carried out by way of deposit accounts maintained by departments, and quarterly returns are received in respect of these showing the amounts advanced and repaid and the amount of interest received. Details of central government borrowing are obtained from the accounts of the Treasury.

With the exception of the return for the National Insurance Funds, the above returns relate to Great Britain. Returns for Northern Ireland are collected and analysed by the Northern Ireland government, which provides a quarterly return of Northern Ireland central government transactions, excluding National Insurance Funds, on a national accounts basis.

5. RELIABILITY

The reliability of the basic data used for the compilation of the central government accounts—nearly all of which are comprehensive and mutually consistent accounting date—is clearly good, in terms of the gradings described on pages 39 to 41. In most cases, the reliability of the annual national accounts statistics is equally good, because the national income accounts are no more than a reclassification of the items shown in the basic accounting data. Some uncertainty arises over the preparation of the figures on a calendar year basis, since it is impracticable to obtain quarterly figures as detailed as the final accounts of a financial year. Moreover, figures for the most recent year shown are subject to revision when detailed accounts become available. Because of the methods used in measuring current expenditure on goods and services (see page 271) the annual, and also the quarterly, estimates of this item are subject to a greater margin of error than the transactions which are satisfactorily measured by cash receipts or payments.

ANNEX 1

GOVERNMENT TRADING ACTIVITIES

The list of government trading bodies, as defined on pages 256 to 258 is given below. Trading bodies not operating after 1954/55 and listed in the previous description of the national accounts[1] are not included. An asterisk denotes those bodies for which commercial accounts are published annually in *Trading Accounts and Balance Sheets*. Accounts for the trading bodies in Northern Ireland (not listed below) are published in *Trading and Other Accounts* (Annex 3, item 76). For other trading activities, commercial accounts are published separately as noted below, or are estimated from the *Appropriation Accounts* and from information from the departments concerned. Except where otherwise stated, the trading surplus or deficit is included in gross trading surplus of central government.

Ministry of Agriculture, Fisheries and Food and *Department of Agriculture and Fisheries for Scotland* (formerly *Ministry of Food*)

*Trading in foods to 31 March 1958. The trading loss of the Ministry, before charging administrative overheads and the cost of milk and welfare food schemes, was treated as a subsidy.

*Agricultural trading services. Pool labour services, agricultural machinery operations, land drainage and water supply operations, pest destruction and farming of land. There were deficits on trading up to 1954/55 which were treated as subsidies.

United Kingdom Atomic Energy Authority

The commercial operations of the Atomic Energy Authority were separated from the rest of their activities from 1 April 1965. Trading accounts are included in the annual reports (see Annex 3, item 24).

Crown Estate Office (formerly *Crown Lands*)

Accounts published as House of Commons papers. The income is included in rent.

Export Credits Guarantee Department

Forestry Commission

Land Commission

From 1967/68 the operations of the Land Acquisition and Management Fund.

Post Office

Postal, telephone and telegraph, etc. services to 31 March 1961. *Commercial Accounts* published annually.

---

[1]*National Income Statistics: Sources and Methods*, Studies in Official Statistics, No. 3, 1956.
* Denotes those trading bodies for which annual trading accounts are included in *Trading Accounts and Balance Sheets*.

Post Office Savings Bank

The Post Office Savings Banks Fund is included. Accounts published separately (see Annex 3, items 26 and 28).

*Royal Mint

Royal Ordnance Factories (formerly *Ministry of Supply*)

When operated by the former Ministry of Supply trading accounts were included in *Trading Accounts and Balance Sheets*. From 1959/60 these accounts are included with the *Defence Appropriation Accounts*.

*State Management Districts

Operation of breweries and public houses in certain areas.

Ministry of Technology (formerly *Ministry of Aviation* and *Ministry of Supply*)

Assistance to private industry by the purchase and leasing of buildings and plant. The income is included in rent.

Board of Trade

*Air navigation services, including *en route* services from 1 November 1964 (formerly Ministry of Aviation). The deficit is treated as a subsidy (see page 339).

*Civil aerodromes (formerly Ministry of Aviation and Ministry of Transport and Civil Aviation). Accounts are included in *Trading Accounts and Balance Sheets* only from 1958/59. Air navigation services are included up to October 1964, and the operation of international airports up to March 1966. The deficit is treated as a subsidy (see page 339).

*Commodity trading divisions (formerly Ministry of Supply and Ministry of Materials).

Building and purchase of factories for sale and leasing to private industry. Accounts are included in *Trading Accounts and Balance Sheets* until 1959/60, after which they are published as House of Commons papers under the Local Employment Acts, 1960 and 1963 (see Annex 3, item 64). The deficit is treated as a subsidy (see page 341). The income is included in rent.

Ministry of Transport (formerly *Ministry of Transport and Civil Aviation*)

Post-war shipping operations—trooping, emigration and commercial services up to 1959/60.

Ministry of Works, Ministry of Housing and Local Government and *Department of Health for Scotland*

Building and renting to local authorities of temporary housing up to 31 March 1962. An imputed income was included under rent and the amount by which this exceeded the receipts from local authorities was treated as a subsidy (see pages 268 and 269).

---

*Denotes those trading bodies for which annual trading accounts are included in *Trading Accounts and Balance Sheets*.

ANNEX 2

GRANT-AIDED BODIES

The list below excludes local authorities and public corporations. The list is not comprehensive and includes only the bodies receiving substantial grants from the central government. Private bodies receiving assistance from the government only in the form of free accommodation are not included. For simplicity, such assistance is ignored in the national accounts; to allow for it would require an imputed grant from the central government to the private sector and imputed expenditure by the private sector.

Treated as part of central government

> Agricultural Research Council
> Arts Council of Great Britain
> British Council
> Commonwealth War Graves Commission (formerly Imperial War Graves Commission)
> Consumer Council
> Criminal Injuries Compensation Board
> Herring Industry Board
> Highlands and Islands Development Board
> Medical Research Council
> National Institute for Research in Nuclear Science
> Natural Environment Research Council
> Race Relations Board
> Regional Hospital Boards and Boards of Governors of Teaching Hospitals
> Science Research Council
> Social Science Research Council
> United Kingdom Atomic Energy Authority
> White Fish Authority

Treated as part of company sector (bodies serving industry)

> Air Registration Board
> British Institute of Management
> British National Export Council
> British Overseas Engineering Services Bureau
> British Productivity Council
> British Standards Institution
> British Travel Association
> Council of Industrial Design
> Home Grown Cereals Authority.
> Industrial Training Boards
> National Building Agency
> National Computing Centre
> Scottish Tourist Board

Treated as part of personal sector

Arts Council of Northern Ireland
British Academy
British Film Institute
Centre for Environmental Research
College of Aeronautics
Commonwealth Institute
Health Education Council
National Central Library
National Committee for Commonwealth Immigrants
National Council of Social Service
National Library of Wales
National Museum of Wales
Private research bodies
Private schools and colleges (including direct grant and special schools and
    voluntary approved schools)
Royal College of Art
Royal Society
Royal Society for the Prevention of Accidents
Ulster Museum
Universities and, from April 1962, colleges of advanced technology
Women's Royal Voluntary Service

ANNEX 3

PUBLISHED SOURCES OF CENTRAL GOVERNMENT ACCOUNTS

The letters (HC) denote that a publication is a House of Commons Paper. The abbreviation (Cmnd.) indicates a Command Paper. Certain of the accounts of grant-aided bodies and funds are appended to the appropriation account of the Vote from which the grant is made, and these therefore appear in the *Appropriation Accounts* referred to in item (9) below; where this is the case it is denoted in the list below by the symbol (AA). The list includes sources providing information from 1955/56 onwards. For sources relevant only for earlier years reference should be made to the first description of the national accounts[1]. A separate list of trading bodies, with a note of the sources of their accounts is given in Annex 1 on page 296.

EXCHEQUER ACCOUNTS

Note: These sources relate to the years up to 1967/68 before the establishment of the National Loans Fund.

(1) *Finance Accounts of the United Kingdom* (HC). This document is published about November of each year and relates to the financial year ended the previous March, with corresponding figures in some tables only for the preceding financial year. Apart from giving the account of the Consolidated Fund as a whole it contains a detailed statement of tax receipts, of miscellaneous sources of revenue, and of issues for Consolidated Fund standing services, and a summary statement of Exchequer issues for supply services. It gives details of transactions in connection with the national debt, of other Exchequer receipts and issues, and of Exchequer assets and liabilities.

(2) The weekly return of *Exchequer Receipts and Issues*. This summary of Exchequer transactions is similar in form of presentation to the *Finance Accounts*, and was published in the *London Gazette*. An abbreviated version of the weekly return was published in the *Monthly Digest of Statistics* and in *Financial Statistics*.

(3) *Financial Statement* (HC). This is published each year on the day the Budget is presented to Parliament. It contains a summary of the estimates of revenue and expenditure for the coming financial year and a statement of proposed tax changes and of their estimated effect on revenue. Figures of the estimates and out-turn for the financial year just ended, or ending, are also given.

(4) *National Debt Return* (Cmnd.). An annual account is published in October, providing a detailed account of transactions during the year and of financial liabilities. For details of financial assets, reference must be made to the *Finance Accounts*.

REVENUE

(5) *Annual Report of the Commissioners of H.M. Inland Revenue* (Cmnd.). This is published about the beginning of the year, for example the 110th Report for 1966/67 was published in February 1968. It contains a detailed statement of revenue from income tax, surtax, profits tax, death duties, stamp duties, and other sources for a series of financial years including the year ended on the

---

[1] *National Income Statistics: Sources and Methods*, Studies in Official Statistics, No. 3, 1956.

previous 31 March. In addition it contains data of general economic interest derived from tax assessments about the financial operations of companies, the distribution of personal income, and estates assessed for death duties.

(6) *Annual Report of the Commissioners of H.M. Customs and Excise* (Cmnd.). This is published about January, for example the 58th Report for 1966/67 was published in January 1968. It contains full details of revenue from Customs and Excise duties, which cover most of what are treated in the national accounts as taxes on expenditure, together with some account of the reasons for changes in their yield.

(7) The *Monthly Digest of Statistics* and *Financial Statistics* give monthly figures of net receipts by the Inland Revenue and Customs and Excise, with an analysis under the main heads of revenue.

SUPPLY SERVICES

(8) *Estimates* (HC). The estimates of expenditure in the financial year beginning on the following 1 April are published in February or March; details of estimated departmental receipts, other than taxes collected by the revenue departments are also shown. They also repeat the *Estimates* for the year then ending, including any supplementary estimates approved during the year. Revised or supplementary estimates are published as House of Commons Papers as they arise. The *Estimates* are published in two groups: those for the defence departments and those for civil departments, the latter being divided since 1962/63 into eleven classes.

(9) *Appropriation Accounts* (HC). These are audited statements of expenditure and of receipts, other than taxes; the estimated expenditure and receipts, as adjusted by any supplementary estimates, are shown for comparison with the actual out-turn. The *Appropriation Accounts* are in somewhat less detail than the *Estimates*. The accounts for each financial year are published in the following January to March.

(10) *Memorandum by the Financial Secretary to the Treasury* (Cmnd.). This is published at the same time as the *Estimates* and contains summary tables and additional information.

(11) *Statement on the Defence Estimates* (Cmnd.). This is published at the same time as the *Estimates* and includes a table showing the estimated expenditure included in the Defence Budget. The content of the Defence Budget as shown in the *Statement on the Defence Estimates* and in the *Financial Statement* differs from that of expenditure on military defence in the national accounts (see page 333).

(12) *Trading Accounts and Balance Sheets* (HC). The accounts of trading activities conducted by government departments are published in an annual volume, the accounts for 1966/67 being published in December 1967. These contain the commercial accounts of the trading activities, as distinct from the cash accounts of their payments and receipts contained in the *Appropriation Accounts* and *Estimates*. The trading bodies for which trading accounts are included are shown in Annex 1 on page 296.

OTHER BODIES, FUNDS AND ACCOUNTS

Only the accounts of the principal bodies and funds, etc. are listed below. They are almost all annual accounts.

(13) National Insurance Funds (HC). The accounts cover the National Insurance Fund, the National Insurance (Reserve) Fund and the Industrial Injuries Fund. Reports by the Government Actuary on the financial condition of the National Insurance Funds are also published (HC).

Grant-aided bodies

(14) Agricultural Research Council (AA).
(15) Arts Council of Great Britain (AA).
(16) British Council (AA).
(17) Commonwealth War Graves Commission (AA).
(18) Herring Industry Board (HC).
(19) Highlands and Islands Development Board (HC).
(20) Medical Research Council (AA).
(21) Natural Environment Research Council (AA).
(22) Regional Hospital Boards, Boards of Governors of Teaching Hospitals, Hospital Management Committees, Executive Councils and the Dental Estimates Board (HC). Summarised accounts are published separately for England and Wales and Scotland.
(23) Science Research Council (AA).
(24) United Kingdom Atomic Energy Authority. An annual report and balance sheet are both published (HC).
(25) White Fish Authority (HC).

Savings Banks

(26) Post Office Savings Banks Account.
(27) Trustee Savings Banks Account. This account shows the amounts invested by the trustees of savings banks through the National Debt Commissioners and details of the securities held by the Commissioners in respect of deposits with their ordinary departments. The trustee savings banks themselves are not treated in the national income accounts as part of the central government. Summarised accounts of the trustee savings banks appear in the annual *Report of the Inspection Committee of Trustee Savings Banks*.
(28) Savings Banks Funds (accounts of the Post Office Savings Banks Fund and the Fund for the Banks for Savings). The income of these funds is the interest on securities held by the National Debt Commissioners on behalf of the banks; the payments from the funds include (a) interest paid to Post Office Savings Bank depositors and to the trustees of savings banks, (b) management expenses of the Post Office Savings Bank, and (c) excess interest paid to the Exchequer. For the items included in the central government current account, see pages 266, 269 and 273.
(29) The National Savings Committee issue weekly and monthly figures of deposits in, and withdrawals from, savings banks and other national savings media. Summaries are reproduced in the *Monthly Digest of Statistics* and *Financial Statistics*.

Lending to local authorities

(30) Local Loans Fund (HC). Details of the purpose for which loans are granted is given in the annual *Report of the Public Works Loan Board*, the body which grants the loans.
(31) Harbours Act, 1964 (HC). Loans to harbour authorities.
See also item 79.

Lending to public corporations

Accounts under the following Acts:
(32) Air Corporations Acts, 1949 to 1966 (HC).
(33) Cinematograph Film Production (Special Loans) Acts, 1949 to 1957 (HC).
(34) Coal Industry Acts, 1946 to 1965 (HC).
(35) Cotton (Centralised Buying) Act, 1947 (HC).
(36) Covent Garden Market Acts, 1961 and 1966 (HC).
(37) Development of Inventions Acts, 1948 to 1965 (HC).
(38) Electricity and Gas Act, 1963 (HC).
(39) Housing Act, 1964 (HC).
(40) Housing (Scotland) Act, 1962 (HC).
(41) Iron and Steel (Financial Provisions) Act, 1960 (HC). Loans to the iron and steel industry, including the private sector as well as public corporations.
(42) New Towns Acts, 1946 to 1965 (HC).
(43) Overseas Resources Development Acts, 1959 and 1963 (HC).
(44) Sugar Act, 1956 (HC).
(45) Transport Act, 1962 (HC).

War damage and Town and Country Planning compensation

Separate accounts are published for:
(46) Town and Country Planning Acts, 1954, 1959 and 1962; Town and Country Planning (Scotland) Acts, 1954 and 1959 (HC).
(47) Town and Country Planning (Planning Payments (War Damage) Schemes, 1949) (HC). This was last published for 1963/64.
(48) War Damage Account (HC), replacing from 1964/65 the War Damage (Land and Buildings) Account (HC) and the War Damage (Business and Private Chattels Schemes) (HC).
(49) War Risks (Marine) Insurance Fund, superseded as from 30 October 1952, by the Marine and Aviation Insurance (War Risks) Fund (AA).
(50) War Damage (Public Utility Undertakings) Account (AA). This was last published for 1958/59.

Other accounts

(51) Acquisition of Guaranteed Securities Fund (AA). This Fund, administered by the Export Credits Guarantee Department, acquires and disposes of foreign government securities and similar securities issued by foreign companies, etc.
(52) Civil Contingencies Fund (HC). This Fund, administered by the Treasury, is used to make temporary advances to departments in anticipation of supply issues.
(53) Colonial Development and Welfare Acts, 1959 to 1965 Accounts (HC).
(54) Crown Estate Abstract Accounts (HC), formerly Crown Lands Abstract Accounts.
(55) Development Fund (HC). Grants and loans are made from this Fund for the purpose of promoting the rural economy and of developing fisheries, etc.
(56) Education (Scotland) Fund (AA). Grants to education authorities and institutions were paid from this Fund; last published for 1958/59.

(57) Forestry Fund (AA). This is the account of the Forestry Commission on a cash basis. Accounts on a commercial basis are included in *Trading Accounts and Balance Sheets* (see item 12 above).

(58) House Purchase and Housing Act, 1959 Accounts (HC). These relate to advances made to building societies.

(59) Housing Act, 1961 and Housing (Scotland) Act, 1962 Accounts (HC). These relate to advances made to private housing associations.

(60) Housing (Temporary Accommodation) Act, 1944 Account (HC). This related to the purchase and erection of temporary houses by the Ministry of Works; last published for 1955/56.

(61) Irish Land Purchase Fund (HC). The account shows the transactions of the National Debt Commissioners in connection with payments of interest on, and the redemption of, stock issued for financing land purchase in Ireland.

(62) Iron and Steel Realisation Account (HC). See page 276. The accounts of the Iron and Steel Holding and Realisation Agency (HC) provide further information.

(63) Legal Aid and Advice Acts, 1949 to 1964 Account (HC).

(64) Local Employment Acts, 1960 and 1963 Accounts (HC). These accounts show the transactions of the Board of Trade, and the management corporations acting on their behalf, in connection with schemes to promote employment in certain areas.

(65) National Land Fund (HC). This Fund is administered by the Treasury; *inter alia*, the Treasury makes payments from the Fund to the Inland Revenue where property is accepted in satisfaction of death duties.

(66) Navy, Dockyard and Production Accounts (AA). These give an analysis of dockyard costs and their division between the principal products. Prior to 1964/65 they were published separately (HC).

(67) Redundancy Fund (HC).

(68) Road Fund (HC). Grants to highway authorities and expenditure on trunk roads were financed from this Fund. The Fund was wound up on 31 March 1956.

(69) Shipbuilding Credit Act, 1964 Account (HC).

(70) Tithe Act, 1936 Redemption Annuities Account (HC). This records transactions in connection with (i) redemption stock issued as compensation when tithes were extinguished, and (ii) redemption annuities paid by landowners released from their tithe rent charge obligations.

(71) Transport Fund (HC). The proceeds of the transport levy were paid into this Fund (see page 265); last published for 1956/57.

NORTHERN IRELAND

Accounts are published by the Northern Ireland government which are similar to those for the United Kingdom. They include:

(72) Finance Accounts.

(73) Financial Statement.

(74) Estimates for supply services.

(75) Appropriation Accounts for supply services.

(76) Trading and Other Accounts.

(77) National Insurance Funds Accounts.

(78) Accounts of Capital Receipts and Payments. This includes details of the

Civil Contingencies Fund, Ulster Land Fund, Reserve and Sinking Funds and Capital Purposes Fund.

(79) Government Loans Fund.

(80) Agricultural Loans Fund.

(81) Road Fund.

(82) Summary of Health Services Accounts.

Chapter X

Local Authorities

1. GENERAL DESCRIPTION

Local authorities are public authorities of limited geographical scope, having power to raise funds by certain forms of local taxation. Substantially all local bodies, other than companies trading for profit, that have powers to levy rates, taxes, tolls or dues, or to require them to be levied, are obliged to make annual returns of income and expenditure under Part XI of the Local Government Act of 1933. In Scotland the relevant Act is the Local Government (Scotland) Act, 1947, and in Northern Ireland the Local Government (Application of Enactments) Order, 1898. It is convenient, therefore, to define the local authority sector as the authorities and bodies making returns under these Acts. The local authority sector thus includes not only the local authorities with general administrative functions in varying degrees—such as the county, borough, district and parish councils, and joint boards and committees formed by two or more councils; it also includes local bodies with special functions—local harbour boards, district fishery boards, drainage boards, river authorities, water boards (including the Metropolitan Water Board) and a variety of bodies such as the conservators of certain commons and the trustees of certain London squares. Some of these local bodies with special functions, such as the Port of London Authority, the Metropolitan Water Board and the Mersey Docks and Harbour Board, are of very substantial size. New Town Development Corporations are not included; they are treated as public corporations. The Metropolitan Police is included in this sector even though it has certain national functions. Up to March 1962 colleges of advanced technology, under the control of local education authorities, are included; from 1 April 1962 these colleges were transferred to the control of independent governing bodies receiving direct grants from the central government and from that date they are treated as private non-profit-making bodies in the personal sector (see page 99).

It should also be noted that the superannuation funds of local authorities are excluded from this sector. The funds are regarded as the property of the members of the superannuation schemes in the personal sector (see page 100) and the transactions of the funds are included with those of financial companies (see page 204). Where part of a superannuation fund is applied by a local authority to finance its capital expenditure, this is treated as lending by financial companies to the local authority sector.

The annual returns made under the Local Government Acts are summarised for England and Wales in *Local Government Financial Statistics* which is published annually by the Ministry of Housing and Local Government. Corresponding summaries are published for Scotland—*Local Financial Returns (Scotland)*—and Northern Ireland—*Local Authority Financial Returns*. The three summaries together have the same scope as the local authority sector, apart from the exclusion of superannuation funds. The three sources provide the greater part of the information required for the local authority sector in the national accounts; they are supplemented by a number of special returns of local authorities' transactions which are available much earlier than the published annual summaries (see Section 3 of this chapter).

The local authority accounts are presented in the same categories as those adopted for the central government. The principles of the classification of transactions are the same and need not be repeated: a detailed discussion is given in Section 1 of Chapter IX. The problems involved in rearranging the published data are, however, fewer[1]. The difficulty of eliminating internal transactions is less because many transfers between one authority and another, for example precepts levied by one authority on another, are already eliminated in the published sources. The distinction between current and capital transactions which is made for the accounting purposes of local authorities is close to that required for the national accounts. The summaries give an analysis of transactions according to the various local authority services, for example education, police, etc., and moreover the services are divided between a group described as 'trading services' and the rest, that is the 'rate-fund' services. It should also be noted that local authorities' accounts are nearly all on a payable-receivable, or an accruals, basis, in contrast with the cash basis used for most central government accounts.

2. THE PUBLISHED TABLES

Two tables for local authorities are published in the Blue Book—a current account (Table 45 of the 1967 Blue Book) and a capital account (Table 46 of the 1967 Blue Book). The following notes describe these tables; except where otherwise stated, the sources from which the estimates are derived are *Local Government Financial Statistics* for England and Wales and the corresponding summaries for Scotland and Northern Ireland. References below to *Local Goverment Financial Statistics* should be read as referring also to the corresponding publications for Scotland and Northern Ireland. In addition, the figures form part of the accounts for combined public authorities and for the public sector which are described in Chapter XI.

CURRENT ACCOUNT

The current account of local authorities in the 1967 Blue Book is presented on the next page.

---

[1]For the analysis of a sample of local authorities' accounts in national accounting terms see J. E. G. Utting, *Social Accounts of Local Authorities*, Cambridge University Press, 1953.

Current account of local authorities, 1966

£ million

Receipts		Expenditure	
Current grants from central government:		Current expenditure on goods and services[1]	2,280
Grants not allocated to specific services	1,166	Housing subsidies	82
Grants for specific services[1]....	313	Current grants to personal sector[1]	208
		Debt interest[1]	600
Total	1,479	Total current expenditure	3,170
Rates	1,353		
Gross trading surplus[2].........	83	Balance: current surplus before	
Rent[1][3]	604	providing for depreciation and	416
Interest, etc.	67	stock appreciation...........	
Total	3,586	Total	3,586

Source: 1967 Blue Book, Table 45
[1]These items are subdivided in the Blue Book table as described in the notes below.
[2]Before providing for depreciation and stock appreciation.
[3]Before providing for depreciation.

Current grants from central government

Grants from the central government comprise both non-specific grants and grants towards specific services, such as roads, police, etc. Since the introduction of the general grant system in April 1959 grants not allocated to specific services have accounted for about three-quarters of the total; prior to this they accounted for only about one-sixth. In addition to the general grant, those grants not allocated to specific services include rate deficiency grants from April 1959, and equalisation and transitional grants. These non-specific grants were superseded in 1967 by the new system of rate support grants. Figures of non-specific grants include receipts from local taxation licence duties which are collected and retained by local authorities but treated as central government taxes (see page 265). They also include from 1965 grants under the Rating (Interim Relief) Act, 1964, and from 1966 grants towards the cost of rate rebates and reimbursements to local authorities in respect of selective employment tax paid on their employees (see page 312). Payments under the Tithe Act, 1936 (about £1 million per annum) which ceased from April 1959 are also included in the figures of non-specific grants.

After the introduction of the system of general grants in 1959, and until 1967, the main services for which specific grants were made were roads, police, school meals and milk. From 1967, under the rate support grant system, the specific grants for current expenditure on roads and school meals and milk ceased and police remained the only major service continuing to receive a specific grant. The specific grants are analysed in the Blue Book table according to service; the services are as defined in Chapter XI, except that grants shown under the heading 'Education' include grants towards the current cost of school meals and milk. Grants for education also include the cost of the salaries of school teachers paid directly by the government of Northern Ireland, which are treated as being paid by local education authorities. Since housing is treated as a trading service, grants towards housing are excluded and regarded as a subsidy paid to the operating account of local authorities. However, grants towards the cost of local authorities' loan charges incurred on grants for conversions and improvements of privately-owned housing accommodation are included.

The figures of current grants derived from *Local Government Financial Statistics* differ somewhat from those derived from the central government *Appropriation Accounts*; this can probably be explained by the central government recording actual payments while the local authorities record amounts due and by local authorities treating as current receipts central government grants towards capital expenditure met from revenue. For the consistency which is essential in a system of national accounts, the figures from the local authority accounts have been adjusted to accord with those given by the central government accounts. This adjustment is partly reflected in the residual item in the capital account 'Miscellaneous financial receipts (net) and changes in cash balances'.

Rates

Local rates, which include land drainage rates, are treated as a tax on expenditure, being related to the particular activity of using land and buildings (see pages 259 and 260). The central government, Post Office, and nationalised railway and electricity undertakings are not liable to pay rates but make instead contributions in lieu of rates; these are included here. Water rates paid by water consumers are not included, but are treated as operating receipts of a trading service. Income from rates is recorded on an accruals basis; it is the estimated amount of rates due in respect of the period. The difference between cash receipts and accruals is included in the capital account under the heading 'Miscellaneous financial receipts (net) and changes in cash balances'. From 1966 income from rates was reduced by the rate rebate scheme for low income households.

Gross trading surplus

The trading activities of local authorities are those shown as such in *Local Government Financial Statistics*, with the addition of housing, income from which appears under the separate heading 'Rent' (see below). The gross trading surplus is the balance of trading income over operating expenditure, before allowing for depreciation and interest charges. In conformity with the treatment of trading bodies elsewhere in the national accounts, income from the ownership of buildings and plant used for trading services (other than housing) is included in the gross trading surplus. While it is recognised that not every local authority trading service (outside housing) may be operated broadly to cover its costs including depreciation and interest, in no case is any surplus treated as a tax on expenditure derived from the exercise of monopoly, nor is any loss (except in the case of housing) treated as a subsidy, as it is for some central government trading bodies (see page 258).

Trading income consists chiefly of revenue from sales, for example from passenger transport, or from various fees, dues and rents which may (as in dock and harbour undertakings) or may not (as in the case of water rates) be precisely related to the extent to which the service is used by the payer. Receipts towards deficiencies from rate-fund accounts and from reserve funds and the small amount of government grants in respect of these services are not regarded as subsidies and are excluded. Operating expenditure consists of the working expenses, but, as for other trading bodies, loan charges are not treated as an operating expense. Transfers in aid of rates, transfers to reserve funds and transfers to capital accounts are also excluded from trading expenses but the expenditure, other than transfers, of trading reserve funds is included. The data relating to these items are set out in *Local Government Financial Statistics*, although certain adjustments, which are partly estimated, must be made in respect of the transfers to and from other accounts and funds.

The composition of the gross trading surplus for 1964/65 is as follows:

	£ million
Water supply	36
Road passenger transport	11
Harbours, docks and piers	13
Civic restaurants, markets, slaughterhouses	2
Other (including general corporation estates, cemeteries and aerodromes)	6
Total	68

Before nationalisation in 1948 and 1949 municipal electricity and gas undertakings in Great Britain were, of course, included and the scope of local authority trading services was much greater. Corresponding undertakings in Northern Ireland are still included.

Rent

Rent from the ownership of dwellings and rent from the ownership of non-trading property, such as schools and offices, are shown separately in the Blue Book table. Provision of housing is treated as a trading activity, in which the price of the product, that is the rent charged to tenants, is as a matter of policy less than its cost. In conformity with the principles set out on pages 255 to 258 the deficit on housing revenue account is therefore treated as a subsidy, and income from rent is taken to equal the annual loan charges; these loan charges are the equivalent of interest on capital and depreciation. Rent income from houses is therefore an imputed measure related to the economic rent. However, in so far as the loan charges are related to the original cost of the houses and not to their current replacement cost, the rent income as measured here is related to less than the full economic rent and does not reflect current market values. The Blue Book table on housing subsidies, Table 49 of the 1967 Blue Book (see page 326), shows how rent income from local authority houses, as here defined (£410 million in 1966), may be equated with the sum of rents received (£369 million), central government subsidies (£100 million) and local authorities' own subsidies (£82 million) *less* the cost of repairs and other expenses (£141 million).

The estimate of rent from non-trading property is also an imputed figure. Some of the difficulties encountered in attempting to measure imputed rent are discussed in the context of the central government sector on pages 267 and 268. With the two exceptions listed below imputed rent from local authorities' non-trading assets is measured, as for local authority housing, by reference to the loan charges incurred in providing these assets. The exceptions are:

(i) imputed rent from local authority schools and colleges is based on the assessments of rateable values made by the valuation office of Inland Revenue; this is consistent with the method adopted for national health service hospitals in the central government accounts (see page 268).

(ii) no imputation is made in respect of the assets employed in local authority road and public lighting services, which is consistent with the treatment of trunk roads in the central government accounts (see page 267).

Imputed rent from non-trading property is balanced by the inclusion of an equal amount in current expenditure on goods and services.

Interest, etc.

This item of income consists of interest received on loans for house purchase and interest received on the invested balances of sinking funds, consolidated loans funds and certain other special funds. The investment income of superannuation funds is excluded; such income is deemed to accrue to the members of the schemes. Receipts from the central government and nationalised industries in respect of loans for which these bodies have accepted responsibility are included (see page 313). Most of the figures are derived from *Local Government Financial Statistics*. No attempt is made to exclude interest received from other local authorities but in the mid-1960's this is estimated to have amounted to only about £6 million a year.

Current expenditure on goods and services

This item represents the general expenditure on revenue account of rate-fund services other than housing *plus* imputed rent (see below) *less* certain expenditure which is treated as grants to the personal sector (scholarships, grants to universities, expenditure on school meals and milk, and legal aid). The parts of expenditure on rate-fund services revenue account representing transfers to capital account, transfers towards deficiencies on trading services, transfers to certain special funds (for example reserve funds) and certain expenditure on renewals, are excluded from current expenditure on goods and services; but the expenditure, other than transfers, of the reserve, etc. funds is included. Fees and recoupments—such as school fees, contributions by the beneficiaries towards the cost of welfare services, entrance fees to museums, and recoveries of expenditure—are deducted from the corresponding expenditure. However, the parts of the heading 'Fees and recoupments, etc.' shown in *Local Government Financial Statistics* which represent transfers from certain special funds, for example reserve funds, and interest on loans for house purchase (small dwellings acquisition) are not deducted in arriving at current expenditure on goods and services. Up to March 1962 current expenditure on colleges of advanced technology was included (see page 306). From September 1966 an estimate of the selective employment tax payable in respect of local authority employees is also included with current expenditure on goods and services. All the figures are derived from *Local Government Financial Statistics* except the estimates of grants to the personal sector (see page 313) and payments of selective employment tax.

It should be noted that the figures include employers' superannuation contributions in respect of all local authority employees except police and firemen. Such contributions are paid to special superannuation funds managed by local authorities (see page 306) or, in the case of the teachers' pension scheme, to the central government. In the case of the contributory pension schemes for the police and fire services, there are generally no separate pension funds and no identifiable employers' contributions; the pensions paid to retired members of these services *less* employees' contributions, are included in current expenditure on goods and services. This treatment is consistent with the definition of income from employment (see Chapter VI, Section 3).

Except for road and public lighting services, the figures of current expenditure on goods and services include imputed payments of rent for the use of the assets employed in providing local authority services. This is balanced by the inclusion of an equal amount in rent income, the basis of measurement of which is explained on page 310. The imputed rents included in expenditure on each service for public authorities as a whole are given in the table analysing public authorities' current expenditure on goods and services (Table 48 of the 1967 Blue Book).

Local authorities receive reimbursements for their payments of selective employment tax, except for employees engaged on new construction work; but for national accounts purposes the tax is regarded as falling on their expenditure on goods and services and reimbursements of the tax are included with current grants from central government. The amount of the tax included in expenditure on each service for public authorities as a whole is given in the table analysing public authorities' current expenditure on goods and services (Table 48 of the 1967 Blue Book).

Current expenditure on goods and services is analysed in the Blue Book according to service; the classification is the same as that used for the analysis of the combined expenditure of the central government, local authorities and public corporations (Table 53 of the 1967 Blue Book). The definitions of the services, in terms of the classification used in *Local Government Financial Statistics*, are given in Chapter XI.

Housing subsidies

This is the only expenditure regarded as a subsidy in the presentation of local authority accounts. It represents the deficit on housing services, that is the excess of expenditure, including loan charges, repairs and other expenses on all housing revenue accounts over the amounts received in rents from tenants and in central government contributions. Actual repair expenditure charged to statutory housing repairs accounts is included, rather than provision for repairs charged to housing revenue accounts. The part of expenditure on housing revenue accounts representing transfers to capital account and to reserve funds is excluded. The derivation of the figures is shown in the Blue Book table on housing subsidies (Table 49 of the 1967 Blue Book, see page 326). Except for the years 1957 and 1958 nothing is included in local authority subsidies in respect of emergency housing, since in all other years the central government reimbursements to local authorities have been approximately equal to the net cost incurred by them in providing such housing.

Current grants to personal sector

(a) *Scholarships and grants to universities, colleges, etc.* Scholarships comprise cash payments to pupils and students in respect of fees and maintenance allowances; they account for nearly all of this item.

(b) *School meals and milk.* The cost to local authorities of providing school meals and milk, after deducting receipts from parents. This is treated as a grant to persons, rather than expenditure on goods and services, in the same way as milk and welfare foods provided by the central government (see page 105). The cost of school milk has been borne by local education authorities since October 1954 when it was transferred from the Ministry of Food; the central government grant towards the cost of the education service was increased by an equal amount.

(c) *Legal aid*. The cost to local authorities of legal aid in criminal cases in courts other than magistrates' courts. This is reimbursed by a current grant from the central government.

Figures of these items are not given in *Local Government Financial Statistics;* figures for (a) and (b) are derived from returns made by local education authorities to the education departments and for (c) from the amount of the grants made by the Home Office to local authorities for legal aid.

Debt interest

This is the interest paid on rate-fund and trading services revenue accounts. Payments of debt interest which are financed from interest received on the invested balances of consolidated loans funds are also included although this element of debt interest does not appear in *Local Government Financial Statistics*. Interest on loans in respect of hospitals and gas and electricity undertakings now taken over by national bodies is included; the reimbursements made by the central government and nationalised industries are included in the item showing interest received. No attempt is made to exclude interest paid to other local authorities, which is also included in receipts; in the mid-1960's this is estimated to have amounted to only about £6 million a year. Interest payments are shown gross, before deduction of income tax, which is regarded as falling on the recipients of the interest.

Interest paid on loans from the central government is shown separately from other payments of interest; the figures are taken from the central government accounts.

United Kingdom taxes on income

The annual current account in the 1967 Blue Book includes no item for payments of United Kingdom taxes on income. Local authorities are liable to tax on certain of their trading activities but the amounts involved are relatively minor and the small amounts of tax paid have been ignored. However, local authorities also make payments to the Inland Revenue in respect of tax deducted from their payments of interest and, as in the case of other sectors, figures of tax payments are taken to be the amounts paid to the Inland Revenue *less* the tax withheld from interest paid. In each calendar year up to 1966 the amounts paid to the Inland Revenue have been taken to be equal to the tax withheld but the quarterly figures have varied considerably (see page 316).

CAPITAL ACCOUNT

The capital account for local authorities, covering both trading and non-trading services, is set out below. The problem of separating capital from current items is much simpler than for central government; the distinction made for accounting purposes by the local authorities and summarised in *Local Government Financial Statistics* is close to that required here.

L

Capital account of local authorities, 1966

£ million

Receipts		Payments	
Current surplus before providing for depreciation and stock apprec-iation......................	416	Gross domestic fixed capital for-mation: Housing	636
		Other trading services[1]	134
Capital grants from central govern-ment[1]	82	Non-trading services[1]	560
Net borrowing from central govern-ment	546		
Other identified borrowing (net)...	408	Capital grants to personal sector..	18
Miscellaneous financial receipts (net) and changes in cash balances....	−97	Net lending for house purchase...	7
Total	1,355	Total	1,355

Source: 1967 Blue Book, Table 46

[1]These items are subdivided in the Blue Book table, as described in the notes below.

Capital grants from central government

This comprises grants towards capital expenditure on specific services, a number of which are shown separately. From 1955 to 1966 the principal item has been grants for roads (£47 million in 1966). Grants for education (£10 million in 1966) relate mainly to capital expenditure on canteens for the school meals service. The definitions of the services are given in Chapter XI. War damage compensation is also included in this item and combined with other grants for the service concerned; the total is shown separately in the central government capital account. War damage compensation was paid mainly in the early post-war years and by 1954 it was only £2 million a year and from 1959 to 1966 it was only £1 million. This item includes lump sum contributions by the Northern Ireland government towards the cost of newly-built houses.

Capital grants from central government are shown in *Local Government Financial Statistics*. The figures differ from those in the central government accounts; the latter have been used in order to achieve consistency, as in the case of current grants from the central government (see page 309). Certain grants made specifically towards capital expenditure met from revenue and treated by local authorities as current receipts are included.

Net borrowing from central government

Borrowing from central government is not distinguished in *Local Government Financial Statistics* from borrowing from other sources. The figures are taken from the central government accounts. They relate to advances *less* repayments from:

(i) the Local Loans Fund through the agency of the Public Works Loan Board;
(ii) the Consolidated Fund to harbour authorities;
(iii) the Northern Ireland Government Loans Fund;
(iv) the Votes of certain government departments, for example Ministry of Transport, providing loan finance for local authorities' capital expenditure, principally on tunnels and bridges.

Other identified borrowing (net)

From 1961 estimates of local authority borrowing are available covering borrowing by means of quoted securities, other long-term borrowing and temporary borrowing. They are derived from quarterly returns made by virtually all local authorities in the United Kingdom. A detailed analysis of borrowing by source, period to maturity, etc. based on returns from all the larger and selected smaller authorities is published in *Financial Statistics*. Before 1961 this item is combined with 'Miscellaneous financial receipts (net) and changes in cash balances'.

Miscellaneous financial receipts (net) and changes in cash balances

This is the residual item in the accounts of local authorities which reflects changes in cash balances, debtors and creditors, etc. together with any errors or adjustments in the other items shown—for example, the adjustments to the figures of grants from the central government made in order to conform with the accounts of the central government (see pages 309 and 314). The excess of rates received over the amount accrued, which assumes greater significance in the quarterly accounts where it is shown separately (see page 316), is also included under this heading. Before 1961 this item is combined with 'Other identified borrowing (net)', covering borrowing from sources other than the central government.

Gross domestic fixed capital formation

Estimates of fixed capital formation for all years but the most recent are derived mainly from *Local Government Financial Statistics* and to some extent from the capital payments returns referred to on page 318. The whole of expenditure on capital account shown in *Local Government Financial Statistics*, other than re-payment of debt, has been treated as expenditure on fixed assets, apart from expenditure on loans for house purchase, improvement grants and clean air grants. In addition, certain expenditure on renewals charged directly to revenue account is included. Capital receipts from 'Other sources', except those under the headings 'Small dwellings acquisition' and 'Improvement grants', are assumed to relate to sales of fixed assets and have been deducted from the corresponding expenditure.

The Blue Book table shows the division of gross domestic fixed capital formation between the various non-trading services, corresponding to the analysis of current expenditure on goods and services, and the following trading services:

Housing
Road passenger transport
Harbours, docks and aerodromes
Gas and electricity
Water
Other

The estimates for education include the cost of the school canteens referred to on page 314. Further information on the definitions of the services and content of the items is given in Chapter XI. The estimates of fixed capital formation are further described in Chapter XII.

Capital grants to personal sector

This mainly represents grants by local authorities for the conversion and improvement of housing under the Housing (Financial Provisions) Act, 1958, the House Purchase and Housing Act, 1959, the Housing (Scotland) Act, 1949 and the Housing (Miscellaneous Provisions) and Rent Restriction Law (Amendment) Act (N.I.), 1956. Grants by local authorities in Northern Ireland towards the cost of privately-built houses under the Housing and Local Government (Miscellaneous Provisions) Act (N.I.), 1946, and Housing (No. 2) Act (N.I.), 1946 are also included. The estimates are based on information provided by the Ministry of Housing and Local Government, the Scottish Development Department and the Ministry of Finance, Northern Ireland. From 1960/61 information in respect of improvement grants appears in *Local Government Financial Statistics* for England and Wales only. Grants under the Clean Air Act, 1956 and the Clean Air Act (N.I.), 1964 are also included.

Net lending for house purchase

This is expenditure on capital account other than repayment of debt *less* capital receipts from 'Other sources' shown under the heading 'Small dwellings acquisition' in *Local Government Financial Statistics*. Calendar year estimates are derived in part from the quarterly returns to the housing departments of new advances mentioned on page 318.

QUARTERLY TABLES

Quarterly estimates are compiled for both the current and capital accounts of local authorities. The current account is published quarterly in *Economic Trends* and each month in *Financial Statistics*; the figures have been published from 1961. The capital account is also published in *Financial Statistics* and the estimates also date from 1961.

Rates

In the national income accounts rates are recorded on an accruals basis but payments of rates to local authorities are generally made half-yearly. Quarterly variations in cash payments of rates have an important effect on local authority borrowing requirements. The quarterly current account therefore shows both cash receipts of rates and the adjustment necessary to bring rates on to the accruals basis consistent with the accounts for other sectors. The counterpart of this adjustment also appears as an item in the quarterly capital account.

United Kingdom taxes on income

Tax deducted from interest paid is estimated on the basis of interest payments other than to the central government. The tax is paid to the Inland Revenue mainly towards the end of the financial year and there are therefore considerable quarterly fluctuations in the net figure shown in the quarterly account as 'Payments of United Kingdom taxes on income' (see page 313).

3. STATISTICAL SOURCES

Annual sources

The basic source of information for the local authority accounts is the statutory annual returns which are summarised for England and Wales in *Local Government Financial Statistics*, for Scotland in *Local Financial Returns (Scotland)* and for Northern Ireland in *Local Authority Financial Returns*.

Two problems arise in the construction of the accounts of the local authority sector which are similar to problems already discussed in connection with the central government accounts (page 288); firstly the preparation of calendar year figures from financial year data, and secondly estimation for the most recent year or years for which published accounts are not yet available.

The published summaries of local authorities' accounts all relate to financial years, which end on 31 March in England and Wales and in Northern Ireland, and, with some exceptions, on 15 May in Scotland. Calendar year estimates are derived from the financial year data by using a number of special returns which form the basis of the quarterly accounts compiled for the local authority sector; these returns are described below.

The collection and publication of the statutory returns from local authorities are not complete in time to provide statistics for the most recent years. Thus at the time the 1967 Blue Book was prepared, the latest published material related to 1964/65. Figures for the latest two years are estimates based mainly on the information obtained from the special quarterly returns described below. For the latest year but one the Ministry of Housing and Local Government provide estimates based on a tabulation of a sample of local authorities' annual returns. The Scottish Development Department and other government departments with special responsibilities for particular local authority services also provide information for estimates for the latest two years.

The statutory annual returns do not, however, provide the full information required for the national accounts. Although one important element of expenditure on revenue account, namely loan charges (that is, interest on borrowed moneys, repayments of principal other than out of sinking funds, and payments into sinking funds), is shown separately, the economic categories of expenditure on goods and services and grants to the personal sector are not distinguished. Hence other sources of information have to be used for the estimates of current grants to the personal sector, and there can be no certainty that all classes of local authority grants to the personal sector have been identified. The principal source is more detailed information on local education authorities' expenditure collected by the education departments of the central government. In the case of expenditure on capital account, the statutory returns show separately capital moneys assigned to the repayment of debt, but for the most part capital transfers and financial transactions, such as lending, are not distinguished from expenditure on fixed assets. Nor are increases in the value of stocks identified. Except for expenditure on conversion and improvement grants, clean air grants and loans for house purchase for which information is provided separately, the whole of the entry showing expenditure on capital account, other than the repayment of debt, has therefore been treated as expenditure on fixed assets. It has been assumed that increases in the value of stocks, capital transfers and lending, other than those mentioned, are sufficiently small to be ignored, although in fact some trading stocks must be held.

Central government grants and loans to local authorities are taken directly from the central government accounts, for which government sources provide quarterly figures of cash payments. Similar information is available for payments of debt interest by local authorities to central government.

Quarterly sources

The following special returns are available and are also used for the annual estimates until the annual data become available.

(i) A quarterly sample inquiry on wages and salaries paid in England, Wales and Scotland which was instituted from the beginning of the financial year 1956/57 and which provides the main basis for quarterly and calendar year estimates of current expenditure on goods and services. In this inquiry wages and salaries in England and Wales are analysed under eight headings—police, education, roads, other non-trading services, housing, other trading services, capital account and agency services. The Scottish returns provide less detail. Wages and salaries account for about three-quarters of total current expenditure on goods and services by local authorities. Payments of imputed rent (see page 312) can be regarded as having no seasonal variation. No information is at present available about the quarterly pattern of other current expenditure on goods and services by local authorities and smooth quarterly changes are assumed. The estimates for the latest periods take into account the latest financial year forecasts.

(ii) A half-yearly capital payments return from all authorities. This return distinguishes between all the main local authority services and between payments for different types of fixed asset. From 1956 it is supplemented by a quarterly return for the June and December quarters in much less detail, now collected with (iv) below.

(iii) Quarterly returns by authorities in England and Wales to the Ministry of Housing and Local Government of conversion and improvement grants and loans for house purchase.

(iv) From 1961 a quarterly return from virtually all authorities of total borrowing *less* repayments and a detailed analysis from all the larger authorities and selected smaller authorities. Borrowing is analysed according to whether it is temporary or longer-term, its source, and its period to maturity. In addition, with this return, the sample authorities have reported from 1961 the amount of rates collected, and from 1964 receipts and payments of interest.

The quarterly estimates of tax deducted from interest paid are based on the estimates of interest payments other than to the central government; Inland Revenue records are the basis for the estimates of amounts paid. The quarterly estimates for current grants to the personal sector take account of the normal incidence of payments of scholarship awards, etc. and seasonal changes in the demand for school meals and milk. The remaining items—gross trading surplus, income from rent, receipts of interest, etc. and expenditure on housing subsidies —are all assumed to follow smooth quarterly changes, estimates being based on the latest figures for financial years, including a forecast for the current financial year.

4. RELIABILITY

The basic data are accounting data and their reliability, in terms of the gradings described on pages 39 to 41, is good. The adjustments to a calendar year basis and the other adjustments required do not substantially affect the reliability of the estimates. An element of uncertainty arises in the figures for the latest two years shown which are partly based on estimates and projections. The reliability of the figures for the last two years is less than for the figures compiled for the central government; the figures should not be regarded as more than fair.

Clearly, those items in the quarterly accounts for which a smooth quarterly trend is assumed may be subject to a greater margin of error than those for which quarterly data are available. These possible errors are unlikely to be significant, however. The assumption made in the case of rent, for example, is matched for non-trading assets by a similar assumption in the estimates for current expenditure on goods and services. Receipts of interest on local authority loans for house purchase can quite reasonably be assumed to be paid regularly. The assumption of a smooth quarterly trend for gross trading surplus may be less justifiable, but since this item is relatively small any error is unlikely to be important.

Chapter XI

Public Authorities and the Public Sector

1. GENERAL DESCRIPTION

Public authorities

Public authorities comprise the two sectors central government and local authorities, as defined in the two preceding chapters. For certain purposes it is convenient to combine the accounts for central and local government in order to show the total of government activity. This is necessary when considering the development of services to which both central and local government bodies contribute, for example the national health service, education, and the roads programme. It is also necessary, for example, when considering the extent of taxation, since local rates are an important part of total taxes on expenditure. The public authorities sector is the 'general government' sector of the United Nations system of national accounts[1]. It is appropriate for international comparisons as it is not affected by differences in the division of responsibilities between central, state and local government bodies.

Public sector

The public sector comprises the three sectors central government, local authorities and public corporations, as defined in the three preceding chapters. For many purposes it is convenient to treat the public sector as a whole and to draw a distinction between the publicly controlled and privately controlled sectors of the economy. Although public corporations are productive enterprises, the products of which are sold commercially, their policy is affected by social and political as well as commercial considerations. The financial affairs of public corporations are interlocked with those of the central government, upon which they depend for their financing. It is important to include the operations of public corporations when considering the impact of public expenditure on the economy, since investment by public corporations is an important element of public expenditure.

Consolidation of accounts

In preparing the accounts for public authorities and the public sector, transactions within the sector have generally to be eliminated. The principles followed in this process of consolidation are the same as those followed in preparing the accounts for the central government sector (see page 253). In principle, all transactions are eliminated except those in which the payment by one part of the sector falls within a different economic category from the receipt by the other part. Thus, transactions which enter into gross national expenditure at market prices are not affected by the consolidation. Payments for the products of public enterprises which form part of current expenditure on goods and services

---

[1]*A System of National Accounts and Supporting Tables*, United Nations, New York, 1964.

are not eliminated, because to the enterprises they are part of operating receipts. Similarly, payments of subsidies from the central government current account which are part of the operating receipts of public corporations are not eliminated. Taxes on expenditure levied by the central government which fall on local authorities' expenditure and payments by the central government in lieu of local authority rates are also not eliminated. By retaining transactions which enter into expenditure on goods and services at market prices, the accounts for the public sector are kept on a comparable basis with those for the private sector; and the sum of public sector and private sector transactions is the total transactions for the economy as a whole. But all transfers and payments which form part of the same economic category are, as far as possible, eliminated. Examples of transactions eliminated from the accounts of the public sector are the grants from central government to local authorities, taxes on income paid by public corporations and interest payments by local authorities and public corporations to the central government. In some cases, however, the consolidation is not complete because of lack of information; for example receipts of interest by local authorities on their holdings of government securities are not eliminated.

2. THE PUBLISHED TABLES

Published estimates of the transactions of public authorities combined and of the public sector as a whole are generally restricted to calendar or financial years. Consolidated current and capital accounts are not published on a quarterly basis but from the information given in the quarterly tables it is possible to construct most of the consolidated estimates. The annual estimates in the 1967 Blue Book are presented in eight tables which are described below. For public authorities there is a combined current and capital account; an analysis of current expenditure on goods and services; an analysis of housing subsidies; an allocation of taxes on expenditure and subsidies by type of expenditure; and an analysis of taxes on income, national insurance contributions and taxes on capital by sector, type of income and property. The public sector section of the 1967 Blue Book includes a current and capital account and a functional analysis of public expenditure. The corresponding Treasury analysis of public expenditure for financial years is given at the end of the notes to the Blue Book.

In addition, the financial accounts section of the Blue Book gives an analysis of the transactions in financial assets of the public sector and an analysis of the sectors acquiring these assets. The transactions in financial assets of the public sector are also published on a quarterly basis in *Financial Statistics*. The financial accounts are described in Chapter XIV.

Current and capital accounts for the public sector, on the same basis as those in the Blue Book, are also given in the *Financial Statement* presented to Parliament on the day of the Budget. These tables relate to the financial year just ended and the coming financial year.

PUBLIC AUTHORITIES: COMBINED CURRENT AND CAPITAL ACCOUNT

The account presented in the 1967 Blue Book is shown on the next page. The table consolidates and summarises the current and capital accounts of the central government and local authorities (Tables 41, 42, 45 and 46 of the 1967 Blue Book). The following transactions between central government and local

Public authorities' combined current and capital account, 1966

£ million

Receipts		Expenditure	
Current account		*Current account*	
Taxes on income:		Goods and services:	
Central government	4,449	Central government	4,111
Taxes on expenditure:		Local authorities	2,280
Central government	4,243		
Local authorities [1]	1,353	Subsidies and grants:	
National insurance and health		Central government	3,423
contributions:		Local authorities	290
Central government	1,797		
Gross trading surplus:		Debt interest:	
Central government	15	Central government	1,041
Local authorities	83	Local authorities	429
Rent:			
Central government	96		
Local authorities	604	Total	11,574
Interest and dividends, etc.:			
Central government	502		
Local authorities	67		
		Capital account	
Total	13,209	Goods and services [3]:	
		Central government	366
Capital account		Local authorities	1,330
Taxes on capital:		Grants:	
Central government	317	Central government	169
Changes in financial assets and		Local authorities	18
liabilities [2]:		Financial assets [4]:	
Central government	654	Central government	1,027
Local authorities	311	Local authorities	7
Total	1,282	Total	2,917
Combined current and capital account		*Combined current and capital account*	
Total receipts	14,491	Total expenditure	14,491

[1] Rates.   Source: 1967 Blue Book, Table 47
[2] Other than those shown on the expenditure side of the capital account.
[3] Comprises gross domestic fixed capital formation and increase in value of stocks.
[4] Comprises net lending to the private sector and public corporations, loans to overseas governments, drawings from United Kingdom subscriptions to international lending bodies, other net lending abroad and cash expenditure on company securities (net).

authorities have been eliminated in this table:

(a) debt interest on loans by the central government to local authorities;
(b) central government and capital grants to local authorities;
(c) net landing by the central government to local authorities.

The figures for certain years also exclude the notional transactions of the central government connected with writing-off debt of public corporations. But the process of consolidation has not been carried to its furthest extent (see page 320). Transactions which enter into gross national expenditure at market prices have not been eliminated, and some transactions have not been eliminated for lack of information.

PUBLIC AUTHORITIES:
ANALYSIS OF CURRENT EXPENDITURE ON GOODS AND SERVICES

The table presented in the 1967 Blue Book on the next page. It provides an analysis by service of current expenditure on goods and services between wages, salaries, etc., selective employment tax, imputed rents and all other payments (net).

Wages, salaries, etc.

These figures include employers' national insurance and health contributions and employers' contributions to pension funds or actual pension payments (see pages 270, 311 and 312) and are thus equal to income from employment. In conformity with the definition of central government employed in the national accounts, the figures for the central government include wages and salaries paid by the Atomic Energy Authority, Regional Hospital Boards and Boards of Governors of Teaching Hospitals, etc. Hospital consultants' fees are included, but not the remuneration of general practitioners and dentists in the national health service who are regarded as being self-employed; this corresponds with the Inland Revenue distinction between Schedules E and D (see Appendix III). The figure for military defence includes Forces' pay in cash and kind and the related employers' contributions (£609 million in 1966).

The estimates of wages and salaries given in the table relate to wages and salaries forming part of current expenditure on goods and services. Estimates of total wages and salaries and employers' contributions paid by public authorities, including payments to those employed in trading services, those directly employed on capital works, and other wages and salaries not treated as current expenditure on goods and services, are given in a footnote to the Blue Book table and are shown for 1966 below.

Total wages, salaries, etc. paid by public authorities, 1966

	£ million
Total shown in Table 48 of the 1967 Blue Book	3,544
Wages, salaries, etc. in trading services:	
Central government	53
Local authorities	264
Wages, salaries, etc. charged to capital account:	
Central government	6
Local authorities	62
Other wages and salaries, etc.	53
Total income from employment	3,982

Wages and salaries charged to the central government capital account include payments by the Regional Hospital Boards from 1963; for earlier years these payments were not separately identified and are included with current expenditure on goods and services. The item 'Other wages and salaries, etc.' consists of expenditure on wages and salaries which forms part of grants, in particular expenditure on the provision of school meals and some overseas aid; the expen-

Analysis of public authorities' current expenditure on goods and services, 1966

£ million

	Wages, salaries, etc.	Selective employ- ment tax	Imputed rents	Other payments (net)
Defence:				
Military defence	946	7	5	1,204
Civil defence	10	—	—	11
External relations	37	1	—	59
Roads and public lighting	139	2	—	89
Transport and communication	8	—	—	4
Employment services	31	—	—	6
Other industry and trade	17	—	—	44
Research	47	1	14	29
Agriculture, fishing and food	33	—	3	11
Housing and environmental services:				
Sewerage and refuse disposal	69	2	54	27
Public health services	23	1	2	8
Parks, pleasure grounds, etc.	47	1	8	4
Other[1]	113	2	31	−18
Libraries, museums and arts	29	1	2	22
Police	162	2	7	40
Prisons	18	1	—	11
Parliament and law courts...............	29	—	1	14
Fire service...........................	39	1	4	8
Social services:				
Education[2].........................	808	11	71	273
National health service	642	12	26	605
Local welfare services.................	31	1	7	10
Child care............................	17	1	1	23
Social security benefits	58	1	—	59
Finance and tax collection	111	1	—	47
Records, registrations and surveys	16	—	—	3
Other services	64	—	35	−66
Total current expenditure on goods and services	3,544	49	271	2,527
of which				
Central government	1,960	23	75	2,053
Local authorities	1,584	26	196	474

Source: 1967 Blue Book, Table 48

[1]Including housing, land drainage and coast protection, and miscellaneous local government services.

[2]Including the administrative costs of school meals, milk and welfare foods.

diture is attributed to other sectors in the national accounts and regarded as being financed by the grants to them. The amounts included for the Post Office up to 1961 include wages, etc., charged to capital account but exclude the remuneration of sub-postmasters who are regarded as being self-employed.

The estimate of income from employment given above is that shown in the analysis of gross national product by sector and type of income (Table 13 of the 1967 Blue Book). However, it is considerably larger than the estimate which can be derived from the analysis of the gross domestic product by industry (Table 17 of the 1967 Blue Book) under the headings 'Public administration and defence', 'Public health services' and 'Local authority educational services'. The difference is due mainly to (a) public authorities' trading undertakings which are classified to other headings in Table 17, (b) some central government non-trading establishments which are classified to other headings in Table 17, principally the Atomic Energy Authority, the Stationery Office, Navy Department shipbuilding, engineering and explosives establishments, R.E.M.E. establishments, Air Force maintenance units, government research establishments, and (c) local authorities' building and contracting establishments which are classified to construction in Table 17.

The classification by service is described in detail in Section 3 of this chapter. Attention is drawn to one point in the classification by service of central government expenditure on wages and salaries. Wages and salaries paid by a government non-trading department A (for example, Ministry of Labour) in providing services for another department B (for example, Ministry of Social Security) have been classified according to the category of public service provided by A (that is against 'Employment services' and not against 'Social security benefits'). The payments made by B to A for these services, whether actual or imputed as allied services (see page 331), then appear in the column headed 'Other payments (net)'—positively against the service provided by B and negatively against the service provided by A. The most important examples are wages and salaries paid by the Ministry of Public Building and Works and the Stationery Office, which appear against the heading 'Other services' in the table and not against the public services receiving office accommodation, stationery, etc., from these two departments. This explains why the figures in the columns headed 'Other payments (net)' shown against certain services are negative.

From 1963/64, the figures of central government wages and salaries have been provided by departments. For earlier years they were compiled mainly from an analysis of the published *Estimates*, *Appropriation Accounts*, *Trading Accounts and Balance Sheets*, summary accounts of Regional Hospital Boards, and so on. It follows that the statistics of central government wages and salaries before 1963/64 exclude wages and salaries not identified as such in these publications, for example any wages included under the heading of maintenance.

The figures for local authority wages and salaries are derived from the wage and salary table in *Local Government Financial Statistics* for England and Wales, an approximate addition being made to cover Scotland and Northern Ireland. The results of the quarterly inquiry on wages and salaries, referred to on page 318, have also been used.

Selective employment tax
This is the tax payable from 5 September 1966 in respect of the civilian employees of public authorities; the estimates are on the same basis as those for wages,

salaries, etc. It should be noted that since the figures for 1966 cover less than four months of the year they are not typical. Figures for central government employees are provided by departments. Figures for local authority employees have been estimated on the basis of repayments made by the Ministry of Housing and Local Government, the Scottish Development Department, the Welsh Office and the Ministry of Development, Northern Ireland.

Imputed rents

The basis of these imputed payments is explained on pages 267 and 310. Imputed rents in respect of government-owned office accommodation are included under the heading 'Other services'. The imputed payments for this accommodation also appear in the column 'Other payments (net)'—positively against the services using the accommodation and negatively against the heading 'Other services'. This treatment corresponds with that for certain wages and salaries, described above.

PUBLIC AUTHORITIES: HOUSING SUBSIDIES

Expenditure on housing subsidies by public authorities is presented in the 1967 Blue Book as in the table below. These subsidies are described on pages 272 and 312.

Housing subsidies, 1966

	£ million
Central government	
Permanent housing:	
Subsidies to local authorities	100
Subsidies to public corporations	8
Temporary housing:	
Annuities	—
less Receipts from local authorities	−1
Emergency housing: net payments to local authorities	1
Net subsidies	108
Local authorities	
Emergency housing:	
Expenses *less* Rents, etc.	1
less Receipts from central government	−1
Other housing:	
Loan charges	410
Payments to central government for temporary houses	1
Other expenses	140
less Rents, etc.	−369
less Subsidies from central government	−100
Net subsidies	82
Combined public authorities	190

Source: 1967 Blue Book, Table 49

Central government subsidies to local authorities include amounts paid, by way of local authorities acting as agents, to private housing associations, etc. This expenditure is included in the local authorities' section of the table under 'Other expenses'. Temporary housing annuities, which ceased from April 1962, were repayments of principal and interest from housing Votes to the Consolidated Fund in respect of advances for the construction of temporary houses. These annuities are treated as rent income of the central government (see page 268) and the excess of this amount over the corresponding receipts from local authorities is regarded as a subsidy. From 6 June 1955 local authorities, which had until then acted as agents of the central government in the management of emergency housing, took over full responsibility for requisitioned premises. All emergency housing transactions have therefore been shown in the local authority section of the table. However, except for the years 1957 and 1958 central government reimbursements have been approximately equal to the net cost incurred by local authorities in providing emergency housing.

TAXES ON EXPENDITURE AND SUBSIDIES: ALLOCATION BY TYPE OF EXPENDITURE

For estimating each form of final expenditure at factor cost, the total taxes on expenditure and subsidies must be split between the different forms of final expenditure. Certain taxes and subsidies can fairly clearly be allocated to specific forms of final expenditure; examples are Customs and Excise duties on drink and tobacco, betting tax, some purchase tax and the greater part of the food subsidies. Difficulty arises however in the allocation of taxes (and of certain subsidies) falling, not directly on some specific form of final expenditure, but wholly or partly on intermediate products. Thus tax on motor fuel, in so far as it falls on fuel used by business vehicles is a tax on an intermediate product, and in so far as it falls on fuel used by private motorists is a tax on consumers' expenditure. Local rates on business properties are another example of a tax which is spread over a wide variety of final expenditure.

In making the estimates for this table (Table 50 of the 1967 Blue Book) each tax and subsidy is examined and where possible allocated to a specific category of final expenditure. Details of those allocated to consumers' expenditure are given on page 117. Payments of selective employment tax in 1966 were allocated to the categories of final expenditure largely on the basis of input-output statistics for 1963. The remaining amounts of taxes and subsidies are then distributed proportionately between the categories of final expenditure according to their value after the deduction of readily identifiable components which contain no unallocated indirect taxes. The components of final expenditure which are deducted are consumers' expenditure on rent, rates and water charges, domestic service, wages, salaries, etc. paid by private non-profit-making bodies and expenditure abroad; and public authorities' expenditure on wages, salaries, etc. and the associated selective employment tax, and imputed rents. This method of allocating the remaining taxes and subsidies to the category of final expenditure on which they ultimately fall is inevitably arbitary and not much significance can be attached to the precise results. Generally between one quarter and one third of the total taxes *less* subsidies is allocated in this way.

TAXES ON INCOME, NATIONAL INSURANCE CONTRIBUTIONS AND TAXES
ON CAPITAL: ALLOCATION BY TYPE OF INCOME, PROPERTY AND SECTOR

This table (Table 51 of the 1967 Blue Book) brings together the different forms
of direct taxes on income and capital, and analyses them according to the type of
income or property on which they fall. The figures refer to payments in the year,
and not to the provision for tax arising from the income earned during the year,
nor to the tax legally payable to the government during the year.

The allocation of taxes on income by type of income presents some difficulty
because the taxpayer is assessed on his total income, irrespective of its source.
Hence if an individual receives both a wage or salary and an investment income
the questions arise (a) whether the tax-free allowances should be set against his
salary or his investment income, (b) whether, if he is liable to surtax on the top
slice of his total income, the surtax should be regarded as falling on his salary or
his investment income. These questions can be answered only arbitrarily, and the
theoretical basis generally adopted is that the tax on a mixed income should be
allocated *pro rata* to its various constituents. However, after the introduction of
the special earned income allowance for surtax in the Finance Act, 1961, this
procedure is not appropriate and from 1963 no allocation of surtax between
employment and other incomes has been made. An exception to the general
procedure of allocating tax proportionately to the various types of income is
made in the case of certain transfer incomes which are regarded as marginal
incomes bearing the rate of tax chargeable on the topmost slice of income. Such
transfer incomes include family allowances and certain small pensions, but
exclude dividends and interest.

Full data for this calculation are not available. The method of charging income
tax under Schedules enables a rough allocation of gross income tax collected
between types of income. The various income tax Schedules are described in
Appendix III. It is believed that the income tax appropriate to civil employment
income and pay of the Forces follows very closely that actually paid under
Schedule E by civilians and the Forces respectively, for whom separate accounts
are kept. The income tax appropriate to rent up to 1963 is taken as amounts paid
under Schedule A together with an estimate for taxes on excess rents charged
under Schedule D; from 1964 the amount is estimated from the income tax
collected under Case VI and Case VIII of Schedule D. Estimates can be made
for taxes on the transfer incomes previously mentioned. There is no good basis,
however, for imputing a division of Schedule C and Schedule D tax between
profit incomes and interest and dividends and the table therefore gives combined
figures for income from dividends and interest and trading incomes. A particular
difficulty with these estimates arises because repayments of tax are not analysed
by the Schedule to which they refer; for example it is not known how much of
the tax which is deducted at source from dividends and interest is repaid to recipients not liable at the standard rate on all the income. The apportionment of
surtax is more difficult; up to 1962 it is based on information from the Inland
Revenue surveys of the distribution of incomes.

The estimates of tax payments by the various sectors of the economy are also
shown in this table; the estimates are described in the various sector chapters.
In allocating taxes on income by sectors the broad position from 1966 is that
income tax and surtax are borne by persons and corporation tax by companies

and public corporations. For earlier years income tax collected under the various Schedules had to be apportioned between the sectors; profits tax was borne by companies and public corporations. Tax deducted at source from payments of dividends and interest is regarded as falling on the recipients of the dividends and interest. The method of collecting income tax by deduction at source leads to differences in any given period between the tax suffered by deduction and tax receipts. In so far as any sector deducts at source more than it hands over to the Inland Revenue during a period, this is treated as a negative tax payment by that sector; the sum of tax payments by all sectors thus equals the total receipts by the Inland Revenue. These differences are difficult to estimate and there are also difficulties in apportioning repayments of income tax between sectors. For both these reasons, despite the introduction of corporation tax, there are still difficulties in estimating the tax payments by the various sectors.

The table also provides a breakdown of taxes on capital, showing the types of property on which death duties are paid. These estimates are provided by the Inland Revenue. Up to 1966 taxes on capital other than death duties comprise the special contribution and taxes on capital gains. The special contribution was a once for tax levied in 1948/49 and assessed on the basis of investment income. The estimated tax collected on short-term capital gains, levied from 1962/63 under income tax Schedule D is included together with amounts collected under the capital gains tax introduced in 1965/66 and any amounts on capital gains collected under corporation tax. From 1967 the betterment levy on the development value of land is included. The special charge levied on investment income in 1968/69 is also regarded as a tax on capital.

PUBLIC SECTOR: CURRENT AND CAPITAL ACCOUNTS

The accounts for the public sector as a whole presented in the 1967 Blue Book are shown on the next page. The table summarises the transactions of central government, local authorities and public corporations. In addition to the consolidation carried out for public authorities in the table described above (see pages 321 and 322), the following transactions between central government and public corporations (for which accounts are given in Tables 37 and 38 of the 1967 Blue Book) have been eliminated:

(a) taxes on income paid by public corporations;
(b) debt interest on loans by the central government to public corporations;
(c) central government capital grants to public corporations;
(d) net lending by the central government to public corporations.

Payments of subsidies by the central government to public corporations are not eliminated (see page 321).

Additional detail on the item 'Net borrowing, changes in debtors, creditors and cash balances' for the central government is available in the capital account of the central government (Table 42 of the 1967 Blue Book) which is described in Chapter IX. Total public expenditure is further analysed by functional and economic categories in Table 53 of the 1967 Blue Book, described in the following section of this chapter.

Public sector current and capital accounts, 1966

£ million

Receipts		Expenditure	
Current account		*Current account*	
Taxes on income	4,418	Current expenditure on goods and	
Taxes on expenditure:		services	6,391
Central government	4,243	Subsidies......................	558
Local authorities (¹)	1,353	Current grants to personal sector	2,973
National insurance and health con-		Current grants abroad	182
tributions	1,797		
Gross trading surplus:		Total current expenditure exclud-	
Central government and local		ing debt interest	10,104
authorities	98	Debt interest:	
Public corporations	1,038	Central government	1,041
Rent	745	Local authorities	429
Interest and dividends, etc.:		Public corporations	105
Central government	131		
Local authorities	67	Total current expenditure	11,679
Public corporations	54	Current surplus (²)	2,265
Total	13,944	Total	13,944
		Capital account	
		Gross domestic fixed capital for-	
		mation:	
Capital account		Central government	341
Current surplus (²)	2,265	Local authorities	1,330
Taxes on capital	317	Public corporations	1,447
Capital transfers from private sector	9		
Receipts from certain pension		Total	3,118
'funds' (net)	64	Increase in value of stocks:	
Loan repayments by overseas		Central government	25
governments..................	30	Public corporations	41
Net borrowing, change in debtors,		Capital grants to private sector...	185
creditors and cash balances:.....		Net lending to private sector.....	35
Central government:		Loans to overseas governments...	95
Net balance	534	Drawings from U.K. subscriptions	
Other financial receipts (net)..	26	to international lending bodies.	10
Local authorities:		Other net lending and investment	
Identified borrowing (net)....	408	abroad......................	8
Miscellaneous financial receipts		Cash expenditure on company	
(net).......................	−97	securities, etc. (net)..........	55
Public corporations	16		
		Total capital expenditure........	3,572
Total	3,572		
		Combined current and capital	
Combined current and capital account		*account*	
Receipts on current account......	13,944	Current expenditure excluding	
		debt interest	10,104
Receipts on capital account	1,307	Capital expenditure	3,572
		Total public expenditure excluding	
		debt interest	13,676
		Debt interest	1,575
Total	15,251	Total public expenditure	15,251

Source: 1967 Blue Book, Table 52

(¹)Rates.

(²)Before providing for depreciation, stock appreciation and additions to reserves.

3. ANALYSIS OF PUBLIC EXPENDITURE

The total of public expenditure analysed in Table 53 of the 1967 Blue Book is the sum of the expenditure on current and capital account of the public sector, which is shown on the expenditure side of the account described above. Total public expenditure comprises the current and capital expenditure of central government and local authorities and the capital expenditure of the nationalised industries and other public corporations. All operating expenditure by trading bodies is excluded; but where trading receipts are less than operating expenditure and the deficit is covered by a subsidy, the amount of the subsidy is included in total public expenditure. Expenditure on lending and the acquisition of financial assets by the public sector are included. Debt interest, although part of total public expenditure, was not included in the analysis in the 1967 Blue Book. Expenditure on debt interest cannot be satisfactorily allocated between the various services and has been omitted from the Treasury surveys of future expenditure because the forecasting of it is dependent on assumptions about future levels of expenditure, taxation and interest rates.

The Blue Book table provides a two-fold analysis of total public expenditure by function and economic category. The analysis into twelve economic categories is the same as that shown in the table on page 330. Thirty functional or service categories are distinguished in the analysis; they are each described below. Not every item of expenditure falls unambiguously into one or other of the functional categories and the functional classification of expenditure is to a certain extent arbitrary. For example, expenditure by the Agricultural Research Council might be included under 'Agriculture, fisheries and food' rather than under 'Research'.

Central government departmental expenditure is divided into Votes, each Vote bringing together the expenditure connected with a particular object or purpose. In classifying central government expenditure by functional category it is found that in most cases the whole of a Vote can be allocated to one service. Where this is not so, the allocation of the expenditure on a single Vote to two or more services is carried out on the basis of the separate sub-heads of expenditure in the Vote. Some sub-heads, for example those covering wages and salaries and other administrative costs, have to be dealt with in an arbitrary way, either by allocating them to the major service provided by the Vote or splitting them in fairly arbitrary proportions. As an example, expenditure by the Ministry of Transport is divided between (a) civil defence (provision of equipment at docks, etc.), (b) roads and public lighting, (c) transport and communication, and (d) finance and tax collection (the cost of collection of motor vehicle licence duties). The main bulk of expenditure on these services can be segregated because it is shown in separate Votes or separate sub-heads, but the general administrative costs of the Ministry of Transport cannot readily be allocated by type of service since they fall on a single sub-head and they have to be divided between the four services in fairly arbitrary proportions.

In the case of current goods and services provided free, that is without cash reimbursement, by one department for another the cost has been debited to the service receiving these free facilities. In consequence, almost the whole of the current cost of providing certain common services is allocated to the various public services making use of them. These common services are principally office and other accommodation costs borne by the Ministry of Public Building and Works, the stationery and printing costs of the Stationery Office, the expenses of the Central Office of Information, rates on government property which are charged to a single Vote, and the cost of civil service superannuation which for a large section of the service is charged to a single Vote. The allocation is based on the statements of the cost of allied services given at the end of the estimate for each supply Vote. There are no corresponding statements in the *Appropriation Accounts* showing the actual costs of providing allied services. Consequently the analysis of allied services derived from the published *Estimates* has to be used with an approximate adjustment where the actual expenditure on common service Votes differs from the expenditure on those Votes shown in the *Estimates*.

In the classification of central goverment expenditure the composition of the items is as far as possible consistent in all years despite changes in responsibility when departments have been reorganised. References to particular departments should be taken to include where relevant the departments providing similar services in years before 1966.

For local authorities, the analysis of expenditure by type of service has been obtained by grouping as appropriate the various services separately specified in *Local Government Financial Statistics*; details of the grouping are given in the following paragraphs of this chapter. References to *Local Government Financial Statistics* should be taken to include also *Local Financial Returns (Scotland)* and the Northern Ireland *Local Authority Financial Returns*. Some additional information has also been used to provide a finer breakdown.

For public corporations, the four industry groups described on page 245 are each allocated to one service. The expenditure of 'Other corporations' is allocated to various services as appropriate.

The description of individual items in the analysis of public expenditure which follows refers only to the principal elements within each category. References to public services in Great Britain should be taken to include where applicable the corresponding services in Northern Ireland. The descriptions given in general cover the whole of the period 1953 to 1966, the period for which analyses on the basis described below have been published. As far as possible the classification adopted is consistent for all years.

The analysis by service of public sector gross domestic fixed capital formation given in this table is similar to the detailed analysis by industry for all sectors combined given in the section of the Blue Book on capital formation (Table 60 of the 1967 Blue Book). The main differences in classification are as follows:

(a) So far as possible the industry analysis follows the *Standard Industrial Classification, 1958*, which differs from a classification by service. For example, expenditure by all establishments falling within the definition of 'Manufacturing' is included under 'Manufacturing' in Table 60 whatever service is involved. Examples are Royal Ordnance Factories, which are classified in Table 53 to 'Military defence', and railway workshops which are classified in Table 53 to 'Transport and communication'.

(b) In the industry analysis all expenditure on new housing, except the cost of land, is included under 'Dwellings', but in Table 53 expenditure on housing provided for specific public services, for example married quarters for the Forces and houses for police, is included under the service concerned.

(c) The figures for each industry in Table 60 exclude purchases *less* sales of land and existing buildings, but these are included under the appropriate service in Table 53.

Certain other small differences of classification are referred to below in discussion of individual items.

MILITARY DEFENCE

The term military defence used in the national income accounts corresponds, so far as practicable, with the internationally agreed definition used by the North Atlantic Treaty Organisation. This definition is wider than that used in the Defence Budget. In order to show its relationship to the Defence Budget, presented in the annual White Paper *Statement on the Defence Estimates*, it is convenient to describe it in terms of the following groups.

(a) *Defence Budget*. The Defence Budget, as presented for 1966/67, consists of expenditure by the Ministry of Defence and expenditure on military account by the Ministry of Technology, the Ministry of Public Building and Works, and the Atomic Energy Authority. It is treated as a whole for purposes of financial control. The scope of the Defence Budget has changed somewhat over the years; for example part of the expenditure of the Atomic Energy Authority is now included, while expenditure on the superannuation of civil employees of the service departments is no longer included. However, the scope of military defence expenditure is the same in all years and the content of the other items of military defence listed below incorporates compensating adjustments where necessary for earlier years.

(b) *Purchasing services*. Payments by the Army Department and Ministry of Technology for defence equipment through the Purchasing (Repayment) Services Votes and the Purchase of United States Aircraft Vote in excess of the amounts recouped from the service departments (included in the Defence Budget) and from other customers.

(c) *Other military defence expenditure*. For 1966/67 this comprises:
(i) military aid to overseas countries, including the cost of internal security in certain overseas territories;
(ii) common services, including civilian superannuation, rendered without charge to the Ministry of Defence and the Ministry of Technology;
(iii) part of the imputed rent of the Atomic Energy Authority.
Expenditure by the Air Department on meteorological services, which is included in the Defence Budget, is excluded from expenditure on military defence and is deducted. In earlier years other items, not then included in the Defence Budget, are included here.

The figures of military defence expenditure up to 1958 include purchases of equipment financed by Defence Aid from the United States; the receipts of Defence Aid were deducted in the Defence Budget but in the national income accounts appear separately as an item on the receipts side of the central government current account (see page 270). However, military defence expenditure excludes local supplies provided without charge by overseas governments.

All public expenditure on military defence is expenditure by the central government.

Current expenditure on goods and services

Expenditure on military services overseas is recorded partly on a net basis, that is, it excludes the cost of local supplies and services provided for United Kingdom Forces without charge. In the years 1955/56 to 1960/61 when contributions in cash were made by the German Federal Republic towards meeting the costs of the United Kingdom forces stationed in Germany, these were treated as a deduction from expenditure.

Where the transfer without charge of buildings and other fixed assets to overseas countries on independence does not form part of economic or military aid, and is therefore not included in current grants abroad, no deduction has been made from current expenditure on goods and services.

The item comprises:

(a) Expenditure, both at home and abroad, by the Ministry of Defence, apart from the meteorological service of the Air Department (see page 354). It includes expenditure on new equipment of all descriptions, none of which is classified as fixed capital formation. It also includes expenditure on North Atlantic Treaty Organisation infrastructure projects, such as airfields and communications. Purchases from Royal Ordnance Factories are valued at cost, including provision for depreciation and interest.

(b) Expenditure, both at home and abroad, by the Ministry of Public Building and Works on buildings and works for defence purposes, such as barracks and airfields. Expenditure on the construction of married quarters at home is excluded and classified as fixed capital formation.

(c) Expenditure by the Ministry of Technology on research and development, inspection, storage, hostels, etc., for defence purposes, including costs of administration of these services.

(d) Payments by the Ministry of Technology and Army Department for defence equipment in excess of the amounts recouped from the service departments, and from other customers purchasing equipment through the Purchasing (Repayment) Services Votes. The effect of adding this item to the service departments' expenditure (item (a) above) is to include in defence expenditure, not the service departments' payments to the Purchasing (Repayment) Services Votes but the payments to defence contractors by the Ministry of Technology and Army Department.

(e) Part of the expenditure of the Atomic Energy Authority; the rest of the Authority's expenditure is classified to 'Research' and 'Other services'.

(f) Expenditure by the Ministry of Labour on the call-up of National Service men, which ceased after 1960/61.

Gross domestic fixed capital formation

This comprises:

(a) Purchases of land and existing buildings in the United Kingdom by the service departments.

(b) The building of married quarters for the Forces by the Ministry of Public Building and Works.

(c) Expenditure by the Ministry of Technology on land, buildings, works and plant for research and development, inspection, storage, hostels, etc. for defence purposes.

(d) Purchases of land, buildings, works and plant for Royal Ordnance Factories.

(e) Expenditure under Ministry of Technology capital assistance schemes, where buildings and plant are purchased by the Ministry and leased to firms engaged on defence contracts.

(f) Purchases *less* sales of machine tools by the Ministry of Supply from 1951 to 1955 for setting up a pool of equipment for use in connection with the defence programme. It includes machine tools intended for use in Royal Ordnance Factories and in capital assistance schemes, including those imported from the United States up to 1953 under the Mutual Defence Assistance (M.D.A.) scheme.

Sales of land and existing buildings by the service departments and Ministry of Technology in the United Kingdom are deducted in arriving at the figures.

Increase in value of stocks

The estimated change in the value of stocks and work in progress at Royal Ordnance Factories.

Current grants to personal sector

From 1950 to 1962 this item consists of National Service grants. The National Service grants were payments made to service personnel to relieve financial difficulty in cases where service emoluments were insufficient to meet the men's obligations to their families, etc.

Current grants abroad

This item consists of cash grants to overseas governments for military purposes, the cost of goods and services of a military nature provided to overseas countries without charge, and subscriptions to international military agencies such as the North Atlantic Treaty Organisation.

Capital grants to private sector

Compensation paid by the service departments for losses and damage arising from traffic accidents, training, etc.; and royalties and awards to inventors paid by the Ministry of Technology. Figures prior to 1957 include gratuities for service in Korea.

CIVIL DEFENCE

The central government component of this service comprises:

    (a) The civil defence services of the Home Office and the Scottish Home and Health Department, and civil defence expenditure incurred by the following departments in connection with the public services indicated.

        Ministry of Housing and Local Government, Scottish Development Department, Welsh Office: water and sewerage, care of the homeless
        Health departments: health services
        Ministry of Transport: railways, ports, etc.
        Ministry of Power: storage and distribution of petroleum
        Ministry of Agriculture, Fisheries and Food: food distribution
        Ministry of Public Building and Works: buildings and equipment

    (b) Expenditure in connection with the procurement and maintenance of strategic reserves of food and raw materials; these costs are borne mostly on the Votes of the Board of Trade and the Ministry of Agriculture, Fisheries and Food.

The local authority component of civil defence consists of the service identified in *Local Government Financial Statistics* as civil defence. Most of the local authority expenditure is current expenditure on goods and services. Capital expenditure on civil defence by public corporations (Post Office; British Broadcasting Corporation; railway, gas and electricity undertakings) is excluded; it is included with other expenditure by the corporations under the service with which they are concerned.

Current expenditure on goods and services

Central government. The cost of administration and training of, and the cost of stores for, the civil defence services described at (a) above; the handling and storage costs of the strategic reserves described at (b).

Local authorities. The running costs of civil defence establishments.

Gross domestic fixed capital formation

Central government. Expenditure on buildings, vehicles, vessels and electronic equipment for the home departments' civil defence services; reserve equipment, etc. for the water and sewerage services and ports; provision of emergency accommodation at hospitals; provision of petroleum storage and distribution installations; and provision of emergency food distribution facilities. Capital expenditure at ports for civil defence purposes is included here but in the industry analysis of fixed capital formation it is included under the heading 'Harbours, docks and canals'.

Local authorities. Expenditure on buildings and vehicles for civil defence establishments and capital expenditure on civil defence measures in connection with water and sewerage.

Increase in value of stocks

Purchases *less* sales of strategic reserves of food and raw materials by the central government.

Some capital grants to the private sector were attributed in error to this service in the 1967 and previous Blue Books; up to 1966 no capital grants were made to the private sector in this connection.

EXTERNAL RELATIONS

The main element comprises the group of services, both at home and abroad, administered by the Foreign Office, the Commonwealth Office and the Ministry of Overseas Development. Certain expenditure by these departments on the maintenance of internal security, however, is classified under 'Military defence' (see page 333). There is no local authority element, but the item 'Other net lending and investment abroad' includes certain expenditure by public corporations (see below).

Current expenditure on goods and services

In addition to the expenditure of the departments mentioned above, current expenditure by the Secret Service, the British Council, the Commonwealth War Graves Commission, the former Trade Commissioner establishments of the Board of Trade and expenditure by the Ministry of Public Building and Works on public buildings overseas are included. Payments to the British Broadcasting Corporation for its external services, regarded as trading receipts of the Corporation, are also included under this heading.

Gross domestic fixed capital formation

Fixed capital formation by the British Broadcasting Corporation in connection with its external services.

Current grants abroad

The principal components of this heading are:
    (a) multilateral economic aid through the agency of the United Nations and other international organisations;
    (b) subscriptions to certain international organisations;
    (c) bilateral economic aid to the developing countries comprising cash grants and technical assistance in the form of goods and services, including education and training and the provision of facilities in Britain;
    (d) other cash grants to overseas countries.
Military aid is not included under this heading but is shown under 'Military defence'.

Loans to overseas governments

This comprises the whole of the item of central government capital expenditure described on page 285.

Drawings from United Kingdom subscriptions to international lending bodies

This item, which is described on page 285, relates to central government transactions with the International Bank for Reconstruction and Development, the International Development Association, the International Finance Corporation and the Asian Development Bank.

Other net lending and investment abroad

The main component of this series is lending by the Commonwealth Development Corporation for the financing of development projects overseas. Also included are capital expenditure overseas by the British Broadcasting Corporation in connection with its external services; loans *less* repayments by the former Commonwealth Relations Office to Bailey (Malta) Ltd., towards the capital cost of conversion of the naval dockyard to a commercial ship repairing yard; and the purchases *less* redemptions of United Nation bonds by the Foreign Office. The figure for 1966 includes the servicing of Rhodesian debt to the International Bank for Reconstruction and Development.

    More detailed figures of expenditure on economic aid by the United Kingdom government are published in the *Annual Abstract of Statistics* for financial years and in *Financial Statistics* for quarters.

ROADS AND PUBLIC LIGHTING

The central government component of this heading covers the administrative activities of the Ministry of Transport, the Scottish Development Department and the Welsh Office in connection with roads in general and the direct responsibilities of the ministries for the provision and maintenance of trunk roads and motorways. Local authorities act as agents of the ministries in maintaining trunk roads and motorways, but the expenditure is included with that of the central government. The costs of collecting motor vehicle licence duties and of motor vehicle registration are not included; they are allocated to 'Finance and tax collection'. The accounts of the Road Fund were consolidated within this heading prior to its abolition in April 1956.

The local authority element consists of the services identified in *Local Government Financial Statistics* as roads other than trunk roads (including scavenging), parking of vehicles and public lighting. Expenditure on private street works, which is generally reimbursed by the private interests concerned, is included under 'Miscellaneous local government services'.

Current expenditure on goods and services

Central government. Administrative expenditure of the departments mentioned above in connection with roads; cost of surveys and research, including expenditure by the Road Research Laboratory; maintenance, minor improvement and lighting of trunk roads.

Local authorities. Cost of maintenance and minor improvement of roads other than trunk roads and motorways, parking of vehicles and public lighting. Separate figures for roads and for public lighting are given in the current account of local authorities.

As explained on page 267, no imputed payment is included for the use of the fixed assets employed.

Gross domestic fixed capital formation

Central government. Cost of construction and major improvement of trunk roads and motorways, including purchases of land.

Local authorities. Cost of construction and major improvement of roads other than trunk roads and motorways, including purchases of land; capital expenditure on car parks and public lighting.

TRANSPORT AND COMMUNICATION

The central government component covers (a) the activities of the Ministry of Transport, other than its functions in relation to roads and civil defence, (b) the activities of the Board of Trade in respect of civil aerodromes and air navigation services, including related expenditure on works and buildings by the Ministry of Public Building and Works, and (c) the responsibilities of the Board of Trade for coastguards and services to shipping. Prior to April 1961 capital expenditure by the Post Office was also included in the central government component, but from that date it forms part of the capital expenditure by public corporations which is included under this heading.

The local authority component covers trading undertakings operating road passenger transport, aerodromes, harbours and docks.

Capital expenditure by the following public corporations is included here: British Railways Board, London Transport Board, British Transport Docks Board, British Waterways Board and the Transport Holding Company (all of which prior to January 1963 formed the British Transport Commission), Ulster Transport Authority, National Dock Labour Board, National Ports Council, British Overseas Airways Corporation, British European Airways, British Airports Authority, Post Office (from April 1961) and Cable and Wireless Ltd.

Current expenditure on goods and services

Central government. The administrative and other expenses of the Ministry of Transport, other than the part attributable to the Ministry's responsibilities for roads and civil defence; expenditure by the Board of Trade on services to transport and communication. Expenditure by the former Ministry of Aviation on air navigation services is included before 1 November 1964; from that date they are regarded as a trading activity and the expenditure is excluded. The costs of running civil aerodromes are also excluded as they are regarded as trading expenses.

Gross domestic fixed capital formation

Central government. The two components (a) civil aerodromes, including air navigation services, and (b) up to March 1961 the Post Office, are shown separately in the capital account of the central government.

Local authorities. Land, buildings, works, vehicles and plant for (a) road passenger transport and (b) harbours, docks and aerodromes. Separate figures for (a) and (b) are given in the capital account of local authorities.

Public corporations. Fixed capital formation by the corporations listed above.

Increase in value of stocks

Central government. The change in the value of the stocks of the Post Office prior to April 1961.

Public corporations. The change in the value of stocks held by the corporations listed above.

Subsidies

Central government. These comprise:

(a) Grants towards the revenue deficits of the British Transport Commission from 1960 to 1962, the British Railways Board and British Waterways Board from 1963 and the London Transport Board from 1966. The compensation paid to the London Transport Board for loss of revenue in 1965 and subsidies paid to the Ulster Transport Authority are also included. These subsidies are shown separately in the central government current account.

(b) The Board of Trade deficit on the operation of civil aerodromes, including aerodrome navigation services, and from November 1964 on all air navigation services, being the excess of operating costs including interest and depreciation over revenue from landing fees, rents receivable, etc.

(c) From 1965 grants to road passenger transport operators in relief of additional costs arising from increased tax on fuel.

(d) Before 1956 grants towards the operating losses of the airways corporations.

Current grants abroad

Subscriptions to international transport and civil aviation organisations.

Cash expenditure on company securities, etc. (*net*)

Expenditure by the public corporations listed above. This expenditure has been identified only from 1964.

EMPLOYMENT SERVICES

The central government component comprises the services administered by the Ministry of Labour, including services to the disabled, and the transactions of the Redundancy Fund. Expenditure on youth employment and sheltered employment services by local authorities is included, although the figures are not shown separately in *Local Government Financial Statistics.* Estimates of these items are made by the Ministry of Labour. Expenditure by the Ministry of Labour on (a) the call-up of National Service men, which ceased after 1960/61, is included under 'Military defence' and (b) subsidies to National Service hostels, which ceased after 1956/57, is included under 'Housing'.

Current expenditure on goods and services

Central government. The administrative and other expenses of the Ministry of Labour and the Redundancy Fund with the exceptions noted above. The costs of vocational training courses and industrial rehabilitation borne on the National Insurance and Industrial Injuries Funds are excluded. Grants towards the administrative costs of industrial training boards are included.

Local authorities. The running costs of youth employment services and sheltered employment services for handicapped persons.

Current grants to personal sector

Central government. Travelling and maintenance allowances to transferred workers, trainees and persons under rehabilitation; fees for training courses; grants to Remploy Ltd. and to voluntary bodies for the training of severely disabled persons. Figures from 1966 include rebates paid to employers from the Redundancy Fund.

Current grants abroad

Subscriptions by the central government to the International Labour Organisation.

OTHER INDUSTRY AND TRADE

Broadly, the central government component comprises most of the services administered by the Board of Trade other than civil aviation and shipping, the Export Credits Guarantee Department, and most of the services administered by the Ministry of Power. It also includes expenditure on civil aircraft projects and assistance to the shipbuilding industry by the Ministry of Technology. The procuring and maintenance of strategic reserves of materials by the Board of Trade is excluded; this expenditure is included under 'Civil defence'. From 1967, the payments by the Ministry of Labour of selective employment premiums, including regional employment premiums, in excess of the original tax payments are included under this heading.

The following trading activities are included under this heading (see Chapter IX, Annex 1):

(a) the Exports Credits Guarantee Department;

(b) the provision by the Board of Trade of factories for lease, etc. in development areas and the provision of factories by the Ministry of Commerce in Northern Ireland;

(c) trading in raw materials and other commodities by the Board of Trade;

(d) the State Management Districts.

The local authority component of this service relates to the trading undertakings not included under other services. These undertakings appear in *Local Government Financial Statistics* under the descriptions: cemeteries, civic restaurants, markets, slaughterhouses, general corporation estates and miscellaneous trading. Gas and electricity services in Northern Ireland are also included.

Capital expenditure by public corporations in the fuel and power, and iron and steel industries is included here. These comprise the National Coal Board, Electricity Council, Central Electricity Generating Board, Area Electricity Boards, North of Scotland Hydro-Electric Board, South of Scotland Electricity Board, Electricity Board for Northern Ireland, Gas Council and Area Gas Boards, and the Iron and Steel Holding and Realisation Agency and its subsidiaries. From 1967 capital expenditure by the British Steel Corporation is included. In addition, the capital expenditure of certain other corporations is included, as noted below.

Current expenditure on goods and services

Central government. Current expenditure on the development and proving of transport aircraft; administrative costs and other expenses in connection with the central government services described above. Payments to certain grant-aided bodies regarded as serving industry, such as the British Travel Association, are included (see page 261 and Chapter IX, Annex 2).

Gross domestic fixed capital formation

Central government. Mainly land, buildings and equipment for factories built by the Board of Trade and by the Ministry of Commerce in Northern Ireland.

Local authorities. Land, buildings and equipment for the local authority trading services referred to above.

Public corporations. Fixed capital formation by the corporations referred to above.

Increase in value of stocks

Central government. The change in the value of the stocks of raw materials held by the trading divisions of the Board of Trade.

Public corporations. The change in stocks and work in progress of the corporations referred to above.

Subsidies

Central government. The principal components of this item for recent years are the deficit on letting of factories by the Board of Trade and the subsidy on fuel paid by the Ministry of Commerce to certain industrial undertakings in Northern Ireland. In 1966 the item included assistance to Beagle Aircraft Ltd. pending acquisition of the company by the government.

Capital grants to private sector

Central government. Grants by the Board of Trade to industrial and other undertakings under the Local Employment Acts, 1960 and 1963; grants and compensation under the Cotton Industry Act, 1959, paid mainly in 1960 and 1961; and grants in earlier years towards the re-equipment of the cotton spinning and other industries. From 1967 payments of investment grants are included under this heading.

Net lending to private sector

Central government. Loans *less* repayments under the Local Employment Acts, 1960 and 1963 and earlier legislation for the assistance of industry in areas of high unemployment; lending under the Ship Building Credit Act, 1964;

lending to Colvilles Ltd. under the Iron and Steel Financial Provisions Act, 1960; lending by the Ministry of Power for the installation of fuel saving equipment; net advances to the British Sugar Corporation Ltd. until March 1957; and net advances to the Potato Marketing Board from April 1955 to March 1960. Sales of factories on mortgage terms, which are treated as being financed by loans to the private sector, are included here.

Public corporations. Loans *less* repayments by the National Film Finance Corporation, the Sugar Board and, from 1967, the Industrial Reorganisation Corporation.

Cash expenditure on company securities, etc. (net)

Central government. All expenditure by the central government on company securities is included here. In 1966 this comprised the expenditure of £31 million on British Petroleum shares and £1·5 million on shares and loan stock of Fairfields (Glasgow) Ltd.

Public corporations. Expenditure by the corporations referred to above. From 1967 expenditure by the Industrial Reorganisation Corporation is also included.

RESEARCH

This covers central government expenditure on civil research and development by the Atomic Energy Authority, the Ministry of Technology, the research councils (Agricultural Research Council, Medical Research Council, Science Research Council, etc.) and the Department of Education and Science. Certain expenditure of the National Research Development Corporation is also included.

Current expenditure on goods and services

This comprises the running costs of the central government establishments referred to above, together with expenditure by these departments on research and development carried out by industry, etc. on their behalf. Imputed rent for the use of fixed assets by the Atomic Energy Authority is included.

Gross domestic fixed capital formation

Land, buildings, plant and equipment for the central government establishments referred to above. The amount of fixed capital formation by the Atomic Energy Authority allocated to civil research is necessarily somewhat arbitrary, since assets may not be specifically purchased for civil research.

Subsidies

Grants to the National Research Development Corporation in relief of interest liability.

Current grants to personal sector

This covers grants to persons and institutions engaged in research paid by the Ministry of Technology, the research councils and the Department of Education and Science.

Current grants abroad

This comprises contributions towards international atomic energy projects by the Atomic Energy Authority and subscriptions to international organisations concerned with nuclear and space research.

Capital grants to private sector

This covers grants towards capital expenditure by institutions engaged in research by the departments and research councils referred to above.

Net lending to private sector

The financial support of research and development projects by the National Research Development Corporation.

AGRICULTURE, FORESTRY, FISHING AND FOOD

Most of the expenditure under this heading is accounted for by the central government, although there is some local authority expenditure on the provision of allotments and smallholdings, and on animal health and the control of pests, The central government element covers the services administered by the Ministry of Agriculture, Fisheries and Food, the Department of Agriculture and Fisheries for Scotland, and the Forestry Commission. Expenditure by the White Fish Authority, the Herring Industry Board and the Development Fund is also included; these bodies are treated as part of central government. Expenditure by the agricultural departments on field drainage is included, but expenditure by them and by local authorities on land drainage, including arterial drainage, and sea defences is excluded from this heading and is included under 'Land drainage and coast protection'. The costs of procuring and maintaining a strategic reserve of foodstuffs and of providing emergency food distribution facilities are excluded; they are included under 'Civil defence'.

Certain trading services are included under this heading (see Chapter IX, Annex 1):

(a) the Forestry Commission and Northern Ireland government forestry operations;

(b) agricultural trading services, including the farming and management of land, by the Ministry of Agriculture, Fisheries and Food and the Department of Agriculture and Fisheries for Scotland;

(c) trading in foods by the former Ministry of Food to 31 March 1958.

Current expenditure on goods and services

Central government. The administrative and other expenses of the non-trading activities of the departments and authorities detailed above. The administrative costs of the former Ministry of Food at headquarters and at regional and local food offices, apart from the costs of administering the welfare food schemes, were part of this item.

Local authorities. Net current expenditure on allotments, smallholdings. animal health, control of pests, etc.

Gross domestic fixed capital formation

Central government. Land, buildings, works and equipment for forestry and for the trading activities of agricultural departments. Capital expenditure on experimental centres and the provision of fixed assets for agricultural colleges is included. The cost of planting and maintaining forests is included under the heading 'Increase in value of stocks'.

Local authorities. Land and buildings for allotments and smallholdings.

Increase in value of stocks

Central government. After 1957 this is the increase in the balance sheet value of the forests and other stocks, valued at historical cost, of the Forestry Commission and Northern Ireland government forestry operations. In earlier years the item also included changes in the trading stocks of the Ministry of Food, and of the other trading bodies listed above.

Subsidies

Central government. This comprises subsidies paid mainly by the agricultural departments and the other authorities detailed above to the agriculture, forestry and fishing industries. The principal items are listed below.

(a) Agricultural price guarantees under schemes for wheat and rye, barley, oats and mixed corn, cattle, sheep, pigs, eggs, wool and potatoes.

(b) Fertilizer and lime subsidies.

(c) Grants and subsidies for ploughing of grassland; cultivation of certain crops (acreage payments); maintenance of attested herds (bonus payments); rearing of calves, farrowing sows, hill sheep, hill cattle and beef cows; improvement of livestock; compensation for slaughter of diseased animals *less* proceeds of sales of carcases; production on marginal land; improvement programmes for small farms.

(d) Subsidies to the white fish industry and the herring industry.

(e) Grants by the Forestry Commission to owners of private woodlands.

(f) Deficits on the trading activities of the agricultural departments.

Up to 31 March 1958 subsidies include the trading losses of the Ministry of Food as defined in their published trading accounts, which regard interest on capital and depreciation as current costs *less* the part thereof attributable to (a) the cost of the milk and welfare food schemes, which are treated as a current grant to persons (see page 352) and (b) administrative expenses at headquarters and regional and local food offices, which are included in current expenditure on goods and services.

Current grants to personal sector

Central government. Grants to agricultural colleges and research institutions; agricultural scholarships and maintenance allowances; and grants from the Development Fund to promote the rural economy and to develop fisheries.

Current grants abroad

Subscriptions by the central government to the Food and Agriculture Organisation of the United Nations and certain other international bodies.

Capital grants to private sector

Central government. Grants to farmers for field drainage and water supply, farm improvements, and the improvement of land; grants by the White Fish Authority and Herring Industry Board; grants to horticulture; and grants to crofters. From 1967 investment grants paid to farmers are included.

Net lending to private sector

Central government. Net lending by the White Fish Authority and Herring Industry Board for the purchase of boats, engines, etc.; net lending to the Agricultural Mortgage Corporation Ltd.; loans to smallholders. From 1963 to 1966 loans were offset by repayments.

HOUSING

This service relates to the provision of housing for the general public, including temporary housing and emergency housing. It excludes houses provided by public authorities for their employees, which are shown against the service concerned—for example married quarters for the Forces, which are included under 'Military defence', and houses for the police. The ownership by public authorities of houses intended for the general public is regarded as a trading activity, since the ownership of dwellings is included within the boundary of production. All capital expenditure by the housing and new town corporations is included.

Temporary housing consists of prefabricated structures which were manufactured and erected at central government expense on sites provided by local authorities; the local authorities let the accommodation and make an annual payment to the central government as a form of rental. Emergency housing was accomodation provided in requisitioned premises and in ex-Service hutted camps, etc.; the local authorities let the accomodation as the agents of the central government, and the government reimbursed to the local authorities the full net cost incurred. From 6 June 1955 responsibility for requisitioned premises, but not hutted camps, etc., was transferred to local authorities and from 1 April 1956 the central government reimbursed to the local authorities most, though not all, of the net cost of providing this accommodation.

Current expenditure on goods and services

This item refers to the expenses of the Ministry of Housing and Local Government, the Scottish Development Department, the Welsh Office and the Ministry of Development, Northern Ireland in the administration of their housing responsibilities. Local authorities' administrative expenses are excluded; these are treated as operating costs in the housing trading account, and hence enter into the figure of local authorities' housing subsidies.

Gross domestic fixed capital formation

Central government. The cost of manufacture and erection of temporary houses, which was negligible after 1951.

Local authorities. Purchases of land for housing and the cost of construction of permanent dwellings, including site development. Sales of land and houses are deducted.

Public corporations. All fixed capital formation by New Town Development Corporations, the Commission for the New Towns, Scottish Special Housing Association, Nothern Ireland Housing Trust, and Coal Industry Housing Association. The expenditure is mainly on purchases of land and the construction of dwellings but some expenditure on factories and commercial buildings by new town corporations is included.

Subsidies

The composition of the total is shown in the table on housing subsidies, described on page 326. Grants to the National Service Hostels Corporation are included up to 1954.

Capital grants to private sector

Local authorities. This is the whole of the item 'Capital grants to personal sector' in the capital account of local authorities, described in detail on page 315.

M

Net lending to private sector

Central government. Net lending to building societies and private housing associations under the House Purchase and Housing Act, 1959, the Housing Act, 1961 and Housing (Scotland) Act, 1962.

Local authorities. This is the whole of the item 'Net lending for house purchase' in the capital account of local authorities, described on page 316.

Public corporations. Net lending by the Housing Corporation to housing societies.

WATER, SEWERAGE AND REFUSE DISPOSAL

The whole of the expenditure shown is incurred by local authorities. Water supply is treated as a trading service. Expenditure on civil defence measures in connection with water and sewerage is excluded; it is included under 'Civil defence'.

Current expenditure on goods and services

The current cost of the sewerage and refuse disposal services, including an imputed rent equal to loan charges for the use of the fixed assets employed.

Gross domestic fixed capital formation

Land, buildings, works, water mains, plant and vehicles for local authorities' water undertakings, and for sewerage and refuse disposal services.

PUBLIC HEALTH SERVICES

This comprises expenditure by local authorities shown in *Local Government Financial Statistics* under the headings 'Port health service', 'Public conveniences' and 'Public health: Other items'. It covers the salaries of Medical Officers of Health and sanitary inspectors, and expenditure in connection with the inspection of food and drugs and the notification of diseases.

Current expenditure on goods and services

The current cost, including an imputed rent equal to loan charges, of the services described above.

Gross domestic fixed capital formation

Land, buildings, plant and vehicles for the services described above. In the industrial analysis of gross domestic fixed capital formation this expenditure is included under the heading 'Health services'.

LAND DRAINAGE AND COAST PROTECTION

Expenditure by local authorities, mainly river authorities. Up to 1966 there was no significant expenditure by the central government, except for grants to local authorities which do not appear in this table. Field drainage is excluded; it is included under 'Agriculture, fisheries and food'.

Current expenditure on goods and services

The current cost of maintaining arterial drainage systems, sea defences, etc.

Gross domestic fixed capital formation

The capital cost of land drainage schemes and sea defences. Reconstruction work arising from the East coast floods of February 1953 gave rise to a substantial increase in expenditure in 1953, which is also reflected in the figure for current expenditure on goods and services. The distinction made by local authorities between current and capital expenditure on reconstruction is probably somewhat arbitrary.

PARKS, PLEASURE GROUNDS, ETC.

This comprises central government expenditure on Royal parks and pleasure gardens, and the preservation of historic buildings and ancient monuments; together with local authority expenditure on parks, pleasure gardens and open spaces, baths, wash-houses and open bathing places.

Current expenditure on goods and services

Central government. Current expenditure by the Ministry of Public Building and Works on salaries, maintenance and running expenses at Royal parks and pleasure gardens, and the cost of maintaining, repairing and excavating ancient monuments.

Local authorities. The current cost, including an imputed rent for the use of fixed assets, of the local authority services referred to above. Receipts from the public, for example admission charges at swimming baths, are deducted.

Gross domestic fixed capital formation

Local authorities. Land, buildings, etc. for the local authority services referred to above.

MISCELLANEOUS LOCAL GOVERNMENT SERVICES

The central government component of this item consists of the administrative costs of the Ministry of Housing and Local Government, Scottish Development Department, Welsh Office and Ministry of Development, Northern Ireland, other than those which have been allocated to specific services, such as housing and roads.

The local authority element mainly comprises expenditure on the services shown in *Local Government Financial Statistics* under the headings 'Town and country planning', 'Private street works, etc.', 'Council elections', 'Weights and measures', 'Miscellaneous' and 'General administrative expenses'.

Current expenditure on goods and services

Central government. The administrative costs referred to above. The administrative costs of the Central Land Board are included up to 1958/59.

Local authorities. In addition to the current costs of the local authority services referred to above, the expenditure, other than transfers, of certain special funds is included; these are shown in *Local Government Financial Statistics* as 'Other reserve funds', 'Insurance funds', 'Trust or charity funds' and 'Other special funds'. Only part of the expenditure of 'Other special funds' is included, however, since not all the transactions of these funds can be regarded as purchases of goods and services by the non-trading part of local authorities. An imputed rent equal to loan charges is included.

Gross domestic fixed capital formation

Local authorities. Land, buildings, etc. purchased in connection with the local authority services referred to above, including local government offices. Receipts from sales are deducted.

LIBRARIES, MUSEUMS AND ARTS

The central government component covers expenditure on national libraries, museums and art galleries, expenditure by the Arts Council of Great Britain, and other grants for the arts. Local authority expenditure on local libraries and museums is also included.

Current expenditure on goods and services

Central government. The cost of maintaining certain national libraries, museums and art galleries, the most important of which are the British Museum, Science Museum, Victoria and Albert Museum, National Gallery and Tate Gallery; (for a full list see *Civil Estimates* 1967/68 Class VIII). The administrative costs of the Arts Council, which is treated as part of the central government, are also included.

Local authorities. The current costs, including an imputed rent equal to loan charges, of local libraries and museums; receipts from fees, fines, etc. are deducted.

Gross domestic fixed capital formation

The whole of this item relates to local authorities, central government expenditure being insignificant.

Current grants to personal sector

Central government. Grants to private bodies concerned with the arts, for example the British Film Institute and the Royal Opera House, Covent Garden. Grants to the National Library of Wales and the National Museum of Wales, which are treated as part of the personal sector, are included (see Chapter IX, Annex 2).

POLICE

Current expenditure on goods and services

Central government. Cost of certain police services, for example training centres, administered by the Home Office; and the cost of the Royal Ulster Constabulary.

Local authorities. Cost of police forces in Great Britain, including the Metropolitan police. The cost of pensions paid to former members of the police *less* employees' superannuation contributions is included (see page 311).

Gross domestic fixed capital formation

Central government. Buildings, including houses, equipment and vehicles for Home Office establishments and the Royal Ulster Constabulary.

Local authorities. Buildings, including houses, equipment and vehicles for police forces in Great Britain.

PRISONS

This is entirely central government expenditure on the current cost of prisons (current expenditure on goods and services) and on prison buildings and equipment (gross domestic fixed capital formation).

PARLIAMENT AND LAW COURTS

Current expenditure on goods and services

Central government. Administrative and other costs of the House of Lords, House of Commons, Privy Council Office, Supreme Court of Judicature, County Courts, Courts of Law in Scotland and Supreme Court of Judicature in Northern Ireland.

Local authorities. Current expenditure shown under the heading 'Administration of justice' in *Local Government Financial Statistics.*

Current grants to personal sector

These are grants for legal aid by the central government and local authorities.

FIRE SERVICE

Expenditure incurred by local authorities. Up to 1966 there was no significant expenditure by the central government except for grants to local authorities, which do not appear in this table.

Current expenditure on goods and services

The current cost of maintaining the fire service. It includes pensions paid to retired members of the fire service *less* employees' superannuation contributions (see page 311).

Gross domestic fixed capital formation

Land, buildings, vehicles and equipment for the fire service.

EDUCATION

This service comprises education in schools, technical institutions and universities. Physical training and the school health service are included. The current costs of providing school meals and school milk, apart from central government administrative costs, are excluded and appear under a separate heading in this table (see page 352); but the central government administrative costs of providing school meals and school milk and the capital costs of school canteens are included here.

Current expenditure on goods and services

Central government. The main items are the administrative and other costs of the Department of Education and Science and the Scottish Education Department. The excess of the repayment annuities, which until March 1962 were paid by the education departments to the Ministry of Works in respect of the construction costs of temporary school accommodation, over receipts from local authorities for the use of this accommodation is included (see page 268).

The net cost to the central government of teachers' pensions, that is pensions paid to teachers *less* pension contributions received from teachers and their employers, is not included. It is regarded as the repayment of a liability and is included in the item 'Receipts from certain pension 'funds' (net)' in the central government capital account (see page 276).

Local authorities. The current cost of education, apart from the cost of school meals and school milk and of scholarships and grants to universities and colleges, which are treated as current grants to the personal sector. Prior to April 1962 expenditure on the colleges of advanced technology was included here, but from that date they are treated as private non-profit-making bodies in the personal sector. The rent imputed for the use of local authority schools and colleges is based on rateable values (see page 310).

Gross domestic fixed capital formation

From 1950 the whole of this item relates to local authority expenditure, central government expenditure being insignificant. It includes expenditure on school canteens and their equipment financed by the Department of Education and Science and the Scottish Education Department; the payments by the two departments are treated as capital grants to local authorities.

Current grants to personal sector

Central government. Scholarships and maintenance allowances; current grants to universities, colleges, technical institutions and schools other than those maintained by local education authorities, including grants to colleges of advanced technology from April 1962. Separate figures for scholarships and maintenance allowances, grants to universities, colleges, etc. and grants to other private non-profit-making bodies are given in the current account of the central government.

Local authorities. Scholarships paid to pupils and students in respect of fees and maintenance allowances and grants to universities, colleges, etc.; these grants are given in the current account of local authorities.

Capital grants to private sector

Central government. Grants towards the cost of buildings and equipment in universities, and from April 1962 colleges of advanced technology; grants to voluntary (aided and special agreement) schools and colleges of education in Great Britain and voluntary schools in Northern Ireland. Separate figures for grants to universities, colleges, etc. are given in the capital account of the central government.

Net lending to private sector

Central government. Loans *less* repayments to universities, colleges and schools in the private sector.

NATIONAL HEALTH SERVICE

The expenditure shown under this heading relates almost entirely to the national health service which came into existence on 5 July 1948. Central government expenditure covers the hospital service, payments to general practitioners and the net cost of the pharmaceutical, dental and ophthalmic services. Other central government expenditure included here relates to the administrative and other expenses of the Ministry of Health and the corresponding expenses of the Scottish Home and Health Department and the Northern Ireland Ministry of

Health and Social Services. Expenditure on civil defence measures is excluded; it is included under 'Civil defence'.

The local authority part of the national health service corresponds to the item 'Individual health' in *Local Government Financial Statistics*. This service relates to the provision of health centres, health visiting and home nursing, care of mothers and young children, ambulance services, vaccination and immunisation, etc. Local authority expenditure on port health and other public health services is included under 'Public health services'.

Current expenditure on goods and services

Central government. An imputed rent is included for hospitals (see page 268). The figures of current expenditure on goods and services include the contributions paid by Regional Hospital Boards, etc. towards staff superannuation, and not the net cost of health service pensions, that is the actual payments of pensions *less* the contributions received from employees (see pages 270 and 276). The cost of collection of national health contributions is also included.

Local authorities. Current expenditure on the services listed above, including an imputed rent based on loan charges.

Gross domestic fixed capital formation

Central government. Land, buildings, plant and equipment for the national health service.

Local authorities. Capital expenditure on health centres, ambulances, etc.

Current grants to personal sector

Central government. Patients' allowances and pocket money paid in hospitals and payments towards the costs of running motor invalid chairs and cars.

Current grants abroad

Subscriptions by the central government to the World Health Organisation.

Capital grants to private sector

Compensation paid by the central government to doctors for the loss of right to sell medical practices, paid mainly on retirement or death.

LOCAL WELFARE SERVICES

This is entirely local authority expenditure shown in *Local Government Financial Statistics* under the heading 'Care of the aged, handicapped and homeless'. The part of this expenditure which relates to sheltered employment service is, however, excluded; it is included under 'Employment services'.

Current expenditure on goods and services

The current cost, including an imputed rent equal to loan charges, of providing these services. Receipts, such as charges to persons in homes for old people, are deducted.

Gross domestic fixed capital formation

Mainly the purchase of land and buildings for the housing of old people.

CHILD CARE

This service is mainly provided by local authorities, though voluntary bodies in the private sector, who receive government grants towards their costs, are also of importance. The local authority component is shown in *Local Government Financial Statistics* under the heading 'Protection of children'. It covers approved schools, remand homes, children's homes and other services for the care and welfare of children.

Current expenditure on goods and services

Local authorities. The current cost, after deducting such receipts as parents' contributions, of the services referred to above. An imputed rent, equal to loan charges, for the use of buildings owned by local authorities is included.

Gross domestic fixed capital formation

Local authorities. Land, buildings, etc. purchased in connection with the services referred to above.

Current grants to personal sector

Grants by the central government towards the current costs of voluntary approved schools, etc.

Capital grants to private sector

Grants by the central government towards the capital expenditure of voluntary approved schools, etc.

SCHOOL MEALS, MILK AND WELFARE FOODS

In the national income accounts the net cost to public authorities, after deducting receipts from those receiving meals, milk, etc., is treated as a current grant to persons, and the full cost of the food is included in consumers' expenditure. The central government administrative costs of school meals and school milk are included in public expenditure under the heading 'Education', together with capital expenditure on school canteens and equipment.

Current expenditure on goods and services

The cost to the central government of administering the welfare foods scheme•

Current grants to personal sector

Central government. The net cost of providing milk and vitamin foods at reduced prices to children and expectant mothers. Before 1 October 1954, the cost of milk in schools maintained by local education authorities was borne directly by the Ministry of Food.

Local authorities. The net cost of providing school meals and, from 1 October 1954, of providing school milk.

SOCIAL SECURITY BENEFITS

This is entirely central government expenditure comprising the services now administered by the Ministry of Social Security, including the national insurance schemes.

Current expenditure on goods and services

The administrative costs of the Ministry of Social Security, and administrative and other expenditure charged to the National Insurance Funds. The running costs of reception centres are included.

Current grants to personal sector

The composition of these grants is shown in the current account of the central government as follows:

National insurance benefits. Further details of the composition of this item are given in the current account of the National Insurance Funds. Benefits paid to non-residents are excluded; they are included under 'Current grants abroad'. Payments of extended unemployment benefit, which ceased on 5 July 1953, are included.

War pensions and service grants. Payments of pensions, gratuities and allowances for disablement or death arising out of war, or out of service in H.M. Forces after 2 September 1939. Pensions, etc. paid in respect of the mercantile marine and civilians are included. Payments to those no longer resident in the United Kingdom are excluded; they are included under 'Current grants abroad'.

Non-contributory pensions. Non-contributory old age pensions, paid through the National Assistance Board, ceased after 26 November 1966 and were replaced by supplementary benefits.

Supplementary benefits. Non-contributory benefits supplementing the national insurance scheme. Up to 26 November 1966 the series related to assistance grants paid by the National Assistance Board.

Family allowances.

Current grants abroad

Central government. Payments of national insurance benefits and war pensions to those not resident in the United Kingdom.

FINANCE AND TAX COLLECTION

Current expenditure on goods and services

Central government. Administrative and other expenses of the Treasury, the Board of Inland Revenue, Customs and Excise, the Exchequer and Audit Department and the National Savings Committee; management expenses of the national debt, other than cash payments on conversion of stock and prize money on premium savings bonds; payments to local authorities and the Post Office for expenses incurred in the registration of motor vehicles and collection of motor vehicle licence duties; cost of collection of selective employment tax. The purchase by central government of new coin at cost is included (see page 266). From 1967 the expenses of the Land Commission in collecting the betterment levy are included.

Local authorities. Cost of rate collection and valuation expenses.

Current grants to personal sector

Payments by central government of post-war credits, including interest.

Capital grants to private sector

Central government. Post-war refunds of excess profits tax (see page 283); and cash payments to holders of government securities on conversion into other government securities.

M*

RECORDS, REGISTRATION AND SURVEYS

Expenditure under this heading consists only of current expenditure on goods and services.

Current expenditure on goods and services

Central government. Current costs of the Ordnance Survey, Charity Commission, Friendly Societies Registry, Land Registry, Office of the Registrar of Restrictive Trading Agreements, Public Record Office, Scottish Record Office, Offices of the Registrars General and Department of the Registers of Scotland.

Local authorities. Current expenditure under the headings 'Registration of electors' and 'Registration of births, deaths and marriages' in *Local Government Financial Statistics*.

WAR DAMAGE AND TOWN AND COUNTRY PLANNING COMPENSATION

This heading covers only central government capital grants to the private sector under the war damage and town and country planning compensation schemes. These items are shown separately in the capital account of the central government and are described on pages 282 and 283.

OTHER SERVICES

This item is mostly central government expenditure by various departments whose activities do not fall into any of the functional headings already described; certain investment expenditure of public corporations is also included. From 1967, the transactions of the Land Acquisition and Management Fund of the Land Commission, which is treated as a trading body, are included under this heading.

Current expenditure on goods and services

The most important component under this heading is the current expenditure on goods and services, including imputed rent, of the Atomic Energy Authority other than that included under 'Military defence' and 'Research'. This fluctuates quite substantially from year to year since it represents the remaining net purchases of goods and services, other than fixed assets, by the Authority, and reflects changes in stocks and work in progress arising in the course of all its activities except, from April 1965, the commercial activities for which separate accounts are kept.

Other items included are the current costs of the Meteorological Office of the Air Department, Cabinet Office, Civil Service Commission, Department of Economic Affairs, Office of the Parliamentary Commissioner, Royal Commissions, Government Actuary and Public Trustee; that part of the administrative and other costs of the Home Office and Scottish Home and Health Department not included elsewhere; the Civil List; law charges; and pensions of the Royal Irish Constabulary.

Gross domestic fixed capital formation

Central government. Capital expenditure by the Ministry of Public Building and Works on land, buildings, furniture and equipment for public buildings in the United Kingdom; expenditure on fixed assets by the Atomic Energy Authority other than that classified under the heading 'Research'.

Public corporations. Expenditure on fixed capital formation by the British Broadcasting Corporation in connection with its home services, Independent Television Authority, Bank of England and the Covent Garden Market Authority.

Current grants to personal sector

Miscellaneous grants. The main components of this item in 1957 and 1958 were payments to or in respect of British subjects who had to leave Egypt, or who were dependent upon assets in Egypt, and were in distress.

Net lending to private sector

This covers miscellaneous loans *less* repayments to the private sector under the Land Settlement Acts and Trade Facilities Acts, Northern Ireland land purchase annuities, etc.

Other net lending and investment abroad

Loans *less* repayments by the Atomic Energy Authority to certain uranium producers in South Africa and Australia.

TREASURY ANALYSIS OF PUBLIC EXPENDITURE

The Treasury analysis of public expenditure, given at the end of the notes to the 1967 Blue Book, provides an alternative analysis of total public expenditure to that given in the table in the section on the public sector, which is described above. Instead of giving an analysis of expenditure by functional and economic categories which are the same in all years, expenditure is analysed largely in terms of the programmes for which departments are responsible. These programmes may be affected by changes in the departments responsible for certain services and variations in the extent to which services are provided free by one department to another, but they are the basis for the formulation of policy. This analysis is on much the same basis as that used by the Treasury for surveys of future expenditure. The analysis relates to financial years and figures are given from 1959/60 only.

The classification is essentially the same as that used in Table II of the *Memorandum by the Financial Secretary to the Treasury* on the Estimates presented to Parliament each year. It is applied there, however, to net expenditure on Votes, whereas here it is applied to total public expenditure. The Vote element within this total differs from net Vote expenditure. Grants to local authorities and other bodies within the public sector are excluded and so are some financial transactions. Differences also arise from differences in the treatment of receipts, such as national health contributions, and in the treatment of transactions of trading bodies. These differences are explained in Chapter IX.

The totals of expenditure analysed in the Treasury table are consistent with the calendar year totals shown in the analysis of public expenditure given in the section of the Blue Book on the public sector (Table 53 of the 1967 Blue Book). The Treasury analysis differs from the functional analysis in Table 53 in the following respects.

(a) The classification in the Treasury analysis is more detailed. In the right-hand column of the table are shown the headings under which the expenditure is classified in Table 53.

(b) Expenditure by Northern Ireland authorities is shown in the Treasury analysis as a separate heading. All other headings therefore relate to expenditure, wherever it may occur, by bodies comprising the public authorities sector of Great Britain only. In Table 53, each heading, and not just the grand total, relates to the United Kingdom.

(c) 'Allied services' expenditure, that is expenditure shown at the end of Votes as connected with the service provided by a department (for example accommodation, stationery and printing) is generally not allocated to other headings in this table. The major exception is defence. In Table 53 'Allied services' expenditure is always classified with other expenditure under the heading concerned.

(d) Capital expenditure by the nationalised industries, etc., which is shown separately at the end of the Treasury analysis, covers the expenditure of all the industries dealt with in the White Papers on the nationalised industries[2], together with that of the British Broadcasting Corporation, Independent Television Authority, Covent Garden Market Authority and, up to 1966/67, the nationalised iron and steel undertakings. The capital expenditure of other bodies classified as public corporations in the national income accounts is allocated to the relevant heading. In Table 53 the investment of all public corporations is allocated to individual headings. There is a difference in the classification of investment expenditure by new town corporations which in the Treasury analysis is divided between the headings 'Roads', 'Housing', 'Water supply', 'Sewerage' and 'Miscellaneous local government expenditure'; in Table 53 all investment expenditure by the new town corporations is classified to 'Housing'.

(e) In the Treasury analysis in the 1967 Blue Book expenditure on fixed assets is included under each heading without deducting amounts realised from sales except in the case of the expenditure on fixed assets of the nationalised industries, etc. The total amount so realised is deducted in the item 'Statistical adjustments'. In Table 53 receipts from sales of fixed assets are deducted from each heading concerned. In future issues of the Blue Book receipts from sales will be deducted from each heading in the Treasury analysis also.

(f) The heading 'Statistical adjustments' in the 1967 Blue Book includes (i) a negative item for sales of fixed assets and (ii) the other small differences remaining between the sum of the figures used for the Treasury analysis and the total used in the national accounts.

4. PUBLIC AUTHORITIES' CURRENT EXPENDITURE ON GOODS AND SERVICES AT CONSTANT PRICES

For the estimation of gross domestic product at constant prices, the estimates of public authorities' current expenditure on goods and services are revalued at constant prices.

The Blue Book table on expenditure and output at constant prices (Table 14 of the 1967 Blue Book) shows estimates for four separate functional categories, namely 'Military defence', 'National health service', 'Education' and 'Other'.

---

[2]See *The Financial and Economic Obligations of the Nationalised Industries*, Cmnd. 1337, and *Nationalised Industries—A Review of Economic and Financial Objectives*, Cmnd. 3437. From 1967/68 the British Steel Corporation is included with these industries.

Quarterly estimates of public authorities' current expenditure on goods and services revalued at constant prices are published only in total and date from 1955. The estimates are published quarterly in *Economic Trends* and in the *Monthly Digest of Statistics*. The series is seasonally adjusted.

The principles involved in revaluing public authorities' expenditure on goods and services are discussed in Chapter III. In general, the methods of revaluation assume that there is no increase in the productivity of those employed in public services (see pages 44 and 45). The estimates are as far as possible consistent with the estimates of output at constant prices, described in Chapter V.

The methods of revaluation used fall into two groups:
(a) the deflation of expenditure figures by indices of pay and prices;
(b) the use of volume indicators.

Over three-quarters of expenditure is revalued by the first method, including about two-fifths of expenditure which is on wages and salaries deflated by an index of changes in rates of pay. Both methods are used for quarterly and annual estimates but the annual calculations are carried out in greater detail. The table below shows the extent to which categories of public authorities' current expenditure on goods and services are revalued separately for the annual estimates and the methods of revaluation adopted. It will be seen that for expenditure on goods, which is deflated by a price index, the index often relates to costs rather than to the price of the product, because of the variable nature of the goods.

The reliability of the estimates for a year three or four years away from the base year can be regarded only as fair in terms of the gradings described on pages 39 to 41, because of the difficulty of revaluing at constant prices the goods and services bought by public authorities (see pages 51 and 52).

Methods used for revaluing at constant prices public authorities' current expenditure on goods and services

	Method of revaluation	Expenditure at current prices, 1966 £ million
Central government		4,111
Military defence:		2,162
Forces' pay	Volume indicator: index of strength of armed forces	609
Civilian wages and salaries, including locally engaged staff overseas but excluding payments of pensions	Deflation by base-weighted index of wage and salary rates	344
Superannuation (payments of pensions)	Volume indicator: the index of civilian strength implied by estimates of deflated expenditure on the preceding item	
Research and development (excluding wages and salaries of government employees)	Deflation by price index for input costs of research and development	
Aircraft	Deflation by price index based on input costs for aircraft	
Shipbuilding (excluding wages and salaries of government employees)	Deflation by price index for ships	

	Method of revaluation	Expenditure at current prices, 1966 £ million
Other major equipment and munitions	Deflation by price indices mainly based on input costs for aircraft	
Construction	Deflation by price index for costs of new construction other than dwellings	1,209
Petroleum products	Deflation by index for world petroleum prices	
Transport	Deflation by appropriate section of the retail price index	
Maintenance and repair of buildings	Deflation by appropriate section of the retail price index	
Other expenditure	Deflation by price index implied for all categories above, other than wages and salaries	
National health service:		1,158
Hospital services, etc.	Deflation by base-weighted index of wage and salary rates for (a) Medical, professional and administrative staff (b) Nursing staff (c) Industrial staff Deflation by price index for other hospital expenditure	759
General medical services	Volume indicator: number of doctors on Executive Council services list	108
Pharmaceutical services: Ingredient cost	Deflation by wholesale price index for products of manufacturing industries other than food, drink and tobacco sold on the home market	161
Dispensing cost	Volume indicator: number of prescriptions dispensed	
Dental services	Volume indicator: number of courses of treatment completed	65
Ophthalmic services	Volume indicators: number of sight tests carried out and number of pairs of spectacles paid for	13
Imputed rent for hospitals	Volume indicator: rateable value of hospitals	21
Other expenditure	Deflation by specially constructed base-weighted price index for general central government administrative costs	31
Other:		791
Maintenance of trunk roads and motorways	Deflation by price index for maintenance of roads	28
Other expenditure	Deflation by specially constructed base-weighted price index for general central government administrative costs	763

	method of revaluation	Expenditure at current prices, 1966 £ million
Local authorities		2,280
Education:		1,151
Imputed rent for local authority schools and colleges	Volume indicator: rateable value of local authority schools and colleges	71
Other expenditure	Deflation by specially constructed base-weighted price index covering wage and salary rates and other costs	1,080
Other:		1,129
National health service	Mainly volume indicators for various local authority health services	127
Local welfare services	Volume indicator: number of persons resident in local authority homes	49
Child care	Volume indicators: mainly number of children boarded out and number in local authority homes	42
Maintenance of roads other than trunk roads and motorways	Deflation by price index for maintenance of roads	178
Public lighting	Volume indicator: consumption of electricity and gas for public lighting	24
Fire service	Volume indicator: index of strength of the fire service	52
Police	Volume indicator: index of strength of police forces in Great Britain	203
Other expenditure	Deflation by specially constructed base-weighted price index for general local authority administrative costs	454

Chapter XII

Gross Domestic Fixed Capital Formation

1. CONCEPTS

Additions to the nation's wealth are divided into three categories: the acquisition of fixed assets in the United Kingdom, the acquisition of stocks and work in progress, and net investment abroad. The first of these three forms of investment is considered in this chapter, investment in stocks is dealt with in the next chapter and net investment abroad is described in Chapter XV. Investment in fixed assets and stocks is described as capital formation, to distinguish it from investment in financial assets. Investment in financial assets adds to national wealth only in so far as claims on the rest of the world are increased; within the nation financial liabilities offset financial claims.

Fixed capital formation represents additions to physical productive assets that yield a continuous service beyond the period of account in which they are purchased. In contrast, capital formation in stocks and work in progress represents additions to completed goods not yet sold, materials and fuel not yet used and partly finished products awaiting completion. Examples of fixed capital assets are machinery, equipment, vehicles, buildings, civil engineering works and land. Gross domestic fixed capital formation is that part of a country's final output, including imports, which is not consumed, exported or added to stocks during the accounting period, but represents an addition to its stock of fixed assets. The contribution of land to the total of gross domestic fixed capital formation is limited to the costs incurred in the transfer of land from one owner to another.

Scope of gross domestic fixed capital formation

Since gross domestic fixed capital formation relates to productive assets, its scope is restricted by the definition of the boundary of production already discussed in Chapter I. All expenditure on fixed assets by trading bodies, whether companies, public sector enterprises or unincorporated businesses, is included. Also included is expenditure on land and dwellings by persons, since the provision of housing is included within the boundary of production. Expenditure on other goods which yield a continuous service to consumers, such as household durable goods and cars, is not included because the goods are regarded as being consumed when they are purchased. The ownership of land and buildings by the non-trading branches of public authorities and by certain private non-profit-making bodies is included within the production boundary and expenditure on these assets is part of gross domestic fixed capital formation. Certain other expenditure by these institutions on fixed assets, such as office and research equipment, is also included in gross domestic fixed capital formation in order to achieve comparability with similar expenditure by private industry.

360

The word 'gross' in the term 'gross domestic fixed capital formation' denotes that nothing is deducted for wear and tear, obsolescence and accidental damage. The net addition to the stock of fixed assets is gross domestic fixed capital formation *less* that part of the physical assets used up in the course of production. But fixed capital formation is shown gross both because of the difficulty of estimating capital consumption and because the gross addition to assets is of importance in itself—replacement of assets can, to some extent, be postponed. Estimates of capital consumption on the basis required for the national accounts are made; these are described in Section 5 of this chapter. Estimates of depreciation as obtained from Inland Revenue data are described in the annex to this chapter. Gross domestic fixed capital formation is, however, net of amounts realised from the sale of fixed assets; when a fixed asset is sold for scrap, for export or to a consumer, the proceeds are deducted from purchases of fixed assets to obtain gross domestic fixed capital formation. Expenditure on second-hand assets is included but, of course, transfers of existing fixed assets between one producer and another contribute to gross domestic fixed capital formation only to the extent of any transport, legal or other costs of transfer.

The significance of the word 'domestic' is that the fixed assets concerned are confined to assets located in the United Kingdom. Fixed assets held abroad are excluded since the concept of fixed capital formation is designed to measure changes in the physical capacity for production in the United Kingdom. Also, not enough is known about changes in either fixed assets owned by United Kingdom residents and located overseas, or those owned by non-residents and located in the United Kingdom, for these assets to be separately distinguished. Ships and aircraft are an exception to the general rule of classification on the basis of physical location, however; all ships and aircraft owned by United Kingdom residents are included irrespective of their location, and all those owned by non-residents are excluded.

For the sake of brevity, throughout the remainder of this chapter the term fixed capital formation is used to refer to gross domestic fixed capital formation.

The capital assets entering into fixed capital formation are valued at the cost to their purchaser. Expenditure incurred in the course of their acquisition on such things as transport, installation, stamp duties and the services of agents, solicitors, architects, and consulting engineers are therefore included. Interest charges incurred during long periods of construction which have been capitalised are also included. But expenditure on arranging the supply of finance, for example the costs of share issues, stamp duties and other costs on the transfer of financial assets, are not included. They are regarded as part of current or operating expenditure.

Expenditure on the acquisition of the fixed and other assets of another enterprise (or part of an enterprise) as a going concern is treated as the purchase of a financial asset and is not included in fixed capital formation. Thus, when an unincorporated business is bought by a company or when a company is nationalised, the estimates of fixed capital formation do not include the take-over.

In principle, expenditure on improvements to existing fixed assets should be included in fixed capital formation; extensions and structural alterations to buildings, for example, should be included. On the other hand, expenditure on maintenance and repairs to keep the assets in running order should not be included but should be regarded as an operating expense, except in so far as it may incidentally entail improvements. In practice it is usually impossible to distinguish such improvements; as the United Nations recommendations put it '. . . expenditure on repairs over and above what is needed to keep the capital goods in a state of constant repair should be included. As a practical solution, however, it will often only be possible to include instead the costs of major alterations and renewals'[1]. In the industrial and commercial field the part of repair and maintenance expenditure included in fixed capital formation is in practice determined by the accounting conventions adopted by businesses in allocating their expenses between capital and current expenditure. Thus fixed capital formation includes extensive repairs amounting to reconstruction of assets but excludes day to day repairs and the replacement of parts. In the case of privately-owned dwellings it is impracticable to separate the extensive conversion and major improvement of existing dwellings from ordinary repairs and maintenance; hence, except for grant-aided expenditure on conversions and improvements, which is estimated from grants paid by local authorities, expenditure on existing privately-owned dwellings is excluded from fixed capital formation.

There are certain problems of demarcation between fixed capital formation and work in progress, which arise in the case of assets with long periods of construction. Usually the purchaser makes progress payments to the manufacturer or contractor during the course of construction, and this expenditure will normally be recorded as fixed capital formation by the purchasing industry. In general, therefore, the estimates of fixed capital formation include progress payments and can be taken to approximate to the value of work done in the year on the production of fixed assets. It should be noted, however, that although estimates on this basis approximate to the demands made on the economy by the production of fixed assets, they may not reflect changes in the country's productive capacity, which would be measured more closely in principle if fixed assets were included only on becoming available for use.

Fixed capital formation by public authorities

Expenditure on the replacement of, and additions and major improvements to, the land, buildings and equipment of public authorities, both for their trading and non-trading branches, is included in fixed capital formation. The principle followed in deciding what expenditure of these authorities is to be included is that each item of expenditure is treated so far as possible in the same way as a similar item of expenditure would be treated in estimating fixed capital formation in the private sector; this means departing in some cases from the definitions adopted for accounting purposes by the particular authority, for example where the renewal of a fixed asset is charged to revenue in the authority's own accounts.

The United Nations recommendations[1], to which the United Kingdom statistics broadly conform, are that fixed capital formation should include all expenditure of a capital nature by central and local government, except for most of that on military defence. In the United Kingdom statistics, nearly all expenditure on buildings and equipment for the Forces is excluded from fixed capital formation and treated as central government current expenditure. Exceptions to this rule are made, however, in the case of expenditure on (a) land for the Forces, (b) married quarters for members of the Forces, (c) buildings

---

[1] *A System of National Accounts and Supporting Tables*, United Nations, New York, 1964.

and plant for research and development establishments, and (d) buildings and plant for the manufacture of armaments. Categories (a) and (b) are treated as fixed assets on the grounds that they would be usable for other purposes if no longer required for military use. Categories (c) and (d) are types of assets which are purchased as fixed assets by private industry. Expenditure of a capital nature on civil defence, for example on fire-fighting equipment, is also treated as fixed capital formation.

2. THE PUBLISHED TABLES

Fixed capital formation is analysed in three ways: by industry (agriculture, coal mining, etc.), by type of asset (ships, buildings, etc.), and by institutional sector (companies, local authorities, etc.).

ANNUAL TABLES

Analysis by industry

The most detailed of the Blue Book tables (Table 60 of the 1967 Blue Book) gives an analysis of fixed capital formation by industry and by type of asset, distinguishing forty-five industries cross-classified by three types of asset. In an abridged version of this table (Table 58 of the 1967 Blue Book) the figures for all fixed assets are condensed into eleven industry groups. Estimates for these eleven industry groups are also given at constant prices (Table 59 of the 1967 Blue Book).

The classification by industry mainly follows the *Standard Industrial Classification, 1958*. Detailed differences of coverage from this classification for the forty-five industries separately distinguished are described in Section 3 of this chapter. The eleven industry groups given in the summary tables are defined as in the *Standard Industrial Classification, 1958* except as follows:

(a) The industry group 'Transport and communication' corresponds to Order XIX of the *Standard Industrial Classification, 1958* except that it excludes road haulage contracting, miscellaneous transport services and, prior to 1960, taxi and private hire car businesses.

(b) Ownership of dwellings is treated as a separate industry, in line with other tables in the national accounts. All dwellings are grouped together under one heading, which covers owner-occupied dwellings and dwellings for renting, and includes any dwellings built by industries for their employees.

(c) 'Other service industries' covers the headings 'Insurance, banking and finance' and 'Other transport and services' as defined in Section 3.

(d) 'Social services' covers the headings 'Universities, colleges, etc.', 'Other education', 'Health services' and 'Local welfare services' as defined in Section 3.

(e) 'Other public services' covers the headings 'Roads, etc.', 'Sewerage and land drainage' and 'Other public services' as defined in Section 3.

The classification by industry from 1956 is on the basis of the business unit (enterprise or part of an enterprise) and not the establishment (usually the individual factory or workshop). From 1959 the annual census of production returns, except for detailed census years, and the annual Board of Trade inquiries into the distributive and service industries, have been made on a business unit basis and the estimates have been adjusted to this basis from 1956. They are therefore not entirely comparable with the analysis by financial units of company profits, and the analysis by establishment of income from employment, given elsewhere in the Blue Book and used for the analysis of gross domestic product by industry (Table 17 of the 1967 Blue Book).

A difficulty in the analysis by industry arises from the growing practice of leasing assets. In most cases data can only be collected from the owners of assets and information is not available as to their industrial use. Examples include the leasing of vehicles or plant, such as computers, to other industries. The figures for 'Insurance, banking and finance' also include buildings owned by insurance companies, banks and property companies but rented wholly or in part by other industries. Thus the industrial classification of fixed capital formation does not provide a precise analysis by industry of use.

In principle, land and existing buildings should be treated similarly to other types of asset in the analysis by industry, but the data available for some industries, particularly agriculture and the ownership of dwellings, are insufficient to allow this. The figures for each industry therefore exclude expenditure on land and existing buildings. The net expenditure by all industries on land and existing buildings, that is transfer costs of land and buildings, is shown as a separate item in the industry tables.

Analysis by sector

The most detailed table (Table 55 of the 1967 Blue Book) shows fixed capital formation for the five main institutional sectors cross-classified by five types of asset. A condensed version of this table (Table 54 of the 1967 Blue Book) in which the sectors are combined into the two sectors, private and public, gives estimates at constant as well as at current prices. For all assets combined the public sector is also divided between public corporations and public authorities.

In Table 55, fixed capital formation of the central government and local authorities is subdivided between trading and non-trading activities. Provision of housing, except in conjunction with a non-trading service such as police or prisons, is regarded as a trading service. A full list of central government trading bodies is given on page 296. The main trading activities of local authorities are listed on page 310.

The institutional sectors are the sectors used throughout the national accounts and the allocation of fixed capital formation to a particular sector is on the basis of ownership, which may differ from the sector of use. In using the sector analyses it needs to be remembered that the series are affected by changes in the scope of the sectors as well as in the rate of capital formation.

The sector figures, unlike those for industries, include purchases *less* sales of land and existing buildings. Separate figures for these transactions are given in the detailed sector table. The private sector is subdivided only for 1959 and subsequent years, the only years for which the figures are at all reliable.

Fixed capital formation by the personal sector comprises:
(a) fixed capital formation of unincorporated businesses (professional persons, farmers and other sole traders and partnerships); it is this element which accounts for nearly all capital formation by the personal sector in vehicles and plant machinery and most of that in buildings other than dwellings;
(b) fixed capital formation by persons in dwellings, land and existing buildings;

(c) fixed capital formation by certain private non-profit-making bodies serving persons, such as universities.

Fixed capital formation by the life funds of life assurance companies and by superannuation funds is not included even though their funds are regarded as the property of the personal sector; it is included with that of financial institutions in the company sector (see pages 206 and 413).

Additional details of fixed capital formation by sector are given in other sections of the Blue Book. Separate figures for industrial and commercial companies and financial companies are given in their respective capital accounts in the section on companies. The fixed capital formation of public corporations is analysed by five industry groups in the section on public corporations. And the fixed capital formation of public authorities and the public sector is analysed by service in the sections on central government, local authorities and the public sector. The latter estimates are described in Chapter XI.

Analysis by type of asset

The most detailed analysis of fixed capital formation by type of asset (Table 56 of the 1967 Blue Book) distinguishes five types of vehicle (which are shown as a single category in other tables), plant and machinery, dwellings, other new buildings and works, and transfer costs of land and buildings. These series are translated into constant prices in Table 56, amalgamating the figures for railway rolling stock, ships and aircraft.

The different types of asset are defined below.

(a) *Vehicles, ships and aircraft.* These comprise:

(i) *Buses and coaches.* Vehicles included in the fixed capital formation of the road passenger transport industry other than that of taxi and private hire car businesses. This is assumed to cover vehicles such as buses, coaches, trolley-buses and trams.

(ii) *Other road vehicles.* All other vehicles intended mainly for use on public roads. This category includes various road vehicles with specialised uses, for example ambulances, street cleansing vehicles; it excludes vehicles used in such places as warehouses or railway goods depots, mobile cranes with road licences, road-making vehicles and agricultural tractors, all of which are classified as plant and machinery. Cars for business use are included but those purchased by consumers are excluded from fixed capital formation.

(iii) *Railway rolling stock.* Locomotives, coaching vehicles, wagons and containers. Railway wagons for use on private sidings are included, but trucks and wagons for use in mines, quarries, cement works, etc. are classified as plant and machinery.

(iv) *Ships.* Vessels of all descriptions purchased by businesses resident in the United Kingdom. The figures include expenditure on ships transferred from overseas to United Kingdom ownership, and sales of second-hand ships to non-resident owners are deducted.

(v) *Aircraft.* Civil aircraft of United Kingdom ownership. The figures exclude expenditure borne by the government on the development of prototype civil aircraft.

(b) *Plant and machinery.* The term 'plant and machinery' is an abbreviation of 'plant, machinery and equipment'. The distinction between plant and machinery and vehicles or buildings is not always clear-cut. It is sometimes difficult to distinguish buildings from plant and machinery, for example in parts of the steel and chemical industries. Agricultural tractors, road-making vehicles, rolling stock used in mines and quarries, oil-rigs, mobile cranes and vehicles used within warehouses, railway goods depots, etc. are classified as plant and machinery. Machinery and equipment forming an integral part of buildings and works, for example lifts, heating and ventilating plant, is in general included in buildings; railway track and gas and water mains are also included in buildings and works, but electricity and telephone lines and cables are classified as plant.

(c) *Dwellings*. Houses, bungalows, flats and maisonettes. All expenditure on the construction of new houses and flats, including architects' and quantity surveyors' fees is treated as capital formation. Conversions and improvements to private sector dwellings are included in fixed capital formation only if they are grant-aided; otherwise they are included in consumers' expenditure. The estimates for public sector dwellings include all expenditure on conversions and improvements, however financed. The figures include, so far as is possible, items of equipment which are an integral part of the completed house or flat, such as boilers, and moveable equipment installed by landlords, for example cookers; but moveable equipment installed by tenants and owner-occupiers is included in consumers' expenditure.

(d) *Other new buildings and works*. Buildings other than dwellings, most civil engineering and construction work. Both new construction and extensions and improvements to existing buildings and works are included. Machinery and equipment forming an integral part of buildings and works, for example lifts, heating and ventilating plant, is in general included. The distinction between buildings and plant is sometimes difficult to draw (see above); in such cases the normal accounting practice for distinguishing buildings and plant is generally followed. Railway track and gas and water mains are included under this heading, but electricity and telephone lines and cables are classified as plant. Architects' and surveyors' fees are included, but not fees and costs incurred in transferring the ownership of land and buildings.

(e) *Purchases less sales of land and existing buildings; Transfer costs of land and buildings*. Figures of purchases and sales, given for each sector, cover the capital cost of freeholds purchased, the capital cost of premiums payable for leaseholds acquired, associated professional fees and other transfer costs. Over all sectors these transactions net out to equal transfer costs only. Transfer costs cover stamp duties, legal fees, dealers' margins, agents' commissions and other costs incurred in connection with the transfer of ownership of land and buildings. Land development charges levied under the Town and Country Planning Acts, 1947 are included in the years 1948 to 1960.

In a footnote to the table analysing fixed capital formation by type of asset estimates are given of the total value of expenditure on repairs and maintenance to buildings and works, including conversions and improvements to dwellings. Such expenditure is regarded as expenditure on current or operating account and not as a part of fixed capital formation, apart from public sector and grant-aided private sector conversions and improvements to dwellings. The figures are, however, given because variations in the amount of this expenditure may be of some importance and, since some other countries (including formerly the United Kingdom) treat such expenditure as a part of fixed capital formation in their national accounts, estimates of the amounts involved may help international comparisons where figures adjusted to the standard international definitions are not available.

In the quarterly tables published in the *Monthly Digest of Statistics* and quarterly in *Economic Trends* the eleven industry groups shown in the Blue Book are further condensed into eight groups; the analysis by type of asset is in terms of four categories with separate figures for private and public sector dwellings; and the analysis by sector distinguishes between the private sector, public corporations and public authorities. All these series are shown at current prices, at constant prices and at constant prices seasonally adjusted, and have been published from 1955. In addition, quarterly current price series for the five main institutional sectors are published quarterly in *Economic Trends* and in their respective capital accounts in *Financial Statistics*. These estimates have all been carried back to 1961. In *Financial Statistics* figures are also given separately for industrial and commercial companies and financial companies, a division which has been published from 1962. The estimates for the central government have been published from 1958.

3. STATISTICAL SOURCES

GENERAL METHODS OF ESTIMATION

There are two alternative methods for estimating fixed capital formation, the expenditure and the commodity flow or supply (output *plus* imports *less* exports) method. The expenditure method uses the records which accountants keep of the purchases of capital goods by particular enterprises and public authorities. The commodity flow method uses statistics of production and imports of particular commodities and distinguishes the flow into fixed capital formation from the flows into consumption, exports, stockbuilding and intermediate expenditure.

The alternative methods each have distinct advantages and disadvantages. Capital expenditure figures can be collected according to definitions which are consistent with figures of operating costs taken into account in estimating the profits of the enterprises incurring capital expenditure. To this extent they are consistent with estimates of saving in a way that estimates of capital formation based on output data are not. This consistency fits in with the requirements of the financial accounts which show, *inter alia*, how fixed capital formation is financed. Furthermore, expenditure statistics allow, as output statistics do not, analyses by purchasing industries and sectors. On the other hand, expenditure figures do not as a rule allow more than a summary split of fixed capital formation by type of asset—buildings, plant, vehicles, etc.—whereas estimates from the commodity flow method are naturally available in considerable commodity detail. The commodity flow method also has the advantage of allowing close adherence to the strictly logical definition of a capital good as a good which lasts for more than one accounting period. Accountants usually treat as fixed assets only those items which last several years or more and are costly; they often charge to operating account such things as hand tools and jigs for use in a production run of a few years. Using the commodity flow method all office equipment, for example, can be treated as capital goods, whereas no one can tell how much office equipment is included in the aggregate of capital expenditure since sometimes it is charged to capital account and sometimes to operating account.

However, whilst the commodity flow method allows the consistent application of precise definitions, it requires detailed information about the use of commodities and however much detail is available some guesswork is unavoidable. Intermediate goods, that is goods charged to operating account, have still to be distinguished from goods charged to capital account; intermediate goods include replacement parts as well as parts such as electric motors which may be bought by a producer for incorporation in his more elaborate product. Also, a distinction has to be drawn between goods which are part of fixed capital formation and goods which are part of consumption; a single product may be used for a variety of purposes: a car would be consumers' expenditure if sold to an individual consumer but fixed capital formation if sold to a business or a public authority. The more detailed the production or delivery figures which are available, the easier it is to distinguish fixed capital formation from other uses. The separate delivery figures for the three types of refrigerating machinery (domestic, industrial and commercial) make reasonably accurate distinction possible between fixed capital formation and consumers' expenditure on this item. Industrial plant and steelwork are almost entirely capital goods and there is a wide range of general mechanical engineering products which are virtually all intermediate goods. But it is very difficult to assess the amount of scientific instruments, electrical machinery, insulated wire and cables, radio and electronic goods, etc. which are capital as opposed to consumer or intermediate goods. Offices are furnished with carpets as well as with commodities identifiable as exclusively office furniture; carpets are also bought by hotels but are mostly consumer goods. The commodity flow method requires that these divisions be quantified. The commodity flow method also requires estimates of changes in dealers' stocks, of transactions in used assets and of the costs incurred in the purchase of capital goods after they leave the producer—such things as transport costs, dealers' margins, import and excise duties. For the most part these are difficult estimates to make. However, changes in producers' stocks do not present a problem where, as in this country, the commodity flows are mainly measured by delivery rather than by production figures.

The choice of methods depends upon the circumstances in which they are to be applied, particularly on what data are available. In countries which import most of their machinery, trade statistics provide much of the information required and the commodity flow method is more suitable than in countries such as the United Kingdom which largely manufacture their own capital goods. Ideally, of course, both methods would be used. Most countries use some combination of the two. In this country the expenditure method now predominates but is supplemented by the output approach in two categories of fixed capital formation for which expenditure figures are non-existent or not comprehensive, namely private dwellings and agriculture.

An overall estimate from production data is available for the United Kingdom for the year 1958[2]; it is 12 per cent higher than the expenditure-based estimate in the 1967 Blue Book of £3,492 million. The difference reflects the inclusion in the former estimate of small or short-lived assets and also of an estimated allowance for conversions and extensions to private dwellings, other than those which are grant-aided. The difference may also be due to errors in either or both estimates.

---

[2]G. Dean, 'Fixed Investment in Britain and Norway: An Experiment in International Comparison', *Journal of the Royal Statistical Society*, Series A (General), Volume 127, Part 1, 1964.

Censuses and inquiries by the Board of Trade

A description of the censuses of production and distribution, and the annual inquiries into the distributive and service industries by the Board of Trade is given in Appendix II. For manufacturing and the distributive and service industries the collection of data is now organised in a three-tier structure of inquiries. First, for all but certain service industries, a comprehensive or bench-mark inquiry is undertaken at intervals of about five years; secondly, a simple annual census or inquiry, usually on a sample basis, is carried out for the intervening years; and thirdly, information is collected either monthly or quarterly from a more limited number of businesses.

The quarterly inquiry was started by the Board of Trade in July 1955 and figures were collected from the first quarter of that year. The inquiry is on a voluntary basis and returns are collected mainly from the larger companies, which account for about two-thirds of the fixed capital formation of manu-facturing industry and rather more than one-third of that in the distributive and service industries. The results of the inquiry are published each quarter in the *Board of Trade Journal* and are also given in the *Monthly Digest of Statistics*.

The annual censuses and inquiries ask for separate details of capital expendi-ture on different types of asset, together with figures of proceeds from the sale of assets (other than normal trading sales). An extract from the census of pro-duction form for 1966 is given in Appendix II. The quarterly inquiries ask for the same information.

Returns from public corporations and public authorities

Most public corporations make quarterly returns of their transactions which include details of expenditure on fixed assets in the United Kingdom and proceeds from sales separately for each type of asset. Central government departments also submit quarterly returns analysing their income and expendi-ture in national accounting terms, which provide the necessary data for esti-mating fixed capital formation by industry and type of asset. The returns made by local authorities in respect of fixed capital formation comprise:

(a) returns of capital payments for the half-years ending in March and Sept-ember, which distinguish between all the main local authority services and between payments for different types of asset;

(b) from 1956 returns of capital payments for the quarters ending in June and December which give very limited service or asset detail.

These local authority returns provide no information on sales of fixed assets.

Published accounts for public corporations and public authorities

In addition to the special returns described above, annual information on fixed capital formation in the public sector is provided by published accounts. These accounts do not, however, give all the information required, and are available only after some delay. In particular, the published accounts do not provide the necessary breakdown of fixed capital formation by type of asset. Where in the published accounts of public corporations certain expenditure on renewals has been charged to revenue and not to capital account, the quarterly returns provide the information for the necessary adjustments. The *Appropriation Accounts* and *Trading Accounts and Balance Sheets* of the central government do not give the required detail which is provided separately by departments. *Local Government Financial Statistics* for local authorities in England and Wales and similar publications for Scotland and Northern Ireland are the main source of the financial year estimates of total expenditure on fixed capital formation by local authorities, and they are the only source of information on sales of fixed assets by local authorities. But in these accounts also some expenditure on renewals is charged direct to revenue instead of to capital account and adjustments need to be made to the published figures.

Estimates of building output

Quarterly estimates of building output in Great Britain have been made since 1955 by the Ministry of Public Building and Works from returns from a sample of contractors. The value of work done is divided for both the public and private sectors between housing, other new work, and repairs and maintenance. Private sector fixed capital formation in dwellings is not measured from expenditure statistics, mainly because of the difficulty and cost of tracing most of the purchasers and the estimates of building output for private sector dwellings are used as the main source of both the quarterly and annual estimates. In addition, the output estimates relating to public sector buildings are used as an indicator to assist in assessing short-term changes in fixed capital formation by local authorities in dwellings and other new buildings and works. It should be noted, however, that the coverage of the output figures for housing and other new work is not the same as that of expenditure on new buildings and works. The main differences arise because the asset analysis of expenditure is based on a distinction made by the purchaser of the asset, and because his expenditure covers items in addition to the output of the construction industry, such as the work done by architects and surveyors.

Published company accounts

The annual statements of accounts which public companies are required to lodge with the Registrar of Companies might appear to be a potential source of information about capital expenditure but are not in fact used. Capital expenditure on fixed assets is not stated directly in the company accounts but could be derived from the accounts by taking the increase in the written-down value of fixed assets *plus* the depreciation charged in the year; this should give total purchases, new and second-hand, *less* the book value of assets sold or scrapped. The results would however have several defects from the point of view of the national accounts: the absence of any distinction between types of asset, and differences in the definition of capital expenditure. In addition there are some further substantial difficulties:

(a) the accounts of most private companies were not lodged for public inspection until the Companies Act, 1967 came into operation;

(b) adjustments are required if there has been a revaluation of assets during the year;

(c) no distinction is made, as a rule, between domestic and overseas fixed assets;

(d) allowance must be made for newly consolidated subsidiaries;

(e) any industrial analysis would have to be in terms of enterprises, not establishments or business units.

ESTIMATES FOR INDIVIDUAL SECTORS

Private sector

The separate figures of fixed capital formation by the personal and company sectors are obtained by aggregating the relevant components within each industry and adding on the estimates of each sector's transactions in land and existing buildings. The individual industry components are not always separately identifiable, however, and sometimes they are estimated indirectly by reference to Inland Revenue data on incomes or depreciation allowances which distinguish between companies and unincorporated businesses. The sources of the personal and company sector estimates within each industry are described below.

From 1959 estimates for purchases *less* sales of land and existing buildings by companies are based on data collected by the Board of Trade in the course of the various inquiries into fixed capital formation (see above). Figures for industrial and commercial companies in the latest year are very rough. After identifying public sector transactions in land and existing buildings and estimating the total transfer costs of land and buildings, the figures for the personal sector are then derived as a residual, since transfers of land and buildings must net out when aggregated for the country as a whole to equal the legal and other costs involved in such transfers. The figures for the personal sector so obtained are subject to a large margin of error, particularly as the estimate of total transfer costs from which they are derived is unreliable. Sales exceed purchases and the full extent to which they do so is to some degree masked by the transfer costs which are involved in the buying and selling of existing, as opposed to new, houses which take place within the personal sector. Information is not available for the years before 1959 to separate transactions in land and existing buildings for the personal and company sectors. Rough estimates have been made, however, in order to provide figures of total fixed capital formation by these two sectors.

Public sector

The estimates of fixed capital formation by public corporations, central government and local authorities are obtained from the returns and accounts described on page 369. These returns and accounts provide information on transactions in land and existing buildings as well as on purchases and sales of other fixed assets.

ESTIMATES FOR INDIVIDUAL INDUSTRIES

In this section a more detailed description of the estimates for each industry is given. The industries are listed as far as possible in the order of the *Standard Industrial Classification, 1958*. The descriptions cover the analysis by type of asset and by institutional sector for each industry.

Agriculture

The estimates for vehicles are based on regular censuses of equipment in use on farms; cars are included. The estimates for machinery are made principally from statistics of imports and deliveries to the home market; tractors are included. New buildings and works includes farm ditching, drainage, water supply and soil improvement. The estimates are based almost entirely on government grants for such capital improvements and on periodic surveys of expenditure by farmers. Domestic premises are excluded; they are covered by the estimates for dwellings. Changes in the value of livestock and growing crops are excluded from fixed capital formation and are included in stocks and work in progress.

In line with the treatment of agriculture elsewhere in the accounts, private sector fixed capital formation by agriculture is attributed entirely to the personal sector, even though some is carried out by farming companies (see page 142).

Forestry

The estimates relate to roads, buildings and equipment; changes in the value of growing timber are included in work in progress. The sources are returns for the Forestry Commission and central government forestry in Northern Ireland. Nothing is included for private forestry.

Fishing

Figures of fixed capital formation are estimated annually by the Ministry of Agriculture, Fisheries and Food on the basis of returns collected from firms in the industry. A small proportion is allocated to the personal sector on the basis of very rough estimates of net output, relative to that of companies, based on Inland Revenue statistics of wages, salaries and profits.

Coal mining

The estimates cover capital expenditure in connection with deep-mined coal only. Fixed capital formation in connection with ancillary manufacturing activities is classified to manufacturing and opencast coal mining is classified to the construction industry in accordance with the *Standard Industrial Classification, 1958*. The source is the quarterly return of capital expenditure from the National Coal Board.

Other mining and quarrying

The source is the annual census of production, which gives figures of capital expenditure. A small proportion is allocated to the personal sector on the basis of very rough estimates of net output, relative to that of companies, based on Inland Revenue statistics of wages, salaries and profits.

Manufacturing

This covers fixed capital formation by both public and private sector enterprises classified to Orders III to XVI of the *Standard Industrial Classification, 1958*. It includes some expenditure by public enterprises whose main activities lie outside manufacturing, for example fixed capital formation in railway workshops and in coke ovens and brickworks owned by the National Coal Board. In addition to fixed capital formation at its own manufacturing establishments, expenditure by the central government allocated to manufacturing industries includes:

(a) Expenditure by the Board of Trade and Northern Ireland Ministry of Commerce on the erection of factory buildings for lease to private firms.

(b) Expenditure on capital assistance to contractors, including the purchase of imported machine tools intended for loan to contractors. These schemes are now of little significance, but were important during the years 1951 to 1953. Expenditure on factory building for lease to private firms by New Town Development Corporations is also included. Expenditure on buildings, plant and vehicles at naval dockyards and repair depots is excluded from fixed capital formation since it is part of expenditure on defence (see page 362).

There is a break in comparability between 1955 and 1956, when the unit of classification changes from the establishment, usually the individual factory or workshop, to the business unit (enterprise or part thereof). From the 1959 census of production onwards, returns have been made on a business unit basis which in general relates to the whole of a company or group of companies. The exceptions are that any subsidiary companies operating mainly overseas are excluded and that, where a firm is engaged in a number of quite different activities, separate returns are collected for each main activity. Capital expenditure in 1958 was estimated by the Board of Trade on both bases by substituting figures from firms which provided quarterly returns on a business unit basis during 1958 for their figures on an establishment basis returned in the census of production for that year. This indicated that for manufacturing as a whole capital expenditure was only about 4 per cent higher on the business unit basis, although for some industry groups expenditure was even higher (as much as 15 per cent in the case of food, drink and tobacco) and in a few industries the business unit estimate was lower[3]. The estimates for 1956 and 1957 are the result of *pro-rata* adjustments to estimates for establishments using the estimates for 1958 made on both bases.

The principal sources are the Board of Trade annual census of production and quarterly sample inquiry into capital expenditure. 1948 was the first year for which capital expenditure figures were collected in a census; for each subsequent year except 1950 the census has included similar questions; expenditure in 1950 was covered by a special sample inquiry. A description of the census and extracts from the 1966 census form are given in Appendix II. The quarterly sample inquiry was started by the Board of Trade in July 1955 and provides information from the first quarter of that year. Unlike the census, it is on a voluntary basis. Returns are collected mainly from the larger companies and cover about two-thirds of total fixed capital formation by manufacturing. The quarterly returns provide the basis for the latest annual estimates until the annual data become available. Expenditure by the public sector on factory buildings for lease to private industry is estimated from departmental returns and published accounts. It is allocated by industry using statistics of factory space completed.

In the detailed industry table of the Blue Book fixed capital formation in manufacturing is analysed by eighteen industry groups. The industrial analysis for the latest year, however, is less detailed, as are the quarterly estimates published in the *Board of Trade Journal* and the *Monthly Digest of Statistics*, because the quarterly returns on which it is based do not permit reliable estimates for smaller industrial groups until supplemented by the returns from other firms which are collected in the census of production. The statistics published quarterly in the *Board of Trade Journal* and in the *Monthly Digest of Statistics* include an analysis by type of asset for manufacturing as a whole.

The estimates for individual industries may have considerable margins of error when based on only a sample census of production, but the detailed results for private manufacturing are probably accurate in years when based on a full

---

[3]For further details see *The Report on the Censuses of Production for 1959, 1960, 1961 and 1962*, 1964.

census of production. The figures for years prior to 1958 are less reliable than those for later years. The basic data for 1949 and 1950 do not distinguish between the aircraft, motor vehicle and other vehicle industries. There may also be substantial errors in the analysis of government-financed expenditure which could significantly affect the estimates for 1948 and 1951 to 1953, particularly in the engineering, motor vehicle and aircraft industries.

The proportion of private investment allocated to the personal sector, indicated by rough estimates based on Inland Revenue data on depreciation allowances, has been taken as about 6 per cent in the early post-war years reducing to 2 per cent by 1964.

Construction

Fixed capital formation by building and civil engineering establishments of central government, local authorities, and public utilities such as the electricity boards are not included. Fixed capital formation in connection with opencast mining by the National Coal Board is included. There is a break in comparability in 1956 when the unit of classification changes from an establishment to a business unit basis but it is of little significance.

The main source is census of production figures of capital expenditure, supplemented for the latest year and for the years 1945 to 1950 for which census estimates are not available, by production data for civil engineering contractors' plant. Small firms employ about a third of the labour force and do not make returns for the census of production. The Board of Trade held special inquiries into the capital expenditure of small firms in 1958 and 1963 which serve as a basis for grossing up the figures for the larger firms in other years. Inevitably the estimates for small builders, and to a lesser extent for the industry as a whole, are subject to a substantial margin of error.

The proportion of private investment allocated to unincorporated businesses is based on Inland Revenue data on depreciation allowances; this was about 40 per cent in the early post-war years falling to 25 per cent by 1964.

Gas; Electricity

Initial expenditure on nuclear fuel elements for power stations is regarded as fixed capital formation in plant and machinery. Transmission lines and purchases of meters and appliances for hire are also included in plant and machinery. Gas mains are included under buildings and works. Quarterly returns of capital expenditure are supplied by the various boards.

Water

Expenditure on water mains is included under new buildings and works. Local authorities' fixed capital formation is estimated from the returns and published accounts described on page 369. The census of production is the source of the figures of fixed capital formation by companies.

Railways

Expenditure on fixed capital formation in railway manufacturing and repair establishments is excluded from this industry and included in the estimates for manufacturing. Certain renewals of works and structures, although charged to revenue in the published accounts of the relevant public corporations, have been included in fixed capital formation. Expenditure by nationalised transport undertakings on fixed capital formation in shipping is included here for the years prior to 1964; from that date, however, such expenditure (£4 million in 1964) is included under 'Shipping' in accordance with the *Standard Industrial Classification, 1958*. The sources of the estimates are quarterly returns provided by the relevant public corporations.

Road passenger transport

Local authority fixed capital formation is estimated from the returns and published accounts described on page 369. Public corporations (from 1963 the London Transport Board and the Transport Holding Company) submit quarterly returns of their capital expenditure distinguishing this and other industries. Private capital formation is estimated by the Board of Trade from capital expenditure returns as part of their inquiries into the distributive and service industries (see page 369); the first full inquiry into road passenger transport was for 1960. Taxi and private hire car businesses are included from 1960; in earlier years they are included under 'Other transport and services'. The estimates for buses in years prior to 1960 are based on registrations and average prices.

Shipping

Oil company fleets are included, but not that small proportion of ships which is used by industries other than the shipping industry itself, in particular fisheries. Fixed capital formation in shipping by nationalised transport undertakings is included from 1964; prior to that date it is included under 'Railways'. Progress payments on new ships are included, whether they are under construction at home or abroad.

From 1956 the estimates have been made by the Board of Trade from either annual or quarterly inquiries into the capital expenditure of shipping companies. The pre-1956 figures are based on the commodity flow method by adding imports and subtracting exports from estimates of home production. A full inquiry into capital expenditure by shipping companies was made for the year 1956 and quarterly figures were subsequently collected from a sample of roughly two-thirds of the industry. For 1956 the figures of expenditure on ships constructed or under construction in United Kingdom shipyards compared well with estimates of the value of work done on such ships from production data but thereafter they diverged widely. However, another full inquiry was made in 1960 and the coverage of the quarterly returns has been extended to the point where nearly all companies are included.

Harbours, docks and canals

Local authority expenditure is estimated from the returns and accounts described on page 369. Quarterly returns of capital expenditure are supplied by the British Transport Docks Board and the British Waterways Board. Expenditure by private companies is estimated by the Board of Trade from annual returns from a sample of companies. Estimates for private companies for years preceding 1956 are mere extrapolations of the later figures.

Air transport

British European Airways, British Overseas Airways Corporation and the British Airports Authority supply quarterly returns of their capital expenditure. The Board of Trade collects annual returns of capital expenditure from a sample of private companies. The Board of Trade provides quarterly figures of its expenditure on aerodromes and air navigation services and annual estimates of local authority expenditure. Central government expenditure on the development of prototype aircraft is not included; it is regarded as current expenditure.

Postal, telephone and radio communications

Quarterly returns of capital expenditure are supplied by the Post Office. Expenditure on rearranging telephones and wiring is treated as maintenance expenditure and not as fixed capital formation. Telephone cables and ducts are included under plant and machinery.

Wholesale distribution; Retail distribution; Insurance, banking and finance; Other transport and services

The figures for 'Wholesale distribution' cover Minimum List Headings 810, 831 and 832 in the *Standard Industrial Classification, 1958*. 'Retail distribution' covers Minimum List Heading 820, and 'Insurance, banking and finance' covers Order XXI. 'Other transport and services' comprises road haulage contracting (Minimum List Heading 703) and miscellaneous transport services and storage (Minimum List Heading 709); professional and scientific services (Order XXII) except for educational, medical and dental services (Minimum List Headings 872 and 874); and miscellaneous services (Order XXIII) including cinemas and theatres, hotels and restaurants, laundries and dry cleaners, garages and petrol stations, and head offices of industrial enterprises with mixed activities or activities mainly abroad. Up to and including 1959 taxi and private hire car businesses are included; from 1960 they are included under 'Road passenger transport'.

There is a break in comparability in 1956 on account of the change from an establishment to a business unit basis; the effect of this difference is the obverse of that in manufacturing, the business unit estimates for this group of industries in 1958 being less by about 7 per cent than they would be on an establishment basis.

The estimates for 1956 and subsequent periods have been made by the Board of Trade from returns of capital expenditure collected mainly from private businesses through various inquiries into particular industries, supported by quarterly returns from a panel of voluntary contributors. The estimates incorporate figures for the public sector collected by departments for the Central Statistical Office. Annual inquiries on a sample basis were started using, for lack of a more comprehensive register, a list of companies. These inquiries were developed where practicable by extending the coverage to unincorporated businesses: the inquiry for 1959, for example, covered all wholesalers; correspondingly the census of distribution for 1961 contained questions on capital expenditure. In these ways reliable estimates have become available for retail and wholesale distribution. Similarly, by extending the inquiry in particular years, reliable estimates for the motor trades, catering, and property companies have been obtained. The inquiries are described in Appendix II. Rather more than a third of total private fixed capital formation in this group of industries is covered by quarterly returns.

The difficulties in this field stem largely from two causes: first, many of the units are small and therefore, because their accounting is not so detailed, find it difficult to provide the right kind of information, particularly on a quarterly basis; second, there are wide variations in expenditure between one unit and another. It is on account of these difficulties in particular that separate estimates cannot yet be published for road haulage contracting; company investment is estimated by sampling but investment by unincorporated businesses, which is substantial, has been estimated roughly from initial and investment allowances, which are themselves estimated from total allowances by sampling. The estimates of fixed capital formation by unincorporated businesses represent about one-tenth of the total for 'Wholesale distribution', and one-fifth of the total for both 'Retail distribution' and 'Other transport and services'. The estimates of private sector fixed capital formation by 'Insurance, banking and finance' relate wholly to companies.

The pre-1956 estimates are based on the commodity flow method, except for public investment, for which expenditure figures are available. The sources of the pre-1956 estimates of private investment are:

(a) building—Ministry of Public Building and Works estimates of new non-industrial building work for private owners; until the end of 1951 monthly returns were made by contractors of the value of work done at each site on which a licensed or authorised job over £2,000 was proceeding; these returns were supplemented by quarterly and annual returns covering all jobs, returns which were maintained in a somewhat revised form when licensing ended in 1954 (see page 370);

(b) plant and machinery—extrapolations from the expenditure estimates for 1956 and subsequent years using production data;

(c) vehicles—extrapolations from the expenditure estimates for 1956 and subsequent years using a series of estimated total investment in road vehicles based on registrations and average prices *less* expenditure in other industries.

Quarterly figures for wholesale distribution, retail distribution, shipping, and other industries (construction, road passenger transport and other transport and services) are published quarterly in the *Board of Trade Journal* and in the *Monthly Digest of Statistics*; the statistics published include an analysis by type of asset.

Dwellings

Private sector fixed capital formation in dwellings is not measured from expenditure data because most of the purchasers are individuals who are difficult to trace and who, if they were traced, could not state their expenditure excluding land. There is, however, much statistical information about production. Statistics of the numbers of houses and flats started, completed and under construction are collected monthly by the Ministry of Housing and Local Government and Scottish Development Department and quarterly by the Ministry of Development, Northern Ireland from returns made by local authorities. They are published in the *Monthly Digest of Statistics*, partly on a monthly and partly on a quarterly basis. Quarterly estimates of building output in Great Britain have been made separately for public and private housing since 1955 by the Ministry of Public Building and Works from returns from a sample of contractors; they are published in the *Monthly Digest of Statistics*.

Since 1955 there have thus been two ways in which private fixed capital formation in new dwellings can be estimated: first, by adding to the figures of the value of output an allowance for expenditure in Northern Ireland, for expenditure on architects' and surveyors' fees, for the cost of irremoveable equipment not installed by builders and for expenditure by private housing associations; second, by converting the numbers of starts, completions and dwellings under

N

construction into an estimate of the numbers of equivalent completions in the period and multiplying by average prices per dwelling. The estimates for 1948 to 1954 are necessarily based on the latter method since separate figures of housing output were not collected until 1955; the average prices used were obtained from builders' site returns, a source which was lost when building licensing ended in 1954. Figures of average prices were then collected from building societies; these prices, however, include unknown amounts for land and no sound estimate is available of the average prices of the other new houses bought outright or financed by loans from insurance companies or banks. There are also difficulties in estimating equivalent completions for lack of detail as to the type of dwelling (whether four-bedroomed houses, five-storey flats, etc.). Although the value of output figures collected from builders provide a reasonably reliable measure of changes in private fixed capital formation they are difficult to use as a measure of the absolute level of fixed capital formation because the amounts which need to be added cannot be accurately determined. The solution adopted has been to estimate fixed capital formation in 1955 by reconciling estimates made by both methods and thereafter to extrapolate by the value of output series.

The Ministry of Housing and Local Government supplies figures of conversion and improvement grants made by local authorities, which cover half the cost of such work; the total cost of these conversions and improvements is included in private sector fixed capital formation. The cost of conversions and improvements which are not grant-aided cannot be measured at all accurately and is not included; expenditure by occupiers is included in consumers' expenditure along with other house repairs.

Annual figures of property companies' capital expenditure on new dwellings have been collected by the Board of Trade and are the sole source for the series for the fixed capital formation of companies in new dwellings.

Public sector fixed capital formation in dwellings is mainly by local authorities, both acting as housing authorities and in providing accommodation for certain staff such as police. Also included are expenditure on dwellings by New Town Development Corporations and certain other public corporations, central government expenditure on new married quarters for the Forces, and expenditure by the central government on dwellings built for civilian employees, for example prison staff. The estimates are mainly based on the sources described on page 369. The figures of output of new housing for the public sector, already mentioned, are used to estimate quarterly changes.

Universities, colleges, etc.

The whole of fixed capital formation under this heading falls within the personal sector, though most of it is financed by central government grants. Expenditure by colleges of advanced technology is included from April 1962 (£4 million in 1963); in earlier years it is covered by the estimates for 'Other education'. Expenditure on both new building work and plant and equipment is included. The estimates for Great Britain are based on quarterly returns provided by the University Grants Committee of expenditure financed by government grants, together with very rough estimates for expenditure financed from other sources. Estimates of expenditure by Queen's University, Belfast are derived from the *Appropriation Accounts* for Northern Ireland.

Other education

Expenditure on approved schools, remand homes and children's homes is included. Local authority expenditure is estimated from the sources described on page 369. Grant-aided private expenditure is estimated from grants paid by the education departments of the central government. Other private expenditure is assumed to be small and the estimates are little more than guesses.

Health services

The figures for expenditure by Regional Hospital Boards and other public authorities are obtained from returns from the authorities concerned (see page 369). Expenditure by doctors and dentists on equipment, including cars, is estimated from Inland Revenue depreciation allowances.

Local welfare services

This covers local authority expenditure on care of the aged, handicapped and homeless; the sources are described on page 369.

Roads, etc.

Expenditure on street lighting and car parks is included. The estimates cover expenditure on major road improvements but minor improvements are generally excluded. Purchases of road-making equipment by local authorities are included, but purchases by civil engineering contractors engaged in road works are included in the fixed capital formation of the construction industry. Local authority expenditure is estimated from the sources described on page 369. Central government expenditure covers trunk roads and motorways; the figures are taken from departmental returns.

Sewerage and land drainage

Local authority expenditure is estimated from the sources described on page 369. Expenditure by New Town Development Corporations is also included; it is estimated from their accounts. Expenditure on sewers is included under the heading 'New buildings and works'.

Other public services

The main items under this heading are: police, prisons, fire service, town and country planning, public buildings and central government office machinery. Local authority expenditure is estimated from the sources described on page 369. Central government expenditure is estimated from returns made by the government departments concerned.

Transfer costs of land and buildings

This covers stamp duties, legal fees, dealers' margins, agents' commissions, etc. incurred in connection with the transfer of ownership of land and buildings. Land development charges levied under the Town and Country Planning Acts, 1947 are included in the years 1948 to 1960. Figures for stamp duties are published by the Inland Revenue. The other transfer costs can be estimated only very roughly from the stamp duty figures and the scale of solicitors' fees.

REVALUATION OF FIXED CAPITAL FORMATION
AT CONSTANT PRICES

It is not possible to do more than indicate general trends in fixed capital formation at constant prices because of the well-known problems in measuring movements in the prices of capital goods. The main difficulties lie in the variable nature of capital goods; although some of them are of a fairly standard type, many are unique. The limited extent to which capital expenditure figures can be analysed by type of asset also restricts the accuracy of the revaluation. On the one hand it is difficult to revalue particular categories of capital goods and on the other it is difficult to identify expenditure on the particular categories even in those cases where a consistent measure of price changes is available. The price indices available have to be adapted for use in connection with the asset analysis which can be made of expenditure.

For vehicles, ships and aircraft five different indices compiled by the Board of Trade are used. These relate to cars, buses and coaches, other road vehicles, railway rolling stock and ships. There is no specific index for aircraft, and the index mentioned below for engineering capital goods is used. Since the available capital expenditure data do not usually distinguish one kind of road vehicle from another, the car component can be estimated only very roughly.

Fifteen different indices are used to deflate expenditure on plant and machinery. The indices are prepared by the Board of Trade by weighting indices for specific types of capital goods derived from returns of prices collected from producers. The commodity flow method is used to estimate the asset composition within total investment in plant and machinery for the years in which detailed statistics of production are available from the census of production, thus giving a set of weights for each industry, or group of industries, from which composite price indices can be constructed. The industry groups are as follows: agriculture; coal mining; other mining and quarrying; food, drink and tobacco; chemicals and allied industries; metal manufacture; vehicles; engineering and electrical goods, shipbuilding and marine engineering, metal goods not elsewhere specified; textiles, leather, leather goods and fur, clothing and footwear; paper, printing and publishing; other manufacturing; construction; electricity; postal, telephone and radio communications; distributive trades, insurance, banking and finance, professional and scientific services, miscellaneous services. It can be seen that there are some industries for which no specific index is available but apart from the gas industry their expenditure on plant and machinery is small.

The conceptual problems are particularly acute when attempting to revalue expenditure on building work at constant prices. The variable nature of the goods purchased renders the measurement of price changes extremely difficult, and in practice indices of changes in costs are used. The indices are constructed by combining with fixed weights an index of building materials prices, an index of labour costs, and an indicator of changes in overheads and profits. Labour costs are calculated from an index of earnings and an index of productivity which is based on the simple assumption that materials used per man is a measure of output per man. The indices are available only for the two large categories 'Dwellings' and 'Other new buildings and works'. Hence, in deflating the current price estimates for industry groups it has to be assumed that price movements are the same for all types of new construction other than dwellings; this limits the degree of industry detail in which constant price estimates can be given with any confidence. Similarly, for the sector of ownership estimates it has to be assumed that construction costs move in step for the public and the private sectors.

Only a very rough assessment can be made of price changes in transfer costs, apart from stamp duties. This is true also of land, which is a significant item in the sector estimates although it is not included in the industry estimates.

4. RELIABILITY

An attempt to assess the reliability of the annual estimates of fixed capital formation for each industry is made in the table below. The gradings relate to the later years, except for the most recent. The estimates for the most recent year are less reliable than those for previous years because they are based on incomplete data.

The estimates for public corporations, central government and local authorities, including those relating to purchases *less* sales of land and existing buildings, can each be regarded as within category A since they are based on direct returns and accounts with complete coverage. In total the private sector estimates are in category B, but the division between the company and personal sectors is approximate and the resulting estimates must therefore be regarded as in category C only. The estimates for transactions in land and existing buildings by these two sectors are particularly unreliable.

For both the industry and sector estimates the quarterly estimates are less reliable than the annual ones.

These reliability gradings do not take account of a factor which affects the accuracy of the short-term changes in the estimates, rather than the accuracy of their absolute values. Most of the estimates are expenditure figures and reflect amounts paid or charged to capital account; they may not correspond closely to the value of work done or deliveries. Normally expenditure is charged to capital account on receipt of a bill at some time after the actual work is done and this period of time can vary, particularly for buildings and for large projects like power stations. In these cases progress payments are usually made covering most of the work done but leaving a percentage of each stage to be paid for on completion, when there often remains a further amount outstanding to be agreed at a final settlement. The standard accounting period being a year, the final quarter's figure often reflects the attempt to settle accounts before the end of the accounting year. But any quarter's figure may be higher than another merely because it happens to include more progress payments or final settlements. Moreover, in some industries where the distinction between capital and current expenditure is not clear-cut substantial amounts of expenditure are not divided between capital and current spending until the end of the accounting year, when the whole capital amount is attributed to the final quarter. In so far as expenditure is regularly above average in the final quarter of an enterprise's accounting year, the seasonal adjustments which are calculated will allow for these fluctuations.

The estimates at constant prices are much less reliable than those at current prices because of the difficulties of revaluation of expenditure on fixed capital formation, discussed above. For a year three or four years away from the base year the estimate of total fixed capital formation at constant prices must be regarded as within category C.

Reliability of annual estimates of fixed capital formation at current prices[1]

A ± less than 3 per cent
B ± 3 per cent to 10 per cent
C ± more than 10 per cent

	Grading	Fixed capital formation at current prices, 1965 £ million
Agriculture	C	169
Forestry	B	3
Fishing	B	9
Coal mining	A	75
Other mining and quarrying	C	34
Manufacturing..............................	B	1,401
Construction	C	144
Gas	A	103
Electricity	A	654
Water	B	69
Railways	B	120
Road passenger transport	C	41
Shipping	A	100
Harbours, docks and canals	B	27
Air transport	A	65
Postal, telephone and radio communications	A	196
Wholesale distribution	B	146
Retail distribution...........................	B	235
Insurance, banking and finance	A	228
Other transport and services	C	363
Dwellings:		
Private	B	713
Public	A	572
Universities, colleges, etc.	B	78
Other education	B	199
Health services	B	101
Local welfare services........................	A	13
Roads, etc.	B	192
Sewerage and land drainage	A	80
Other public services	A	131
Transfer costs of land and buildings	C	58
Total gross fixed capital formation	B	6,319

[1]For the significance of the reliability gradings see pages 39 to 41.

5. CAPITAL CONSUMPTION AND CAPITAL STOCK

Official estimates of capital consumption and of the gross and net capital stock were first published in the 1956, 1964 and 1966 Blue Books respectively. It is convenient to consider them together because they are calculated jointly.

Concepts

The amount of fixed assets currently consumed in production cannot be measured directly, for it is primarily the services of fixed assets that are used up and their consumption is not observable. Moreover the measurement of capital consumption requires judgements about the timing of the services expected from capital. Most owners of fixed assets provide for depreciation in their accounts but these provisions are not suitable for the national accounts because generally they are based on original cost and take no account of changes in prices since the time of purchase; nor are they necessarily on a consistent basis between one enterprise and another as regards the periods over which assets are written off. For the national accounts depreciation, like other transactions, needs to be measured at current prices and, in the general absence of such measurement by enterprises themselves, it has to be specially estimated.

In order to make the estimates it is necessary to make broad assumptions about the expected lives of fixed assets and their pattern of utilisation. It is rarely feasible to take into account changes in expectation of life due to obsolescence. Obviously there are limits to the degree of detail in which the calculations can be made and to the amount of knowledge available centrally on lengths of life and the pattern of utilisation. Assets are assumed to render their services, and in this sense to be consumed, in equal amounts in each year of their life—the 'straight line' basis of depreciation. This will be a better approximation for some assets than for others. Clearly the estimates of capital consumption can only be rough; they are not likely to be much affected, however, by errors in the assumed lengths of life. If the length of life is underestimated capital consumption in respect of each relevant asset in a particular year will be overstated but the error is likely to be offset by the allowance for capital consumption being made in respect of too few assets.

Another source of error is the difficulty of measuring the current costs of replacing assets. Capital consumption should be valued at the cost of replacing capacity but so far it has only been possible to value it at the estimated cost of replacing existing fixed assets with identical assets. Consequently the capital consumption estimates fail to allow for technological change.

The estimates of capital consumption can be deducted from the estimates of gross fixed capital formation to give estimates of net fixed capital formation.

Net fixed capital formation, like gross fixed capital formation, reflects the two-dimensional nature of capital—quantity and future life—and neither gross nor net fixed capital formation measures the change in annual productive capacity. Future research may improve knowledge of the length of life of assets, the pattern of their utilisation and their replacement costs. The general method described below, however, appears to be the best way of making comprehensive estimates from the information at present available.

The capital stock comprises investments from many past years and consequently consists of assets which vary in age, in the intensity with which they have been used and the extent to which they have become obsolete. In aggregating the assets of which the stock of capital is composed these disparities ought to be taken into account; it has not so far proved possible to do so in a way relevant to the measurement of capital as a factor of production, which is the main aim of the national accounts estimates. Assets become less valuable as the stock of unexpired services which they represent diminishes but any decline in productivity with age would rarely correspond to this decline in value. In view of this, estimates of the capital stock net of accrued capital consumption are not published for particular industries. Net capital stock estimates are made for sectors, however, and constitute that part of sector balance sheets relating to reproducible fixed assets, for which valuation at written-down replacement cost is a suitable approximation to market value. For the reasons given above in respect of capital consumption, neither the gross nor net capital stock estimates make any allowance for technological change.

Methods of calculation

The method used for estimating both capital consumption and the gross capital stock is mainly the perpetual inventory method first applied to United Kingdom data by Redfern[4]. The official estimates are a development of those made by Redfern and by Dean[5]. The calculations are described in detail in the papers by these authors.

The perpetual inventory method of calculation is as follows. Estimates or assumptions are made about the average length of life of each class of asset separately distinguished. Gross fixed capital formation is then estimated for each class of asset for L years prior to Y, where L is the average life of the class of asset in question and Y is the year for which capital consumption and the gross stock are to be estimated. Price indices are applied to these estimates to convert them to constant prices. The estimates at constant prices are then aggregated for L years to obtain the estimate of the capital stock. Division of the capital stock by L gives the estimate of capital consumption at constant prices. The price indices are then used to convert to whatever price basis is required; for example current prices in year Y for capital consumption.

The estimates of net capital stock (capital stock *less* accrued capital consumption) are also first calculated at constant prices and then converted to current prices. The net capital stock at the end of 1958 was estimated at constant prices for the various industries and the resulting total capital stock was then analysed by sector. These base-year estimates were then projected to earlier and later years by estimates of net fixed capital formation by sector at constant prices. The resulting estimates are converted to current prices to obtain estimates at current replacement cost.

The published tables

Capital consumption is analysed by type of asset at both current and constant prices (Table 61 of the 1967 Blue Book), and by institutional sector at current prices (Table 62 of the 1967 Blue Book). The corresponding estimates of net fixed capital formation (gross fixed capital formation *less* capital consumption) are also shown (Tables 63 and 64 of the 1967 Blue Book).

---

[4]P. Redfern, 'Net investment in Fixed Assets in the United Kingdom, 1938-1953', *Journal of the Royal Statistical Society*, Series A (General), Volume 118, Part 2, 1955.

[5]G. Dean, 'The Stock of Fixed Capital in the United Kingdom in 1961', *Journal of the Royal Statistical Society*, Series A (General), Volume 127, Part 3, 1964.

Capital consumption is also deducted from gross national product (in Tables 1 and 14) to arrive at an estimate of national income or net national product. It should be noted that there are certain items of imputed income in gross national product with which the estimates of capital consumption at current prices are not strictly comparable. These items are the gross incomes imputed to the central government and to local authorities in respect of (a) non-trading properties (offices, schools, etc.) owned by them and (b) those trading activities for which the deficiency is treated as a subsidy (for example housing) or for which the surplus is treated as a tax on expenditure (the Post Office until March 1956). The imputed incomes in these cases are represented either by the loan charges payable on the assets or by an amount based on the rateable value of the assets. In neither case are the imputations comparable with the corresponding figures of capital consumption which are based on the current cost of replacing the existing assets. For comparability with the figures of capital consumption, some addition should be made to these imputed incomes, which would have the effect of slightly increasing the national income. Also, in general no income is imputed in the accounts in respect of non-trading assets, other than buildings, owned and used by public authorities, although these assets are covered by the estimates of capital consumption; the amounts involved are relatively small. No attempt is made to adjust the figures in the national accounts for these inconsistencies.

Net capital stock at current replacement cost is analysed by sector and type of asset (Table 65 of the 1967 Blue Book). The total gross capital stock at constant replacement cost is analysed by twenty-six industries and by five types of asset (Table 66 of the 1967 Blue Book). In addition, separate figures for buildings and for plant and machinery are given for eight industrial groups comprising manufacturing excluding textiles, for construction, and for distribution and other services (Table 67 of the 1967 Blue Book). The estimates of capital stock relate to the end of the year.

Estimates of depreciation are also given in the notes at the end of the Blue Book. These figures cannot be used in conjunction with the statistics of gross fixed capital formation because, with few exceptions, they are based on the original cost of the assets concerned. As pointed out above, such estimates are not appropriate to national income measurement. The depreciation allowances for unincorporated businesses, companies and, up to 1964, local authorities are the statutory allowances for income tax, including investment allowances; the allowances are described in the annex to this chapter. These depreciation allowances are significant in the national accounting context because taxes on income have been levied on the basis of the net profits after deducting these allowances; they may differ from the depreciation provisions shown in the enterprises' own accounts and they are subject to substantial changes from year to year due to changes in the rates of allowance. Figures for the two latest years are subject to amendment. The figures for public corporations and the central government are the sum of the depreciation provisions shown in the published trading accounts *plus* estimates of the renewals of certain fixed assets that were charged to revenue in some of these accounts.

Statistical sources

From 1948 the estimates of fixed capital formation used in the perpetual inventory are the latest estimates made for the national accounts. Estimates for the earlier part of the period were last published in the 1963 Blue Book.

N*

The principal sources for years before 1948 are:
   (a) capital expenditure statistics for local authorities and public utilities;
   (b) estimates of capital expenditure in manufacturing and construction, distribution and other services prepared by the Department of Applied Economics of Cambridge University[6]; these estimates are based on samples of company accounts;
   (c) Dean's projections of (b) back into the nineteenth century;
   (d) Dean's estimates of fixed capital formation in the second world war;
   (e) statistics of the number of houses built for private owners.

Since the publication of Dean's paper separate estimates have been made for 'Timber, furniture, etc.' and 'Construction'. Estimates of fixed capital formation prior to 1948 do not distinguish between these two industries and the division of the capital stock in 1948 has been made on the basis of indirect evidence on the relative importance of the two industries and is very rough. However, by the end of 1966 investment prior to 1948 accounted for only about 30 per cent of the capital stock for 'Timber, furniture, etc.' and some 10 per cent for 'Construction'.

The price indices for the years before 1948 are as described in Redfern's paper, except for plant and machinery in manufacturing and construction, distribution and other services, for which an index from Feinstein's monograph is used; this index was constructed by averaging engineering wage rates and the cost of materials. The price indices for years from 1948 are those used in estimating fixed capital formation at constant prices, which are described in Section 3 above.

Lengths of life

The average lives are intended to take into account accidental damage by fire or other causes. Assets destroyed in the war are eliminated so far as possible from the capital stock.

For manufacturing, construction, distribution and other services, the average lives used in the calculation of the capital stock and of capital consumption are those estimated by Dean from the gross stock estimates for 1938 in Feinstein's monograph and the estimates of fixed capital formation in years prior to 1939 referred to above. The average life estimated for buildings is 80 years; for five groups of plant and machinery the estimated average lives are 16, 19, 25, 34 and 50 years respectively. The basis of these estimated average lives and their relationship to those implied by Inland Revenue depreciation allowances are described in Dean's paper. Except for textiles, the estimates of the gross capital stock obtained using these average lives compare reasonably closely with Barna's direct estimates based on fire insurance values[7]. Only rough estimates have so far been made for textiles which has therefore been included in the residual group 'Other industries'. For dwellings an average life of 100 years is assumed. For coal mining, gas, electricity, railways and the Post Office the lengths of life assumed are generally those employed by the undertakings concerned in estimating depreciation for their own accounts. An assumed life of 100 years is used for railway track, buildings and works, for which no provision for depreciation is made in the railways' accounts. An estimated life of 40 years is used for mine-workings.

---

[6]C. H. Feinstein, *Domestic Capital Formation in the United Kingdom 1920-1938*, Cambridge University Press, 1965.

[7]T. Barna, 'The Replacement Cost of Fixed Assets in British Manufacturing Industry in 1955', *Journal of the Royal Statistical Society*, Series A (General), Volume 120, Part 1, 1957.

Some roadwork lasts indefinitely and does not depreciate, while some needs to be renewed periodically. In the national accounts, however, nothing is included for roads in the estimates of capital consumption. Since no imputation for the use of roads is made in measuring the gross national product (see page 267) no deduction is made for depreciation of roads in estimating the national income

Reliability

The capital consumption estimates may all be regarded as falling within category C of the gradings described on pages 39 to 41, that is as having a margin of error of more than 10 per cent. For the grading of the capital stock estimates it is useful to extend the three categories generally used in this volume, for while most of the estimates may be classified to category C, some of them are much less reliable than others. A further limit at 20 per cent is therefore used; category C is limited to errors of up to 20 per cent and a fourth category, D, is used for errors of more than 20 per cent.

Reliability of estimates of gross capital stock at constant replacement cost[1]

A ± less than 3 per cent
B ± 3 to 10 per cent
C ± 10 to 20 per cent
D ± more than 20 per cent

	Grading	Gross capital stock at 1958 replacement cost at end 1966 £ thousand million
Agricultural plant and machinery	B	0·8
Mining and quarrying	D	1·5
Manufacturing, excluding textiles	B	22·9
Construction	C	1·3
Gas	C	1·3
Electricity	C	7·0
Water	D	2·3
Railways	D	5·5
Road passenger transport	C	0·4
Shipping	B	2·5
Harbours, docks and canals	D	1·0
Air transport	C	0·6
Postal, telephone and radio communications	C	2·4
Distribution and other services.................	D	11·8
Private dwellings	D	21·5
Public dwellings	C	10·8
Roads[2]	D	2·5
Other public and social services	C	7·1
Other industries..............................	D	4·5
Total gross capital stock	C	107·7

[1]For the significance of the reliability gradings see pages 39 to 41.
[2]Excluding the non-renewable element more than 75 years old.

ANNEX

INLAND REVENUE DEPRECIATION ALLOWANCES

For the purposes of income tax, corporation tax and, previously, profits tax, there is a system of allowances for capital expenditure on a number of classes of fixed assets incurred in a trade or business or in connection with agriculture or forestry. The qualifying assets include plant and machinery, vehicles (including ships and aircraft) and industrial buildings, but exclude dwellings, commercial buildings, such as hotels, shops and offices, and non-trading assets of the government and local authorities. But from 1965/66 there are no allowances in respect of local authorities' trading assets because local authorities ceased to be liable to income tax and are not charged to corporation tax. The system which applies to expenditure incurred on or after 17 January 1966 provides for:

(a) An initial allowance at a specified percentage of the cost of the asset for the year in which the expenditure is incurred, that is becomes payable. The initial allowance is not given when a relevant grant is paid for expenditure under one or other of the several schemes providing for the payment of investment grants.

(b) Annual writing-down allowances which are given until these, together with any initial allowance, have completely written off the original cost of the asset *less* any relevant grant or until the asset is sold or ceases to be used in the trade. For industrial buildings, the allowance is normally at the rate of 4 per cent of the cost of construction (2 per cent for expenditure incurred on or before 5 November 1962). For plant and machinery, the allowance is normally given by the reducing-balance method at a rate of either 15, 20 or 25 per cent of the written-down value. For expenditure incurred on or before 5 November 1962 the writing-down allowances vary according to the type of plant concerned.

(c) A final balancing allowance or balancing charge to adjust the total of initial and writing-down allowances to agree with the cost of the asset to the taxpayer *less* the proceeds of its resale.

For expenditure incurred before 17 January 1966, the system also provided for investment allowances which were given, at a specified percentage of the cost of the asset, *in addition* to the other depreciation allowances for the year in which the expenditure was incurred.

Under the scheme for free depreciation, which operated during the period from 3 April 1963 to 16 January 1966, a trader could take what writing-down allowance he chose in respect of expenditure incurred on plant and machinery used for industrial purposes in specified development districts. Free depreciation in respect of expenditure incurred on ships was introduced from 6 April 1965 and continued to be available after 16 January 1966.

The following table gives the rates of initial and investment allowances from 7 April 1954 to 5 April 1968 for industrial buildings and most plant, machinery and vehicles. There are other rates which apply, for example to new ships, new mining work, and scientific research assets.

Rates of initial and investment allowances

Percentage

Date expenditure incurred	Industrial buildings		Plant, machinery and vehicles	
	Initial allowance	Investment allowance	Initial allowance	Investment allowance [1]
7 April 1954 to 17 February 1956	—	10	20[2]	20
18 February 1956 to 14 April 1958	10	—	20	—
15 April 1958 to 7 April 1959	15	—	30	—
8 April 1959 to 5 November 1962	5	10	10[3][4]	20
6 November 1962 to 16 January 1966	5	15	10	30
17 January 1966 to 5 April 1968....	15	—	30[5]	—

[1]Not on ordinary motor cars.
[2]On private cars and second-hand plant only.
[3]30 per cent on private cars and second-hand plant.
[4]Restricted after 16 April 1961 for cars costing more than £2,000.
[5]Where no investment grant.

Chapter XIII

Capital Formation in Stocks and Work in Progress

1. CONCEPTS

Two classes of assets are distinguished in the estimates of capital formation. First, physical productive assets which yield a continuous service beyond the period of account in which they are purchased; these assets are termed fixed assets and are dealt with in the preceding chapter. Secondly, assets for use in future production, which can be used only once, and goods awaiting purchase which constitute stocks and work in progress. Typical examples are coal awaiting consumption, goods awaiting sale in shops and factories and partly finished products awaiting completion in factories. Both stocks and work in progress are to be regarded as included in the term stocks, which is used throughout this chapter for the sake of brevity.

With the exception noted below, the stocks taken into account here are limited to those which are held by trading enterprises and entered as assets in their balance sheets, so that increases in such stocks are added to receipts from sales in arriving at figures of trading profits. Expenditure incurred by persons, and by the non-trading branches of the central government and local authorities in increasing the quantities of goods they hold, is treated as consumers' expenditure or as current expenditure of public authorities. These conventions are adopted on grounds of convenience rather than of principle; it would be quite impracticable to attempt to measure changes in household stocks of durable or other consumer goods, and estimates of changes in public authorities' stocks in such commodities as paper or road-making materials cannot be derived from the accounting records normally kept.

The exception to this rule is expenditure by the central government on building up stocks of food and raw materials for strategic reasons, which is here treated as capital formation in stocks. Also, for the years before 1953, sales of surplus government stores located in the United Kingdom were treated as negative capital formation because of their importance and special nature. These stores accumulated during the war were mostly sold by the end of 1952, and subsequent sales of government stores are treated as an offsetting item to central government current expenditure on goods and services, which includes purchases of stores.

A difficulty arises in the treatment of stocks held abroad. For consistency with the definition of company profits, capital formation in stocks should include all changes in stocks held by businesses operating in the United Kingdom whose profits are included in domestic factor incomes, including changes in stocks which they hold abroad. Changes in stocks held by businesses operating overseas should be excluded, their profits being part of net profit income from abroad and any change in their stocks being part of net investment abroad. The figures of stock changes are collected on this basis, but this leads to an inconsistency with the balance of payments statistics where imports are normally

390

recorded, not when the change of ownership occurs, but when they enter the United Kingdom. Where stocks held abroad are eventually imported the inconsistency is one of timing, but where a business holds stocks abroad permanently the inconsistency between changes in stocks and imports remains uncorrected. Although inconsistencies of timing, which are further discussed at the end of this section, may sometimes be significant, particularly in the quarterly accounts, the long-term discrepancy between changes in stocks and imports is not thought to be serious, since one would not expect businesses operating mainly in the United Kingdom to engage in substantial stockbuilding overseas.

The valuation of stock changes

The appropriate valuation of stock changes gives rise to both conceptual and practical problems. In times of rising prices commercial accounting data, from which most of the available statistics of stock changes are derived, record greater investment in stocks, and correspondingly greater profits, than seems justifiable on the principles adopted for national income accounting; in times of falling prices, commercial accounting methods show lower investment in stocks and lower profits. A method of adjusting the accounting data is therefore adopted for the measurement of national income and expenditure; this adjustment requires an equal subtraction—described as stock appreciation—from accounting figures of profits and from the change in the book value of stocks when prices are generally rising, and an addition when prices are generally falling. The origin of the problem, and the method of dealing with it are described in general terms in the following paragraphs. A more detailed account of the method of statistical adjustment is given in Section 4 of this chapter.

The national income has been described in Chapter I as the resources available for consumption or adding to wealth. Part of this addition to wealth may consist of an increase in stocks and work in progress, but the essential feature of stock changes is that they represent uncompleted and unrealised transactions. Thus, in contrast to the valuation of most other final expenditures, which can be valued at the prices at which those goods and services are sold, the method of valuing stock changes must within certain limits be a rather arbitrary process.

The problem may be put another way. The trading surplus of a manufacturing enterprise is its receipts from sales *less* its operating costs. The problem then is how that part of its operating costs which represents materials used should be valued. Again, the valuation must be arbitrary because the use of materials is not in itself an actual market transaction. The internal transfer of materials from stock into the manufacturing process is a notional transaction, the valuation of which affects the measurement of the trading surplus or profits and the measurement of the change in stocks.

These two questions—the valuation of materials used which affects profits, and the valuation of the change in stocks—must be answered consistently. The problem of valuing these imputed transactions is common to both commercial accounting and the measurement of national income and expenditure. For either purpose, the solution must be to some extent arbitrary.

Accounting valuations and national income concepts

It is thought that the solution most commonly adopted for commercial accounting is to value the stock of unused materials and work in progress at cost or realisable value, whichever is the lower. The stock is deemed to consist of the most recent acquisitions, since it is assumed that materials are used in the order of their acquisition on the 'first in, first out' or FIFO convention. Thus, the value of materials charged to operating account is their original cost of acquisition *plus*, when prices are falling, the loss arising on unused materials between the time of acquisition and the time of their valuation at current prices. It is not of course necessary explicitly to put a valuation on each unit of material used; the same result is reached by reckoning profits as receipts from sales *less* actual expenditure *plus* the closing stocks valued at cost or realisable value, whichever is lower, *less* the opening stocks valued at cost or realisable value, whichever is lower. The closing stocks may be regarded as an imputed sale to the following period of account, the opening stocks as an imputed purchase from the preceding period of account.

The effect of this method of commercial accounting is that when prices are rising operating costs attributed to materials used in production in a period are less than the average costs of replacing during the period the quantity of materials used. When prices are falling the converse is true but in addition, by valuing the stock of unused materials at realisable value which will be lower than original cost, the contribution of materials to operating costs is further increased above the average costs of replacing the quantity of materials used.

For national accounting purposes it is appropriate, because it is generally more consistent with the valuation of all transactions (actual and imputed) at the prices current in the period of account, to treat as a current cost all expenditure required to maintain intact the physical quantity of stocks. Hence the internal or imputed transactions of using materials should for national accounting purposes be valued at the current, or replacement, prices; this implies that profits should be the excess of receipts from sales over operating costs, valuing the materials incorporated in the sales at replacement prices. Profits should be recorded after charging to operating account the replacement cost of maintaining intact the physical quantity of stocks. By contrast, in systems of commercial accounting, what is charged to operating account is usually the cost of maintaining intact the money value of stocks.

In the national accounts, every change in stocks throughout a period should strictly be valued at current replacement prices to match a corresponding valuation at current replacement prices of materials used; changes in the value of stocks would then reflect only changes in physical quantities. That part of any rise in assets shown by commercial accounting which reflects a rise in the prices at which stocks are valued should be regarded from the point of view of national income accounting as a capital gain—an imputed and unrealised capital gain—not as income. Conversely, when prices are falling the loss on stock values, which is part of trading losses in commercial accounting, should be treated for national accounting purposes not as an offset to income, but as an imputed capital loss.

As mentioned in Chapter II, the valuation of total stocks held at the beginning and end of the period of account for national and sector balance sheets should theoretically be made at replacement prices. Stocks revalued at replacement prices are likely to be equivalent to stocks at book values when prices are falling, but the two will usually differ when prices are rising. The extent of this difference depends upon the extent to which prices are rising and the period for which stocks are held. The difference is unlikely to be large, however, and would normally be well within the margin of error in the estimates of the book value figures.

Method of adjustment

It follows from the objectives of the national accounts set out above that, in an ideal system of accounts, the internal transactions occurring when materials are used in production and when goods are finished and transferred temporarily to stock, would be valued at the prices current at the time of use or transfer. If all such internal transactions could be recorded, all additions to, and withdrawals from, stock would be accounted for as they occurred, and the need for valuing stocks at a point in time would not arise in compiling the accounts of transactions.

In practice, of course, the information does not exist from which estimates on these principles could be compiled. An indirect approach must therefore be made by seeking to measure the physical change in stocks, using chiefly the data relating to the accounting values of stocks at the beginning and end of a period of time. The method adopted in the United Kingdom—similar methods are used in other countries facing the same statistical problem—is to revalue the accounting figures of both opening and closing stocks, by the use of price indices, at the average market prices of the period. The difference between the revalued opening and closing stocks is then treated as the net investment in stocks at current prices for national accounting purposes.

It must be emphasised that this method of adjustment does not give the same result as would a complete revaluation at replacement prices of materials added to, or withdrawn from, stock. It would give a close approximation if the quantity of stocks held rose or fell at a uniform rate throughout the period. The difference arises from the fact that the simple average of prices during a period is unlikely to be the same as an average of, say, daily prices weighted by the increments or decrements in stocks of each day. The method outlined, however, seems to be the nearest practicable approach to the result that would be secured if the imputed transaction of transferring materials from or to stock were to be valued at the replacement prices current at the time. The use of quarterly data relating to stocks which are now widely available gives a rather better approximation to the theoretically ideal basis than was possible when annual data only were available.

The difference between investment in stocks, or the value of the change in the physical quantity of the stocks, measured in this way, and the value of the change in stocks shown by the accounting data, is the amount of stock appreciation, which may be positive or negative. The statistical methods employed for the revaluation are described in more detail in Section 4 of this chapter.

Consistency with other forms of national expenditure

The problem of securing consistency of data is particularly acute in connection with statistics of stocks. The basic information about stock changes is obtained from what are essentially accounting data and relates to the change in the value of stocks consistent with the estimates of trading profits. The statistics may be complete and accurate, but recorded at a different stage of distribution, or at a different time, from the statistics of other forms of national expenditure. For instance, estimates of consumers' expenditure are sometimes derived, not from data referring directly to consumers' retail purchases, but from statistics of supplies available as shown by production and import data; they do not therefore take account of changes in stocks at all points in the chain of distribution. Hence an increase in supplies of a particular commodity may appear in the estimates of national expenditure as a rise in consumers' expenditure and also be double-counted as a rise in distributors' stocks.

The problem of consistency also arises in connection with the recording of imports and exports. As mentioned at the beginning of this section, imports and exports are recorded in the balance of payments statistics when they enter and leave the United Kingdom and this leads to inconsistency with the statistics of stocks, which include changes in stocks on the basis of ownership. Stocks acquired abroad by businesses operating mainly in the United Kingdom will be included in imports only when they enter the United Kingdom. For example, annual crops such as tobacco may be bought and included in stocks at the time of auction but imported into the United Kingdom throughout the year as they are required. At times when the level of imports (or exports) is changing rapidly there may well be very substantial inconsistency between imports (or exports) and the stocks estimates. Some conjectural adjustments are made for obvious known cases of inconsistency although precise correction is impracticable. For example, an adjustment is included in the stockbuiding of 'Other industries' in the second and third quarters of 1966 to allow for goods for export held up at the docks by the seamen's strike. The goods were excluded from manufacturers' stocks some time before they were included in exports, and the unusual delay had a significant effect on the consistency of the quarterly figures.

A further instance of the way in which the difficulty of achieving consistency may arise is in the manufacture of goods with long periods of production. Usually the purchaser of such goods makes progress payments to the manufacturer during the course of production, and this expenditure is recorded as fixed capital formation by the purchasing industry or, in the case of equipment for military defence, as current expenditure on goods and services by public authorities. It is not generally possible, however, to collect from producers data on the value of the work in progress after deducting progress payments received from customers and including progress payments made to sub-contractors and out-workers. Where these transactions are of particular importance, therefore, as in shipbuilding and construction, special estimates are made which attempt to achieve consistency. These are described in Section 3 of this chapter.

2. THE PUBLISHED TABLES

ANNUAL TABLES

The annual tables which relate specifically to stocks show analyses of stock changes and of the total book value of stocks held at the end of the most recent year by industry and by sector. In the case of manufacturing stocks, there is also a breakdown by type of asset, that is materials and fuel, work in progress and finished products.

Analysis by industry

The classification by industry is based on the *Standard Industrial Classification, 1958*. The analysis by industry is given in three tables of the Blue Book (Tables 68 to 70 of the 1967 Blue Book), the first of which shows both the book value of the stocks held at the end of the most recent year, and the annual changes in book value for the following industrial groups: (a) agriculture; (b) forestry; (c) mining and quarrying; (d) manufacturing—(i) food, drink and tobacco,

(ii) chemicals and allied industries, (iii) metal manufacture, (iv) engineering, shipbuilding and vehicles, (v) textiles, leather and clothing, (vi) other manufacturing; (e) gas, electricity and water; (f) retail distribution; (g) wholesale, distribution (from 1957 only)—(i) wholesale distributors, (ii) dealers in coal, industrial materials and machinery; (h) other industries (including wholesale distribution for years up to 1956)—included here are estimates which cover construction, transport and communication, and miscellaneous services; details of the composition of these estimates are given on pages 399 and 400; and (j) central government—these estimates cover (i) those central government trading bodies not included with their appropriate industries and (ii) strategic stocks; the coverage is described on page 400.

The table includes one overall estimate for stock appreciation, which is that part of the change in the book value of stocks which arises from increases in the prices at which stocks are valued. The estimate is not shown separately for each industry because of the uncertainty of the figures, although industry estimates are implied by the difference between the figures of the change in the book value and the value of the physical increase for each industry.

The two other tables show estimates of changes in the physical quantity of stocks, measured at current prices and at constant prices. From 1956 onwards these figures are given separately for the manufacturing industries listed above and for retail distribution; figures for wholesale distribution are shown from 1957 onwards. Estimates for all the remaining industries combined are also given. Figures for years prior to 1956 have been published only for total manufacturing and all other industries combined.

From 1956 estimates for manufacturing, retail and wholesale distribution are on a business unit basis; the estimates for earlier years are on an establishment basis, although the difference is of little importance in the case of retail distribution. The business unit generally relates to the whole of a company or group of companies, but where a firm is engaged in a number of different activities separate returns are collected for each main activity. Thus where a company is engaged in both retailing and other activities it would make separate returns for its retail stocks if retail distribution is a distinguishable part of its operations. Classification by the business unit rather than the establishment nevertheless increases the stocks classified as held by manufacturing industry rather than wholesalers or retailers and brings within the scope of the figures stocks not held at establishments in the United Kingdom, but held abroad or afloat.

It should be noted that the analysis of manufacturing stocks by type of asset is an economic rather than a commodity classification. It relates to the classification of the status of stocks in the business of the stockholder. The same kind of items may be reported as finished products by one manufacturer but as materials by another, and the aggregate of the figures for both materials and fuel and for finished products, as well as that for work in progress, contains a high proportion of intermediate goods.

Analysis by sector

One table (Table 71 of the 1967 Blue Book) shows the change in book value, the stock appreciation and the value of the physical increase for the stocks of each sector. An estimate is also given of the total book value of the stocks held at the end of the most recent year by these sectors, that is by the personal sector, companies, public corporations and the central government.

The estimates of stocks held by the personal sector represent exclusively stocks held for business purposes by farmers, professional persons and other sole traders and partnerships.

The changes in stocks held by public corporations do not include transfers of stocks resulting from the acquisition or re-acquisition of undertakings. The figures for the central government relate to the stocks of all the trading bodies listed on page 296 and to stocks purchased under the strategic stockpiling programme.

Although the trading enterprises of local authorities must hold some stocks, no information relating to them is included in *Local Government Financial Statistics* and they are assumed to be sufficiently small to be ignored.

QUARTERLY TABLES

Quarterly estimates of changes in the value of the physical increase in stocks are published quarterly in *Economic Trends* and each month in the *Monthly Digest of Statistics*. In the *Monthly Digest of Statistics* the estimates are given both at current prices and at constant prices seasonally adjusted in respect of manufacturing industry, retail distribution, wholesale distribution and other industries. The estimates for manufacturing industry are shown separately for the industries listed above and are also subdivided by type of asset. The figures for manufacturing and the distributive trades are first published each quarter in the *Board of Trade Journal*. Estimates of the book value of stocks held are also given in this table for each category separately distinguished. The table published in *Economic Trends* shows four industry groups only—manufacturing, retail distribution, wholesale distribution and all other industries—with no analysis by type of asset, but the constant price series before seasonal adjustment for each of these industry groups is also given and the series (apart from the separation of the distributive trades) have been published from 1955.

Quarterly estimates of total stock appreciation, to which no seasonal adjustment is made are also published quarterly in *Economic Trends* and in the *Monthly Digest of Statistics*. This series also has been published from 1955.

Quarterly estimates of changes in the book value of stocks by sector are included in the tables published in *Financial Statistics*. Estimates for the personal sector, companies, public corporations and central government are given in their respective capital accounts.

3. STATISTICAL SOURCES

Until the results of the first post-war census of production for 1948 became available, it was impossible to attempt to build up brick by brick an estimate of the total change in the value of stocks. Although there was always a certain amount of fragmentary information about particular categories of stocks, serving to some extent as a check on the total, the change in total stocks was necessarily obtained as a residue. For 1948 onwards, however, the estimates have been derived from information relating to each significant stockbuilding industry. The sources of the book value figures for individual industries are described below.

ESTIMATES FOR INDIVIDUAL SECTORS

The analysis by sector has been obtained by subdividing between the different sectors each of the items in the analysis by industry, and aggregating the results in order to obtain sector totals. The estimates for public corporations are derived from quarterly returns of their transactions made by the main corporations and from their published annual accounts. Changes in stocks held by the central government are estimated from published accounts and quarterly returns made by the appropriate departments. The division of the increase in the value of stocks of private enterprises between companies on the one hand and unincorporated businesses on the other is in most cases based on estimates of the relative net outputs of companies and unincorporated enterprises; for this purpose the ratio of wages, salaries and profits for companies to the corresponding sum for unincorporated enterprises is taken. This method of dividing the increase in the stocks of private enterprises may be subject to a considerable margin of error.

ESTIMATES FOR INDIVIDUAL INDUSTRIES

Agriculture

The estimates of agricultural stocks arise from the annual calculation of income from farming, which is made for the farm year from June to May (see page 143). The raw materials included are feedingstuffs and fertilisers purchased from merchants or manufacturers; work in progress comprises livestock and growing crops, grass and cultivations as recorded in the annual agricultural census; stocks of finished products consist of harvested hay, potatoes and cereals. Feedingstuffs and fertilisers are valued at prices paid to suppliers, net of subsidy where applicable; the other items are valued at estimated average unit costs of production.

Changes in the value of stocks for farm years are converted to calendar years by taking 5/12 and 7/12 of the changes in the appropriate farm years. This cannot be regarded as a satisfactory method of estimating the change in stocks during the calendar year, but the figures obtained in this way are consistent with the farmers' income figures. Quarterly estimates are generally a smooth interpolation of the calendar year figures.

Forestry

Annual figures are taken from the trading accounts of the Forestry Commission and central government forestry in Northern Ireland; they represent the net cost, including interest, of growing timber during the year. Calendar year and quarterly estimates are smooth interpolations of the financial year figures taken from the trading accounts. In estimating the level of forestry stocks, the cumulation of such costs is supplemented by an estimate of the value of standing timber in private woodlands, made by the Forestry Commission.

Mining and quarrying

Quarterly estimates for coal mining are provided by the National Coal Board. For other mining and quarrying, the source is the census of production. Coal stocks are valued at selling prices *less* specific provisions for loss, degradation, lifting and marketing expenses and general provisions assessed in the light of all the circumstances.

Manufacturing

Data on the value of stocks held by manufacturing industries are collected by means of various inquiries carried out by the Board of Trade. The structure of these inquiries is broadly similar to those for retail distribution and wholesale distribution. Firstly, a comprehensive census or benchmark inquiry is undertaken at intervals of about five years; secondly, a simple annual census or inquiry usually on a sample basis, is carried out for the intervening years; and thirdly, information is collected either monthly or quarterly from a more limited number of businesses on a voluntary basis.

The basic source of information about the stocks of manufacturing industry is the census of production. The first post-war census in which information was collected was for 1948 and the census has included similar questions in each subsequent year. A description of the census and extracts from the census form for 1966 are given in Appendix II. The reporting unit in a detailed census is the establishment. The sample censuses from 1959 onwards are on a business unit basis, though earlier sample censuses were on an establishment basis. The census of production asks for figures of opening and closing stocks divided between (a) materials and fuel, (b) work in progress and (c) stocks of finished products. The figures for stocks of materials and fuel in the food, drink and tobacco industry include tobacco held in bonded warehouses.

The quarterly sample inquiry was started by the Board of Trade in 1954; unlike the census, it is on a voluntary basis. The businesses reporting the value of their stocks and work in progress each quarter account for about two-thirds of total manufacturing stocks but the selection is not fully representative; businesses holding large stocks are necessarily over-weighted in the sample. The statistics from the annual census are generally not available until about twelve months after the end of the year; until then the annual, as well as the quarterly figures, are based on the results of the quarterly inquiry.

The problem of measuring work in progress consistently with other forms of national expenditure has already been mentioned in Section 1 of this chapter. For shipbuilding, unpaid for work in progress is assumed to be nil, so that the change in work in progress is assumed to be charged to the customer's capital account and included in the estimates of fixed capital formation by the shipping industry. The change in work in progress on ships for overseas customers is also counted as nil, although progress payments for such work are not included in the estimates for exports. Some element of duplication may occur in other industries, particularly in respect of work in progress in the heavy engineering and aircraft industries. The 1968 census of production includes questions to provide information for estimates free of this duplication in all manufacturing industries.

Gas, electricity and water

Quarterly and annual figures of changes in the values of stocks held, divided between fuel—mostly coal—and other goods, are supplied by the nationalised gas and electricity corporations. Stocks of domestic appliances held for sale through the electricity and gas showrooms are excluded since they are included in retail stocks.

Retail distribution

Changes in retailers' stocks are estimated by means of the three-tier structure of statistical inquiries mentioned under 'Manufacturing'. In the first place, the census of distribution, taken at intervals of about five years, provides a benchmark estimate of the level of retailers' stocks; secondly, the annual inquiry into the distributive and service industries collects information each year, except when a census of distribution is being taken, from a substantial sample of larger retail companies and unincorporated businesses; and thirdly, information is collected monthly from retailers who are able to provide a monthly figure of stocks, and this limited information is used in conjunction with the results of the other two inquiries to compile estimates of the monthly movement of total retail stocks. The annual inquiries are described in Appendix II. Retailers providing monthly figures account on average for about one-fifth of total retailers' stocks, but the coverage differs from one kind of business to another. The monthly returns provide the basis of the annual estimates until the annual data become available.

Wholesale distribution

In the present context, wholesale distribution comprises Minimum List Headings 810, 831 and 832 of the *Standard Industrial Classification, 1958*. This includes wholesaling, that is the function of buying from a manufacturer or another wholesaler and selling to a retailer or another wholesaler; dealing, either wholesale or retail, in coal, builders' materials, grain and agricultural supplies; and dealing in industrial materials such as timber and metals.

The wholesale trades are covered by the annual inquiries into the distributive and service industries, which are described in Appendix II. Benchmark inquiries into the wholesale trades were made for 1959 and 1965; smaller, sample inquiries have been made for all other years from 1956. In these inquiries reporting is on a business unit basis. Quarterly information on the change in the value of the stocks held by the wholesale trades is derived from a voluntary inquiry begun at the end of 1956; distributors providing quarterly figures account for about 40 per cent of total wholesalers' stocks. The quarterly returns provide the basis of the annual estimates until the annual data become available.

Other industries

Construction. The estimates should in principle cover builders' stocks of materials and fuel, and any work in progress not included in the estimates of fixed capital formation. Estimates of unpaid for work in progress are made each quarter from figures of the construction industry's output collected by the Ministry of Public Building and Works. The estimates are based on the assumption that output normally precedes payment by some six weeks in the case of new work other than housing and by about four weeks in the case of repairs and maintenance work. No estimate is included in respect of work in progress on dwellings, since the estimates for this category of fixed capital formation are recorded in principle at the same time as output. At present changes in builders' stocks of materials and fuel are ignored.

Transport and communication. Quarterly estimates are provided by the Post Office and by the British Railways Board. Stocks and work in progress in engineering workshops are excluded from the latter, since they are already covered by the census of production and are included in the estimates for manufacturing. For other public corporations, annual figures are taken from their published accounts; the changes are very small. Rough estimates for the level of stocks held by companies, sole traders and partnerships engaged in road passenger transport and sea transport have been derived from an analysis made by Inland Revenue; changes in the level of these stocks are assumed to be negligible.

Miscellaneous services. The principal groups included in this category are motor traders, and hotels and caterers. Estimates of the stocks held by these two industries are derived from 1962 and 1960 respectively from the annual inquiries carried out by the Board of Trade (see Appendix II). Quarterly figures are a smooth interpolation of the annual estimates.

Central government trading bodies. The stocks of central government trading bodies represent the stocks held by the trading bodies listed on page 296, other than those mentioned below. The estimates are derived from the published trading accounts and quarterly returns supplied by departments. After excluding forestry which is given separately in the analysis by industry in the Blue Book, and omitting the Royal Mint, Royal Ordnance Factories and certain Atomic Energy Authority establishments whose stocks are covered by the census of production and included in the estimates for manufacturing, the stocks of the remaining central government trading bodies are now principally represented by the non-strategic stocks of the Board of Trade, although these are of little significance. In the early post-war years, however, included here were stocks held by the Ministry of Food and commodity trading divisions of the Board of Trade, which were of considerable importance.

Central government strategic stocks. These are stocks of food and raw materials purchased under the programmes for procuring strategic reserves. The figures are taken from direct returns from the departments concerned of the value at cost of stocks purchased *less* receipts from sales. No adjustment for stock appreciation is therefore required.

INDICATORS OF PRICE CHANGES

Prices of virtually all the important items held in stock as materials and fuel or finished goods and a very wide range of the smaller items are collected regularly by the Board of Trade, the Ministry of Agriculture, Fisheries and Food, and the Ministry of Power. These prices are, in general, prices paid by manufacturers for materials and fuel and prices received by them for finished goods which are included in the wholesale price indices prepared and published by the Board of Trade. Notes on the coverage and definition of these wholesale price indices are given in an annual article published in the *Board of Trade Journal* each year, usually in February. On the whole, for materials and fuel the prices collected for the wholesale price indices will be related to the prices at which manufacturers value their stocks. The wholesale price information is, however, based on quoted market prices and various arrangements, for example long-term contracts and special prices, may cause some divergence from prices at which stocks are valued.

For those industries for which work in progress is revalued on the assumption that figures reflect labour costs as well as material costs, the changes in labour costs are estimated from Ministry of Labour data on earnings and wage rates.

4. THE MEASUREMENT OF THE VALUE OF THE PHYSICAL CHANGE IN STOCKS AND WORK IN PROGRESS

It has been shown above that an adjustment is required to the accounting data of changes in the value of stocks in order to secure an estimate of the change in stocks which is consistent with the general principles of national accounting. The method adopted was described on page 393 as the revaluation of the accounting figures of both opening and closing stocks, by the use of price indices, at the average market prices of the period. The difference between the revalued opening and closing stocks is treated as the net investment in stocks at current prices; the difference between this figure of net investment and the change in the book value shown by the accounting data is treated as stock appreciation.

The steps in the revaluation of the opening and closing stocks at the average price of each period, usually the quarter, are described below. The description, which applies primarily to manufacturing industry, is set out in greater detail in the August 1960 issue of *Economic Trends*. For industries other than manufacturing the calculations are on a more summary basis, as considered appropriate on the merits of each case.

In addition to the necessity for making basic assumptions about the valuation underlying the accounting data, the process of revaluation requires information or assumptions about:
  (a) changes in prices;
  (b) the period over which stocks are assumed to have been built up; and
  (c) the commodity composition of the stocks, that is the types of commodities and products included in the stocks that are being revalued and their relative importance.

Accounting conventions adopted

In order to revalue the accounting levels of stocks, it is necessary to come to some conclusion about the accounting conventions adopted by companies in making the estimates which they return to the Board of Trade. The general principle is to value stocks at cost or net realisable value, whichever is the lower (or in certain circumstances at replacement price if that is lower), but various methods are accepted and used by accountants in applying this principle, particularly in the determination of cost. The cost of acquiring the stocks may be exactly known by recording the date and price at which each item was bought, or it may be estimated conventionally. Some systems accept the convention that the materials acquired at the most distant date are first drawn from store for processing and consequently that the stocks consist of the most recently acquired items. This is the 'first in, first out' or FIFO convention, described on page 392. The opposite assumption is also possible—that the materials drawn from store are the most recently acquired and that stocks consist of the items first purchased; the 'last in, first out' or LIFO convention. This comes closer to the national accounting concept of charging materials at replacement price, when stock appreciation would not arise. When the volume of stocks is falling the materials deemed to be used at any time are valued at the prices of an earlier time, which is usually a time less distant than would be assumed on the FIFO convention. Some stock appreciation may arise, but probably less than under a FIFO system. The valuation of the unused stocks under the LIFO system, however, is admittedly arbitrary; so long as the physical volume of stocks is unchanged, it is valued at the same prices as the opening stocks, and no change in prices during the accounting period is reflected in a change in the value of stocks. But when the volume of stocks changes, the valuation put on the change is not necessarily based on current prices.

Another system is to keep a running figure of the value of stocks by adding purchases at their actual cost and deducting issues at the average cost per unit of the stocks in hand before the issue is made; the average cost per unit is recalculated either continuously, as fresh purchases and issues are made, or at fixed intervals. Another method is to value stocks, or some part of them, at a standard cost which may be changed annually or even less frequently.

It is thought that the great majority of firms determine cost by adopting the 'first in, first out' convention and value stocks at cost, as so determined, or net realisable value (or in certain circumstances replacement price), whichever is the lower. Most of the alternative methods in use are generally likely, in practice, to be fairly close to this method. The 'last in, first out' method is likely to give the most significantly different results but it seems to be rarely used.

For the purposes of revaluing materials and fuel and finished goods, therefore, the assumption is made that all manufacturers use the FIFO convention and value their stocks at the lower of cost or realisable value. Although this assumption must result in some error in the estimates, the error is likely to be small since it is shown by the census of production that in none of the industrial groups do stocks of finished goods amount to much more than one month's production, or stocks of materials to much more than three months' purchases, and generally to only one or two months' purchases.

An accountant using the 'first in, first out' method thereby assumes that the stocks held at any time are those most recently bought or produced. He will accordingly value them either at the costs of the most recent period, going back far enough for the total purchases in the period exactly to equal the stocks in hand, or at the current realisable value, whichever is lower, in order to produce a book value figure. To deflate the book value figure, therefore, the correct price to use is either the average over the most recent period or the current realisable value, whichever is the lower, and this is the method employed in producing the estimates of the value of the physical increase in stocks.

Assumptions must also be made about the accounting methods which underlie the valuation of work in progress. The method commonly adopted by accountants is to value work in progress at the cost of materials and fuel used, together with direct labour costs *plus* a percentage or a fixed amount for overheads. In the majority of trades, the time during which work in progress is accumulated is short and the amount of work in progress is small. The unit cost will lie between the unit cost of materials and fuel and that of finished goods. For these trades, therefore, the assumption is made that little error in the estimates as a whole will result from a revaluation carried out by means of a simple unweighted arithmetic average of the price index numbers of materials and fuel and finished goods. For the mechanical and electrical engineering and aircraft manufacturing industries, however, in which work in progress is accumulated over a considerable period and the amount of work in progress is therefore large, the corresponding revaluations are carried out on a more refined basis, with separate indices of material costs and labour costs weighted together in a way which reflects general accounting practice.

Periods over which stocks have been built up

Before the items held in stock can be revalued either at the average prices of the period or at base year prices, it is necessary to arrive at the average prices assumed to underlie the accounting valuations. The first stage in assessing these

average prices involves estimating the period of time over which the level of the
stocks is assumed to have been built up. For materials and fuel this means the
months during which the stocks were purchased, and for finished goods and for
work in progress the months during which stocks were produced. A broad
indication of these turnover periods, for the categories for which stocks figures
are available, can be obtained from the detailed censuses of production, which
show, as well as the level of stocks in each trade, the purchases of materials and
fuel and the sales of goods during the year.

The above method of assessing the period over which stocks of materials and
fuel and finished goods have been built up is not adequate for work in progress
in such trades as mechanical, electrical and marine engineering and aircraft
production, in which the production process extends over a long period of time,
perhaps up to several years. In such cases it can be shown that a high proportion
of the amount of the work in progress has been done in the most recent months
and only a small proportion in earlier months. An appropriate cost index is
therefore compiled by combining together the relative monthly cost indices
using a succession of increasing weights.

Assume that a company has four projects in hand, that each takes four months
to complete (and then, of course, passes out of work in progress), that each
project is begun at the beginning of the month and that an equal amount of work
is done on each project each month. If W_1 represents the value of work done on
each project in the past month, W_2 represents the value of work done in the
previous month and so on, and the projects are numbered in the order in which
they are started, then the amount of work in progress at the end of any month is
made up as follows:

Project 1 W_1 *plus* W_2 *plus* W_3 *plus* W_4
Project 2 W_1 *plus* W_2 *plus* W_3
Project 3 W_1 *plus* W_2
Project 4 W_1

and the total of work in progress consists of $4W_1$ *plus* $3W_2$ *plus* $2W_3$ *plus* W_4.
In this simplified example the cost index appropriate to work in progress for the
most recent month should have a weight of four, that for the previous month a
weight of three, and so on.

Since in practice there is no means of arriving at an exact pattern, the sequence
of natural numbers is taken as an approximate representation of the relative
build-up of the work in progress in those trades in which the period of accumulation is long and the level of work in progress is sufficiently large to justify this
refinement to the calculation. These trades together account for nearly two-thirds
of all work in progress in manufacturing industries.

Commodity composition of stocks

Ideally, one would like to know the composition of stocks at the end of each
period, and use a current-weighted index of price changes to adjust the level of
stocks each quarter. But with the exception of some items of basic materials,
the commodity composition is not known. The only systematic information
about the make-up within industries of manufacturers' stocks of materials and
fuel, and products on hand for sale, is provided by the results of the census of
production in respect of 1948. But relatively few items of stocks were shown
separately and 1948 was still in the period of post-war recovery, with distortions

in the patterns of stockholding caused by shortages and controls. This information is therefore not used and, for the most part, the commodity composition of stocks of materials and fuel and of finished goods held by each industry is taken as being similar to the pattern of purchases and of sales, respectively, in the latest year for which this information has been collected in the census of production. Composite price indices can then be formed by weighting together the price indices of the individual commodities according to the assumed composition of the stocks in the industry concerned.

For materials and fuel, the solution is not wholly satisfactory as, apart from the fact that the commodity composition of stocks changes over time, the number of months' purchases normally held in stock will vary to some extent from item to item and the relative importance of items as purchases will not be the same as their relative importance as items of stocks. It is, however, the most appropriate assumption to make in view of the information available and is not likely to lead to serious error in the price indices used for adjusting the levels of stocks.

Some of the larger errors that might have been introduced by this assumption have been avoided, however, because certain of the more important basic materials and commodities are treated separately from the rest of the stocks of those industry groups in which they occur. The items concerned are imported wheat, cocoa, sugar, home grown barley, several steel products, raw cotton, raw wool, natural rubber, and wood pulp. For these commodity items regular quarterly information is available on the quantities held in stock by manufacturers and is used to estimate their book value; these amounts are excluded from the reported book value figures and revalued separately. Although their total value is only about one-tenth of the total value of materials and fuel held in stock by manufacturing industry, the importance of their separate treatment lies in the fact that the quantities of these basic materials held in stock, or their prices—and sometimes both—are subject to greater than normal variations. Their separate treatment introduces a fairly important element of current weighting into the calculations.

In assessing the commodity composition of the stocks of finished goods, data on the pattern of sales in the separate trades distinguished in the census of production have been combined using the stocks held by the trades as weights to provide weights for the price indices for the broad groups used in these calculations. This is exactly analogous to what has been done for materials and fuel and although the procedure is not ideal, it is generally likely to be more accurate than in the case of materials and fuel.

The calculations on these lines are made separately for materials and fuel, work in progress and finished goods for each of about twenty groups in manufacturing industry.

Method of adjusting the data

The price indices described above are set out for each category of stocks for each quarter as follows:

(a) price index at the end of the quarter; the index for the last month is used and is assumed to represent the market price at the end of the quarter;

(b) the average price index for the latest period covered by the number of months' purchases, or sales, held in stock; this is assumed to relate to the original cost of the closing stocks;

(c) the average price index for the whole quarter.

The value of the closing stocks in each category at the end of each quarter is then adjusted by the ratio of (c) to (a) or (b), whichever has the lower value in each case. For example, if the values of the index are (a) 135 for the market price at the end of the quarter, (b) 133 for the cost price and (c) 132 for the average price in the quarter, then the value of the closing stocks is multiplied by 132/133 as in the table below. The value of the opening stocks is similarly adjusted by the ratio of (c) for the current quarter to (a) or (b) for the preceding quarter, whichever is the lower.

The following table illustrates how the method of revaluation is carried out.

Revaluation at current prices of stocks change in the fourth quarter

	£ thousand
1 Book value of stocks	
(a) end of fourth quarter	1,600
(b) end of third quarter	1,000
(c) increase in book value during fourth quarter	600
	Number
2 Number of months purchases in stock	2
3 Composite price index for stocks held	
(a) December	135
(b) Average for November and December (assumed to be price underlying 1(a) because it is less than 3(a))	133
(c) Average for fourth quarter	132
(d) September (assumed to be price underlying 1(b) because it is less than 3(e))	126
(e) Average for August and September	127
(f) Average for base year	100
	£ thousand
4 Stocks revalued at average prices of fourth quarter	
(a) Stocks at end of fourth quarter	
$1(a) \times \dfrac{3(c)}{3(b)}$	1,588
(b) Stocks at end of third quarter	
$1(b) \times \dfrac{3(c)}{3(d)}$	1,048
5 Value of physical increase in stocks during the fourth quarter at current prices	
$4(a) - 4(b)$	540
6 Stock appreciation in the fourth quarter	
$1(c) - 5$	60

Revaluation at constant prices

The value of the change in the physical quantity of stocks, estimated by the methods described above, is a measure in terms of the average prices obtaining in the quarter. For estimates of national expenditure at constant prices, a further revaluation is required, at base-year prices. This revaluation is performed for each category of stocks by essentially the same methods as the revaluation at current prices. The following table illustrates how the physical increase calculated above is revalued at base-year prices.

Revaluation at base-year prices of stocks change in the fourth quarter

	£ thousand
7 Stocks revalued at base-year prices	
(a) Stocks at end of fourth quarter	
$1(a) \times \dfrac{3(f)}{3(b)}$	1,203
(b) Stocks at end of third quarter	
$1(b) \times \dfrac{3(f)}{3(d)}$	794
8 Value of physical increase in stocks during the fourth quarter at base-year prices	
$7(a) - 7(b) = 5 \times \dfrac{3(f)}{3(c)}$	409

5. RELIABILITY

Change in book value

The following comments relate to the estimates of the annual change in the book value of stocks, not to those of the value of the physical change which are dealt with separately. The reliability is assessed on the criterion that the value of stocks changes should be recorded in a manner consistent with the figures of profits, whatever the accounting conventions adopted by the enterprises concerned.

For the central government and public corporations, comprehensive accounting data are used; the estimates can be regarded as in category A of the gradings described on pages 39 to 41. The estimates for the company and personal sectors, however, can be regarded as in category C only.

The data for manufacturing industry are mainly derived from the census of production. The basic figures in the census may be regarded as accounting data, but estimation is involved for small establishments and the basic figures may relate to the accounting year and not to the calendar year. Hence the estimates are classified as in category B. The large margin of uncertainty about the estimates for 'Other industries' arises partly from the incomplete coverage of the information available.

There are inherent difficulties in interpreting these gradings arising from the very variable size of stocks changes. It is clearly not implied, for example, that in the extreme case when the stocks change is nil, there is no error in the estimate. Such a literal interpretation of the gradings is not intended. The gradings should be regarded as relating not to the absolute change in any one year but rather to the average change over a number of years, as shown in the table.

In all cases the estimates for the latest year are less reliable than those for the earlier years. The quarterly estimates are less reliable than the annual ones, not only because of the limited coverage of the quarterly inquiries but also because stockholders are unlikely to carry out a proper valuation of stocks each quarter.

Reliability of annual estimates of change in book value of stocks[1]

A ± less than 3 per cent
B ± 3 per cent to 10 per cent
C ± more than 10 per cent

	Grading	Average annual change in book value, 1962 to 1966 £ million
Agriculture and forestry	B	61
Mining and quarrying	A	−8
Manufacturing...............................	B	351
Gas, electricity and water	A	13
Wholesale and retail distribution	C	131
Other industries.............................	C	55
Central government	A	−4
Total change in book value	C	599

[1]For the significance of the reliability gradings see pages 39 to 41.

Value of physical change

The process of revaluation followed in estimating the value of the physical change in stocks has been outlined in the preceding section of this chapter. A major uncertainty arises on the validity of the basic assumptions about the nature of the accounting valuations. Apart from this, the chief statistical weaknesses in the revaluation process are as follows:

(a) The element of estimation in the commodity composition of stocks, and in the number of months' purchases it represents; the latter affects the extent of lagging in the price indices used.

(b) The doubt surrounding the implied equality in movements of the market prices used for the price indices and of actual prices paid during the period; long-term contracts at special prices are a case in point.

(c) The unavoidable assumption that the average prices of the period, as shown by the price indices, represent the average price of all actual or imputed stocks transactions. The inherent assumption in the calculation is that stocks change at a uniform rate throughout the period; this is unlikely to be the case when prices are fluctuating.

(d) The difficulty of obtaining appropriate price indices for some categories of stocks.

The difficulties of making accurate estimates are great and at a number of stages in the estimation, approximations and assumptions have to be made. By the nature of the basic data it is virtually impossible to obtain estimates of a high degree of reliability in this field and the estimates of the value of the physical change in stocks and stock appreciation should be regarded as subject to a wide margin of error.

Chapter XIV

Financial Accounts

1. GENERAL DESCRIPTION

Financial accounts are designed to set out the financial transactions of each of the different sectors of the economy systematically and in a convenient form. They provide a statistical framework for considering financial transactions and enable the transactions of one sector to be directly related to those of other sectors.

Financial transactions cover all transactions in financial assets and liabilities, including currency, which is regarded as a liability of the central government. Examples of assets are loans made, bank deposits, Treasury bills, company shares and unit trust units. Examples of financial liabilities are borrowing, hire purchase debt incurred, shares issued and trade debts. Financial assets are in every case balanced by a corresponding liability. A share is an asset to the owner but a liability to the company issuing it; a bank deposit is an asset to the depositor but a liability to the bank. When the country is considered as a whole, financial transactions between residents cancel out and only transactions between residents and non-residents remain. The sum of these transactions is the country's net acquisition of financial claims on the rest of the world. For convenience, physical assets held abroad are included with financial assets and the sum of the financial transactions for the country as a whole is equal to its investment in overseas assets or its net investment abroad (see Chapter XV).

CLASSIFICATION OF SECTORS

The classification of sectors used in financial accounts is more detailed than that used in the rest of the national accounts. This is because it is necessary to separate out the transactions of financial intermediaries from those of other enterprises. The company sector is therefore divided between industrial and commercial companies and financial companies. In the financial accounts, financial companies are further subdivided into the three sectors described below.

Not all financial intermediaries are companies and the financial companies sector, which is also described as the financial institutions sector, is not entirely comprehensive. The financial activities of the public sector which are excluded are the Post Office Savings Bank, apart from the Investment Account, the management of the funds of the ordinary departments of the trustee savings banks and the Exchange Equalisation Account; these are an integral part of the financing operations of the central government. However, in the financial accounts, the Bank of England Banking Department is included in the banking sector and not in the public corporations sector, as elsewhere in the national accounts (see below). Stockbrokers and jobbers are included almost entirely in the personal sector and are excluded from the financial institutions sector. But the financial transactions of life assurance companies and superannuation schemes are included with those of financial institutions, even though in the national accounts their funds are regarded as the property of the personal sector and relatively few superannuation funds have corporate status (see page 206)

The banking sector

Owing to its size, its key role in government financing, the flexibility of its lending operations, and because its deposit liabilities form the major part of the money supply the banking sector is shown separately. The banking sector comprises the United Kingdom offices of three main groups of banks: (a) deposit banks, including the Bank of England Banking Department, (b) accepting houses and overseas banks and (c) the discount market. In all, about 170 separate institutions are covered. A complete list of the banks included at 31 December 1966 is given in Annex 1 to this chapter.

It is convenient in practice to include the transactions of the Banking Department of the Bank of England with those of the banking sector, and to record all transactions between the central government and the Banking Department as a single net figure under the heading 'Net Exchequer indebtedness to the Bank of England Banking Department'. There are two minor disadvantages to this treatment. One is that it gives rise to a slight inconsistency, because the figures of saving and of gross domestic fixed capital formation for public corporations include those for the whole of the Bank of England. The second is that in the account for the banking sector, all transactions between the Bank of England Banking Department and the rest of the sector are netted out.

Insurance companies and superannuation funds

Insurance companies and superannuation funds are shown as a separate sub-sector both because of their importance and because their liabilities are rather different in nature from those of other financial institutions. Except for their non-life funds and reserves, the assets of insurance companies and the funds of superannuation schemes are regarded as the collective property of policy holders and the members of the schemes (see page 100).

The superannuation funds cover schemes for employees in the public and private sectors. For those public sector schemes for which no separate fund is kept, the excess of contributions from employers and employees over the pensions actually paid to retired employees is treated as if it were a loan from a pension fund to the central government.

Other financial institutions

The institutions covered by this sub-sector are: hire purchase finance companies, the special investment departments of trustee savings banks, the Investment Account of the Post Office Savings Bank, building societies and certain other institutions which accept deposits, unit trusts, investment trusts quoted on the London Stock Exchange, and certain special finance agencies which are quoted public companies engaged in the provision of medium and long-term finance to industry, such as the Agricultural Mortgage Corporation and the Industrial and Commercial Finance Corporation. A list of special finance agencies is given in Annex 2 to this chapter. Property investment companies and other similar organisations deriving their income from ground rents or from owning and letting are not included; in this respect the financial companies sector differs from companies within the industry group 'Insurance, banking and finance'.

o

CLASSIFICATION OF ASSETS

An important feature of financial accounts is the classification of assets in a uniform way. The classification may be based on two different criteria: the relative degree of liquidity of the assets and the institutional sector on which the asset is a claim. The most liquid assets are notes and coin and bank deposits, and the least liquid are long-term assets such as loans and mortgages. But it is not always easy to decide on the relative liquidity of different assets; an asset may have a long period to maturity but be a liquid asset in the sense that it is readily marketable, although at some risk of capital loss. A classification by sector is particularly useful for financial accounts because each asset is a financial liability of only one sector. Ideally, the classification of financial assets would incorporate both methods of classification.

The classification used in the United Kingdom financial accounts makes use of both criteria but is not comprehensive. For example, British government and government guaranteed securities are not divided according to their period to maturity, which may vary from less than a year to indefinite. Again, company and overseas securities are grouped together and no distinction is made between the securities of financial companies, industrial and commercial companies and overseas companies; nor are these securities divided between debentures, preference shares and ordinary shares. But overseas assets are generally classified on a sector basis because of their importance in considering international capital movements. And public sector liabilities are also distinguished in order to analyse the financing of the public sector deficit.

In general, as much detail as possible is included in the published tables in order to make possible different groupings of the assets. More comprehensive classifications of transactions than the classification given in the financial accounts are published in *Financial Statistics*, including in some cases the distinctions mentioned in the previous paragraph, in particular for the transactions of financial institutions.

VALUATION AND TIMING OF TRANSACTIONS

In the financial accounts, each transaction should be valued at the price at which the asset is exchanged. When an asset is sold the value recorded should be the amount received from the sale; when an asset is acquired, the value should be the amount paid by the purchaser. Transactions are thus recorded on a cash value basis. As each sale is matched by a purchase (including the sales and purchases of dealers and of non-residents) the total of the value of the sales of an asset *less* the total of the value of the purchases should be nil. However, for transactions in securities there is a difference between the amount paid by the purchaser and the amount received by the seller—their costs in making the transaction. This is equal to any stamp duties paid by the purchaser *plus* the sum of the commissions paid by the purchaser and by the seller. So far, no adjustment has been made to the figures to eliminate this inconsistency. It follows that where a sector's transactions are estimated as a residual they include as a sale any costs included in the figures of net purchases by the other sectors.

Capital gains and losses, whether or not realised, are not recorded in the financial transactions accounts. A person may sell a block of shares for £1,000 after having paid, say, £900 for them at an earlier date and so make a capital gain of £100. The financial accounts will record only the cash transactions—the purchase of stock for £900 and the corresponding sale for the same amount at the first date, and the sale of stock for £1,000 and the corresponding purchase for £1,000 at the second date. The capital gain of £100 will not be recorded.

Capital gains and losses do, of course, affect the behaviour of the individuals and institutions making them, but this is not sufficient reason for including them in the transactions accounts. In practice some gains and losses are included because it is not always possible to record all the transactions on a cash value basis and some transactions are estimated from changes in the value of holdings. For short-term assets there is no problem because their market price does not change, or moves only within narrow limits, so that information on cash transactions for these assets can be derived satisfactorily from changes in the value of holdings. But for securities changes in the value of holdings between the beginning and end of a period will not necessarily be equal to the net acquisition of assets at cash values. It is generally possible to record transactions on a cash value basis only when returns are made direct by buyers and sellers. Balance sheet data provide details of holdings of securities at either book value, nominal value or market value. Changes in the market value of holdings of securities, for example, would reflect any capital gains or losses made, both realised and unrealised.

The transactions in the financial accounts should be recorded on a consistent timing basis. In the national accounts transactions are generally recorded on an accruals, or payable-receivable, basis. This procedure gives rise to some complications in the financial accounts where the differences between accruals and cash flows need to be allowed for as a short-term credit or debit. As far as possible the transactions in any one asset are recorded consistently, preferably according to the date of contract. But even when all transactions are recorded in the same way the difficulty of dealing with items in transit still arises; this gives rise to the large 'unallocated' item for deposits with the banking sector. There may be inconsistencies of timing between the figures for transactions taken from the balance of payments accounts, which are based mainly on the registers of paying agents, and the figures for the domestic sectors. The problem is discussed in greater detail in a paper by Berman [1].

2. THE PUBLISHED TABLES

Financial accounts for different sectors of the economy were first presented as an integral part of the United Kingdom system of national income accounts in the 1964 Blue Book. Previous Blue Books had included financial accounts for the public sector only, and some details of the financial transactions of the personal sector had been included in its capital account since the 1955 Blue Book. Wherever possible, the figures cover the full eleven years of the Blue Book but the accounts are comprehensive only from 1963, when direct returns were first available from all the major financial institutions. Quarterly financial accounts were published for the first time in the December 1964 issue of *Financial Statistics* and now appear regularly in that publication. The accounts have been prepared from the first quarter of 1963.

The development of financial accounts was made possible by the substantial increase in the range of financial statistics which followed the recommendations of the Radcliffe Report [2]. The Committee in its recommendations laid emphasis on increasing the range of available financial statistics and on ensuring that the

[1] L. S. Berman, 'The Flow of Funds in the United Kingdom', *Journal of the Royal Statistical Society*, Series A (General), Vol. 128, Part 3, 1965.
[2] *Report of the Committee on the Working of the Monetary System*, Cmnd. 827.

statistics should be made more consistent and comprehensive. The subsequent developments were described in articles in the September 1962 and February 1964 issues of *Economic Trends*.

The tables in the Blue Book show only transactions in financial assets and do not show holdings at the beginning or end of the year. Some information on holdings by financial institutions is given in *Financial Statistics*, but no comprehensive official estimates have been prepared. Sector balance sheets, giving details of the total assets and liabilities of each sector of the economy have, however, been compiled by Revell and his associates for the years 1957 to 1961[3] and are being brought up to date by them.

Net acquisition of financial assets

Financial accounts are linked to the income and expenditure or appropriation accounts in the table on the net acquisition of financial assets which provides a summary of the capital accounts of each of the different sectors (Table 72 of the 1967 Blue Book). Figures for 1966 are summarised below.

Net acquisition of financial assets, 1966

£ million

| | Private sector | | | Public sector [1] | Overseas sector | Residual error |
	Personal sector	Industrial and commercial companies	Financial companies			
Saving before providing for depreciation, stock appreciation and additions to reserves	1,879	2,899	253	2,265		
Capital transfers, including taxes on capital (net receipts)	−162	21	—	141		
less Gross domestic fixed capital formation	−916	−2,418	−183	−3,118		
less Increase in value of stocks and work in progress	−91	−403	—	−66		
Net acquisition of financial assets	710	99	70	−778	59	−160

Source: 1967 Blue Book, Table 72

[1]Public corporations, central government and local authorities are shown separately in the Blue Book.

This table shows the saving and receipts from capital transfers of each sector and how far these are matched by expenditure on fixed assets and the increase in the value of stocks and work in progress. The extent to which each sector on balance contributes by way of lending to the capital formation of the other sectors and to net investment abroad, or draws on the savings of other sectors is shown by the sector's net acquisition of financial assets. The net acquisition of financial assets is obtained as a residual between saving, capital transfers and

[3]Jack Revell, assisted by Graham Hockley and John Moyle, *The Wealth of the Nation*, Cambridge University Press, 1967.

capital formation. It represents the net balance of very large flows of transactions in financial assets and liabilities; details of these transactions, in so far as they can be identified, are set out systematically in each sector's financial transactions account. The aggregate of the net acquisition of financial assets for all sectors, including the overseas sector, should in theory be nil. This is because an increase in the financial assets of one sector is always matched by a reduction in the financial assets or an increase in the liabilities of another sector, or sectors. In practice the aggregate is not nil because there is a statistical discrepancy in the national accounts between the estimates of total saving and of total investment by all sectors. This discrepancy is the 'Residual error', which arises because the gross domestic product is estimated by two different methods (see page 39).

The individual items in this table are defined in the sector chapters where the capital accounts are described. The estimates of gross domestic fixed capital formation and the increase in the value of stocks and work in progress are described in Chapters XII and XIII respectively. One difference in presentation from the income and expenditure accounts in the Blue Book should be noted. Saving in this table is reckoned before providing for additions to tax, dividend and interest reserves. This provides a simpler analysis, which can be used in both the quarterly and annual accounts; the additions to reserves are a temporary source of finance.

The net acquisition of financial assets for companies includes the overseas investment in physical and financial assets by companies resident in the United Kingdom, including investment in their overseas branches and subsidiaries.

The net acquisition of financial assets for financial companies includes as a negative item an amount equal to the gross domestic fixed capital formation by the life funds of life assurance companies and the funds of superannuation schemes. These funds are regarded as the property of the personal sector and the whole of the increase in the funds is included in the saving of persons and not of companies. It could be argued that their capital formation should be attributed to the personal sector but this has not been done since the choice between investment of the funds in fixed assets or financial assets rests with the companies and schemes and not with the policy holders and members. All of the increase in the funds is included in the net acquisition of financial assets by the personal sector on the grounds that this represents the claim by persons on financial institutions.

The treatment can, perhaps, be explained best by the following figures, which relate to 1966:

	£ million
Net increase in life assurance and superannuation funds	1,198
Gross domestic fixed capital formation by life assurance and superannuation funds	121

The contribution of these figures to those in the table on page 412 is:

Personal sector:	
Net acquisition of financial assets	1,198
Financial companies:	
Net acquisition of financial assets	−121
made up of:	
Increase in liabilities (−)	−1,198
Increase in financial assets (+)	1,077

This helps to explain why the table on page 417 shows a net decrease of £170 million in the total identified assets acquired by insurance companies and super-annuation funds.

The net acquisition of financial assets by the overseas sector equals, apart from the change in sign, net investment abroad by the United Kingdom. This is equal to the balance of payments surplus on current account *plus* any transfers received from overseas residents and included in the capital account of the balance of payments. In recent years there have been no such capital transfers from abroad and the net acquisition of financial assets of the overseas sector has therefore been equal, with sign reversed, to the balance of payments surplus on current account.

Transactions in financial assets: analysis by sector

In the Blue Book, financial transactions accounts are presented for the different sectors of the economy. These accounts give details of the financial assets and liabilities acquired by each sector for a series of calendar years. Accounts are given for the personal sector, industrial and commercial companies, the banking sector, financial institutions other than banks, the public sector and the overseas sector (Tables 74 to 79 of the 1967 Blue Book). The public sector is considered as a whole because of the financial interdependence of public corporations, the central government and local authorities; most of the items are also given in the detailed capital accounts for each of these three sectors. As far as possible the accounts cover the full eleven years of the Blue Book, but insufficient information is available to provide accounts before 1960 for industrial and commercial companies and for financial companies other than banks. Similar accounts on a quarterly basis are published in *Financial Statistics*.

An analysis by sector is also given of transactions in the assets and liabilities of the public sector. This shows the extent to which the different sectors of the economy contribute towards financing the public sector deficit.

Estimates of the total net acquisition of financial assets (or liabilities) by each domestic sector can be obtained in two ways: (a) as the balancing item in the sector's capital account, or (b) by aggregating the various items in each sector's financial transactions account. In the United Kingdom accounts, the first method is used. For each domestic sector the estimate of its net acquisition of financial assets is obtained as shown above from saving *plus* net receipts of capital transfers *less* expenditure on capital formation. In theory, the two methods of estimation should give identical results but in practice they do not. For each sector the difference between the two is shown against the heading 'Unidentified items' (see table on page 417). The difference arises partly because it is not yet possible to identify all the different transactions in financial assets, partly because of differences in valuation and timing and other statistical discrepancies in the estimates of financial transactions, and partly because the estimates of saving and of investment in physical assets given in the various sector capital accounts are subject to error [4].

The financial transactions account for the overseas sector covers all financial flows between residents and non-residents; it is shown on page 450. A description of this account and of its relationship to the balance of payments accounts is

---

[4] For further discussion see: L. S. Berman, 'The Flow of Funds in the United Kingdom', *Journal of the Royal Statistical Society*, Series A (General), Vol. 128, Part 3, 1965.

given in Chapter XV. These financial transactions are recorded partly in the long-term capital account of the balance of payments accounts and partly in the account of monetary movements. The classification in the overseas sector's financial account is a classification of assets and liabilities and cuts across that followed in the balance of payments accounts: transactions in one financial asset, for example government securities, may appear in both the long-term capital account and under monetary movements. In theory, the sum of the transactions included under these two headings should be equal, with sign reversed, to the balance of payments surplus on current account; in practice it is not. The statistical difference between the two is the so-called 'Balancing item' in the balance of payments accounts, which is shown as the unidentified item in the financial transactions account for the overseas sector.

Transactions in financial assets: analysis by sector and type of asset

The Blue Book contains a flow of funds table (Table 73 of the 1967 Blue Book) which brings together in the form of a matrix the various financial transactions accounts of the different sectors in the latest year. Flow of funds tables for calendar quarters, and from time to time for calendar years, are also published in *Financial Statistics*. The first calendar year for which such a table has been published is 1963, and the first calendar quarter, the second quarter of 1964.

This table provides a two-way classification of assets and sectors and gives details of the transactions in each of the various kinds of financial assets by each of the different sectors. Assets and liabilities are classified in a uniform way so that it is possible to relate the acquisition of a particular financial asset by one sector to the associated changes in the assets and liabilities of that sector and of each of the other sectors. The flow of funds matrix for 1966 is reproduced on pages 416 and 417. The final row in the matrix shows the total net acquisition of financial assets or liabilities by each sector; it is also the final row in the financial transactions account for each of the various sectors.

3. STATISTICAL SOURCES: SECTORS

Personal sector; Industrial and commercial companies

No direct returns are made by these two sectors and the estimates of their financial transactions are generally based either on information provided by other sectors or on information about the particular financial asset. For example, estimates of their lending to local authorities are based on the analysis of the source of their borrowing provided by local authorities; deposits with and borrowing from banks and other financial institutions are based on information provided by these institutions. Details of how the estimates are made are given in the next section, which describes the estimates made for each type of asset.

Transactions by the personal sector might be estimated in various ways. A sample survey of the transactions of households would provide information on the transactions of individuals, but not on the transactions of private non-profit-making bodies and private trusts, which have large holdings. Also, it is difficult to obtain reliable information in this way because of the need to include a relatively large number of households in the higher income groups. Some information is obtainable from the analysis of the total wealth of individuals made by the Inland Revenue from information obtained from estate duty figures. But

Transactions in financial assets[1]
Analysis by sector and type of asset, 1966

£ million

	Private sector — Personal sector	Private sector — Industrial and commercial companies	Financial institutions — Banks	Financial institutions — Insurance companies and superannuation funds	Financial institutions — Other	Public sector	Overseas sector	Unallocated
Notes and coin	37	29	82	—	—2	—148	—	—
Treasury bills	—	—16	—209	—4	—	10	221	—
British government and government guaranteed securities	—4[2]	—	119	59	64	—230	—8	—
National savings:								
Deposits	94	—	—	—	—167	73	—	—
Certificates and bonds	—129	—23	85	—	—	129	—	—
Tax reserve certificates	17	—	—	—	—	—79	—	—
Net Exchequer indebtedness to Bank of England Banking Department	—	—	44	—	—	—44	—	—
Local authority debt:								
Temporary borrowing	5	—58	81	—4	55	17	—30	—
Quoted securities and negotiable bonds	..	..	}	2	38	—106	—8	97
Other long-term borrowing	131	—23	—	—	113	—310	742	138
Deposits with banking sector	260	—7	—1,212	—	66	13	—	—
Deposits with building societies	726	—2	—	—	—724	—	—5	—
Deposits, etc. with hire purchase finance companies	18	6	—	—	—19	—	36	—
Deposits with other financial institutions	—	—	—	—	—36	—	—	—
Bank lending (except to local authorities):								
Advances and loans	97	—204	1,040	—	56	—14	—975	—
Commercial bills	—	—40	74	—	—7	—	—27	—
Money at call and short notice	—31	—3	37	—	—	—	—3	—
Hire purchase debt	102	—13	—	—	—72	—17	—	—
Trade debt (net) of public corporations	—28	114	—	—	—	—86	—	—

(Braces in the original join the "Temporary borrowing" and "Quoted securities and negotiable bonds" rows for the Banks (81), Insurance companies and superannuation funds (2), Overseas sector (—8) and Unallocated (97) columns.)

Loans for house purchase:								
Local authorities	-7	—	—	—	—	7	—	—
Other public sector	-11	—	—	—	—	11	—	—
Financial institutions	-709	-18	-19	61	667	—	—	—
Other loans by public sector to private sector	-2	—	—	—	3	17	—	—
Loans by superannuation funds to parent organisation	—	-8	—	84	—	-76	—	—
Other loans and mortgages by financial institutions (excluding banks)	-33	-143	—	81	95	—	—	—
Unit trust units	105	—	—	—	-105	—	—	—
Company and overseas securities:								
Capital issues	-574[2]	-568	-20	-11	-95	—	16	—
Other	1,198	321	26	670	130	55	50	—
Funds of life assurance and superannuation schemes	-21	-32	—	-1,198	—	53	—	-79
Miscellaneous short-term home assets (net)	..	..	2	89	4	-16	—	—
Other identified home assets	—	—	—	—	—	—	—	—
Gold and currency reserves	—	—	—	—	—	-282	282	—
Inter-government loans	—	—	—	—	—	62	-62	—
Transactions with International Monetary Fund, etc.	—	—	—	—	—	26	-26	—
Other identified overseas assets:								
Short-term	—	-14	—	—	3	34	-23	—
Long-term	—	112	—	1	—	7	-120	—
Total identified assets	1,241	-590	130	-170	67	-894	60	156
Unidentified items	-531	689	43 *(cols. 3–5 combined)*			116	-1[3]	-316
Net acquisition of financial assets[1]	710	99	70 *(cols. 3–5 combined)*			-778	59	-160[4]

Source: 1967 Blue Book, Table 73

[1] Acquisition of assets or reduction in liabilities is shown positive; sale of assets or increase in liabilities negative.
[2] Residual, including unidentified transactions by industrial and commercial companies.
[3] The Balancing item in the balance of payments accounts.
[4] The Residual error in the national income accounts.

o*

the figures are subject to very large errors, especially on the year-to-year changes, and again do not cover the private non-profit-making bodies and private trusts.

The only information obtained direct from companies is that given in their published balance sheets and that collected from a number of large companies about their overseas transactions for balance of payments purposes. Published balance sheets of companies are analysed regularly by the Board of Trade. For 1965 this analysis covered about 2,350 large companies whose shares are quoted on a United Kingdom stock exchange and also nearly 900 large non-quoted non-exempt companies, all of which are engaged in manufacturing, construction, transport (excluding shipping), distribution, property owning and miscellaneous services. The results of this analysis are published in *Economic Trends* and in *Financial Statistics*. The income of these companies is equal to about one half of the total income of all industrial and commercial companies. The figures obtained for them relate to a mixture of accounting years, and the figures of changes in holdings of marketable securities and of trade investments relate to changes in book values which are affected by changes in valuation. This information, however, is used only for the estimates of cash expenditure on trade investments and for cash expenditure on subsidiaries over the years 1960 to 1962. Figures of capital issues by quoted companies are compiled by the Bank of England.

Banking sector

Statistics of assets and liabilities for the banking sector are compiled by the Bank of England from returns made by the individual banks. Comprehensive returns have been made only from the second quarter of 1963; the amount of estimation for 1963 is therefore negligible. For earlier years the published figures are partly estimated and do not cover a number of important banks, in particular the United Kingdom banking offices of certain overseas banks. The returns provide details of assets and liabilities at the end of each calendar quarter including an analysis by sector of deposits and of advances and loans.

Information is available and published in *Financial Statistics* for the three parts of the banking sector: deposit banks including the Bank of England Banking Department, accepting houses and overseas banks, and the discount market.

Insurance companies and superannuation funds

Details of the transactions in financial assets by insurance companies and friendly societies have been collected quarterly by the Board of Trade since 1963 [5]. The figures of transactions in financial assets by insurance companies cover all members of the British Insurance Association whose parent company is registered and whose head office is in the United Kingdom. An allowance is made so that the figures also cover members of the Association of Collecting Friendly Societies which are not members of the British Insurance Association (generally the smaller societies). But the figures do not cover Commonwealth companies which are members of the Association and United Kingdom branches of overseas registered insurance companies. The funds managed by Lloyd's underwriters are also not covered. The figures include assets held in respect of money remitted by overseas branches and subsidiaries but they exclude direct investment by a

---

[5] See *Board of Trade Journal*, 19 July 1963.

United Kingdom company in its overseas branches or subsidiaries as well as financial assets held by or on behalf of these branches, even if held in the United Kingdom.

The quarterly figures of transactions in financial assets by superannuation schemes for those employed in the private sector are compiled from quarterly returns received from a sample of self-administered pension funds. The assets of the funds making returns are estimated to amount to about 80 per cent of the assets of all private pension funds. Estimates are included for funds which do not make returns. The figures have been compiled by the Board of Trade since 1963[6].

The figures for superannuation schemes for those employed in the public sector are compiled from direct returns giving similar information for superannuation funds of local authorities and of the various nationalised industries. They also include some from pre-nationalisation funds and certain other funds, namely: the British Council Superannuation Scheme, the Commonwealth War Graves Commission Superannuation Scheme, Indian Family Pensions Fund, Royal Seamen's Pension Fund and National Industrial Fuel Efficiency Service Superannuation Scheme.

Net receipts by the central government from those public sector superannuation schemes for which no separate fund is kept are taken from the government accounts (see page 276).

Separate quarterly figures of transactions in financial assets by insurance companies, private superannuation funds, and local authority and other public sector superannuation funds, together with figures of their holdings of assets at the end of the year, are published regularly in *Financial Statistics*.

The estimated increases in the liabilities of life assurance and superannuation funds relate to all funds; the estimates are described on page 113. Statistics of transactions in financial assets are not fully comprehensive and there is therefore a difference in coverage between the identified increases in the assets of life assurance and superannuation funds and the estimated increases in their liabilities.

Other financial institutions

Figures of transactions in financial assets by other financial institutions are compiled from quarterly returns made by them. For unit trusts and investment trusts quarterly returns have been made to the Bank of England since 1961; hire purchase finance companies have made returns to the Board of Trade since 1962[7]; the special investment departments of the trustee savings banks and the Investment Account of the Post Office Savings Bank make returns to the National Debt Office; and building societies have made quarterly returns of their transactions in financial assets to the Building Societies Association and the Central Statistical Office since 1960. Detailed quarterly figures of transactions by each of these groups of institutions are published in *Financial Statistics*. For the special finance agencies, quarterly returns are not available and their annual accounts are used to provide figures, quarterly figures being interpolated and extrapolated where necessary.

Building societies have made quarterly returns from 1954 and monthly returns from 1965 of changes in shares and deposits and mortgage advances. Nearly 100

---

[6]See *Board of Trade Journal*, 26 July 1963 and 10 July 1964.
[7]See *Board of Trade Journal*, 19 October 1962.

societies made monthly returns in 1966 and they accounted for nearly 90 per cent of the total assets of all building societies. Changes in the liabilities of hire purchase finance companies are taken from the same quarterly returns which provide details of their transactions in financial assets. For unit trusts, monthly figures of sales of units are provided by the Association of Unit Trust Managers. For investment trusts, hire purchase finance companies and special finance agencies, figures of capital issues are compiled by the Bank of England. Monthly figures of changes in deposits with the Investment Account of the Post Office Savings Bank and with the special investment departments of the trustee savings banks are compiled by the National Savings Committee. The detailed figures are published regularly in *Financial Statistics*.

Public sector

The figures of financial transactions for public corporations are based on quarterly returns made by the main corporations and on the corporations' annual accounts. Further details are given in Chapter VIII.

Details of financial transactions by the central government are based on quarterly departmental returns and are taken from the detailed capital account published for the central government. Further details of these sources are given in Chapter IX.

From 1961 local authorities have made quarterly returns covering their borrowing. Virtually all the local authorities in the United Kingdom provide figures of net borrowing, that is borrowing *less* repayments, divided between (a) temporary borrowing, (b) loans from the Public Works Loan Board and Northern Ireland Government Loans Fund, and (c) other long-term borrowing. In addition, a sample of all the larger authorities and selected smaller authorities, including those whose net borrowing in the quarter exceeds £100,000, provide an analysis of their borrowing by period to maturity and, except for quoted securities, by source. Long-term borrowing for which no analysis is given amounted to only 1 per cent of the total change during 1966.

Overseas sector

Except for the figures obtained specially from financial institutions, the items appearing in the financial transactions account for the overseas sector are taken from the balance of payments accounts, set out in detail in the annual publication *United Kingdom Balance of Payments*. The sources are described in Chapter XV, Section 3. A reconciliation between the financial accounts and the balance of payments accounts for 1966 is given on pages 451 to 454.

4. STATISTICAL SOURCES: FINANCIAL ASSETS

This section describes each of the financial assets shown in the table on pages 416 and 417 and gives the sources of the figures. The statistical sources which provide the figures for calendar years generally provide also the figures for calendar quarters.

Notes and coin

The issue of notes and coin is a source of finance for the central government. The figures for the public sector relate to the increase in the fiduciary note issue *plus* the increase in coin issued *less* the increase in holdings of notes and coin by the Bank of England Banking Department. The latter is included in the item 'Net Exchequer indebtedness to the Bank of England Banking Department', described below.

The figures for the banking sector relate to changes in their holdings of notes and coin *less* changes in Scottish and Northern Ireland notes issued. The former are an asset of the banking sector, the latter a liability.

Changes in holdings of notes and coin by other sectors are, for convenience, arbitrarily divided equally between industrial and commercial companies and the personal sector, apart from a special adjustment made to allow for the fact that the amount of notes and coin held by companies varies with the day of the week. On Thursdays and Fridays their holdings are normally higher than they are on Tuesdays and Wednesdays. The adjusted figures are provided by the Bank of England.

Treasury bills

These are market Treasury bills. They comprise Treasury bills other than those held by the National Debt Commissioners, the Exchange Equalisation Account, central government departments and the Bank of England. The counterpart of most transactions between central banks in support of the reserves in the form of swaps against sterling is included, but bills held by the Bank of England as the sterling equivalent of foreign currency deposits arising from central bank assistance are excluded.

Net sales by the public sector are equal to the increase in market Treasury bills outstanding *less* identified purchases by public corporations and local authorities. Information is available about changes in the holdings of market Treasury Bills by the banking sector, by other financial institutions and by non-residents. As holdings by the personal sector are believed to be relatively small, all the residual difference between identified sales and purchases is attributed to industrial and commercial companies. The figures for the overseas sector up to 1962 relate to overseas official holdings only.

British government and government guaranteed securities

These comprise British government and government guaranteed marketable securities. Public sector sales are equal to total cash issues *less* redemptions, including the purchases by government sinking funds, *less* net purchases by the Bank of England and the National Debt Commissioners, and *less* identified purchases by public corporations and local authorities.

The figures for the banking sector do not relate to cash transactions but to changes in holdings valued at book or nominal values or at cost. The figures for other financial institutions relate to cash transactions and are derived from the quarterly returns made by each of the various groups of institutions. The figures for the overseas sector relate to changes in holdings recorded in the balance of payments statistics of external liabilities and claims *plus* other identified portfolio investment in British government securities. Up to 1959 the figures relate to overseas official holdings only. An adjustment is made to convert the figures of external liabilities from a nominal to a cash transactions basis (see page 465). The residual difference between identified purchases and sales is arbitrarily attributed to the personal sector, as it is believed that net changes in the holdings of industrial and commercial companies are relatively small.

National savings

This comprises the following items.

 (a) *Deposits.*

 (i) Increases in outstanding deposits, including estimated accrued interest, with the ordinary departments of the Post Office Savings Bank and trustee savings banks.

 (ii) Increases in deposits, including estimated accrued interest, with the Investment Account of the Post Office Savings Bank and with the special investment departments of the trustee savings banks.

 (b) *Certificates and bonds.* Net receipts from sales of premium savings bonds, defence bonds, national development bonds and national savings certificates *plus* the increase in accrued interest on national savings certificates. Net receipts from sales of Ulster savings certificates and development bonds are not included.

Items (a) (i) and (b) represent financial claims by the personal sector on the public sector, and are shown in the central government capital account. Item (a) (ii) represents a financial claim by the personal sector on the financial institutions sector.

Tax reserve certificates

For the public sector this represents net receipts from issues of tax reserve certificates. Transactions by local authorities and by public corporations are known to be unimportant. The figures of net purchases by the personal sector and by the banking sector (from 1966 only) are taken from Bank of England records. All other net purchases are attributed to industrial and commercial companies, the figures for which therefore include unidentified net purchases made by financial institutions. The small amounts of net purchases reported by building societies, on which information is available, will be allocated to other financial institutions in the 1968 Blue Book.

Net Exchequer indebtedness to Bank of England Banking Department

All transactions between the central government and the Bank of England Banking Department, which is included in the banking sector, are recorded under this heading. The item comprises the sum of the increases in the following assets of the Banking Department: ways and means advances, holdings of notes and coin, tax reserve certificates, British government and government guaranteed securities, Treasury bills and Treasury interest-free notes; *less* increases in the balances of the Exchequer and Paymaster General at the Bank of England.

Changes in this item largely reflect movements in the net claims of the rest of the banking sector on the Banking Department. For example, during 1966 bankers' deposits with the Banking Department fell by £31 million; special deposits with the Banking Department increased by £102 million; and advances by the Banking Department to the discount market increased by £48 million. The banking sector's net claim on the Banking Department therefore increased by £23 million. This largely matched the increase of £44 million in the Exchequer's net indebtedness to the Banking Department.

Local authority debt

The figures for the public sector relate to all borrowing by local authorities from outside the public sector. They include borrowing from the banking sector and from local authorities' own superannuation funds.

From 1961, the figures are based on returns made quarterly by local authorities in the United Kingdom (see page 420). For the years before 1961, direct information from local authorities is not available and the total increase in local authority borrowing from outside the public sector is taken to be equal to the residual item shown in the local authority capital account (Table 46 of the 1967 Blue Book) *less* debt redemption by public corporations.

Local authority debt is divided between temporary borrowing, quoted securities and other long-term borrowing. Temporary borrowing covers money repayable in less than twelve months, including borrowing on bills and bank overdrafts. Quoted securities and negotiable bonds are securities quoted on a United Kingdom stock exchange and all negotiable bonds, some of which are unquoted. Loans by local authority superannuation funds to the parent authority are included in figures for other long-term debt acquired by insurance companies and superannuation funds.

Local authority debt acquired by the banking sector comprises advances and loans *plus*, from 1963, their acquisition of local authority bills and of quoted and unquoted securities. The figures are based on returns provided by the banking sector.

Local authority debt acquired by the overseas sector covers identified transactions, some of which are classified in the balance of payments accounts as 'Portfolio investment' in the long-term capital account and others which are classified as 'External liabilities in sterling' in monetary movements. The figures are based partly on returns by local authorities and partly on balance of payments returns (see pages 420 and 465).

Deposits with banking sector

These are current and deposit accounts held with institutions classified to the banking sector. These accounts include:

(a) deposits with the Bank of England Banking Department, other than bankers' deposits and the balances of the Exchequer and Paymaster General;

(b) funds borrowed by the discount market from outside the banking sector;

(c) the banking sector's net liabilities to offices abroad and deposits and advances from banks abroad.

They exclude banks' own internal funds and all transactions between institutions classified to the banking sector. The increase in the banking sector's liability to other sectors is equal to the increase in other sectors' deposits with the banking sector *plus* any increase in credits in course of transmission *less* any increase in cheques in course of collection and *less* any increase in items in transit between offices of the same bank. These three adjustments for items in transit are not allocated by sector. They probably largely reflect changes in liabilities to companies.

From 1963 a full analysis by sector is obtained from information provided by the institutions classified to the banking sector, and is compiled by the Bank of England. For earlier years the information is incomplete. The figures of net bank deposits for the personal sector for the years up to 1962 relate to deposits, *less* advances, of persons with the London clearing banks. They relate to persons as individuals and exclude accounts known to be used by unincorporated businesses, for example the accounts of shopkeepers, farmers and professional men.

Deposits with building societies

These cover both shares and deposits with building societies. Increases in deposits are equal to receipts of principal *plus* interest credited and not paid out *less* withdrawals of principal. The figures cover all building societies in the United Kingdom.

The annual figures are based on statutory returns made to the Registrar of Friendly Societies and summarised in the *Report of the Chief Registrar of Friendly Societies, Part* 5. Monthly and quarterly returns are made by a sample of building societies to the Building Societies Association and the Central Statistical Office. Since 1965 nearly 100 societies have made monthly returns; they accounted for nearly 90 per cent of the total assets of all building societies in 1966.

Deposits, etc. with hire purchase finance companies

This comprises deposits with, and other borrowing except from banks by, hire purchase finance companies. Bills discounted with banks are not included in this item but in 'Bank lending: commercial bills'. The figures are based on returns from all the largest hire purchase finance companies and a selection of the smaller ones. The returns cover companies with about nine-tenths of the business of all hire purchase finance companies. Estimates are included for companies not making returns.

Deposits with other financial institutions

These are deposits received from overseas residents by financial institutions not classified to the banking sector. The series is compiled from returns made in connection with balance of payments statistics (see page 466).

Bank lending

All transactions between institutions classified to the banking sector are excluded. Lending to local authorities is excluded; it is recorded against the heading 'Local authority debt'.

(a) *Advances and loans.* These include overdrafts. The analysis by sector is obtained from the returns made to the Bank of England by the institutions classified to the banking sector. Loans for house purchase are now identified and in some tables, including that on pages 416 and 417, are excluded from this item and included with loans for house purchase (see page 425).

(b) *Commercial bills.* These are commercial bills drawn on United Kingdom and overseas residents and discounted by banks. They also include Treasury bills of the Northern Ireland, Commonwealth and foreign governments. The figures for 'Other financial institutions' relate to bills discounted by hire purchase finance companies and are obtained from quarterly data provided by these companies. The figures for the overseas sector are obtained from returns made by the banks. The figures for industrial and commercial companies are obtained as a residual. No information is available on changes in holdings by the personal sector and these are ignored.

(c) *Money at call and short notice.* The estimated allocation by sector is based on information provided by the banks.

Hire purchase debt

The figures relate for all years to debt outstanding on instalment credit transactions to durable goods retailers (including gas and electricity showrooms), department stores and hire purchase finance companies; from 1961 co-operative societies, general mail order houses and other general stores are also covered. The figures also include the personal loan business of hire purchase finance companies. Excluded are non-instalment credit, such as monthly charge accounts, and sales against credit checks of check-issuing companies. Debt owed to finance companies, though not that owed to retailers, is reckoned after deducting unearned finance charges, that is the interest element which will accrue to finance companies from future repayments under instalment credit contracts. The estimates are derived from regular returns made to the Board of Trade [8] by retailers in the kinds of business listed above and by hire purchase finance companies.

The figures for the public sector relate to credit given by public corporations through gas and electricity showrooms. The figures for other financial institutions include agreements block discounted with finance companies by retailers. The figures for the personal sector relate only to the debt of individual consumers and therefore exclude credit given to professional persons, farmers, and other unincorporated businesses; this is included in the residual figures for industrial and commercial companies.

Trade debt (net) of public corporations

Information on trade credit given or received is available only for public corporations. The figures are derived from the annual accounts of the corporations and from quarterly returns provided by them. The sector allocation is based on a very rough analysis of the figures in the published annual accounts.

Trade credit given or received on overseas transactions by industrial and commercial companies is included under the heading 'Other identified overseas assets: short-term'. Other trade credit is not identified in the financial accounts.

Loans for house purchase

(a) *Local authorities.* Loans made for 'Small dwellings acquisition'. Financial year figures are obtained from *Local Government Financial Statistics* and the corresponding publications for Scotland and Northern Ireland. Quarterly figures are obtained from returns made to the housing departments.

(b) *Other public sector.* Loans made by the central government under the Housing Act, 1961 and Housing (Scotland) Act, 1962 to private housing associations, and loans made by the Housing Corporation to housing societies.

(c) *Financial institutions.* Mortgage advances made by building societies, loans by insurance companies and, in some tables, loans by banks. Figures for building societies are based on figures for accounting years from the *Report of the Chief Registrar of Friendly Societies, Part 5* and monthly and quarterly returns made by a sample of building societies to the Building Societies Association and the Central Statistical Office. Estimates for insurance companies up to 1962 have been made using figures presented to the Committee on the Working of the Monetary System and the annual analysis of company reports summarised by the Board of Trade. From 1963 the figures are taken from quarterly returns made by insurance companies. Quarterly figures for banks are compiled by the Bank of England; the 1967 Blue Book included figures from 1963 only but figures from 1960 have been published subsequently.

---

[8] See *Board of Trade Journal*, 12 February 1965.

Other loans by public sector to private sector

The figures relate to net lending by the central government to building societies under the House Purchase and Housing Act, 1959 (allocated to other financial institutions), to industry and trade (allocated entirely to industrial and commercial companies) and other miscellaneous loans for education and other services (allocated entirely to the personal sector). Also included is net lending by public corporations to the private sector, other than for house purchase (allocated to industrial and commercial companies). The figures are taken from the detailed capital accounts of the central government (see page 283) and of public corporations (see page 245).

Loans by superannuation funds to parent organisation

This includes loans made by their superannuation funds to public corporations and companies. Figures are taken from returns made by the superannuation funds. Loans made by local authorities' superannuation schemes to local authorities are excluded; they are recorded against the heading 'Local authority debt'. This item also includes net receipts by the central government from those public sector schemes for which no separate pension fund is maintained. These figures are taken from the capital account of the central government, where they are described as 'Receipts from certain pension "funds" (net)'.

Other loans and mortgages by financial institutions (excluding banks)

Loans and mortgages other than hire purchase debt, loans for house purchase, and loans made to their parent organisation by superannuation funds. These loans are made mainly by insurance companies and by special finance agencies. The figures for the personal sector before 1963 represent loans made by insurance companies established in Great Britain as shown by reports summarised by the Board of Trade. The figures include some loans made to non-residents but do not include similar loans to United Kingdom residents made by companies established outside Great Britain.

Unit trust units

Sales *less* repurchases of unit trust units, provided by the Association of Unit Trust Managers. All transactions are assumed to be with the personal sector.

Shares of retail co-operative societies

These figures relate to purchases of shares in retail co-operative societies. They are obtained from the *Report of the Chief Registrar of Friendly Societies, Part 3.* The figures are shown separately in the tables for industrial and commercial companies and the personal sector, but because the amounts are small they are included with 'Company and overseas securities' in the flow of funds table (see page 427).

Company and overseas securities

(a) *Capital issues.* New money raised by issues of ordinary, preference and loan capital; the figures cover public issues, offers for sale, issues by tender, placings and issues to shareholders and employees *less* redemptions. The figures relate to quoted public companies in the United Kingdom and to overseas public companies and overseas public authorities. Issues to shareholders are included only if the sole or principal share register is maintained in the United

Kingdom. Issues in foreign currencies are included where United Kingdom institutions take a leading part in arranging them. Estimates of issues are based on the prices at which securities are offered to the market. Subscriptions are included in the periods in which they are due to be paid. It is not possible to provide an analysis of capital issues by the sector acquiring them; these acquisitions are included with other transactions in company securities.

The estimates are prepared by the Bank of England [9] and are published monthly in *Financial Statistics*.

(b) *Other*. These are all other transactions in quoted and unquoted securities which can be identified, including the acquisition of capital issues.

Transactions by the public sector are taken from the capital accounts of the central government and of public corporations. They comprise cash expenditure on company securities, etc. (net) by the central government and by public corporations *less* net cash receipts by the central government from iron and steel disposals (see pages 286, 245 and 276).

Figures for the banking sector relate to the published changes in the book value of their holdings of 'Other securities' *less* changes in the book value of their holdings of local authority securities. Figures for life assurance and superannuation funds and other financial institutions are purchases *less* sales of both quoted and unquoted securities valued at cash values. These are based on their quarterly returns of cash transactions.

For the overseas sector, figures of total transactions in company and overseas securities are taken from balance of payments statistics. The derivation of the figures for 1966 is shown in the table on page 453. The difference between total transactions and the figure of capital issues for the overseas sector taken from the Bank of England series described above is allocated to this item.

Information about transactions in company and overseas securities by industrial and commercial companies is not complete. The figure given in the flow of funds table relates only to their estimated cash expenditure on acquiring other businesses as going concerns and trade investments, which are described below (£315 million in 1966), and to the issue of shares of retail co-operative societies, described above (£6 million in 1966). When a subsidiary is acquired, or a trade investment is made, by way of a share exchange, no transaction needs to be recorded in the financial accounts because no other item is affected. But if the acquisition is paid for, or partly paid for, in cash, then the cash part of the transaction needs to be recorded, because the cash payment will be reflected in other items in the accounts. No allowance is made for portfolio investment by industrial and commercial companies. To this extent the estimates may be understated.

Cash expenditure on acquiring subsidiaries and trade investments. The figures relate to three items:

(a) Cash expenditure on acquiring businesses as going concerns in the United Kingdom (£183 million in 1966). Quarterly information is available from the reports on bids and deals published in the press. Not all deals are reported and an allowance needs to be made for this. An allowance also has to be made for cash expenditure on acquiring unincorporated businesses as going concerns. In order to obtain an indication of the amounts involved, the Board of Trade carried out a limited inquiry at the end of 1964, covering about 1,500 large

---

[9] See *Bank of England Quarterly Bulletin*, June 1966.

companies engaged in distribution, catering and property owning. Even if a generous allowance is made for industries not covered by the inquiry, the results suggest that cash expenditure on acquiring unincorporated businesses in 1963 and 1964 amounted to no more than £10 to £20 million in each year. Quarterly estimates of cash expenditure on subsidiaries were first prepared in the Central Statistical Office, but by agreement the preparation of these estimates was taken over by the Bank of England in 1965[10].

(b) Cash expenditure on trade investments in the United Kingdom (£78 million in 1966). The estimates are based on the Board of Trade analysis of the accounts of large quoted and non-quoted companies (see page 418) and on an analysis of the accounts of a number of other large companies operating in industries such as shipping which are not covered in the Board's regular analysis. This estimate is very uncertain as it is based on changes in book values and on incomplete information. For the latest year, no information is available from published accounts and it is assumed that expenditure on trade investments is the same as in the previous year, because the figures show no definite trend. Quarterly figures are obtained simply by dividing the annual figures by four.

(c) Net acquisition of share and loan capital in overseas companies (£54 million in 1966). The series forms part of private investment abroad in the balance of payments accounts. The figures exclude net investment by oil companies, which is included under 'Other identified overseas assets: long-term'.

The estimates of transactions in company and overseas securities by the personal sector, given in the table on page 417, are derived as a residual. They are obtained as the difference between the aggregate of the sales and purchases of all the other sectors. Because of this, they are subject to a wide margin of error. In particular, any errors in the estimates for the acquisition of securities by industrial and commercial companies, which could be large, are reflected in the residual figure for the personal sector. Also included are any errors arising from the inclusion of costs of transactions in the figures of net acquisitions by financial institutions. But the estimates have the important advantages of being comprehensive and of being available quarterly as well as annually [11].

Monthly figures of turnover in securities on the London Stock Exchange have been collected and published since September 1964. The figures are classified by category of security but not by sector and hence do not provide any help in dividing transactions between those of companies and the personal sector. Even if a sector analysis were provided it would be of limited value because of the extensive use of nominees.

The estimated figure of net sales of company and overseas securities by the personal sector, obtained as a residual, is very large indeed. This result is broadly confirmed by a detailed analysis of company share registers carried out by Revell and Moyle which provided a direct estimate of sales of ordinary shares by the personal sector for the year 1963 [12].

A substantial proportion of the sales of securities by the personal sector represents a switching from direct holdings of securities to indirect holdings through the agency of financial institutions. In particular, purchases of annuities and

---

[10] See the article 'Company acquisitions', *Bank of England Quarterly Bulletin*, December 1966.

[11] See 'More Light on Personal Saving', *Economic Trends*, April 1965.

[12] J. Revell and J. Moyle, *The Owners of Quoted Ordinary Shares: A Survey for 1963*, A Programme for Growth, No. 7, Department of Applied Economics, Cambridge, 1966.

single premium bonds (£190 million in 1964) and purchases of unit trust units (£105 million in 1966) are often considered close substitutes to direct holdings of company securities. In addition, there has been a steady increase in contractual saving through life assurance and superannuation schemes and this has been associated with substantial purchases of company securities by these institutions.

The figures of sales by the personal sector include sales by company directors and their associates when their businesses 'go public'. It is important to note here that the acquisition of securities by the personal sector arising from the incorporation of businesses is not recorded in the financial accounts. Although this represents a change in the composition of the assets of the personal sector it does not involve a cash transaction and hence cannot be recorded. But the subsequent sale of any shares held by the personal sector to other sectors is recorded. Thus it is possible for the financial accounts to record continuing sales of company securities by the personal sector without any reduction in the total market value of their holdings. Similarly, continuing sales of securities may arise from the realisation of capital gains. When market prices are rising sales of securities by the personal sector can take place without any reduction in the total market value of their holdings. As has been indicated already, capital gains and losses are not recorded in the financial accounts.

Some sales by the personal sector may be associated with the payment of death duties (the latter amounted to £309 million in 1966) and the breaking-up of personal estates; others may be the counterpart of investment in dwellings, which is in part financed out of existing savings.

Finally, it should be repeated that because the estimate of sales of company and overseas securities by the personal sector is calculated as a residual, the figures of sales are overstated to the extent that costs of arranging transactions, that is stamp duty *plus* commissions, are included in the estimates of the net acquisition of securities by financial institutions.

Funds of life assurance and superannuation schemes

The annual estimates of the net increase in the funds of life assurance and superannuation schemes are taken from their revenue account (Table 24 of the 1967 Blue Book) which is described on page 113. The quarterly estimates are based on the quarterly returns of investments made by insurance companies and superannuation funds, which are described on pages 418-9. The net increase in the funds is regarded as a claim by the personal sector on financial institutions (see page 413).

Miscellaneous short-term home assets (net)

The national accounts are generally on an accruals basis whereas transactions in the financial transactions accounts are on a cash basis. This item is designed to link the two. It represents the difference between accruals and the corresponding cash payments for local authority rates, purchase tax and some interest charges, which are recorded on an accruals basis in the income and expenditure and appropriation accounts (see pages 309, 277 and 217. The allocation of the difference to other sectors is approximate.

Other identified home assets

For the public sector this item comprises the following transactions:

(a) net sales of securities and increases in other debt by the Northern Ireland central government;

(b) coal compensation in cash;

(c) purchases of silver;

(d) certain miscellaneous capital receipts, such as gifts, by the Exchequer;

(e) redemptions *less* issues of stock of the Electricity Board for Northern Ireland.

For financial institutions this item comprises:

(a) increases in assets and liabilities which are not separately identified in the returns made by financial institutions;

(b) changes in the balances of agents for insurance companies;

(c) investment in land, property and ground rents, which is identified in the returns made by certain financial institutions *less* the estimated gross domestic fixed capital formation by these institutions.

In the table on pages 416 and 417 the matching transactions are not allocated to other sectors and are shown as unallocated. It is hoped to allocate them in subsequent Blue Books.

Gold and currency reserves

The net change in the official holdings of gold, dollars and other foreign currencies, both convertible and non-convertible. Up to 1959 the change in the United Kingdom balance in the European Payments Union was also included. Further details are given on page 455.

Inter-government loans

The entries under this item comprise drawings on and repayments of loans made by the United Kingdom government to overseas governments and to the United Kingdom government by overseas governments. From 1959 the figures include repayments of debt created as a consequence of the winding-up of the European Payments Union, when the outstanding debts were converted into bilateral long-term loans.

The figures also appear in the detailed capital account of the central government and are described on pages 280 and 285.

Transactions with International Monetary Fund, etc.

This comprises the following central government transactions with non-territorial financial organisations:

(a) drawings from United Kingdom subscriptions to international lending bodies;

plus

(b) capital subscriptions to the International Monetary Fund and European Fund;

less

(c) increase in holdings of interest-free notes by the International Monetary Fund.

The figures also appear in the detailed capital account of the central government and are described on pages 285 and 281.

Other identified overseas assets: short-term

This comprises the total of monetary movements in the balance of payments accounts *less* all the items which are identified separately in the flow of funds table. This item is shown separately for the private and public sectors in the table on page 450 and described on pages 456 and 457. The figure for the public sector includes bills held by the Bank of England as the sterling equivalent of foreign currency deposits arising from central bank assistance. The figure for other financial institutions is taken from the returns made by the institutions. The remainder of the private sector figure is arbitrarily attributed to industrial and commercial companies.

Other identified overseas assets: long-term

This covers those transactions from the balance of payments long-term capital account which are not allocated elsewhere in the financial accounts.

For the public sector this item consists of net changes in overseas assets held by the United Kingdom central government, including the Atomic Energy Authority, and public corporations such as the Commonwealth Development Corporation. The purchase by the United Kingdom government of United Nations bonds in 1962 and subsequent redemptions are included in this item. Also included in 1966 is the servicing of the loan by the International Bank for Reconstruction and Development to Rhodesia, guaranteed by the United Kingdom government.

For financial institutions the figures relate to loans and mortgages by insurance companies. For financial institutions and industrial and commercial companies combined the item represents private investment abroad, other than in securities, *less* the corresponding private investment in the United Kingdom. The un-remitted profits of overseas branches and subsidiaries and all investment abroad by oil companies are included in this item. The relationship between the figure in the flow of funds table and the figure of total private direct investment in the balance of payments accounts is shown in the table on page 454.

Unidentified items

A number of financial assets are not covered by the estimates given above. The main omissions are trade credit of private businesses, and loans made by those not making comprehensive financial returns, that is mainly loans between industrial and commercial companies and the personal sector.

This item is also the balancing item in the financial account and includes any errors and omissions in the identified transactions in financial assets and in the estimates of the total net acquisition of financial assets (see page 432).

5. RELIABILITY

Net acquisition of financial assets

The estimates of saving are the residual item in the sector income and expenditure and appropriation accounts and the reliability of the annual estimates depends upon the reliability of the other items, discussed in the chapters on the individual sectors. Generally, the estimates of saving for the public sector are better than those for the private sector. Figures for the former are obtained almost entirely from comprehensive accounting data, except those for the most recent year or two, whereas those for the latter are not. In terms of the reliability gradings described on pages 39 to 41, financial year figures for the public sector are good, but those for calendar years are less reliable. The figures for the private sector as a whole are probably at best fair, but the division of the total between the personal and company sectors is less reliable and, in particular, the estimates for the personal sector are poor.

The figures of net acquisition of financial assets are obtained as a balancing item in the sector capital accounts. The reliability of the annual estimates of expenditure on fixed capital formation is described in Chapter XII and on stocks in Chapter XIII. For the public sector, the annual figures of the net acquisition of financial assets are fair but the figures for the private sector and for the overseas sector are poor. The reliability of the figures for the overseas sector is discussed in Chapter XV.

The quarterly estimates are in all cases less reliable than the annual ones.

Financial transactions

Most of the figures of transactions by the public sector are good, as they are taken from accounting data.

Figures for the banking sector from 1963 are generally good. The figures are based on returns made by the banks themselves. One difficulty is that the number of institutions making returns has been increased from time to time. However, the figures for securities do not relate to cash transactions but to changes in book or nominal values. Most of the British government securities held by banks have a fixed and relatively early redemption date so the margins of error here are probably not large. But this may not be the case for their holdings of other securities.

Figures of transactions by other financial institutions are mostly good. They are based mainly on returns made by the institutions themselves and generally relate to cash transactions in each quarterly period. The main errors here are probably those associated with sampling, as the coverage of the smaller institutions is limited.

Many of the figures for industrial and commercial companies and for the personal sector are derived indirectly from information provided by the public sector and by financial institutions. For example, returns for the banking sector give details of the amounts advanced to and deposits received from each of the different sectors. Similarly, returns from insurance companies and building societies give details of loans made to the personal sector. A difficulty here is to ensure that the transactions attributed to the personal sector or to industrial and commercial companies relate to the same point in time as the estimates of saving and investment given in their capital accounts. Figures for calendar years obtained in this way are considered good. Figures obtained as residuals are considered poor; examples are transactions in securities by the personal sector and transactions in Treasury bills by industrial and commercial companies.

The reliability of the figures of transactions with non-residents is discussed on pages 471 and 472.

The size of the 'Unidentified items' in each sector's financial transactions account (shown at the end of the table on page 417), provides only a very partial indication of the reliability of the estimates of the aggregate of transactions in financial assets which are identified. Transactions in some financial assets are not identified and the unidentified items reflect also the residual error in the national income accounts, the balancing item in the balance of payments accounts, and errors in the estimated distribution of saving and of capital formation between the different sectors.

ANNEX 1

BANKING SECTOR

As at 31 December 1966

Afghan National Bank Ltd.
African Continental Bank Ltd.
Alexanders Discount Co. Ltd.
Allen, Harvey & Ross Ltd.
The American Express Company Inc.
Anglo-Israel Bank Ltd.
Anglo-Portuguese Bank Ltd.
Arbuthnot Latham & Co. Ltd.
Australia and New Zealand Bank Ltd.
Banco de Bilbao
Banco Español en Londres S.A.
Bangkok Bank Ltd.
The Bank of Adelaide
Bank of America National Trust and Savings Association
Bank of Baroda Ltd.
Bank of Ceylon
Bank of China
Bank of Cyprus (London) Ltd.
Bank of England Banking Department
The Bank of India Ltd.
Bank of Ireland
The Bank of Kobe Ltd.
Bank of London & South America Ltd.
Bank of Montreal
Bank of New South Wales
Bank of New Zealand
The Bank of Nova Scotia
Bank of Scotland
Bank of Tokyo Ltd.
Bank Saderat Iran
Bankers Trust Company
Banque Belge Ltd.
Banque Belgo-Congolaise S.A.
Banque de l'Indochine
Banque de Paris et des Pays-Bas Ltd.
Banque Nationale de Paris
Barclays Bank D.C.O.
Barclays Bank Ltd.
Baring Brothers & Co. Ltd.
Belfast Banking Company Ltd.
Wm. Brandt's Sons & Co. Ltd.
British and Continental Banking Co. Ltd.

British and French Bank Ltd.
The British Bank of the Middle East
The British Linen Bank
Brown, Shipley & Co. Ltd.
Canadian Imperial Bank of Commerce
Cater, Ryder & Co. Ltd.
Central Bank of India Ltd.
The Chartered Bank
Charterhouse Japhet & Thomasson Ltd.
The Chase Manhattan Bank N.A.
Chemical Bank New York Trust Company
Clive Discount Co. Ltd.
Clydesdale Bank Ltd.
The Commercial Bank of Australia Ltd.
Commercial Bank of the Near East Ltd.
The Commercial Banking Company of Sydney Ltd.
Commonwealth Trading Bank of Australia
Continental Illinois National Bank and Trust Company of Chicago
Co-operative Wholesale Society Ltd., Banking Department
Coutts & Co.
Crédit Industriel et Commercial
Crédit Lyonnais
Dai-Ichi Bank Ltd.
Daiwa Bank Ltd.
District Bank Ltd.
The Eastern Bank Ltd.
The English, Scottish and Australian Bank Ltd.
First National Bank of Boston
First National Bank of Chicago
First National City Bank
French Bank of Southern Africa Ltd.
Fuji Bank Ltd.
Gerrard & Reid Ltd.
Ghana Commercial Bank
Antony Gibbs & Sons, Ltd.

Gillett Bros. Discount Co. Ltd.
Glyn, Mills & Co.
Guinness Mahon & Co. Ltd.
Habib Bank (Overseas) Ltd.
Hambros Bank Ltd.
The Hibernian Bank Ltd.
Hill, Samuel & Co. Ltd.
C. Hoare & Co.
The Hongkong and Shanghai Banking
  Corporation
International Credit Bank Geneva
Ionian Bank Ltd.
Irving Trust Company
Isle of Man Bank Ltd.
Israel-British Bank Ltd.
Italo-Belgian Bank
Jessel, Toynbee & Co. Ltd.
Leopold Joseph & Sons Ltd.
Keyser Ullmann Ltd.
King & Shaxson Ltd.
Kleinwort, Benson Ltd.
Lazard Brothers & Co. Ltd.
Lewis's Bank Ltd.
Lloyds Bank (Europe) Ltd.
Lloyds Bank Ltd.
Malayan Banking Ltd.
Manufacturers Hanover Trust
  Company
Marine Midland Grace Trust
  Company of New York
Martins Bank Ltd.
Mercantile Bank Ltd.
Midland Bank Ltd.
Midland and International Banks Ltd.
Mitsubishi Bank Ltd.
Mitsui Bank Ltd.
Samuel Montagu & Co. Ltd.
Morgan Grenfell & Co. Ltd.
Morgan Guaranty Trust Company of
  New York
Moscow Narodny Bank Ltd.
The Munster & Leinster Bank Ltd.
Muslim Commercial Bank Ltd.
National and Grindlays Bank Ltd.
The National Bank Ltd.
The National Bank of Australasia Ltd.
National Bank of Greece
The National Bank of Ireland Ltd.
The National Bank of New Zealand Ltd.
National Bank of Nigeria Ltd.

National Bank of Pakistan
National Commercial Bank of Scotland
  Ltd.
National Discount Co. Ltd.
National Provincial Bank Ltd.
Netherlands Bank of South Africa Ltd.
Nippon Kangyo Bank Ltd.
Northern Bank Ltd.
Ottoman Bank
Overseas Union Bank Ltd.
Provincial Bank of Ireland Ltd.
Rafidain Bank
Ralli Brothers (Bankers) Ltd.
Rea Brothers Ltd.
N. M. Rothschild & Sons
The Royal Bank of Canada
The Royal Bank of Ireland Ltd.
The Royal Bank of Scotland
Sanwa Bank Ltd.
E. D. Sassoon Banking Co. Ltd.
J. Henry Schroder Wagg & Co. Ltd.
Scottish Co-operative Wholesale
  Society Ltd., Banking Department
Seccombe, Marshall & Campion Ltd.
Singer & Friedlander Ltd.
Smith, St. Aubyn & Co. Ltd.
Société Centrale de Banque
Société Générale
The Standard Bank Ltd.
The Standard Bank of West Africa Ltd.
State Bank of India
Sumitomo Bank Ltd.
Swiss Bank Corporation
Swiss-Israel Trade Bank
Tokai Bank Ltd.
The Toronto-Dominion Bank
Trade Development Bank
Ulster Bank Ltd.
Union Discount Co. of London Ltd.
United Bank Ltd.
The United Bank of Kuwait Ltd.
United Commercial Bank Ltd.
S. G. Warburg & Co. Ltd. (incorporat-
  ing Seligman Brothers)
Westminster Bank Ltd.
Westminster Foreign Bank Ltd.
Williams Deacon's Bank Ltd.
Yorkshire Bank Ltd.
Živnostenská Banka National
  Corporation

ANNEX 2

SPECIAL FINANCE AGENCIES

As at 31 December 1966

Finance Corporation for Industry Ltd.
Industrial and Commercial Finance Corporation Ltd.
Agricultural Mortgage Corporation Ltd.
Commonwealth Development Finance Co. Ltd.
Scottish Agricultural Securities Corporation Ltd.
Ship Mortgage Finance Co. Ltd.
Private Enterprise Investment Co. Ltd.
Charterhouse Industrial Development Co. Ltd.
Technical Development Capital Ltd.
Insurance Export Finance Co. Ltd.

Chapter XV

International Transactions

1. GENERAL DESCRIPTION

The national income, product and expenditure of the United Kingdom are the income, product and expenditure of those persons, enterprises and institutions which are regarded as United Kingdom residents. They are not the same as the income and product originating within the geographical boundaries of the United Kingdom or the expenditure occurring there (see Chapter I). Hence international transactions must be defined as those between the residents of the United Kingdom and non-residents. The measurement of the outcome of all transactions between residents of the United Kingdom and non-residents is the object of the balance of payments accounts. In the balance of payments accounts the United Kingdom is taken to include the Channel Islands and the Isle of Man as well as Great Britain and Northern Ireland. The inclusion of the Channel Islands and the Isle of Man gives rise to a minor inconsistency since income and expenditure in the Channel Islands and the Isle of Man are not included in the domestic accounts; there is thus a small and fairly regular discrepancy between the two sets of figures for which no adjustment is made.

Residents of the United Kingdom comprise private individuals living in the United Kingdom; the United Kingdom central government and local authorities; and all business enterprises and non-profit-making organisations located in the United Kingdom, including branches and subsidiaries of overseas companies but excluding overseas branches and subsidiaries of United Kingdom companies. Agencies of the United Kingdom government operating abroad, such as embassies or military units, are regarded as residents of the United Kingdom, and conversely, the agencies of foreign governments in the United Kingdom are regarded as overseas residents.

Definition of residents

The definition of residence for an individual is relatively straightforward, although discrepancies may arise in the estimates because of differences in the treatment of those who live in the United Kingdom for relatively short periods. The rules defining residence for tax purposes determine the estimates of total domestic income. Broadly speaking, persons are resident in the United Kingdom for tax purposes if they maintain a place of abode in the United Kingdom and visit it at any time during the year or if they are in the United Kingdom for six months or more during the year or if they visit the United Kingdom regularly for substantial periods. Persons who fulfil any of these conditions are subject to United Kingdom tax in respect of the whole of their income wherever originating, with only certain minor exceptions. United Kingdom government officials and Forces stationed abroad are regarded as United Kingdom residents; they are subject to United Kingdom income tax and are covered by the Inland Revenue figures. Similarly, officials and Forces of other governments stationed in the United Kingdom are excluded.

In the balance of payments accounts, there is a distinction for individuals other than government officials and Forces between migrants, who change residence, and visitors, who do not. It is based on the intention to stay abroad for one year or more. A United Kingdom resident leaving the United Kingdom for one year or more is regarded as an emigrant. Similarly, an overseas resident arriving in the United Kingdom with the intention of staying here for one year or more is regarded as an immigrant. This definition therefore differs from that used for income tax purposes but is fairly close to it. It is not possible to estimate the practical effect of this difference, but it is thought to be not large.

Neither the definition used in determining the residence of individuals for tax purposes nor the definition adopted in the context of migration necessarily corresponds exactly to the definition in the international recommendations for balance of payments statistics, where 'centre of interest' is given as the determining factor in marginal cases [1]. It should be noted that in a few cases an individual may satisfy the criteria for residence in more than one country. And in practice an individual may be regarded as a resident only in so far as his income and expenditure arise in the country.

The definition of residence for a business is more complicated. For income tax purposes a company, wherever registered, is treated as resident in the United Kingdom if the central management and control of the business is exercised in the United Kingdom; its profits, wherever originating, are then liable to United Kingdom tax. Thus some companies are subject to tax as United Kingdom residents although most of their assets are abroad: for instance many mining companies and rubber plantations. 'Resident' for Inland Revenue purposes also includes branches and subsidiaries of overseas companies operating in the United Kingdom and in this respect is practically identical with the concept required for national income and balance of payments purposes.

For the national income accounts, an enterprise which is a United Kingdom resident but whose trading operations take place wholly or partly abroad is in principle divided into two parts: (i) overseas branches or subsidiaries earning trading profits on overseas operations and (ii) a head office and branches earning trading profits on operations in the United Kingdom, if any. Branches are treated as residents of the country in which they are located and subsidiaries where they are registered. The profits of overseas branches and subsidiaries contribute to national income not as part of domestic income but as income from abroad. Correspondingly, the United Kingdom branches and subsidiaries of overseas companies contribute to domestic income but not to national income, their profits being part of income paid abroad.

For the estimates of the gross trading profits of companies operating in the United Kingdom, which form part of total domestic income, the Inland Revenue provides figures of the total profits of resident companies whose operations are mainly in the United Kingdom, including resident branches and subsidiaries of overseas companies. These figures exclude all of the profits of companies with operations mainly abroad, and dividends received from overseas subsidiaries

---

[1] *Balance of Payments Manual*, Third Edition, International Monetary Fund, Washington, D.C., 1961.

which are taken into account in the overall assessment to tax of a resident parent company. An approximate adjustment is made to exclude any trading profits earned abroad by companies operating mainly in the United Kingdom and include any profits earned in the United Kingdom by companies operating mainly abroad, but the overall difference from the required concept is thought to be small. It should be noted that enterprises engaged in operating British ships and aircraft are treated as operating in the United Kingdom irrespective of where the ships or aircraft are located; the incomes earned by their crews and the gross trading profits of the companies are regarded as part of domestic product. Similarly, the operations of oil rigs on the United Kingdom part of the North Sea Continental Shelf are regarded as operations within the United Kingdom.

To estimate the national income, the profits of overseas branches and subsidiaries of United Kingdom companies have to be included and the profits of United Kingdom branches and subsidiaries of non-resident companies excluded. These estimates are based on the Board of Trade direct investment inquiry, made for the balance of payments accounts. In this inquiry the definition of an overseas branch is a permanent establishment as defined for the purpose of United Kingdom tax in the Statutory Instruments relating to double taxation relief. It is thus consistent in principle with the estimation of profits arising in the United Kingdom. In addition to allowing for the profits of overseas branches, the profits of overseas subsidiaries are also allowed for in proportion to the degree of ownership of the parent company, whether the profits are remitted or not. The profits of trade investments in associated companies are similarly allowed for. Other operations abroad of the parent company which do not fall within these definitions are regarded as part of the operations of the parent company. If the parent company employs an overseas agent, the transactions arranged by the agent are regarded as being made directly with the parent company and only the commissions, etc. paid to the agent for his services accrue to the country of residence of the agent.

Thus, as far as possible, the balance of payments and national income accounts employ the same definition of residence for companies although there may be some inconsistencies in the treatment of profits earned from operations abroad which form a minor part of the total operations of the company. Discrepancies may also arise from differences in the assessments of profits by the Inland Revenue and the amounts of profits reported in the direct investment inquiry.

Principles of the balance of payments accounts

In principle, transactions are recorded in the balance of payments accounts when the ownership of goods or assets changes and when services are rendered. This conforms with the payable-receivable or accruals basis generally used in the national accounts. But in practice in the balance of payments accounts it is not always possible to keep precisely to this principle; the main departure from it is in the recording of imports and exports of goods (see page 441).

Transactions in the balance of payments are classified in three main accounts:
(a) the current account covers imports and exports of goods and services, property income and transfers;
(b) the long-term capital account covers inter-government loans, other official capital transactions and private investment;
(c) monetary movements cover the remaining financial transactions, that is changes in the gold and convertible currency reserves, transactions with the

International Monetary Fund, changes in banking liabilities and claims, and other capital transactions of a monetary nature.

It should be noted that the balance of payments current account combines transactions which may be included in a production account, an income and expenditure account or a capital account within the national income accounts (see Chapter II). Thus, imports of goods by United Kingdom residents which are included in the current account of the balance of payments may be intermediate goods, goods for current consumption or fixed capital assets. Also, except in the case of certain special grants, no distinction is made in the balance of payments accounts between current and capital transfers, which are both included in the current account. The current balance in the balance of payments accounts, apart from these special capital grants, is equal to net investment abroad. In the balance of payments accounts the term 'capital' is used to describe only transactions in overseas assets and liabilities, including physical assets held abroad; in the national income accounts physical assets held abroad are for convenience included with financial assets in the financial accounts, and the long-term capital account and the monetary movements section of the balance of payments correspond to the financial account for the overseas sector (see page 449). Thus the 'capital' transactions of the balance of payments accounts correspond to 'financial' transactions within the national income accounts.

The balance of payments accounts include all transactions between residents and non-residents; every transaction in principle involves both a credit and a debit and so should be entered twice and the accounts should balance exactly. Thus, when a United Kingdom firm exports goods, the value of the goods is shown as a credit under visible trade in the current account. But this sale will be accompanied by another entry representing the payment for the exports. If a remittance is made in a foreign currency, there is an increase in the gold and convertible currency reserves; but if the foreign importer pays from balances already held in sterling there is a decrease in United Kingdom sterling liabilities to overseas residents. Both these types of payment will be reflected in the balance of monetary movements. The second entry can also appear under other headings. For example, if no payment is to be received for the goods, as for gift parcels or for exports financed by official grants, the matching debit entry will appear as a transfer payment, private or official, in the current account. If trade credit is provided from the United Kingdom, the matching debit entry reflecting the lending by the exporter or by a United Kingdom bank will usually appear in monetary movements. The repayment of such trade credit provides an example of a double entry for which both items are within a single heading of the accounts —monetary movements—one representing the reduction in lending and the other representing the payment received.

In the balance of payments accounts, the two entries made in respect of each transaction are derived from separate sources in almost every case. Moreover, the methods of estimation are not completely accurate and some items are missing. Hence the accounts do not balance exactly and in order to bring them into balance an additional entry, the balancing item, is required to offset the sum of all the errors and omissions in the other items of the accounts.

2. THE PUBLISHED TABLES

There are two tables in the Blue Book devoted entirely to international transactions, the summary table on international transactions (Table 7 of the 1967 Blue Book) and the table on overseas transactions in financial assets (Table 79 of the 1967 Blue Book). Both tables are consistent with the annual balance of payments Pink Book, *United Kingdom Balance of Payments*, published at about the same time, in which full details of the balance of payments are given.

To close the system of sector accounts, non-residents, in respect of their transactions with the United Kingdom, may be regarded formally as a sector of the United Kingdom economy. The summary table on international transactions combines elements of a production account, income and expenditure account and capital account for the overseas sector. The table is a re-arrangement, in summary form, of the current account of the balance of payments as shown in the published balance of payments accounts. The table on financial transactions is the financial account for the overseas sector; it analyses the changes in the United Kingdom assets and liabilities of the overseas sector and is a re-arrangement of the long-term capital and monetary movements sections of the balance of payments accounts.

INTERNATIONAL TRANSACTIONS

Transactions are grouped in this table so as to separate three categories of transactions distinguished throughout the national accounts: transactions in goods and services, property income payments and transfer payments. The Blue Book table is set out as follows:

International transactions, 1966

£ million

United Kingdom credits		United Kingdom debits	
Exports and re-exports of goods	5,110	Imports of goods	5,262
Exports of services	1,829	Imports of services	1,863
Property income from abroad ..	1,496	Property income paid abroad .	774
U.K. taxes paid by non-residents on portfolio income	15	Foreign taxes paid by U.K. residents	556
U.K. taxes paid on profits due abroad	190	Imports and property income paid abroad	8,455
Exports and property income abroad	8,640	Current transfers:	
		From personal sector	183
		From central government ...	182
Current transfers:		Investment and financing:	
To personal sector	121	Net investment abroad......	−59
To central government	—	*less* Capital grants from overseas governments (net) ...	—
Capital transfers from abroad ..	—	Total[1]	−59
Total	8,761	Total	8,761

Source: 1967 Blue Book, Table 7

[1] Equals the current balance in the balance of payments accounts.

This table is also published quarterly in *Economic Trends* but without any subdivision of United Kingdom taxes paid by non-residents. The quarterly table has been prepared from 1961. Seasonally adjusted estimates and quarterly estimates back to 1958 for the series other than tax payments are available from the balance of payments accounts.

Exports and re-exports, and imports of goods

These items are identical with exports and re-exports, and imports in the balance of payments accounts. Both exports and imports are valued 'f.o.b.', or free on board, that is excluding all freight and insurance charges. Purchases of shipping and insurance services by or from non-residents are included in exports and imports of services. With some exceptions, the most important of which is recent purchases of military aircraft from the United States (see page 460), they represent the value of merchandise crossing the United Kingdom boundary. The figures of exports and imports of goods are based mainly on the monthly *Overseas Trade Accounts of the United Kingdom* (*Trade Accounts*) but certain adjustments are made to convert the *Trade Accounts* to a balance of payments basis. The adjustments are described in Section 3 of this chapter.

To achieve consistency with the basis for estimating other transactions in the national accounts, exports and imports of goods should be recorded at the time when the ownership of the goods changes. In practice, however, the compilation of the *Trade Accounts* and therefore, in general, of the balance of payments and national income accounts is geared to the declarations made by exporters and importers which are received in the statistical office of H.M. Customs and Excise. With certain exceptions, traders are allowed a short period of grace before documents have to be presented at the ports. Export documents are commonly presented after shipment; the normal period of grace is six days, but this may be extended. There is a further interval before copies reach the statistical office. The effect of these lags is accentuated since the monthly processing of the exports statistics begins before the end of the calendar month. Importers are usually required to present their documents before they can obtain customs clearance and remove the goods. Moreover, the monthly total for imports includes those recorded in documents relating to the month which reach the statistical office up to the third working day after the end of the month. The imports statistics therefore correspond more closely than the exports statistics to movements through the ports during the calendar month. No single definition can be given of the time when ownership changes, but on the assumption that on average it occurs at some time between the departure of goods from the exporting country and their arrival in the importing country, United Kingdom exports and re-exports are recorded at various times around the time of change of ownership, whilst imports tend to be recorded in arrears of change of ownership. In general, no adjustment is made to the figures for any differences in timing between the recording in the *Trade Accounts* and the change of ownership.

Exports and imports of services

These comprise transactions in services between United Kingdom and overseas residents together with certain transactions in goods not crossing the United Kingdom boundary, such as purchases for local use by the Forces overseas, purchases by tourists, ships bunkers and stores, etc. The estimates are taken

P

from the figures of invisibles in the balance of payments, exports and imports of services in the national accounts being equivalent to credits and debits respectively in the balance of payments accounts. As far as possible these items are measured consistently with the definitions required for the national income accounts. But there are difficulties in drawing the distinction between payments for factor services, to be included here, and interest payments which form part of property income. Also, it is often difficult to distinguish the resident status of those rendering or receiving the services and thus to decide whether the payments should be included in transactions with overseas residents. The balance of payments items included are government (other than transfer payments), transport (shipping and civil aviation), travel and other services. In line with international recommendations [2] the system of classification in the balance of payments accounts is a functional one and this criterion is given precedence where necessary over a classification by economic sector.

(a) *Government.* Exports and imports of services under the balance of payments item 'Government' cover both military and non-military items and include all transactions in services of the United Kingdom government, and its employees stationed abroad, with overseas residents, and certain transactions in goods (see above) which are not appropriate to other items in the balance of payments accounts or which cannot be allocated to them because of lack of information. Transactions between United Kingdom private residents and overseas governments are not included in this item.

Exports of services include receipts by the United Kingdom government from the United States and Canadian Forces stationed in the United Kingdom for supplies and services, receipts from the United States government in respect of goods supplied to the United Kingdom Forces (offshore sales), contributions from overseas governments towards common defence projects and various other miscellaneous receipts from overseas countries. The value of goods held abroad and transferred to overseas countries by the United Kingdom Forces as part of military aid is also included, together with the value of services provided in the United Kingdom to overseas residents by government departments under military training schemes and under the United Kingdom government programme of economic aid to overseas countries. Where no charge is made, the entries representing the value of goods or services provided are offset by grants abroad. But where the transfer of buildings and other fixed assets to overseas governments on independence does not form part of economic or military aid, and is therefore not included in grants abroad, nothing is included in this item. In the central government current account (Table 41 of the 1967 Blue Book) government exports of services are a deduction in arriving at current expenditure on goods and services.

Imports of services comprise wage and salary payments to the locally engaged staff of United Kingdom government offices and military bases abroad; the personal expenditure abroad of United Kingdom Forces, diplomatic staff and other staff engaged from the United Kingdom; the operating costs of overseas military bases, embassies, high commission offices and consulates, including local purchases of food, equipment, fuel and services; and contributions towards common defence projects. Expenditure overseas is recorded partly on a net basis, that is after deducting receipts arising locally. In particular, in the years from

---

[2] *Balance of Payments Manual*, Third Edition, International Monetary Fund, Washington, D.C., 1961.

1955/56 to 1960/61, when contributions in cash were received from the German Federal Republic towards meeting the costs of the United Kingdom Forces stationed in Germany, these receipts were deducted from expenditure.

These imports of services form part of current expenditure on goods and services in the central government current account, but the latter includes the total wages and salaries, etc. of United Kingdom Forces and government employees stationed abroad and not just their personal expenditure. The wages and salaries are the income of individuals regarded as residents and that part of their income which they spend overseas is included in consumers' expenditure as part of 'Consumers' expenditure abroad' (see page 185).

(b) *Transport: shipping.* The shipping estimates cover both dry cargo and tanker transactions. Exports of services include the earnings of the United Kingdom shipping industry from the carriage of United Kingdom exports, and from freight on cross-trades; receipts from chartering ships to overseas residents; and receipts of passenger fares from overseas residents. Also included are the disbursements of foreign ships in United Kingdom ports. Imports of services comprise payments by United Kingdom residents to overseas shipping companies for passenger fares; freight payments to foreign shipping companies for carrying United Kingdom imports; payments to overseas residents for chartering; and the disbursements abroad of United Kingdom shipping companies. Disbursements include payments for bunkers, canal dues, maintenance of shore establishments, port charges, agency fees, handling charges, crews' expenditure, pilotage and towage, repair work, ships' stores, light dues and other miscellaneous port expenditure abroad.

(c) *Transport: civil aviation.* Exports of services comprise receipts by British Overseas Airways Corporation, British European Airways and the British independent airlines of passenger fares from overseas residents, and their earnings from the carriage of United Kingdom exports, from freight on cross-trades and from the carriage of mail on behalf of overseas postal authorities; receipts by the British airlines of sums due from overseas airlines as settlements under pooling arrangements; receipts from chartering aircraft to overseas residents; and disbursements in the United Kingdom by overseas airlines. Imports of services comprise the corresponding payments by United Kingdom residents to overseas airlines and the disbursements abroad of British airlines. Disbursements include airport landing fees, handling charges, crews' expenditure, purchases of fuel and oil and catering supplies, commissions to agents, advertising and the operating costs of overseas offices.

(d) *Travel.* Exports comprise expenditure in the United Kingdom by overseas visitors; imports comprise expenditure by United Kingdom residents on visits to overseas countries. Expenditure on business account is included. The cost of sea or air travel from and to the United Kingdom is not part of this item; payments to shipping and airline companies affecting the balance of payments are included in 'Transport'. But other payments for transport by overseas visitors within the United Kingdom and by United Kingdom residents travelling within or between overseas countries are included in this item.

Personal expenditure overseas by United Kingdom residents, not on business account, is included in consumers' expenditure and is part of the item 'Consumers' expenditure abroad'. The rest of that item comprises expenditure by United Kingdom Forces and government employees stationed abroad (see above). Expenditure on business account is not shown separately; it is part of the operating costs of businesses. The estimates of the separate categories of consumers' expenditure (shown in Table 27 of the 1967 Blue Book) include the amount spent on each of the items by overseas residents in the United Kingdom. But since the estimates of total consumers' expenditure must exclude all purchases by overseas residents, a negative adjustment is made to exclude total expenditure by overseas visitors on both personal and business accounts, expenditure by the Forces and employees of overseas governments and expenditure of other non-residents (see page 186). The latter should cover expenditure by non-resident journalists and overseas students, which is included in exports of 'Other services' (see below). However, in the 1967 Blue Book no deduction was made for the expenditure of overseas students and the expenditure estimates of gross domestic product were too high on that account.

(e) *Other services.* This item includes all transactions in services between United Kingdom private residents and overseas residents (both government and private) which are not appropriate to other items in the account or which cannot be allocated to these items for statistical reasons. Components include payments and receipts for financial and allied services, telecommunications and postal services, films and television, use of royalties (including licence fees and payments for technical 'know-how'), services rendered between related companies (including management and head office expenses), advertising and other commercial services between non-related companies, work done by architects and consultant engineers, building and civil engineering work, and temporary work overseas such as by entertainers, journalists and domestic workers. Financial and allied services cover earnings of banks and other financial institutions for brokerage, merchanting, arbitrage, banking services, underwriting and other insurance; but not interest payments or receipts or the profits of the overseas branches, subsidiaries and associates of banks and other financial institutions. In line with the treatment of dividends and interest in the national accounts, the latter categories are included in property income received from or paid abroad. However, up to 1962 the earnings of United Kingdom insurance companies from their overseas branches, subsidiaries and associates were not distinguishable from other insurance earnings from abroad and they therefore form part of exports of services. This break in continuity does not affect the estimates of gross national product, but it does affect its division between gross domestic product and net property income from abroad. For years up to 1962 there was probably on average an overstatement of gross domestic product of about £20 million a year on this account.

Exports of services also include receipts, other than by the United Kingdom government, from overseas government agencies, foreign military establishments and international organisations located in the United Kingdom. The personal expenditure of their employees recruited overseas is also included. Personal expenditure by non-resident students and journalists is also included here and not under 'Travel'. For temporary work overseas, only remitted earnings are taken into account. Gold purchased for industrial use is included in imports of services.

More detailed definitions of the components of 'Other services' are given in the annual balance of payments Pink Book, *United Kingdom Balance of Payments.*

Property income

Property income consists of the income entitled 'Interest, profits and dividends' in the balance of payments accounts. In order to maintain consistency with the treatment of domestic incomes, property income from abroad is measured in the national income accounts before deduction of taxes on income levied by overseas governments. In the balance of payments accounts however, interest, profits and dividends are recorded after deduction of all overseas taxes. In the national accounts the tax payments are entered again on the opposite side of the account so that the balance between payments and receipts in the balance of payments accounts is preserved. The payment of tax to an overseas government on income accruing to United Kingdom residents is thus regarded as a payment of property income by the United Kingdom and vice versa. United Kingdom taxes paid by non-residents on portfolio income relate to income tax paid on receipts of dividends and interest from portfolio investment in United Kingdom securities. United Kingdom taxes paid on company profits due abroad relate to corporation tax, income tax, profits tax and excess profits tax paid on profits earned in the United Kingdom by overseas-owned branches and subsidiaries. Foreign taxes paid by United Kingdom residents are those levied by central governments on the basis of income; taxes which are regarded as part of operating expenses, including most mining royalties, are excluded.

Property income from abroad is estimated before providing for stock appreciation but after deduction of depreciation allowances, as in the balance of payments accounts, and in the latter respect it is inconsistent with the treatment of domestic incomes. The discrepancy arises on both the gross flow and the net flow, but in so far as the depreciation allowances are an appropriate measure of capital consumption the estimates of national income, as opposed to gross national product, are not affected.

In the national income accounts, property income received from and paid abroad are included in the accounts of the appropriate domestic sector. The only components separately identified, however, are the income from abroad of companies and public corporations and that part of income paid abroad represented by company profits. In the balance of payments accounts the components of interest, profits and dividends are grouped into direct, portfolio and other investment income.

(a) *Direct investment income.* Direct investment is defined as investment by United Kingdom companies in their overseas branches, subsidiaries or associated companies; and investment by overseas companies in branches, subsidiaries or associated companies in the United Kingdom. Income from direct investment includes branch profits, interest on loans and dividends remitted by subsidiaries, together with the parent companies' share of unremitted profits retained for reinvestment. The latter item is included also in the financial accounts as an increase or decrease in 'Other private sector assets: long-term'. The overseas earnings of oil companies are excluded from this item and included in 'Other investment income'. Up to 1962 the income of United Kingdom insurance companies from the operations of their overseas branches, subsidiaries and associates is also excluded (see page 444).

In the national income accounts, direct investment income from abroad including taxes paid abroad is included in 'Income from abroad' in the appropriation accounts of companies and public corporations; nearly all of this income is received by companies. The whole of direct investment income paid abroad is included in the item 'Profits due abroad net of United Kingdom tax' in the appropriation account of companies.

(b) *Portfolio investment income.* The payments of interest and dividends on portfolio investment, both to and by the United Kingdom, relate solely to the remitted proceeds. Interest on British government securities held by overseas banks, central monetary institutions and the Note Security and General Funds of the Crown Agents is excluded from this item and included in 'Other investment income'. Prior to 1963 interest on British government securities held by certain other official bodies in the overseas sterling area and interest on the Crown Agents' investments in United Kingdom local authorities were also included in 'Other investment income' instead of 'Portfolio investment income'.

The proportion of portfolio investment income from abroad which is received by United Kingdom companies is approximately 60 per cent of the total. The estimate of receipts by companies *plus* the corresponding taxes paid abroad is included in 'Income from abroad' in the company appropriation account. Portfolio income paid abroad is included in the figures of total dividends and interest paid by the domestic sectors and payments abroad by each sector are not separately identified.

(c) *Other investment income.* Included under this heading are the earnings of oil companies. Broadly speaking, oil credits represent the surplus on the current transactions of United Kingdom companies resulting from their operations overseas although this surplus differs in various ways from an accounting measure of the profits earned overseas. It includes, for example, the value of services rendered between parents, overseas subsidiaries and associated companies, such as current expenditure in the United Kingdom on marketing, headquarters expenses, research, etc. Also, for some companies they are arrived at after taking account of payments of taxes overseas, rather than of the accrued liability for overseas taxation. Oil debits consist of the interest, profits and dividends paid abroad by the United Kingdom subsidiaries and associates of overseas oil companies and the profits retained by these companies for reinvestment in the United Kingdom. These oil credits and debits are earned and paid entirely by companies.

Other transactions under this heading include interest receipts and payments on inter-government loans and other official investment, including interest received on the reserves and interest (or dividends) on the Treasury portfolio of dollar securities; charges on drawings from the International Monetary Fund; interest on external banking liabilities and claims in sterling and sterling area currencies, including interest on British government securities held by overseas banks, central monetary institutions and the Note Security Funds of the Crown Agents (see note on 'Portfolio investment income' above); any other interest charged to overseas importers on trade credit extended by United Kingdom residents; income from real estate owned abroad, other than through the overseas subsidiaries of property companies; and income from trust funds invested abroad to the benefit of United Kingdom resident individuals or institutions.

In the national income accounts, investment income from abroad in the form of interest on sterling claims, discounts on bills and other interest received on trade credit is included, gross of any taxes paid abroad, in the estimate of 'Income from abroad' in the company appropriation account. Some income on overseas investments is received by public corporations and included in the estimate of their 'Income from abroad'. Interest received on trusts and annuities is included indistinguishably in the rent, dividends and net interest received by the personal sector, whilst the remainder (interest on inter-government loans, the reserves, etc.) forms part of the total interest received by the central government. 'Other investment income' paid abroad is included indistinguishably in the figures of total dividends and interest paid by the domestic sectors and payments abroad by each sector are not separately identified.

Current transfers

(a) *Personal sector.* Current transfers to and from the personal sector shown in the national income accounts are the same as credits and debits under private transfers in the balance of payments accounts. Private transfers comprise cash gifts and the value of goods transferred and services rendered between United Kingdom private residents and overseas residents without a *quid pro quo.*

Examples of the types of transaction giving rise to entries under this heading are gifts of goods sent by parcel post, payments by United Kingdom residents to their dependants overseas and other cash gifts, transfers of funds by missionary societies and charitable institutions, legacies and transfers of assets by migrants other than their personal and household belongings. As far as possible, the total wealth of a migrant is included to correspond with the treatment in the long-term capital account or monetary movements section of the balance of payments, where the assets are recorded or re-classified in accordance with the new resident status of the migrant, even if the assets are not removed to or from the United Kingdom at the time of migration.

Some of these private transfers may be received or made by companies but, in the absence of any detailed information, they are attributed entirely to the personal sector. The error involved through this mis-classification is not likely to be large. Mis-classification also arises in the national accounts because transfers of assets by migrants and also any legacies included, should properly be treated as capital and not current transfers; but the available data do not permit a satisfactory separation to be made.

(b) *Central government.* Current transfers to the central government occurred only in periods before 1959 and consisted almost entirely of defence aid. This was assistance provided, mainly by the United States government, for the purchase of raw materials, machinery and equipment (see page 270).

Current transfers from the central government are the same as the government transfers debits in the balance of payments current account, which are divided into four groups: economic grants, military grants, subscriptions and contributions to international organisations, and other transfers. Economic grants comprise cash grants made to the less developed countries to assist in their economic development and the value of goods and services provided to these countries without charge by the United Kingdom government. Military grants consist of cash grants for military purposes and goods and services of a military nature provided to overseas countries by the United Kingdom government without charge. Where economic or military aid is not involved, no entry is made either under transfers or under government receipts, in respect of fixed assets transferred without charge to overseas countries. Subscriptions and contributions include United Kingdom subscriptions to the United Nations and other international bodies to meet the administrative expenses of these organisations, similar payments to international military agencies (South-East Asia Treaty Organisation, Central Treaty Organisation, etc.) and United Kingdom contributions to international organisations for multilateral economic assistance to the less developed countries and other international projects. Subscriptions to the International Finance Corporation, the International Development Association, the European Fund and the International Monetary Fund are not included under this heading since they are regarded as creating a financial asset. Other transfers are mainly national insurance benefits and war pensions paid to overseas residents.

Capital transfers from abroad

This item includes a variety of capital receipts arising from government operations abroad. In the early post-war years the main constituents were sales of surplus war stores held abroad and the settlement of debts and claims arising out of the war. The item comprises items (b) and (c) on pages 274 and 276 where further details are given. Receipts were last recorded in 1955.

Apart from certain special grants which form a separate category (specified below), no distinction is made in the balance of payments accounts between current and capital transfers. All of these transfers are included as part of government receipts from transfers in the current account of the balance of payments.

Investment and financing

(a) *Capital grants from overseas governments* (*net*). These occurred in the years 1947 to 1951 and were included in the balance of payments accounts in a separate category outside the current and long-term capital accounts. They included:

(i) Grants to the United Kingdom from the United States under the European Recovery Programme, including conditional aid *less* the United States share of the sterling counterpart.

(ii) Aid in foreign currency received from European countries, under the Intra-European Payments Agreement, *less* grants to those countries of the sterling counterpart of conditional aid under the European Recovery Programme either in the form of drawing rights or in the form of the initial debit balance allotted to the United Kingdom under Article 10 of the Agreement for the Establishment of a European Payments Union.

(iii) Gifts made to the United Kingdom in 1947 and 1949 by Australia and New Zealand in order to reduce the level of overseas sterling holdings.

(iv) Revaluation payments made on the sterling holdings of certain countries following the change in the value of sterling on 18 September 1949 were deducted from this item. Entries arising from revaluations on devaluation in 1967 are included elsewhere in the accounts.

The gross transfers were included in the central government capital account (see pages 274 and 284).

(b) *Net investment abroad*. This represents the net increase in the value of overseas assets acquired by United Kingdom residents *less* the net increase in the value of assets in the United Kingdom acquired by non-residents. It is the third main form of additions to the national wealth shown in the combined capital account for the United Kingdom (Table 6 of the 1967 Blue Book, see page 64). Overseas assets include investment in physical assets, financial assets and gold and foreign currency reserves. In the national income accounts, physical assets held abroad are included with financial assets in the financial accounts and net investment abroad is equal, apart from the change in sign, to the net acquisition of financial assets by the overseas sector. The table on transactions in financial assets by the overseas sector, which is described below, therefore provides an analysis of the form of net investment abroad.

Net investment abroad is equal to the current balance in the balance of payments accounts except in the years 1947 to 1951 when capital grants from overseas governments have to be added to the current balance to arrive at net investment abroad. It is also equal, apart from the change in sign, to the balance of the long-term capital account in the balance of payments *plus* the balance of monetary movements *plus* the balancing item. An alternative measure of net investment abroad is given by the sum of the balance of the long-term capital account and of the balance of monetary movements, with sign reversed. The difference between the two measures, the balancing item, is thought to contain a recurrent positive element probably representing an understatement of credits on current account, an overstatement of debits, or quite probably a combination of both (see page 472). But this element, which cannot be precisely identified, is excluded from the measure of net investment abroad shown in the tables and the whole of the balancing item is presented as unrecorded financial transactions.

Net investment abroad is estimated net of depreciation provisions (see page 445) and the figures differ in this respect from those of domestic capital formation, which is estimated gross, before deduction of capital consumption.

TRANSACTIONS IN FINANCIAL ASSETS: OVERSEAS SECTOR

The financial account of the overseas sector is a regrouping of transactions from the long-term capital account and the monetary movements section of the balance of payments accounts according to the types of assets and liabilities exchanged. The net acquisition of financial assets by the overseas sector is equal, with sign reversed, to net investment abroad (see above) and the table shows the form of that investment.

The presentation of the financial account of the overseas sector in the 1967 Blue Book is shown on the next page. A similar presentation has been prepared quarterly from 1963 and is published in *Financial Statistics*.

The assets distinguished in the financial accounts are defined in Chapter XIV, to which reference should be made. Additional details of central government financial transactions are given in Chapter IX. The following notes amplify where necessary the description of those items which are taken directly from the balance of payments accounts and explain some of the differences in coverage between other items in the financial account of the overseas sector and the corresponding item in the balance of payments accounts. A reconciliation of the figures for 1966 in the financial accounts with the items in the balance of payments accounts is shown in the table on pages 451 to 454.

Treasury bills

These include the counterpart of most inter-central bank transactions in support of the reserves in the form of swaps against sterling. When swaps are made the foreign currencies received are added to the holdings of the Exchange Equalisation Account and thus augment the gold and convertible currency reserves. There is a corresponding increase in external liabilities in sterling to central monetary institutions. The sterling is held on behalf of the central monetary institutions undertaking the swap and is usually invested in Treasury bills, leading to an increase in Treasury bills held by overseas residents. Bills held by

P*

Transactions in financial assets(1): overseas sector, 1966

£ million

Treasury bills	221
British government and government guaranteed securities	−8
Local authority debt	−38
Gold and currency reserves	282
Inter-government loans (net)	−62
United Kingdom subscriptions to International Monetary Fund and European Fund	−175
Drawings from United Kingdom subscriptions to international lending bodies	−10
Holdings of interest-free notes by International Monetary Fund	159
Other public sector assets and liabilities:	
Short-term	−34
Long-term	−7
Deposits with banking sector	742
Deposits with other financial institutions	31
Bank lending:	
Advances and loans	−975
Commercial bills	−27
Money at call and short notice	−3
Company and overseas securities	66
Other private sector assets:	
Short-term	11
Long-term	−113
Unidentified items(2)	−1
Net acquisition of financial assets(1)(3)	59

Source: 1967 Blue Book, Table 79

(1)Acquisition of assets or reduction in liabilities by the overseas sector is shown positive; sale of assets or increase in liabilities negative.

(2)The balancing item in the balance of payments accounts.

(3)Equals, apart from the change in sign, the current balance in the balance of payments accounts.

the Bank of England as the sterling equivalent of foreign currency deposits arising from central bank assistance are however excluded; these are included in 'Other public sector assets: short-term'. Up to 1962 the figures relate to overseas official holdings only.

British government and government guaranteed securities

In the balance of payments accounts, transactions in government and government guaranteed securities by overseas banks and central monetary institutions are treated as transactions in liquid liabilities which are included in monetary movements. Those by other holders where the liabilities are regarded as less liquid, are included in the long-term capital account as part of private investment. Up to 1959 the figures relate only to the overseas official holdings included in monetary movements.

Local authority debt

In the balance of payments accounts changes in overseas holdings of local authority temporary money are treated as monetary movements, while changes in holdings of securities and mortgages are included in the long-term capital account as part of private investment.

Reconciliation between financial accounts and balance of payments accounts, 1966

£ million

Transactions in financial assets: overseas sector[1]		Balance of payments accounts[2]	
Treasury bills	221	External liabilities in sterling: Treasury bills	221
British government and government guaranteed securities ...	−8	Private investment: British government stocks	20
		External liabilities in sterling: British government stocks ..	−28
		Miscellaneous capital: Adjustment of external liabilities to transactions value	—
			−8
Local authority debt...........	−38	External liabilities in sterling: Deposits with local authorities	−30
		Private portfolio investment: Local authorities—securities and mortgages	−8
			−38
Gold and currency reserves	282	Gold and convertible currency reserves	−34
		Transfer from dollar portfolio to reserves	316
		Official holdings of non-convertible currencies	—
			282
Inter-government loans (net)....	−62	Inter-government loans (net)...	−62
United Kingdom subscriptions to International Monetary Fund and European Fund	−175	Other official long-term capital (net): Subscriptions to European Fund	—
		Account with International Monetary Fund: Subscription in gold and sterling.....	−175
			−175
Drawings from United Kingdom subscriptions to international lending bodies	−10	Other official long-term capital (net): Subscriptions to international lending bodies	−12
		External liabilities in sterling: Change in these bodies' holdings of non-interest bearing notes	−2
		Timing and rounding differences (a)	4
			−10

See footnotes on page 454.

£ million

Transactions in financial assets: overseas sector [1]		Balance of payments accounts [2]	
Holdings of interest-free notes by International Monetary Fund.	159	Account with International Monetary Fund (net)	−2
		less Subscription to International Monetary Fund ...	175
		less Deposits in International Monetary Fund current and deposit account	−2
		less I.M.F. gold deposits in U.K.	−12
			159
Other public sector assets and liabilities: short term	−20 [3]	Liabilities in non-sterling currencies: Deposits by overseas central banks	14
		Miscellaneous capital: Official assets and liabilities (not elsewhere included)...	−34
		less Adjustment to transactions value of British government stocks	—
		plus Transactions of public corporations	—
			−20
Other public sector assets and liabilities: long-term	−7	Other official long-term capital (net)......................	−19
		less Subscriptions to international lending bodies and European Fund	12
			−7
Deposits with banking sector....	742	Liabilities in non-sterling currencies: U.K. banks	878
		Liabilities in overseas sterling area currencies............	−45
		less Commercial bills drawn in non-sterling or overseas sterling area currencies on U.K. residents	6
		External liabilities in sterling: Current and deposit accounts	38
		less Identified deposits with financial institutions other than banks and hire purchase finance companies ..	−36
		Account with International Monetary Fund: I.M.F. current and deposit account	2
		I.M.F. gold deposits in U.K. .	12
		Timing and coverage differences (b)	−113
			742

See footnotes on page 454.

£ million

Transactions in financial assets: overseas sector [1]		Balance of payments accounts [2]	
Deposits with other financial institutions	31	External liabilities in sterling: Deposits with hire purchase finance companies	11
		Identified deposits with other financial institutions	36
		Differences in timing and coverage of hire purchase finance companies' transactions (c) ..	−16
		Private investment: Other overseas borrowing by hire purchase finance companies.....	—
			31
Bank lending: Advances and loans .... Money at call and short notice	} −978	Claims in non-sterling currencies: U.K. banks	−1,040
		Claims in overseas sterling area currencies	—
		less Commercial bills drawn in non-sterling or overseas sterling area currencies on overseas residents and held by banks on behalf of their U.K. customers	7
		External claims in sterling: Advances and overdrafts ...	—
		Timing and coverage differences (d)	55
			−978
Bank lending: commercial bills	−27	External claims in sterling: Commercial bills and promissory notes	−111
		Acceptances	26
		less Bills lodged with banks by U.K. customers	36
		Timing and coverage differences (e)	22
			−27
Company and overseas securities	66	Private direct investment: Net acquisition of share and loan capital by U.K.	−54
		Net acquisition of share and loan capital in U.K........	69
		Private portfolio investment by U.K.	112
		Private portfolio investment in U.K.—Company securities	−61
			66

See footnotes on page 454.

£ million

Transactions in financial assets: overseas sector [1]		Balance of payments accounts [2]	
Other private sector assets: short-term......................	−3 [3]	Miscellaneous capital:	
		Trade credit (not elsewhere included)...............	⎫
		Other identified commercial short-term transactions ..	⎬ −12
		less Transactions of public corporations.............	⎭ —
		Liabilities and claims in non-sterling and overseas sterling area currencies:	
		Commercial bills drawn on U.K. residents	−6
		Bills drawn on overseas residents and lodged with U.K. banks	−7
		External liabilities and claims in sterling:	
		Commercial bills drawn on U.K. residents	10
		Bills drawn on overseas residents and lodged with U.K. banks	−36
		less Timing and coverage differences in other items, (a)+(b)+(c)+(d)+(e)	48
			−3
Other private sector assets: long-term......................	−113	Private investment:	
		Direct investment by the U.K.	−314
		less Acquisition of share and loan capital	54
		Direct investment in the U.K.	224
		less Acquisition of share and loan capital	−69
		'Other' private investment by the U.K.	−115
		'Other' private investment in the U.K.	107
		less Overseas borrowing by hire purchase finance companies	—
			−113
Unidentified items.............	−1	Balancing item...............	−1
Net acquisition of financial assets	59	Current balance (sign reversed)	59

[1] Acquisition of assets or reduction in liabilities by the overseas sector is shown positive; sale of assets or increase in liabilities negative.

[2] United Kingdom assets: increase −, decrease +. United Kingdom liabilities: increase +, decrease −.

[3] These figures incorporate corrections made after publication of the 1967 Blue Book. The table on page 450 shows the figures given in the 1967 Blue Book.

Gold and currency reserves

This item comprises (a) changes in the reserves of gold and convertible currencies held in the Exchange Equalisation Account, (b) changes in official holdings of non-convertible currencies, (c) up to 1959 changes in the United Kingdom balance in the European Payments Union, and (d) transfers (£316 million in 1966) from the government portfolio of dollar securities to the reserves of gold and convertible currencies held in the Exchange Equalisation Account. In the balance of payments accounts these four components are shown separately. In the national income accounts only the combined figure is shown and the transfers to the reserves do not affect this total because they represent a transfer within the central government.

Currency is valued at par rates and gold at the sterling equivalent (at parity) of $35 per ounce fine. Until a par value for the Canadian dollar was established on 2 May 1962 holdings of this currency were valued at the appropriate exchange rates. The balance at the liquidation of the European Payments Union in 1959 was converted into bilateral debts due to and by member countries and the debts were funded so that they now form part of inter-government lending. Most of the process of changing the composition of the government portfolio of dollar securities from holdings mainly in equities into holdings mainly in liquid assets had taken place by the end of 1965 and the portfolio of dollar securities had long been regarded as nearly equivalent to a reserve asset.

Drawings from United Kingdom subscriptions to international lending bodies

The figures in the financial accounts are derived from Exchequer records. In the balance of payments accounts, subscriptions to the international lending bodies and changes in the bodies' holdings of sterling are shown separately. The difference between the figures in the financial accounts and the net total of those in the balance of payments accounts is due partly to rounding and partly to differences in timing between Exchequer records and the Bank of England records from which the balance of payments figures are derived.

Holdings of interest-free notes by International Monetary Fund

Holdings of interest-free notes by the International Monetary Fund represent the counterpart of (a) the unused balance of the sterling portion of the United Kingdom subscription to the Fund, which is deposited in the United Kingdom against the issue of interest-free notes by the Exchequer and is available for drawings from the Fund in sterling by other countries; and (b) United Kingdom drawings from the Fund. When drawings are made from the Fund by the United Kingdom the foreign currencies drawn are purchased for sterling and the Fund lends back the sterling to the Exchequer on the security of interest-free notes.

In the balance of payments accounts, the subscriptions in gold and in sterling to the Fund and changes in holdings of interest-free notes are included in the account with the I.M.F., which also includes changes in the Fund's current and deposit accounts held in the United Kingdom. Also included in the years 1965 to 1967 is the gold deposited in the United Kingdom by the Fund to alleviate the impact of gold purchases from the United Kingdom by other Fund members in order to pay the increase in their gold subscriptions.

In the financial accounts, the deposits in the current and deposit accounts of the I.M.F. and the gold deposited in the United Kingdom are classified as 'Deposits with banking sector'.

Other public sector assets and liabilities: short-term

The main recurrent components of this item are changes in non-sterling currency balances held in official funds, other than the Exchange Equalisation Account, including the Trust Fund set up to finance the United Kingdom share of the cost of developing and producing Polaris missiles; and changes in the deposits by the German Federal Republic against future expenditure in this country, made to offset part of the foreign exchange costs of stationing Forces in Germany. Also included are changes in official liabilities in non-sterling currencies in the form of deposits by overseas central banks. These deposits are made under the reciprocal credit facilities established with the central banks of the United States, Canada, Japan and a number of European countries. The other main forms of drawing under these facilities, the swap transactions, are reflected in the item 'Treasury bills'.

Other public sector assets and liabilities: long-term

This item includes net changes in long-term overseas assets, other than inter-government loans, held by the United Kingdom central government, including the Atomic Energy Authority, and public corporations such as the Commonwealth Development Corporation. Items included are the purchase by the United Kingdom government of United Nations bonds in 1962 and subsequent redemptions, and the servicing in 1966 of the loan by the International Bank for Reconstruction and Development to Rhodesia, guaranteed by the United Kingdom government.

Deposits with banking sector; Bank lending

The figures of bank deposits and bank lending in the financial accounts are derived from returns covering both domestic and overseas liabilities and assets made by those institutions classified to the banking sector. In the balance of payments accounts, however, bank deposits and bank lending are included in the series of external liabilities and claims in sterling and in other currencies. Part of the difference between the two series arises because some institutions contribute to the external liabilities and claims series but are not included in the banking sector; some are regarded as other financial institutions and some are industrial and commercial companies. Also, some branches of banks with relatively little overseas business supply figures for the banking sector statistics, but not for the external liabilities and claims series. The external liabilities and claims series include commercial bills held by banks on behalf of customers which are not bank lending; changes in these are entered under 'Other private sector assets: short-term', together with the residual difference between the two sets of statistics.

Deposits with other financial institutions

This item combines two series. The figures for hire purchase finance companies are based on returns made by hire purchase finance companies to the Board of Trade and, as in the banking statistics, the coverage differs from the series included in the balance of payments under external liabilities. The figures for other financial institutions are taken from the balance of payments statistics.

Company and overseas securities

The figures for this item are available only from 1960. They are taken entirely from the balance of payments accounts and include that part of private direct investment classified as net acquisition of share and loan capital, portfolio investment overseas by United Kingdom residents and portfolio investment by overseas residents in United Kingdom company securities.

Direct investment comprises investment by United Kingdom companies in their overseas branches, subsidiaries or associated companies and investment by overseas companies in branches, subsidiaries or associated companies in the United Kingdom. Oil and, up to 1962, insurance companies are excluded; from 1963 investment by United Kingdom insurance companies in their overseas branches and subsidiaries is included.

Overseas portfolio investment includes net transactions of United Kingdom residents in issues of sterling loan stock raised by overseas public authorities on the London market, in overseas government and municipal loans and in stocks and shares of overseas registered companies. Portfolio investment by overseas residents in United Kingdom company securities comprises their net transactions in the stocks and shares of United Kingdom registered companies including issues by these companies on markets abroad.

Other private sector assets: short-term

This item comprises the total of monetary movements in the balance of payments accounts *less* all the items which are identified separately. It includes transactions between United Kingdom and overseas residents in commercial bills, other than bills held by United Kingdom banks on their own account; changes in trade credit outstanding not covered elsewhere in the accounts, that is mainly suppliers' credit to unrelated companies not covered by commercial bills; and other identified short-term lending and borrowing not covered elsewhere in the accounts. Because this is a residual item in the accounts it also contains the counterpart of the timing and coverage differences arising on other items between the figures in the financial accounts and the figures in the balance of payments accounts.

Other private sector assets: long-term

This item includes the remainder of the items in the long-term capital account. It comprises the remainder of private direct investment, that is the unremitted profits of subsidiaries and associated companies, changes in branch indebtedness and changes in inter-company accounts which include changes in trade credit; and other private investment, that is investment by oil companies and other miscellaneous investment. The changes in unremitted profits are estimated net of depreciation provisions (see page 445).

Overseas investment by oil companies is measured on a basis comparable to the estimates for other direct investment. The estimates of overseas investment by the British oil industry thus include the share of oil earnings reinvested overseas attributable to United Kingdom interests. But they exclude the overseas companies' share of investment by 'joint venture oil companies', that is by companies operating in the Middle East which, although registered in the United Kingdom, are jointly owned by the United Kingdom and overseas oil companies.

Other overseas investment by United Kingdom residents includes, as far as identifiable, the purchase of real estate abroad, investment by the Commonwealth Development Finance Company and, before 1963, investment by United

Kingdom insurance companies. Compensation payments to United Kingdom residents in respect of overseas assets which have been nationalised are included as a disinvestment. Other investment in the United Kingdom by overseas residents includes identified investment in real estate and in the insurance industry in the United Kingdom and certain borrowing by United Kingdom companies direct from banks and commercial companies overseas.

Unidentified items

This is equal to the balancing item in the balance of payments accounts; it represents the net total of the errors and omissions in other items in the balance of payments accounts (see page 472).

3. STATISTICAL SOURCES

This section describes the statistical sources and methods used in compiling the items in the national accounts table on international transactions and also those items in the financial accounts which are taken directly from the balance of payments accounts. A general description of the statistical sources for the financial accounts is given in Chapter XIV, Sections 3 and 4.

INTERNATIONAL TRANSACTIONS

Exports and imports of goods

The *Overseas Trade Accounts of the United Kingdom* (*Trade Accounts*), which are published monthly, form the starting point for calculating the balance of payments figures of exports and imports. Although the balance of payments accounts aim to include transactions when the change of ownership takes place, no adjustment is made for timing differences between the declaration of trade by exporters and importers as recorded in the *Trade Accounts* and the time of change in ownership, apart from the important exception of the treatment of purchases of United States military aircraft (see page 460). Differences in timing between payments and the recording by exporters and importers of sales and purchases, for example due to the granting of trade credit, are treated as changes in assets or liabilities and are recorded in monetary movements or as part of direct investment in the long-term capital account. The net effect of unidentified differences in timing is automatically reflected in the balancing item.

A number of adjustments are made, however, in respect of valuation and coverage to convert the *Trade Accounts* to a balance of payments basis. The following are the more important of these adjustments.

(a) *Valuation adjustments*. (i) *Freight and insurance*. Imports in the *Trade Accounts* are valued 'c.i.f.', that is inclusive of the cost of insurance and freight from the country of consignment. For the balance of payments these costs are deducted since freight and insurance payments to foreign shipping, airline and insurance companies are included in the appropriate invisibles account item, and those to United Kingdom concerns are regarded as domestic transactions.

The freight element of the c.i.f. value of dry cargo imports is estimated from the actual freight rates applicable to a large sample of individual commodities imported from various sources. The system of estimating freight on imports of oil is, so far as possible, complementary to the method adopted by oil companies in building up the c.i.f. value of oil imports declared to H.M. Customs and Excise; the estimates of freight are based largely on the Average Freight Rate Assessment (AFRA) of the London Tanker Brokers' Panel. Estimates of payments for air freight and for insurance are based on a sample examination of customs entry forms and supporting invoices augmented, in the case of insurance, by data supplied by the British Insurance Association and Lloyd's.

(ii) *Port charges.* Certain charges associated with the unloading of imports at United Kingdom ports are included in the *Trade Accounts* valuation. These charges are excluded from the balance of payments figures since the payments are made by United Kingdom importers to United Kingdom residents. The deductions made are based on a sample examination of customs entry forms.

(iii) *Customs uplift.* The value of imports recorded in the *Trade Accounts* is based on the price they would fetch on sale in the open market. In certain cases where the transaction is not an open market one, for example some transactions between related companies, the *Trade Accounts* value may exceed that paid or payable to the supplier abroad. As it is the latter value which is appropriate to the balance of payments accounts an adjustment is made to the *Trade Accounts* figures. Estimates of the amounts to be deducted are derived from a sample examination of customs entry forms.

(iv) *Imports on consignment.* Certain classes of goods are imported on a consignment basis, in which case the market value of the goods is not known until they are actually sold. Until the final value is known, a provisional value, which is often above the market value, is entered in the *Trade Accounts*. Where the goods are subject to an *ad valorem* duty the actual market value is eventually declared to H.M. Customs and Excise, thus allowing for a subsequent correction to appear in the trade figures. However, some of the goods imported on a consignment basis, especially fruit and vegetables, are either duty free or are subject to specific duties. In many such instances it appears from a sample comparison of the value as originally declared on the customs entry form and the actual payments as shown by Exchange Control records that there is a tendency for the original higher value to remain in the *Trade Accounts*. A deduction is made from the imports figures to allow for this overstatement.

(v) *Sugar.* An adjustment is included in the balance of payments figures for 1964 and earlier years to take account of the difference between the market value of imported sugar recorded in the *Trade Accounts* and the amounts actually paid by the Sugar Board under the Commonwealth Sugar Agreement. From the beginning of 1965 the values recorded in the *Trade Accounts* have included the amounts paid under the agreement.

(b) *Coverage adjustments.* (i) *Second-hand ships and aircraft.* These are excluded from the *Trade Accounts* but need to be included in the balance of payments figures. The value of trade in second-hand aircraft is obtained mainly from customs records. Details about both purchases and sales of second-hand ships are derived from a number of sources, including information provided by the General Register and Record Office of Shipping and Seamen, government departments and various trade publications.

(ii) *New ships delivered abroad.* Certain ships built abroad for United Kingdom owners are delivered in the first place to overseas ports. These purchases are not always recorded in the *Trade Accounts*, but they are appropriate to balance of payments figures of imports. The details are obtained from the same sources as for second-hand ships.

(iii) *Atomic energy materials*. Imports and exports of certain atomic energy materials, including uranium ore, are omitted from the *Trade Accounts* figures. Details are supplied by the Atomic Energy Authority and included in the balance of payments figures.

(iv) *Exports by letter post*. The *Trade Accounts* do not include exports from the United Kingdom by letter post. Information about the most important element of this trade, the export of books, is obtained from the Publishers' Association. Other details are derived from a sample inquiry made by the General Post Office.

(v) *Tin buffer stock*. Imports of tin into the United Kingdom for the International Tin Council, regarded as an international organisation, are included in the *Trade Accounts*. In the balance of payments accounts, therefore, imports of tin for the buffer stock of the I.T.C. are recorded as having been simultaneously re-exported to the Council. Similarly, when tin is sold in the United Kingdom from the buffer stock, either for retention in the United Kingdom or for export, a corresponding entry for imports is entered in the balance of payments figures.

(vi) *NAAFI*. Goods exported by the Navy, Army and Air Force Institute for the use of United Kingdom Forces abroad are included in the *Trade Accounts* but, since they are for sale to United Kingdom residents, they are deducted from the *Trade Accounts* for balance of payments purposes. The figures are obtained through returns received from the Institute.

(vii) *Returned goods and goods for processing and repair*. The *Trade Accounts* include certain goods which are imported and exported without payment. These are of two types, returned goods and goods for processing and repair. Returned goods include, for example, items such as contractors' plant temporarily exported without changing ownership. The value of these goods is known to H.M. Customs and Excise since duty is normally involved and exemption from this duty can be claimed. The same value is deducted from both imports and exports in the balance of payments accounts at the time of import. This probably results in some error in timing of exports, however, and in this event the error would be reflected in the balancing item. In the case of goods imported for processing and repair, this treatment means that the value added as a result of the processing or repair remains in the export figures. Theoretically, these processing fees more appropriately belong to exports of services (invisibles), but as their precise value is not known, this transfer is not made; the estimates of the gross domestic product and the current balance in the balance of payments accounts are not affected.

(viii) *U.S. military aircraft and missiles*. In 1964 purchase began of a quantity of military aircraft and missiles, together with certain spare parts, from the United States under credit arrangements with the Export-Import Bank of Washington. Payments to the United States manufacturers are made largely in advance of delivery, during the course of production. The bulk of these production payments and the final payments on delivery, are financed through credit provided to the United Kingdom government by the Export-Import Bank of Washington, each drawing of credit being repayable by instalments over seven years. The cost to the current and long-term capital account of the balance of payments occurs as interest payments and capital repayments are made to the Export-Import Bank.

In the *Trade Accounts*, the aircraft and missiles are recorded as imports when they arrive in the United Kingdom. In the balance of payments and national income accounts, however, the purchases are recorded as imports in the period when payments to the United States manufacturers are made and not when the finished products arrive in the United Kingdom. In so far as the payments are financed through drawings from the Export-Import Bank credit, the counterpart of the payments appears in inter-government loans in the capital account of the central government and the long-term capital account of the balance of payments. This treatment is a departure from the usual practice of recording imports when they arrive in this country but is consistent with the treatment of corresponding purchases from United Kingdom manufacturers; central government current expenditure on defence equipment includes progress payments made in advance of the delivery of the equipment.

Certain components, including engines, are being purchased by the United Kingdom government from British manufacturers and supplied to the United States for incorporation in the aircraft. These are included as exports in the *Trade Accounts*, but excluded from the balance of payments figures of exports since they do not leave United Kingdom ownership and no payment is received from overseas. Certain other components, however, are purchased directly by the United States manufacturers from United Kingdom suppliers and are included in the price charged for the aircraft. The value of these components is left in the figures of exports in the balance of payments, and is also included, although not necessarily in the same period, in imports since it forms part of the payment for the complete aircraft.

Details of the necessary adjustments to the *Trade Accounts* figures are derived from H.M. Customs and Excise and other official records.

Exports and imports of services

(a) *Government.* The figures for government overseas expenditure and receipts are derived from returns provided by government departments having transactions with overseas residents.

(b) *Shipping.* (i) *United Kingdom shipping.* Annual statistics relating to the United Kingdom shipping industry are provided by the Chamber of Shipping of the United Kingdom, which conducts a full inquiry generally every five years, and large-scale sample inquiries in the intervening years, into the participation of United Kingdom shipping in overseas trade. Quarterly estimates are based on the volume of United Kingdom and world trade, passenger movements, changes in freight rates, and other appropriate indicators.

(ii) *Overseas shipping.* Estimates of freight on imports, other than oil, paid to overseas residents are obtained by deducting the Chamber of Shipping estimates of the amount earned by United Kingdom ships for carrying United Kingdom imports, from the estimates of total freight on imports by sea used in assessing the f.o.b. value of imports. Estimates of freight on oil imports paid to overseas residents are based on information made available to the Chamber of Shipping by the oil companies. The estimates of the United Kingdom shipping industry's earnings for carrying United Kingdom imports are available only annually, and for quarterly figures it is assumed that the proportion of total freight paid to overseas shipping for carrying United Kingdom imports remains constant. An estimate of passenger fares paid to overseas shipping companies, almost all of which are resident in the non-sterling area, is derived from an analysis of Exchange Control records.

Estimates of port charges, handling charges, agency fees, crews' expenditure and the value of ships' stores, are based on the results of sample inquiries made periodically. Pilotage and towage costs, light dues and expenditure on repairs are assessed from regular returns made to the Board of Trade. The value of oil bunkers lifted in the United Kingdom by foreign flag vessels is estimated from figures of the quantity of oil fuel taken on board.

(c) *Civil aviation.* (i) *United Kingdom airlines.* Estimates of the transactions of BOAC and BEA are derived from quarterly returns supplied by the two cor-porations. Estimates of the transactions of the British independent airlines are based on financial information supplied by some of these airlines to the Board of Trade and on traffic handled and capacity provided.

(ii) *Overseas airlines.* Passenger revenue is estimated by applying average fares appropriate to the various routes to estimates of the numbers of United Kingdom residents travelling on overseas airlines. The latter estimates are derived from the International Passenger Survey conducted by the Government Social Survey for the Board of Trade. Estimates of freight on imports carried by overseas airlines are obtained by deducting the amount earned by United Kingdom airlines for carrying United Kingdom imports from estimates of total freight on imports by air. Estimates of the expenditure in the United Kingdom of overseas airlines are derived from returns from the British Airports Authority, municipal airports and the Board of Trade on the expenditure of overseas airlines at United Kingdom airports for landing fees, use of airport buildings and other airport services; estimates of oil bunkers lifted, based on total deliv-eries of aviation fuel; and information on other expenditure provided by the major overseas airlines operating into the United Kingdom.

(d) *Travel.* The travel estimates for 1962 and later periods are based primarily on the International Passenger Survey of air and sea passengers, conducted by the Government Social Survey for the Board of Trade, which provides infor-mation on the numbers and expenditure of overseas visitors to the United Kingdom and United Kingdom residents travelling abroad. The sample surveys do not cover travel between the United Kingdom and the Irish Republic, for which estimates are derived from statistics published by the Irish Central Statistics Office.

Before the introduction of the sample surveys, estimates of travel expenditure were derived as a product of numbers of passengers and rough estimates of average expenditure per head, supported by information made available by other countries. For some areas the estimates based on the sample surveys showed considerable differences from those based on previous methods and, in order to preserve a reasonably consistent series of estimates, some of the travel figures previously published were revised in the light of the sample surveys.

(e) *Other services.* The estimates for some of the components of this item are obtained from direct inquiries; for other components a variety of sources is used. In some cases accurate estimates can be made, but for miscellaneous transactions and certain other components which present particularly difficult problems of measurement, the estimates are approximate and may be revised as new sources of information become available. For example, the British National Export Council's Committee on Invisible Exports[3] instituted a number of direct inquiries of City and other commercial organisations which

---

[3] *Britain's Invisible Earnings*, Report of the Committee on Invisible Exports, British National Export Council, 1967.

may be capable of development as continuing sources of information. Where regular direct inquiries are already established, the results from them have mostly been available for only a few years and only on an annual basis. In these instances the available results have been used as a guide, in association where possible with other related indicators, in making quarterly estimates and annual estimates for earlier years. The sources currently used for the annual estimates are described briefly below. Further details are given in the annual Pink Book, *United Kingdom Balance of Payments*.

(i) *Financial and allied services*. The estimates of exports of services cover the earnings of British insurance companies, Lloyd's underwriters, insurance brokers, stock exchanges, the Baltic Exchange, the United Kingdom banking sector, organised commodity markets on merchanting, and similar smaller items. The estimates are based mainly on returns by the insurance industry to the Board of Trade and information on other institutions available to the Bank of England.

(ii) *Commissions, etc. on imports and exports*. Commissions on exports to non-sterling areas are obtained from Exchange Control records and those to the overseas sterling area are assumed to be in the same proportion to the value of exports. The estimates of commissions on imports are made by applying appropriate percentages to the c.i.f. values of imports in the various commodity classes; these percentages are based on a sample of customs records and on information from traders.

(iii) *Telecommunications and postal services*. Figures are based on returns by the General Post Office and on Exchange Control records of payments by private cable companies.

(iv) *Films and television*. Figures are derived from the Board of Trade annual inquiries into overseas transactions in respect of production costs, royalties, rentals and purchases of cinematograph films and television material. A deduction is made to eliminate the overlap between this inquiry and the purchases and sales of exposed cinematograph films recorded in the *Trade Accounts* and included in imports and exports of goods.

(v) *Royalties, etc.* (other than film royalties). Figures are taken from the Board of Trade annual inquiry into royalty payments, etc.

(vi) *Services rendered between United Kingdom enterprises and related enterprises overseas*. The estimates are obtained from returns collected annually by the Board of Trade in connection with the direct investment inquiry, which record the net amount debited or credited between parent companies and individual branches, subsidiaries and associates.

(vii) *Advertising, etc.* Statistical reviews of press and television advertising provide a source for measuring advertising expenditure and other sales promotion, which is supplemented by information made available by various bodies including the Institute of Practitioners in Advertising and the International Wool Secretariat, and by information derived from Exchange Control records.

(viii) *Expenditure by overseas students and journalists*. The figures are obtained by applying estimates of average expenditure to the number of overseas students and journalists in the United Kingdom. Some allowance is made for receipts from United Kingdom nationals permanently overseas whose children are being maintained and educated in the United Kingdom.

(ix) *Architects' and consulting engineers' fees and contractors' net earnings*. These are estimated from the values of contracts on hand and returns provided by the construction industry.

(x) *Overseas governments' and non-territorial organisations' expenditure.* The estimates are based on the known number of diplomats stationed in the United Kingdom in conjunction with an assumed average expenditure, and on information provided by the non-territorial organisations.

(xi) *Non-governmental receipts from foreign military Forces.* The figures are derived from information provided by the appropriate military authorities.

Property income

(a) *Direct investment income.* For years from 1958, figures of direct investment income have been obtained from the Board of Trade inquiry into overseas direct investment. Both quarterly and annual returns are obtained; the former are on a sample basis, while the annual returns are substantially complete. Before 1958, figures were obtained mainly from Exchange Control records and from data provided by other countries. The main deficiency in these figures was the omission, both from payments of property income and from the inflow to the United Kingdom in the capital account, of a large part of the profits earned by United Kingdom subsidiaries of overseas companies and subsequently reinvested in this country. A special inquiry was made in respect of the years 1955-57 to identify this element and allowance has been made for it in the published figures of property income and capital investment. The inquiry was not carried back to earlier years, but a rough allowance has been made to bring the figures for these years broadly into line with those for 1955 and subsequent years.

(b) *Portfolio investment income.* Estimates of portfolio income accruing to the United Kingdom are based primarily on Inland Revenue records. Debits are estimated in relation to the outstanding level of liabilities, from Exchange Control records and from information published or made available by overseas sterling area countries.

(c) *Other investment income.* Estimates of oil credits and debits are based on returns made by the oil industry. The method of compiling the estimates for credits starts from the total flow of oil companies' cash remittances to and from the United Kingdom which is then adjusted to take account of oil company transactions entered elsewhere in the balance of payments accounts (that is under exports or imports of goods and services, in the long-term capital account and in monetary movements). Since the figures for other transactions are mostly on a payable-receivable basis, including for example investment out of locally retained profits, the adjusted estimates of credits include earnings other than cash receipts.

Estimates for other items are based mainly on returns of the outstanding assets and liabilities and on other records of the Bank of England, government departments and certain other official bodies.

The estimates of foreign taxes paid on property income from abroad and of United Kingdom taxes on property income paid abroad are based on Inland Revenue data.

Current transfers

Personal sector. Receipts from the non-sterling areas are based partly on Exchange Control information, a source which was lost as the result of the changes in exchange regulations in 1965, and partly on information available from other countries' balance of payments statistics of their transfers to the

United Kingdom. For estimates of United Kingdom transfers to the non-sterling areas, Exchange Control records are used. For the overseas sterling area, information from the balance of payments statistics of the sterling area countries is used to measure both United Kingdom credits and debits. Estimates of the value of the gift element in parcel post trade are provided by the Board of Trade on the basis of a sample inquiry made by the General Post Office.

Central government. Figures are compiled from returns made by government departments.

Capital transfers from abroad; Capital grants from overseas governments (net)

The figures for these items are compiled from government records.

FINANCIAL TRANSACTIONS

Treasury bills

The figures are derived from the balance of payments statistics of external liabilities and claims in sterling. These statistics are compiled from Bank of England records, information supplied by the Crown Agents and returns made by banks and other financial institutions to the Bank of England.

British government and government guaranteed securities

The figures are derived from three main sources. Holdings by United Kingdom banks on behalf of overseas banks and central monetary institutions are reported to the Bank of England as part of the regular series of returns on external liabilities and claims in sterling. Details of holdings by the Crown Agents for Overseas Governments and Administrations are provided by the Crown Agents. The holdings by banks and the Crown Agents are reported at nominal values and an adjustment is made to convert the figures to a cash transactions basis. This adjustment is included in the balance of payments accounts under 'Miscellaneous capital'. A separate inquiry conducted by the Bank of England from 1960 measures changes in the holdings of government and government guaranteed stocks by other overseas residents, that is by holders other than overseas banks and central monetary institutions, whether held directly or through the nominee companies of United Kingdom banks.

Local authority debt

Figures of changes in holdings by United Kingdom banks and other nominee companies on behalf of overseas residents and of changes in holdings by the Crown Agents are derived from the same sources as the figures of government and government guaranteed securities. From 1961 figures of changes in direct holdings of local authority mortgages and temporary money by overseas residents are also included; the figures are obtained from returns made by local authorities (see page 420).

Gold and currency reserves; Inter-government loans (net); United Kingdom subscriptions to I.M.F. and European Fund; Drawings from United Kingdom subscriptions to international lending bodies; Holdings of interest-free notes by I.M.F.; Other public sector assets and liabilities: short-term and long-term

Figures for all of these items are derived from returns from government departments and public corporations or from other official records.

Deposits with banking sector; Bank lending

Figures for these items are not taken from balance of payments statistics. They are derived from returns made by the banking sector to the Bank of England (see page 418).

Deposits with other financial institutions

Figures of deposits with hire purchase finance companies are not taken from balance of payments statistics; they are derived from returns made by the companies to the Board of Trade (see page 420). Figures of deposits with other financial institutions are, however, drawn from the series of returns on external liabilities and claims made by certain financial institutions to the Bank of England, primarily for balance of payments statistics.

Company and overseas securities; Other private sector assets: long-term

(a) *Direct investment.* These figures are obtained from the Board of Trade inquiry into overseas direct investment, referred to on page 464. The returns of investment in this inquiry distinguish between net acquisitions of share and loan capital, the unremitted profits of subsidiaries, changes in branch indebtedness and changes in inter-company accounts. Net acquisitions of share and loan capital are included under 'Company and overseas securities'; the other components of direct investment are included under 'Other private sector assets: long-term'.

(b) *Portfolio investment.* Estimates of overseas portfolio investment by the United Kingdom are based on the Bank of England survey of overseas investment which includes transactions in securities dealt in on the London Stock Exchange and in non-sterling securities quoted abroad. The survey makes use of information obtained from registrars and paying agents in the United Kingdom and from Exchange Control sources. Adjustments based on balance of payments information compiled in other countries are made to cover overseas sterling area securities falling outside the range of the Bank of England survey. Figures of portfolio investment by overseas residents in United Kingdom company securities are based on an inquiry conducted from 1960 by the Board of Trade among large companies which account for 70 per cent of the total market value of issued capital. The inquiry provides information on changes in the holdings of the securities of such companies by overseas residents, including so far as possible holdings by nominees acting on their behalf.

(c) *Other private long-term investment.* Estimates of United Kingdom oil companies investment abroad and of overseas oil companies investment in their United Kingdom subsidiaries are based on information supplied by the oil industry. Estimates for other items are based on records of the Bank of England, information made available by companies and information published or made available by other countries.

Other private sector assets: short-term

(a) *Trade credit (not elsewhere included).* Estimates of trade credit are derived from an inquiry conducted by the Board of Trade since 1963 into the structure of trade credit extended to, or received from, other countries[4]. The inquiry distin-

---

[4]For full description see *Board of Trade Journal,* 17 June 1966 and 21 July 1967.

guishes credit between members of the same company or group, which is included in private direct investment; credit extended under financial guarantees and other credit covered by bills of exchange or promissory notes owned by or lodged with United Kingdom banks, which is covered by the various entries for commercial bills; and other trade credit between unrelated companies in which the banking sector has not participated, which is the trade credit included in this item.

(b) *Other identified commercial short-term transactions (net)*. These estimates are derived from information provided by certain traders and companies to the Bank of England for balance of payments statistics.

(c) *Commercial bills, etc.* These transactions are measured through the system of returns of external liabilities and claims made by financial institutions to the Bank of England.

Also included in 'Other private sector assets: short-term' is the counterpart of the timing and coverage differences between the financial accounts figures and the balance of payments figures arising on other items. The sources of the balance of payments figures are described in greater detail in the annual Pink Book, *United Kingdom Balance of Payments*.

4. INTERNATIONAL TRANSACTIONS IN GOODS AND SERVICES AT CONSTANT PRICES

Estimates are made of the value of exports and imports of goods and services at constant prices for the expenditure estimates of the gross domestic product at constant prices. Net property income is also revalued in order to provide an estimate of gross national product at constant prices. The estimates are given in Table 14 of the 1967 Blue Book.

Exports and imports of goods

Estimates of exports and imports of goods at constant prices are obtained by projecting the estimates for the base year by indices of the volume of trade. Volume index numbers of United Kingdom trade are compiled monthly by the Board of Trade and published in the *Board of Trade Journal* and the *Monthly Digest of Statistics*.

The volume indices are applied to the *Trade Accounts* figures of exports and imports in the base year, adjusted for valuation, but not for coverage, to a balance of payments basis. The estimate for exports and re-exports of goods is projected by the Board of Trade volume index for total exports, adjusted to include provision for re-exports. The calculation for imports is more complicated because the Board of Trade volume index is based on c.i.f. values, whereas for the national income accounts f.o.b. values are required. Ideally the index should be completely re-weighted to f.o.b. values but in practice it has been found that, apart from imports of fuel, variations in the ratio of the f.o.b. to the c.i.f. value for different commodities have little effect on the movement of the volume index for total imports. For this reason, only the relative weights for fuel and for all other commodities together are changed to obtain the volume index by which total imports in the base year are projected. The base year for the Board of Trade volume index numbers (1961) differs from the base year for the national accounts (1958) but no adjustments have been made to the weights of the volume indices for this difference, apart from those which follow from the adjustments described above.

The implied price index for exports derived by these methods is used to revalue at constant prices the balance of payments coverage adjustments applied to the *Trade Accounts* figures of exports and of imports. The same price index is used to revalue the coverage adjustments to exports and to imports since the two sets of adjustments cover much the same types of goods. An exception is made, however, in the case of imports of United States military aircraft where the balance of payments adjustments are converted to constant prices by a specially calculated price index.

Exports and imports of services

Exports and imports of services cannot for the most part be accurately estimated at constant prices. From the data that are obtainable, only rough price indices can be constructed. The main indices used for deflating the shipping estimates are weighted averages of tramp and liner freight rates. For civil aviation, where passenger revenue is relatively more important, the main price index used is a specially calculated index of air fares based on the revenue per passenger mile of United Kingdom airlines. Government expenditure overseas is deflated by very rough price indices for the kinds of goods and services principally purchased. For 'Travel' and 'Other services', extensive use is made of appropriate components of the United Kingdom retail price index and price indices of various countries abroad, together with foreign exchange rates.

Net property income from abroad

It is impossible to make direct estimates of income from abroad at constant prices consistent with other items of national expenditure, without knowing how that income was spent. Property income from abroad may be used to build up financial assets and not spent on goods and services. However, in order to arrive at an estimate of national as opposed to domestic product at constant prices, the United Kingdom accounts adopt the convention of revaluing net property income from abroad by dividing it by the price index implied by the estimates of imports of goods and services at current and constant prices. This procedure gives a measure of the worth of the net income flow for purchasing imported goods and services. In the United Kingdom accounts no attempt is made to revalue separately the gross flows of property income from abroad and property income paid abroad.

5. RELIABILITY

The balance of payments estimates are compiled from a large number of different sources and the degree of accuracy attained varies considerably between items. Some of the errors and omissions may be persistent and tend to be in the same direction in all years. For this reason, the absolute error in the change from year to year is likely to be less than the error in any particular year. In any particular year errors in the various items are likely, to some extent, to offset each other and the proportionate error in major aggregates is likely to be less than the weighted average of the proportionate errors in the components. However, where a balance is drawn between two aggregates and the balance is small in relation to the aggregates, such as the current balance in the balance of payments accounts, the proportionate error attached to the balance is liable to be very substantial. The following notes assess the comparative quality of the individual components of the annual estimates for the later years and the main points at which errors and omissions may arise.

Exports and imports of goods

Customs regulations lay down a formula for the valuing of export and import merchandise on the customs entry forms from which the *Trade Accounts* are compiled. A number of adjustments are made, as described in Section 3 above, for both valuation and coverage to bring the *Trade Accounts* figures on to a balance of payments basis. Some of these adjustments are based on comprehensive returns and others on the results of sample inquiries; any errors in them are thought to be comparatively small. For the most important adjustment, any error in the estimate of total freight on dry cargo imports, which is deducted to bring the value of imports to an f.o.b. basis, will be offset by an equal and opposite error in the estimate for services, since the same estimate is used as the starting point for the calculation of imports of freight services. It is possible, however, that there is some inconsistency between the value of commissions assumed to be included in figures of exports and imports of goods and the estimates for debits and credits on commissions included within 'Other services'. In relation to the large gross value involved the margin of error in the estimates for exports and imports of goods is probably very small, although it is still of significance in relation to the difference between the two estimates.

Exports and imports of services

Figures of government transactions are based on records of government departments and can be considered good; any errors are generally limited to minor timing discrepancies.

The figures relating to United Kingdom shipping are based on the inquiries carried out by the Chamber of Shipping and the margin of error is unlikely to be large. There may, however, be appreciable errors in the quarterly estimates and the preliminary annual estimates produced before the full results of these inquiries become available. Errors in the estimates of freight payments for overseas shipping arise from two sources: errors in the estimates of total freight charges on dry cargo imports and errors in the estimates of the earnings of United Kingdom shipping companies from the carriage of dry cargo imports. The former errors are offset by equal and opposite errors in the estimates of the f.o.b. values of imports. It is therefore only the latter errors which affect the overall estimates of imports of goods and services, and these errors are probably relatively small although they are larger in the preliminary estimate for the most recent year. The estimates for the transactions of United Kingdom airlines are based on regular returns from the airlines and are considered to be reliable; but estimates for overseas airlines are less firmly based.

Estimates of travel expenditure are now based largely on a system of interviews with a sample of passengers leaving or arriving at sea or air ports. Though still subject to some sampling error and to deficiencies in reporting, the estimates are more firmly based than in earlier years.

Estimates for the numerous and heterogenous types of transaction which fall into 'Other services' are of varying quality. The range of estimates which are based on direct inquiries of industry and commerce has been extended in recent years and now covers about half the estimated total value of exports and imports in this category. Exchange Control records remain the basis for other imports from the non-sterling areas and 'partner country' information for much of the imports from the overseas sterling area. The estimates for many export items are still derived from various related indicators and are inevitably no more than rough. Thus the totals for both exports and imports under this heading must be regarded as poor. In particular, errors are likely to arise here in distinguishing transactions between residents and non-residents and the estimates may not be entirely consistent with the estimates of domestic income.

Reliability gradings for the main components of exports and imports of goods and services are given in the table below in terms of the gradings described on pages 39 to 41. The gradings apply to the estimates for the later years as published in the Blue Book and the balance of payments Pink Book. Although less information is available for the latest year, the estimates do not warrant a lower grading.

Reliability of annual estimates of exports and imports of goods and services at current prices[1]

A ± less than 3 per cent
B ± 3 per cent to 10 per cent
C ± more than 10 per cent

	Grading[1]	Exports of goods and services at current prices, 1966 £ million	Imports of goods and services at current prices, 1966 £ million
Goods	A	5,110	5,262
Services:			
Government	A	43	321
Shipping	B	767	744
Civil aviation	B	175	152
Travel	B	219	297
Other services	C	625	349
Total services	B	1,829	1,863
Total goods and services .	A	6,939	7,125

[1]For the significance of the reliability gradings see pages 39 to 41.

Estimates of exports and imports of services in years before 1958 are less reliable than those for later years, but because of the reliability of the *Trade Accounts*, on which estimates of exports and imports of goods are based, a grading of A is probably still appropriate in these earlier years for the combined total of goods and services.

Property income

The interest, profits and dividends, after deduction of overseas taxes, arising from direct investment are thought to be satisfactorily measured both on the receipts and the payments side. Estimates of interest and dividends on portfolio investment are somewhat less reliable, more particularly on the payments side of the account. Earnings from oil, taken in conjunction with the goods and services entries for oil operations and the estimates of private investment, are also thought to measure fully the effect of transactions in oil on the balance of payments, but the figures of oil earnings which are included in property income differ in various ways from the accounting measure which is required of profits earned overseas (see page 446). The estimates for certain other elements of investment income are not directly measured, and may be subject to error, particularly where no precise information is available on the type of liabilities and assets involved.

The gross figures of property income after deduction of overseas taxes can be regarded as in category B. Errors in the gross figures of income from abroad and income paid abroad inevitably have a relatively greater effect on the estimates of net income, and the reliability of the estimates of net property income from abroad is graded as C; that is, the estimates are probably subject to an error of more than 10 per cent.

Transfers

Figures of government transfer receipts and payments are derived from official records and are generally subject to only minor errors.

Estimates of private transfers to the non-sterling areas are based mainly on Exchange Control data and are likely to be substantially complete. Until 1965 certain types of cash transfers from non-sterling areas were eligible for the investment currency premium and this provided a basis for estimating the amounts of the transfers. As a result of changes in Exchange Control regulations in that year, however, this source of information was lost and subsequent estimates have been based on incomplete information from other countries, supplemented by related indicators. Private transfers to and from the overseas sterling area are also estimated from information from other countries and related indicators, such as numbers of migrants. The total estimates of private transfers are therefore only approximate.

Net acquisition of financial assets

The estimate of the current balance in the balance of payments accounts is the net result of the large aggregates of the transactions described above and must be regarded as in category C. Thus the estimation of the net acquisition of financial assets by the overseas sector, which is equal, apart from the change in sign, to the current balance *plus* any transfers from abroad included in the capital account of the balance of payments, is poor.

Financial transactions

The reliability of the estimates of financial transactions varies considerably between the different assets and liabilities. Complete records of inter-government loans and other official capital transactions are available and the estimates are good. The flows of private direct investment are also thought to be adequately measured. The estimates of outward portfolio investment are based partly on changes in holdings of overseas securities having a United Kingdom registrar or paying agent; some transactions in other overseas sterling area securities escape recording although some of the gap is filled by use of information from the other countries concerned. The measurement of inward portfolio investment has been improved, but gaps still exist. Changes in overseas holdings of local authority securities are not yet fully covered and the Board of Trade inquiry on company securities is limited to the major companies. The identification of nominee holdings is a problem and they are only partially identified.

The figures of most private transactions in short-term assets are reliable, being taken from the regular returns made by banks and other financial institutions. The coverage of other changes in short-term assets and liabilities has improved, particularly with the development of the Board of Trade inquiry into trade credit. Some gaps still remain, however, and errors may also arise through failure to recognise non-resident status, especially where nominee accounts are employed.

Balancing item

The balancing item represents the net total of errors and omissions arising throughout the balance of payments accounts and although varying considerably in size from year to year it has been positive in eleven of the fifteen years from 1952 to 1966; over the nine years 1958 to 1966 the average has been about +£50 million. This suggests that there is an underlying tendency for credit entries to be understated or debit entries to be overstated, or quite probably a combination of both.

It is difficult to find reasons for the size of the balancing item and its fluctuations from period to period, but it seems probable that it includes:

(a) a recurrent positive element attributable to deficiencies in the measurement of current account transactions; it is possible that this recurrent element may be growing in line with the scale of current account transactions; it is thought in the mid-1960's to be within the range of +£50-£75 million a year.

(b) a much more irregular element which includes timing differences in the recording of transactions and payments but is probably mainly attributable to unrecorded financial transactions; the latter includes short-term leads and lags in the timing of payments, which, like identified flows of short-term funds, are probably influenced to some extent by the level of interest rates in the United Kingdom relative to those abroad and, on occasion, by speculation about exchange rates.

In so far as the persistent positive element is due to an overstatement of imports of goods and services or an understatement of exports of goods and services, there is an understatement of the gross domestic product measured as a sum of expenditures and, in turn, a persistent negative element in the residual error in the national income accounts. But the average level of the residual error can provide no evidence to support this because it is affected by many other factors. There seems, however, to be some association in the fluctuations of the balancing item and the residual error which suggests that some of the irregular element in the balancing item may be associated with timing differences in recording transactions in goods and services and the corresponding payments. In so far as the balancing item arises solely on financial transactions, there is no effect on the estimates of the gross domestic product or on the residual error.

Appendix I

RENT

General description

Some description has been given of the treatment of rent, considered both as income derived from the ownership of land and buildings and as expenditure by the occupier, in the chapters dealing with the several sectors of the economy. This appendix summarises the treatment of rent income and brings together the various estimates.

Rent is a category of factor income with a special and rather arbitrary definition. It denotes the income derived from the ownership of land and buildings, reckoned after deduction of actual expenditure by the owners on current repairs, maintenance and insurance. Where the owner of property not used for trading purposes is also the occupier, an income is imputed to him which in principle is designed to represent the amount he would receive if he let the accommodation unfurnished under an agreement whereby the tenant undertook the responsibility for rates, all repairs and insurance. In what follows, rent income means the net rent in the sense of expenditure on rent by the occupier, including ground rents in the case of leasehold property, *less* the landlord's expenditure on repairs, etc.

The justification for specifying income from rent separately is practical rather than theoretical, although there is much tradition behind it. The figures given, which relate principally to buildings, certainly do not measure the earnings of the factor of production land as conceived in classical economic theory. Rent is better regarded as a form of trading profits—the surplus on operating account derived from the business of letting real estate—than as the earnings of a specific and distinguishable factor of production. But both the concept of rent income and the available statistics have special features which make it convenient to give separate treatment to rent income. Firstly, a large proportion of land and buildings is owned by their occupiers; hence a correspondingly large proportion of income from rent can be measured only by imputation, being estimated by reference to the market rents actually received for similar property. This imputed income was of course regarded as real enough to suffer income tax under Schedule A. Secondly, much of the statistical material for estimating both actual and imputed rent income is unsatisfactory.

For these reasons it is felt better to state rent income, so far as possible, as a separate item rather than to attempt to add an unsatisfactory allowance for it to the other forms of profit income. However, the distinction between rent income and trading income from the provision of accommodation is not always clear-cut when accommodation is rented furnished or for short periods.

Some general features of the definition of the estimate of rent income should be noted:

(i) One important form of rent income is included in trading profits and excluded from the estimates of rent. This is the income of all trading concerns other than farms (companies, unincorporated businesses, public corporations and trading branches of public authorities) owning the land and buildings which

473

they occupy. The reason for this exception is that there is no satisfactory basis for estimating the rent income. The total trading profits of a concern may reasonably be regarded as including the profits derived from the ownership of its land and business premises and, since the abolition of Schedule A income tax, the total profits have been the basis for the tax assessment. Any attempt to determine how much of the profits is derived from the property, as distinct from the profits earned by the other factors of production employed, would be unrealistic and would not, of course, affect the contribution of the concern to total national income.

(ii) The income from owner-occupied farm land and buildings is, by contrast, treated as rent income. This follows the procedure of the agricultural departments in estimating farmers' income.

(iii) The incomes of concerns owning and letting property as a business, that is the 'real estate' industry, are included in rent income.

(iv) The income from rent of public authorities is estimated on the basis of an economic rent being paid by the tenants. Where payments by tenants do not cover costs, their payments are regarded as being supplemented by a subsidy, which contributes to the rent income derived from the property.

(v) Rent income includes indistinguishably any income arising from the provision of furniture when property is let furnished, and some income from the provision of other ancillary services, such as cleaning, may also be included.

(vi) Rent income, like trading income, is obtained after allowing for the estimated expenditure incurred on repairs and maintenance, etc. The expenditure incurred may differ from the expenditure required to maintain the property in running order. No allowance can be made for this difference.

(vii) Rent income, like trading income, is estimated before providing for depreciation. Estimates of capital consumption are made for dwellings and for other buildings and works (Table 61 of the 1967 Blue Book) but the latter are not comparable with the estimates of rent because they cover owner-occupied trading property.

Estimation of rent

The estimate of total income from rent has been built up by combining the estimated rent income for five groups of property, as described below. Annual estimates up to 1962 and the provisional estimates for later years are based entirely on this method. The quarterly estimates of rent are also built up by interpolation and projection of the annual figures for these five groups of property.

(a) *Land and buildings used by persons as consumers and not owned by public authorities.* This group covers land, houses and other buildings used by households and individuals, as consumers, or by non-profit-making bodies included in the personal sector. All property not owned by public authorities is included, that is property owned by persons, companies and public corporations. Both rented and owner-occupied houses and other properties are included. The trading property occupied by unincorporated businesses is excluded. The main component, of course, relates to privately-owned houses and covers the rent income of both landlords and owner-occupiers.

The measurement of rent income for this group is derived from the estimates of consumers' expenditure on rent, rates and water charges, shown in the analysis of consumers' expenditure (Table 27 of the 1967 Blue Book). The sources of the estimates, which include the imputed rent of owner-occupiers, are described on pages 162 and 163. Where premises are used for domestic and business purposes, an adjustment is made to exclude the business element. From these estimates expenditure on rates and water charges is excluded and an estimate of expenditure by landlords on repairs, maintenance and insurance is deducted. The latter estimate is very rough. It makes use of information on tax allowances for repairs by landlords, expenditure on property maintenance by local authorities and information collected by the Ministry of Public Building and Works on total work done by contractors on private dwellings. The rent income of public authorities from dwellings is then excluded to obtain the income on this group of property.

(b) *Central government property*. This group covers (i) property owned and let; (ii) owner-occupied non-trading property and married quarters for the Forces, for which a rent is imputed. For convenience, some income arising from fixed assets other than land and buildings is included. The methods used in making these estimates are described on pages 267 to 269.

(c) *Local authority property*. This group covers (i) local authority dwellings; (ii) property owned and used by local authorities other than in connection with their trading activities, for which a rent is imputed; this property may include some plant and vehicles. The estimates are described on page 310.

(d) *Farm land and buildings*. For this group, which includes both rented and owner-occupied property, rent income is estimated from the sources used for calculating farm incomes generally (see page 143). The rent income represents an average rent per acre (computed by regular surveys) multiplied by acreage, *less* an estimated deduction for current repairs and maintenance. The figures exclude rent in respect of the domestic use of farmhouses and cottages, which is included under (a).

(e) *Land and buildings rented to trading concerns or public authorities*. The main item is property, other than farms, owned by persons, companies and public corporations and rented for use by both private and public trading enterprises. Owner-occupied properties are excluded. No direct information is available for this group of property and the estimates are poor. The estimates are based on Schedule A assessments, with an addition for assessments under Schedule D in respect of rents in excess of the Schedule A value of the property, and a deduction for maintenance claims in excess of the statutory allowance. Hence, although the Schedule A assessments mainly related to pre-war values, the adjustments result in a rough measure of net rents at current prices. The estimates have been projected and adjusted to reconcile the resulting estimate of total rent for all forms of property with the alternative estimates of total rent described below.

From 1963, after the abolition of income tax under Schedule A, total rent income is also estimated by making use of the information on tax assessments under Case VI and Case VIII of Schedule D. These assessments provide separate figures of income from rent received by persons and by companies and cover nearly all of the income received by the private sector from rented property. With a small allowance for the income not covered by the assessments, and the addition of imputed income from owner-occupied dwellings and farm land and buildings, included respectively in (a) and (d) above, an estimate of rent income is obtained on the basis required for the national accounts. The estimates of rent received by public authorities—(b) and (c) above—are taken from the sector accounts and so are the estimates of rent received by public corporations (see page 241). In this way an estimate of total rent is built up by combining the estimates for each sector instead of for each type of property. These estimates are used for the annual figures of rent from 1963 and for the sector allocation.

The composition of rent income in 1966

The following table shows how the estimate of total rent income was divided in 1966 between the different groups of property separately discussed above.

Composition of rent income, 1966

	£ million
(a) Land and buildings used by persons as consumers and not owned by public authorities:	
Rented property	346
Owner-occupied dwellings	687
(b) Central government property:	
Rent from letting of property	21
Imputed rent from owner-occupied property	75
(c) Local authority property:	
Dwellings	410
Imputed rent from owner-occupied property	194
(d) Farm land and buildings	43
(e) Land and buildings rented to trading concerns or public authorities	173
Total	1,949

The division of rent income by sector is given in the analysis of gross national product by sector and type of income (Table 13 of the 1967 Blue Book, see page 67). Until information became available under Schedule D from 1964/65, the allocation between the personal sector and companies was very rough. The figure for the private sector was obtained as a residual and its allocation between the personal sector and companies was based on a largely arbitrary allocation of income from each group of property, illustrated in the first table on page 477. From 1963, direct estimates are made of the rent income received by the personal sector and companies (see above).

Rent income is analysed also by industry of origin. In the analysis of gross national product by industry (Table 17 of the 1967 Blue Book) rent is treated as originating in three industries only:
(i) agriculture;
(ii) insurance, banking and finance (including real estate);
(iii) ownership of dwellings.
It will be remembered that the income derived from owner-occupied trading property, except farms, is not separately identified; such income is included in the gross trading income of the industries concerned. The allocation by industry of the five groups of property described on pages 474 and 475 is shown in the second table on page 477.

Analysis of rent income by group of property and sector, 1966

£ million

Group of property	Personal sector	Companies	Public corporations	Central government	Local authorities	Total
(a) Land and buildings used by persons as consumers and not owned by public authorities.	932	69	32	—	—	1,033
(b) Central government property	—	—	—	96	—	96
(c) Local authority property	—	—	—	—	604	604
(d) Farm land and buildings	34	9	—	—	—	43
(e) Land and buildings rented to trading concerns or public authorities	38	122	13	—	—	173
Total	1,004	200	45	96	604	1,949

Rent income by industry of origin, 1966

£ million

Agriculture:	
Farm land and buildings—group (d)	43
Real estate industry:	
Land and buildings rented to trading concerns, etc.—group (e)	173
Central government property, other than dwellings—part of group (b)	92
Local authority property, other than dwellings—part of group (c)	194
Ownership of dwellings:	
Land and buildings used by persons and not owned by public authorities—group (a)	1,033
Dwellings owned by central government—part of group (b)	4
Dwellings owned by local authorities—part of group (c)	410
Total	1,949

Appendix II

CENSUSES OF PRODUCTION AND DISTRIBUTION AND THE INQUIRIES INTO THE DISTRIBUTIVE AND SERVICE INDUSTRIES

The estimates of fixed capital formation and stocks and work in progress rest heavily on the statistics provided by the censuses of production and distribution and the annual inquiries into the distributive and service industries. The inquiries are also used for certain estimates of consumers' expenditure and for estimating wages and salaries in individual industries. The main characteristics of these statistics, which affect all uses made of them in the national accounts, are for convenience brought together here. Fuller information is given in the published reports on the various censuses, and in the reports on the inquiries into the distributive and service industries which are published annually in the *Board of Trade Journal*.

The figures derived from the censuses and annual inquiries do not strictly relate to the calendar year, since firms are allowed to make returns for their own accounting year if it is not possible for them to give figures for the calendar year, even on an estimated basis. The resulting aggregates are the sum of returns relating to twelve month periods ending between 6 April in the year to which the census or annual inquiry relates and 5 April in the following year. The spread of accounting periods is such, however, that the figures can be taken as relating on average to the calendar year. Analyses of the census results have shown that, for example for manufacturing and for retail distribution, the mean terminal date was within a few weeks of the end of the calendar year, although substantial variations occur in some individual industries. Also, in the business unit censuses of production and in the annual inquiries, quarterly returns of capital expenditure and stocks from voluntary contributors are used to provide annual data for the firms concerned so that in these cases the estimates relate exactly to the calendar year.

Census of production

For 1948 and each subsequent year a census of production has been taken covering mining and quarrying, manufacturing, construction (except in 1950), gas, electricity and water supply. In the case of coal mining, mineral oil refining, gas and electricity, the inquiries are carried out by the Ministry of Power; the results are reported separately in the Ministry of Power *Statistical Digest* and from 1959 are included in the reports of the detailed censuses only. Separate censuses, but on similar lines, are taken in Great Britain and in Northern Ireland (except in 1948, when there was no census in Northern Ireland).

The censuses taken in respect of the years 1948 to 1951 were full censuses in that an approach was made to all firms within the fields covered by the censuses, although generally the smallest establishments reported only the nature of their business and the number of persons employed. From 1952, sampling procedures have been extensively used, interspersed with full censuses taken for the years

1954, 1958 and 1963. A full census is also being taken for 1968. The inquiries for the years 1952, 1953 and 1955 to 1957 were confined to a sample of establishments, including some of the smaller establishments and all over a certain size. For 1959 no approach was made to businesses employing fewer than twenty-five persons but all larger businesses were covered. Subsequent sample censuses for 1960 to 1962 and 1964 to 1967 also excluded all smaller businesses and included only a sample of the larger ones. The sample censuses for 1964 to 1967 have covered about 75 to 80 per cent of total capital formation in manufacturing industry. Estimates covering the small establishments are mostly based on the figures of numbers employed collected from those establishments as part of a full census. Information about the sampling procedures used is given in the relevant census reports. In the case of the Ministry of Power inquiries, there has been full coverage in all years.

Up to 1958, the censuses were conducted on an establishment basis, information being collected, with certain exceptions, from each establishment or a sample of establishments falling within the scope of the census. The census taken in respect of 1959, and subsequent censuses with the exception of the full census taken in respect of 1963 (and also that for 1968) used the 'business unit' as the reporting unit. The business unit relates to a whole company or group of companies in a particular industry group; any subsidiary companies operating mainly overseas are excluded. One return is made for an entire enterprise, but where an enterprise is engaged in a number of quite different activities separate returns are made for each main activity.

The questions asked in the censuses have varied over the years. However, questions on capital expenditure have been included in all years except 1950, and on stocks and work in progress in all years. Extracts from the 1966 form covering these two topics are given at the end of this appendix. The pattern from 1958 has been to ask for detailed information quinquennially, with the intervening censuses having only a limited question content. In addition to questions on capital expenditure and stocks, the less detailed censuses from 1959 to 1962 also asked manufacturers for information about total sales and work done, and in 1961 for the value of their sales direct to the public. Questions on average employment during the year, wages and salaries paid, details of sales, and information on purchases of materials and fuel have been asked for only in the full censuses for 1958 and 1963; up to 1957 more detailed questions of this kind were included in the census for each year.

Census of distribution

The first census of distribution was taken in respect of 1950; subsequent censuses have related to 1957, 1961 and 1966. The 1950 census covered retail and wholesale distribution, non-residential catering (excluding public houses), hairdressing, funeral furnishing, portrait photography, repairing goods direct for the general public and retail motor distribution and repairing as well as petrol retailing. For 1957 the census was confined to retail distribution, the hairdressing and manicure trades, and boot and shoe repairing direct for the public. The 1961 census covered the same industries as that for 1957 (but included boot and shoe repairing for the trade), together with hiring-out of consumer goods direct to the public and laundries, launderettes and dry cleaners. The industrial coverage of the 1966 census was similar to that for 1961, with the addition of commercial radio and television relay services. All of these censuses related to Great

Britain; the first census of distribution for Northern Ireland was taken in respect of 1965.

The 1950 census was a full inquiry, attempting to cover all establishments and asking the same questions of all except the smallest retail establishments. Subsequent censuses were partly on a sample basis. For 1957 only a sample of small independent traders was included and the smallest of these supplied information on only kind of business, turnover and numbers employed. The 1961 census was a full census but involved an element of sampling among independent traders for most questions other than those on kind of business, turnover and employment. The 1966 census was on a sample basis like that for 1957.

The reporting unit in the censuses of distribution is the establishment for sales, employment and occasionally other items. The 'retail organisation', which is fairly similar to the business unit, is the reporting unit for stocks, capital expenditure, purchases, etc.

All the censuses of distribution have included questions on kind of business, turnover (with a detailed analysis by commodity), stocks, employment (in a specified week) and wages and salaries paid. Questions on capital expenditure have been asked from 1957. Questions on credit sales and book debts have also been included from 1957 and various other questions, for example on methods of trading, membership of voluntary groups, transport costs and floorspace, have also been included at different times.

Inquiries into the distributive and service industries

Statutory annual inquiries into the distributive and service industries have been made by the Board of Trade in respect of each year from 1956 onwards. The trades covered have varied, but have normally included at least wholesale distribution; retail distribution (except in a census year); road transport and road haulage; shipping; insurance, banking, and finance, including property companies; catering; and the motor trades. The inquiries are generally run on a sampling basis. The reporting unit is the business unit throughout the annual inquiries. For the most part, the information collected has been confined to capital expenditure and stocks.

The initial inquiry in 1956 related only to a sample of companies, but the coverage has been improved over the years. In 1956 and 1960 all shipping companies were included and the coverage of this industry is now virtually complete. In 1959 the coverage of the sample for wholesale and retail distribution was extended to unincorporated businesses. In the same year a fuller inquiry was made of property companies. In 1960 the sample was extended to include unincorporated catering businesses. For the years 1960 to 1962 the inquiry covered all taxi and private hire car companies, air transport companies and the larger bus and coach companies. In 1961 the larger unincorporated bus and coach operators were also covered in full, and in 1962 all bus and coach operators were included in the inquiry, whatever their size. In subsequent years the road passenger transport and air transport industries have been covered on a sample basis. In 1962 unincorporated motor traders were also brought into the inquiry. And in 1966 the register of road haulage operators was extended to cover unincorporated businesses as well as companies.

In addition to capital formation, further information, some of which is used in the estimation of consumers' expenditure, has also been collected in certain years, usually as part of major inquiries for industries not covered by the censuses of distribution. For 1959 and 1965 wholesale traders provided figures of their total receipts. For 1960 and 1964 an analysis of turnover was obtained from the catering trades and for 1962 and 1967 motor trades provided information on turnover and purchases.

Extracts from census of production form for 1966

The questions on stocks and capital expenditure are reproduced below.

II. STOCKS† (see notes 5-10)

	At beginning of year	At end of year
5. Materials, stores and fuel	£..	£..................................
*6. Work in progress	£..	£..................................
7. Goods on hand for sale	£..	£..................................

†Not applicable to water undertakings
*Not applicable to mines and quarries
*Shipbuilding—Do not include the value of work in progress on ships in course of construction (see Note 5)

III. CAPITAL EXPENDITURE (see notes 11-15)

Land and buildings

8. Cost of new building work, or other constructional work of a capital nature	£..
9. Cost of land and of existing buildings acquired	£..
10. Proceeds of land and buildings disposed of	£..

Vehicles

11. Cost of new and second-hand vehicles bought	£..
12. Proceeds of vehicles sold or traded in	£..

Plant, machinery, and other capital equipment

13. Cost of new and second-hand items bought	£..
14. Proceeds of items sold or traded in	£..

II. STOCKS

5. All your stocks (except the value of work in progress on ships in course of construction) should be apportioned between the three headings shown. Separate figures should be given for each heading, estimates being made where necessary.

6. The division of stocks between the headings should as far as possible be made in relation to the whole of the business covered by the return. For example, stocks of goods produced which in the main are to be further processed within the business covered by the return should be recorded as work in progress and not as materials and fuel or as goods on hand for sale.

7. The values for the beginning and end of the year should be on the same basis. If a business has been acquired during the year, its stocks should not be included

Q*

for the end of the year unless they can also be included for the beginning of the year.

8. Include:

(a) Any stocks held outside the United Kingdom (but see Note 9).

(b) Any stocks of goods held for merchanting or factoring.

(c) Loose tools, jigs, dies, patterns, moulds and similar items.

(d) Vehicles, plant, machinery, etc., let out on hire only if they were not charged to capital asset accounts when acquired.

(e) Duty in the case of dutiable goods held out of bond.

9. Exclude stocks held by subsidiary companies mainly operating overseas.

10. Progress payments received by you should be ignored, i.e. gross figures should be given for work in progress. Exclude any progress payments made by you to sub-contractors.

III. CAPITAL EXPENDITURE

General

11. Include (except as stated in note 12):

(a) All expenditure charged to the capital asset accounts.

(b) Capital expenditure at any establishments belonging to the business where production had not yet begun.

(c) Capital items bought on hire purchase.

(d) New building work or other capital items produced by you for use in the business covered by the return.

(e) Any expenditure on additions to capital assets which is temporarily being carried forward under other headings, e.g. work in progress on capital assets in course of construction, or deposits or other payments on account of capital assets in process of acquisition.

(f) Expenditure on replacing capital assets destroyed under circumstances (e.g. fire) which have given rise to an insurance claim.

(g) Any expenditure on the replacement of major capital assets where, in lieu of depreciation, these renewals are charged either direct to revenue or against a provision for renewals created out of revenue.

12. Exclude:

(a) The value of any assets acquired in taking over an existing business.

(b) Expenditure on intangible assets such as goodwill, patents and trade marks.

(c) Transfers to capital asset accounts during the year brought forward under other headings (see note 11(e)) from previous years.

(d) Expenditure on any items which are to be used outside the United Kingdom.

(e) Expenditure on loose tools, jigs, dies, patterns, moulds and similar items (see note 8(c)).

Land and buildings

13. Include:

(a) Against heading 8 expenditure on the construction of new buildings, the extension or improvement of old buildings (including fixtures, e.g. lifts, heating and ventilation systems), and on site preparation and other civil engineering work. Include the cost of any newly constructed buildings purchased.

(b) Against heading 9 the capital cost of freeholds purchased and the capital cost or premium payable for leaseholds acquired, and against heading 10 amounts receivable.

(c) Against headings 8 and 9 architects' and surveyors' fees and any legal charges, stamp duties, agents' commissions, etc.

Vehicles, plant, machinery, and other capital equipment

14. Include against headings 11 and 12 ships, aircraft and railway rolling stock as well as motor vehicles, but exclude vehicles, such as fork lift trucks, used within warehouses, factories, etc., and mobile powered equipment such as earth movers, etc. Include against headings 13 and 14 plant, machinery and all capital equipment (e.g. office machinery and furniture) not covered by headings 8 to 12.

15. Do not deduct any amounts received from the Cotton Board under the Cotton Industry Act, 1959, or from the Board of Trade under the Local Employment Acts of 1960 to 1966.

Appendix III

SUMMARY OF TERMS USED IN INLAND REVENUE DATA

Inland Revenue statistics provide the main source of information on the incomes of both persons and companies. The following summary definitions and explanations of the Inland Revenue system are given for reference.

Income tax

Income is charged to tax under Schedules according to the source from which it arises. Under the Finance Act, 1965 the income of corporate bodies is charged to corporation tax instead of income tax (see below).

Schedule A. Income from the ownership of land, buildings and other hereditaments up to 1963/64.

The income charged under Schedule A was determined by reference to the annual rent at which the property was, or could be, let or on the value of the beneficial occupation of the property when the rent fell short of the annual value. The annual value was normally fixed once every five years, but the last revaluation was, in fact, made in 1936. Where property was actually let at a rent which exceeded the Schedule A assessment, the 'excess rent' was charged under Case VI of Schedule D. If, over the past five years, the average expenditure on repairs, maintenance and insurance exceeded the statutory deduction allowed in the assessment, a claim might be made for relief for 'excess maintenance'.

Schedule B. Income from the occupation of lands. Profits arising from lands occupied for farming or other commercial use have, for the years 1949/50 onwards, been wholly assessable under Schedule D. From 1964/65 only income from woodlands managed on a commercial basis is charged under this Schedule.

Schedule C. Interest on certain British government securities and certain securities of governments and public authorities outside the United Kingdom.

Schedule D. Profits and income grouped under the following 'Cases':

Case I. Profits of a trade.

Case II. Profits of a profession or vocation not dealt with under any other Schedule.

Case III. Interest, except interest charged under Schedule C, assessed on the recipient, discounts, annuities and other annual payments.

Case IV. Income, except interest charged under Schedule C, from overseas securities.

Case V. Income from other posesssions abroad, for example dividends from ordinary shares in a foreign company.

Case VI. Income from furnished lettings and other miscellaneous income not charged under any other Case of Schedule D or any other Schedule.

Case VII. Short-term capital gains from 1962/63, that is capital gains arising on the disposal of assets within twelve months of their acquisition (six months up to 1964/65).

Case VIII. Rents and other income from the ownership of property from 1964/65, formerly charged partly under Schedule A and partly under Schedule D, Case VI.

The dates above generally relate to the year the income arises. The income charged under Cases I and II of Schedule D is normally the profits made in the trader's accounting year ending in the preceding year of assessment. Income charged under Cases III, IV, V, VI (other than excess rents) and VII is normally that arising in the preceding year of assessment. Income under Case VI (excess rents) and Case VIII is the actual income of the year of assessment, although under Case VIII the initial assessment is based on the preceding year's income and adjusted later. There are, however, exceptions under all Cases, applying when a business is started or discontinued, or when some other source of income is acquired or disposed of.

Schedule E. Income from an office, employment or pension. Most of the tax collected under this Schedule is deducted by the employer under the 'Pay-as-you-earn' (PAYE) system.

Schedule F. Dividends and other company distributions from 1966/67. Income tax withheld by companies from dividends and other distributions, chargeable under Schedule F, is collected about a month after payment under the provisions of Schedule 12 of the Finance Act, 1965. Under these provisions there is also collected the tax on company payments of interest, royalties, etc. chargeable under Section 170 of the Income Tax Act, 1952. Schedule 12 provides that a company is to make a return at the end of each month of income tax withheld from distributions and payments, and to pay over to the Revenue any tax due. Tax collected thus is known as 'Schedule 12 income tax' and, although collected from companies, most of it is borne ultimately by persons.

The year of assessment for income tax purposes runs from 6 April in one year to 5 April in the next. This period is referred to as the 'fiscal year' or 'income tax year' to distinguish it from the 'financial year', ending on 31 March, which is the period used for the accounts of the central government.

As far as possible, income tax is deducted at the source and collected by the Inland Revenue from the payer rather than from the recipient of the income who ultimately bears the tax. Thus tax deducted by the Bank of England from payments of government interest is assessed under Schedule C; tax deducted by local authorities from their interest payments is assessed under Schedule D, Section 170; tax on company dividends is deducted by the company making the payment and from 1966 accounted for under Schedule F; and tax on wages and salaries is deducted by the employer under the PAYE system.

Surtax

Surtax is a deferred instalment of income tax chargeable upon the total income of a person if it exceeds £2,000 per annum. In general it is payable only by individuals. Since 1961/62 there have been special allowances reducing the liability of earned incomes.

Profits tax

Profits tax, which was in force up to 5 April 1966, was charged on the profits of trades or businesses, including the holding of investments, carried on in the United Kingdom by corporate bodies or carried on abroad by corporate bodies ordinarily resident in the United Kingdom. From 1 January 1947 to 31 March 1958 distributed profits were charged at a higher rate than non-distributed profits. Profits for this purpose were computed on income tax principles, subject to prescribed modifications. It was chargeable by reference to the profits for each 'chargeable accounting period', normally the yearly accounting period of the business.

Corporation tax

Corporation tax, introduced by the Finance Act, 1965, is charged on the trading profits (after deducting capital allowances), other income and chargeable capital gains of corporate bodies, collectively described as their 'profits'. It replaced the income tax and profits tax formerly charged, and falls on the 'profits' of corporate bodies resident in the United Kingdom wherever they arise and whether they are remitted to this country or not. Dividends or other distributions received by one United Kingdom company from another, which have borne income tax under Schedule F, are not subject to corporation tax in the hands of the receiving company. Other income tax deducted at source is allowed for in the corporation tax assessment. Broadly speaking, the profits chargeable to corporation tax are computed according to income tax principles under the Schedules and Cases governing income tax.

The first accounts charged to corporation tax were generally those for the accounting period following that of which the profits had been assessed to income tax for the year of assessment 1965/66; the first major payment of tax was in January 1967.

Capital gains tax

Capital gains tax is payable on capital gains, other than short-term capital gains liable to income tax under Case VII of Schedule D, accruing to individuals on the disposal of assets. The capital gains of companies are charged to corporation tax. The tax was introduced by the Finance Act, 1965, and is charged on capital gains realised after 6 April 1965 but only to the extent that such gains are attributable to the period after that date. The first payments of capital gains tax were received during 1966.

Disposal includes sale, exchange, gift and, generally, any occasion when the owner of an asset derives a capital sum from it. Assets are deemed to have been disposed of at the owner's death, with an exemption for the first £5,000 gains.

Gains arising from certain types of asset are exempt from capital gains tax, the main types being principal private residences occupied as such; tangible moveable property worth £1,000 or less; most life insurance policies; savings certificates, premium bonds, defence bonds and national development bonds. From 1967/68 an individual's gains for any one year are exempt if they do not exceed £50.

Index

Printed in England for Her Majesty's Stationery Office by McCorquodale & Co. Ltd., London.

HM 2183 Dd 137244 K 48   8/68 M^cC. 3309.   SBN 11 630061 2